# Estonia, Latvia & Lithuania

**Nicola Williams**
**Debra Herrmann**
**Cathryn Kemp**

LONELY PLANET PUBLICATIONS
Melbourne • Oakland • London • Paris

**LAHEMAA NATIONAL PARK**
A naturalist's paradise and Estonia's first national park with grand 18th-century manors, picturesque rivers, forests and lakes

**TARTU**
The heart of the 19th-century Estonian national revival and a lively university town where Estonia's move towards independence is celebrated and cultural legacy preserved

**LAKE PEIPSI**
Time travel in an Old Believers' village on the banks of a lake, where local customs and language remain an ancient mix of Estonian and Russian Orthodox

**GAUJA NATIONAL PARK**
Spirit-soaring canoeing and rafting down the majestic blue-green Gauja River

**TALLINN**
One of Europe's most charming capitals with a World Heritage-listed medieval Old Town, historic parklands, beaches and several islands to explore

**RIGA**
The hub of Baltic entertainment by night and a stunning architectural showroom by day displaying Europe's best collection of Art Noveau and a gorgeous medieval Old Town

**HIIUMAA**
Favourite island holiday destination for locals seeking peace, solitude and an Estonian idyll

**LIVONIAN COAST**
Peaceful, untouched homeland of Latvia's ancient Liv people with white-sand beaches, the stunning Slītere National Park and odd little gems like the Museum of Horns & Antlers

FINLAND

RUSSIA

ESTONIA

Gulf of Finland

Lake Peipsi

Gulf of Riga

BALTIC SEA

UST-LUGA
KINGISEPP
NARVA
SLANTSY
Sillamäe
Kohtla-Järve
OSTROV
KRASNOGORODSKOE
PSKOV
PECHORY
Izborsk
Gdov
Spitsyno
Palkino
Obinitsa
VÕRU
RÄPINA
PÕLVA
OTEPÄÄ
Puhja
ELVA
TARTU
JÕGEVA
MUSTVEE
Kallaste
RAKVERE
KUNDA
TAPA
Aegviidu
PAIDE
TÜRI
PÕLTSAMAA
VÕHMA
VÄNDRA
SUURE-JAANI
VILJANDI
KARKSI
TÕRVA
ABja-Paluoja
VALGA
VALKA
Rūjiena
SMILTENE
Strenči
ALŪKSNE
Liepna
Vijaka
BALVI
GULBENE
LUBĀNA
MADONA
LOKSA
KEILA
TALLINN
RAPLA
MÄRJAMAA
Lihula
Kullamaa
PÄRNU
Kilingi-Nõmme
Häädemeeste
Mazsalaca
Aloja
Matiši
VALMIERA
CĒSIS
LĪGATNE
SIGULDA
Limbaži
Rauna
Ve/piebalga
Jaunpiebalga
Mālpils
Suntaži
RĪGA
JŪRMALA
KĀRDLA
Käina
Hiiumaa
Kõpu
Sõru
Orissaare
Kuressaare
Saaremaa
Salme
Muhu
Virtsu
Kõmsu
HAAPSALU
Risti
Vormsi
Riguldi
Kolka
Mazirbe
Mikeltornis
Oviši
VENTSPILS
Pāvilosta
Alsunga
Vārve
KULDĪGA
Kabile
Sabile
STENDE
DUNDAGA
TALSI
Valdemārpils
Mērsrags
Engure
TUKUMS
KANDAVA
Roja
Ragana
Saulkrasti
Skulte
Tūja
Salacgrīva
Staicele
Stacele
Ainaži

FINLAND

50km
30mi
0 25
0 15

22°E 23°E 24°E 25°E 26°E 27°E
59°N 58°N 57°N

**ELEVATION**

300m
240m
180m
120m
60m
0

**PILSRUNDĀLE**
Home to Rundāle Palace, the palatial creation of architect Bartolomeo Rastrelli (who created St Petersburg's Winter Palace in the same mould)

**VISAGINAS**
A surreal Soviet toy town built in the 1970s, home to the controversial Ignalina nuclear power station

**VILNIUS**
Lithuania's graceful and enchanting capital, a skyline of church spires and a World Heritage–listed baroque Old Town

**DZŪKIJA NATIONAL PARK**
Berrying and mushrooming in the forests, a traditional sauna and a Soviet sculpture park

**ORVYDAS GARDEN**
A mystical maelstrom of stone carvings and bizarre creations that survived the Soviet era

**CURONIAN SPIT**
A world of windswept sand dunes, a beachside sauna, pine trees and the fantastical and grotesque carvings on Witches' Hill

**KAUNAS**
Home to the Čiurlionis Museum, an outstanding collection of the romantic painter/musician's work, and one of Europe's last funiculars

LATVIA
LITHUANIA
BELARUS
POLAND
KALININGRAD REGION (RUSSIA)

MINSK

Karšava
Žilupe
Ludza
Rēzekne
Kaunata
Skaune
Dagda
Aglona
Preiļi
Vilāni
Viļāni
Malta
Jēkabpils
Subate
Dzisna
Mēry
Opsa
Braslav
Postavy
Daugavpils
Zarasai
Obeliai
Rokiškis
Svedasai
Anykščiai
Utena
Molėtai
Kaltanėnai
Dūkštas
Švenčionėliai
Švenčionys
Pabradė
Nemenčinė
Vilnius
Smorgon
Oshmyany
Volozhin
Molodechno
Radoshkovichi
Lida

Mežāre
Koknese
Alūksne
Madliena
Mengele
Skaistkalne
Bauska
Ogre
Kegums
Baldone
Birzgale
Jaunjelgava
Vecumnieki
Elgava
Eleja
Kalnciems
Dobele
Auce
Saldus
Skrunda
Aizpute
Liepāja
Priekule

Viesīte
Nereta
Suvainiškis
Biržai
Pandėlys
Kupiškis
Panevėžys
Pasvalys
Linkuva
Radviliškis
Šeduva
Šiauliai
Kelmė
Raseiniai
Kėdainiai
Šėta
Ukmergė
Jonava
Kaunas
Širvintos
Maišiagala
Rūdiškės
Šalčininkai
Baltoji Vokė
Vārena
Eišiškės
Dieveniškės
Druskininkai
Lazdijai
Seiny
Alytus
Suwalki
Marijampolė
Vilkaviškis
Kudirkos Naumiestis
Šakiai
Jurbarkas
Tauragė
Skaudvilė
Telšiai
Plunge
Kretinga
Gargždai
Klaipėda
Priekulė
Palanga
Salantai
Rietavas
Vainutas
Šilutė
Nida
Sovetsk
Vievis
Nesterov
Gusev
Goldap
Wegorzewo
Ketrzyn
Chernyakhovsk
Gvardeysk
Polessk
Mysovka
Baltijsk

**Estonia, Latvia & Lithuania**
**3rd edition** – June 2003
**First published** – September 1997

**Published by**
**Lonely Planet Publications Pty Ltd**  ABN 36 005 607 983
90 Maribyrnong St, Footscray, Victoria 3011, Australia

**Lonely Planet Offices**
**Australia** Locked Bag 1, Footscray, Victoria 3011
**USA** 150 Linden St, Oakland, CA 94607
**UK** 10a Spring Place, London NW5 3BH
**France** 1 rue du Dahomey, 75011 Paris

**Photographs**
Many of the images in this guide are available for licensing from
Lonely Planet Images.
W www.lonelyplanetimages.com

**Front cover photograph**
Winter view towards St John's Church from Gedimino Hill, Lithuania
(Jonathan Smith)

ISBN 1 74059 132 1

# Contents – Text

## 2 Contents – Text

# Contents – Maps

## FACTS ABOUT LITHUANIA

## VILNIUS

## EASTERN & SOUTHERN LITHUANIA

## CENTRAL LITHUANIA

## WESTERN LITHUANIA

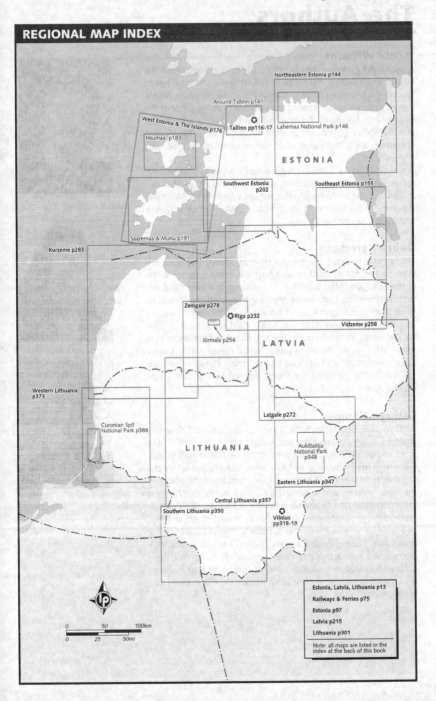

# REGIONAL MAP INDEX

Northeastern Estonia p144

Around Tallinn p141

West Estonia & The Islands p176

Hiiumaa p183

Tallinn pp116-17

Lahemaa National Park p146

**ESTONIA**

Southwest Estonia p202

Southeast Estonia p155

Saaremaa & Muhu p191

Kurzeme p283

Zemgale p278

Riga p232

Jūrmala p254

Vidzeme p258

**LATVIA**

Western Lithuania p373

Latgale p272

Curonian Spit National Park p388

**LITHUANIA**

Aukštaitija National Park p348

Eastern Lithuania p347

Central Lithuania p357

Southern Lithuania p350

Vilnius pp318-19

0  50  100km
0  25  50mi

# The Authors

### Nicola Williams

A journalist by training, Nicola first hit the road in 1990 when she bussed and boated it from Jakarta to East Timor and back again. Following a two year stint at the *North Wales Weekly News*, Nicola moved to Latvia to bus it round the Baltics as Features Editor of the English-language *Baltic Times* newspaper. Following a happy 12 months exploring the Baltics as editor-in-chief of the *In Your Pocket* city-guide series, she traded in Lithuanian *cepelinai* for Lyonnaise *andouillette*.

She updated the Latvian chapters and worked as coordinating author for this edition of *Estonia, Latvia & Lithuania*; and has authored several Lonely Planet titles including *Romania & Moldova*, *Provence & the Côte d'Azur*, *The Loire*, *Milan, Turin & Genoa* and *Russia, Ukraine & Belarus*.

### Debra Herrmann

Debra, who updated the Estonia chapter, started out from the Wimmera region of southeastern Australia, some distance south of the Baltic Sea. After subsisting as a junior in the design and advertising business, copywriting anything from seedy nightclubs to Swedish cars, she soon realised the value of a passport. Over 30 countries proved irresistible in the years that followed and, after a visa-friendly foray into publishing in London, led to the one employer who would regard this as a logical career path - Lonely Planet. Her other contributions to the Lonely Planet list include *Eastern Europe, Europe on a shoestring* and *Lonely Planet Unpacked Again*.

### Cathryn Kemp

Cathryn swapped tabloids for travel to update the Lithuanian chapters. Freelance journalist and feature writer, she went off the press and on the road for this her first Lonely Planet assignment. Cathryn started travelling in 1990 when she studied art at the Moscow Institute of Architecture. Several trips through Russia and the Ukraine later, and a passion for travel was born. She then moved to Barcelona to complete an MA in Fine Art and Photography. After graduating from Winchester School of Art in 1995, and with camera in hand, she became a slave to backpacking across Asia, Europe, Australia, New Zealand and South America – interspersed with a budding career in journalism. For five years Cathryn has written for British national and regional newspapers with some freelance photography thrown in – but travel just keeps getting in the way.

# FROM THE AUTHORS

## Nicola Williams
Many thanks to old friends who made me feel like I'd never left: Nomeda Navickaitė and Reine Ortiz (who made sure I got that train), Renata Šutovaitė and Sco, and Rimas (for yet another nippy little number) in Vilnius; and Grquote irts Upenieks, Māris Petrevics and Mārtiņš Zaprauskis (for ice-hockey and beers at dawn) in Rīga. At home, smiles of gratitude to Ingrida (Ligers) Rogal, my parents Ann & Paul Williams, and husband Matthias Lüfkens. And kisses to Niko and Tomass (that you will use this guide for your Baltic travels). At LP, thanks to my co-authors Cathryn and Debra (for prompt 'n cheery responses to pesky emails); Imogen Franks and Mark Griffiths.

## Debra Herrmann
In Australia, special thanks to Sirje Jõgi for the introduction to Estonian language and culture, recipes and laughter and to Liz Filleul and Mark Griffiths for plotting the course from Footscray to Eurovision. Among many others in the LP community, the efforts of Nicola Williams, Imogen Franks and Louise McGregor deserve more than praise. In Estonia I thank Raivo Tõnissaar for generously sharing his Hiiumaa experience and Marko Kaulder, Tõnu and crew for the adventures east. The inspired work of Ursula Toomri in putting Tartu into perspective will long be remembered as will the intuition of Anne Kurepalu in Lahemaa. Many thanks to Mart Laar for the Forest Brothers insight and for such inspirational efforts in preserving this legacy. Finally, thanks to Steve Kokker for his empathic ear, the brilliant Tiina Laats from the Eesti Institut and to Anne Pilli, Sirje Toom and the many other information experts who have assisted with grace and flair.

## Cathryn Kemp
Lithuania greeted me – and my faltering Russian – with open arms. I humbly thank everyone who came to my rescue along the way. In crazy old Vilnius, the first helping hand arrived before I even got off the plane. Rob and Laima – can I just say ačiū! Thanks to Livijus from the Old Town Hostel for giving me the local gossip (and following my 'backpacker's intuition'). My host family in Vilnius should be applauded for their patience in the face of relentless questions, as should American Paul (finish that book!) and his army of kindly musical and literary friends. Many thanks to everyone at Vilnius TIC, to fabulous Rimas from Rimas-Rent-A-Car and fountain-of-wisdom Sco and his gang from In Your Pocket – both in Vilnius and Kaunas, to Dalia Bardauskienė, advisor to Vilnius Mayor Artūras Zuokas, and to Dr Shimon Alperovitch from the State Jewish Museum for granting me an audience (but not answering my questions).

In Lithuania's heart, thanks to Barry who unravelled Panevėžys' own particular charms, and all in the Kaunas TIC for helping beyond the cause of duty. On Lithuania's magical western shores, good luck and thanks to Jurda at the revamped Travellers Hostel and to Dr Artūras Razinkovas from Klaipėda Univeristy and Antanas Kontautas from the Lithuanian Green Movement for their invaluable ecological know-how. On the spit, gratitude to the excellent Smiltynė and Nida TICs. And no thanks what-so-ever to coordinating author Nicola who only gave me brilliant contacts, excellent advice and a sympathetic ear during this journey into our precious Lithuania.

# This Book

The first edition of this book was written by Nicola Williams. The second edition was updated by three authors: Estonia by Steve Kokker; Latvia by Kate Galbraith; Lithuania by Nicola Williams. The third edition of *Estonia, Latvia & Lithuania* was updated by Nicola Williams, Debra Herrmann and Cathryn Kemp.

## FROM THE PUBLISHER

This third edition of *Estonia, Latvia & Lithuania* was produced in Lonely Planet's Melbourne office by coordinators Kalya Ryan and Lou McGregor (editorial) and Jimi Ellis (mapping). Lou and Kalya were assisted by Melanie Dankel, Nancy Ianni and Tasmin Waby. Jimi was assisted by Jolyon Philcox and Valentina Kremenchut-skaya. Thanks also to Mark Griffiths. Jacqui Saunders took the book through layout and James Hardy designed the cover. Celia Wood was the project manager and Imogen Franks the commissioning editor. Thanks to LPI for photos, Quentin Frayne for the Language chapter and Cathy Viero for the readers' letters.

# Thanks

Many thanks to the travellers who used the last edition and wrote to us with helpful hints, useful advice and interesting anecdotes:

Kasper Anderson, Jeffry Angermann, Glenn Ashenden, Lorna Ashworth, Gunnar Aug, Caroline Auriel, Ray Baker, Ali Baldwin, Michael Beck, Marco Birg, Ilga Blankmeyer, Jason Bloomer, Jeroen Bode, Carmen Boudreau-Kiviaho, Graham Boyd, Lena Bretz, Helen Brock, Andeas Bruckmeier, Cormac Byrne, Bradley Chait, Elspeth Christie, Naomi Clift, Keith Cocks, Abigail Collins, Sam Collins, Brad Costello, Christine Crowther, Fiammetta Curcio, Rob de Raaij, Jean Delforge, Emils Delins, Michael Doburn, Birge Dohmann, András Domany, Gatis Eglitis, Andrew Embick, Philipp Engewald, Mario Falzon, Stephen Fenech, Mauricio Ferandez, James Ferryman, Kimberly Fisher, Keith Fountain, Ludek Frybort, Martin Garvey, Petra Geurts, Andrew Girdler, Patricia Grumberg, Konrad Grygorczyk Morten Hagedal, Gail Hammond, IW Harris, Scott Hegerty, Ms Hellevoetsluis, Henk Hiddinga, Viki Hirst, Dana Frederick Hoch, Alex Hopkins, Marcel Huibers, Jouni Hytönen, Richard Jacques, Rok Jarc, Kay Jaumeers, Bjorn Juliussen, Aino Kald, Alexander Kierdorf, Rob Kingston, Stephen Kinsella, V Kisowski, Gabi Knight, Tony Kokker, Y Koopmans, Erki Kurrikoff, Peter Kim Laustsen, Edward Le Fannu, Bert Leunis, Juha Levo, Marge Lilane, Paul Logman, Richard Mace, Annette Magnusson, Kari Makelainen, Reinhard Mandl, Roberto Manfredi, Ulf Marsen, Alan Martin, Blanche Massey, Roy & Susan Masters, Kristina Mazeikyte, Marjo Meijer, G J Mensink, Gunnar Merbach, Thomas Molnard, Martin Moore, R Morris-Jones, Sally Murphy, J. Mussche, Ludwig Naf, Chloe Newnham, Monique Nomen, Lawrence O Shea, Peter Ogan, Martin Oliver Anders Paalzow, John Patrick, Eduardo Peris, Robertas Pogorelis, James Potter, Ian Prosser, Ieva Pudane, Peter Purland, Brandon Pustejovsky, Suzanne Ravenhall, Thadeusz Rawa, Louise Robinson, Jaroslaw Rudnik, K T Saar, Rhys Sage, Fiona Sanders, Wendy Scaife, Jacco Scheffer, Peter Scheidegger, Frede Scheye, Ursula Schmidz, Sara Schneider, John Segars, Jonathan Seglow, Yury Shatz, Sarah Shey, Tiana Sidey, Mariella Smith, Terry Smith, Anthony Snieckus, Vic Sofras, Johan Sundblad, Laurens Swinkels, Veiko Taavere, David Thomas, Emily Vaivars, Kieran Vaivars, Juha Valimaki, Edwin & Marlies van der Zande, Raf Vermeyen, Diana Walker, Viktor Weisshaupl, Philipp Wendtland, D E Wickham, Maarten Wijnen, Tracey Willmott, Andreas Wocko, Brian Worsley, Whui Mei Yeo, Oliver Zoellner.

# Foreword

## ABOUT LONELY PLANET GUIDEBOOKS

The story begins with a classic travel adventure: Tony and Maureen Wheeler's 1972 journey across Europe and Asia to Australia. There was no useful information about the overland trail then, so Tony and Maureen published the first Lonely Planet guidebook to meet a growing need.

From a kitchen table, Lonely Planet has grown to become the largest independent travel publisher in the world, with offices in Melbourne (Australia), Oakland (USA), London (UK) and Paris (France).

Today Lonely Planet guidebooks cover the globe. There is an ever-growing list of books and information in a variety of media. Some things haven't changed. The main aim is still to make it possible for adventurous travellers to get out there – to explore and better understand the world.

At Lonely Planet we believe travellers can make a positive contribution to the countries they visit – if they respect their host communities and spend their money wisely. Since 1986 a percentage of the income from each book has been donated to aid projects and human rights campaigns, and, more recently, to wildlife conservation.

Although inclusion in a guidebook usually implies a recommendation we cannot list every good place. Exclusion does not necessarily imply criticism. In fact there are a number of reasons why we might exclude a place – sometimes it is simply inappropriate to encourage an influx of travellers.

## UPDATES & READER FEEDBACK

Things change – prices go up, schedules change, good places go bad and bad places go bankrupt. Nothing stays the same. So, if you find things better or worse, recently opened or long-since closed, please tell us and help make the next edition even more accurate and useful.

Lonely Planet thoroughly updates each guidebook as often as possible – usually every two years, although for some destinations the gap can be longer. Between editions, up-to-date information is available in our free, monthly email bulletin *Comet* (W www.lonelyplanet.com/newsletters). You can also check out the *Thorn Tree* bulletin board and *Postcards* section of our website, which carry unverified, but fascinating, reports from travellers.

**Tell us about it!** We genuinely value your feedback. A well-travelled team at Lonely Planet reads and acknowledges every email and letter we receive and ensures that every morsel of information finds its way to the relevant authors, editors and cartographers.

Everyone who writes to us will find their name listed in the next edition of the appropriate guidebook. The very best contributions will be rewarded with a free guidebook.

We may edit, reproduce and incorporate your comments in Lonely Planet products such as guidebooks, websites and digital products, so let us know if you don't want your comments reproduced or your name acknowledged.

**How to contact Lonely Planet:**
Online: e talk2us@lonelyplanet.com.au, W www.lonelyplanet.com
**Australia:** Locked Bag 1, Footscray, Victoria 3011
**UK:** 10a Spring Place, London NW5 3BH
**USA:** 150 Linden St, Oakland, CA 94607

# Introduction

Estonia, Latvia and Lithuania are three small but remarkable countries. Their story is one of centuries of struggle to assert their own idiosyncratic identities, which sparkle brilliantly today.

Dismissed for decades as 'confetti states' on the edge of the Baltic Sea, Estonia, Latvia and Lithuania burst onto the world scene almost from nowhere in the late 1980s as leading players in the break-up of the Union of Soviet Socialist Republics (USSR), of which, the world learned, they had been unwilling members since the 1940s. Previously, for most people, they had been no more than semimythical places that existed in an old atlas or in a grandparent's stamp collection.

A decade on, these proudly independent Baltic countries have shed their Soviet heritage and postcommunism pains, and are locked in a future set firmly in Europe. They hosted the Eurovision Song Contest in 2001 and 2002, and by 2004 all three countries should be fully fledged members of the European Union (EU), thus resolving an age-old question of identity that has haunted them for centuries. Until then, they remain dramatically poised on the edge of Europe, wedged between Scandinavia, Central Europe and the rest of the former Soviet Union.

Cobbled streets, chocolate-box collections of brightly painted houses and a trio of medieval Old Towns sufficiently historic to be included on Unesco's World Heritage list are among the huge trove of treasures that Estonia, Latvia and Lithuania and their capital cities offer. Northernmost Tallinn is an enchanting mix of church spires and turrets, reflected in its summertime white nights and in the sparkling waters of a bay that spills into the Gulf of Finland; a rash of tiny islands pinprick the city's shores and Helsinki is but a short ferry ride away. In Vilnius, Lithuania's capital, the grandeur of a Polish past peers out from the streets of a beautiful Old Town – the largest in Eastern Europe and praised as 'the new Prague' by anyone who has explored its fabulous heritage. The

ESTONIA, LATVIA & LITHUANIA

13

skyline of Rīga – the cosmopolitan big boy of the Baltics – crowns the world's best collection of Art-Nouveau architecture, a market housed in WWI zeppelin hangars, and an elegant coastal resort not far away.

Beyond these graceful cities, the Baltic landscape surprises. While rarely spectacular, it has a gentle, rolling beauty that inspires and fascinates the traveller who takes time to discover and understand its subtle nature. Estonian, Latvian and Lithuanian roots lie very much in the countryside and here, amid a kaleidoscope of ever-changing landscape – sand, sea, bog, marsh, delta – are nations with their own languages, customs, and a wealth of colourful, musical festivals to uncover. Whole sweeps of history and a myriad of legends and myths little known outside the immediate region hide behind each castle, folk costume, forest and lake.

The rapid change that has swept through Estonia, Latvia and Lithuania is equally fascinating to witness. Although independence has brought new opportunities for some with talent, initiative and energy, life for many is even tougher than it was under the Soviet Union. Prices have practically reached Western levels, yet pensioners live on a monthly pension of €100 and the average salary in all three countries hovers around €300 a month. Drab Soviet apartment blocks and dirty factories litter city suburbs and the damage done to social harmony by divisive, initiative-sapping methods of political control and heavy immigration from Russia has yet to be completely resolved.

Yet no-one has revolted against changes brought about by independent governments, because Balts now have hope. Impoverished pensioners know that life for their grandchildren in a new Europe will be 10 times better than the life they have had to endure. And for that reason alone, they cherish the freedom that they, and others, fought for so dearly.

# Facts about the Region

## HISTORY

Until the early 20th century, the ethnic identities of Estonia, Latvia and Lithuania were denied or suppressed. They emerged from the turmoil of WWI and the Russian Revolution as independent countries and enjoyed two decades of statehood until WWII, when all three fell under Soviet influence. Occupation by Nazi Germany in 1941 was followed by Soviet reconquest and the region was forcibly merged with the Union of Soviet Socialist Republics (USSR). In 1991, Estonia, Latvia and Lithuania again won independence.

Ethnically speaking, Latvians and Lithuanians are closely related. The Estonians have different origins, with closer linguistic links to Finland than to their immediate Baltic neighbours. However, in terms of the history of the past 800 years or so, Latvia and Estonia have more in common with each other than with Lithuania.

Lithuania was once a powerful state in its own right – at its peak in the 14th to 16th centuries – but Latvia and Estonia were entirely subject to foreign rule from the 13th to the early 20th century. For much of this time the southern part of modern Estonia and most of modern Latvia were governed as one unit called Livonia. Latvia was not thought of as a political entity in its own right until the 19th century. By the late 18th century the entire region had fallen under Russian rule. Until emancipation in the 19th century, most of its native people had been serfs for centuries.

## Beginnings

**Arrival** Human habitation in the region goes back to at least 9000 BC in the south and 7500 BC in the north. The first forebears of the present inhabitants were Finno-Ugric hunters from the east, who probably reached Estonia and parts of Latvia between 3000 and 2000 BC. Their descendants – the Estonians and now almost-extinct Livs – are related to other Finno-Ugric peoples such as the Finns, Lapps and Hungarians (see Population & People in the Facts about Estonia chapter). The ancestors of the modern Lithuanians and Latvians – known as Balts – probably reached the area from the south east some time around 2000 BC.

**12th-CENTURY TRIBES**

*Approximate Distribution of pre-German Tribal Groups, 12th Century AD*

**Outside Contacts** All these newcomers settled down to agriculture. Well before the time of Christ the region became known as the source of amber. In the first few centuries AD, the tribes of the region traded with German tribes and the Roman Empire. Later they traded with (and fought) Vikings and Russians. From the 8th or 9th century the Viking trade route to Russia and Ukraine was along the Daugava River. Russian armies tried to invade Estonia and Latvia in the 11th and 12th centuries but were defeated. Orthodox Christianity, however, did penetrate parts of Latvia and Lithuania from the east.

**Who Was Who** By the 12th century the Finno-Ugric and Baltic peoples in the region were split into a number of tribal groups – all practising nature religions. Of the Finno-Ugric peoples, the Estonians were divided into eight to 12 districts in Estonia, while the Livs inhabited northern and northwestern coastal parts of Latvia. The Balts on the territory of modern Latvia were

## Baltic Lexicon

**Baltic countries** – Estonia, Latvia and Lithuania.

**Baltic states** – a generic term used to refer to the Union of Soviet Socialist Republics' (USSR) Baltic Sea republics of Estonia, Latvia and Lithuania and one which, since independence, has become a misnomer of convenience. It is considered to be horribly outdated and politically incorrect by many. Avoid.

**Baltic region** – the entire Baltic Sea catchment area, of which Estonia, Latvia and Lithuania make up approximately 11%. Finland, Sweden, Denmark, Germany, Poland and the Kaliningrad Region (Russia) are all in the Baltic region – but are not Baltic countries.

**Balts** – a derivative of the Latin (mare balticum) for 'Baltic Sea' (coined by the German chronicler Adamus Bremen in the 11th century), used to describe people of Indo-European ethnolinguistic groups (Latvians and Lithuanians) who settled in the southeastern Baltic Sea area from 2000 BC.

**Nordic countries** – traditionally understood to be Scandinavia and Finland, but seen by many as including Estonia too, as the former Estonian foreign minister pointed out in the newspaper Eesti Ekspress in January 1998. Toomas Hendrik highlighted Estonia's closer historical and cultural ties to Finland than to Latvia and Lithuania, and concluded by saying that Estonia was Europe's 'only postcommunist Nordic country'.

**Post-Soviet countries** – assumed to be an indisputable tag, yet one that the Lithuanian parliament clearly rejected in early 1999 when it urged the North Atlantic Treaty Organization (NATO) not to describe Lithuania as 'former' or 'post-Soviet'. This, the Seimas (Lithuania's parliament) argued, implied that the Baltics legally belonged to Moscow in the Soviet era, as opposed to being 'illegally occupied'.

**Balkans** – absolutely nothing whatsoever to do with the Baltics, beyond the fact that a shocking number of people confuse the two.

---

divided into the Latgals or Letts in the east, who were grouped into at least four principalities; the Cours or Couronians in the west, with five to seven principalities sometimes united under one king; the Zemgals or Semigallians in the centre, again, sometimes united; and the Selonians in the eastern centre, south of the Daugava. The Cours, Zemgals and Selonians were on the fringes of what is now modern-day Lithuania.

Lithuania had two main groups of its own: the Samogitians (or Žeaičiai) in the west and the Aukštaitiai in the east and southeast. In what is now southwestern Lithuania and neighbouring parts of Poland were the Yotvingians or Sūduviai – also a Baltic people – later to be assimilated by the Lithuanians and Poles. A little farther west, between the Nemunas and Vistula Rivers, were the Prussians, the westernmost Baltic people. Other Balts to the east, in eastern Belarus and neighbouring parts of Russia, were already being assimilated by Slavs.

## Germanic Conquest & Rule
**Latvia & Estonia – the Knights of the Sword** The region was dragged into written history by the *Drang nach Osten* (urge to the east) of Germanic princes, colonists, traders,

missionaries and crusading knights. Having overrun Slavic lands in modern-day eastern Germany and western Poland in the 12th century, the Germanic expansionists turned their attention to the eastern Baltic region. Traders visited the mouth of the Daugava River, near Rīga, in the mid-12th century.

Following papal calls for a crusade against the northern heathen, Germanic missionaries arrived in the area but achieved little until Albert von Buxhoevden was appointed Bishop of Rīga in 1201. Bishop Albert built the first Germanic fort in the Baltic region at Rīga, which became the region's leading city, and in 1202 he established the Knights of the Sword – an order of crusading knights whose white cloaks were emblazoned with blood-red swords and crosses – to convert the region by conquest. The invaders gave the name Livonia (after the Liv people) to the area around the Gulf of Rīga and the territories inland from it.

Despite strong resistance, this unwholesome brood had subjugated and converted all of Estonia and Latvia within a quarter of a century – except for the Zemgals and Cours in western Latvia. Southern Estonia fell to the knights in 1217 with the defeat of the Estonian leader, Lembitu. Denmark, an ally of

Bishop Albert, conquered northern Estonia about 1219, landing on the site of modern-day Tallinn. The knights took control of all of Estonia in 1227, having also subdued the Estonian islands in that year. The Livs had been conquered by 1207 and most of the Latgals by 1214.

**Prussia – the Teutonic Order** In the 1220s another band of Germanic crusaders, the Teutonic order, was invited into Mazovia (in modern-day central-northern Poland) to protect it against raids by the Prussians. Founded in Palestine in 1190 as a charitable organisation, the Teutonic order had developed a military character and begun crusading in Europe. Its method of 'protecting' Mazovia was essentially to exterminate the Prussians and to bring in settlers from the German states. The Prussians resisted until 1283, by which time all their lands were in the hands of the Teutonic order. Among the forts the order founded on the conquered Prussian territory were Memel (which is now Klaipėda in Lithuania) in 1252, Königsberg (now Kaliningrad in Russia) in 1255, and Marienburg (now Malbork in Poland), where the order set up its headquarters in 1306. The few Prussians left were eventually assimilated by their conquerors; they ceased to exist as a separate people by the end of the 17th century.

**Final Subjugation of Estonia & Latvia** The Knights of the Sword, meanwhile, had first earned a ticking-off from the pope for their brutality, then, returning laden with booty from a raid into Samogitia in 1236, were attacked and defeated by Zemgals and Samogitians at Saule.

The next year they were compelled to reorganise as a branch of the Teutonic order and became known as the Livonian order. Northern Estonia was returned to Danish rule in 1238. In 1242 the Russian prince Alexandr Nevsky of Novgorod decisively defeated the Livonian knights on (frozen) Lake Peipsi, in eastern Estonia, curbing their eastward expansion. In the 1260s the knights subjugated Courland, undeterred by the Cours' strategy of making a separate peace with the pope. In 1290 they completed the conquest of Latvian territory by defeating the Zemgals. Eventually the Livonian order settled its headquarters at Wenden (now Cēsis in Latvia). All the

native tribes in the area now known as Latvia, with the exception of a few Livs, were assimilated into one group – the Latgals or Letts – by the 16th century.

The peoples of Estonia, meanwhile, continued to rise up in intermittent revolt, the last and biggest of which was the Jüriöö (St George's Night) Uprising of 1343 to 1346. Denmark, unsettled by this, sold northern Estonia to the Livonian order in 1346. This meant that Germanic nobles were in control of the Baltic seaboard from west of Danzig (modern Gdansk in Poland) all the way to Narva in northeastern Estonia. In addition, they controlled territory up to 250km inland, and the Estonian islands. The major gap in their Baltic domain was Lithuania. Protected by forests, the Lithuanians were able to restrict the invaders to a thin coastal strip despite repeated attacks in the 14th century.

**Germanic Rule** The Germanic rulers divided the region into a number of fiefdoms headed variously by the Prussian-based Teutonic order, the Livonian order and their vassals – the archbishop of Rīga; the bishops of Courland (Kurzeme), Dorpat (Tartu) and Ösel-Wiek (western Estonia), who owed allegiance to the archbishop; the bishop of Reval (Tallinn), who didn't – and the sometimes-free city of Rīga.

The Hanseatic League of traders, which controlled commerce in the Baltic and the North Sea, brought prosperity to German-dominated Hanseatic towns like Rīga, Reval, Dorpat (Tartu), Pernau (Pärnu), Windau (Ventspils), Wenden (Cēsis) and Königsberg (Kaliningrad), all on the trade routes between Russia and the West. But the local Finno-Ugric and Balt inhabitants of Estonia and Latvia were reduced to feudal serfs. The indigenous nobility had been wiped out and the new German nobility dominated Estonia and Latvia until the 20th century.

## Medieval Lithuania
**Mindaugas & Gediminas** In the mid-13th century Mindaugas, the leader of the Aukštaitiai, managed to unify the Lithuanian tribes for the first time. He accepted Catholicism in a bid to defuse the threat from the Teutonic order. Lithuania's first Christian buildings were constructed at this time. Neither the conversion nor the unity lasted, however. Mindaugas was assassinated, most probably

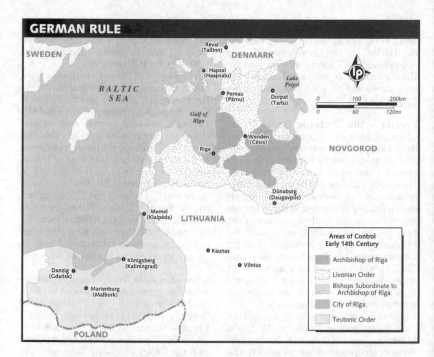

by pagan Lithuanian princes, in 1263, and Christianity was rejected.

Lithuania was reunified in 1290 by Vytenis, who became its grand duke. His brother Gediminas, grand duke from 1316 to 1341, took advantage of the decline of the early Russian state (which had been based at Kyiv) to push Lithuania's borders south and east into Slav-inhabited territory (modern-day Belarus). He invited traders and landowners from around the Baltic region to settle in Lithuania and protected both Catholic and Orthodox clergy. But, like Mindaugas before him, he found his own willingness to accept Christianity opposed by pagan kin. Nor was he able to stop attacks by the Teutonic order.

**Union with Poland**  After Gediminas' death two of his sons shared the realm. Algirdas, based in Vilnius, pushed the southern borders of Lithuania past Kyiv, while Kęstutis, based at Trakai, fought off the Teutonic order. After Algirdas' death in 1377, Kęstutis drove Algirdas' son and successor, Jogaila, from Vilnius and proclaimed himself sole ruler of Lithuania. However, Jogaila captured Kęstutis and his son Vytautas in 1382.

Kęstutis died in prison, some say murdered by Jogaila, but Vytautas escaped.

Jogaila faced conflicting advice from his princes on how to respond to the growing threat from the Teutonic order. The Orthodox among them advised alliance with Moscow, the rising Russian power in the east, and conversion to Orthodoxy, while the pagan princes suggested conversion to Catholicism and alliance with neighbouring Poland. Jogaila's decision to take the latter path was a watershed in Eastern European history. In 1386 he married Jadwiga, crown princess of Poland, forging a Lithuanian-Polish alliance against the German knights. Jogaila became Władysław II Jagiełło of Poland and a Catholic, initiating Poland's 200-year Jagiełłon dynasty and a 400-year bond between the two states – which together became a major power and a rival to the emergent Muscovy. The Aukštaitiai were baptised in 1387 and the Samogitians in 1413, making Lithuania the last European country to accept Christianity. Just a few years earlier, Jogaila's predecessors, Algirdas and Kęstutis, had been cremated according to the practices of the old religion: burnt on pyres with their treasures, weapons, horses and hunting dogs.

**Defeat of the Teutonic Order** Jogaila patched things up with Vytautas, who became Grand Duke of Lithuania on condition that he and Jogaila would share a common policy. Samogitia (occupied by the Teutonic order in 1398) rebelled in 1408, which led to a decisive defeat of the Teutonic order by Jogaila and Vytautas' combined armies at Grünwald (also called Tannenberg or Žalgiris), in modern-day Poland, in 1410.

Kazimir IV of Poland (1447–92), also Grand Duke of Lithuania, went on to reduce the Teutonic order's Prussian realm and to place it under firm Polish suzerainty. In 1525 the order was dissolved by its last grand master, Albert of Hohenzollern, and its lands became his own secular fiefdom under Polish hegemony – the Duchy of Prussia. Its territory was similar in extent to the area inhabited by the old Prussians before the arrival of the order. Its capital was Königsberg, where the Teutonic order's headquarters had been transferred in 1457.

**Lithuanian Expansion** Vytautas (known as 'the Great') extended Lithuanian control farther to the south and east. At the time of his death in 1430 Lithuania stretched beyond Kursk in the east and almost to the Black Sea in the south – the greatest extent it was to reach. Lacking a big population to colonise its acquisitions or the military might to rule by force, Lithuania maintained its territories through diplomacy, allowing conquered lands to keep their autonomy and Orthodox religion.

**Polonisation** Lithuania sank into a junior role in its partnership with Poland, especially after the formal union of the two states (instead of just their crowns) at the Treaty of Lublin in 1569 during the Livonian War with Muscovy, and the end of the Jagiełłon line in 1572. Lithuanian gentry adopted Polish culture and language; Lithuanian peasants became serfs. The joint state became known as the Rzeczpospolita (Commonwealth). The 16th-century religious Reformation sent a wave of Protestantism across the Commonwealth, but this was quickly reversed by the Counter-Reformation, which saw Catholicism gain

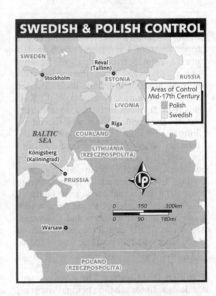

SWEDISH & POLISH CONTROL

ground. Lithuania and Poland remain predominantly Catholic today.

## Swedish, Polish & Russian Rule
**Livonian War** The confederation of all the Catholic, Livonian order and semi-independent towns through which Germans controlled Latvia and Estonia became fatally weakened by the mid-16th century: the Hanseatic League was losing its hold over Baltic commerce; the Reformation threatened the Catholic ecclesiastical states from the 1520s onwards; the Livonian order lost its military strength after the death of its last capable master, Walter von Plettenberg, in 1535; and peasant discontent was growing.

Poland and Lithuania began to cast interested eyes over Livonia and Estonia, but so did other growing regional powers – Muscovy, under Ivan the Terrible, and Sweden. It was Ivan, looking for access to the Baltic Sea, who invaded first. And so, in 1558, began the Livonian War – a 25-year spell of bloodshed, misery and devastation in which Ivan seemingly ravaged, occupied or besieged nearly every town in mainland Estonia and the eastern half of Latvia. Estonia lost two-thirds of its population during this and subsequent wars which lasted until 1629.

The Livonian order, unable to resist the Russian invasion, disbanded. Its territories either sought the protection of neighbouring powers or were battled over by them. Poland-Lithuania fought Russia for Livonia proper (eastern Latvia and southern Estonia), eventually triumphing in 1582 – but not before Ivan had taken, then been expelled from, areas of Lithuania itself. Sweden took 20 or so years to finally expel the Russians from northern Estonia, also acquiring western mainland Estonia and the island Hiiumaa in 1582. The last master of the Livonian order made Courland (western Latvia) and Zemgale (central Latvia) his own personal duchy, owing allegiance to Poland. Even Denmark joined in, taking possession of some ex-church lands in Courland and western Estonia for a while; it held on longest to the island Saaremaa, which was finally transferred to Sweden in 1645. Rīga was independent from 1561 to 1582, then autonomous under Polish rule.

**Swedish Dominance** The Russian menace dealt with for the time being, Protestant Sweden and Catholic Poland-Lithuania settled down in 1592 to fight each other in the Baltic lands. By 1629 Poland had been forced to hand over Rīga and most of Livonia (eastern Latvia and southern Estonia) to Sweden. The only piece of Livonia that stayed in Polish-Lithuanian hands was Latgale, the southeast, which is why Latgale is the stronghold of Catholicism in Latvia today. Sweden successfully defended its gains against Russia and Poland in a couple more wars in the 1650s.

Swedish rule, which consolidated Lutheran Protestantism in Estonia and most of Latvia, is looked back on fondly as it was a relatively enlightened episode in the two countries' long history of foreign oppression. The 17th-century Swedish kings, Gustaf II Adolf and Carl (Charles) XI, tried to raise Estonian and Latvian peasants from serfdom and introduced universal elementary education, translated the Bible into Estonian and Latvian, and founded Dorpat (Tartu) University – but their efforts were severely hampered by frequent wars, plagues and famines.

**Russian Wars** Meanwhile, conflict between Poland-Lithuania and Muscovy continued. Rzeczpospolita forces briefly took Moscow in 1610 and besieged it again in 1617; but in 1654 it was Russia's turn to invade the Rzeczpospolita and take significant territory from it.

Russia finally succeeded in reaching the Baltic shores under its westward-looking tsar, Peter the Great, in the Great Northern War (1700–21), which destroyed Sweden as a regional power. Sweden surrendered its Baltic possessions – Estonia and central and north eastern Latvia – to Russia at the Treaty of Nystad in 1721. The war was another period of devastation for Estonia and Latvia. At the end of it, according to one Russian general, neither bark of dog nor crow of cock could be heard anywhere from Narva to Rīga.

**Prussian Revival** In 1618 Prussia was joined through royal marriage to the powerful north German state of Brandenburg, centred on Berlin. In 1660 Brandenburg purchased suzerainty over Prussia from Poland, and in 1701 the elector of Brandenburg was crowned as the first Prussian king at Königsberg. In the 18th century the Prussia-Brandenburg axis became a major European power, with a military and bureaucratic bent, under Frederick the Great; and cracks appeared in the Polish-Lithuanian Rzeczpospolita, where various factions called in Russian help from time to time.

**Partitions of Poland** Finally the Rzeczpospolita was so weakened that Russia, Austria and Prussia (as the Prussia-Brandenburg state was called) simply carved it up in the Partitions of Poland (1772, 1793 and 1795–96). Most of Lithuania, along with the Polish-Lithuanian possessions Latgale and Courland, went to Russia. A small chunk of western Lithuania went to Prussia, which now stretched uninterruptedly across northern Poland from its original core around Königsberg to its Brandenburg territories.

## The 19th Century

**National Revivals** Russian rule brought privileges for the Baltic-German ruling class in Estonia and Latvia but greater exploitation for the peasants. Finally the Estonian and Latvian peasants were freed, between 1811 and 1819, and were permitted to move freely and own land from the mid-19th century. In Lithuania, which got involved in the Polish rebellion against Russian rule in 1830 to 1831, the peasants were not freed till 1861, the same year as the rest of Russia. Lithuania was also involved in a second Polish rebellion against Russia in 1863. Later, thousands of Lithuanians, and fewer Latvians and Estonians, migrated to the Americas.

The liberation of the serfs enabled the Baltic national revivals of the second half of the 19th century and early 20th century by allowing the native peoples to move into trades, professions, commerce and intellectual circles. In the north the revivals focused particularly around educated Estonians and Latvians at Dorpat (Tartu) University; Vilnius University had been shut down in 1832. Slowly the three native Baltic peoples crawled out from under the doormat of history. They began to express their cultures and senses of nationality; to teach, learn and publish in their own languages; to hold their own song festivals and stage their own plays. Railways were built from Russia to the Baltic ports. By 1914 Rīga had a population of 500,000 and had become an important international port. It also grew, like Tallinn and Narva, into an industrial centre. In Estonia and Latvia there was almost total literacy by 1900.

**Russification** The national movements were strengthened, if anything, by the unpopular policy of Russification that was followed by the Russian authorities, especially towards the end of the 19th century. Estonia, Livonia and Courland were governed as separate provinces, but Lithuania, after the rebellions, was treated as part of Russia itself. Russian law was imposed on the region (as early as 1840 in Lithuania) and the Russian language was used for teaching. Catholicism was persecuted in Latvia and Lithuania. From 1864 books could only be published in Lithuanian if they used the Cyrillic alphabet, while books, newspapers and periodicals in Polish (which was spoken by the Lithuanian gentry) were banned altogether. Lithuanian publishing continued among those living in eastern Prussia (including the first newspaper in Lithuanian) and was smuggled into Lithuania.

## Independence
**Effects of Russian Revolutions** Ideas of Baltic national autonomy and independence were first seriously voiced during the 1905 Russian revolution. When Estonian and Latvian revolutionaries began burning manor houses, there were harsh reprisals, with about 1000 people shot.

During WWI, Germany occupied Lithuania and western Latvia in 1915 but didn't reach Rīga, eastern Latvia or Estonia until late 1917 and early 1918. Baltic nationalists initially hoped the war would bring their nations some kind of improved status within Russia; only with Russia's February Revolution in 1917, which overthrew the tsar, did the idea of full independence really take off. But there were wars and some complicated comings and goings to negotiate first.

In March 1917, Russia passed a bill for Estonian self-government and the first Estonian parliament, the Diet Maapäev, met in July in Toompea Castle, Tallinn. Following the October Revolution in Russia, a communist administration was set up for Estonia, but when the German forces reached mainland Estonia in February 1918, the communists fled. On 24 February the Diet Maapäev declared Estonian independence. Next day, however, the Germans occupied Tallinn. In Lithuania, under German occupation, a Lithuanian national council, the Taryba, had declared independence on 16 February.

In March 1918, Russia's new communist government, desperate to get out of the war, abandoned the Baltic region to Germany in the Treaty of Brest-Litovsk.

**Baltic Independence Wars** On 11 November 1918, Germany surrendered to the Western Allies. The same day, a Lithuanian republican government was set up. In Latvia, peasant, middle-class and socialist groups declared independence on 18 November and the leader of the Farmers' Party, Kārlis Ulmanis, formed a government. The Estonian independence declaration of February was repeated in November. Soviet Russia now launched a military and political campaign to win back the Baltic countries, but this was eventually defeated by both local opposition and outside military intervention – in Estonia's case it constituted a fleet of British ships and volunteer fighters from Scandinavia and Finland. Estonia's prime minister, Konstantin Päts, was able to declare Estonia free of enemies in February 1919.

In Latvia, fighting continued until 1920 between nationalists, Bolsheviks, and lingering German occupation forces and Baltic Germans (under the anticommunist General von der Goltz, who still hoped to bring the Baltic region back under German sway). The Ulmanis government had a communist rival in Valmiera headed by Pēteris Stučka. The Red Army took Rīga in January 1919, and the Ulmanis government moved to Liepāja, where it received British naval protection. In May, von der Goltz drove the Red Army from Rīga but he was then defeated at Cēsis by Estonian and Latvian troops, who drove the Red Army from most of the rest of Latvia. Ulmanis returned to Rīga only to have another army, this time comprised of anticommunist Russians and Germans organised by von der Goltz and led by an obscure adventurer called Pavel Bermondt-Avalov, attack the city in November 1919. The Latvians, however, defeated it, and in December the last German troops left Latvia. The last communist-held area, Latgale, also fell to Latvia.

In Lithuania, things were complicated by the re-emergence of an independent Poland, which wanted Lithuania either to reunite with it or to cede it the Vilnius area, which had a heavily Polish or Polonised population. The Red Army installed a communist government in Vilnius in January 1919, but was driven out of Lithuania by August that year. Polish troops drove the Red Army out of Vilnius on 3–4 January 1919, only for the Red Army to recapture it on 5 January 1919. The Poles occupied the capital for a second time on 19 April, but again were thwarted by the Red Army. Following the Peace Conference of Paris on 1 June 1919, Lithuanian independence was recognised. However, on 9 October 1920 the Poles occupied the city for a third time and on 10 October 1920 annexed Vilnius once and for all. The 'Vilnius issue' was a constant source of Lithuanian–Polish tension. Independent Lithuania's capital was Kaunas. German forces finally left Lithuania in December 1919.

In 1920 Soviet Russia signed peace treaties with the parliamentary republics of Estonia, Latvia and Lithuania recognising their independence in perpetuity.

**The Independence Years** Despite a promising start, the three Baltic republics – caught between the ascendant Soviet Union and, by the early 1930s, an openly expansionist Nazism that glorified the historic German eastward urge – soon lapsed from democracy into authoritarianism. All three republics came to be ruled by regimes that feared the Soviet Union more than the Third Reich. In Estonia the anticommunist, antiparliamentary 'vaps' movement won a constitutional referendum in 1933 but was outflanked in a bloodless coup by Prime Minister Päts, who took over as dictator. In Latvia from 1934, Ulmanis headed a nonparliamentary government of unity which tried to steer between the strong Nazi extreme and the left. Lithuania suffered a military coup in 1926, and from 1929 was ruled by Antanas Smetona along similar lines to Mussolini's Italy.

## WWII & Soviet Rule
**Soviet Occupation** On 23 August 1939, Nazi Germany and the USSR signed the Molotov-Ribbentrop non-aggression pact, which also secretly divided Eastern Europe into German and Soviet spheres of influence. Estonia and Latvia were put in the Soviet sphere and Lithuania in the Nazi one. When Lithuania refused to join the Nazi attack on Poland in September 1939, it was transferred to the Soviet sphere. The USSR insisted on 'mutual-assistance pacts' with the Baltic countries, gaining the right to station troops on their territory. Lithuania's pact regained it Vilnius in October 1939 (the Red Army had taken the city in its invasion of eastern Poland at the same time as Germany had invaded western Poland).

Those Baltic Germans who hadn't left for Germany during the 1920s land reforms departed between 1939 and 1940 in response to Hitler's *Heim ins Reich* (Home to the Reich) summons. By August 1940 Estonia, Latvia and Lithuania had been placed under Soviet military occupation, communists had won 'elections', and the three states had been 'accepted' as republics of the USSR.

The Soviet authorities began nationalisation and purges. Within a year or so of their takeover, according to various estimates, somewhere between 11,000 and 60,000 Estonians were killed, deported or fled; 45,000 Lithuanians suffered the same fate; and in Latvia the figure was about 35,000. Many of the deportees were children or elderly. Many went in mass deportations to Siberia, beginning on 14 June 1941.

**Nazi Occupation** When Hitler invaded the USSR and occupied the Baltic countries in

1941, many in the Baltics initially saw the Germans as liberators. The Nazi-occupied Baltic countries were governed together with Belarus as a territory called Ostland. Some local people collaborated to varying degrees with the Nazi occupation. Some joined in the slaughter of the Jews, gaining a reputation for cruelty at least as bad as that of their German masters. Nearly all of Lithuania's Jewish population – between 135,000 and 300,000 people according to varying estimates – were killed in camps or ghettos. Latvia's Jewish population of perhaps 90,000 was virtually wiped out. An estimated 5000 Jews were killed in Estonia. Thousands of other local people, Jews and those brought from elsewhere, were killed in the Baltic countries by the Nazis and their collaborators.

An estimated 140,000 Latvians, 45,000 Lithuanians and 50,000 Estonians were enlisted in German military units – some voluntarily, some conscripted. Other people were conscripted for forced labour. There was also nationalist and communist guerrilla resistance against the Nazis. Somewhere between 65,000 and 120,000 Latvians, plus about 70,000 Estonians and 80,000 Lithuanians, succeeded in escaping to the West between 1944 and 1945 to avoid the Red Army's reconquest of the Baltic countries. Many others were captured on the way and sent to Siberia. Altogether, Estonia lost something like 200,000 people during the war. Latvia lost 450,000 and Lithuania 475,000.

**Soviet Rule** The Red Army reconquered the Baltic countries, except Courland (which was still in German hands when Germany surrendered in May 1945), by the end of 1944. Many cities were badly damaged in fighting between the advancing Soviet forces and the Nazi occupiers.

Between 1944 and 1952, with Stalin's Soviet rule firmly established, agriculture was collectivised. As many as 60,000 Estonians, 175,000 Latvians and 250,000 Lithuanians were killed or deported between 1945 and 1949, many of them in March 1949 during the collectivisation. Thousands of people – known as 'forest brothers' – took to the woods rather than live under Soviet rule. A few offered armed resistance. They were effectively crushed by 1953, but the last, an Estonian called August Sabe, was not cornered by the KGB until 1978. Sabe

drowned swimming across a lake trying to escape.

With postwar industrialisation, the Baltic republics received such an influx of migrant workers, mainly from nearby regions of Russia, Belarus and Ukraine, that the native Estonians and Latvians feared they would become minorities in their own countries. This further increased the Baltic dislike of Soviet rule. Resentment also grew over issues such as the allocation of housing and the top jobs. Industrialisation shifted the population balance from the countryside, on which the Baltic economies had been based before WWII, to the towns. It helped bring the Baltic countries high living standards, in Soviet terms, but also brought about environmental problems. Religion was repressed and tourism restricted, although Tallinn enjoyed a steady flow of visitors, trade and investment from nearby Finland, a neutral state with a peculiarly close relationship with the USSR. This gained Estonia a reputation as the most westernised of the Baltic countries, both during Soviet rule and in its aftermath.

## Towards New Independence

**First Steps** Through the decades of Soviet rule, the Baltic peoples still hoped for freedom. In the late 1980s, Soviet leader Mikhail Gorbachev began to encourage *glasnost* (openness) and *perestroika* (reconstruction) in the USSR. Pent-up Baltic bitterness came into the open and national feelings surged into mass demands for self-rule.

**The Singing Revolution** The Baltic peoples seriously began to believe in the possibility of independence in 1988. In March some Latvian government members joined a public meeting to commemorate one of the Stalin deportations. Several big rallies on environmental and national issues were held in Latvia, with 45,000 people joining hands along the coast in one antipollution protest. And in Estonia, huge numbers of people gathered to sing previously banned national songs and give voice to their longing for freedom in what became known as the Singing Revolution (see the special section 'The Power of Song'). An estimated 300,000 – about one in three of all Estonians – attended one song gathering in Tallinn. Some 250,000 people gathered in Vilnius to protest on the anniversary of the Molotov-Ribbentrop Pact (23 August).

**Political Steps** Popular fronts, formed in each republic to press for democratic reform, won huge followings. The local communist parties joined them in virtual alliance. Estonia's Popular Front, claiming 300,000 members, called for Estonian autonomy, democracy and cuts in Russian immigration at its first congress in October 1988. All three republics paid lip service to *perestroika* while actually dismantling Soviet institutions. In November 1988, Estonia's supreme soviet (or parliament) passed a declaration of sovereignty, announcing that USSR laws would apply in Estonia only if it approved them.

Lithuania came to lead the Baltic push for independence after its popular front, Sajūdis (The Movement), won 30 of the 42 Lithuanian seats in the March 1989 elections for the USSR Congress of People's Deputies.

On 23 August 1989, the 50th anniversary of the Molotov-Ribbentrop Pact, some two million people formed a human chain stretching from Tallinn to Vilnius, many of them calling for secession. In November, Moscow granted the Baltic republics economic autonomy and in December the Lithuanian Communist Party left the Communist Party of the Soviet Union – a pioneering act which was a landmark in the break-up of the USSR. Equally daringly, Lithuania became the first Soviet republic to legalise noncommunist parties. Estonia and Latvia soon followed.

**Lithuania Declares Independence** Vast proindependence crowds met Gorbachev when he visited Vilnius in January 1990. Sajūdis won a majority in the elections to Lithuania's supreme soviet in February, and on 11 March this assembly declared Lithuania an independent republic. In response, Moscow carried out weeks of troop manoeuvres around Vilnius, then clamped an economic blockade on Lithuania, cutting off fuel supplies. The pressure was finally removed after 2½ months, when Sajūdis leader, Vytautas Landsbergis, agreed to a 100-day moratorium on the independence declaration in exchange for independence talks between the respective Lithuanian and USSR governments. No foreign country had yet recognised Lithuanian independence.

Estonia and Latvia followed similar paths, but more cautiously. In the spring of 1990 nationalists were elected to big majorities in their supreme soviets and reinstated their pre-WWII constitutions, but declared 'transition periods' for full independence to be negotiated. Estonia led the way towards a market economy by abolishing subsidies on some important everyday goods.

**The Events of 1991** Soviet hardliners gained the ascendancy in Moscow in winter 1990–91, and in January 1991 Soviet troops and paramilitary police occupied and stormed strategic buildings in Vilnius and Rīga. Thirteen people were killed in the storming of the Vilnius TV tower and TV centre, five in the storming of the Interior Ministry in Rīga, and hundreds were injured. The parliaments in both cities were barricaded; the people stayed calm; the violence drew Western condemnation of Moscow and the immediate threat subsided.

In referendums in February and March 1991, big majorities in all three states voted in favour of secession from the USSR. However, the West, not wanting to weaken Gorbachev further, gave only lukewarm support to the Baltic independence movements.

Everything changed with the 19 August 1991 coup attempt against Gorbachev in Moscow. Estonia declared full independence on 20 August and Latvia on 21 August (Lithuania had done so back in March 1990). The Western world recognised their independence and so, finally, did the USSR, on 6 September 1991.

On 17 September 1991, Estonia, Latvia and Lithuania joined the United Nations and began taking steps to consolidate their newfound nationhood, such as issuing their own postage stamps and currencies. In 1992 they competed independently in the Olympic Games for the first time since before WWII. The pope visited all three countries in September 1993 but, such landmarks apart, the Baltic countries dropped out of the world's headlines.

After independence, Estonia, Latvia and Lithuania experienced differences over economics and border controls, and the three countries found themselves competing for the same foreign investment and aid. Baltic émigré communities in the West were an important source of investment for all three countries, and influenced politics too. Germany became a big investor, but since the German reunification much investment which might have come to the Baltics has been diverted into the former German Democratic Republic. Estonia's close ethnic, economic and transport links with Finland encouraged a flood of Finnish investment as well as Swedish interest. Latvia looked to Sweden and Denmark. Lithuania took up its old quarrel with Poland where it had left off in 1939, and tried (harder than Estonia and Latvia) to build relationships with the Commonwealth of Independent States (CIS), while also looking to the West. Trade and other forms of cooperation between the Baltic trio, however, have remained relatively minor. Each has its own army and police force, but because of the Baltic region's leaky borders and its location between East and West, smuggling and organised crime dominated by the 'mafias' of the CIS remain a problem.

A general free-trade agreement between Estonia, Latvia and Lithuania was signed in 1993, followed in 1996 by an agricultural free-trade agreement removing all export and import tariffs and quotas on agricultural produce. Free-trade agreements between the former Soviet republics and the European Union (EU) have been effective since 1995.

In 1996 a Russo-US agreement, removing North Atlantic Treaty Organization (NATO) objections to the stationing of 600 Russian tanks and other forces near Baltic borders, caused much resentment within the Baltics. The closure of the Skrunda radar site in Latvia in August 1998 marked the final steps towards ridding the region of the last Russian military personnel stationed on Baltic soil. Latvia formally regained control of Skrunda in October 1999, following which the last remaining Russian 'military experts' left and the site was dismantled.

## Towards Europe
Nervous of Russian sabre rattling and hungry for economic stability, all three Baltic countries are desperate to join NATO and the EU. It is this race towards Europe that prompted the Baltic trio, in the late 1990s, to present a united front to the world at large, thereby dispelling the zealous one-upmanship between the three that marked the immediate postindependence years.

By 1998 the West seemed less concerned about annoying Russia – fiercely opposed to eastward expansion by NATO – than previously, and in January 1998 the USA publicly pledged its support for Estonia, Latvia and Lithuania by signing the US-Baltic Charter of Partnership, in which it gave its support to Baltic integration into Western institutions, including NATO. The three Baltic presidents joined forces again in May 1998 to publicly condemn Russia's political and economic pressure on Latvia, warning it was posing a danger to the region's future unity and integration with Europe. A medal awarded by Latvia to the former Russian president, Boris Yeltsin, for his role in helping Latvia secure its independence was spurned by Yeltsin following Latvia's imprisonment of a former WWII Soviet partisan in January 2000 (see the boxed text 'Purging the Past' later in this chapter).

Estonia kicked off accession talks with the EU in March 1998, with Latvia and Lithuania following suit in October 1999. Full membership for all three should be achieved in 2004 – see the boxed text 'Joining Europe' for more details. The Balts are now busy harmonising their laws with those of Europe. All three countries have addressed the thorny issue of citizenship, abolished the death penalty and are prosecuting Nazi and Soviet criminals (see the boxed text 'Purging the Past'). Estonia and Latvia joined the World Trade Organization (WTO) in 1999, followed by Lithuania in 2001.

The three Baltic countries have also tried to resolve their border disputes, Estonia being the first of the former Soviet republics to finalise border agreements with all of its neighbours (although at the time of writing in late 2002 Russia had still not ratified its 1997 agreement with Estonia). Lithuania is still waiting for the Russian Duma to ratify a border treaty signed by the two countries in 1997 delineating Lithuania's border with the Russian enclave of Kaliningrad and another 50km sea border with mainland Russia.

Lithuania chaired the Council of Europe's Committee of Ministers in 2001 and hosted NATO's spring parliamentary assembly in Vilnius in 2002. At NATO's Prague Summit in November 2002, Estonia, Latvia and Lithuania were formally invited to join the defensive alliance.

## Purging the Past

Local collaboration with Nazi and Soviet occupiers during WWII is being confronted head-on by the Balts, who are prosecuting war criminals. They are the only post-Soviet countries to do so.

Among the first to be tried was Aleksandras Lileikis, former head of Saugumas, the Vilnius security police during the 1941–44 German occupation of Lithuania. The TV images of the feeble 91-year-old defendant appearing in court in 1998, wheelchair-bound and scarcely able to speak, sent shock waves through the international community. Lileikis, who had fled to the US where he remained until 1996 when the US Justice Department stripped him of his American citizenship and expelled him, was accused of turning hundreds of Jews over to Nazi death squads. But his case was dropped a year later after the courts ruled him medically unfit to stand trial. He died in 2000.

Another war criminal, Kazys Gimzauskas, who worked beneath Lileikis as deputy commander of the Vilnius security police, was the first to actually be found guilty (of genocide) in 2001. But following his conviction, the courts ruled the 93-year-old pensioner medically unfit for imprisonment or other sentence.

Lithuanian Antanas Gudelis, a resident of Scotland and member of the 2nd Lithuanian Police Battalion during WWII, did not even make it to court. In 2000 the Scottish authorities ruled him unfit for trial and refused to extradite him; he died two months later.

Neighbouring Estonia has succeeded in doling out one prison sentence. In 1999, 79-year-old Mikhail Neverovski, an Estonian citizen and former KGB agent, was sentenced to four years' imprisonment for his role in deporting 300 Estonians to Siberia in 1949 under the Soviets. Every other decrepit collaborator tried by Estonian courts, however, has been given a suspended sentence.

Ironically, the biggest trial ever in Baltic history, which saw some 4000 witnesses give evidence and took three years to complete, was of Soviet hardliners who stormed the Vilnius TV tower in 1991. In August 1999, leaders of the Lithuanian Communist Party, 59-year-old Juozas Jarmalavičius and his 71-year-old counterpart, Mykolas Burokevičius, were sentenced to eight and 12 years in prison respectively. Four other defendants were jailed for three to six years.

Purging the past of their war criminals remains a painful and controversial process for the Balts. This was dramatically demonstrated in the Kalejs case in 2000, which saw the Latvian government refuse to prosecute 86-year-old Konrad Kalejs, accused of killing thousands of Jews, yet – in the same breath – condemn 77-year-old WWII Soviet partisan, Vasily Kononov, to six years in prison. This was slammed as blatantly hypocritical by Russia and international critics alike.

On no less a serious note, the Balts' singing talents are making Europe sit up and take note. Mocked in music circles it might be, but the kitsch Eurovision Song Contest – hosted by Tallinn in 2002 and Rīga in 2003 – has served as billion-dollar publicity campaigns for the relatively unknown countries. The €8.2 million alone it cost Tallinn to host the show was a small price to pay for bringing small Estonia to the attention of 166 million TV viewers worldwide, not to mention the €5 million of business generated in the capital by the event.

## GEOGRAPHY

It's tempting to sum up the geography of the Baltic countries in two words: small and flat. From the northernmost point of Estonia to the southern tip of Lithuania the distance is only 650km. As for altitude, the land rarely rises much above 300m: Estonia, Latvia and Lithuania's highest points are Suur Munamägi (318m), Gaizinkalns (312m) and Juozapinė (294m) respectively. Parts of Latvia are below sea level.

The coastal regions are the lowest-lying. The whole of western Estonia and most of the Zemgale region of central Latvia are below 50m. Lithuania has a wide central lowland belt, running from north to south and up to 80km across. The low-lying regions are generally the most fertile. However, there's more of geographical interest than these basic facts suggest. The coasts vary from cliffs to dunes to low-lying marshy margins. Inland, the landscape is gently rolling as a result of deposits left behind on the bedrock of the North European Plain by the glaciers that covered the region before about 12,000 BC. The region is crossed by many rivers, some of

## The Baltic Sea

The Baltic Sea is very low in salt as seas go, being fed by so many rivers and with only one narrow, shallow opening to the North Sea (between Denmark and Sweden – a factor which also makes it relatively tide-free). The Baltic is a very young sea. It attained its present character only about 6500 years ago.

The Scandinavian ice sheet of the last ice age covered the whole Scandinavian-Baltic region as far south as the Polish-German coast until about 12,000 BC. The melting of the southern part of the ice sheet created what was the Yoldia Sea. By about 7500 BC, this body of water stretched from the North Sea across southern Sweden, southern Finland and most of the present Baltic region (except the Gulf of Bothnia between Finland and Sweden), and along the Gulf of Finland to Lake Ladoga, east of St Petersburg.

By about 6500 BC, with the ice sheet almost completely melted, water levels dropped. This left a land bridge between Sweden and Denmark/Germany and, behind it, a freshwater 'lake' (Ancylus Lake). This roughly covered the present area of what we now know as the Baltic Sea. The land bridge was breached around 4500 BC, opening up the Baltic region to the open sea once more.

At that time nearly all of the Estonian islands and the western Estonian mainland, along with a slice of Latvia's west coast, were still under water. The earth's crust here has been gradually rising ever since – hence the proliferation of very low-lying islands off Estonia's coast and the flat, low nature of western Estonia. Currently the rate of rise is about 3mm per year (about 1m every 350 years). Local tour agencies like to encourage visitors to keep returning the following year as there will always be more of Estonia to see!

The Baltic Sea is called Läänemeri (Western Sea) in Estonian, Baltijas jūra in Latvian, Baltijos jūra in Lithuanian, and Baltiyskoe More in Russian.

---

which have cut surprisingly deep valleys, and is dotted with thousands of lakes and a range of vegetation.

Estonia, Latvia and Lithuania enjoy about 5000km of coastline between them, the majority of it (3794km) being around the indented fringes of Estonia's mainland and islands. Some stretches of coast are low-lying, reedy and wet – the kind of place where it's hard to tell where land ends and sea begins. There are also lengths of cliff or steep bank, over 50m high in parts, and long stretches of dunes often fronted by sweeping, sandy beaches and covered with pine woods. These create a really refreshing fragrance in combination with the salty sea air.

Little of this coast faces the open Baltic Sea, as much of it fronts the Gulfs of Finland and Rīga or is protected from the open sea by islands. Incredibly, while Estonia boasts over 1000 islands, Latvia and Lithuania have absolutely none. The most extraordinary feature of the coastline is the Curonian Spit, a sand bar 98km long and up to 66m high, but nowhere more than 4km wide.

Something the Baltic trio doesn't lack is lakes. There are around 9000 of them according to some counts, though the distinction between a lake and a pond must be hard to make in some cases! Most of the lakes are small and shallow, and Latvia and Lithuania have the greatest numbers of them, especially in their southeastern and northeastern uplands, respectively. Estonia has the largest lakes: Lake Peipsi (3555 sq km, of which 1529 sq km are in Estonia), which accounts for 54% of the total area of Estonia's inland waters, and Lake Võrtsjärv (271 sq km).

Lots of rivers wind their way across the land. The two biggest, both flowing in from Belarus, are the Daugava (1005km), which crosses Latvia from the southeast to enter the sea near Rīga, and the Nemunas (937km), which crosses southwestern Lithuania then forms the Lithuanian border with the Kaliningrad Region (Russia) for its final 100km or so to the Curonian Lagoon. Other major rivers include the Narva, which flows north from Lake Peipsi to the Gulf of Finland and forms the Estonia-Russia border; the Gauja, looping 452km entirely within eastern Latvia; and the 346km-long Venta, rising in Lithuania and entering the sea in western Latvia.

Not surprisingly in such a low-lying region, there are a lot of bogs, swamps, fens and marshes. These occupy as much as one-fifth of Estonia and one-tenth of Latvia, though you see little of them as you travel

## Amber Trail

Amber was formed in the Baltic region 40 to 60 million years ago. Yet it was not until the mid-19th century that the trail for the region's so-called 'Baltic gold' really began.

An organic substance rather than a mineral, the golden 'stone' that sparkles in sunlight is in fact fossilised resin. During the subtropical climes of the early Cenozoic era, the vast pine forests of Fennoscandia (later to be engulfed by the Baltic Sea) secreted rivers of resin, entombing and preserving insects along the way. Fifteen years later, this sticky resin became buried by ice – kilometres thick – and it was not until the warming of the earth's atmosphere millions of years later that 'Baltic gold' came to light once more.

Early humans used amber as heating fuel (it burns extremely well). In the Middle Ages it was used as cash. For the tribal Prussians inhabiting the southeastern shores of the Baltic Sea around 12,000 BC, rubbing amber was the best way to generate static electricity (hence its ancient Greek name, *elektron*). During the 12th century, this sunny stone was said to contain mystical qualities – amber worn next to the skin helped a person become closer to the spirits. Perhaps not surprisingly, the German crusading Knights of the Teutonic order, who took over the Baltic region in the 13th century, claimed amber as their own; yet they too failed to understand just where and how much more Baltic gold could be found.

Between 1854 and 1855 and in 1860 substantial amounts of amber were excavated close to the shores in Juodkrantė, on the Curonian Spit in western Lithuania. Three separate clusters weighing 2250 tons were uncovered during the 'amber rush' to the sleepy seashore village, yet by 1861 its source had dried up, leaving treasure seekers to find their fortune elsewhere. Since 1869 amber has been mined at the Yantarny amber mine in the Kaliningrad Region of Russia – the source of most amber sold in the Baltics today.

Ironically, 1998 saw treasure seekers trail Juodkrantė's shores once more, this time in search of the legendary Amber Room, a magnificent room made up of 10,000 panels of carved, polished amber (55 sq metres) that was given to Peter the Great by the Prussian king in 1716. For decades opportunists have been trying to track down the missing panels that graced the Catherine Palace near St Petersburg until 1942 when invading Germans plundered the jewel and shipped it either to Königsberg (Kaliningrad) or, as the mayor of Neringa told the world in 1998, to the shores of the Curonian Lagoon, where wartime residents allegedly saw the SS burying large crates. Predictably, the search yielded few results, hence the unsolved mystery regarding the Amber Room's fate.

Amber pieces come in a variety of shades and sizes; some are heated and compressed, which combines small pieces into bigger ones. Old-fashioned ways of treating it include boiling in honey to make it darker, or in vegetable oil to make it lighter. Pieces with 'inclusions' (some would say 'imperfections') such as grains of dirt or vegetation inside are more likely to be original and may be more valuable. The most sought-after pieces are those containing Jurassic Park–style insects. Rīga's A&E gallery, Vilnius' Amber Gallery-Museum and the Amber Gallery in Nida in western Lithuania (see Shopping in the respective destination chapters) design and sell interesting and unique, quality pieces of amber jewellery.

The region's best collection of amber, with dozens of impressive insect inclusions, is in the palace-museum in Palanga's botanical park in western Lithuania. The 14,478-piece exhibition is the world's sixth-largest collection of Baltic amber in the world – those in London's Natural History Museum, Warsaw's Earth Museum and St Petersburg's Zoological Institute (25,000 pieces a piece) are the largest.

those countries' roads. They're a useful resource, especially for their peat.

## GEOLOGY

Amber (fossilised tree resin, millions of years old) has been a source of Baltic prosperity since the earliest times. Five centuries before the birth of Christ it was valued by the ancient Greeks for its medicinal and semimagical properties, and it commands high prices still. Mined from deposits in Estonian and Latvian peat bogs, it remains fairly plentiful. Other geological 'assets' have proved a mixed blessing. Both Estonia and Latvia have large deposits of oil shale, a sedimentary rock rich in hydrocarbons. Opencast shale mining scars the landscape in several places, and the use of oil as a power-plant fuel causes severe air pollution. Meanwhile, offshore oil deposits detected close to the Latvian and Lithuanian coasts in the early 1990s remain a source of friction between the two countries, causing disagreement over coastal borders and undersea mineral rights. The resultant maritime boundary agreement drawn up between the two countries in 1998 remained unratified in 2002.

## CLIMATE
The Baltic climate is temperate, but on the cool and damp side. It verges on the continental as you move inland where, in winter, it's typically 2°C to 4°C colder than on the coasts but in summer may be a degree or two warmer. From May to September, daytime highs are normally between 14°C and 22°C. It's unusually warm if the temperature reaches the high 20s. July and August, the warmest months, are also wet, with days of persistent showers. May, June and September are more comfortable, but late June can be thundery. At these northern latitudes days

are long in summer, with a full 19 hours of daylight at midsummer in Estonia. April and October have cold, sharp, wintry days as well as mild springlike or autumnal ones.

In winter, November to March, temperatures rarely rise above 4°C and parts of the region may stay below freezing almost permanently from mid-December to late February. Winter hours of daylight are short, and sometimes it never seems to get properly light at all. The first snows usually come in November, and there's normally permanent snow cover from January to March in coastal regions – but up to an extra month either side in the inland east. In some coastal areas, some recent winters have been much milder, with no lasting snow cover. Slush under foot is something you have to cope with in autumn, when snow is falling then melting, and spring, when the winter snow cover is thawing.

Annual precipitation ranges from 500mm to 600mm in the lowland areas to 700mm to 900mm in the uplands. About 75% of it usually falls as rain, 25% as snow. Winters can be foggy.

Coastal waters average between 16°C and 21°C in summer – July and August are the warmest months. The Gulfs of Finland and Rīga freeze occasionally, and the straits between Estonia's islands and the mainland usually freeze for three months from mid-January. The open Baltic Sea coast almost never freezes.

## ECOLOGY & ENVIRONMENT
Although it is being curbed, pollution remains one of the disturbing legacies of the Soviet period. Upgrading or replacing sources of pollution – especially sources of power – remains a problem, however. Estonia has stopped mining its large phosphorite reserves, but the continued mining of oil shale – 9.97 million tons were extracted countrywide in 2000 compared with 17 million in 1992 – in the northeast and its use as a fuel for thermal power plants in Narva continues to generate 95% of Estonia's hazardous waste. Municipal waste is an equally dirty business – the average Estonian generates 350kg of waste a year. The Butinge oil terminal near the Latvian Coast in Lithuania remains an environmental thorn for Latvia and Lithuania alike (see Ecology & Environment in the Facts about Lithuania chapter).

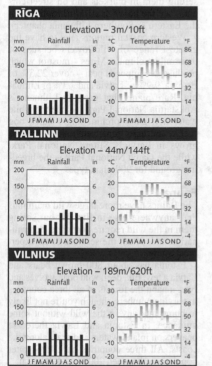

## Clean Beaches

Twenty-seven criteria must be met to get a European Blue Flag (W www.blueflag.org), awarded each year to clean, safe beaches and marinas in Europe. In 2002 the Baltic region scored 12 flags. In Estonia, beaches in Pärnu, Võsu and Pühajärve (near Otepää) were given the thumbs up, as were Lohusala, Pärnu and Romassaare marinas. In Latvia, Jūrmala's sandy Majori and Bulduri beaches, Ventspils beach and marina, and the beach in Liepāja were proclaimed suitably swimworthy; while the central beach at Nida in western Lithuania was awarded a blue flag.

Though the Baltic Sea as a whole is getting cleaner, virtually all Estonian, Latvian and Lithuanian coastal waters are polluted – partly by chemical pollution washing out from rivers and partly by untreated sewage pumped straight into rivers or the sea. Incredibly, the biggest city in the region, Rīga, lacked any kind of modern sewerage system until 1991. Today Rīga has a treatment plant but it can only handle 80% of the city's sewage. Tap water in many parts – including Rīga – is still reportedly tainted by chemical as well as organic pollutants (see under Health in the Regional Facts for the Visitor chapter). Raising the quality of drinking water to EU norms is the goal of a project that will see €106 million pumped into the system by 2010. Sweden has pledged to cooperate with Latvia on a number of environmental projects between 2002 and 2004, including the construction of new wastewater treatment plants in Rīga, Jūrmala, Daugavpils and Liepāja.

Many rivers and ground waters are polluted by industrial wastes, fertilisers and pesticides. In Estonia the Pühajõgi River, which flows through the industrial northeast, is the country's most polluted river. The Nemunas River in Lithuania is among Europe's most polluted rivers.

## FLORA & FAUNA
### Flora
Large portions of the region are forested: 44% of Estonia, 44% of Latvia and 30% of Lithuania. Pine accounts for up to half of the forest cover and is concentrated nearer the

coasts, while inland forests are more often mixed. Birch is the most common deciduous tree. Juniper shrubland is characteristic of parts of Estonia, especially the islands and western mainland. Alvar, a unique habitat of plant communities found on limestone, is common to northern Estonia and to most of its islands.

Northern Vidzeme and northern Kurzeme are the most forested parts of Latvia. The country's oldest forest, in Kurzeme's Slītere National Park and protected since 1921, is a broad-leaf forest with a calcium-rich bog and several rare orchids. This national park alone protects 23 forest types and three types of swamp. In Lithuania, the south – particularly the southwest – is the most densely forested area.

A favourite forest recreation of the local people is gathering the many edible mushrooms and berries that grow in the south in late summer and autumn; you'll see people laden with them returning from the countryside on weekend buses and trains and selling them in markets and on street corners (see the boxed text 'Mushrooming' in the Eastern & Southern Lithuania chapter).

Western coastal regions tend to have the greatest range of wildflowers because of their milder climate. Mires – most of which produce decomposed peat – cover 22.3% of Estonia, 9.9% of Latvia and 7.3% of Lithuania. Rare plants that grow in Lithuania's Aukštaitija National Park include the white water lily, ghost orchid, single-leafed bog orchid and hairy milk vetch. The yew tree grows in Latvia's Slītere National Park, while the Gauja National Park is the breeding ground for 900 plant types.

### Fauna
The Baltics have more large wild mammals than anywhere else in Europe, but seeing them in the wild requires patience, determination and, often, the services of an expert local guide.

Estonia has about 800 brown bears and Latvia a few. Elk, deer, wild boar, wolves and lynx inhabit the forests of all three countries in varying numbers, though you're not likely to bump into any in the wild without some guidance. In Estonia and Latvia there are beavers on inland waters and seals along the coasts. All three countries have large otter populations, between 2000 and 4000 each.

## Storks

The start of spring is marked by the arrival of the majestic stork, which jets in for the summer from its winter home in Africa.

The height of sensibility, this bird of passage usually settles back into the same old nest that it has summered in for years. Large and flat, the nest is always balanced high in the sky – in a tree or straddling a disused chimney or telegraph pole. Some are splayed out across wooden cartwheels, fixed atop tall poles by kindly farmers keen to have their farmstead blessed by the good fortune that the stork is believed to bring. Lithuanians celebrate the stork – one of their national symbols – with Stork Day (25 March), the day farmers traditionally stir their seeds, yet to be planted, to ensure a bigger and better crop.

Measuring some 90cm in height, this beautiful long-legged, wide-winged creature is a breathtaking sight in flight. Equally marvellous is the catwalk stance adopted by this elegant bird when strutting through meadows in search of frogs to feast on. When sleeping, it stands on one leg.

White storks abound in Latvia, home to 6500 breeding pairs. Lithuania, with approximately 13,000 pairs, can lay claim to Europe's highest density of storks. In western Lithuania's Nemunas Delta Regional Park alone, more than 1000 pairs of storks nest each year. By contrast, the rare black stork numbers just seven pairs.

The world's stork population is estimated to be around 166,000 breeding pairs.

Estonia's animal populations include 40,000 deer (of which 10,000 are shot by hunters annually), 400 wolves (also widely culled), 900 lynx (more than in the whole of Western Europe put together), 2600 beavers, 10,000 wild boar (5000 are shot a year) and several thousand elk. It is possible to spot 48 types of mammal in Latvia's Gauja National Park. South of Liepāja, Latvia's branch of the Worldwide Fund for Nature (WWF) has reintroduced konik horses – descendants of the wild horses that once roamed free in Europe – on abandoned farmland around Lake Pape. The organisation's future plans also include releasing European bison and wild cattle into the habitat.

Some of Estonia's islands and coastal wetlands and Lake Žuvintas in southern Lithuania are important breeding grounds and migration halts for water birds. Latvia and Lithuania harbour notably more white storks than in the whole of Western Europe, while the rarer black stork nests in western Lithuania's Nemunas Delta Regional Park and Latvia's Gauja National Park. The eagle owl and white-backed woodpecker – rare in the rest of Europe – also nest in abundance in the latter. For more on storking, see the boxed text 'Storks'.

One species that you're likely to encounter everywhere during the summer months is the mosquito.

## National Parks

There are four national parks in Estonia (total area 120,400 hectares), 58 nature reserves and 255 parks, landscape reserves and other protected areas. By contrast, Latvia has four nature reserves, 240 protected areas and three national parks. Lithuania boasts the highest percentage area of protected territory (some 11% of total), reaping the rewards of five lovely national parks (152,300 hectares), including western Lithuania's Curonian Spit National Park, which is a Unesco-declared World Heritage site, five nature reserves and 394 areas under varying degrees of control.

National parks protect areas of natural, historical, architectural and archaeological importance. Some parts are strict reserves, off limits to everyone except a few specialists, but recreation is encouraged in other sectors. They are all partly inhabited and can be reached by public transport. Most have efficient visitor centres which advise on accommodation possibilities within or around their territory and run nature walks, bird-watching trips and other activities aimed at helping visitors to learn about the park's flora and fauna.

Nature reserves tend to be more remote, harder to reach and less accessible in terms of structured information in English.

Detailed information on individual national parks and nature reserves is included in the Facts about Estonia, Latvia and Lithuania chapters, and the regional chapters.

## All the President's Men & Women

Latvian president Vike-Freiberga (W www.president.lt) and her Lithuanian counterpart until early 2003, Valdas Adamkus (W www.president.lt), marked a new breed of Baltic president. Educated wholly in the West with a lifetime spent outside their land of birth, they embody all that most only dream of a future tied firmly to Europe and the West. Predictably, both bear a chequered past, as eclectic and volatile as their countries' histories.

Politically independent Vaira Vike-Freiberga (1937–) ran for presidency within 24 hours of losing her Canadian citizenship. Born in Rīga, she left Latvia on 31 December 1944, aged seven. She spent her childhood in refugee camps in Germany, her adolescence in Morocco, and her adult years in Canada. Following a glowing career in academia, this multilingual psychology professor returned to Rīga in 1998 as director of the Latvian Institute. A year on, aged 61, Vike-Freiberga became president of Latvia. She also became the first female head of state in post-Communist Europe.

Ousted from his presidential chair by a man 30 years his junior, Kaunas-born Adamkus (born 1926) fled Lithuanian with his family in 1944 and later emigrated to the USA. He climbed from car factory worker to senior official in the US Environmental Protection Agency in the 1970s, returned 'home' in 1998 to retire, and served as president from 1997 until early 2003.

## GOVERNMENT & POLITICS

Estonia was the first to hold elections under its own system, in 1992. It was followed later that year by Lithuania and by Latvia in June 1993. Since then, the political situation has remained fluid (as it has in most post-Soviet countries in Eastern Europe), with a plethora of nationalist parties, social democrats, reformed postcommunist parties (now avowing commitment to democracy and the free market), and a host of splinter groups appealing for votes in each country. None has been able to win a convincing electoral mandate and overall parliamentary majority, and coalition governments seem likely to dominate Baltic politics for the foreseeable future.

A major bone of contention within the Baltic political arena in recent years is the sensitive question of how each of the three countries treat their substantial Russian-speaking minorities, especially in Estonia and Latvia where there's substantial Russian-speaking communities. With EU accession just around the corner, however, it seemed that by 2002 all three countries had addressed the citizenship issue to the satisfaction of the local Russian and international community alike. For more details, see Government & Politics in the Facts about Estonia, Latvia and Lithuania chapters.

The elections of an American-Lithuanian president in Lithuania and a Canadian-Latvian in Latvia in the late 1990s marked a watershed in Baltic politics as electorates opted for a new 'foreign-bred' brand of president. See the boxed text 'All the President's Men & Women'.

All three Baltic presidents are charting a rigorous course towards EU accession. See the boxed text 'Joining Europe' for details.

## ECONOMY

The painful postindependence years, which saw Estonia, Latvia and Lithuania move from a centralised to market economy, have finally paid off for the three Baltic countries, which today enjoy healthy economies characterised by fully stable currencies and low inflation (2.1%, 3.3% and 5.8% in Lithuania, Latvia and Estonia). By 2002 they ranked among the fastest-growing economies in Central and Eastern Europe, with real GDP growth in 2001 clocking in at 5.4% in Estonia, a record 7.6% in Latvia and 5.9% in Lithuania. All three economies were well on target for their country's entry into the EU in 2004 – an achievement that will yield massive financial benefits for the region. See the boxed text 'Joining Europe' later in this chapter for more details.

Achieving this economic stability has been no mean feat for the Balts. As part of the USSR, many Balts enjoyed a higher living standard during the USSR-era than they do today. Hopes for a rapid transition after independence from Soviet-style prosperity to Western standards of living were dashed by the collapse of the Soviet rouble (wiping out most people's meagre savings), runaway

## Joining Europe

The driving force behind Baltic politics is membership of the European Union (EU) in 2004, a step that will yield massive financial benefits. At the time of writing, accession negotiations were yet to be completed, but the Latvian Foreign Ministry, for example, reckons on paying €118 to €128 million into the EU pot a year – and getting out €261 to €447 million a year. Nevertheless, the overwhelming fear for the person on the street is that consumer prices will soar.

The three countries applied for EU membership in 1995 and negotiations began three years later (four and five years later for Latvia and Lithuania, respectively). The harmonisation of local legislation with EU directives is a vast task. Thirty-one chapters addressing everything from agriculture and transport to education, energy and industrial policy must be resolved prior to accession; the basic premise being that applicant countries accept EU law. Lithuania must close both nuclear reactors at Ignalina by 2009 if it wants to join the EU. By mid-2002, Estonia and Latvia had each closed 24 of the 31 chapters opened, and Lithuania 26.

Of the 12 candidate countries currently in negotiations with the EU, the Balts rank among the poorest. Estonian/Latvian/Lithuanian GDP per capita is just 37/28/31% of the current EU average.

Countries can apply to adopt the euro two years after accession – although the strict economic criteria required suggests that the Balts might be keeping their national currencies beyond 2006.

For more information, contact the **Office of European Integration in Tallinn** (☎ 693 52 00; ☎ info@eib.ee; ⓦ www.eib.ee; Tönismägi 2); the **European Integration Bureau in Rīga** (☎ 728 79045; ☎ info@eib.lv; ⓦ www.eib.lv; Basteja bulvāris 14); or the **European Commission Delegation Information Center in Vilnius** (☎ 5-231 4707; ☎ infocentre@eudel.lt; ⓦ www.eudel.lt; Naugarduko gatvė 10).

inflation that topped 1000%, and a harsh introduction to the downside of consumer capitalism – soaring unemployment, plummeting purchasing power, and an end to the rudimentary but universal Soviet social welfare system. The collapse of Latvia's largest commercial bank, Banka Baltija, and the ensuing bank crisis in 1996 – which again wiped out thousands of people's savings – fuelled further turmoil in the region. And in 1998 the region's young and floundering economy was hit by the Russian financial crisis.

The three Baltic countries flexed their muscles fairly successfully to weather the financial storm that ripped across the entire region and battered most of the other post-Soviet economies. Economic restructuring has followed a broadly similar path in all three countries: gradual privatisation of state-owned businesses, property and land; removal of state subsidies to industry, agriculture and consumers; and agreements on economic austerity with the International Monetary Fund (IMF), World Bank and other international financial bodies to attract vital foreign loans and investment. Free economic zones (FEZ) offering foreign investors lucrative tax breaks have been established in all three countries:

Lithuanian FEZ embrace Kaunas and Klaipėda; Estonia has FEZ in Valga and Varu in southeastern Estonia, where unemployment is very high, and in the industrial town of Sillamae in northeastern Estonia; and in Latvia there are special economic zones (SEZ being the Latvian equivalent) in Liepāja and Rēzekne and free ports (which are likewise exempt from tax) at Ventspils and Rīga.

Economic miracles aside, life remains tough for an enormous number of Balts. An estimated one-third of households live below the official poverty line, with average monthly salaries remaining low: €365, €277 and €284 respectively in Estonia, Latvia and Lithuania in 2002. Estonian/Latvian/Lithuanian pensioners struggle to make ends meet on €103/99/93 a month.

The three countries are generally short on natural resources, except for timber. Estonia and Latvia have useful reserves of peat in their bogs, and Estonia has oil shale. Lithuania has an oil refinery and some oil reserves, but virtually all oil and gas has to be imported.

For details on the more recent economic development of each Baltic country, see Economy in the Facts about Estonia, Latvia and Lithuania chapters.

## POPULATION & PEOPLE

In 2002, Estonia had 1.36 million people, Latvia 2.36 million and Lithuania 3.6 million – figures which, since independence, have fallen at a rate that demographers describe as concerning. The natural emigration of Russians back to Russia, coupled with deteriorating living conditions and a disproportionate decrease in the number of women of child-bearing age, account for the region's shrinking – and ageing – population. The ratio of children and teenagers to adults dropped by 10% in the last decade (from 22.8% of the total population in 1990 to 17.8% in 2000).

Ethnic identity remains a sticky issue. In both Latvia and Estonia, ethnic Estonians and Latvians are barely in the majority (65.5% and 57.7% respectively), although Lithuanians in Lithuania rank strongly at 82%. For more on what 'Estonian', 'Latvian' and 'Lithuanian' mean, see Population & People in the Facts about Estonia, Latvia and Lithuania chapters. Other ethnic groups present in smaller numbers include Poles, Jews, Roma, Tatars and Germans (in Lithuania), as well as nationals of the former Soviet Union.

Prior to WWII, Russians only numbered about 8% in Estonia, 10% in Latvia and 3% in Lithuania. Their large numbers today – 28% of the population in Estonia, 29.6% in Latvia and 8% in Lithuania – are a result of immigration during the Soviet period, when many came to work in the new industries being set up in the Baltics. This ethnic Russian population is congregated mainly in the large cities, forming 47% of Tallinn's population, 43.7% in Rīga (compared with 41.2% Latvian) and about one-fifth of Vilnius. The industrial towns of northeastern Estonia and Latgale in Latvia are overwhelmingly Russian, notably Narva and Daugavpils, where Russians form 92.5% and 55.1% of the population respectively. Latvians are a minority in Latvia's seven largest cities.

In order to gain citizenship, non-native residents in Latvia and Estonia are required to learn the local language and pass language and history tests. Lithuanians, with a smaller Russian minority in their midst, don't have the understandable fear of being swamped that Estonians and Latvians feel, hence Lithuania's citizenship policy is more relaxed. Citizenship requirements for each of the three countries are outlined under Population & People in the Facts about Estonia, Latvia and Lithuania chapters.

Somewhat disturbingly, the suicide rate in Lithuania and Estonia has soared by 70% and 46% respectively since independence, making Lithuania's suicide rates the highest in Europe and the two countries among the world's most suicidal nations. Official statistics show that 1533 people in Lithuania – 44 in every 100,000 – committed suicide in 2001. Estonia and Latvia were not far behind with, 33 and 34 respectively out of every 100,000 (compared with 11 in 100,000 in the UK and the US, and an average of 16 in the world). Over 80% of Lithuanian suicides are committed by men and more than half are believed to be alcohol-fuelled – hence the country's recent crackdown on the sale of alcohol and public drinking (see Legal Matters in the introductory Facts for the Visitor chapter).

The difference in life expectancy between men and women is likewise substantially higher than the European norm: Baltic men on average live 10 years less than Baltic women (compared with seven or eight years less in most other countries). Divorce rates have also soared in recent years (to more than 60% in Latvia); more than one-third of children are born out of wedlock.

Before WWII two-thirds to three-quarters of the population of Estonia, Latvia and Lithuania lived in the countryside; today only a quarter to one-third live outside the main cities.

### Lost People

The history of these Baltic countries in the 20th century is studded with groups of people who have disappeared. Emigration for pure economic reasons apart, war, Nazi and Soviet terror, and Soviet deportations have all caused horrifying drops in the countries' populations at various times. Estonia's population fell from 1.14 million in 1939 to 854,000 in 1945; Latvia's from 2.5 million in 1914 to 1.6 million in 1920; and Lithuania's from 3.1 million in 1940 to about 2.5 million in the mid-1950s.

In WWII the Nazis exterminated virtually all the Jews in the region. Estimates vary, but they range between 135,000 and 300,000 Jews killed in Lithuania, 90,000 in Latvia, 5000 in Estonia.

The Baltic Germans, the upper class who dominated Estonia and Latvia for centuries, left for Germany in the mid-1920s when they lost most of their lands in agrarian reforms and in 1939 to 1940 when they were summoned 'home' by Hitler. They had numbered a few tens of thousands. Estonia lost virtually its whole Swedish population of about 8000 when they left for Sweden in 1943 to 1944 under an agreement with the German occupiers.

Some 220,000 Poles, including most of the educated ones, left or were deported from Lithuania to Poland between 1945 and 1958. Those 'Poles' who stayed in Lithuania were mostly Belarusian speakers living in rural areas with Polish Catholic churches – nearly all in the two southeastern districts of Vilnius and Salčininkai. They became the focus of controversy when their regional councils were accused of supporting the August 1991 coup attempt in Moscow and collaborating with the KGB. The Lithuanian parliament imposed direct rule on the two districts in September 1991, dissolving the two regional councils, which caused tensions in Lithuania's relations with Poland. New councils were elected to office in 1993.

## ARTS

Few Baltic artistic figures or works, past or present, are internationally known. Until the 19th century, Estonian, Latvian and Lithuanian cultures were largely foreign-dominated, and when they did emerge in their own right in the 19th and 20th centuries, they remained, with some exceptions, isolated by geographical, linguistic or political barriers or by their chiefly local relevance.

## Folk Culture

Native folklore survived centuries of foreign dominance, thanks largely to a rich oral tradition of songs, verses and chants on subjects like the seasonal cycle, farming and the land, family life, love and myths. It's widely thought that women composed most of these. The Latvian and Lithuanian verses, known as *dainsa*, are often short and poetic and have been compared with the Japanese haiku. The oldest Estonian song type, going back to the first millennium BC, is the *runic* chant, based on lines of eight syllables with a theme gradually developing from line to line. *Runic* verses are still sung at weddings on the island of Kihnu.

In the 19th century, great collections of folk lyrics and tunes were made by people like Krisjānis Barons in Latvia and Jakob Hurt in Estonia; over 1.4 million folk lyrics and 30,000 tunes have been written down in Latvia alone. There's much interest in folk rhymes and music today, with numerous societies and groups devoted to them, but they're also a living tradition with regional variations. Particularly unusual are chants of the Setumaa region in the southeast of Estonia and those known as *sutartinės* in northeastern Lithuania.

More immediately impressive, and evidence of the age-old power of song in the Baltic cultures – although centred more on 19th- and 20th-century songs than the oldest traditions – are the national song festivals that played a great part in awakening national feelings in the 19th century and keeping them alive in the Soviet period. The independence fervour of the late 1980s was christened the Singing Revolution in Estonia because of its song festivals (see the special section 'The Power of Song').

## Music & Dance

Opera bigwigs in Latvia include Jāzeps Vītols (1863–1948), who founded the Latvian National Opera; and the contemporary Andrejs Žagars, who played a major role in the revival of that same opera in the mid-1990s. In Lithuania, composer Kęstutis Antanėlis wrote the first Lithuanian rock opera in 1982.

Drama played a part in the 19th-century national revivals, and Rīga was the preeminent performing arts centre before WWI and between the world wars. Its ballet, which produced Mikhail Baryshnikov among other notables, goes back to the 1920s and was one of the best in the Soviet Union.

Rock and pop thrives, arguably at the expense of the classical performing scene, which was state-funded but has been horribly strapped for cash since independence. Both Estonia and Latvia host big annual rock festivals (see Public Holidays & Special Events in the Facts for the Visitor chapters for these countries), and there are jazz clubs galore in the Lithuanian capital. The region's best-known composer is Estonian Arvo Pärt, who writes mainly choral works; as does the lesser-famed, Estonian composer Velijo Tormis. Musicians-turned-politicians

## Gregarious, Glum & Greatly In-Between

It is always dangerous to generalise about national characters, but there are some clear general differences between Estonians, Latvians and Lithuanians.

Estonians and Lithuanians are usually seen as the two extremes, with Latvians somewhere in between. The stereotypical Estonian is reserved, efficient, short on praise, and polite. Lithuanians are stereotypically more gregarious, welcoming and emotional – and place greater emphasis on contacts and favours than method and calculation.

The independence campaign of the late 1980s and early 1990s puts the contrast in a nutshell. In Lithuania this was romantic, daring, cliffhanging and risky, with at least 20 deaths. In Estonia it was cool, gradual, calculated and bloodless, leading to the unkind saying that 'Estonians would die for their freedom – to the last Lithuanian'. Latvia's path to independence lay, typically, somewhere between the two extremes.

The three countries' introduction of new currencies to replace the Soviet rouble after they gained independence likewise varied enormously. Estonia brought in its *kroon* cleanly, efficiently and with minimum fuss over a single weekend in mid-1992. Not only that, the Estonian government was then smart enough to secretly (and illegally) sell the 70 tons of Soviet rouble banknotes it withdrew from circulation, reportedly to Chechnya for US$1.9 million! Latvia introduced its *lats* gradually in 1993 after an intermediate phase with a transitional currency called the Latvian rouble. Lithuania had to undergo two sets of transitional banknotes, a succession of postponements, and the sacking of the head of the national bank, before its *litas* finally appeared in June 1993. Then the notes had to be reprinted all over again because they were too easy to forge!

But with a much smaller Russian minority in their midst than Latvia or Estonia and a grander history behind them, Lithuanians seem to have a greater confidence in their national identity – and are all the more fun for it! Of the three Baltic countries, it is the only one where its toppled Lenin is still displayed in its full glory, albeit in a Soviet sculpture park in the backwaters of southern Lithuania. In contrast, authorities in Latvia and Estonia keep the communist's whereabouts a closely guarded secret. Likewise, the unveiling of a memorial statue to the American rock singer Frank Zappa, legendary for his antiestablishment songs, or the proclamation of a republic in the capital, is something that only the Lithuanians would dare do.

Bureaucracy certainly seems its most Byzantine in Latvia, where armed Guards of Honour still stand, as rigid as stone, in front of the freedom monument in Rīga from sunrise to sunset come rain,

include acclaimed pianist and independence leader, Vytautas Landsbergis, in Lithuania; and Raimonds Pauls, in Latvia. Pauls composed pop hits during the Soviet era, served as culture minister in 1989 and went on to form the politically centrist New Party and run for president in the late 1990s. Another interesting name to look for is Lithuanian composer Bronius Kutavičius (born 1933), who fuses modern, classical and folk traditions in his music.

Latvia's surprise victory in the 2002 Eurovision Song Contest – all the more remarkable given that Latvia didn't qualify originally (it only took part after Portugal dropped out) – proved once and for all to the world that the Balts' singing revolution and previous Estonian victory in the 2001 Eurovision Song Contest were not one-off events: Balts really can sing.

Eurovision-type pop and dance music remain the dominant force in the Baltics' young music scene, where ground-breaking rap and hip-hop have yet to make much noise. The somewhat-mocked song contest was won by Estonian duo Tanel Padar and Dave Benton in 2001 and by Marija N, a Rīga Russian soloist, in 2002. Marija N had released several albums prior to her Eurovision victory with the Latin-inspired *I Wanna*, as had Estonia's female soloist Sahlene, who came third in 2002. Lithuania's original Eurovision hopeful, boy band B'Avarija, was disqualified after prereleasing its song *Mes Cia (We All)* on its new album *Is Visos Sirdies* (2001). Another promising voice to listen out for is 15-year-old Estonian soloist Kerli Ko, winner of the 2002 Fizz Superstar, a Baltic song contest sponsored by Universal Records.

## Gregarious, Glum & Greatly In-Between

hail or 10 feet of snow. Following the example set by the enterprising, predominantly Russian population (in Rīga at least), Latvians have perhaps the best-developed entrepreneurial sense of the three peoples. Given the ethnic tensions that run equally high between Latvians and Russians, however, it is fair to say that Latvians are also the least at ease with foreigners.

Some people find the Estonian reserve frustrating. An invitation to an Estonian's home – unless you're a relative – is a rare treat. But such an attitude can also be seen as an admirable form of self-reliance. Certainly the Estonian modesty and embarrassment about advertising is a joy to anyone who likes to make up their own mind about where to stay, eat and so on. You'll hardly ever find anyone trying to pressure you into some particular choice.

There are some traits that all three peoples share. One, which many visitors find disconcerting, is the outwardly glum, pessimistic, sometimes brusque bearing of many people. This can be put down to at least three things. One is that life has never been easy for the majority of people in this part of the world. Another is the weather – long, dark, cold winters never make anybody very happy (there's a marked brightening of everybody's mood in spring and summer). A third factor is the legacy of the Soviet era, when trust in strangers could be risky.

But in happy contrast to all this – and all the more pleasing because of it – you'll find that once you break the ice, people are often only too pleased to do what they can to help a visitor.

A powerful trait the Baltic peoples share is a very strong feeling for their land; even those who live in cities frequently abandon them to visit family, friends or their own cottages in the country. The universal custom of taking flowers when visiting someone's home is one reflection of this love of nature. Flower stalls and markets are in every town, often open ridiculously late, and travellers nurture bunches of blossoms for hours and hours on crowded buses in order to present them to their host upon arrival.

The strong attachment to local roots and traditions is, perhaps, also a cause of the Baltic peoples' surprisingly sparse contact with each other. Although the outside world tends to think of the three Baltic countries as one combined group, each is actually very much its own little world. There are obviously neighbourly connections between the three countries, but it is a good deal less common than at first you might expect for Estonians, Latvians and Lithuanians to speak each other's languages; do business with each other; or visit, have friends in – or even know much about – each other's countries.

---

For more on the arts and culture of each Baltic country, see the Facts about Estonia, Latvia and Lithuania chapters. For more on traditional song and music, see the special section 'The Power of Song'.

## Literature

Baltic literature draws heavily on the rich folklore heritage of each of the native peoples. Modern Estonian and Latvian literature got going with the writing of national epic poems in the mid-19th century – *Kalevipoeg* (Son of Kalev) in Estonia and *Lāčplēsis* (The Bear Slayer) in Latvia. These epic poems were based on legends and folk tales which had been part of the oral tradition over preceding centuries. The giants of 20th-century literature in these countries are the Estonian novelist Anton Hansen Tammsaare (1878–1940) and the Latvian poet and playwright

Jānis Rainis (1865–1929), who spent much of his life in exile in Siberia and Switzerland for his trenchant criticisms of tsarist social and political oppression. He has been compared with Shakespeare and Goethe. More recently, Estonians Jan Kross, a novelist, and Jaan Kaplinski, a poet, have received international acclaim.

The first major fiction in Lithuanian was the poem *Metai* (The Seasons) by Jonas Mačiulis (1862–1932), describing the life of serfs in the 18th century. Jonas Mačiulis, known as Maironis, is regarded as the founder of modern Lithuanian literature for his poetry written early in the 20th century. Lithuania also shares the credit for some major Polish writers who grew up in Lithuania, including contemporary Nobel laureate Czesław Miłosz.

In the Soviet years many leading writers and artists went into voluntary or forced exile and most other talent was stifled. In the post-Soviet era, the cultural scene has changed so fast and there has been such a flood of outside influences that writers, artists and musicians in all three countries seem to have been somewhat stunned, with many still struggling to assimilate their new freedoms.

The literature of each of the Baltic countries is discussed in more detail in the Facts about Estonia, Latvia and Lithuania chapters.

## Visual Arts

The art scene is pretty active in the region and there are lots of galleries and museums in the capital cities displaying past and present art, although few Baltic artists have caused a stir internationally.

There was a flowering of many national artists around the turn of the 19th century, under Western influences like impressionism, which was followed by decades of experimentation and uncertainty in the early 20th century and forced conformity in the Soviet era. Like some other art forms, the visual arts initially struggled to find new directions after the Soviet straitjacket, which shaped their approach for so long even in rebellion, had been removed.

Lithuania in particular has a thriving visual arts scene, epitomised by the tongue-in-cheek Republic of Užupis proclaimed by bohemians living in the artsy quarter in 1998. Only Lithuanians would be bold enough to turn sessions of NATO's spring parliamentary assembly, hosted in Vilnius in 2002, into a visual arts object – encasing the proceedings in glass walls so that the public could view what was happening. Outside the capital, contemporary art installations by Baltic artists are displayed at the Centre of Europe Museum, the highlight being the world's largest TV sculpture – a maze of 3000 second-hand TV sets which leads to a statue of Lenin when followed to the bitter end – by Lithuanian sculptor Gintaras Karosas. As with many works conceived by the region's artists today, it is the Baltics' Soviet past that inspired the work: the TV maze portrays the absurdity of Soviet propaganda transmitted by TV and communism's ultimate burial by the Balts.

Across the region, some good modern work is in the field of applied art and handicrafts, often influenced by folk art.

## SOCIETY & CONDUCT

Postindependent Estonia, Latvia and Lithuania are young societies in every sense of the word. Large chunks of all three economies are in the hands of pushy young men (mostly, as this is still a very male-dominated society) with mobile phones and smart German cars. A few of the older generation even look back with a certain nostalgia to the Soviet era when a certain equality of poverty prevailed. Some business visitors find the young dynamos obnoxiously cocky, but there's no doubt that youth lends the Baltics energy.

That said, most people are quite formal – it takes a while to get onto first-name terms. Don't expect big smiles all round – but don't mistake a reserved attitude for indifference or hostility. Estonians are especially poker-faced – one national motto goes: 'May your face be as ice'. At the other extreme, Lithuanians are seen by other Balts as hot-headed, romantic and unpredictable, while Latvians are reported to be warmer than Estonians but more cool-headed than Lithuanians (see the boxed text 'Gregarious, Glum & Greatly In-between' earlier).

## Dos & Don'ts

Baltic people do not greet each other with a hug or kiss. Men always shake each other's hands and some women will shake hands too. Flowers are a universal greeting, but only give odd-numbered bouquets as even-numbered offerings (including a dozen red roses!) are for mournful occasions. If you are invited to a private home, take flowers or a bottle – but never money – as a gift for your host. Take your shoes off when you enter and do not shake hands across the threshold. Do not whistle inside either. Both actions bring bad luck and will be severely frowned upon.

Muttering just a few words in the local language will raise instant smiles. In Latvia and Lithuania, speaking Russian as a foreigner is generally (but not always) acceptable. In Estonia, you should try every other language you know first – be it English, German or Finnish – as speaking Russian can be met with a hostile response, or no response at all.

Prostitution is rife in the capitals, particularly in Rīga. Prostitution is illegal in Estonia and Lithuania. In Latvia, it is legal but 'taking advantage, for purpose of enrichment, of

## Easter Traditions

Traditionally, Shrove Tuesday, falling seven weeks before Easter, was always celebrated in Estonia, Latvia and Lithuania. It marked the end of a harsh Baltic winter and was a day for baking pancakes and barley bread in preparation for the strict Lenten fast to follow. Cattle, penned up all winter, would be let loose to run free in the fields. In Estonia, the remains of the Christmas *kringel* bread would be fed to the cows to fortify them for the coming season. In all three countries, children would go on long sled rides; the longer their journey the taller the flax would grow that year. In Lithuania, doing the washing or dragging a block of wood on a rope also contributed to a better harvest.

Today in Estonia and Latvia the traditional food is still shared at the table, although in Estonia cream-filled buns seem to have usurped the more meagre flour-and-eggs diet. In Lithuania, the much-loved tradition of parading through the streets in a masked disguise in return for sweets and small gifts is still very much alive. Accompanying the masked revellers in the carnival is the traditional *Morė*, an effigy dressed in women's clothes and dragged along, fixed to a cartwheel. In Vilnius, the *Morė*, symbolising winter, is still taken to the top of Taurus Hill and set alight.

Easter itself is very much an 'egg holiday' for all three Baltic countries, although if you're hoping for a commercially wrapped chocolate egg in a flash cardboard box, forget it. The age-old tradition of hard-boiling eggs and then painting or dying them a rainbow of colours is an integral part of the Balts' Easter celebrations. Friends, families and work colleagues exchange painted eggs with great enthusiasm. Various egg games are always played, ranging from the smash and run variety to playing boules with them down a hill.

In Estonia and Latvia, the Easter Bunny has hopped his way into town since the 16th century. In Lithuania, the Easter Granny arrives on her horse made from wax, pulling a cart filled with eggs, which she hides in the trees. By sunrise she has gone (her horse would melt otherwise).

person engaged in prostitution' is punishable by up to four years in prison. Incidents do occur where Western clients are drugged, robbed and left lying in the gutter – literally. For your personal safety and for the sake of the young girls at hand, often forced by their parents to work the streets, it is better not to engage in this activity.

Women should refrain from wearing revealing clothing as this can attract undue attention.

## Treatment of Animals

Limited hunting of species including the brown bear, wolf and lynx is, very sadly, permitted and could pose a threat to their future, especially if it continues to not be strictly regulated (see Fauna under Flora & Fauna earlier in this chapter).

## RELIGION

After decades of persecution and discouragement under Soviet rule, religion – which chiefly means Christianity – enjoys full freedom again and is currently experiencing a revival. It was an important element in the national independence movements of the 1980s and '90s.

The leading faith among Estonians is Lutheranism, although they are a rather irreligious people – no more than 30% adhere to any specific religious conviction. Lutheranism is also the leading faith among Latvians but there's a significant Roman Catholic community too, especially in Latgale, the southeastern region. Lithuanians are mostly Roman Catholics and are more enthusiastic about their creed than the Lutherans to their north. The Catholic Church generally is a conservative force in Lithuanian society. Russian Orthodoxy is the faith of most Russian believers throughout the region, which makes it important in places with big Russian populations such as Tallinn, northeastern Estonia and several Latvian cities. There are also, particularly in Lithuania, some Old Believers – a schismatic sect of the Russian Orthodox church which has come in for intermittent persecution since it rejected a number of church reforms back in the 17th century.

Many customs and beliefs connected with the land and the seasons survive – perhaps most notably the 23 June midsummer celebrations (see Public Holidays & Special Events and the boxed text Midsummer

## Paganism vs Christianity

Czech bishop Albert Waitiekus, the first Christian missionary to venture into the Baltics, came here at the end of the 10th century. Unfortunately for him, he wandered into a forest dedicated to pagan gods and was killed – leaving paganism to run rife in the region for another two centuries.

Quite a lot is known about the pre-Christian religions of the Latvians and Lithuanians, who shared similarities as members of the Balt group of peoples. Less is known about the religion of the old Estonians, who came from the entirely different Finno-Ugric religious tradition.

Paralleling the importance of Latvian and especially Lithuanian among Indo-European languages, the old Latvian/Lithuanian religion apparently shares many similarities with Vedic ideas from India and beliefs from ancient Iran. There are also similarities between the metric structure of the Baltic folk rhymes known as *dainas* and the verses of the old Indian sacred text the *Rig Veda*.

To the old Latvians and Lithuanians the sky was a mountain and many of the leading gods lived on it, among them: Dievs the sky god, Saule the sun god (a female), Perkūnas (Latvian: Pērkons) the thunder god, who was particularly revered, and Mēness the moon god. There was also an earth mother figure called Žemyna in Lithuania and Zemes māte in Latvia. In Latvia the Christian Virgin Mary has many of the attributes of Žemyna, and the two figures seem to be combined in the mythological figure of Māra. Also important were Laima the goddess of fate, the forest goddess (Meža māte in Latvia, Medeinė in Lithuania), and the guardian of wizards and sages (Latvian: Velns; Lithuanian: Velnias), who was transformed into the devil in the Christian scheme of things. Many lesser deities presided over natural phenomena and objects, or human activities.

Today, there are still pagans in the Baltic region who adhere to this system of belief. In Latvia, there is just a handful of pagan followers known as *Dievturība* (literally 'holding the Gods'). However, in Lithuania it is a different story. Lithuania was the only part of Europe not Christianised by the end of the 12th century and existed as the last European stronghold of paganism until 1385. Today, the pagan gods are enjoying a marked revival in worshippers.

The Romuva movement has congregations in Vilnius, Kaunas (a membership of some 200) and among Lithuanian communities in Canada and the USA. It is named after an ancient temple site near Chernahovsk (in today's Kaliningrad Region) that attracted Lithuanian, Latvian and Prussian worshippers alike prior to Christianity's arrival in the Baltics. The movement works towards rekindling Lithuania's ancient spiritual and folklore traditions. Romuva (W www.romuva.lt) was founded as an organised pagan revival movement in 1967, was banned under the Soviet regime in 1971, and was revived again under the jurisdiction of the 'Society for Ethnic Lithuanian Culture' in 1988.

Madness' in the introductory Facts for the Visitor chapter).

Orthodoxy made some inroads into the region from the Slav regions to the east before Catholicism took over from the west in the 13th and 14th centuries (after desultory efforts since the 10th century). The brutal conversion of Estonia and Latvia by German crusaders, as well as the atheist influences of the Soviet period when even Christmas celebrations were banned for a long time, make it hardly surprising that support in those countries for the Lutheran Church, to which the German ruling class turned with the Reformation in the 1520s, is still lukewarm. Lithuania fought off the German knights but its leaders eventually accepted Catholicism as part of the deal with Poland which led to the knights' long-term defeat. Still, as late as 1377 and 1382, the Lithuanian princes Algirdas and Kęstutis were cremated in rituals of the old religion – dressed in silver and gold and burnt on pyres with their treasures, weapons, horses and hunting dogs.

The Reformation that swept across Europe in the 16th century triumphed in Estonia and most of Latvia, where Lutheranism became established under German or Swedish rule. But Catholicism survived in Lithuania and Latgale, controlled by Poland. The local churches – Lutheran and Catholic – endured oppression under Russian rule in the 19th century as well as in the Soviet periods.

# Facts for the Visitor

## HIGHLIGHTS

Savouring the bright white nights Estonia shares with St Petersburg; scouring the Baltic coastline for amber; scaling the sand dunes of Nida; and sampling the local cuisine, including Lithuania's infamous Zeppelin, Latvia's disgusting black Balzāms or Estonia's sickly sweet Vana Tallinn – these are but some of the joys the Baltic countries offer.

Vilnius has Eastern Europe's largest old town, a bohemian republic, the unmatched church of SS Peter and Paul's with its thousands upon thousands of stuccoed statues, a statue of Frank Zappa and a TV tower you can bungee jump from. Rīga has the world's finest collection of Art-Nouveau architecture, a central market housed in six WWI zeppelin hangars and one of the cheapest (drinkable) champagnes around the globe. Elegant Estonia, meanwhile, has a coastline studded with 1521 beautiful islands and inland bogs to explore.

In all three Baltic countries, while their Soviet past has been well and truly dumped, quirky reminders of former Soviet days have been rekindled: a Soviet sculpture park; retro nightclubs; the world's largest TV sculpture, portraying Soviet propaganda's insanity; an underground Soviet missile base; and an antenna that poked its nose into Western satellite communications during the Cold War, are all part of the act. It's all a Baltic show that should not be missed.

## SUGGESTED ITINERARIES

Here are some suggested itineraries ranging from a week-long stay to an enviable, one-month stint.

**One week** A whistlestop tour of the three capitals, Vilnius, Rīga and Tallinn

**Two weeks** A whistlestop tour of the three capitals, with a couple of day trips to the Lithuanian, Latvian or Estonian coast; the Gauja National Park in Latvia, the islands or the Lahemaa National Park in Estonia, or the Nemunas Delta Regional Park in Lithuania

**One month** Vilnius to Nida, via Klaipėda and the Curonian Spit; up to Rīga taking in äiauliai and the Hill of Crosses en route; from Rīga, day trips to Jūrmala and the Gauja National Park; to Pärnu, Haapsalu and across to the Estonian islands; up to Tallinn, with a day trip to Paldiski through the Lahemaa National Park to Narva, and back down the eastern realm through Tartu and Daugavpils to Vilnius

## PLANNING
### When to Go

Summer and spring are far and away the best times of year to visit. The weather is warm, the days are longer and there's an abundance of fresh food in the markets. People seem to smile more, cottage gardens blossom with flowers, and the cultural calendar oozes fun festivals and outdoor events. Baltic summers are short but sweet. July and August, the warmest and busiest months, are also among the wettest and there can be days of persistent showers, particularly in July. May, June and September, while a bit cooler, are often more comfortable.

The spingtime months of April and May in particular convey a real magic; it's when the stork – believed to bring good luck – returns to his nest for another year, and when the land and the people open up after the long, dark winter. June is the month of midsummer celebrations and festivities that bring home the Baltic peoples' close ties to nature and remind us of their pagan past.

Winter (December to February) is very much a second-best season for travellers. Though there'll usually be a picturesque sprinkling (or more) of snow on the ground and in the trees, there may also be only a few hours of semi-daylight every 24 hours. If you dress warmly there's no reason why you can't enjoy ice-fishing and skating on the frozen lakes, tobogganing (wherever you can find a slope), and skiing. Theatre and concert-going peaks in winter.

Wet and soggy March is a month to avoid, as the snow thaws, bringing with it slush galore.

### Maps

Decent regional and country maps are widely available outside the region, as are quality city maps in each country.

**Regional Maps** A map covering the three Baltic countries is useful for planning: *Lithuania Estonia Latvia* (Cartographia;

w www.cartographia.hu), *Estonia, Latvia, Lithuania* (Bartholomew World Map Travel Series; w www.bartholomewmaps.com) and *Baltische Staaten* (Ravenstein Verlag, Bad Soden am Taunas; w www.reisebuch 24.de) are very similar 1:850,000-scale maps of the three countries.

Estonia, Latvia and Lithuania have their own map publishers producing excellent maps and atlases. Estonia's leading map publishers are **E O Map** (☎ 626 6210, 660 4800, fax 646 6216; e eomap@eomap.ee; w www.eomap.ee; Rävala pst 8, EE10143 Tallinn); and **Regio** (☎ 738 73 00, fax 738 73 01; e regio@regio.ee; w www.regio.ee; Riia 24, EE51010 Tartu), with its own **map shop** (Narva maantee 13a; open 10am-6pm Mon-Fri) in Tallinn. Both publishers also issue a regional map, *Baltimaad – Baltic States* (1:1000,000).

In Latvia, map publisher **Jāņa sēta** (☎ 731 75 40; e kartografi@kartes.lv; w www.kartes .lv; Stabu iela 119, LV-1009 Rīga), also with its own **shop** (☎ 709 22 88; e veikals@ kartes.lv; Elizabetes iela 83/85, LV-1050 Rīga; open 10am-7pm Mon-Fri, 10am-5pm Sat), is the market leader. Its pocket-size, spiral-bound, 252-page *Baltic States Road Atlas* (1:500,000) contains 71 city and town maps as well as 24 double-page road maps covering the entire region. Its *Baltic States* (1:700,000) road map is equally indispensable.

In Lithuania, *Eesti, Latvija, Lietuva* (1:750,000), as well as the motoring map *Via Baltica – Baltic States Road Map* (1:1,000,000), with coverage from Helsinki to Warsaw, are recommended. **Briedis** (☎ 5-270 6479, fax 270 6627; e info@briedis.lt; w www.briedis.lt; Parodų gatvė 4, LT-2043 Vilnius) is the publisher. On the Internet, w www.maps. lt is a digital map resource.

**Country, City & Town Maps** The spiral-bound road atlases for Estonia and Latvia published by Regio and Jāņa sēta respectively are particularly useful for anyone exploring the countries by car. Both publishers also produce country-specific road atlases on CD-ROM, with free Web-downloadable upgrades; E O Map, Regio and Briedis each publish a variety of country and city maps for their respective country. But Jāņa sēta is the only Baltic map publisher to produce maps for all three countries, including individual *Eesti, Latvija* and *Lietuva* country

maps (1:500,000) with several city-map insets; and a whole array of top-quality town maps (scale 1:15,000, 1:7000 or 1:25,000), costing between €1.50 and €3.20 each. Jāņa sēta maps are well distributed throughout the region.

With the exception of a couple of detailed national park maps, hiking maps don't exist yet. Jāņa sēta does, however, stock topographical and satellite sheet maps of Latvia, and satellite sheet maps of Estonia – all scaled at 1:50,000. See Maps in the country-specific Facts for the Visitor chapters for more details on these and other map titles.

## What to Bring

Don't bring too much. If you only plan to stay in the larger towns and cities, you can buy anything or everything when you arrive. If you intend travelling around a lot, a backpack is the easiest way to carry your things. A light day-pack is also useful. Unless you plan to camp or sleep out, a sleeping bag is not necessary. A towel and soap will be useful if you're staying in cheap hotels, which don't always provide them. A universal sink plug is very useful (a squash ball suffices just as well), as are an adaptor plug for electrical appliances and a good wad of tissues or toilet paper – to be carried in your pocket at all times.

In summer, bring a light waterproof garment or an umbrella to protect you from the odd shower or three. Cold snaps do punctuate spring and autumn, so bring some warm headgear, gloves, a coat (or at least a warm leather or padded jacket) and either thermal underwear or some very warm trousers. In winter, there are mountains of snow, so bring waterproof boots (equally handy for when that slushy thaw sets in). Your clothing should be able to cope with permanent subzero temperatures, and thermal underwear is essential. Whether it rains, hails or shines, an indestructible pair of shoes or boots tough enough to combat the most invincible of cobblestones and icy sidewalks is an absolute must.

Bring any special medicines you might need. Western toiletries are readily available, although you might want to bring condoms (locally produced condoms are available; quality not guaranteed). A small torch (flashlight) and an alarm clock might also come in handy. In summer bring mosquito repellent or coils. An electric water-heating element will enable you to purify suspect tap water by boiling it and to make your own hot drinks. A Swiss Army Knife never goes astray. If you like your food spicy, bring your own Tabasco sauce.

## RESPONSIBLE TOURISM

Environmental protection was not one of the legacies of Soviet rule. However, ever-swelling tourist numbers coupled with local property development and an increasing drive towards commercialism have finally prompted action to be taken in an effort to protect the region's fragile ecosystems, biological diversity and natural (relatively unspoiled) treasures. Ways to avoid placing pressure on the environment include conserving water and electricity, not littering or burying your rubbish, and taking care not to disturb wildlife. If you intend to camp or hike, seek permission to camp from the landowner or, in the case of national parks and protected nature reserve, only pitch your tent in designated areas. Forests – which carpet both 44% of Estonia and Latvia and 30% of Lithuania – are especially vulnerable. Do not light fires or discard cigarette butts in these areas, and stick to assigned paths. Always observe the rules and regulations set by park and forest authorities.

Erosion and fire pose a huge threat to the unique sand spit and dunes on the Curonian Spit National Park in western Lithuania, prompting Unesco in 2000 to list the spit as a World Heritage natural treasure in need of protection. When walking in the dunes, do not leave existing tracks to blaze a new trail across virgin sand; and avoid removing the plant life that keeps the top sand in place.

The historic old towns of Rīga, Tallinn and Vilnius are also included on Unesco's list of World Heritage cultural and natural treasures. Pay them the respect they deserve.

## TOURIST OFFICES

All three capitals, plus most cities, towns and seaside resorts, sport an efficient tourist office of sorts which doles out accommodation lists and information brochures, many in English. These tourist offices are coordinated by each country's national tourist board, listed under Tourist Offices in the Facts for the Visitor chapter for each country.

Overseas, the three tourist boards are represented by the following, pan-Baltic organisations:

**Finland** (Latvia only, ☎ 09-278 47 74, fax 687 426 50; ℮ latviatravel@kolumbus.fi) Mariankatu 8B, SF-00170 Helsinki

**Germany** (☎ 0251-21 50 742, fax 21 50 743; ℮ info@gobaltic-info.de; W www.baltic-info.de, www.gobaltic.de) Salzmannstrasse 152, D-48159 Münster

**Russia** (Lithuania only, ☎/fax 095-203 6790; ℮ litinfo@gol.ru) Borisoglebskij per 13, Building 2, RUS-16109 Moscow

**USA** (Lithuania only, ☎ 718-281 1623; ℮ latvia travel@kolumbus.fi) 40–24 235th St Ste 100, Douglaston, New York NY 11363

## VISAS & DOCUMENTS

Your number-one document is your passport. Make sure it's valid until at least two months after the end of your Baltic travels.

### Visas

Estonia, Latvia and Lithuania each issue their own visas. However, all three adhere to 'common visa space', meaning – for most Western nationalities at least – if you have a visa for one of the countries, it is good (for the term of its validity) for the other two as well.

All three countries have lengthening lists of nationalities that don't need visas. Citizens of most European Union (EU) and Schengen countries don't need a visa, although it is always wise to check the latest visa developments before leaving home – the websites of the **Ministries of Foreign Affairs for Estonia** (W www.vm.ee), **Latvia** (W www.mfa.gov.lv) and **Lithuania** (W www.urm.lt) are the best sources.

In late 2002, nationalities that could travel visa-free (for most, up to 90 days in a six-month period) included those from the following countries.

**Estonia** Andorra, Australia, Austria, Belgium, Bulgaria, Costa Rica, Chile, Croatia, Cyprus, Czech Republic, Denmark, Finland, France, Germany, Greece, Hong Kong, Hungary (up to 30 days only), Iceland, Ireland (90 days single stay only and no more than 180 days a year), Israel, Italy, Japan, Korea, Latvia, Liechtenstein, Lithuania, Luxembourg, Macao, Malta, Monaco, Netherlands, New Zealand, Norway, Poland (up to 30 days), Portugal, San Marino, Singapore (for 14 days only), Slovakia, Slovenia, Spain, Sweden,

Switzerland, UK (up to six months but not more than 180 days a year), USA, Vatican City

**Latvia** Andorra, Austria, Australia, Belgium, Bulgaria, Canada, Croatia, Cyprus, Czech Republic, Denmark, Estonia, Finland, France, Germany, Greece, Hong Kong, Hungary, Iceland, Ireland, Israel, Italy, Japan, Liechtenstein, Lithuania, Luxembourg, Malta, Monaco, Netherlands, New Zealand, Norway, Poland, Portugal, Romania, Slovakia, Slovenia, Spain, Sweden, Switzerland, UK, USA, Vatican City

**Lithuania** Andorra, Australia, Austria, Belgium, Bulgaria, Canada, Chile, China (up to 30 days), Croatia, Cyprus, Czech Republic, Denmark, Estonia, Finland, France, Germany, Greece, Hong Kong, Hungary, Iceland, Ireland, Israel, Italy, Japan, Kaliningrad Oblast (Russia; up to 30 days), Korea (up to 15 days), Latvia, Liechtenstein, Luxembourg, Macao, Malta, Monaco, Netherlands, New Zealand, Norway, Poland, Portugal, San Marino, Slovakia, Slovenia, Spain, Sweden, Switzerland, UK (up to six months), Uruguay, USA, Vatican City, Venezuela

**Types of Visas** Estonia, Latvia and Lithuania issue transit, single-entry and multiple-entry visas. Fees vary enormously – check the Ministries of Foreign Affairs websites mentioned earlier for updated prices.

Transit visas are non-extendable, allow single, double or multiple entry and are valid for 48 hours. Transit visas are issued by an embassy or consulate – no Baltic country issues transit visas at its borders. Costs vary between countries: Estonia charges €13/20 for a single-/double-entry visa; a Lithuanian single-entry visa costs €10 and a double- or multiple-entry visa costs around €25; while a Latvian single- or double-entry transit visas costs €9.40 and a multiple-entry visa valid for three/six/12 months costs €14/28/37.50.

Embassies and consulates issue single-entry visas for periods up to a usual maximum of 30 days for Estonia (€13) and Latvia (€14) and 90 days for Lithuania (€20). You can buy a 10-day visa upon arrival at Rīga airport or port (€20), Vilnius airport (€10) or Klaipėda sea port (€10). Estonia does not issue visas at any of its borders.

Because of the Baltics' common visa space, a single-entry visa for any of the three countries allows you to travel back and forth across the Estonian–Latvian and Latvian–Lithuanian borders as many times as you like within its term of validity,

provided you don't leave the Baltics during that time.

Multiple-entry visas are issued for various periods up to 12 months, but are only available from embassies and consulates – not on arrival. An Estonian multiple-entry visa, allowing 90 days stay within 12 months, costs €65; a Latvian equivalent valid for three/six/12 months costs €28/47/75; and a Lithuanian multiple-entry visa valid for three months costs €22.

**Applying for Visas** You can get visas in advance at Estonian, Latvian and Lithuanian embassies and consulates in most countries. On arrival in Latvia, you can buy a 10-day single-entry visa at the port or airport. On arrival at Vilnius airport or Klaipėda sea port in Lithuania, only citizens of countries belonging to the EU or people arriving from a country where there is not a Lithuanian consulate will be issued with a 10-day single-entry visa. Neither Latvia nor Lithuania issues visas at any other borders. Estonia does not issue visas at any of its borders.

When applying at an embassy or consulate you need to supply your passport, a completed application form, and one photo. Applications often have to be accompanied by an invitation from a registered organisation or proof of hotel/return airfare booking from the tour operator with whom you are travelling.

**Visa Extensions** Single-entry visas can be extended in the Baltics. In Estonia go to the Tallinn office or a regional branch of the **Migration and Citizenship Board** (English service ☎ 612 69 78, fax 631 37 44; e kma@mig.ee; w www.mig.ee; Endla tänav 13, EE15179 Tallinn). In Latvia there is a visa office inside the **Department of Citizenship and Migration Affairs** (☎ 721 96 39, fax 733 11 23; e pmlp@pmlp.glv.lv; w www.pmlp.gov.lv; Raiņa bulvāris 5, LV-1181 Rīga). In Lithuania make your embassy or the immigration department inside the **Ministry of Internal Affairs** (☎ 5-271 8695, 271 8785; w www.vrm.lt; Sventaragio gatvè 2, LT-2600 Vilnius) your first port of call.

**Russian Visas** Lithuania's neighbour, Kaliningrad Region, is part of Russia; St Petersburg is just a train trip from any of the Baltic capitals – and all Western visitors need a visa to enter Russia.

Obtaining the visa can be a very time-consuming task and is best dealt with before leaving home. A tourist visa requires proof of prebooked accommodation to support its application. The Russian embassies in Rīga, Tallinn and Vilnius are all notoriously bureaucratic and issue visas for a price, but only after an extraordinary length of time. See Embassies & Consulates in each country's Facts for the Visitor chapter.

**Belarussian Visas** Trains between Poland and Lithuania, unless on the direct Suwałki–Sestokai route, pass across about 60km of Belarusian territory. If you're taking one of these trains you need a Belarusian visa; border guards will gladly march you off the train to the immigration office to buy a transit visa for around €50. Visas are *not* issued at road borders. Belarusian embassies in all three Baltic capitals issue visas (see Embassies & Consulates in each country's Facts for the Visitor chapter).

## Travel Insurance
A travel-insurance policy to cover theft, loss and medical problems is a good idea. There is a wide variety of policies available, so check the small print.

You may prefer a policy which pays doctors or hospitals directly rather than you having to pay on the spot and claim later. If you have to claim later make sure you keep all documentation. Some policies ask you to call back (reverse charges) to a centre in your home country where an immediate assessment of your problem is made.

Check that the policy covers ambulances or an emergency flight home.

## Driving Licence & Permits
If you are planning to drive to or in the region, an International Driving Permit (IDP) will be useful, although, if you don't have one, your own national licence (if from a European country) should suffice – see Car & Motorcycle in the introductory Getting There & Away and Getting Around chapters. However, British driving-licence holders should note that licences not bearing a photograph of the holder have been known to upset traffic police, so try to get an IDP before you arrive. You will also need your vehicle's registration document. Accident insurance is compulsory in all three countries.

## Hostel Cards
A Hostelling International (HI) card yields discounts of up to 20% in affiliated hostels in the region. Filaretai Hostel in Vilnius (see Accommodation in the Lithuania Facts for the Visitor chapter) issues these cards, valid for one year, for just 30 Lt (€8.50) – among the cheapest in the world. Alternatively, contact your national **Youth Hostel Association** (YHA; **w** www.iyhf.org) before leaving home.

## Student & Youth Cards
An International Student Identity Card (ISIC) can pay for itself through half-price admissions, discounted air and ferry tickets, and cheaper cinema and theatre tickets. Many stockists – generally student-travel agencies – stipulate a maximum age, usually 25. If you're aged under 26 but not a student, you can apply for an International Youth Travel Card (IYTC) instead, which entitles you to much the same discounts as the ISIC. Both cards are administered by the **International Student Travel Confederation** (**w** www.istc .org) and issued by student travel agencies. Within the region, ISIC cards are sold at branches of Student & Youth Travel in Rīga, Tallinn and Vilnius – listed under Travel Agencies in the Information section of the respective city chapters later in this book.

## Seniors Cards
There are few discounts available to older people – a handful of museums in Tallinn reduce the entrance fee and seniors aged over 80 travel for free on Rīga trolleybuses and trams. But that is about it.

## Copies
All important documents (passport data page and visa page, credit cards, travel-insurance policy, air/bus/train tickets, driving licence etc) should be photocopied before you leave home. Leave one copy with someone at home and keep another with you, separate from the originals.

## EMBASSIES & CONSULATES
Estonia, Latvia and Lithuania each have numerous diplomatic missions overseas. Likewise, many countries have their own embassies or missions in the Baltic capitals, details of which can be found under Embassies & Consulates in the relevant Facts for the Visitor chapters later in the book.

It's important to realise what your own embassy – the embassy of the country of which you are a citizen – can and can't do to help you if you get into trouble. Generally speaking, it won't be much help in emergencies if the trouble you're in is remotely your own fault. Remember that you are bound by the laws of the country you are in. Your embassy will not be sympathetic if you end up in jail after committing a crime locally, even if such actions are legal in your own country.

## CUSTOMS

All three Baltic countries ban the import and export of firearms, ammunition, explosives, drugs or narcotics without special permission. Latvia and Lithuania also prohibit the import and export of pornography. Beyond that, customs rules vary and are subject to change. Baltic embassies and consulates should be able to tell you the latest if there's anything you're concerned about. The customs departments in Estonia (W www.customs.ee) and Lithuania (W www.cust.lt) have highly detailed websites spelling out all the latest rules and regulations.

Customs forms are available at border points if you're bringing in anything you think might be queried when you take it out again – such as hordes of money, works of art, furs or jewellery. If you think that a painting or other cultural object you want to buy in one of the Baltic countries may attract customs duty or require special permission to export, check with the shop or seller before you buy.

Further details on customs restrictions for Estonia, Latvia and Lithuania see Customs in the relevant Facts for the Visitor chapters later in the book.

## MONEY
## Currency

Baltic travel will improve your mental arithmetic, given that you will end up using three different currencies – Estonian kroon (EEK), Latvian lati (Ls) and Lithuanian litų (Lt). Since 1992 when the kroon was introduced and 1993 when the lati and litų were introduced (following the dumping of the Soviet rouble), all three have remained completely stable.

Lithuania and Estonia have pegged the litų and kroon to the euro since 2002. Even after joining the EU – slated to happen around 2004 (see the boxed text 'Joining Europe' in the Facts about the Region chapter) – Estonia, Latvia and Lithuania will conserve their national currencies. They could well trade in their own currencies for the euro one day, however, a move that can only happen once strict economic criteria have been met.

Within the region, Western currencies are perfectly acceptable and can be exchanged easily. Exchange rates for Polish *złoty*, Russian roubles, Ukrainian *hrivna* and other Eastern European money remain poor. Within the Baltic region, it is easy to change one Baltic currency into another, although rates are not always as favourable as for US dollars.

### Exchanging Money

See under Money in the individual country chapters for that country's currency exchange table.

**Cash** Make sure whatever currency you bring is in pristine condition. Marked, torn or very used notes will be refused. US-dollar notes issued before 1990 are not generally accepted either.

Every town has somewhere you can change cash. Usually it's a bank, exchange office or kiosk doing nothing but currency exchange. The latter crop up in all sorts of places, particularly transport terminals – airports, bus stations and train stations. Rates vary from one outlet to another. Exchange places are generally open during usual business hours.

**Travellers Cheques** A limited amount of travellers cheques are useful because of the protection they offer against theft. It is difficult to find places to exchange them, though, once you are out of the cities; most banks charge 4.5% commission. Most banks accept Eurocheques too.

American Express (AmEx) has a representative in each capital:

**Estravel** (☎ 626 62 66, fax 626 62 02,
  e sales@ estravel.ee, W www.estravel.ee)
  Suur-Karja tänav 15, EE10140 Tallinn
**Latvia Tours** (☎ 708 50 01, fax 782 00 20,
  e hq@latviatours.lv, W www.latviatours.lv)
  Kaļķu iela 8, LV-1050 Rīga
**Lithuanian Tours** (☎ 5-272 4154, fax 272 1815,
  e contact@lithuaniantours.com, W www.lithuaniantours.com) Šeimyniškoi gatvė 18, LT-2005 Vilnius

**ATMs** Automatic teller machines (ATMs) accepting Visa and/or MasterCard/Eurocard are widespread in cities and larger towns. Some are inside banks and post offices but the majority are on the streets, outside banks and at bus and train stations, enabling you to get cash 24 hours a day. Most ATMs are multilingual, using the five main European languages.

**Credit Cards** Especially at the upper end of the market, credit cards are widely accepted in hotels, restaurants and shops. Visa, Master Card/Eurocard, Diners Club and AmEx all crop up. One thing they are essential for is renting a car. With the liberal spread of ATMs, fewer banks are prepared to give cash advances on Visa and MasterCard/Eurocard – those that do, mainly in cities and larger towns, tack a 2% to 5% commission onto the amount of a cash advance. They also want to see your passport before agreeing to make the advance.

**International Transfers** Direct bank-to-bank wire transfer is possible at major banks, although you may need to open a bank account to do so. Usually a commission of up to 5% is charged on the amount you want to transfer; the service takes about five days.

### Security
Pickpockets are rife in the Baltic capitals and larger cities, and any Westerner attracts attention. A moneybelt worn inside your clothing is a good idea. Also, always divide your money up and carry it in several different places on your person and in your baggage. Leaving a secret stash in your hotel room is *only* a good idea if you're staying in an expensive hotel.

### Costs
Ex-Soviet republics they might be, but life on the cheap in the Baltic countries is but a distant memory these days. Latvia and Estonia are the most expensive of the trio, touting prices comparable to those of Scandinavia. Accommodation, particularly in the Latvian capital and throughout Estonia, is pricey and will be the biggest cost for most travellers. Goods in the shops vary from Helsinki-priced (read: among the most expensive in Western Europe) to cheap, but the variation applies to the quality too.

Eating out in Lithuania is still quite cheap – by far the cheapest of the Baltic countries. Overland travel in all three remains pleasantly affordable.

**Accommodation** In the capital cities, at the very bottom of the barrel, you can scrape a night's sleep with shared bathroom for €5.75/10.50/6.95 (dorm bed) in a hostel in Tallinn/Rīga/Vilnius and €19.50/12/14.50 (single room) in a hotel. Comfortable B&B accommodation in Tallinn/Rīga/Vilnius starts at €17/32/20 per person, including breakfast, while a night's stay in a single room in a mid-range hotel will set you back about €35/45/20.

Prices are considerably lower in the countryside – in all three countries, count on paying about €10 for budget accommodation and €35 for a mid-range room.

Top-end prices are in the capitals can be as sky-high as €200 per double – best suited to a corporate bank account.

**Food** In Rīga and Tallinn the cost of eating out is practically on a par with Western European city prices, although Vilnius still offers cheaper dining. In more provincial towns of all three Baltic countries, you'll rarely pay more than €6 for the same meal. Everywhere, you can cut costs to the bone – €4 or less – by eating at a cheap canteen or cafeteria, or by buying some of your own food at markets and shops.

**Transport** Fares vary a bit from country to country but, very roughly, €3 will take you 100km by bus or train. A bus or train from Tallinn to Vilnius – the length of the region – costs about €25 in mid-2002. Things get horribly expensive if you take to the air, but you probably won't need to unless you're in a big hurry.

In mid-2002, Western-grade petrol cost around €0.40 per litre.

### Tipping & Bargaining
It's fairly common, though not compulsory, to tip waiters 5% to 10% by rounding up the bill. A few waiters may try to tip themselves by 'not having' any change.

Some bargaining (but not a lot) goes on at flea markets. Savings are not likely to be more than 10% to 20% of the initial asking price.

## POST & COMMUNICATIONS
### Post

Letters and postcards from any of the three countries take about two to four days to Western Europe and seven to 10 days to North America. Occasionally, as in any other country, a letter or parcel might go astray for a couple of weeks but generally everything arrives.

Buy your stamps at a post office (Estonian: *postkontor*; Latvian: *pasts*; Lithuanian: *pastas*) and post your mail there too. Postal rates are listed under Post & Communications in the country-specific Facts for the Visitor chapters; alternatively, check the websites of the postal companies: in Estonia – **Eesti Post** (Ⓦ *www.post.ee*), Latvia – **Latvijas Pasts** (Ⓦ *www.riga.post.lv*) and Lithuania – **Lietuvos Paštas** (Ⓦ *www.post .lt*). Expensive international express-mail services are available in the capital cities.

The way in which addresses are written conform to Western norms, that is:

Kazimiera Jones
Veidenbauma iela 35-17
LV-5432 Ventspils
Latvia

Veidenbauma iela 35-17 means Veidenbaum Street, building No 35, flat No 17. Postcodes in Estonia are the letters EE plus five digits, in Latvia LV- plus four digits, and in Lithuania LT- plus four digits. For people wanting to receive mail on the move, there are poste-restante mail services in the main post offices in Tallinn and Vilnius, and at the post office next to Rīga train station. All three keep mail for a month. Address letters to Estonia with the full name of the recipient followed by: Poste Restante, Peapostkontor, EE10101 Tallinn, Estonia. Letters to Latvia should be addressed as follows: Poste Restante, Rīga 50, LV-1050, Latvia. Letters to Lithuania: Poste Restante, Centrinis Pastas, Gedimino prospektas 7, LTo-2000 Vilnius, Lithuania.

### Telephone

Nowhere is the region's startling transformation from Soviet stagnation to postcommunist capitalism more obvious than in its telephone systems. New exchanges, allowing direct digital connections to the rest of the world, have replaced the slow and decrepit, analogue Soviet system that once painfully routed all calls through Moscow.

Calling to/from Estonia, Latvia and Lithuania is just like calling to/from anywhere else in the West. International calls can be made from practically every private phone, as well as the public cardphones, liberally scattered around the Baltic capitals, cities and towns. Throughout this book, city codes are listed under the relevant town heading, with the exception of Latvia, which does not use city codes. Precise details on how to call are included under Post & Communications in the respective Facts for the Visitor chapters.

Mobile phones are massively popular in the region; many places to eat and drink listed in this guidebook favour mobile telephones over fixed phone lines. Estonia, Latvia and Lithuania all use GSM 900/1800 – compatible with the rest of Europe and Australia, but not with the North American GSM 1900 or the totally different system in Japan. Assuming your phone is GSM 900-/1800-compatible, you can buy a SIM card package from a choice of mobile-phone providers in all three countries. See Post & Communications in the relevant Facts for the Visitor chapter for details.

**International Country Codes** The international country code for Estonia is ☎ 372. In Latvia the code is ☎ 371 and in Lithuania it's ☎ 370.

### ekno Communication Service

Lonely Planet's ekno global communication service provides low-cost international calls – for local calls you're usually better off with a local phonecard. ekno also offers free messaging services, email, travel information and an online travel vault, where you can securely store all your important documents. You can join online at Ⓦ www .ekno.lonelyplanet.com, where you will find the local-access numbers for the 24-hour customer-service centre. Once you have joined, always check the ekno website for the latest access numbers for each country and updates on new features.

### Fax

Practically every hotel and organisation is contactable by fax. There are reasonably priced public fax services, both outgoing and incoming, at post offices and in most major hotels in the main cities throughout the region.

## Email & Internet Access

The Internet has boomed in Estonia, Latvia and Lithuania in recent years which, according to reports on the region's so-called 'Tiger Leap', saw '…society sitting in front of computers at lightning pace, almost straight from the Stone Age'. Estonia leads the way, with 33% of Estonians regularly using the Internet, followed by 13% of Latvians and 9% of Lithuanians.

Practically every hotel, restaurant and commercial enterprise is happily hooked up, with email communication; numerous hotels accept email bookings.

Public Internet access is available in all three capitals and most provincial towns int the region. Expect to pay around €2 an hour.

## DIGITAL RESOURCES

Email account holders can subscribe for free to a host of online discussion groups. These include **Radio Free Europe/Radio Liberty** (RFE/RL; ⓦ www.rferl.org), which mails out daily news reports on Eastern Europe and Russia, including Estonia, Latvia & Lithuania; **Estonia Today** (ⓦ www.europeaninternet.com/estonia), a weekly review of Estonian news; and the twice-monthly newsletter **Latvians Online** (ⓦ www.latviansonline.com), which runs some excellent Latvian-related features and lots of news.

Within the region, all three countries are well up to speed digitally. The presidents and parliaments each have their own websites; all three have their national auction house online where you can shop; there are webcams galore; and most places to stay and eat have a site of sorts. Estonia, Latvia and Lithuania's Internet country codes are .ee, .lv and .lt; see Digital Resources in the individual Facts for the Visitor chapters for websites specific to each country.

Useful Baltic-related websites include:

**Baltic Shop.com** (ⓦ www.balticshop.com) The digital place to buy everything from Latvian rye bread to summer-solstice greeting cards and amber, as well as Baltic-related books, videos and CDs.
**The Baltic Times** (ⓦ www.baltictimes.com) Features news and views from the region's weekly English-language newspaper, covering all three countries.

**Baltics Worldwide** (ⓦ www.balticsww.com) Website of the Tallinn-based City Paper, this is a well-organised and eye-catching site, with updated news, discussion forums, links to Baltic dictionaries and telephone directories, and extensive archives to search.
**In Your Pocket** (ⓦ www.inyourpocket.com) Includes the entire contents of the Tallinn, Pärnu, Rīga, Vilnius and Kaunas/Klaipėda In Your Pocket city guides, bar the paper-version coloured maps.
**News about the Baltics, Central & Eastern Europe, World** (ⓦ www.ciesin.ee/NEWS) Provides dozens of links to English-language media sources, including local newsagencies ETA (Estonia), LETA (Latvia) and ELTA (Lithuania), plus Baltic News Service (BNS; ⓦ www.bns.ee), with daily news in English.

## BOOKS

Estonia, Latvia and Lithuania have numerous bookshops, many of which stock foreign-language books.

In the USA, **The Baltic Bookshelf** (☎/fax 410-721 34 11; ⓔ balticbook@aol.com; ⓦ www.geocities.com/balticbook; PO Box 3314, Crofton, MD 21114) specialises in books on the Baltics, albeit mainly Lithuania.

In Britain, try **Zora Books** (☎ 020-7602 1691, fax 7610 4255; ⓔ zorabooks@btinter.net.com), a Russian, Central and Eastern European book specialist. The company, which functions by mail order, issues regularly updated book lists. London's **Travel Bookshop** (☎ 020-7229 5260; 13-15 Blenheim Crescent, London W11 2EE) stocks Baltic travel literature; its small second-hand section occasionally throws up some real treasures.

Titles focusing solely on Estonia, Latvia or Lithuania are listed under Books in the respective Facts for the Visitor chapters.

### Lonely Planet

If you're following the Scandinavian route via the Baltics, *Scandinavian & Baltic Europe* is recommended, as are *Eastern Europe* and *Europe*, both of which include Estonia, Latvia and Lithuania. Lonely Planet's *Baltic States phrasebook* and *Scandinavian Europe phrasebook* are handy and portable.

### Travel

*Among the Russians* by Colin Thubron, an Englishman's account of driving everywhere he could in the pre-*glasnost* Soviet

Union, takes in Tallinn and Rīga, and captures the gloomy, resigned mood of the time.

If you can manage to track it down, *Russia* by JG Kohl includes a quite lengthy section on the Baltic states among its German author's account of his travels in the tsarist empire in the 1840s.

Laurens Van Der Post's *Journey into Russia*, an account of the author's travels through Soviet Russia in the 1960s, also relates his visits to Rīga, Vilnius and Tallinn at that time.

*The Singing Revolution* by Clare Thomson traces Estonia, Latvia and Lithuania's path towards independence through an account of travels there in 1989 and 1990. It also provides background on the Soviet and earlier periods of outside rule.

## History & Politics

Old hat as it might seem, *The Baltic Revolution* by Anatol Lieven remains a classic in its field. The author, who is half Irish and half Baltic German (of a family which traces its lineage back to Germanised Liv chieftains), grew up in London but spent the early 1990s as the Baltic correspondent for the London *Times*. His book entertainingly and thoroughly surveys both the past and present of the region, and is full of unique insights and startling information (eg, the phrase 'going to Rīga' is a Lithuanian colloquialism meaning 'to vomit').

Another solid history told from a very personal perspective is *Walking Since Daybreak: A Story of Eastern Europe, World War II and Heart of the Century* by acclaimed historian Modris Eksteins (1998). In 272 pages, the author – who was born in Latvia in 1943 and spent most of his childhood in displaced persons camps – relates his family history up to WWII.

The other classic works in English on Baltic history are two weighty tomes: *The Baltic States: The Years of Independence 1917–40* by Georg von Rauch and *The Baltic States: Years of Dependence 1940–1980* by Romualdas Misiunas & Rein Taagepera, covering the Soviet era. These books have lengthy bibliographies if you're interested in following things up. *The Baltic States and Weimar Ostpolitik* (2002) by John Hiden is a more recent work which focuses on European politics in the region in the post-WWI period.

The 1980 winner of the Nobel prize for literature, Czesław Miłosz, who grew up in Vilnius in a part-Polish, part-Lithuanian family, occupies a leading position in modern Polish literature. The last chapter of his *The Captive Mind*, written in 1951–52, deals with the Soviet occupation of the Baltic states.

Partly autobiographical, *Walking Since Daybreak* (2000) by Modris Eksteins combines true stories from the author's own family with black-and-white facts on Estonia, Latvia and Lithuania during and after WWII.

The *Guide to Jewish Genealogy in Latvia and Estonia* (2001) by Rosemary E Wenzerul is published by the Jewish Genealogical Society of Great Britain and makes for a fascinating, if unsettling, read.

Robert G. Darst's *Smokestack Diplomacy* (2001) tackles the whole dirty issue of environmental protection in five former Soviet states, including Estonia, Latvia and Lithuania. A polluted Baltic Sea, nuclear power production and air pollution are the author's main gripes. Pollution of the Baltic Sea is likewise the focus of *Managing a Sea* by Ing-Marie Gren, R. Kerry Turner & Frederick Wulff.

*Bandits, Gangsters and the Mafia: Russia, the Baltic States and the CIS since 1991* by Martin McCauley, as the title suggests, delves into the darker side of Russian and Baltic life.

*Advice Not Welcomed* (2001) by Vadim Poleshchuk looks at the words of wisdom of the first OSCE High Commissioner on national minorities, Max van der Stoel, and his role in stabilising the Baltic region – not that his formal recommendations in Estonia and Latvia were necessarily followed.

Another contentious political issue is addressed in *Which Identity for Which Europe*, edited by Antje Herrberg. The book in part analyses the implications the Baltic countries' Soviet past might well have on a future Europe. Read this, plus *The Baltic States* (2002) by Signe Maria Landgren – which addresses the security debate surrounding the Baltics since independence – for a strong background on the two big political issues facing the region today.

## Fiction

*The Good Republic* by William Palmer tells the story of a young man in a Baltic country who, more by accident than design, gets involved in a minor way in the Nazi bureaucracy during WWII. He escapes to exile in London but returns 'home' decades later to suffer unexpected nightmarish consequences from his past. The book conjures up well the atmosphere of the pre-WWII Baltics, the Soviet and Nazi occupations, and the feel of emigre life. It also lays bare the moral dilemmas facing the occupied peoples in the war years.

For a sense of the atmosphere of 1930s Latvia and Estonia, track down *Venusburg* (1992), one of Anthony Powell's early novels. First published in 1932, it tells the amusing tale of an English journalist trying unsuccessfully to make his name as a foreign correspondent amid the exiled Russian aristocrats, Baltic German intellectuals, and earnest local patriots of the era.

## Art

Modern art is looked at from two very different perspectives in *Peeling Potatoes, Painting Pictures* (2001) by Renee Baigell & Matthew Baigell and *Art of the Baltics*, edited by Alla Rosenfeld & Norton C Dodge. The former takes an enlightened look at how female artists in Estonia, Latvia and Russia perceive themselves in this post-Soviet era (the conclusion after 60-odd interviews being that art in the region remains staunchly male-dominated); the latter looks at the fight for artistic expression during the Soviet era (1945–91).

## NEWSPAPERS & MAGAZINES

There is a small but rather select choice of English-language publications in the Baltics, most of which are a useful information source for the increasing number of English-speaking locals as well as the active expat community. For newspapers and magazines specific to Estonia, Latvia and Lithuania see Newspapers & Magazines in the respective Facts for the Visitor chapters.

The weekly *Baltic Times*, online at w www.baltictimes.com, is published in Rīga every Thursday and enjoys moderate success as the only English-language newspaper to cover all three Baltic countries. It has a fair balance of news and business stories, features, entertainment listings and some useful classifieds.

Tallinn-based *City Paper*, published every two months, is a news magazine and

Baltic city guide rolled into one. It contains some fine analytical pieces on Baltic politics, and lots of news and views.

*Baltische Rundschau*, a German-language newspaper with a website at w www.rundschau.lt, is published monthly and available in all three capitals.

The *Baltic Review*, online at w www.tbr.ee, is a quarterly English-language journal, containing in-depth features and political analysis on affairs in the three Baltic countries.

For a more practical orientation there is a clutch of locally produced guides, including those by In Your Pocket, which produces exceptional city guides to the three capitals; see the relevant regional chapters later in this guidebook for details.

With the exception of the latter, all the above-mentioned publications can be received outside the region by subscribing to them; full details are on their websites.

Imported English-language newspapers and magazines including London's *Guardian*, *Times* and the *International Herald Tribune* can be easily picked up in the capitals. The same goes for *Time*, *Newsweek* and the *Economist*. German papers are available in Rīga and Vilnius, and Finnish ones are sold in Tallinn.

Details of local-language publications and country-specific publications are given in the relevant Facts for the Visitor chapters later in this book.

## RADIO & TV

Most mid-range, all top-end and some budget hotel rooms tout a TV. Only those in top-end hotels – and some Western-style bars and restaurants – receive CNN, BBC, Eurosport, MTV and other Western satellite stations. Further details are given under Radio & TV in the relevant Facts for the Visitor chapters.

## VIDEO SYSTEMS

PAL and Secam are the two main systems used in the region. However, things are changing all the time and it is best to check on arrival which is the 'in' system. PAL is not compatible with Secam.

## PHOTOGRAPHY & VIDEO

Sunlight can be a rarity in the Baltic region. Some fast film, ASA 400 or more, is useful if you want to try taking photos in dim light. Carry spare camera batteries, especially in winter when the cold can make them sluggish.

Kodak, Agfa and Fuji film and basic accessories like batteries are widely available in towns and cities from hotels and specialist outlets. There are plenty of quick print-processing outlets. Not all places sell slide or B&W film so you might want to bring your own to save running out at that vital moment. Film for your camcorder is readily available in the three capitals and large cities.

## TIME

Estonia, Latvia and Lithuania are on Eastern European Time (GMT/UTC + 2). In 2002 only Estonia and Latvia adhered to daylight saving, applicable from the last Sunday in March to the last Sunday in October.

The 24-hour clock is used for train, bus and flight timetables. Dates are generally listed the American way: the month first, followed by the day and the year; ie, 02/03/71 refers to 3 February 1971, not 2 March 1971.

## ELECTRICITY

The region runs on 220V, 50Hz AC. Most appliances that are set up for 240V will handle this happily. Sockets require a European plug with two round pins.

## WEIGHTS & MEASURES

The three countries all use the metric system, sometimes to amusing excess: some menus still spell out the weight of bread, meat and fish per 10g (a 100g hot dog in a 50g bun doused with 10g of ketchup is written on the menu as 100/50/10). More common is the practice of serving drinks by weight – a standard shot of spirits is 50g and a glass of wine 200g.

## LAUNDRY

All top hotels tout a laundry service, at a price of course. There are laundrettes in all the major cities.

## TOILETS

Public toilets in Tallinn are well signposted, clean and a sheer pleasure to use compared with the vile, stinking black holes you will generally encounter elsewhere in the Baltics. Regardless of their lack of cleanliness, in public toilets you are obliged to pay a small fee on entry in exchange for a few sheets of exceedingly rough toilet paper or squares of newspaper. Many Baltic sewerage systems can't cope with toilet paper. If a bin or basket is placed in the cubicle, put toilet paper in there. Bring your own toilet paper and be prepared to squat.

Smelly public toilets can be found at every bus and train station in the Baltics. You can also stroll into a large hotel in the major cities and use their toilets without upsetting the staff too much. Alternatively, do what everyone else does and pop into the nearest McDonald's.

The letter 'M' marks a men's toilet in Estonian, 'V' in Latvian or Lithuanian. 'N' indicates a women's toilet in Estonian, 'S' in Latvian and 'M' in Lithuanian. Some toilets sport the triangle system: a skirt-like triangle for women and a broad-shouldered, upside-down triangle for men.

## HEALTH

The Baltic region is, on the whole, a pretty healthy place to travel around, though medical care is not entirely up to Western standards.

## Predeparture Preparations

Make sure you're healthy before you start travelling. If you are going on a long trip make sure your teeth are OK. If you wear glasses take a spare pair and your prescription.

If you require a particular medication take an adequate supply, as it may not be available locally. Take part of the packaging showing the generic name rather than the brand, which will make getting replacements easier. It's a good idea to have a legible prescription or letter from your doctor to show that you legally use the medication to avoid any problems.

Bring any pharmaceuticals you think you'll need – including condoms or other contraceptives. These are available (chiefly in the main cities) but you cannot rely on getting any particular thing where and when you need it. Take plenty of mosquito repellent in summer.

**Immunisations** No immunisations are required for Estonia, Latvia or Lithuania. If you intend to spend a lot of time in forested areas, however, it is advisable to get a vaccine against tick-borne encephalitis. All along the Latvian coastline in Jūrmala, there are large 'tick' signs warning you where ticks are rife.

You might also consider vaccination against hepatitis A. Make sure your tetanus, polio and diphtheria vaccinations are up to date.

**Health Insurance** Make sure that you have adequate health insurance. See Travel Insurance under Visas & Documents earlier in this chapter for details.

## Basic Rules

**Food** There is an old adage that says: 'If you can cook it, boil it or peel it you can eat it...otherwise forget it'. Vegetables and fruit should be washed with purified water or peeled where possible. Beware of ice cream which is sold in the street or anywhere it might have been melted and re-frozen; if there's any doubt (eg, a power cut in the last day or two), steer well clear.

If a place looks clean and well run and the vendor also looks clean and healthy, then the food is probably safe. In general, places that are packed with travellers or locals will be fine, while empty restaurants are questionable. The food in busy restaurants is cooked and eaten quite quickly, with little standing around, and is probably not reheated.

**Water** Take care with water – both the tap and sea varieties. Tap water in several places *is* unclean. Definitely in Rīga, and probably in Vilnius, it needs to be boiled before you drink it. In other places check with locals whether the tap water is safe to drink or not. If in any doubt boil it or drink something else (mineral water is a cheap, widely available substitute). To purify water thoroughly you should boil it for 10 minutes. Alternatively, you can do it chemically. Chlorine tablets kill many but not all pathogens. Iodine is very effective and is available in tablet form (such as Potable Aqua) but follow the directions carefully as too much iodine can be harmful.

Sea water is similarly dodgy because of pollution – chiefly untreated sewage although there's chemical pollution as well. Every so often, various environmental groups issue warnings not to swim in the sea, although beachgoers still venture into the water. Many inland lakes are cleaner than the sea waters, but you should take local advice anywhere.

## Medical Problems & Treatment

Self-diagnosis and treatment can be risky, so you should always seek medical help. An embassy, consulate or five-star hotel can recommend a local doctor or clinic. Antibiotics should ideally be administered only under medical supervision. Take only the recommended dose at the prescribed intervals and use the whole course, even if the illness seems to be cured earlier. Stop immediately if there are any serious reactions and don't use the antibiotic at all if you are unsure that you have the correct one. Some people are allergic to commonly prescribed antibiotics such as penicillin; carry this information (eg, on a bracelet) when travelling.

Practically all pharmacies in the capitals and larger towns stock imported Western medicines – see Medical Services under the town and city sections.

There are few alternatives to the local medical system, which is short on both facilities and training should you have the misfortune to need serious attention. Private clinics offer Western-standard, English-speaking medical care in the capitals but they are very expensive. In an emergency seek your hotel's help first (if you're in one) – the bigger hotels may have doctors on call. Emergency care is free in all three countries.

## Infectious Diseases

**Diarrhoea** Simple things like a change of water, food or climate can all cause a mild bout of diarrhoea, but a few rushed toilet trips with no other symptoms is not indicative of a major problem.

Dehydration is the main danger with any diarrhoea, particularly in children and the elderly, as dehydration can occur quite quickly. Under all circumstances *fluid replacement* (at least equal to the volume being lost) is the most important thing to remember. Weak black tea with a little sugar, soda water, or soft drinks allowed to go flat and diluted 50% with clean water are all good. With severe diarrhoea a rehydrating solution is preferable to replace minerals and salts lost. Urine is the best guide to the adequacy of replacement – if you have small amounts of concentrated urine, you need to drink more. Keep drinking small amounts often. Stick to a bland diet as you recover.

**Fungal Infections** Occuring more commonly in hot weather, fungal infections are usually found on the scalp, between the toes (athlete's foot) or fingers, in the groin and on the body (ringworm). You get ringworm (which is a fungal infection, not a worm) from infected animals or other people. Moisture encourages these infections.

To prevent fungal infections wear loose, comfortable clothes, avoid artificial fibres, wash frequently and dry yourself carefully. If you do get an infection, wash the infected area at least daily with a disinfectant or medicated soap and water, and rinse and dry well. Apply an antifungal cream or powder like tolnaftate. Try to expose the infected area to air or sunlight as much as possible and wash all towels and underwear in hot water, change them often and let them dry in the sun.

**Hepatitis** This general term for inflammation of the liver is a common disease worldwide. Symptoms include fever, chills, headache, fatigue, feelings of weakness and aches and pains, followed by loss of appetite, nausea, vomiting, abdominal pain, dark urine, light-coloured faeces, jaundiced (yellow) skin and yellowing of the whites of the eyes. People who have had hepatitis should avoid alcohol for some time after the illness, as the liver needs time to recover.

**Hepatitis A** is transmitted by contaminated food and drinking water. You should seek medical advice, but there is not much you can do apart from resting, drinking lots of fluids, eating lightly and avoiding fatty foods.

**Hepatitis B** is spread through contact with infected blood, blood products or body fluids, for example through sexual contact, unsterilised needles and blood transfusions, or contact with blood via small breaks in the skin. Other risk situations include having a shave, tattoo or body piercing with contaminated equipment. The symptoms of hepatitis B may be more severe than type A and the disease can lead to long-term problems such as chronic liver damage, liver cancer or a long-term carrier state.

There are vaccines against hepatitis A and B, but there are currently no vaccines against the other types of hepatitis.

**HIV & AIDS** Infection with the human immunodeficiency virus (HIV) may lead to acquired immune deficiency syndrome (AIDS), which is a fatal disease. Any exposure to blood, blood products or body fluids may put the individual at risk. The disease is often transmitted through sexual contact or dirty needles – vaccinations, acupuncture, tattooing and body piercing can be potentially as dangerous as intravenous drug use. HIV/AIDS can also be spread through infected blood transfusions. If you do need an injection, ask to see the syringe unwrapped in front of you, or take a needle and syringe pack with you.

Fear of HIV infection should never preclude treatment for serious medical conditions.

**Sexually Transmitted Infections (STIs)**
HIV/AIDS and hepatitis B can be transmitted through sexual contact – see the above sections. Other STIs include gonorrhoea, herpes and syphilis; sores, blisters or rashes around the genitals and discharges or pain when urinating are common symptoms. In some STIs, such as wart virus or chlamydia, symptoms may be less marked or not observed at all, especially in women. Chlamydia infection can cause infertility in men and women before any symptoms have been noticed. Syphilis symptoms eventually disappear completely but the disease continues and can cause severe problems in later years. While abstinence from sexual contact is the only 100%-effective prevention, using condoms is also effective. The treatment of gonorrhoea and syphilis is with antibiotics. The different sexually transmitted diseases each require specific antibiotics.

## Insect-Borne Diseases
**Encephalitis** From May to September there is a risk of tick-borne encephalitis in forested areas. Encephalitis is inflammation of the brain tissue. Symptoms include fever, headache, vomiting, neck stiffness, pain in the eyes when looking at light, alteration in consciousness, seizures and paralysis or muscle weakness. Correct diagnosis and treatment require hospitalisation. Ticks (see under Cuts, Bites & Stings, following) may be found on the edge of forests and in clearings, long grass and hedgerows. A vaccine is available (see Immunisations earlier in this section).

## Cuts, Bites & Stings

**Cuts & Scratches** Wash well and treat any cut with an antiseptic such as povidone-iodine. Where possible avoid bandages and Band-Aids, which can keep wounds wet.

**Bedbugs & Lice** Bedbugs live in various places, but particularly in dirty mattresses and bedding, evidenced by spots of blood on bedclothes or on the wall. Bedbugs leave itchy bites in neat rows. Calamine lotion or a sting-relief spray may help.

All lice cause itching and discomfort. They make themselves at home in your hair (head lice), your clothing (body lice) or in your pubic hair (crabs). You catch lice through direct contact with infected people or by sharing combs, clothing and the like. Powder or shampoo treatment will kill the lice and infected clothing should then be washed in very hot, soapy water and left in the sun to dry.

**Bites & Stings** Bee and wasp stings are usually painful rather than dangerous. However, in people who are allergic to them severe breathing difficulties may occur and require urgent medical care. Calamine lotion or a sting-relief spray will give relief and ice packs will reduce the pain and swelling.

**Ticks** You should always check all over your body if you have been walking through a potentially tick-infested area, as ticks can cause skin infections and other more serious diseases. If a tick is found attached, press down around the tick's head with tweezers, grab the head and gently pull upwards. Avoid pulling the rear of the body as this may squeeze the tick's gut contents through the attached mouth parts into the skin, increasing the risk of infection and disease. Smearing chemicals on the tick will not make it let go and is not recommended.

## WOMEN TRAVELLERS

The Balts have some fairly traditional ideas about gender roles, but on the other hand they're pretty reserved and rarely impose themselves upon other people in an annoying way. Women are not likely to receive aggravation from men in the Baltics, although unaccompanied women may want to avoid a few of the sleazier bars and beer cellars. Many women travel on overnight buses and trains alone but if you're travelling on a train at night, play safe and use the hefty metal lock on the inside of the carriage door.

In larger cities in Latvia particularly, some Russian women walk around with skirts so short you can practically see their bottoms – much to the delight of many male travellers who come to the Baltics mistakenly assuming that *all* young Baltic women are desperate for their attention. Unfortunately, tourists who copy this scanty attire risk being treated as prostitutes. In some tourist hotels prostitution is a fact of life, and a woman sitting alone in a lobby, corridor or café might be propositioned.

### Organisations

Lithuania's **Women's Issues Information Centre** (WIIC; ☎ 5-262 9003, fax 262 9050; e wiic@undp.lt; Jakšto gatvė 9, room 303/315, LT-2001 Vilnius) is a fabulous source of information and can put you in touch with other women's organisations in the region. Hot issues of the day for Baltic women are addressed in its quarterly *Women's World* magazine and in other English-language publications.

## GAY & LESBIAN TRAVELLERS

There is a fairly active gay and lesbian scene in the three capitals – and practically nothing elsewhere. Latvia was the first Eastern European country to host a lesbian wedding, in 1995, but same-sex marriages remain unrecognised in all three countries. Rīga is the most gay-friendly capital but public expressions of affection are treated with contempt by some. While gay bars, nightclubs and saunas in Rīga and Tallinn happily publicise their venues, the scene in Catholic Vilnius is a little more coy. Permanent gay and lesbian venues (of which there was just one in Rīga and Vilnius, and three in Tallinn, in late 2002) are listed under Entertainment in the respective city sections.

### Organisations

The website w www.gaybaltics.com is the best source of information covering all three countries.

Estonia's key gay organisation is the **Estonian Gay League** (e gayliit@hotmail.com; PO Box 142, EE10502 Tallinn). **Estonian Gay Planet** (w www.gay.ee) lists party venues in Estonian only.

The Latvian association **Latvian Gay & Lesbian** (☎ 959 22 29; ⓔ gay@gay.lv; ⓦ www.gay.lv, www.gaybaltics.com; Pastkaste iela 380, LV-1001 Rīga) offers advice on gay issues. Its English-language website is crammed with practical information.

The **Lithuanian Gay League** (LGL; ☎/fax 5-233 3031; ⓔ lgl@gay.lt; ⓦ www.gay.lt; PO Box 2862, LT-2000 Vilnius) runs a video library and organises weekend parties, as does the **Lithuanian Lesbian League** (Sappho; ⓔ sphinfo@is.lt; ⓦ www.is.lt/sappho; PO Box 2204, LT-2049 Vilnius).

## DISABLED TRAVELLERS

With its cobbled streets, rickety pavements and old buildings, the Baltic region is not user-friendly for travellers with disabilities. In Estonia the **Social Rehabilitation Centre** (☎ 655 94 42; ⓔ srk@ngonet.ee; Männiku tee 92, EE01077 Tallinn) gives out advice to travellers with disabilities. In Lithuania, contact the **Disability Information and Consultation Bureau** (☎ 5-261 7277; Teatro gatvė 11/8-13, LT-2001 Vilnius).

Latvia scores oodles of brownie points from travellers with disabilities the world over for the Baltics' most disabled-friendly hotel, adjoining Jūrmala's seaside **Vaivari National Rehabilitation Centre** (☎ 776 61 22/25, fax 776 63 14; ⓔ nrc3@nrc.lv; Asaru prospketas 61, LV-2008 Jūrmala), which acts as an information centre, too, for travellers with disabilities. Single/double hotel rooms cost 14.60/22.12 Ls (12.78/19.66 Ls in low season). Elsewhere it's only really upmarket hotels that have rooms equipped with disabled travellers in mind.

Some beaches on the western Lithuanian coast in Nida and Palanga have ramps to allow wheelchair access to the sand, as does the above-mentioned hotel.

## TRAVEL WITH CHILDREN

If you intend travelling across the region by public transport with young children, take every opportunity to break up the journey. Bus and train journeys between regional cities and the three Baltic countries can be long and arduous, with little to make the journey pass quickly. Take sufficient food and drink supplies, as once you're on the bus from Vilnius to Rīga, you're stuck on it! Despite some drivers' nasty glares, if you smile sweetly they will generally stop by the roadside for a quick loo break. Many of the larger hotels have family rooms or will put an extra bed in the room for you. And remember, Rīga has the only permanent circus in the Baltics! See Lonely Planet's *Travel with Children* for more information.

## DANGERS & ANNOYANCES
### Crime

Crime has increased markedly since independence, but that's starting from a pretty low level. Guard against theft from hotel rooms by keeping valuables with you or in a hotel safe. Be extra careful when walking along poorly lit city streets at night. Some prostitutes working in tourist hotels rob their customers.

Car theft is rife in all three Baltic capitals. Don't leave anything valuable in your car when it is parked. Stripping the inside bare of its stereo and all personal belongings is still not sufficient to deter some thieves who are into stealing car batteries, door locks, tyres and even windscreen wipers.

You're sure to hear about the 'mafia' while you're in the region. But don't be alarmed – the Baltic mafia does not bother with dull tourists. Rather, it's into any sort of third-rate activity that will turn a few bucks, including arms dealing, drugs, metals smuggling, prostitution, buying up state businesses on the cheap by frightening off other potential buyers, and extortion from any profitable business they can get their claws into. The most you'll encounter of the mafia, if any, is a slob-like presence – a small knot of thick-set men sporting five o'clock shadows and cheap leather jackets – at a taxi rank or in a restaurant or café.

### Service

Most of the surly, rude, obstructive goblins employed in service industries in the Soviet era have miraculously changed character now that pleasing the customer has become worthwhile, but there are still one or two hangovers from the bad old days. When you encounter them, all you can do is grit your teeth and persist until you've got what you need. In budget and upmarket restaurants alike, service on the whole remains frustratingly slow.

### Rip-Offs

Taxi drivers may cheat foreigners the world over and those in the Baltic cities, especially at airports and outside the main tourist hotels, are no exception. A few hints on avoiding rip-offs are given in the city sections.

## Drunks

Drunks on the streets and in hotels can be a nuisance in the evenings, especially at weekends. In Tallinn they're as likely to be foreign tourists as locals. Steer clear and don't get involved!

## Border Guards

Baltic border guards are not out to rip you off. They are just suckers for stamps – and for the old Soviet way of doing things, which means service without a smile. At road borders these stamp-obsessed, snail-paced creatures are at their meanest – the longer the line, the colder they are. Smile sweetly and make sure you have your paperwork ready.

## Ethnic Attitudes

Some Estonians, Latvians and Lithuanians have a 'send-'em-home' attitude towards Russians and other ex-Soviet nationalities in their midst. Anti-Semitic statements are likewise not unknown to pass from some Balts' lips. In 2000 President Adamkus warned against growing radicalism in Lithuania, adding that his government would not tolerate 'anti-Semitism or hatred of other cultures'. Jewish cemeteries in all three countries are constantly under attack from vandals, and in 1998 a bomb exploded outside the synagogue in Rīga (the second since 1995). A reader's letter warns following a trip to Lithuania in 2001: 'I met with a level and intensity of latent anti-Semitism in Lithuania that I have never come across in the West. Equally, I met some truly remarkable Lithuanians, some of whom I felt comfortable disclosing my religious (Jewish) background to'.

## LEGAL MATTERS

If you are arrested you have the same basic legal rights as anywhere else in Europe. You have the right to be informed of the reason for your arrest (before being carted off to the police station) and you have the right to inform a family member of your misfortune (once you have been carted off). You cannot be detained for more than 72 hours without being charged with an offence, and you have the right to have your lawyer present during questioning.

In Rīga, you can be fined on the spot for straying from public footpaths onto the neatly mowed grass lawns in city parks. In Vilnius, you can sit/lie/sunbathe on the grass in city parks but you can't sleep; police patrol on horseback to check that your eyes aren't shut.

In Latvia it is illegal to buy alcohol anywhere except restaurants, cafés, bars and clubs between 10pm and 8am. In Lithuania and Estonia, public drinking anywhere except licensed premises is likewise illegal – downing a beer on a park bench in Vilnius warrants a €15 on-the-spot fine and repeat offenders can be jailed.

Tobacco advertising was only illegalised in Lithuania in 2000 (Estonia and Latvia banned it in 1993 and 1998 respectively), while public gambling was only legalised in Lithuania in mid-2001.

## BUSINESS HOURS

Shops open weekdays from 8am, 9am or 10am to 6pm, 7pm or 8pm; and Saturday from 8am, 9am or 10am to some time between 1pm and 5pm. Some close for lunch, or on Monday. Shops are generally closed on Sunday (though in all three capitals many open on Sunday for several hours).

Cafés open from about 9am to 8pm; restaurants, from noon to around midnight. Museums often close on Monday and Tuesday. Businesses tend to work from 8am or 9am to 4pm or 5pm Monday to Friday.

## PUBLIC HOLIDAYS & SPECIAL EVENTS

Estonia, Latvia and Lithuania all enjoy fat festival calendars encompassing everything from religion and music, to song, art, folk culture, handicrafts, film, drama and more. Summer is the busiest time of year, although each of the three Baltic countries celebrates a couple of truly magical festivals at other times of year too: the remarkable Day of Setu Lace in the heart of Setumaa in South eastern Estonia on 1 March and the colourful Kaziukas crafts fair in Vilnius to mark St Casimir's Day on 4 March are two that immediately spring to mind.

Most festivals are annual, others are one-off – see under Public Holidays & Special Events in the relevant Facts for the Visitor chapters for details. Public holidays vary

## Happy Christmas

The most important day of the year in the Baltic calendar is 24 December. Traditionally it is a day when the family stays at home; celebrations with friends and neighbours are only enjoyed on 25 December. In Estonia, Latvia and Lithuania, the family table is covered with straw, and the culinary feast is served upon it. Places are also laid for any deceased relatives. In Lithuania, the feast comprises 12 vegetarian dishes, collectively known as *kucios*. Meat is only eaten on the 25th. In Estonia, pepper biscuits and a German-style knotted bread with nuts known as *kringel* are the order of the day. Blood sausages, traditionally with a small gift inside, are also served. Various fortune-telling games are played throughout the region.

Today, the red-cheeked, white-bearded Santa Claus is a celebrated figure. The gifts he bears are opened on Christmas Eve. During the Soviet era, he did not exist, however. Children had to go to school on Christmas Eve and Christmas Day, and Santa Claus was replaced by the soulless Father Frost, who dropped gifts down chimneys on New Year's Eve instead.

between countries and are also listed under Public Holidays & Special Events in the relevant Facts for the Visitor chapters. Estonia, Latvia and Lithuania also celebrate a number of commemorative days, when shops, apartment blocks and offices are obliged by law to fly their national flag.

Above all, however, it is three regular events that are absolutely outstanding: the Baltic song festivals (see the special section 'The Power of Song'), the midsummer celebrations and the Baltika folk festival.

### Baltika Folklore Festival

The Baltic folk festivals, particularly the annual Baltika festival, provide a prime opportunity to catch folk songs, music and dance as well as the colourful traditional costumes which are one of the few instantly recognisable trademarks of Estonia, Latvia and Lithuania. The Baltika annual international folklore festival, dating from 1987, takes place in each Baltic capital in turn (usually in mid-July). The week-long festival is a potent splash of music, dance, exhibitions and parades focusing on Baltic and other folk traditions. In 2003 the Baltika will be held in Latvia; in 2004 it's due in Estonia; and in 2005 in Lithuania.

Regional costumes vary, although women generally sport long and colourful skirts, embroidered blouses, jackets or shawls, and an amazing variety of headgear ranging from neat pillboxes to vast, winged, fairy-tale creations. Male gear is plainer and more obviously a product of peasant existence.

Folk music and dance performances are also regularly held at Rocca al Mare in Tallinn, the Open-Air Ethnography Museum in Rīga, and the Lithuanian Country Life Museum at Rumšiškės near Kaunas.

### ACTIVITIES

The Baltic region is rich in its earthy offering of things to do. Be it berrying or bird-watching, skiing or sweating it off in a steaming sauna, the region's diverse activities certainly allow you to discover some of the wilder, more beautiful parts of the region.

The **Estonian Rural Tourism Association** (☎ 600 99 99, 625 62 73, ☎/fax 641 12 03; e eesti@maatourism.ee; Lai tänav 39-41, EE10133 Tallinn) is a coordinating body of tour organisers and travel agencies, and arranges a fabulous wealth of activity tours focusing on everything from canoeing, cross-country skiing and cycling to horse riding, nature photography, animal- and bird-watching. Rīga-based **Countryside Holidays** (Poilsis kaime; ☎/fax 5-272 6554; e turfond@is.lt; Rotundo gatvė 4, LT-2001 Vilnius) offers the equivalent for Latvia.

### Cycling

Cycling is a pretty cool way to traverse the Baltic region given that it's so damn flat. There are some fun cycling tours on the market and plenty of places to rent bicycles, particularly around seaside hot spots (such as the Curonian Spit and Palanga in western Lithuania), where special cycling paths hug the coastline.

Mountain biking – as in downhill – does not exist, given the region's flat nature. But there are plenty of off-road trails through forests and along dirt tracks. Most are marked on the cycling maps (1:500,000) covering the three countries, published in 2001 by Estonia, Latvia and Lithuania's leading cycling organisations: Estonia's Tartu-based **Vänta Aga cycling club** *(fax 07-42 25 36; Lunini 3, EE50406 Tartu)*; the **Latvian Bicycle Tourism Information Centre** *(VIC; ☎ 750 70 41, fax 7205355; ℮ velokurjers@velokurjers.lv)*; and the **Lithuanian Cyclists' Community** *(LDB; Du Ratai Bicycle Information Centre; ☎ 0685-77 195, fax 46-38 0650; ℮ info@bicycle.lt; ⓦ www.bicycle.lt; PO Box 190, LT-5800 Klaipéda)*. Every year the three clubs organise BaltiCCycle, a Baltic bicycle tour starting in Haapsalu (Estonia) and ending in Kaliningrad (Russia), south of Lithuania. Cyclists cover between 40km and 70km a day and camp in tents.

In Latvia, Sigulda's Eži hostel and bike shop publishes the excellent *Velo-Hanza: Travel Guide for Bikers*, which maps out nine biking routes around Sigulda, Cēsis

and Līgatne. The club helps cyclists with individual itineraries, rents equipment, runs a guide service and overall is an invaluable information source for those poodling or powering round Latvia by pedal. A cycling track links Rīga with Jūrmala, while the Lithuanian capital is the only Baltic city to date to sport cycling tracks around town.

For information on cycling to/from the region, see Bicycle in the Getting There & Away chapter. See also Bicycle in the Getting Around chapter.

## Winter Sports

Skiing (mainly cross-country), ice-skating and tobogganing are all popular. Otepää in southeastern Estonia is the main skiing centre – there are downhill runs, a ski jump and hire outlets where you can get all the gear. In Latvia the Gauja Valley is a winter sports centre; there's a bobsleigh run at Sigulda and a ski jump at Valmiera. Again, you can

## Midsummer Madness

In pagan times it was a night of magic and sorcery when witches would run naked and wild, bewitching flowers and ferns, people and animals. In the agricultural calendar, it marked the end of the spring sowing and the start of the summer harvest. In Soviet times, it became a political celebration; a torch of independence was lit in each capital and its flame used to light bonfires throughout the country.

Today Midsummer Day, summer solstice or St John's Day, falling on 24 June, is the Balts' biggest party of the year. On this night darkness barely falls – reason alone to celebrate in a part of the world with such short summers and such long, dark winters. In Estonia it is known as *Jaanipäev*, in Latvia as *Jāni* or *Jānu Diena*, and in Lithuania as *Joninės* or *Rasos* (the old pagan name).

Celebrations start on 23 June, particularly in Latvia, where the festival is generally met with the most gusto. Traditionally, people flock to the countryside to celebrate this special night amid lakes and pine forests. Special beers, cheese and pies are prepared and wreaths strung from grasses, while flowers and herbs are hung around the home to bring good luck and keep families safe from evil spirits. Men adorn themselves with crowns made from oak leaves, and women with crowns of flowers.

Come midsummer eve, bonfires are lit and the music and drinking begins. No-one is allowed to sleep until the sun has sunk and risen again – anyone who does will be riddled with bad luck for the coming year. Traditional folk songs are sung, dances danced and those special beers, cheese and pies eaten! To ensure good luck, you have to leap back and forth over the bonfire. In Lithuania, clearing a burning wheel of fire as it is rolled down the nearest hill brings you even better fortune. In Estonia, revellers swing on special double-sided Jaanipäev swings, strung from trees in forest clearings or in village squares.

Midsummer night is a night for lovers. In Estonia the mythical *Koit* (dawn) and *Hämarik* (dusk) meet but once a year for an embrace lasting as long as the shortest night of the year. Throughout the Baltic region, lovers seek the mythical fern flower, which only blooms on this night. The dew coating flowers and ferns on this night is held to be a purifying force, a magical healer, and a much sought-after cure for wrinkles! Bathe your face in it and you will instantly become more beautiful, more youthful. However, beware the witches of Jaanipäev/Jāni/Joninės, who are known to use it for less enchanting means.

hire equipment once you arrive. The north-eastern Aukštaitija National Park attracts cross-country skiers.

There is an outdoor ice-skating rink in Rīga, open when it is below –3ĢC; and an indoor rink on the edge of Vilnius in the Akropolis shopping mall (see the Vilnius chapter for details).

## Bird-Watching

In Estonia, the Vilsandi National Park on Saaremaa (see that chapter) arranges bird-watching tours on an island off the western coast of Saaremaa. The Hiiumaa Islets Landscape Reserve and the Matsalu Nature Reserve, both in western Estonia, are other unique birding opportunities. The **Estonian Ornithological Society** (Eesti Ornitoloogiaühing; ☎ 07-422 195, fax 422 180; e eoy@eoy.ee; w www.eoy.ee; PO Box 227, EE50002 Tartu), with an office in Tartu at Veski tänav 4, can guide watchers to birds.

Some 270 of the 325 bird species found in Lithuania can be spotted at the Nemunas Delta Regional Park (see the boxed text 'Nemunas Bird Life' in the Western Lithuania chapter). The park authorities and the information centre in Rusnė help organise bird-watching expeditions during the migratory seasons mid-September and late October, and March to mid-May. Both also assist travellers wanting to get a behind-the-scenes look at the nearby ornithological station, where birds are ringed, in Ventės Ragas – the edge of the world. Some 200 different bird species fly around the Curonian Spit National Park, also in western Lithuania. If you can speak Lithuanian, contact the **Lithuanian Ornithological Society** (☎/fax 5-213 0498; e birdlife@post.5ci.lt; w www.birdlife.lt; Naugarduko gatvė 47/3, LT-2006 Vilnius) for information.

In Latvia, some of Europe's rarest birds can be spotted in the Gauja National Park in the Vidzeme region; around Kurzeme's Lake Kaņieris in the Ķemeri National Park and Lake Engure, a bird reservation, a little further north; and around Lake Pape, south of Liepāja near the Lithuanian border. Places that list bird-watching expeditions are listed under the relevant sections in the regional chapters. On the Internet, **Latvian Birding** (w www.putni.lv) is a highly informative site in English with exhaustive lists of birds common to Latvia, recent sightings of species, bird-watching spots in the country etc.

## Canoeing & Rafting

Canoeing and rafting are particularly popular in Latvia: the Gauja, Salaca and Abava Rivers all offer uninterrupted routes over several days. For information on organised canoeing expeditions in Vidzeme, see the boxed text 'Canoe Trips' in that chapter. In the capital, **Campo** (☎ 922 23 39, fax 750 53 22; e campo@laivas.lv; w www.laivas.lv; Blaumaņa iela 22-24, LV-1011 Rīga) is a good starting point. The club organises canoeing trips in Latgale, Zemgale, Kurzeme and Vidzeme and has all the gear to rent, too.

In Lithuania, the northeastern Aukštaitija National Park is equally excellent canoeing terrain, with a big network of interconnected lakes. The park's tourism centre, 5km southwest of Ignalina, organises trips and rents equipment (see the Eastern & Southern Lithuania chapter). In the Dzūkija National Park, canoeing trips along the Ūla River are arranged through friendly staff at the hostel in the ethnographic village of Zervynos, near Druskininkai. In Vilnius, the Old Town Hostel and Filaretai Hostel (see Places to Stay in the Vilnius chapter) both arrange canoeing expeditions.

Canoe or traditional *haabja* is the primary means of exploring the Soomaa National Park in southwestern Estonia. **Karuskoe** (☎ 050-61 896; e matkad@soomaa.com; w www.soomaa.com), in Tohera, just outside the park's northwestern boundary, arranges canoeing and boating trips on the national park's rivers and bogs between April and September. A day's canoeing/boating in a *haabja* costs upwards of €18/32 and, more unusually, you can canoe at night (€32) or sweat it out in a floating sauna (€32/64/96 per morning/afternoon/evening).

## Berrying & Mushrooming

The Balts' deep-rooted attachment to the land is reflected in their obsession with berrying and mushrooming – national pastimes for all three countries. Accompanying a local friend into the forest on a berrying or mushrooming expedition is an enchanting way to appreciate this traditionally rural occupation. Alternatively, most ecotourism organisations can arrange trips: Latvia's **Country Tourism Association** (Lauku Ceļotājs; ☎ 761 76 00, fax 783 00 41; e lauku@celotajs.lv; w www.traveller.lv, w www.celotajs.lv; Ku-u iela 11,

## Some Like it Hot

In a region snow-covered for months each year, it is not surprising that the sauna is an integral part of Baltic culture. Most hotels have one and there are public bathhouses with saunas in some cities. But the ones that silently smoulder next to a lake or river, by the sea or deep in the forest, provide the most authentic experience.

Balts split their saunas into two categories: Russian, and Finnish or Swedish. A 'Russian' or 'smoke' sauna is the more traditional and is very much modelled on the great Russian *bahnia*. The sauna is housed in a one-room wooden hut; bathing begins when the open wood stove has roared for some three to four hours – turning the interior of the hut black with soot and the heated rocks smouldering red. When taking a sauna, the often boisterous bathers throw water onto the sizzling rocks to ensure the wood-perfumed air remains thick with steam (and sweat).

The 'Finnish' or 'Swedish' sauna, by comparison, can be a clinical, second-rate affair. This Nordic terminology refers to the clean and smokeless modern sauna that sprang up in the 1990s (despite the fact that, until the 1950s, it was the smoke sauna that Finns favoured). Electric heaters are generally used to heat the modest mound of stones, contained in a small rack at one end of the neat, bench-clad sauna.

Balts use a bunch of birch twigs to lightly switch the body, irrespective of which sauna type they're sweating in. This gentle beating is said to increase perspiration, tingle the nerve ends and add to the overall sense of relaxation and revitalisation that a sauna is intended to bring. Cooling down is an equally integral part of the sauna experience: most Finnish-style saunas have showers or pools, while the more authentic smoke saunas are usually next to a lake or river. In the depths of winter, cutting out a square metre of ice from a frozen lake in which to take a quick dip is not unheard of.

An invitation to share a sauna – said to come close to a religious experience on occasion – is a hospitable gesture and one that should be treated with great respect. Public or hotel saunas demand an hourly fee of around €4 and there are plenty of small, private saunas which groups can rent out for €8 to €15 per hour. In Estonia a Finnish-style sauna, noteworthy for its stunning views, is the Hotel Olümpia's glass-windowed sauna in Tallinn. For a sootier, smoke-sauna experience try Kalma Saun in Tallinn; or Mihkli Farm Museum in Malvaste, Hiiumaa, which has a traditional Russian-style sauna dating from 1915 to rent (see West Estonia & the Islands chapter).

In southern Lithuania, there is a sauna at the Zervynos Hostel, in the forests of the Dzūkija National Park (see the Eastern & Southern Lithuania chapter). The larger, Russian-style saunas at Karčema, a rustic farmstead in Agluonėnai, midway between Šilutė and Klaipėda in western Lithuania, are other definite 'sauna highlights'.

---

LV-1048 Rīga), **Countryside Holidays** (*Poilsis kaime;* ☎/fax 5-272 6554; e turfond@is.lt; *Rotundo gatvė 4, LT-2001 Vilnius)* in Lithuania and Estonia's **Estonian Rural Tourism** (☎ 600 99 99, 625 62 73, ☎/fax 641 12 03; e eesti@ maatourism.ee; *Lai tänav 39-41, EE10133 Tallinn)* all offer rural accommodation with hosts who take their guests mushrooming, berrying, or both. On the Estonian island of Saaremaa, the Mere travel agency (see Estonia under Organised Tours in the Getting Around chapter) also arranges berrying and mushrooming trips.

### Fishing
In the dark depths of the Baltic winter there is no finer experience than dabbling in a touch of ice-fishing along with the local,

vodka-warmed fishers on the frozen Curonian Lagoon, off the west coast of Lithuania. Tourist offices throughout the region can advise you on the best spots to fish and on permits etc.

In western Lithuania, the park information office of the Nemunas Delta Regional Park (for more information see Bird-watching earlier) issues angling permits (€3.50/ 30 a day/month) and can assist you with all the gear.

In northeastern Estonia, the **Lahemaa National Park Visitors' Centre** (☎ 032-95 555; e info@lahemaa.ee; w www.lahemaa .ee) in Palmse should be able to help. Elsewhere along the Estonian coastline you need a fishing permit to fish; again, ask at the closest tourist office.

## Aerial Sports

In Latvia, the **Cēsis Flying Club** *(Cēsu Aeroklubs;* ☎ *41 22 639, 94 59 578)* in Cēsis arranges flying and gliding lessons and trips over the Gauja National Park. If you want to fly in a hot-air balloon, contact **Altius** *(☎ 76 11 614, fax 78 60 206;* **w** *www.altius.lv)*.

The fearless can plunge 43m into the Gauja Valley from the cable car in Sigulda or, in Lithuania, leap a heart-stopping 170m from Vilnius TV Tower. Both bungee jumps are organised by the **LGK Bungee Jumping Team** *(***w** *www.bungeezone.com)*. More details are listed in the respective destination chapters.

## Horse Riding

Most tourist farms in Estonia have horses and arrange treks. Contact any of the regional tourist information centres for details.

In Latvia, the Liepāja tourist office doles out a useful list in English of horse-riding opportunities in its region; riding costs around €5 per hour.

In Lithuania, a particularly lovely spot for a canter is around Anykščiai; the **Horse Museum** *(☎ 381-51 722)*, 10km northwest of Anykščiai in Niūronys village, offers jaunts in a traditional horse and cart along the Anykščiai Stallion Path, a 12km trail snaking along the banks of the Šventoji River and through Ramulduva forest.

## COURSES
### Language

Vilnius University runs Lithuanian-language courses. An intensive two-/four-week summer course (50/110 hours) costs €345/ 530, plus €27 registration fee. Accommodation in a student dormitory/with a local family can be arranged for an additional €22/112 a week. One-year courses are also available. For more details contact the **Department of Lithuanian Studies at Vilnius University** *(☎/fax 5-261 0786;* **e** *stud@flf.vu.lt;* **w** *www .vu.lt; Universiteto gatvė 3, LT-2734 Vilnius, Lithuania)*.

In Estonia, the **International Language Services** *(☎ 646 42 58, fax 641 1047;* **e** *info@ ils.ee;* **w** *www.ils.ee; Tolli 1, EE10133 Tallinn)* is one of several schools in the capital to run Estonian-language courses. An intensive five-week course, comprising 40 hours of tuition (three classes a week), costs €155. In Tartu, occasional Estonian-language

courses aimed at foreign students are available at the Department of Estonian and Finno-Ugric Linguistics, inside the **Faculty of Philosophy** *(☎ 07-375 341, fax 372 345;* **e** *filosqut.ee; room 224-229, Lossi tänav 3, EE51003 Tartu)* at the University of Tartu. Contact the **International Student Office** *(☎ 07-375 150;* **e** *proffice@ut.ee;* **w** *www .ut.ee; Ülikooli tänav 18a)* or drop by the university's **information centre** *(☎ 375 100; open 8am-4pm Mon-Fri)*, to the left after entering the main doors.

Those wanting to twist their tongue around Latvian can contact the **Public Service Language Centre** *(☎ 721 22 51, fax 721 37 80;* **e** *vmc@latent.lv;* **w** *www.vmc.lv; Smilšu iela 1-3, LV-1050 Rīga)*, which has a second school *(☎ 731 42 36, fax 731 42 60;* **e** *vmcb@ la tent.lv; K Barona iela 64/2)*; or **Satva** *(☎ 722 66 41;* **e** *satva@mailbox.riga.lv;* **w** *www.satva .lv; A Kalniņa iela 1, LV-1050 Rīga)*.

## Sculpture

Lithuania has the unique **Centre of Europe Museum** *(Europos centro muziejus;* ☎ *5-237 7077;* **e** *hq@eurosparkas.lt;* **w** *www.euro posparkas.lt)* which runs an artists' residency programme whereby artists from around the world can brainstorm with one another at the open-air sculpture park, near Vilnius. Several programmes are held each year and are open to anyone with an interest in applied art or sculpture. Applications have to be accompanied by a curriculum vitae and must be submitted two months prior to courses starting.

## WORK

The Baltic region has enough difficulties keeping its own people employed, meaning there's little temporary work for visitors. Most Westerners working here have been posted by companies back home. However, these are times of change and opportunity, and there is some scope for people who want to stay a while and carve themselves a new niche – though, in Western terms, you could not expect to get rich doing so. The English language is certainly in demand, and you might be able to earn your keep (or part of it) teaching it in one of the main cities. In the UK, **Travel Teach** *(☎ 0870-789 8100;* **w** *www.travelteach.com; St James's Buildings, 79 Oxford St, Manchester M1 6FR)* arranges short- and long-term teaching placements for undergraduates, graduates and postgraduates in Lithuania; it charges a UK£495 placement fee.

Various volunteer placements – teaching or working in a summer camp, for example – are occasionally advertised on websites such as W www.escapeartist.com, an employment overseas index which advertises international jobs and volunteer placements. Very occasionally jobs for English speakers are advertised locally in the *Baltic Times*.

## ACCOMMODATION

The region offers a wide range of accommodation and you'll probably get most out of your trip by trying a variety of types. A few nights in private homes will bring you closer to the people and their way of life than a couple of weeks in hotels.

Book ahead wherever you plan to stay, as vacancies, particularly during summer, can be scarce. Agencies in other countries as well as in the three Baltic countries can make bookings for you but they work mainly with the more expensive hotels and may charge a commission.

### Camping

In the Baltics, a camping ground (Estonian: *kämpingud*; Latvian: *kempings*; Lithuanian: *kempingas*) consists of permanent wooden cottages or, occasionally, brick bungalows, with a few spaces to pitch tents, too. Many are in quite pretty, remote spots, often overlooking a lake or river but often hard to reach unless you have a private vehicle. Cabins vary in shape and size but are usually small one-room affairs with three or four beds. Showers and toilets are nearly always communal and vary dramatically in cleanliness. Many camping grounds have a bar and/or cafeteria, and sauna.

Camp sites usually open from some time in May or June to the end of August or mid-September. A night in a wooden cottage typically costs €10 to €20 per person, but there are a few superior, recently built places – like Piejūras Kempings in Ventspils – which charge up to €25 for a four-person cottage with shower and kitchen.

### Hostels

Lithuania's hostel network has developed in leaps and bounds in the past couple of years, although rooms still get massively booked up in summer and if you don't book in advance, it can be impossible to get a bed for the night. Estonia has the most advanced network, followed by Lithuania, while Latvia has very few. All three are affiliated to Hostelling International (HI). See under Accommodation in the relevant Facts for the Visitor chapters for details.

### B&Bs

Sharing the breakfast table with your host family each morning will give you more of an idea of local life than any number of nights in a hotel could. Sampling traditional cooking is another joy, hard to find elsewhere.

Several agencies, both within and outside of the Baltics, arrange accommodation in private homes in several cities in Estonia, Latvia and Lithuania:

**American-International Homestays** (☎ 303-258 3234, fax 258 3264, ℮ ash@igc.apc.org, W www.aihtravel.com/homestays) PO Box 1754, Nederland, CO 80466, USA – Homestay accommodation with dinner, transportation and an English-speaking guide in any of the Baltic capitals for US$100/175 in a single/double room.

**Gateway Travel** (☎ 02-9745 3333, fax 9745 3237, ℮ agent@russian-gateway.com.au, W www .russian-gateway.com.au) 48 The Boulevarde, Strathfield, NSW 2135, Australia – Baltic homestays.

**Litinterp** (☎ 5-212 3850, fax 212 3559, ℮ vilnius@litinterp.lt, W www.litinterp.lt) Bernardinų gatvė 7-2, LT-2000 Vilnius, Lithuania – B&B with local families in Klaipėda, Nida, Palanga and Kaunas for €22/32 singles/ doubles per night; arranges car and bicycle rental, too. Bookings can be made via the Internet.

**Rasastra Bed & Breakfast** (☎/fax 661 62 91, ℮ rasastra@online.ee, W www.bedbreakfast.ee) Mere puiestee 4, EE10111 Tallinn, Estonia – Rasastra can set you up in people's homes in Latvia and Lithuania for €22 per person, plus €6 breakfast; singles/doubles/triples in central Tallinn cost €17/31/42 and breakfast is €2.

Information on agencies dealing only with the cities where they are located is given in the relevant city/town sections. Rīga in particular has a clutch of B&B agencies which organise B&B accommodation in hotel-style apartments (ie, with a reception and without a host) rather than family homes.

## Hotels

There are hotels to suit every price range, although budget hotel accommodation in the increasingly glam capitals has become disheartengly scarce. As more cheap hotels make the effort to brighten up their image, so nightly rates are being yanked up too.

That is not to say, however, that delightfully horrible dinosaur relics from the Soviet era – offering cheap accommodation in a glum and shabby setting – don't exist. Head into any town in provincial Latvia, for example, and you'll almost immediately stumble upon a towering concrete block whose stereotypical customer – once upon a time – was a man in a vest, lying on his bed quaffing vodka, chain-smoking and watching TV. Rooms tout the most disgusting colour scheme you're ever likely to encounter, and toilet and wash facilities are nothing short of grim. The outside appearance of some is so shockingly rundown and dilapidated that it is hard to believe the hotel still functions: Daugavpils' Hotel Latvija or the Baltija in Jūrmala are prime examples.

The mid-range – both in and outside of the capitals – is marked by a refreshing breed of small, family-run hotels. The only downside of these places is that they get booked up quickly, given the limited number of cosy rooms they offer. Most larger hotels in this range are of the high-rise, concrete variety – former communist-era hotels since renovated and furnished top to toe with all the modern trappings. A rare handful of these places – like Rīga's Hotel Viktorija – still have one or two unrenovated floors with cheaper rooms and shared bathrooms.

Top hotels are a dime a dozen. Many are under Western management or are part of a recognised, international hotel chain, while others – such as Konventa Sēta in Rīga, the Radisson-SAS Astorija in Vilnius and the St Petersbourg in Tallinn – are housed in exquisitely renovated, historic buildings dating to the 13th to 19th centuries. More contemporary architectural creations – like Kaunas' avant-garde Daniela (owned by Lithuanian basketball god Arvydas Sabonis) or Hotel Kaunas – sport suites equipped with everything from dataport to computer with Internet access, printer or fax machine. A double room in these very top hotels can command anything from €150 (€250 in the case of the capitals) upwards a night.

## Farmstays

Farmhouse accommodation comprising a private room in farmhouse, rural manor or cottage is one of the region's most attractive types of accommodation. Accommodation consists of a private room in a farmhouse, manor or cottage in a rural or coastal area. Host families can provide home-cooked meals and arrange fishing, boating, horse riding, mushroom and berry picking in the forest, and other activities – all for an extra fee, naturally. Each of the Baltic countries has its own rural tourism association through which accommodation countrywide can be booked and rural activities arranged:

**Countryside Holidays** (Poilsis kaime; ☎/fax 5-272 6554, e turfond@is.lt, w www.travel-lithuania .com) Rotundo gatvė 4, LT-2001 Vilnius – Countryside arranges accommodation in farmhouses and rural cottages throughout Lithuania for €6 to €25 per person per night. Bookings can be made direct at the farmhouse of your choice online or via Countryside Holidays at the Lithuanian Tourism Fund.

**Estonian Rural Tourism** (☎ 600 99 99, 625 62 73, ☎/fax 641 12 03, e eesti@maatourism.ee) Lai tänav 39-41, EE10133 Tallinn – An umbrella organisation for 220-odd rural tourism organisations in Estonia. The full range of accommodation – from camping and B&B to palatial palace and castle hotels – can be booked through it. Most B&Bs are on farms and costs from €15.

**Latvian Country Tourism Association** (Lauku Ceļotājs; ☎ 761 76 00, fax 783 00 41, e lauku@ celotajs.lv, w www.traveller.lv, w www.celotajs .lv) Ku-u iela 11, LV-1048 Rīga – Arranges B&B accommodation in a variety of rural settings all over Latvia for €12 to €35 per night; it also lets whole farmhouses and cottages, and takes advance bookings for camping grounds, hotels and motels across Latvia.

Many travel agencies also arrange countryside accommodation – see Organised Tours in the introductory Getting Around chapter and Travel Agencies under Information in the city chapters.

## Holiday Homes & Sanatoriums

Many of the holiday homes that in Soviet times were reserved for members of particular organisations are open to general trade and are as good as decent hotels (the odd one is, admittedly, still a tad tatty and institutional).

The better ones give an idea of the rewards that awaited those who succeeded in the communist system. Prices in such places vary widely but often include full board. A holiday home is likely to be called a *puhke-baas, puhkekodu, puhkemaja* or *pansion* in Estonia; a *pansionāts* in Latvia; a *poilsio namai* in Lithuania.

## FOOD
The Baltic capitals burst with sophisticated restaurants, funky eateries, American-style diners and snug and cosy bistros. Cuisines abound and there's ample choice, be it Armenian or Mexican, Italian or Soviet you're seeking. Places dishing up the Balts' meaty national cuisines are equally prevalent, with prices to suit budgets both big and small.

The eating scene has yet to be revolutionised in rural pockets of Estonia, Latvia and Lithuania, where simply finding somewhere to dine can, astonishingly, still be hard to find still. Few eat out, or can afford to eat out, in the countryside, where people continue to live off the land as their ancestors did generations before.

The Language chapter at the back of this book includes words and phrases you will find useful when ordering food and drink.

### Types of Eateries
You easily pay Western city prices in Rīga and Tallinn, but in Vilnius and elsewhere eating remains relatively cheap. Restaurants abound in the capitals and larger towns: most accept major credit cards and tout bi- or multilingual menus which – accurately, amusingly, or both – describe in English what you can expect to eat. Count on paying anything from €10 to €150 for a three-course meal in these places.

For budget travellers, a tasty alternative to a proper restaurant is the new canteen-style places – usually with an attractive rustic interior and buzzing with local city dwellers – which have made a splash in recent years. These places rarely have menus, but this is absolutely irrelevant given that what's cooking is displayed, allowing you to simply point at what you want. While some of the food dished up is no gourmet's delight, it's perfectly palatable and – in the case of the hugely successful Latvian-run Lido chain of cafeterias in Rīga, for example – can be a joy to eat. A lot of the food

served is local cuisine and, best of all, you can fill up for €3 to €6.

In provincial towns, the dining scene is more limited and travellers who spend any length of time exploring the country will more often than not find themselves eating in a small TV-clad place that has clearly been around for several decades. Service could well be snail-slow and the menu will be limited and in the local language only. But the upside is you'll pay no more than €5 to eat.

All three capitals enjoy vibrant café scenes, with a variety of dynamic, offbeat and more traditional places serving up good coffee, fresh and very delicious breads and pastries, as well as alcoholic drinks and light hot meals. In Estonia and Lithuania, international fast-food chains have made their mark in most larger towns and cities, although Latvia – with its own clutch of *pelmeņi* and *pīrāgi* (meat dumpling and pasty) places – has yet to welcome Western chains with open arms; one or two are in Rīga, but that is about it.

### Types of Food
In cities you can get anything you fancy, be it Chinese, Indian, Mexican or Hungarian. Restaurants and cafés specialising in world cuisines have sprung up left, right and centre. However, because many food products are imported, coupled with the fact that the Baltic diet is not particularly hot on spices, you might find that what you end up eating is simply a tasteless, tamed-down version of the same ethnic dish you'd be served back home.

A typical main course in a provincial restaurant usually consists of a piece of grilled or fried meat or fish, along with french fries and small amounts of a couple of boiled vegetables. However, this is only a pallid reflection of real local diets, and you won't truly experience what Baltic people eat unless you're lucky enough to enjoy some home cooking. If you do, the care with which it's prepared and the variety of tastes and textures which can be extracted from some pretty ordinary ingredients will be a pleasant surprise. Notes on some local specialities are given in the Estonia, Latvia and Lithuania Facts for the Visitor chapters.

Common food items throughout the region include pancakes, which come with different fillings – fruit, meat, curd, cheese, jam, sour cream etc – and in a variety of sizes; sausage, usually cold and sliced; and dairy products – milk is turned to curd, sour cream and cottage cheese as well as plain old butter, cream and cheese. Four common ways of cooking meat of almost any kind are as a *shashlik* (kebab), *carbonade* (officially a chop but in practice it could be almost any piece of grilled meat), *beefsteak* (any piece of fried meat), and stroganoff (cubes of meat in sauce or gravy). Dill is liberally used to flavour everything, be it a soup, salad or packet of crisps!

In all three capitals decent vegetarian restaurants have sprouted, but have yet to take root elsewhere.

## Self-Catering
Practically every town has a daily market with a surprising range of fruit and vegetables sold at good prices. Bread is easy to get from bakeries at under €1 a loaf and everything else can be bought at a supermarket or – in the case of the provinces – the village shop.

## DRINKS
## Nonalcoholic Drinks
Tap water can be dodgy – see Basic Rules under Health earlier in this chapter. A good cheap substitute (a few euro cents a bottle) is mineral water, of which there are numerous brands. Be wary of some locally produced ones, though (usually the ones in beer-size glass bottles), which are so salty it is comparable to drinking sea water. Tea, coffee, fruit juices and fizzy drinks are easy to get throughout the region.

## Alcoholic Drinks
Good beer is brewed in the Baltics and is available in most restaurants and cafés, alongside more expensive imported German and Scandinavian beers (and even Guinness in some bars). Local beer is also sold in shops, kiosks, bars and Western-style pubs. It normally comes in half-litre bottles which cost about €2 in shops and kiosks, and for around €3.50 in most bars. You can also buy the mostly inferior draught ale, with which people fill cans at kiosks, some shops and breweries.

Most Baltic beer is light, fairly flat and of medium strength. Utenos, Kalnapilis (the brewery of which you can visit in Panevėžy – see the Central Lithuania chapter), Ragutis and Gubernija are Lithuania's best brews, all from the north of the country; the light Saku beer and the heavier Saare beer from the island of Saaremaa are Estonia's prime choices; Aldaris is Latvia's most popular. Here and there you can get good strong stout – known in Latvia as *tumsais* and in Lithuania as *porteris*. Vodka, brandy and champagne, all from various areas of the ex-USSR and the West, are served everywhere too.

Some Estonian cafés and bars serve tasty, warming hõõgvein (mulled wine). Latvia's speciality is Rīga Black Balsam (Rīgas Melnais Balzāms), a thick, dark, bitter and potent liquid with supposedly medicinal properties. In Lithuania you may find midus (mead) or jolly little fruit liqueurs called *likeriai*. See Food & Drink in the respective country chapters for more food and drink delights.

# Getting There & Away

The fact that you can travel direct to Estonia, Latvia and Lithuania and on to their western and eastern neighbours, with minimal fuss, is the ultimate proof that Soviet writ no longer rules here. There are so many ways of travelling into the Baltic countries that the choice is mind-boggling. And there is certainly no need to stick with the same form of transport. It's perfectly feasible to fly or take a bus to Warsaw and then enter Lithuania by train, or fly to Helsinki and sail from there to Estonia, for example. Within the Baltics, distances are relatively small.

## AIR

Details of interregional flights between the capitals and other Baltic cities are listed under Getting There & Away in the respective destination chapters.

### Airports & Airlines

The three Baltic-capital airports – Tallinn, Rīga and Vilnius – are served by several international carriers, including national carriers **Estonian Air** (W *www.estonian-air.ee*), Latvia's **airBaltic** (W *www.airbaltic.com*), which works in partnership with **SAS Scandinavian Airlines** (W *www.scandinavian.net*), and **Lithuanian Airlines** (*LAL, Lietuvo savialinijos;* W *www.lal.lt*). Outside the capitals, Palanga and Kaunas in Lithuania are the only airports to be billed as international, although few destinations are connected by direct flights. Most short- and long-haul flights advertised require a change of plane in Hamburg, Oslo, Billund and Kristianstad – the only places served by direct flights to these regional airports by the independent airline **Air Lithuania** (*Aviakompanija Lietuva;* W *www.airlithuania.lt*).

For details of these airports and how to travel to/from the town centres, see Air under Getting There & Away and To/From the Airport under Getting Around in the relevant destination chapters.

All four Baltic airlines post updated schedules and fares on the Internet. Estonian Air has offices in the three Baltic capitals (listed under Air in the Getting There & Away sections of the city-specific chapters) and offices abroad. These include:

**Belgium** (☎ 02-712 64 35, e pax.resa@air agencies.be) c/o Air Agencies Belgium, Vilvoordelaan 153 A, B-1930 Zaventem

**Canada** (☎ 1-800 397 1354, 905 677 4295, e canada@estonian-air.ee) Aviareps, c/o Aibridge International Inc, 5955 Airport Rd, Suite 137, Toronto international airport, Mississauga, Ont L4V 1R9

**Denmark** (☎ 70 23 04 73, e sales@estonian-air.dk) Maersk Air, Copenhagen airport south, DK-2791 Dragoer; (☎ 45 70 100 410, e cphhz1@maersk-air.dk) Maersk Air Reservation Centre, DK-7190 Billund airport; (☎ 45 32 31 41 00) Terminal 3, Copenhagen airport

**Germany** (☎ 06105-20 60 70, e yfranta@aviareps.com) c/o Aviareps GmbH, Hessenring 32, D-64546 Mörfelden-Walldorf, Frankfurt

**Netherlands** (☎ 010-208 36 70, e rtm.sales@airagencies.nl) c/o Air Agencies Holland, PO Box 12010, NL-3004 GA Rotterdam

**Sweden** (☎ 08-545 046 55, e ee.se@Estonian-air.ee) c/o Maersk Air A/S, Birger Jarlsgatan 34, S-11429 Stockholm

**UK** (☎ 020-7333 0196, e lon@maersk-air.com) c/o Maersk Air, Terminal House, 52 Grosvenor Gardens, London SW1W OAU

**USA** (☎ 1-800 397 1354, e us@estonian-air.ee) 6355 NW 36th St, Suite 602, Virginia Gardens, Miami, FL-33166

Tickets for airBaltic are sold on the Internet (W *www.airbaltic.com*) – at the time of writing only for journeys originating in Rīga – and at SAS (W www.scandinavian .net) offices worldwide.

The international sales offices of LAL (W www.lal.lt) also sell tickets for Air Lithuania (W www.airlithuania.lt), both of which accept bookings via the Internet. Offices include:

**Denmark** (☎ 32 52 81 50, e lithuanian.airlines@ get2net.dk) Copenhagen airport, DK-2770 Kastrup

**Germany** (☎ 089-5525 33 41, e resteger@ aviareps.com, W www.lithuanian-airlines.de) Landsbergerstr 155, D-80687 Munich; (☎ 01805-73 80 25, 0160-520 62 06, e salesteger@aviareps.com) Hessenring 32, D-64546 Morfelden-Walldorf

**Finland** (☎ 09-622 622 99, e paivi@paivi .pp.fi) Punavuorenkatu 4, SF-00120 Helsinki

**Netherlands** (☎ 020-316 40 66, e lal.ams@ ision.nl) World Trade Centre, Tower A, 7th floor, Schipholl Boulevard 201

**UK** (☎ 01293-57 99 00, e lithair@globalnet .co.uk) Room 1025, 1st floor, North Terminal, Gatwick airport, West Sussex RH6 0PJ

## Buying Tickets
Travel agents, as well as the airlines themselves, can sell you tickets for scheduled flights. Single flights at regular fares are usually as expensive as, or more than, returns. But open-jaw tickets (on which you fly into one city and out of another) are quite widely available for the Baltic capitals. On SAS, single youth fares between Scandinavia and the Baltic capitals can be combined to form the equivalent of open-jaw tickets. Lufthansa likewise offers open-jaw tickets to/from Rīga and Vilnius, allowing you to fly in to one capital and out of the other at no extra cost. The budget-conscious should bear in mind when planning their departure that Tallinn has no airport tax.

Of the national Baltic airlines, Estonian Air and Lithuanian Airlines offer youth fares to travellers under 25. These fares, not valid on all routes, are 20% to 25% cheaper than a regular economy fare. Lithuanian Airlines' special 'summer fares' can work out cheaper than a youth fare, however, so make sure you check what options are available to you. Both airlines give 50% discount to children under 12; toddlers under two pay 10% of an adult fare. The Kaunas-based Air Lithuania gives 30% discount to students

with an ISIC card, and 25% discount to travellers under 28 and over 55/60; it also offers a 35% discount on a family ticket to those travelling together (a married couple with no children qualifies).

## Travellers with Special Needs
If they're warned early enough, airlines can often make special arrangements for travellers, such as wheelchair assistance at airports or vegetarian meals on the flight. Children under two years of age travel for 10% of the standard fare (or free on some airlines), as long as they don't occupy a seat; they don't get a baggage allowance. 'Skycots', baby food and nappies should be provided by the airline if requested in advance. Children aged between two and 12 can usually occupy a seat for around two-thirds of the full fare, and do get a baggage allowance.

The disability-friendly website W www .everybody.co.uk has an airline directory that provides information on the facilities offered by various airlines.

## Scandinavia
**To/from Estonia** Estonian Air and **Finnair** (W www.finnair.com) codeshare on five to seven flights daily between Tallinn and Helsinki. Flying time is only 40 minutes but the trip often ends up being no quicker than a hydrofoil (which is substantially cheaper), due to the time spent getting to/from and at airports. Return fares start at €155 (Sunday-night rule, maximum stay three months).

To/from Stockholm, Estonian Air codeshares with SAS on daily flights to/from the Swedish capital, with return fares starting at €290 (with Sunday rule). The cheapest Tallinn–Stockholm return fare is offered by Finnair, with a change of plane in Helsinki; return fares start at €245.

It is likewise cheaper to fly via Helsinki to get to/from Copenhagen. Finnair offers a €430 return fare (Sunday rule, maximum stay three months), whereas Estonian Air's cheapest return fare – albeit it on a direct flight departing two or four times daily – would leave little change from a €500 bill.

**To/from Latvia** AirBaltic flies five times a week between Rīga and Helsinki, while Finnair flies the same route once or twice. Return fares with either, with the Sunday-night rule, start at around €350.

## Fair Cop

If money is no option and time is of the essence, you can always 'copter it between the Estonian and Finnish capitals. **Copterline** *(in Helsinki ☎ 0200-18181, 09-68 11 670, fax 68 11 6767; ℮ contact@copterline.com; ⓦ www.copterline.com; Hernesaari helicopterterminal, Hernematalankatu 2 • in Tallinn ☎ 610 1818, fax 610 1819; ℮ copterline @copterline.ee; ⓦ www.copterline.ee; Mere puiestee 20)* flies every hour between 8am/8.30am and 9pm/9.30pm Monday to Saturday from Helsinki/Tallinn. Flying time is 18 minutes and the cheapest single fare (available on the Internet) is €49/770 EEK; return fares are twice the price.

SAS and airBaltic codeshare on daily Stockholm–Rīga–Stockholm flights. air-Baltic's return Rīga–Stockholm fare (two weeks in advance, maximum stay 21 days) cost €295 at the time of writing. SAS and airBaltic likewise codeshare on six flights daily to/from Copenhagen; airBaltic's cheapest return fare is €350 (same restrictions as flights to/from Stockholm).

**To/from Lithuania** LAL flies once or twice daily between Helsinki and Vilnius, with return fares notching in at €360 (Sunday rule, maximum stay three months). Cheaper summer/youth fares are also often available.

LAL likewise services Copenhagen to/from Vilnius (once or twice a day Sunday to Friday) and Stockholm (six a week); while SAS operates twice-daily flights between the Lithuanian and Danish capitals.

Air Lithuania flies from Kaunas, via Palanga, to/from Kristianstad (four a week), Oslo (once a week in summer) and Billund (five a week).

### Poland

Lithuanian Airlines is the only national airline to fly to/from Warsaw from Vilnius; beyond that, a change of plane in Copenhagen is required to reach the Polish capital from the Baltics.

### Germany

In addition to the scheduled flights mentioned here, charter flights may be an economical option from Germany to the Baltics. Lufthansa has excellent open-jaw fares combining Rīga and Vilnius at similar or identical rates to there-and-back fares.

**Lufthansa** (ⓦ www.lufthansa.com) doesn't fly to/from Tallinn. Estonian Air flies between Tallinn and Frankfurt/Hamburg four times a week. A return fare at the time of writing was €299/278 (both 21 days' advance purchase, obligatory Saturday-night stay, valid one month), with youth fares available to both cities. From Rīga, there is a daily flight to/from Frankfurt (airBaltic/Lufthansa); return tickets start at €590 (ticket purchase at least three days in advance, valid one month).

Lithuania, meanwhile, enjoys daily flights to a host of German cities, between Vilnius and Berlin or Frankfurt with LAL or Lufthansa; a daily flight to/from Kaunas via Palanga to Hamburg with Air Lithuania; and, between mid-May and mid-September, once-weekly flights from Palanga to/from Berlin and Frankfurt. Sample return fares at research included Palanga–Frankfurt €435, Palanga–Berlin €395 and Vilnius–Frankfurt €435 (all minimum seven days' advance purchase, obligatory weekend stay, valid one month).

### The UK

Estonian Air has six weekly flights between London and Tallinn, costing UK£231 return at the time of writing (28 days' advance purchase, maximum stay one month), with a youth single/return costing UK£111/ 222 (valid one month). **British Airways** (ⓦ www.britishairways.com) flies London–Rīga–London four times weekly (from around UK£220/250 in low/high season).

LAL operates a daily flight to/from London and Vilnius. Its cheapest return, available year-round, is UK£234 if purchased 14 days before (obligatory Saturday night stay, maximum stay one month). At the time of writing, a single/return youth fare – UK£168/234 – yielded little saving. Flying with SAS, there are flights via Copenhagen to each of the Baltic capitals from London, Manchester and Edinburgh. The big advantage of SAS is that it offers student and youth fares.

For all three Baltic capitals, fares offered by specialist agents are usually cheaper than the airlines' own. Some of the best are on

SAS or Finnair flights via Scandinavia, or with Lufthansa via Frankfurt.

## Elsewhere in Europe

The world is almost your oyster as far as direct weekly flights from each of the Baltic capitals to other European cities are concerned. Popular routes include Amsterdam to/from Vilnius (LAL, once or twice a day); Budapest (airBaltic, four a week) and Geneva (airBaltic, once a day) to/from Rīga; Paris–Vilnius (LAL, three a week); Prague to/from Rīga (České Aerolinie (ČSA; w www .csa.cz) once to three times daily) or Vilnius (ČSA, once or twice a day); Vienna to/from Rīga, Vilnius or Tallinn (both on Austrian Airlines (w www.aua.com), five to seven a week); and Rīga–Zurich (airBaltic, two to three a day).

## Russia, Ukraine, Transcaucasia & Central Asia

There are one to four flights daily between Moscow and each of the Baltic capitals including Estonian Air from Tallinn; Aeroflot (w www.aeroflot.com) from Rīga; and LAL or Aeroflot from Vilnius. In Moscow flights use Sheremetevo I airport.

At the time of writing Air Lithuania was offering return fares from Vilnius to Moscow for €280 (minimum three-day stay); Estonian Air was offering summer promotion fares from Tallinn to Moscow for €110 (minimum Saturday-night or three-day stay, 14 days' advance purchase, maximum stay 14 days).

From Tallinn, Estonian Air operates three weekly flights to/from Kyiv (return fares from €138). From Latvia, there are five weekly flights between Rīga and Kyiv with airBaltic. Lithuanian Airlines flies Kyiv–Vilnius–Kyiv three times weekly (€280 return, including obligatory Saturday-night stay in Kyiv and maximum one-month stay).

You can also get to and from dozens of other places in Russia, Transcaucasia and former Soviet Central Asia via a connection at Moscow with Aeroflot or one of its successors – book all the way through in one go.

## The USA & Canada

Any journey to the Baltics entails a flight to Scandinavia or another European transport hub, from where there are ferry or plane connections to the region. **Airhitch** (☎ 212-864 2000; w www.airhitch.org) specialises in cheap stand-by fares.

**Council Travel** (☎ 800 226 8624; w www .counciltravel.com), America's largest student-travel organisation, has some 60 offices in the USA. Call for the office nearest you. **STA Travel** (toll-free ☎ 800 781 4040; w www.statravel.com) has offices in Boston, Chicago, New York, Philadelphia, San Francisco and other major cities.

In Canada, try **Travel CUTS** (☎ 800 667 2887; w www.travelcuts.com).

## Australia & New Zealand

Airlines such as **Thai Airways International** (THAI; w www.thaiair.com), **Malaysia Airlines** (w www.malalysiaairlines.com.my), **Qantas Airways** (w www.qantas.com.au) and **Singapore Airlines** (SIA; w www.singapore.air.com) have frequent promotional fares to Europe. A round-the-world ticket from Australia and New Zealand that takes in a Scandinavian city will cost you around A$2299/NZ$2550.

Two well-known agents for cheap fares are **STA Travel** (☎ 1300 360 960 Australiawide; w www.statravel.com.au; 224 Faraday St, Carlton, Melbourne), with offices in major cities and on many university campuses; and **Flight Centre** (☎ 131 600 Australiawide; w www.flightcentre.com.au; 82 Elizabeth St, Sydney), with dozens of offices throughout Australia.

In New Zealand, **Flight Centre** (☎ 0800 243 544; w www.flightcentre.co.nz; National Bank Towers, cnr Queen & Darby Sts, Auckland) has a large central office in Auckland, while **STA Travel** (☎ 0800 874 773; w www .statravel.co.nz) has its main and other offices, as well as offices in Hamilton, Palmerston North, Wellington, Christchurch and Dunedin.

## LAND
## Border Crossings

Travelling from north to south, Estonia shares borders with Russia and Latvia; Latvia shares borders with Russia and Belarus, Estonia and Lithuania; while Lithuania borders Belarus, Poland and the Kaliningrad Region (also part of Russia).

The Baltic borders with Belarus and Russia continue to be the most rigorously controlled. You need a visa in advance to cross these points (none issued at land borders) and you can expect to wait in line up to an hour regardless of whether you are travelling by bus or car. Entering Russia (including the Kaliningrad Region) or Belarus, you are required to fill in a declaration form, specifying how much cash (in any currency) and what valuables you are taking into the country.

At Narva–Ivangorod on the Estonian–Russian border particularly long queues form. The Kaliningrad Region enjoys quieter road borders with Lithuania at Panemunė/Sovietsk, between Kybartai (Lithuania) and Nesterov, and on the Curonian Spit along the Klaipėda–Zelenogradsk road. Queues are known to occur at Lithuania's two border crossings with Poland – between Ogrodniki (east of Suwałki, Poland) and Lazdijai (Lithuania); and on the road from Suwałki, Szypliszki and Budzisko (Poland) to Kalvarija and Marijampolė (Lithuania). Don't be persuaded to do a slight detour through Belarus instead, however; you will be delayed at least four to five times as long and have to fork out for a Belarusian visa (not available at any border). Only Belarus' road borders with Lithuania at Salčininkai, Medininkai and Lavoriskės are open to Westerners.

Inter-Baltic borders cause little aggravation these days. Public buses get priority over private vehicles and cross immediately, and most trains chug across rail borders without stopping (customs and immigration checks are dealt with on board, while in motion).

If you are travelling by car, don't be alarmed by the kilometres of lorries waiting in line that you see as you approach most crossings. At every border there are separate queues for cars and lorries. You should usually only have to wait in line behind three or four cars, depending on the time of day. The whole procedure should not take more than 30 minutes or so. At the Latvian and Lithuanian borders, you also have to deal with the unnecessarily complicated affair of obtaining a variety of stamps on a little scrap of paper that is given to you by a border guard when you enter the border zone and which is taken away from you by another border guard when you leave. The reasoning behind this procedure is yet to be fathomed.

Border agreements are in place between all three Baltic countries, meaning you only get your passport stamped by the border guard of the country you are entering. Latvian border guards are the least aware of who needs visas and can sometimes be troublesome; Estonian border guards diligently stamp most Western passports; while Lithuanians are completely nonchalant about the whole affair (many even smile).

## Bus

With a few exceptions, buses are the cheapest but least comfortable method of reaching the Baltics. There are direct buses to/from Austria, Belgium, Czech Republic, France, Germany, Netherlands, Poland, Russia, Ukraine and Belarus. From much of the rest of Europe you can reach the Baltics with a single change of bus in Warsaw.

Most international services to/from the Baltics are operated by Eurolines. Updated schedules and fares are posted on the Internet – see the websites listed in the office contact details below. Passengers aged under 26 or over 60 qualify for a 10% discounted fare on Eurolines buses (except those between Lithuania and Poland, which offer no discount, and those between Lithuania and Germany, which offer 12% discount to those under 26). Children aged under four pay 20% of the full fare, and those aged four to 11 pay 50%. Return tickets cost substantially less than two one-way tickets. Passengers are allowed to transport two pieces of luggage per person; a €7.60 fee is charged for each additional bag.

Eurolines has ticketing offices worldwide, including **Eurolines UK** (☎ 08705 143 219; 4 Cardiff Road, Luton LU1 1PP), and in the Baltics:

**Estonia** (☎ 680 09 09, e mreis@delfi.ee, w www.eurolines.ee) Tallinn bus station, Lastekodu 46; (☎ 07-340 075) Tartu bus station, Turu tänav 2
**Latvia** (☎ 721 40 80, e info@eurolines.lv, w www.eurolines.lv) Riga bus station, Prāgas iela 1
**Lithuania** (☎ 5-215 1377, e info@eurolines.lt, w www.eurolines.lt) Vilnius bus station, Sodų gatvė 22; (☎ 45-582 888, e panevezys@eurolines.lt) Panevėžys bus station, Savanorių aikštė 5; (☎ 37-320 2020, e kaunas@eurolines.lt, w www.kautra.lt) Kaunas bus station, Vytauto prospektas 24

**Poland & the Czech Republic** Eurolines runs one bus weekly in each direction between Warsaw and Tallinn (€40/74 one way/return, 14½ hours), via Pärnu (€38/69, 12 hours); and an overnight bus to/from Vilnius (€23 return, 9 hours) via Kaunas (7½ hours), and Rīga (12½ hours). There is also an overnight bus from Vilnius to/from Gdansk (€26 return, 12 hours).

In Warsaw buses depart from the **western bus station** *(Warszawa Zachodnia; ☎ 822 48 11; al Jerozolimskie 144)*. Tickets are sold at the international *(miedzynarodowa)* ticket window at the bus station.

The Czech Republic has weekly bus links with both Latvia and Lithuania. From Rīga, a bus departs on Sunday from the central bus station at 7am, arriving in Prague 26 hours later at 9am the following day; the return bus leaves Prague on Friday. From Vilnius, a bus leaves on Monday, Wednesday and Friday at 9.30pm, arriving in Prague the next day at 11pm. A return Vilnius–Prague fare is €46.

**Western Europe** Eurolines operates four buses a week to/from Vilnius and Paris, stopping en route in Kaunas and Marijampolė in Lithuania, and Strasbourg, Metz and Reims in France. Buses depart from Vilnius at 7pm on Monday, Wednesday, Thursday and Sunday, and arrive in Paris the following morning at 7.30am or 9.30am. Return buses depart from the French capital on Tuesday and Friday at 9pm, and on Wednesday and Saturday at 7pm. A single/return fare from Vilnius, Kaunas or Marijampolė is €127/228. From Paris, there is a connecting bus to London; a single/return Vilnius–London ticket costs €144/243.

Another Eurolines bus runs every Wednesday and Sunday at 7pm from Vilnius, again via Kaunas and Marijampolė, to Vienna. The return bus leaves Vienna on Wednesday and Saturday at 3pm. Journey time is 22½ hours and a one-way Vilnius/Kaunas–Vienna ticket is €86. From Vienna, there are connections with Bratislava, Sofia and Budapest.

A handy route is the three-times weekly Rīga–Kaunas–Amsterdam–Brussels service, departing from Rīga/Kaunas on Tuesday, Thursday and Saturday at 7.15am/1.20pm and arriving in Amsterdam the following day at 4.35pm, Antwerp at 7.45pm and Brussels at 9pm. In Rīga tickets are sold by Ecolines (see under Belarus & Ukraine, following). A single fare from the Latvian

capital to Amsterdam/Brussels costs around €102/107.

There are direct buses galore between all three Baltic countries and Germany. German towns and cities well served by Eurolines to/from Vilnius include Berlin, Bremen, Bremerhaven, Dresden, Frankfurt, Hamburg and Stuttgart. Sample return fares to Vilnius include €65 from Berlin and €84 from Frankfurt. Ticketing offices in Germany include **Berlin bus station** *(☎ 030-3061 9898; Masurenalee 4-6, D-14057 Berlin)*; and **Deutsche Touring** *(☎ 069-79 03 50; e service@deutsche-touring.com; Am Römerhof 17, D-60486 Frankfurt am Main)*.

From Tallinn, there are twice-weekly Eurolines buses to/from Frankfurt (€107/189) via Berlin (€86/156); Cologne (€107/189) via Hannover, Essen and Düsseldorf; and once weekly to/from Münich (€107/189). All these buses stop in Rīga and Panevėžys. Additional Germany-bound services originating in the Latvian capital include a once-weekly bus to/from Stuttgart (€90/155) and a twice-weekly service to/from Bremen (€107/189) operated by Ecolines – see under Belarus & Ukraine, following, for contact details. **TAK Reisid** *(in Tallinn ☎ 6314 444, in Pärnu ☎ 044-73 777, in Rīga ☎ 721 24 02, in Kiel ☎ 0431-666 222; w www.takreisid.ee)* operates a once-weekly bus from Tallinn to Kiel, stopping en route in Pärnu, Rīga, Berlin and Hamburg. A single/return Tallinn–Kiel fare costs €102/184.

**Russia** Estonia, Latvia and Lithuania all have bus links with the Kaliningrad Region (Russia) and the Russian motherland.

From Tallinn, Eurolines runs one bus nightly (departs 6pm) to Kaliningrad, via Pärnu, Rīga, Siauliai and Sovietsk (15 hours). A single Tallinn–Kaliningrad fare is €19. From Rīga, there is one other daily bus to Kaliningrad (€10 one way), also via Siauliai (10 hours). From Vilnius and Kaunas, there are two buses daily; journey times are eight to nine hours and 5½ hours respectively and a single fare costs around €6. Several buses also travel along the Curonian Spit between Klaipėda and Kaliningrad.

To/from Moscow, Latvia's Ecolines (see under Belarus & Ukraine, earlier) runs two buses a day, one of which is an express (departing Rīga at 7pm and arriving the next morning at 10am); and Eurolines in

Estonia operates a service three times weekly (departing Tallinn at 2pm and arriving the next morning at 8.39am), via Tartu. A Tallinn–Tartu–Moscow one-way fare is €28/25.50.

To/from St Petersburg, there are two daily Eurolines buses to/from Rīga (13½ hours), and three daily to/from Tallinn, passing through Narva en route and arriving in St Petersburg about nine hours later. A single fare from Rīga/Tallinn is €19/16. At the time of writing, the Kaunas–St Petersburg service had been suspended.

**Ukraine & Belarus** There are daily buses to/from Minsk from each of the Baltic capitals – twice daily to/from Vilnius (€6.50 return, 4¼ hours), one of which continues to/from Kaunas; three weekly to/from Tallinn (5½ hours) via Tartu; and two daily to/from Rīga (12 hours), one of which stops in Daugavpils. There is also a daily bus between Minsk, Klaipėda and Palanga (11 hours).

Ukraine-bound buses also pass through Belarus. Latvian-based Ecolines (Norma-A) runs a four-times-weekly service between Rīga and Kyiv (17½ hours). Twice a week, the bus continues a farther five hours to Odesa. In Rīga, **Ecolines** (☎ 721 45 12; e eco lines@ecolines.lv; w www.ecolines.lv) at the bus station sells tickets. **Norma-A** (☎ 727 44 44; A Čaka iela 45) sells tickets too. A single/return fare to Kyiv costs €38/69 and to Odesa €50/92.

Between Estonia and Ukraine, **Ostlines** (☎ 646 44 92) at Tallinn bus station runs a weekly service to/from Tallinn and Kyiv (€32, 13 hours).

All Western travellers need a visa to travel through Belarus and Ukraine.

## Train

Travelling by train can be an interesting way of reaching the region – cheaper than flying and less boring than by bus. Two of the world's most memorable rail journeys figure among the approaches to the Baltics: the Trans-Siberian and the briefer Suwałki–Sestokai railway from Poland to Lithuania.

The *Thomas Cook European Timetable* is the trainophile's bible, giving a complete listing of train schedules, supplements and reservations information. It is updated monthly and is available from Thomas Cook outlets. In the USA, call ☎ 800-367 7984.

On the Internet, you can search in English through the timetables of Latvian and Lithuanian Railways at w www.ldz.lv and w www.litrail.lt respectively. Their Estonian counterpart had yet to post its timetable online at the time of writing.

**Rail Passes & Youth Tickets** Estonia, Latvia and Lithuania are not, at present, included in the Inter-Rail, Eurail, ScanRail or other European pass network, so if you're travelling with one of these you won't get any benefits in the Baltics. No rail passes are available within the region either.

The three countries are not included in the Wasteels/BIJ (Billets Internationales de Jeunesse) ticket network. Wasteels/BIJ tickets are sold in the region, but only for Western European destinations from Warsaw onwards, meaning you still pay the full fare between Latvia/Lithuania and Warsaw. Student- and youth-travel offices (listed under Travel Agencies in the Information section of the city chapters), and some travel agencies, sell tickets and can give you more information.

**Poland** There are no direct rail links between Poland and Estonia or Latvia, leaving Baltic-bound travellers with little choice but to travel from Warsaw to Vilnius, from where there are bus and rail links to the other two Baltic capitals.

Between Warsaw and Vilnius (11½ hours), there is one direct overnight train every second day (departing Vilnius/Warsaw on even/odd days). It passes through Belarus – for which you'll need a visa – en route. At the Poland–Belarus border the train sits motionless for hours – apart from an incredible amount of lurching, vibrating and clanking – while the bogeys are changed to fit the broader-gauge tracks of the former Soviet Union.

Another less sane option is the legendary 50km track between Sestokai and Suwałki, linking Lithuania with Poland. There is one daily Sestokai–Suwałki train, but its times change quite frequently. From Suwałki there are a couple of Warsaw trains or combination of trains (such as a Suwałki–Sokóka train) that will get you to Warsaw in the end. At Sestokai, there is a daily Vilnius train that connects with the Sestokai–Suwałki service. It departs Vilnius at 9.25am, arriving at

Kaunas at 11.12am and Sestokai at 1pm. It leaves Sestokai at 2.15pm, arrives at Kaunas at 4.14pm and reaches Vilnius at 6pm.

The tickets for each leg of the journey (Vilnius–Sestokai, Sestokai–Suwałki, and Suwałki–Warsaw) can only be bought at the point of departure. Expect to queue at each departure point for a ticket and don't be surprised if you end up missing the only train going your way that day. If you get on a train without a ticket, you will be fined heavily. If it is a toss-up between the ticket and catching the train though, get the train!

**Russia, Ukraine & Belarus** The old Soviet rail network still functions, with little change, over most of the former USSR. Trains linking Moscow and St Petersburg with all the main Baltic cities enable you to combine the Baltics with a Trans-Siberian trip or other Russian or Central Asian travels. For information on types of train, classes of accommodation, how to understand timetables and so on, see Train in the Getting Around chapter.

The Tallinn–St Petersburg (nine hours) service, reinstated in mid-2002, runs every second day, departing on even/odd days from Tallinn/St Petersburg. A one-way fare in couchette/compartment class costs €15/ 25 and advance bookings are advised – the overnight train fills up quickly.

The Tallinn–Moscow train chugs the 16 to 20 hours once a day between the two capitals. Single fares in compartment/1st class cost around €46/93. In Moscow it arrives at/departs from St Petersburg station.

Belarus-bound travellers can travel between Tallinn and Minsk twice weekly. Trains depart from Tallinn on Tuesday and Saturday, and a place in general seating/ compartment/1st class costs €15/25/44.

The *Latvijas Ekspresis* (Latvia Express) trundles the 16¼ hours daily between Rīga and Moscow (Rīga train station), departing from Rīga/Moscow at 4.15pm/7.11pm. A second train, the daily *Jūrmala*, services the same route, while the overnight *Baltija* links the Latvian capital with St Petersburg (12¾ hours, once a day). At the time of writing a single Rīga–Moscow fare in general seating/couchette/compartment/1st class costs €19/ 40/62/105 and equivalent Rīga– St Petersburg fares were €17.20/34.40/ 53.50/86.

From Moscow's Belarus train station there are also three daily trains to/from Vilnius (13 to 16½ hours); one terminates in Kaunas (Lithuania) and the other two in Kaliningrad (Russia). The daily St Petersburg–Kaliningrad train likewise stops in Vilnius, as do the services between the Russian enclave and Ukraine (Kaliningrad–Kharkov) and Belarus (Kaliningrad–Gomel), both of which depart every second day. Two trains daily link Vilnius with the Belarusian capital of Minsk (five hours).

Another way of getting to/from Ukraine is with the direct Rīga–Lviv service, which does, in fact, stop in Vilnius en route. Departures are twice weekly, journey time to/ from Rīga is 21 hours and a single ticket in general seating/couchette/compartment costs €22.50/38/50; there is no 1st-class carriage. From Rīga there is also a direct train to/from Odesa (twice a week) via Gomel in Belarus, and another to/from Gomel (every second day). Fares in a couchette/compartment typically cost €53.50/72 to/from Odesa and €38/50 to/from Gomel.

Other places in the Baltics with direct rail services to/from Russia, Ukraine and Belarus include: Daugavpils and Rēzekne in Latvia (Moscow, Chernivtsi); Sigulda in Latvia (St Petersburg); Narva in Estonia (St Petersburg, Moscow); and Valga and Võru in Estonia (St Petersburg).

**Western Europe** There are direct services to/from Warsaw from London, Paris and elsewhere. Alternatively, you can head for Prague, Budapest or Sofia and take a train to Vilnius through Ukraine. Tickets to Vilnius bought in Western Europe will route you through Belarus. London–Vilnius takes a little under two days, with a change of trains in Warsaw.

**Trans-Siberian** If you have the time and inclination for it, the Trans-Siberian railway will carry you much of the way between the Baltics and eastern Asia. The 9297km Trans-Siberian (proper) runs between Moscow's Yaroslavl station and Vladivostok on Russia's Pacific Coast. In summer at least, there are steamers between Vladivostok and Niigata in Japan. Straight through without stopping, the ride takes 5½ to 6½ days, but you can break it at places like Irkutsk, Ulan-Ude and Khabarovsk and

# RAILWAY & FERRY ROUTES

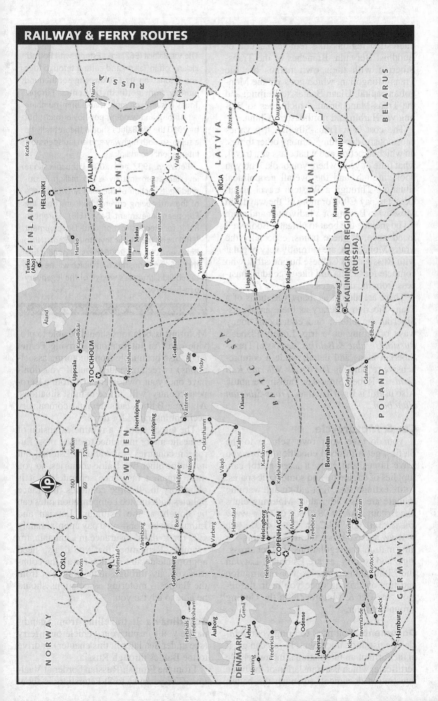

make side trips to beautiful Lake Baykal and interesting regions like remote Yakutia or Buddhist Buryatia. Branches of the Trans-Siberian with their own names are the Trans-Mongolian, which goes via the Mongolian capital, Ulaan Baatar, to Beijing; and the Trans-Manchurian, which goes to Beijing via Harbin and northeastern China.

The cost of a Trans-Siberian trip varies enormously, depending, among other things, on which direction and what class you travel, what time of year, where you book, who you book through, and the overall geopolitical situation. Through a Western travel agent, expect to pay €900 or more all the way from Moscow to Beijing or Vladivostok and more if you include the boat to Niigata. Book well in advance, as these trains, especially the Trans-Mongolian, are currently very popular with Russian and Chinese businessfolk who compete for tickets and like to conduct business from the carriages.

There are almost as many variations of a Trans-Siberian itinerary as there are Trans-Siberian travellers, and equally as many ways of setting up a trip. Lonely Planet's *Russia, Ukraine & Belarus* has lots of Trans-Siberian ideas and detail, while a comprehensive resource is *The Trans-Siberian Rail Guide* by Robert Strauss & Tamsin Turnbull. Also useful is Bryn Thomas' *Trans-Siberian Handbook*.

## Car & Motorcycle

If you do take your own vehicle to the Baltics, get it in good condition before you leave home, and carry a large petrol can, supplies of engine oil and some basic spares. A fire extinguisher, first-aid kit and warning triangle are also advisable. Motoring clubs like Britain's **AA** (☎ *0870 600 0371;* ⓦ *www.theaa.com*) and **RAC** (☎ *0906 4701 740;* ⓦ *www.rac.co.uk*) are worth contacting for information on regulations, border crossings, and so on – as are Estonian, Latvian and Lithuanian embassies. For information and tips on driving once you're in the region, see Car & Motorcycle in the Getting Around chapter.

**Documents** You need to bring your vehicle's registration document. If you can get it in the form of an international motor vehicle certificate, which is a translation of the basic registration document, so much the better.

---

### A Long & Winding Road

The Via Baltica (E67) links Estonia with Poland, kicking off in Tallinn and cutting through Rīga and Kaunas on its 670km-long southbound journey from northern to Central Europe. Today it is nothing more than a bum-numbing set of long and winding pot-holed roads, but by 2010 the Via Baltica should theoretically be a super-smooth highway and an indispensable international road link.

Between 1997 and 2000 Lithuania alone invested approximately €125 million in upgrading its section of the road network, 34% of the latter being covered by loans from the European Investment Bank (EIB), European Bank for Reconstruction and Development (EBRD) and the Nordic Investment Bank (NIB). Between 2002 and 2006 it has pledged a further €547 million, much of which will be used to rebuild Lithuania's wedge of the legendary pan-Baltic road.

---

Motoring associations should be able to provide one. An International Driving Permit (IDP; also obtainable from motoring associations) is recommended, but if you don't have one, your own licence (if from a European country) will suffice in most situations. All three Baltic states demand compulsory accident insurance for drivers.

The Green Card – a routine extension of domestic motor insurance to cover most European countries – is valid in Estonia, but *not* in the other two Baltic countries, so you must organise insurance separately – it is obligatory in all three countries. Insurance policies with limited compensation rates can be bought at the Estonian, Latvian and Lithuanian borders – you pay approximately €22 for 15 days' insurance in Lithuania, for example. Remember that you'll also need appropriate documentation for all the countries you pass through on the way to or from the Baltics – motoring associations should be able to advise you.

**Scandinavia** If travelling from Scandinavia, you can put your vehicle on a ferry (see under Sea later in this chapter) or drive to the Baltics through Russia.

From the Finnish/Russian border at Vaalimaa/Torfyanovka to St Petersburg is about

220km; from St Petersburg to the Russian/ Estonian border at Ivangorod/Narva is 140km. You could do it in a day but there's little point coming this way unless you want to look at St Petersburg on the way through. Don't delay on the Finland–St Petersburg road, as it's said to be plagued by bandits.

**Poland & Germany** Bringing a vehicle into the Baltics from the south entails either a ferry trip from Kiel (Germany) to the Lithuanian port of Klaipėda (ferry details are listed under Sea later in this chapter); a 30-minute to one-hour wait at the Ogrodniki (Poland)–Lazdijai (Lithuania) border or the border on the road from Suwałki, Szypliszki and Budzisko (Poland) to Kalvarija and Marijampolė; or a hellish trip through Belarus.

Suckers for punishment opting for the third – and least rosy – motoring option should not attempt to even approach the border or set foot in Lukashenko land without a Belarusian transit visa, only available at Belarusian embassies. No visas are sold at any Belarus border. Those sufficiently privileged to have their visa application accepted can then expect to wait several hours, at least, at the border. Possible routes include from Białystok, Poland, to Grodno in northwestern Belarus, then on to Merkinė in Lithuania; Brest–Lida–Vilnius or Brest–Minsk–Vilnius.

### Bicycle
Bicycles can be carried cheaply (or for free) on the ferries from Scandinavia and Germany to the Baltics; see under Sea, following, for details. Peddlers through Poland face the same choice of routes as drivers; see Car & Motorcycle, earlier.

### SEA
The Baltics – particularly Estonia with its many islands and deeply indented coast – attract hundreds of private yachts a year, mainly from Finland and Scandinavia. The **Estonian Marine Tourism Association** (EMTA; ☎/fax 2-641 1417; ⓦ http://old.artun.ee/ sadamad; Pikk 71, EE0001 Tallinn) can give you advice on sailing to the region and recommends guest harbours.

The harbour at Pärnu was the first in Eastern Europe to be awarded the blue flag in 1992. Blue flag is a green 'eco' label awarded to beaches, harbours and marinas for their cleanliness and amenities. Customs facilities

**Pedal Power**

Along the Estonian coast, road signs ensure cyclists following the so-called 'Hansa Route' stay on track. Signposted in 2001, the 980km-long coastal route forms part of Eurovelo No 10 – one of a dozen trans-European cycle routes mapped out by the **European Cyclists' Federation** (ECF; ⓦ www.ecf.com).

The Hansa Route, also called the Baltic Sea Cycle Route, takes cyclists on a 7930km-long circular journey around the Baltic Sea, from Gdansk (Poland) to the Russian enclave of Kaliningrad, through to Klaipėda (Lithuania), Rīga (Latvia), the Estonian islands of Saaremaa and Hiiumaa, Tallinn and on to St Petersburg in mainland Russia, and beyond.

Another route, the 'East Europe Route' (No 11), also passes through the region on its 5964km-long southbound trek from North Cape to Athens. Baltic pit stops north of Warsaw include Vilnius (Lithuania), Daugavpils (Latvia), the Valga–Valka crossing, Tartu, Tallinn (Estonia) and Helsinki (Finland).

All 12 Eurovelo routes should be signposted and up and pedalling by 2011. Within the region, Estonia is the only country to have a national cycling network mapped out – four primary trails and six secondary, covering 2086km. For maps, contact the Tartu-based cycling club, **Vänta Aga** (fax 07-42 25 36; Lunini 3, EE50406 Tartu).

are available at Pirita, Dirhami, Haapsalu, Kuivastu, Kunda, Lehtma, Narva-Jõesuu, Nasva, Paldiski-North, Pärnu, Ruhnu, Roomassaare, Triigi, Vergi and Veere. Approaches to Orjaku, Triigi, Mõntu, Kihnu and Ruhnu should only be made in daylight.

The EMTA offers useful information, harbour-berth booking, and visa services for yachties. In Helsinki contact the **Estum Sailing Agency** (☎ 09-629 299, fax 629 390; Vuorimiehenka 23a, SF-00140 Helsinki).

It's also possible to rent yachts throughout the region – see Yacht under Boat in the Getting Around chapter.

You can sail directly from Finland to Estonia; from Germany to Latvia, Lithuania and Estonia; from Denmark to Lithuania; and from Sweden to all three Baltic countries. This can be one of the most enjoyable ways to reach the Baltics. The Tallinn–Helsinki

## Surf 'n' Sail

The ferry and hydrofoil companies that sail the Baltic Sea all have websites. Most feature updated schedules and fares – indispensable to travellers wanting to surf and sail – and accept bookings online.

| operator | route | transport | website |
| --- | --- | --- | --- |
| Eckerö Line | Tallinn–Helsinki | ferry | W www.eckeroline.fi |
| Hanza Maritime Agency | Rīga–Kiel | ferry | W www.hanza.lv |
| Krantas Shipping | Klaipėda–Århus | cargo | W www.shipping.lt |
| | Klaipėda–Åbenraa | cargo | |
| Lisco Lines | Klaipėda–Karlshamn | ferry | W www.lisco.lt |
| | Klaipėda–Stockholm | ferry | |
| | Klaipėda–Copenhagen | cargo | |
| Lisco Lines/Scandlines | Klaipėda–Mukran | ferry | W www.scandlines.de |
| Lisco Lines/Scandlines | Klaipėda–Kiel | ferry | |
| Linda Line | Tallinn–Helsinki | hydrofoil | W www.lindaline.fi |
| Nordic Jet Line | Tallinn–Helsinki | catamaran | W www-eng.njl.fi |
| Rīgas Jūras Līnija | Rīga–Nynashamn | ferry | W www.rigasealine.lv |
| Silja Line | Tallinn–Helsinki | ferry | W www.silja.com |
| | Tallinn–Rostock | ferry | |
| Tallink | Tallinn–Helsinki | ferry & hydrofoil | W www.tallink.ee |
| | Tallinn–Stockholm | ferry | |
| | Paldiski–Kapellskär | ferry | |
| Terrabalt | Liepāja–Karlshamn | ferry | W www.terrabalt.lv |
| | Liepāja–Rostock | ferry | |
| VV Line | Ventspils–Västervik | ferry | W www.vvline.com |
| | Tallinn–Västervik | ferry | |

route has so many competing services that you should have no difficulty in getting a passage any day, but some of the other services – notably Tallinn from Stockholm and the cargo ferries to Denmark – can get booked up far in advance.

Schedules and fares change frequently – double-check both when you are planning your trip. Most ferry and hydrofoil operators publish updated schedules and fares on the Internet (see the boxed text 'Surf 'n' Sail').

Between Helsinki and Tallinn, most operators offer special deals for families and serial tickets for frequent sailers. A return Tallinn–Helsinki ticket with Nordic Jet yields a 50% discount on any return ticket with Finnish Railways VR.

### Finland

**To/from Estonia** A fleet of ferries now carries nearly two million people each year back and forth across the 80km Gulf of Finland between Helsinki and Tallinn. At least

five or six crossings are made each way every day (ships 3½ hours year-round; hydrofoils 1½ hours May to October only). Prices change frequently. Port taxes are included in prices quoted.

In addition to the regular fares, you can also take 23-hour or half-day cruises from Helsinki to Tallinn (or vice versa) with Tallink or Silja Line – floating parties for Swedes and Finns, basically. Cruise tickets cost around €35/45 for 23-hour cruises departing Saturday to Thursday/Friday. Most cruises do not allow passengers to disembark from the ferry upon arrival in Helsinki/Tallinn.

Unlike most other cruises, the Tallinn–Helsinki–Tallinn day cruises offered by Nordic Jet allow you to get off the boat in Helsinki, making it a cheap way to day-trip it to the Finnish port. Day-cruise fares in Tallinn/Helsinki start at 560 EEK/€37. Nordic Jet also offers weekend golfing packages from Helsinki to the 18-hole green in

Niitvälja, 33km southwest of Tallinn (€98 to €108, including green fees, port transfer and overnight accommodation); and family packages from Tallinn to the Särkanniemi amusement park and aquarium in Tampere, 175km from Helsinki (3100 EEK for car and four passengers, including family admission fees and overnight hotel accommodation).

**Tallink** Year-round, Tallink runs the large passenger and vehicle ferries the m/s *Fanta-asia*, m/s *Meloodia*, m/s *Vana Tallinn* and m/s *Romantika*. All four make one crossing in each direction daily (3½ hours), using Terminal A in Tallinn and West Terminal in Helsinki. Fares vary depending on the season, day and time you sail: tickets are cheaper on weekdays (except Friday) and if you leave after 6.30pm from Tallinn or before 1pm from Helsinki. In high season (July to mid-August) a single fare is €22 for a deck seat regardless of which sailing you take, and a berth in a cabin costs from €9.

Tallink also operates two hydrofoils, the *Tallink Express*, which only transports foot passengers, and the *Tallink AutoExpress*, which takes vehicles too. Between them, they make seven Tallinn–Helsinki crossings each way daily April to November (1½ hours). A single fare for a deck passenger costs €19-27, depending on the day of the week and season, and a bicycle/motorcycle/car costs €8.40/10/15. Sailings are prone to cancellation in windy or rough weather. In Tallinn, note that these hydrofoils depart from Terminal D.

For all these services, students and seniors pay 10% less, and those aged between six and 17 years pay 50% of the adult fare. In Helsinki, Tallink ferries and hydrofoils use West Terminal. You can get tickets at the **Tallink office** (☎ 09-228 311, fax 649 808; e tallink@tallink.fi; w www.tallink.fi) within two hours of departure; otherwise from its **Travel Shop** (☎ 09-228 311; Erottajankatu 19, SF-00130 Helsinki). For Tallink's main booking offices in Tallinn, see Getting There & Away in the Tallinn chapter.

**Silja Line** Silja Line's *SuperSeaCatFour* travels at 38 knots six to eight times daily between Tallinn's Terminal D and Helsinki's Olympic Terminal (1¾ hours). Out of season (January to May and September to December) fast *Finnjet* makes the sea crossing twice a week (3¾ hours). In Helsinki it uses the Katajanokka (Finnjet) Terminal.

Fares vary depending on which ferry you take at what time and on what day. It is more expensive to sail on Friday evening and Saturday. Children under six travel for free, and students and seniors get a small discount.

Helsinki ferry departures are from the Olympia Terminal. Tickets can be bought here within two hours of departure at **Silja Line** (☎ 09-180 4555, fax 180 4311; w www.siljaline.se) or in town at **Silja Line's city office** (☎ 09-180 41, fax 180 4279; Mannerheimintie 2, 00100 Helsinki). For Silja Line offices in Tallinn, see Getting There & Away in the Tallinn chapter.

**Eckerö Line** Eckerö Line's *Nordlandia* ferry, big enough to hold 2000 passengers and 450 cars, sails once daily back and forth from Tallinn to Helsinki year-round (3½ hours), departing/arriving in Tallinn at Terminal B and in Helsinki at West Terminal. A single deck fare costs €17 (€20 on Saturday and Sunday) and a place in a cabin is €25-70, depending on how much luxury you plump for. Students and seniors pay €13 and six to 11 years pay €11 for a regular seat. It costs €5/17 one way to transport a bicycle/car.

Tickets are sold in Tallinn at **Eckerö Line** (☎ 631 8606; e info@eckeroline.ee; w www.eckeroline.ee; Sadama tänav 29, Harbour 25-3) in Terminal B; and in Helsinki at **Eckerö Line** (☎ 09-228 8544; Hietasaarenkuja 8, Building L4) at the West Terminal.

**Nordic Jet Line** Nordic Jet runs two sleek, 450-seat jet catamarans, *Nordic Jet* and *Baltic Jet*, between Tallinn and Helsinki. They sail early May to November/December (depending on the weather); and there are six crossings a day (1½ hours), docking at Terminal C in Tallinn. A one-way deck-passenger fare from either city costs €18, €32 or €37 depending on time of departure (morning sailings from Helsinki and afternoon sailings from Tallinn are the priciest). Students and seniors pay 20% less, and children aged between two and 12 are half price. Transporting a bicycle/motorcycle/car costs €5/11/10.28.

In Helsinki, **Nordic Jet** (☎ 09-681 770; e booking@njl.fi) uses the catamaran harbour at Kanava Terminal (Kanavaterminaali). For Nordic Jet's office details in Tallinn, see the Tallinn chapter.

***Linda Line Express*** The prettily named Linda Line Express is a small, independent hydrofoil company whose vessels plough the waters between Tallinn and Helsinki (1½ hours) six to eight times daily May to September. Its speedy *Foilcat*, in service since May 2002, nips between the capitals in just under one hour – at a racy speed of 55 knots. All Linda Line vessels stop sailing in October when the waters ice over. A single/return fare costs €20/30 (€22/32 mid-June to mid-August) and those aged between five and 15 years pay 50% less when travelling with an adult. It costs €12 one way to transport a bicycle.

Linda Line Express hydrofoils arrive and depart from the Linnahall Terminal in Tallinn and the South Port (Makasiinterminaal) in Helsinki. In the Finnish capital contact **Linda Line** (☎ 09-668 9700, fax 668 97070; e *sales@lineline.fi;* w *www.lindaline.fi*). See Getting There & Away in the Tallinn chapter for details of ticketing agents in Tallinn.

## Sweden

**To/from Estonia** There are direct sailings daily from Stockholm and Västervik to Tallinn, and a cargo ship that accepts passengers between Paldiski and Kapellskär, northeast of Stockholm and linked to the Swedish capital by a bus service.

***Tallink*** Tallink's m/s *Regina Baltica* and m/s *Fantaasia* sail every second day (once a day May to September) between Tallinn and Stockholm. Both ferries make the 13-hour crossing year-round. Ferries use Terminal D in Tallinn and the Tallinn terminal at the Frihamnen (Free Harbour) in Stockholm. A one-way adult fare from Tallinn costs 500/650/550 EEK in low/mid/high season (November to May/September to October/June to August); those aged six to 17 years pay 55 to 100 EEK less, depending on the season. Transporting a bicycle/car costs 200/900 EEK. Equivalent one-way adult fares from Stockholm are 300/385/325 Skr and 120/400 Skr for two/four wheels.

Tallink also operates a daily ferry between Paldiski, 52km west of Tallinn, and Kapellskär, northeast of Stockholm. Boats depart from Paldiski at 9am and arrive in Kapellskär at 8am; returning at 9.30am to arrive in Paldiski at 7.30am. A one-way deck-seat fare costs 175/265/210 Skr in low/mid-/high season, and cabin berths start at 120 Skr – and peak at 1500 Skr!

Tallink gets heavily booked, so make your reservation a month or two ahead. See Getting There & Away in the Tallinn chapter for ticket agents in Tallinn and Paldiski. Alternatively, contact **Tallink's Swedish office** (☎ 08-666 60 01, fax 666 60 52; e *booking@ tallink.se;* w *www.tallink.se;* Klaraberdsgatan 31, Box 27295, SE-10253, Sweden).

**To/from Latvia** Between mid-April and mid-September the *Max Mols* ferry sails every second day between Nynäshamn, 60km south of Stockholm, and Rīga. The overnight sailing takes 11 hours and a one-way 1st-/2nd-class deck seat (there are no cabins) costs 39/49 Ls; students, seniors and those aged between five and 12 pay 15% less. Transporting a motorcycle/car one way costs 15/36 Ls; bicycles travel free. The service is operated by **Rīgas Jūras Līnija** *(RJL; Riga Sea Line;* ☎ 720 54 60, fax 720 54 61; e *booking@rigasealine.lv;* w *www.rigasealine .lv; Eksporta iela 3a*). In Sweden tickets are sold at **Rīgas Jūras Līnija** (☎ 08-663 46 40, fax 545 88 159; e *booking@rigasealine.lv; Magasin 2, SF-11556 Frihamnen*).

VV Line (see earlier) operates ferries to/ from Ventspils and Nynäshamn, 57km from Stockholm, in Sweden. Ferries depart five times weekly from both ports and sailing time is 10½ hours. A single/return fare in a three- or four-person cabin costs 800/1400 SEK (54/95 Ls) and transporting a car one way/return costs 1000/1800 SEK (68/122 Ls), including driver. In Nynäshamn tickets are sold at **VV Line** (☎ 08-524 00 850, ticket bookings 08-524 00 855, fax 08-524 00 856; e *office@vvline.com; Hamnterminalen, SE-14921 Nynäshamn*).

**Terrabalt** (☎ 34 25 756, fax 34 81 454; e *info@terrabalt.lv;* w *www.terrabalt.lv; Pier 46, LV-3405 Liepāja*) runs ferries from Liepāja to Karlshamn three times weekly (17½ hours). See under Liepāja in the Kurzeme chapter for details.

**To/from Lithuania** From Stockholm, the *Palanga* ferry sails three times weekly to Klaipėda (17 hours). A simple Pullman seat costs 500/900 Skr single/return, berths start at 720/1298 Skr, and a car costs 472/879 Skr. Departures are from the **Baltic Terminal** (☎ 08-66 75 235, fax 66 75 236) at Stockholm's

Freeport; tickets are sold here too. In Klaipėda, contact Lisco Lines or Krantas Shipping (see following).

Ferries between Klaipėda and Karlshamm (18 hours) are operated by Lisco Lines, also called **Lisco Baltic Service** (☎ 46-393 616, fax 393 618; e passenger@lisco.lt; w www .lisco.lt; Janonio gatvė 24, LT-5813 Klaipėda). Two ferries, the Palanga and the äiauliai, make the crossing five times a week and a single fare for a Pullman deck seat/bed in a three-berth cabin costs 305/590 Lt, including breakfast (400/600 Lt June to August). It costs 20/100/ 250 Lt to transport a bicycle/motorcycle/car one way. In Lithuania, tickets can be bought direct from Lisco Lines or from its agent, **Krantas Shipping** (☎ 46-395 051, fax 395 053; e passenger@krantas.lt; w www.krantas.lt; Perkėlos gatvė 10, LT-5804 Klaipėda), at the ferry terminal, or **Krantas Travel** (☎ 46-395 111, fax 395 222; e travel@ krantas.lt; Lietuvininkų gatvė 5) in town. In Sweden, its agent is **DFDS Tor Line AB** (☎ 0454-33 680, fax 33689; e karlshamn@ dfdstorline.com; Sodra Stillerydsvagen 127, S-374 93 Karlshamn).

## Denmark
**To/from Lithuania** From Århus, the cargo ferry Sea Corona sails via Åbenraa (also in Denmark) to Klaipėda twice weekly. If it has room it takes passengers and cars, but it gets booked up quickly. Book as many months in advance as you can. In Lithuania, contact Lisco Lines or Krantas Shipping.

Lisco Lines' once-weekly cargo ferry between Klaipėda and Copenhagen likewise offers a very limited amount of car and passenger space. Tickets must likewise be bought months in advance from any Lisco Lines or Krantas Shipping office.

## Germany
**To/from Estonia** Between June and early September, Silja Line's passenger ferry, Finnjet (one of the world's fastest ferries), sails three times weekly between Tallinn and Rostock. It departs from Tallinn (Terminal D) on Tuesday, Thursday and Saturday, and arrives in Rostock 20 hours later. In Germany, contact **Silja Line** (☎ 0381-350 4350, fax 350 4359; w www.siljaline.de; Am Warnowkai 8, D-18147 Rostock). Silja Line's offices in Tallinn are listed under Getting There & Away in the Tallinn chapter.

**To/from Latvia** A ferry sails twice weekly in each direction between Rīga and Kiel (13 hours). Contact **Hanza Maritime Agency** (☎ 732 3569, fax 732 5751; e hanza@hanza .lv; w www.hanza.lv; Eksporta iela 10, LV-1045 Rīga) or see Getting There & Away in the Rīga chapter for details. In Germany, tickets are sold by **Baltic Seaways** (☎ 0431-239 8511, fax 239 8529; Ostuferhafen 22, D-24149 Kiel). From Rīga there is also a twice-weekly ferry to/from Lübeck. **Latlines** (☎ 734 9527, ticket bookings ☎ 735 35 23, fax 734 95 75; e booking@latlines.lv; w www.latlines .lv; Zivju iela 1, LV-1015 Rīga) operates a twice-weekly ferry to/from Lübeck, departing from Rīga on Monday and Friday, and from Lübeck on Wednesday and Saturday. The overnight crossing takes nine hours and a single/return fare in a four-bed cabin costs 85/163 Ls or €130/250. Transporting a car one way/return costs 65/124 Ls or €100/ 190. In Lübeck tickets are sold at **Latlines** (☎ 0451-709 9697, fax 0451-709 9687; e info@ latlines.de; Luisenhof 13, D-23569 Lübeck).

Terrabalt runs ferries to/from Liepāja and Rostock, also two times a week each way. See Liepāja in the Kurzeme chapter for details.

**To/from Lithuania** From Kiel, Lisco Lines and Scandlines run a joint daily service aboard the Vilnius, Kaunas, Petersburg or Greifswald to Klaipėda (30 hours). Single/return fares start at €55/110 (€60/120 May to mid-June), €63/130 mid-June to August) for a seat, and from €110/188 (€155/264 May to mid-June, €166/282 mid-June to August) for a berth in a cabin. Each ferry has space for just 40 cars – transporting a car one way/return costs €112/190 (€6/10 for a bicycle and €46/92 for a motorcycle). Tickets should be booked well in advance, particularly if you are taking a vehicle.

In Klaipėda, contact **Lisco Lines** (Lisco Baltic Service; ☎ 46-393 616, fax 393 618; e passenger@lisco.lt; w www.lisco.lt; Janonio gatvė 24, LT-5813 Klaipėda), **Krantas Shipping** (☎ 46-395 050, fax 395 052; e passenger @krantas.lt; w www.krantas.lt; Perkėlos gatvė 10, LT-5804 Klaipėda), or Scandlines (☎ 46 310 561). In Kiel, go to **Lisco Baltic Service** (☎ 0431-209 76 400, fax 209 76 555; e passage@lisco-baltic-service.de; w www.lisco -baltic-service.de; Ostuferhafen 15, D-24149 Kiel).

Lisco Lines' *Klaipéda* cargo and passenger ferry sails every two days between Mukran (Sassnitz) and Klaipéda (18 hours). A berth in a double cabin is €105/190 (those aged under 18 €85/150). Cars on a single/return trip are €107/214. In Klaipéda, contact Lisco Lines or Krantas Shipping. In Germany, tickets are sold by **Lisco Baltic Service** (☎ *0383-92 22 681, fax 91 22 493; Zweigniederlassung Mukran Hafen, D-18546 Mukran*).

## ORGANISED TOURS

With independent travel in the Baltics being so straightforward these days, an organised tour is unlikely to take you along paths you can't tread alone. But if you want to lap up luxury in a multistar hotel, whirlwind through the capitals at breakneck speed, poodle around by pedal power or discover the greener side of Baltic life, a package might just save time, money or both. Tour operators include the following.

### Australia
**Gateway Travel** (☎ 02-9745 3333, fax 9745 3237, e agent@russian-gateway.com.au, w www.russian-gateway.com.au) 48 The Boulevarde, Strathfield, NSW 2135 – Baltics, ex-USSR and Trans-Siberia specialists offering tours of Eastern Europe, taking in Latvia en route.
**Red Bear Tours** (☎ 03-9867 3888, fax 9867 1055, e passport@travelcentre.com.au, w www.travelcentre.com.au) Passport Travel, Suite 11, 401 St Kilda Rd, Melbourne, Vic 3004 – Australia's Russian budget travel specialist, offering cheap Trans-Siberian packages.

**Well Connected Travel** (☎ 02-9975 2355, e info@wctravel.com.au, w www.wctravel.com.au) 89 Ferguson St, Forestville NSW 2087 – Boasts some interesting 'Baltic connections', including an opera and ballet tour taking in Estonia.

### Germany
**Ost-Reise Service** (☎ 0521-417 33 33, 0521-417 33 44, e ors@ostreisen.de, w www.ostreisen.de) Am Alten Friedhof 2, D-33647 Bielefeld – Baltic specialists
**Schnieder Reisen** (☎ 040-380 20 60, fax 388 965, e info@schniederreisen.de, w www.schniederreisen.de) Schillerstrasse 43, D-22767 Hamburg – Touts a big range of tours and individual bookings to the Baltics, offering everything from eight-day tours of Riga to fly-and-drive or sail-and-drive packages.

### UK
**Regent Holidays** (☎ 0117-921 1711, fax 925 4866, e regent@regent-holidays.co.uk, w www.regent-holidays.co.uk) 15 John St, Bristol BS1 2HR – Britain's Baltic specialist, with regular tours as well as one-off special-interest tours.

### USA & Canada
**Baltic DesignTours** (☎ 888-226 36 28, 416-221 9212, fax 2216989, w www.baltic-design-tours.on.ca) 5650 Yonge St, Toronto, Ontario M2M 4G3 – Offers city, country and regional tours and Baltic Sea cruises.
**Vytis Tours** (☎ 718-423 6161, 800-778 9847, fax 718-423 3979, e vyttours@earthlink.net, w www.vytistours.com) 40-24 235th St, Douglaston, New York NY 11363

# Getting Around

## AIR

There are plenty of scheduled flights between the three Baltic capitals, listed in the relevant city and town Getting There & Away sections. Flights are reliable but expensive.

Within each country, domestic flights are minimal – Lithuanian Airlines flies between Palanga and Vilnius once weekly mid-May to mid-September, and Air Lithuania operates Kaunas-Palanga flights daily. Air Livonia operates weekly Pärnu–Ruhnu–Kuressaare and Tallinn–Kuressaare flights; Avies flies also several times weekly to/from Tallinn and Kuressaare; and ELK Airlines flies between the Estonian capital and Kärdla. More details are listed in the respective city and town Getting There & Away sections.

There were no domestic flights within Latvia at the time of writing, although the anticipated transformation of Ventspils airport into a commercial transport hub within the next five years could change this.

## BUS

The region is well served by buses, although services to off-the-beaten track villages are infrequent. Direct bus services link the three capitals – Tallinn, Rīga and Vilnius – and there are plenty of other cross-border services between main towns. To get to Tallinn from Kaunas, you have to change in Panevėzys.

Buses are generally faster than trains and, on the whole, slightly cheaper. Those used for local journeys, up to about two hours long, offer few comforts. Dating from some prehistoric time, many appear to be only fit for the scrap heap. To ensure semisurvival, avoid window seats in rainy, snowy or very cold weather; travel with someone you're prepared to snuggle up to for body warmth; and sit in the seat allocated to you to avoid tangling with a merciless babushka who wants *her* seat that *you're in*. Some shorter routes, however, are serviced by nippier and more modern microbuses, holding about 15 passengers and officially making fewer stops than their big-bus counterparts.

By contrast, buses travelling between the Baltic countries are equal to any long-distance coach anywhere else in Europe. Eurolines has its appointed agents in each Baltic capital. Its buses are clean and tout a heating system that functions and can be moderated. Most have a toilet, hot drinks dispenser and TV on board. Many scheduled buses to/ from Tallinn, Rīga and Vilnius run overnight – a convenient and safe way of travelling, even for lone women.

On buses, you carry your luggage on board with you – unless it is too large, in which case you can ask the driver to stash it in the underneath baggage compartment for a small fee.

### Tickets & Information

Ticket offices/windows selling national and international tickets are clearly marked in the local language and occasionally in English too. Tickets are always printed in the local language and easy to understand once you know the words for 'seat', 'bus stop' etc (see the Language chapter).

For long-distance buses originating from where you intend to leave, tickets are sold in advance. For local buses to nearby towns or villages, or for long-distance buses that are in mid-route ('in transit'), you normally pay on board. This may mean a bit of a scrum for seats if there are a lot of people waiting.

Most bus and train stations in towns and cities have information windows with staff who generally speak some English. Very occasionally, they charge (per question) for their services.

### Timetables & Fares

Timetables can be checked before leaving home on the respective bus company websites (see the boxed text 'Electronic Timetables') or, upon arrival in the region, by calling a local English-language telephone information hotline, prevalent throughout Estonia, in Vilnius and Rīga. The In Your Pocket city guides to the capitals (see Newspapers & Magazines in the introductory Facts for the Visitor chapter) include fairly comprehensive domestic and pan-Baltic bus schedules, updated every two months.

At bus stations, large comprehensive timetables are posted in the main ticket hall. A rare few need careful decoding. Most simply list the departure time and the days (using either Roman or Arabic numerals, the digit one being Monday) on which the service runs.

Fares vary little between the three countries. For a 100km domestic trip you pay

## Electronic Timetables

Domestic bus and train timetables can be checked on the Internet:

**Buses**

| | |
|---|---|
| Estonia | W www.bussireisid.ee |
| Latvia | W www.autoosta.lv |
| Lithuania | W www.toks.lt |

**Trains**

| | |
|---|---|
| Estonia | W www.evr.ee |
| Latvia | W www.ldz.lv |
| Lithuania | W www.litrail.lt |

around 1.50 Ls (€2.60) in Latvia, 11.50 Lt (€3.35) in Lithuania and 55 EEK (€3.50) in Estonia; fares differ slightly between bus companies, reflecting the speed of the bus and time of day it arrives/departs. Pan-Baltic trips are marginally more expensive – around €4.50 per 100km.

## TRAIN

Estonia, Latvia and Lithuania are well covered by railways, although services have been cut in recent years.

Trains are slow and cheap, but they do offer a greater comfort of sorts. You can almost never open the windows, which can make things stuffy (and smelly, depending on your travelling companions), while you stand equal chances of freezing or baking, depending on whether the heating is turned on or not. Lower trains, known as suburban or electric, are substantially slower and make more frequent stops than long-distance trains, of which there are three types – 'fast' (international routes only), passenger and diesel.

No rail passes are available within the region.

## Tickets & Information

Tickets can be bought in advance and immediately before departure at train stations. In larger train stations, such as Rīga, you can only buy tickets for certain types of trains or destinations at certain windows. See under Train in the relevant city and town Getting There & Away sections for details.

Tickets – upon boarding a long-distance train between the Baltics and elsewhere – must be surrendered to the carriage attendant, who will safeguard it for the journey's dura-tion and return it to you 15 minutes before arrival at your final destination (a handy 'alarm clock' if you're on an overnight train).

Local-language words for 'carriage', 'seat' etc – always marked on train tickets – are included in the Language chapter at the back of this book.

## Timetables & Fares

Latvia and Lithuania both publish updated train schedules on their websites (see the boxed text 'Electronic Timetables'), but Estonia has yet to do so. Those displayed at train stations generally list the number of the train, departure and arrival times, and the platform from which it leaves. Some list the return journey schedules, the number of minutes a train waits in your station or the time a train left the place it began its journey. Always study the small print on timetables, too, as many trains only run on certain days or between certain dates.

Train fares vary. In general seating you can go 100km for about 42 EEK (€2.68) in Estonia, 1.20 Ls (€2) in Latvia and 9.80 Lt (€2.80) in Lithuania. Once you get into compartment class, fares start rising – 100km costs about 55 EEK (€3.50) in Estonia, 12 Lt (€3.50) in Lithuania and 3 Ls (€5) in Latvia. Generally, 1st class costs about twice as much as compartment class, while couchette fares are midway between general seating and compartment class.

## Routes

Between the capitals, the only direct train is a slow overnight chugger between Vilnius and Rīga, prompting most people to take the speedier bus instead; there is no direct rail link between Tallinn and Rīga.

The Rīga–St Petersburg train stops at Sigulda, Cēsis, Valmiera, Lugaži, Valga and Võru, then Pechory (Petseri) on its way to St Petersburg. The Tallinn-Moscow *Tallinn Express* train makes stops at Rakvere, Jõhvi and Narva on its way to the Russian border.

Other lines include Tallinn-Narva; Tallinn–Pärnu, Tallinn–Tartu, Tallinn–Viljandi, Rīga–Ventspils, Rīga–Rēzekne, Rīga–Daugavpils, Rīga–Liepāja, Vilnius–Daugavpils–Rēzekne (some terminating at St Petersburg), Vilnius–Druskininkai; Vilnius–Ignalina, Vilnius–Kaunas and Vilnius–Klaipėda. There are several other local railways fanning out from the main cities.

## Classes

There are four classes of train accommodation, only some of which will be found on any one train.

The cheapest, most bum-numbing class is general seating, an unreserved bench-type seating which is the only class available on local 'electric' trains and some 'diesel' trains too. This is what you'll travel on if you train it from Rīga to the seaside in Jūrmala.

One rung up the ladder is 'couchette' class, carriages with three tiers of hard bunks in sections that are partitioned, but not fully closed off from each other. Travelling in them is certainly a communal experience and can be pretty grubby and stuffy.

Better still is compartment class – the equivalent of a Western couchette – with plastic seats and an inside lock on the door. Clean, starched linen and blankets are provided for the bunks at an extra charge (usually around €2 in the local currency), which is collected by the carriage attendant once on board. 'Fast' and 'passenger' trains have compartment carriages and you can get places in them even if you're not travelling at night; in daytime they provide a numbered seat in a space that shouldn't be too crowded. Compartment and couchette classes together form what is referred to as 2nd-class accommodation.

First class, also called 'soft class', is only available on some 'fast' international trains.

Compartments have upholstered seats and convert to comfortable sleeping – lockable – compartments for two or four people. Your beds are usually made up for you and the carriage attendant brings you tea for free.

## CAR & MOTORCYCLE

Driving or riding your own vehicle is an attractive option if you are able to bring or rent a car or motorcycle. It makes some of the region's most beautiful – and remote – places far more accessible, enabling you to discover spots that a 'chug-chug' bus or train just would not get you to in a limited amount of time – or at all. Indeed, driving in the countryside is a world apart from the capital cities' manic motorists – zigzag along gravel roads, admire the movie-style dust trail in your mirror and wonder where on earth that solitary passer-by you just passed is walking to.

Main roads linking the cities and towns are generally good, distances are not too great and traffic is far from congested. The number of cars per capita in Latvia is among the lowest in Europe, unlike in Estonia, where car owners toppled the European average (280 cars per 1000 inhabitants). In more remote areas there are many gravel roads and dirt tracks, but with a wide range of quality road maps with the different grade roads marked you can easily avoid the rougher roads if you don't feel your suspension is up to it.

## Road Distances (km)

|            | Tallinn | Tartu | Pärnu | Narva | Valka/Valga | Rīga | Liepāja | Daugavpils | Ventspils | Vilnius | Kaunas | Klaipėda | Panevė ys | Šiauliai |
|------------|---------|-------|-------|-------|-------------|------|---------|------------|-----------|---------|--------|----------|-----------|----------|
| Tallinn    | ---     |       |       |       |             |      |         |            |           |         |        |          |           |          |
| Tartu      | 190     | ---   |       |       |             |      |         |            |           |         |        |          |           |          |
| Pärnu      | 130     | 205   | ---   |       |             |      |         |            |           |         |        |          |           |          |
| Narva      | 210     | 194   | 304   | ---   |             |      |         |            |           |         |        |          |           |          |
| Valka/Valga| 276     | 86    | 140   | 268   | ---         |      |         |            |           |         |        |          |           |          |
| Rīga       | 310     | 253   | 180   | 435   | 167         | ---  |         |            |           |         |        |          |           |          |
| Liepāja    | 530     | 473   | 400   | 655   | 387         | 220  | ---     |            |           |         |        |          |           |          |
| Daugavpils | 540     | 377   | 410   | 559   | 291         | 230  | 450     | ---        |           |         |        |          |           |          |
| Ventspils  | 510     | 453   | 380   | 635   | 367         | 200  | 119     | 430        | ---       |         |        |          |           |          |
| Vilnius    | 600     | 543   | 470   | 725   | 457         | 290  | 465     | 167        | 584       | ---     |        |          |           |          |
| Kaunas     | 575     | 523   | 460   | 715   | 447         | 280  | 230     | 267        | 349       | 100     | ---    |          |           |          |
| Klaipėda   | 620     | 538   | 490   | 745   | 477         | 310  | 155     | 477        | 274       | 310     | 210    | ---      |           |          |
| Panevė ys  | 460     | 403   | 330   | 585   | 317         | 150  | 270     | 168        | 350       | 140     | 110    | 235      | ---       |          |
| Šiauliai   | 465     | 383   | 310   | 565   | 297         | 130  | 192     | 387        | 330       | 220     | 140    | 155      | 80        | ---      |

There are petrol stations, run by major oil companies such as Statoil, Shell and Neste, open 24 hours along all the major roads. Western-grade fuel, including unleaded, is readily available region-wide; count on paying around €0.40 per litre.

You can take your own vehicle to the Baltics by ferry from Finland, Sweden, Denmark or Germany; or by road from Poland, Belarus or Russia (see the Getting There & Away chapter). Alternatively, you can rent a car once in the region – see Rental later.

## Road Rules

The whole region drives on the right. In Lithuania, driving with any alcohol at all in your blood is illegal – don't do so after even a sip of a drink. In Estonia a blood-alcohol level of 0.02% (which means you still can't drink) is the legal limit; in Latvia it is marginally higher at 0.05%. Seat belts are compulsory for drivers and for front-seat passengers. Speed limits in built-up areas are 50km/h in Latvia and Estonia, and 60km/h in Lithuania. Limits outside urban areas vary from 90km/h to 110km/h. In Estonia and Latvia you always have your headlights switched on when driving on highways, even during the day. In Lithuania, you have to have them on during the day – wherever you are driving, be it a city, village or open highway – for a period of about four weeks starting from 1 September (apparently timed to coincide with the 'going back to school' rush).

Traffic police are fearsome beings who don't need any reason to pull you over. Expect to be asked to stop at least twice on a trip between Rīga and Vilnius. Traffic police are particularly stringent about speeding. Fines are collected on the spot by the police officer who books you. Fines vary dramatically and the only way you can ensure an officer is not adding a little pocket money for himself onto the official fine is to ask for a receipt. In Latvia, the fine for exceeding the speed limit by up to 20km/h is around €10, up to 50km/h around €15 and more than 50km/h anything up to €100. If you do not have enough cash to pay, your passport and car documents can be confiscated until you have paid the fine at the police station stipulated by the penalising officer.

Note that in Latvia it is illegal to use a mobile phone while operating a vehicle; chatting to your mates while driving warrants a hefty fine.

Parking meters exist in the capitals and larger cities – they generally eat around €0.80 an hour, payable in 15-minute blocks. If you do not feed the meter your car will be wheel-clamped. If there's no meter, there is usually a bibbed attendant lurking somewhere close to ensure you pay before leaving your car.

There is an hourly fee of 5 Ls to drive into the Old Town of Rīga, and you need a 48 EEK parking permit to enter Tallinn Old Town by car. Driving into the Old Towns in Vilnius and Kaunas is free but you have to pay an hourly fee of 2 Lt to park between 8am and 8pm Monday to Saturday in Vilnius, and 1 Lt per hour in Kaunas. Motorists must also pay a small entrance fee to drive into Latvia's prime seaside resort, Jūrmala (1 Ls year-round). National parks such as Trakai (5 Lt) and the Curonian Spit in Lithuania (5 Lt per car and driver, 3 Lt each additional passenger) also demand an entrance fee from motorists.

Take care driving near trams, trolleybuses and buses in towns. Passengers may run across the road to catch them while they're still in motion. Traffic behind a tram must stop when it opens its doors to let people in and out. Trolleybuses often swing a long way out into the road when leaving a stop.

## Rental

Tallinn, Rīga and Vilnius are naturally the easiest places to rent cars, although there are small outlets elsewhere. The major international car-rental companies all have offices in the capitals, often both in town and at the airport – listed in the city and town Getting There & Away sections.

If you are driving across all three Baltic countries, it is cheaper to rent a car in Vilnius. Some companies, such as Avis and Hertz, allow you to pick up a car in one city and drop it off in another.

A variety of different packages and weekend specials is available, so it is worth shopping around. Deals apart, expect to pay around €50 (unlimited mileage) a day in Estonia, and anything from €115 a day (unlimited mileage) with a major rental company to €25 a day with a small private company in the other two capitals.

**Documents** If you're renting a car you need a passport and a suitable driving licence – normally an International Driving Permit (IDP), but a national licence from a European country is often acceptable. Some rental companies have minimum ages (usually 19 or 21, but 22 at some places in Estonia) and stipulate that you must have held your licence for at least a year. A major credit card is essential too, as some companies insist on it as the method of payment. Even if they don't, you'll have to leave a very large deposit or make a heavy cash prepayment. See Car & Motorcycle under Land in the Getting There & Away chapter for more on licences and other documents you need if you bring your own vehicle.

## BICYCLE

The flatness and small scale of Estonia, Latvia and Lithuania and the light traffic on most roads make them good cycling territory. On the Estonian islands particularly, you will see cyclists galore in summer. Most bring their own bicycles but there are a plenty of places where you can rent a bicycle too – including Hiiumaa, Kärdla, Palmse, Pärnu, Sagadi, Tartu and Vormsi in Estonia; Rīga, Jūrmala, Cēsis, Sigulda, Valmiera and Kurzeme's Kolka, Kandava and Sabile in Latvia; and in Vilnius, Trakai, Kaunas, Palanga, Nida, Žemaičių Naumiestis (for exploring the Nemunas Delta Regional Park), Druskininkai and Palūšė (in the Aukštaitija National Park) in Lithuania.

Cyclists should certainly bring waterproof clothing, and perhaps a tent if you're touring, since you may not find accommodation in some out-of-the-way places. Some bike-rental places, such as Valmiera's Eži hostel in Latvia, rents tents, sleeping bags and any other gear you might need when out peddling.

Several travel agencies and organisations, both within and outside the region, organise cycling tours. See Organised Tours later in this chapter.

## HITCHING

Hitching is never entirely safe in any country in the world, and we don't recommend it. Travellers who decide to hitch should understand that they are taking a small but potentially serious risk. People who do choose to hitch will be safer if they travel in pairs and let someone know where they are planning to go.

Locally, hitching is a popular means of getting from A to B. The **Vilnius Hitchhiking Club** (VHHC; ☎ 5-278 3025; e info@auto stop.lt; w www.autostop.lt; Umedzių gatve. 98-19, Vilnius) reckons the Baltic hitcher's average speed to be between 55km/h and 60km/h. It provides practical information and contacts to travellers hoping to hitch a ride in all three Baltic countries.

## BOAT
### Ferry

Combined passenger and vehicle ferries sail from the Estonian mainland to the islands of Muhu (which is linked by a road causeway to Estonia's biggest island, Saaremaa), Hiiumaa and Vormsi. In summer there are also ferry services between Saaremaa and Hiiumaa, and between Saaremaa and Vilsandi Island. It is also possible to take boat trips to the tiny islands of Saarnaki and Hanikatsi, off southeastern Hiiumaa, and to Abruka and Vahase off Saaremaa's southern coast. Full details of all of these services are in the West Estonia & the Islands chapter.

From Pärnu, you can take boat excursions to Kihnu and Ruhnu Islands – see the Southwest Estonia chapter. In summer you can sail from Tallinn to its surrounding islands of Aegna and Naissar; from Paldiski to the Pakri Islands; and from Leepneeme Harbour, 18km northwest of Tallinn to Prangli (see the boxed text 'Islands' in the Tallinn chapter for full details).

Boating opportunities within Latvia are few, although you can catch a car ferry across the Gauja River to/from Līgatne in the Gauja National Park; details are included in the Vidzeme chapter.

Ferries year-round make the five-minute crossing from Klaipėda to Smiltynė in western Lithuania. In southeastern Lithuania, a steam boat ploughs the Nemunas River between Druskininkai and Liskiava in the Dzūkija National Park. There is also a seasonal hydrofoil daily along the Nemunas River and the Curonian Lagoon between Kaunas and Nida; in summer it is easy to charter a boat along part of the hydrofoil route or from Nida to Klaipėda. You can also hire boats to explore the Nemunas Delta.

## Yacht

Private yachting is a popular way to get around the Baltic Coast – particularly Estonia's coast with its many islands and bays. Yachts can be rented with or without a skipper from the **Pirita marina** (☎ 639 8981; Regati puiestee 1, EE0001 Tallinn). For information and advice on Estonia's dozens of harbours, contact the **Estonian Marine Tourism Association** (EMTA; ☎/fax 2-641 1417; W http://old.artun.ee/sadamad; Pikk 71, EE0001 Tallinn). It publishes the annual By Pleasure Boat to Estonia guide, which includes harbour maps, details of local sea-rescue operations including shortwave radio channel listings and telephone numbers of the different regional emergency rescue services. The EMTA also sells updated navigation charts of the Estonian Coast, sold at most Estonian harbours and in Finland at the **Estum Sailing Agency** (☎ 09-629 299, fax 09-629 390; Vuorimiehenka 23a, SF-00140 Helsinki).

In Latvia, Rīga's **Andrejosta Yacht Club** (☎ 732 32 25, 950 82 75; e support.rsc@apollo.lv; Eksporta iela 1a) rents yachts and assists sailors wanting to navigate the country's other nine yacht ports. Detailed information on these can be found on the website **Yacht Harbours of Latvia** (W http://yacht.rsc .lv) and in the Yacht Ports of Latvia guide, sold at the Jāņa sēta bookshop in Rīga. Navigation charts for Latvian waters are sold by the hydrographical service of the **Latvian Maritime Administration** (☎ 706 21 01; W www.maritimeadministration.lv; Trijādības iela 5, LV-1048 Rīga); a full list of charts is posted on its website.

See Sailing Yourself in the Getting There & Away chapter for information on recommended harbours in Estonia.

## LOCAL TRANSPORT
## Bus, Tram & Trolleybus

A mix of trams, buses and trolleybuses (buses run by electricity from overhead wires) provides thorough public transport around towns and cities in all three countries (except there are no trams in Lithuania – until sometime around 2007, that is, when shiny new trams will glide around the capital). All three types of transport get crowded, especially during the early-morning and early-evening rush hours, when so many people cram themselves in that the doors

don't shut properly – in Kaunas, some 400 students from the university once squashed into one bus as a publicity stunt to highlight the need for more services!

Trams, trolleybuses and buses all run from about 5.30am to 12.30am, but services get pretty thin in outlying areas after about 7pm. In Estonia, the same ticket is good for all three types of transport; in Lithuania and Latvia, you need different tickets for each type. In all three countries, you pay for your ride by punching a flat-fare ticket in one of the ticket punches fixed inside the vehicle. Tickets are sold from news kiosks displaying them in the window and by some drivers (who are easier to find but charge a little more for tickets). Buy five or 10 at once – a single ticket costs 10 EEK in Estonia, 0.20 Ls in Latvia and 0.80 Lt in Lithuania. Weekly and monthly travel passes are also available. The system depends on honesty and lends itself to cheating, but there are occasional inspections, with on-the-spot fines being flung in your face if you're caught riding without a punched ticket.

Travelling on all trams, trolleybuses and buses requires a certain etiquette. If you are young, fit and capable of standing on one foot for the duration of your journey, do not sit in the seats at the front – these are only for babushkas and small children. Secondly, plan getting off well ahead of time. The moment the bus/tram rolls away from the stop prior to the one you are getting off at, start making your way to the door. Pushing, shoving, stamping on toes and elbowing are, of course, allowed. Thirdly, feel free to take anything you like on any form of public transport – squawking chickens will scarcely raise a second glance.

City buses are supplemented by the route-taxi (liinitakso or marsruuttakso in Estonian, marsruta taksobuss or mikroautobuss in Latvian, and masrutinis in Lithuanian) – minibuses that drop you anywhere along a fixed routes for a flat fare: 15 EEK in Tallinn, 0.20 Ls to 0.30 Ls in Rīga and 2 Lt in Vilnius.

All airports are served by regular city transport as well as by taxis.

## Train

Suburban trains serve the outskirts of the main cities and some surrounding towns and villages. They're of limited use as city transport for visitors, as they mostly go to

## Street Names

|  | Estonian | Latvian | Lithuanian |
| --- | --- | --- | --- |
| street | tänav | iela | gatvė |
| square | väljak or plats | laukums | aikstė |
| avenue or boulevard | puiestee | prospekts or bulvāris | prospektas or bulvaras |
| road | tee | ce|š | kelias |
| highway | maantee | lielce|s or soseja | plentas |
| bridge | sild | tilts | tiltas |

residential or industrial areas where there's little to see. But some are useful for day trips to destinations outside the cities.

### Taxi

Taxis are plentiful and usually cheap: They officially cost 5 EEK to 7 EEK per km in Estonia, 0.30 Ls per km in Latvia, and 0.65 Lt to 1.30 Lt in Lithuania; night-time tariffs, which generally kick in between 10pm and 6am, are higher.

To avoid rip-offs, insist on the meter running. If not, agree on a fixed price before you set off. In some places, such as Vilnius, it is substantially cheaper to order a cab by phone.

## ORGANISED TOURS

Single-city, two- or three-city, country, island and so on tours and excursions are a dime a dozen in all three countries. Key operators include:

### Estonia

**Estonian Holidays** (☎ 641 25 04; e holidays@ holidays.ee, w www.holidays.ee) Lai 5, EE10133 Tallinn. Organises thematic group tours, including an Estonian cultural heritage tour, a 'crown tour' featuring the sights depicted on Estonian banknotes, North Estonian manor houses, wildlife and agricultural tours.

**Estonian Rural Tourism** (☎ 600 99 99, 625 62 73, ☎/fax 641 12 03; e eesti@maatourism.ee) Lai tänav 39-41, EE10133 Tallinn. Organises more alternative four- or five-day tours with farmhouse accommodation, aimed at 'green' travellers into nature and the great outdoors.

**Haapsalu Travel Service** (☎ 047-47 24 180; e info@travel-service.ee, w www.travel-service .ee) Karja tänav 5, EE90502 Haapsalu (☎ 047- 33 188; e info@travel-service) Tallinna maantee 1, EE90507 Haapsalu. Organises tours of six Estonian cities, western Estonia, Vormsi Island as well as a thematic tour of former Soviet military sites in Estonia, and camping and ecological tours through nature reserves across Estonia.

**Mere Travel Agency** (☎ 045-33 610; e mere@ tt.ee, w www.saaremaa.ee/mere) Tallinna maantee 27, EE93811 Kuressaare, Saaremaa. Arranges a variety of ecologically oriented tours, including a weekend in the country with a farm lunch, sauna and some local brew; a two-day trip down memory lane to Grandma's and Grandpa's; crayfish parties; and thematic tours of Saaremaa (military, ancient, maritime etc). It runs boat trips and nature tours, too.

### Latvia

**Country Holidays** (Lauku ce|otājs; ☎ 761 76 00, ☎/fax 783 00 41; e lauku@celotajs.lv) Ku-u iela 11, LV-1048 Rīga. Organises bird-watching, walking, berry-picking and a host of other nature-loving expeditions around Latvia.

**Latvia Tours** (☎ 708 50 01; e hq@latviatours.lv, w www.latviatours.lv) Ka|ķu iela 8. Runs a bounty of tours, including a classic seven-day coach tour of the three capitals. From May to September it runs daily day trips from Rīga to Sigulda (13 Ls) or Rundāle (18 Ls), both departing at 10am and returning at 3.30pm; and day trips along the Daugava River to Aglona, Rezēkne and a Latgalian potter's workshop (25 Ls including lunch); and to Kurzeme (21 Ls) every second Thursday, departing at 8am and returning at 10pm.

### Lithuania

**Baltic Travel Service** (☎ 5-212 0220; e lcc@bts .lt) Subačiaus gatvė 2, Vilnius. Specialises in countryside tourism, running bird-watching tours, Nemunas Delta trips and the like.

**Krantas Travel** (☎ 5-231 3314, fax 5-262 9120; e Vilnius@krantas.lt) Pylimo gatv 4, LT-2001 Vilnius. With branch offices in Kaunas and Klaipėda, Krantas organises cycling, culinary, walking and bird-watching tours in Lithuania's national and regional parks.

**Liturimex** (☎ 5-279 1416, fax 5-279 1417; e center@liturimex.lt, w www.liturimex.lt) Basinavičiaus gatve 11/1, LT-2009 Vilnius. Organises weekend breaks and spa tours to Druskininkai.

# THE POWER OF SONG

Song is the soul of the Balts. And nowhere is this expressed more eloquently than in the national song festivals that unite Estonians, Latvians and Lithuanians worldwide in a spellbinding performance of song. The crescendo is a choir of up to 30,000 voices, singing its heart out to an audience of 100,000 or more, while scores of folk dancers in traditional dress throw a bewitching kaleidoscope of patterns across the vast, open-air stage.

Although the first song festival did not take place in the Baltic region until the late 19th century, the Balts' natural lyricism and love of singing is deep-rooted in folklore and can be traced to pre-Christian times. Ancient Baltic beliefs in the pagan powers of the sky god (*dievas*), the god of thunder *(Perkūnas)* and the mythological family of the sun, moon and stars found their way into Baltic folk rhymes which, when recorded on paper by the likes of Latvian folk song collector Krisjānis Barons (1835–1923) were called *dainas*. The lyrics of these ancient *dainas*, passed down orally between generations, reflected the Balts' age-old marriage with nature. Lines such as 'once we sang so that the fields resounded with our songs' and choral titles like *Song of Pain and Sun Disc* (Ester Mägi), *Lilac, Do You Bring Me Luck* (Olav Ehala) and *Blow Wind, Blow* still feature in the festival song repertoire today.

With the turn of the 19th century and the inscription of these songs and legends, proverbs and sayings, so the Baltic art of song became a political tool. Influenced by the example set by their German overlords who had hosted German song festivals in Tallinn (1857, 1866) and Rīga (1861) with great success, the Estonians decided to follow suit with a festival of their own. The first Estonian song festival in Tartu in 1869 was inspired by the Estonian national awakening and showed Estonians that they could emulate their German overlords. The simultaneous national revival in Latvia likewise gave birth to the first Latvian song festival (1873) in Rīga which, in turn, inspired Latvians to resist the Russification sweeping through their country. In neighbouring Lithuania, the first song festival did not happen until much later, primarily because of the 1830 to 1831 Polish

**Left:** A Lithuanian folk group in traditional costume

JONATHAN SMITH

rebellions which resulted in Russian law being more strictly imposed on the region with Cyrillic replacing the Latin alphabet. It was only after Baltic independence was briefly achieved in 1920 that the first Lithuanian song festival (1924) took place in Kaunas, the interwar capital.

The Balts' recent campaign for independence from the USSR was also driven by the power of song. It was known as the 'Singing Revolution'. More recently, the Balts' drive towards Europe was epitomised in its entry for the 2002 Eurovision Song Contest – *I wanna be* ('part of Europe' might as well have been included in the title of Marija N's Latin-inspired song).

# Early Festivals

Estonia's early festivals were a strictly male affair, with just a handful of male voice choirs accompanied by a small wind orchestra or brass band taking part. Incredibly the very first festival in 1869 featured just two original Estonian songs, both of which remain in Estonia's festival repertoire today (see the boxed text 'Estonian Fatherland' following). This was primarily to avoid German overlords in Estonia banning the event.

The song festivals were originally annual affairs, then took place every five years after 1918 when Estonia achieved its independence for the first time. Women could sing in mixed festival choirs from 1894, but it was not until 1933 that female choirs were allowed to participate. The song festivals in Latvia from 1873 and in Lithuania from 1920 followed a similar pattern to those of their Baltic neighbour.

During the early Soviet era, songs praising Stalin and later the USSR replaced many of the original Baltic songs (including Jannsen's *My Native Land*), considered too nationalistic by the Soviet authorities. At the Latvian song festival in Rīga in 1948, songs such as *Latvians Sing Praise to Stalin* and *May the Land of Soviets be Glorified* were sung.

It was during this period also that an element of dance was added to the festival programme. As deep-rooted in folklore as its choral

## Estonian Fatherland

Estonia's national anthem, *Eesti Hümn* (My Fatherland, My Native Land, My Pride and Joy), is (somewhat predictably) a set piece of the song festival and is always sung at its start. Sung to a melody composed by Finnish composer Frederik Pacius (1809–91), the lyrics were written for the first festival by festival pioneer Johann Voldemar Jannsen who actually did nothing more than adapt the Finnish anthem lyrics *Maamme* (Our Land). Serving as the national anthem of independent Estonia in 1918 to 1940, it was consequently banned by the Soviet authorities and not reinstated until 1990.

Ironically *My Fatherland is All My Joy*, an original poem also written for the first song festival by Estonian poet, Lydia Koidula, and put to music by Aleksander Kunileid-Saebelmann (1845–75), was never banned. Thus it became the unofficial anthem during the Soviet era. It was set to a new musical score by eminent Estonian composer Gustav Ernesaks (1909–93) and – as tears stream down the cheeks of most – passionately sung at the emotional close of each festival. Ernesaks conducted every festival from 1947 to 1990.

counterpart, traditional dance in all three Baltic countries is inspired by the agrarian cycle and relies on a simplistic choreography and moderate tempo. Circles (ring dances), lines (line dancing) and other symmetrical formations (bridges, chains) are formed by pairs of dancing couples. In the 'fisherman dance', giant stylised ocean waves sweep across the stage. A modest 1500 dancers performed at the first Estonian dance festival in 1934 which, 50 years on, was luring as many as 10,000 dancers.

# Singing for Independence

WWII and the consequent exile, deportation or death of thousands upon thousands of Latvians, Lithuanians and Estonians dealt a bitter blow to the national psyche and its singing soul. Three chief conductors of Estonia's 1950 song festival were arrested, just months before the event, and sentenced to 25 years imprisonment. Yet throughout the numerous refugee camps that sprang up in Germany, it was song that displaced Balts turned to for solace. The first song festival outside the Baltics was held in 1946 for the estimated 120,000 Latvian people in the United Nations (UN) camps in Germany. Throughout the Soviet era, the loss (and love) of homeland was the dominant thread that ran through the symphony of festivals celebrated among Baltic emigrants in the US, Canada and elsewhere.

The power of song reached fever-pitch in 1990 at the Estonian and Latvian national song festivals – two highly charged affairs climaxing with some 30,000 choralists from 700 choirs singing in unison. The return of many Baltic exiles for the first time since WWII to the subsequent festivals in 1993 and '94, the first since independence, proved equally emotive.

# Festivals Today

The months leading up to a song festival are studded with nationwide run-off heats to see which of the three countries' hundreds of choirs can actually compete. Only the best (usually about 800 different choirs, of about 30 voices each) go through to the national song festival. Several guest choirs from émigré Latvian, Lithuanian and Estonian communities abroad are also invited.

In Latvia, the week-long song and dance festival sees choral concerts and folk dance performances fill various venues in the capital city, peaking with the grand finale at the open-air song bowl in Mežaparks on the seventh day. On that last morning, the choirs march through the streets of Rīga to the tree-clad park where, come dusk, they sing homage beneath the night stars to their mythological and folkloric roots in a concert of traditional Latvian song. A sea of flickering candles provides light and warmth for the bewitched, 100,000-strong audience.

Song festivals are a more modest three- or five-day affair in Lithuania. They peak with *dainų diena* (song day) when 11,000 singers parade along the streets from Vilnius Cathedral to Vingis Park where they gather on the open-air stage to sing.

In Estonia the festival, held in Tallinn since 1896, opens with *Koit* (Dawn) by Mihkel Lüdig (1880–1958):

'Voices are ringing now
with the sweet sound of singing... '

## Modern Voices

Notable choirs include the Tallinn Philharmonic Chamber Choir (a professional choir and Estonia's most famous); the Estonian National Female Choir (Tallinn-based professional choir); the Laulik Mixed Choir (also Tallinn-based); and the opera choir from Tartu's Theatre Vanu. In Latvia, Ave Sol is in the limelight; in Lithuania the professional Kaunas State Choir, Ažuoliukas boys' choir and Ėglė (amateur female choir) are well known.

The week preceding the three-day festival is marked by the journey of the centenary flame, traditionally lit in Tartu and brought by horse-drawn carriage to Tallinn. Festival highlights include the first-day symphonic choral concert and the second-day traditional concert which opens with the stirring sound of a 1500-piece brass band.

# Contemporary Composers

Leading Estonian composers whose choral works are a regular festival feature include Eduard Tubin (1905–82) whose folkloric *Santa Maria* starred at the 1999 song festival; Maart Saar (1882–1963); Anu Tali and Veljo Tormis, best known for his beguiling folkloric chants such as *Põhjavaim* (Northern Spirit) and large-scale choral compositions like *Estonian Calendar Songs* (1967) which was based on age-old folkloric melodies.

The hauntingly exquisite Magnificat by Arvo Pärt, Estonia's only composer to achieve true worldwide fame, and Rudolf Tobias's musical interpretation of Psalm 42 are often selected as set pieces that competing choirs sing at the International Choir Festival.

Latvian festival classics, spontaneously sung by a roused audience irrespective of whether they are on the official festival programme or not, include *The Light Castle, Blow Wind Blow* and *The Singer from Beverin*. Pieces by present-day politician Raimonds Pauls were a predominant feature of the 1998 song festival in Rīga, as was the work of Jāzeps Vītols (1863–1948), Latvia's most beloved composer who founded the Latvian national opera and also taught Prokofiev in St Petersburg. Imants Kalniņš is another name to watch for. In Lithuania, many choral symphonies are composed by Algirdas Martinaitis.

The 1980s saw Baltic rock emerge as a powerful means of protest against Soviet rule. In Lithuania, Kęstutis Antanėlis composed the first Lithuanian rock opera *Love and Death in Verona* in 1982, followed after independence by Peer Gynt (1997). Alfred Kalniņš followed suit in 1988 with Latvia's first rock opera *Baņuta,* based on the Latvian epic *Lāčplēsis* (about a bear slayer defending his homeland). It was an instant hit. In Estonia it was Alo Mattiisen who stoked the independence drive and stirred the national consciousness with his sparky rock lyrics.

# Sound of the Music

Traditional musical instruments accompany many folk songs. The Balts each have their own version of the zither – the *kannel* in Estonia, the *kokle* in Latvia and the *kanklės* in Lithuania. Playing this ancient string instrument was believed to protect the musician from death. Crafted

## Folkloric Treasure Trove

The Balts' treasure trove of oral folklore is considered the largest collection in the world. Latvia alone boasts more than 1.5 million folk songs, many of them recorded by folk song collector Krišjānis Barons (1835–1923).

The first folkloric musical score was published in 1634 in Lithuania, guardian of some 600,000 folk songs and stories today. Barons' counterparts in Estonia were Jakob Hurt (1835–1907), and Friedrich Kreutzwald (1803–82) who authored the folkloric epic *Kalevipoeg* (Son of Kalev) in 1857 to 1861.

from maple, ash or linden, the wood had to felled and cut on the day a loved one died, thereby inviting the deceased soul to penetrate the five- to 12-string instrument. The zither is used mainly to accompany dances.

Bells, pipes, flutes and fiddles also feature. In Lithuania you may see the *birbynė*, a small pipe made from straw, feather, or willow reed, with finger holes and an animal horn attached. The long wooden trumpet called the *daudytė* was made from wood or wrapped alder bark (rolled from a long strip into an elongated cone) and served as a shepherd's or herdsman's horn. *Molinukai* are small, child-sized clay whistles lovingly made in different animal shapes.

The *skudučiai*, found only in the northeast, is like a set of five wooden pan pipes with each note produced by a different player, playing a different pipe. The pipes – traditionally played only by men – are hollowed from a plant stem or branch of wood.

Equally unique to the Aukštaitija region is *ragas*, a horn made from two wooden half-cones, bound together with flax then encased in birch bark. As with the *skudučiai*, *ragai* (plural of *ragas*) come in sets of five and are used to play age-old five-part melodies. Alternatively, they accompany the region's famed *sutartinės*, an ancient polyphonic song for two, three or five voices and sung only by women.

The harmonica, banjo, mandolin, violin, guitar, 16th-century bagpipe and *džingulis* (a two-forked staff hung with bells and rung to summon guests at weddings) are other popular folkloric instruments. The richest collection in the Baltics can be found at the Folk Music & Instruments Museum in Kaunas, central Lithuania (see that chapter).

# Dates & Tickets

Estonia, Latvia and Lithuania theoretically host their national song festival every four or five years, but this does change. Song festivals will be held in Rīga in 2003 (June 27–July 6), in Tallinn in 2004 (July 2–4) and in Vilnius in 2006.

Tickets cost €15 to €80. For tickets and information for Estonia's festivals contact the Estonian Song & Dance Foundation (☎ 644 9262, 644 9152, fax 644 9147; ⓦ www.laulupidu.ee; Suur-Karja 23, EE10148 Tallinn); or Eesti Konsert (☎ 614 7700, fax 614 7769; ⓦ www.concert.ee; Estonia puiestee 4, EE10148 Tallinn).

In Lithuania contact the Lithuanian Folk Culture Centre (☎ 5-261 1190, 261 2540; fax 261 2607; ⓦ www.lfcc.lt; Barboros Radvilaitės gatvė 8, LT-2600 Vilnius).

The Latvian festival is organised by the culture department of Rīga City Council (☎ 704 36 48, fax 704 36 71; ⓦ www.culture.lv/rdkp; K Valdemāra iela 5; LV-1010 Rīga).

JONATHAN SMITH

## HIGHLIGHTS

- Indulge yourself year-round in Tallinn with culture, history, nightlife and fine menus

- Cure your ills in a marvellous mud bath at the old health resort town of Haapsalu

- Confront Soviet-era military installations and a WWII battle site on Saaremaa

- Call in on grand manor houses and take to the trails in Lahemaa National Park

- Connect with mythical giants Kalevipoeg, Peko or Leiger around Soomaa, Setumaa or Hiiumaa

# Facts about Estonia

Estonia's strategic location ensured that throughout history it would be seen as an appealing acquisition for the region's superpowers. Sharing a similar latitude with Stockholm and St Petersburg, it has been subject to both Swedish and Russian rule, with periods under Danish and German influence. Just 80km across the Gulf of Finland from Helsinki and 130km away from St Petersburg at its most eastern point, the culture, climate and landscape of Estonia exhibit a distinctive blend of the eastern and Nordic.

Estonia (Eesti), even before independence, was known as the most western of the Soviet republics, partly because of its strong links with Finland. Estonians and Finns are ethnically related, although historically there has been no greater influence on Estonia than that of Russian rule.

In the 10 years since regaining independence, Estonia's transformation has been remarkable. As the former defensive frontline of the Soviet Union, much of the country was off-limits to tourists until the early 1990s. Today Estonia welcomes visitors with a well-organised tourism infrastructure that typifies the country's willingness to embrace all things European. Some believe that Estonia's European accession was cemented when it won that most European of events, the Eurovision Song Contest, in 2001. The following year Estonia hosted the event, and 160 million viewers tuned in worldwide.

Tallinn, the capital, bears the imprint of its rich heritage as a port along historic trade routes between east and west. The city now represents a cosmopolitan Estonia, poised to integrate with Europe. Tallinn's many attractions and extensive transport links makes it a practical starting point for a trip through the region. Tartu, the second city, has retained a more uniquely Estonian flavour, infused with the energy of its large student population. The islands off the western coast and Lahemaa National Park, near the capital, appeal as distinctly Estonian destinations, while the exotic lands to the east, whose inhabitants are culturally bound to neighbouring Russia, will reward an in-depth exploration.

Visitors to Estonia should not expect to be bowled over by stark contrasts or spectacular grand-scale beauty. The Estonian landscape is poetically subdued; its appeal lies in the gentle nuance of colour, defined by the elements and often redefined by political imperiousness. The pleasures of this land are many for those who have finely tuned their senses.

The subtleties of the landscape are worth bearing in mind when you come across the pensiveness, reservedness and shyness of its people. For centuries Estonians were an agrarian folk with an intimate relationship with the natural world, and this is still evident today with almost all family names derived from an element in nature. Some 120 nationalities supposedly live in Estonia, although the outward homogeneity of its populace and culture is striking. Travelling eastwards the cultural complexity is revealed; alongside native Estonians live Orthodox Estonians (the Setus, whose language differs from that spoken in the north and west) and Russian Old Believers with centuries-old connections to the land.

This chapter contains information specific to Estonia. For a more general introduction to the history, geography and culture of the Baltic countries, see the introductory Facts about the Region chapter.

## HISTORY

The country held its first general election under the new constitution in 1992, choosing the conservative Fatherland Alliance with nationalist, anti-communist and free-market policies. In May 1993, Estonia (along with Lithuania) was one of the first ex-Soviet states to be admitted to the Council of Europe. Estonian anxiety over Russia's remaining military forces was relieved when the last Russian garrisons withdrew in 1994.

Estonia's at times bitter, at times stubborn border dispute with Russia eased after an agreement in 1997 that remains unratified. Russia recognised Estonian independence, but Estonia had to give up its claim to two frontier areas: a slice of land east of the Narva River and a larger area of the Setumaa region around Pechory (Estonian: Petseri), across Estonia's existing southeastern border. These pieces of land, totalling 2333 sq km, had been in Estonia's possession only between the wars, after the signing of the 1920 Tartu Peace Treaty.

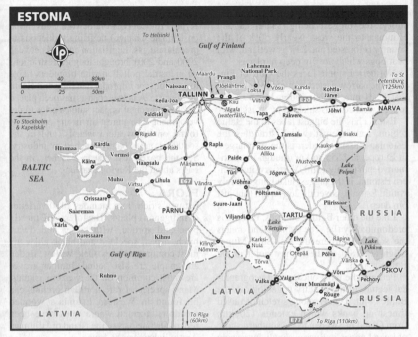

Now that the flush of nationalism that inspired all aspects of society in the 1980s and '90s has subsided, Estonians are defining their place in today's Europe. The issue of Estonian identity is still being explored. Historical and archaeological work of the 1990s (some would have been impossible during Soviet times) aimed to establish a more secure national identity and to reveal deep roots in the land.

Relative political stability has also allowed objective assessment of the country's past. The interwar government, led by President Konstantin Päts, long revered as an Estonian hero, is being held up for public questioning. In late 1999 a small scandal erupted when proof was discovered in Moscow archives that Päts (along with Latvian and Lithuanian politicians) had been receiving large sums of money from Moscow throughout the 1920s and '30s to safeguard some of Russia's interests. This, and the still sensitive issue of Päts' mini-dictatorship in the 1930s (including the proscription of all political parties, even democratic ones), is part of the process of coming to terms with history.

Estonia was the first Baltic country to start direct accession talks with the EU, which commenced in March 1998. Latvia followed in December 1999 and Lithuania in 2000.

Much to the delight of Estonia's politicians, Estonia's European accession has been confirmed for 2004. Some Estonians aren't quite as certain that quick-as-possible integration with all Western structures will provide the brightest future, and there has been a well-organised (but fruitless) resistance to EU membership. Nevertheless, results of an EMOR (Estonian Market Opinion Research) survey in November 2002 indicated that 57% of the population are in support of EU membership, and most Estonian laws have been harmonised with EU objectives. A referendum scheduled for September 2003 must meet with majority approval before Accession is formalised.

## GEOGRAPHY

Estonia is the smallest Baltic country at 45,227 sq km – slightly bigger than Holland, Switzerland or Denmark. It borders Russia in the east and Latvia in the south. Tallinn is on the north coast. Islands (there are 1521 of them) make up nearly 10% of Estonian territory, the biggest being Saaremaa and Hiiumaa to the west. Nearly 50% of the country is forested and 22% is wetland, with peat bogs which are 7m deep in places.

Northern Estonia faces the Gulf of Finland, the narrow eastern arm of the Baltic Sea that leads into St Petersburg. Much of Estonia's west coast is shielded by its islands.

Estonia has the biggest lakes in the Baltic region; Lake Peipsi, which straddles the Estonian-Russian border, is the fifth largest in Europe, at 3555 sq km (though its maximum depth is only 15m). Võrtsjärv, in southern Estonia, is the biggest lake lying entirely within Estonia, covering 266 sq km (but just 6m deep).

Like the other Baltic countries, Estonia is predominantly flat. The main upland area is the southeast where the hill Suur Munamägi, at 318m, is the highest point in the Baltic region.

Perhaps the most outstanding geographical feature of the country is geological: the Baltic Glint. This is a long stretch of raised limestone banks which extends 1200km, from Öland in Sweden to the southern shore of Lake Ladoga in Russia, slowly increasing in height on the way. Some 500km of this lies underwater, part of it rests on the mainland where it's barely noticeable, and some stretches form impressive cliffs along the coast. In these areas, it's possible to see its multicoloured cross sections, each formed in different periods of its 60 million year development. The limestone is softer towards the bottom than at the top of a cliff, and this gives it its unique and picturesque form, with hard patches of rock jutting out to hang over lower, already crumbling stone (see Lahemaa National Park in the Northeastern Estonia chapter).

## ECOLOGY & ENVIRONMENT

While relatively few environment-friendly programmes, such as extensive recycling, are in place yet in Estonia, the staggering disregard for ecology of the Soviet regime left a populace traditionally bound to nature with a heightened sensitivity to the dangers of pollution and the need for ecological conservation. Large-scale clean-up programmes, often foreign-funded, have greatly reduced pollution as well as the concentration of dangerous emissions in industrial areas throughout the

1990s. Estonia is a signatory to the 1997 Kyoto Protocol (UN Framework Convention on Climate Change) targeting reductions in greenhouse gas. Legislation enacted between 2000 and 2001 brought tougher restrictions on industrial pollution with offenders liable to penalties for improper handling and clean-up of waste. A new emphasis has been placed on environmental impact studies prior to development. The purest air in the country is found on the western islands, and in the southeast, areas barely touched by industry. See the boxed text 'Clean Beaches' in the Facts about the Region chapter.

## FLORA

Estonia's rich flora includes 1470 varieties of indigenous plants. The forests are mostly pine and spruce, with silver and dwarf birch, aspen, speckled and black alder the most common species. Oak, willow, linden and maple are also found. Juniper groves are most common on the western islands. Many species of rare northern orchids can be found in Western Estonia's wooded meadows, formed where trees have been felled. On one part of the island of Hiiumaa, Arctic lichen can be found.

## FAUNA

Estonia has large populations of European mammals. There is more information about these in the Facts about the Region chapter. Roe deer, wild boar and elk are commonly hunted and may appear on the menu in more expensive restaurants. Exotic species, introduced for their fur, include the North American muskrat, mink and raccoon dog, all of which are potential threats to native wildlife. The American mink, for example, has completely decimated the previous population of European mink.

### Endangered Species

As well as large mammals, Estonia has 10 species of rare and protected amphibian. A number of large raptors, including the golden eagle, white tailed eagle, spotted eagle and eagle owl, are also protected, as is the rare black stork. A rare sight in the forest is the European flying squirrel.

## NATIONAL PARKS & RESERVES

Some of Europe's few remaining original landscapes have been preserved within

Estonia, much of this inadvertently through isolation under the Soviet regime. Large tracts of land are now protected areas, which brings many opportunities to appreciate the abundant wildlife and to indulge in a favourite Estonian activity, the pursuit of peace and solitude. Estonia has four national parks, three of them established since independence, and a number of nature reserves. More information on these can be found in the relevant chapters; useful contact details and information can also be found on the Union of Protected Areas of Estonia website w www.ekal.org.ee. Following is a list of some of these:

**Endla Nature Reserve** Around the Endla järv, east of Paide – wetlands, nature trails

**Hiiumaa Protected Areas** The area surrounding the island of Hiiumaa (formerly the Biosphere Reserve of the West Estonian Archipelago), together with the Hiiumaa Islets Landscape Reserve – shelters rare grey and ringed seals, black storks, cranes, boar, lynx, marten and raccoon dog

**Karula National Park** Founded in 1993, 103 sq km of southern forest and lakeland, with a battlefield from the Great Northern War in 1708

**Lahemaa National Park** Estonia's oldest national park (founded in 1971), comprising 1120 sq km of typical Estonian coast and unspoiled hinterland east of Tallinn – beaches, rivers, lakes, waterfalls, walking trails

**Matsalu Nature Reserve** On the west coast – wetland and major water bird habitat, guided trips available

**Nigula State Nature Reserve** In the southwest near Latvian border – bog

**Silma Nature Reserve** Covering the islands and the region around Haapsalu in Western Estonia

**Soomaa National Park** Founded in 1993, protects a 367 sq km expanse of mid-Estonian swamplands and flat meadows

**Väinameri Nature Reserve** Islets off southeast Hiiumaa – bird and plant habitat

**Viidumäe Nature Reserve** On Saaremaa – forested area around the island's highest point, observation tower

**Vilsandi National Park** Small islands off western Saaremaa – a bird sanctuary with many species of rare orchid

## GOVERNMENT & POLITICS

Estonia's constitution was approved in June 1992 by a referendum. The law-making body is a 101-seat parliament called the Riigikogu (National Council), elected every four years. The head of state is the president, elected by the Riigikogu in a secret ballot. The government is headed by the prime minister, who is nominated by the president and must be approved by a majority in the Riigikogu. The prime minister chooses the cabinet.

The first elections under the new constitution were held in September 1992. The Fatherland Alliance won a narrow majority after campaigning under the slogan 'Cleaning House', which meant removing from power those who were associated with communist rule. Fatherland's leader, 32-year-old historian Mart Laar, became prime minister. The alliance later formally united as the Fatherland (Isamaa) Party (a nod to Päts' interwar party, the Fatherland League). Its stated policies included free-market economics, privatisation, and reduction of state bureaucracy and monopolies.

In presidential elections held at the same time as those for Riigikogu, Arnold Rüütel, the former head of Estonia's Soviet parliament, and president under the semi-democratic system in place since 1990, won 42% of votes but did not get an overall majority.

Without a clear majority, the law determined that the Riigikogu elect the president. Its choice was the writer, film maker and former foreign minister, Lennart Meri, who narrowly won a second term in 1996. Repeating the chaotic pattern of the interwar years, government has passed through the hands of a series of coalitions with no single party gaining a clear majority.

Estonian political parties come and go and critics say most are over-committed to narrow ideologies and sectional interests at the expense of national progress. All have been dogged by various scandals. In March 1997, the non-partisan Mart Siimann was sworn in as prime minister at the head of a minority coalition government, which lasted until general elections in March 1999. Mart Laar then became prime minister for a second time as leader of a centre-right coalition (between the Pro Patria Union, the Reform Party and the Moderates). Laar's main agenda was European integration and NATO membership, but a split in the coalition prompted his resignation in 2002 after concerns that a destabilised government would delay progress towards EU accession. The ensuing election brought the reluctant Siim Kallas to power, leading a coalition between the Centre and Reform party. Kallas met with controversy when he was accused of embezzlement during his time as head of the Bank of Estonia, but was later cleared. The next parliamentary elections are due in late 2006.

A popular and charismatic president, Lennart Meri brought stability to the political scene until his term of office expired in 2001 (a third presidential term is barred by the constitution). Arnold Rüütel, who oversaw the transition from Soviet rule to independence, was elected president in what many fear to be a return to past ideologies. Rüütel maintains a pro-Europe stance, albeit cautiously. The next presidential elections are scheduled for 2004.

## ECONOMY

Estonia is the outstanding economic success story of the Baltic region, having made a remarkable transition to capitalism. The freely convertible kroon (EEK) replaced the virtually valueless Soviet rouble in June 1992. Formerly pegged to the German mark, now officially to the euro, it has proved surprisingly resilient. Beginning in 1993 the government has privatised most state-owned enterprises with fairly positive results.

Estonia proved more willing than its neighbours to bite the free trade bullet, and has virtually no customs tariffs and minimum restrictions on foreign investment. In January 2000 it also abolished corporate tax. As a result of this free market, money poured into the country, mainly in the finance, manufacturing and transport sectors, and 80% of funds were localised within the Tallinn region. Sweden has now replaced Finland as Estonia's biggest investor, although in 2002 Finland was still Estonia's largest trading partner, followed by Sweden and Germany. Estonia's main exports are machinery, timber and wood products, textiles, base metals and prepared foods.

Despite a diminished dependence on the Russian market, the August 1998 financial crisis in Russia made its mark in Estonia. Of 12 banks registered in 1997, only the six strongest were left by early 1999. However, this corrected an inflated banking scene. Some industries, in particular fish processing and dairy, were also badly shaken. After the full impact of the Russian situation had registered, the economy as a whole slowed down, from an incredible performance in 1997 when GDP growth was 10.6% to

negative 1.1% in 1999. Local and international experts accurately predicted another upswing, with growth of 6.9% in 2000 and 5.4% in 2001. Today Estonia's economic strength has the country firmly on course for EU accession. See the boxed text 'Joining Europe' in the introductory Facts about the Region chapter.

In 2001, inflation stood at 5.8%, and average monthly salaries continued to rise. In early 2002, they were €365, higher than in Latvia and Lithuania. However, one-third of Estonian households live under the official poverty line, with some 50% of its citizens earning (officially) under €100 a month. In early 2002, official unemployment stood at 11.2%, a preliminary indication of an improvement on the previous year. According to year-end estimates from the Bureau of Statistics, GDP is estimated at 7% and inflation down to 3%. The average monthly wages is estimated to be approximately €375 and unemployment is estimated at 9.1%.

## POPULATION & PEOPLE

Only 68% of the 1.36 million people living in Estonia are ethnic Estonians. Russians make up 26% of the population, with 3.5% Ukrainian or Belarusian and 1% Finns. In 1934, Estonians had comprised 91.7% of the population, and after the population shifts of WWII and the redrawing of the border in 1944, this proportion rose to 94%. Yet during the Soviet period Estonia had the highest percentage of 'foreign-born' inhabitants of any USSR republic, which goes some distance in explaining the sensitivity to the continued Russian presence. Ethnic populations are not evenly distributed throughout the country: 47% of Tallinn, for instance, is Russian, while in Narva the figure is 92.5% and in Kuressaare it is just 3%.

The Estonians are one of the Finno-Ugric peoples, an ethno-linguistic group whose members are scattered from the Arctic to Central Europe, halfway across Siberia, and along the River Volga. This sets them apart from the Latvians and Lithuanians, who are Indo-European. Wars and famines have not been kind to Estonians. Whereas in 1550 there were approximately an equal number of Finns and Estonians, today Finns outnumber Estonians by about 5:1.

It's believed that the land that is now Estonia was settled immediately following the end of the last ice age, approximately 10,000 years ago. The oldest archaeological sites, at Pulli, near Pärnu and Kunda, east of Tallinn, bear this out. The long-held notion that the ancestors of the Estonians and Finns arrived in a mass migration of Finno-Ugric tribes from beyond the Ural mountains is now largely discounted by most historians and archaeologists. It has been replaced by a so-called 'contact theory', stressing small-scale migrations (likely to be northwards as opposed to westwards) and cultural intermingling between Finno-Ugric and other tribes.

Research and expeditions to Finno-Ugric tribes in Siberia, archaeological digs and genetic experiments have given no real answers to the origins of the Estonian people. While much archaeological work was permitted in the Soviet period, often evidence of ancient Finno-Ugric presence on these lands was de-emphasised, and research, even about the origins and spread of the Slavs, had to fulfil certain ideological exigencies.

The question of identity, ancestry and 'settledness' is an important one. Within the Finno-Ugric group, the Estonians are closely related to such peoples as the Finns, the Samis, the Karelians (who live in Finland and neighbouring parts of Russia) and the Livs, who used to inhabit coastal Latvia but are now on the verge of extinction as a separate people. Other Finno-Ugric peoples include the Samoyeds along the Russian shores of the Arctic Ocean; the Ostyaks and Voguls, east of the Urals; the Magyars (Hungarians); the Votyaks and Zyryans, west of the Urals; and the Mordvins and Cheremis, along the Volga.

Estonians today continue to decline in numbers. In 2002 the overall population fell 0.7%, due largely to the country's traditionally low birth rate. An estimated 60,000 Estonians live in Russia, many of them in the Setumaa region. Around 80,000 live in other countries as a result of emigration around the start of the 20th century and mainly following the outbreak of WWII. The main overseas Estonian communities are in North America and Sweden but there are others in Britain, Australia and elsewhere.

## Citizenship

When Estonia regained independence, not every resident received citizenship. People who were citizens of the pre-1940 Estonian Republic and their descendants were automatically citizens. Other people must be naturalised, a process which includes a language test (with questions about the constitution); so far, some 115,000 Russians and other nationalities have become citizens in this way. Anyone living in Estonia before 1 July 1990 can apply for citizenship automatically; anyone who arrived after that date must hold a residency permit for five years before applying. However, anyone born in the country after 26 February 1992 is an automatic citizen. Only citizens may vote in parliamentary elections. Noncitizens can vote in local government elections providing they have legal residency.

As of early 2002, there were still some 269,500 people classified as 'foreigners' living in Estonia, 88,500 of whom held Russian passports, and the remainder holding a so-called 'alien's passport' (dubbed 'grey passport'). The latter gives legal residency in Estonia and freedom to travel to most countries but essentially renders the holders stateless – unless they choose to become naturalised or take up Russian or other citizenship.

One reason Russians do not apply for citizenship is their easier, visa-free travel to Russia to visit relatives (Estonian passport holders need visas). Another deterrent for young Russian men is that they avoid Estonian army service if they are not citizens until after the age of 27.

One deterrent to Russian speakers learning enough Estonian to pass a language test has been a perceived lack of goodwill on the part of the government to encourage them to learn. The Estonian government has spent relatively little on language immersion and integration programmes, the funding for which has largely come from foreign sources. Instead, efforts have concentrated on discouraging the 'illegal' use of Russian. The Language Department enforces laws which forbid the display of foreign-language words (excluding trademarks) in public places like billboards and store-front windows (inside a store is allowed in certain cases). Another law regulates the minimum Estonian language requirements in all public and private enterprises (even including a Russian cultural centre in Narva, which is 92% Russian). As the majority of Russians are far from proficient in Estonian, this has prompted concern from the United Nations over limitations on freedom of speech and reduced opportunities for advancement and representation for many of Estonia's Russian speakers. The Estonian government has now committed to an extension of the timeframe for phasing out Russian language tuition (see the following Education section), and has requested assistance both politically and financially from organisations such as the EU to implement larger-scale language and integration programmes.

## EDUCATION

Education has long held importance to the country which boasted one of the world's highest literacy rates by the turn of the 20th century. The primary concerns of the education system in the 1990s were the redressing of historical questions de-emphasised or disallowed during Soviet times (with a resulting increase in Estonian history and culture in the curriculum) and the establishment of a firm language policy that will see a decline in Russian language education and emphasis on bilingual or Estonian language tuition. Although Russian language tuition is set to continue in all levels, primary level education in Russian will be phased out after 2007.

Estonia is also racing to increase access to computers and the Internet in every school throughout the country. The *Tiger Leap* programme, established in 1996, aims to equip schools with the necessary infrastructure to further the skills of teachers and students. Tallinn's new IT college will release its first graduates in 2003.

## SCIENCE & PHILOSOPHY

During the Soviet era, scientific research was in many respects quite advanced in Estonia. The Cybernetics Institute of the Estonian Academy of Sciences, founded in 1960, saw Estonia take a leading role in the development of computer technology. Even today, despite tight funding, new initiatives in research and development have been launched. Many are based in Tartu, such as the Genome Project Foundation, which aims to database genetic records of the Estonian population by 2007, for use in diagnostics and improving treatment of prevailing medical conditions.

## ARTS
## Music

Estonia is widely known for its serious classical music tradition, and most notably its choirs. The Estonian Boys Choir has been acclaimed worldwide. Hortus Musicus, formed in 1972, is probably Estonia's best known ensemble, and performs mainly Middle Age and Renaissance music. The group regularly appears in Tallinn, and attending one of their concerts is a cultural highlight.

The main Estonian composers of the 20th century all wrote music dear to the heart of the people, and remain popular today. Rudolf Tobias (1873–1918) wrote influential symphonic, choral and concerto works as well as fantasies on folk song melodies. Mart Saar (1882–1963) studied under Rimsky-Korsakov in St Petersburg but his music shows none of this influence. His songs and piano suites were among the most performed pieces of music in between-war concerts in Estonia. Eduard Tubin (1905–82) is another great Estonian composer whose body of work includes 10 symphonies. Contemporary composer Erkki-Sven Tüür (1959–) takes inspiration from nature and the elements as experienced on his native Hiiumaa.

Estonia's most celebrated composer is Arvo Pärt (1935–), the intense and reclusive master of hauntingly austere music many have misleadingly termed minimalist. Pärt emigrated to Germany during Soviet rule, and his *Misererie Litany*, *Te Deum* and *Tabula Rasa* are among an internationally acclaimed body of work characterised by dramatic bleakness, piercing majesty and nuanced silence. His music draws inspiration from prayers or Bible passages and corresponds with a time in the Middle Ages when performers and composers were not celebrated as individuals for their creations but driven to find expression for collective aspirations. Pärt himself refers to his music as the tintinnabular style, a sparse method of creating tension and beauty with outwardly simple but actually complex, even mathematical, structures. Many believe his musical structures are like none other before.

Internationally renowned Tõnu Kaljuste, director of the Estonian Philharmonic Chamber Orchestra, has frequently recorded the music of Arvo Pärt. Neeme Järvi, Estonia's most heralded conductor, is now the director of the Detroit Symphony Orchestra.

## Radio Free Estonia

Leading musicians in Estonia today have been influenced by close ties with neighbouring countries (covertly during Soviet times) and from Western music trends in the years since independence.

Dance music rules in Estonia, as it does throughout Europe. The biggest Estonian techno groups are 2 Quick Start and Caater. There is also a thriving underground dance scene whose vibes have been influenced by New York and Chicago house.

Ultima Thule is one of the country's longest-running and most beloved bands on the rock and blues scene. Jäääär are also somewhere at the top. Groups like Venaskond, Tuberkuloited, and the U2-style Mr Lawrence have a rougher edge.

Singer Vinger have been light-rock kings for years, much praised for their lyrics. Excellent folk bands include Untsakond and Väikeste Lõõtspillide Ühing.

Estonians also seem to have a taste for broad comedy with their music. The Kuldne Trio have been a staple at multi-group concerts for over 20 years and their parody sometimes borders on slapstick.

Despite perennial gibes, the popularity of Eurovision and Estonia's success have given Estonian music an international audience and raised awareness worldwide of this small nations' vast musical traditions. Many of Estonia's best emerging musicians perform at the Pühajärve beach festival in Otepää each July, which now rates as one of the Baltic-Scandinavian region's favourite music festivals.

In jazz, the duo of saxophonist Villu Veski and piano accordionist Tiit Kalluste incorporate elements of Nordic music and lore into their work. Violinist Camille fuses classical with pop music. In the world of New Age, Kirile Loo, who mixes sparse folk music with incantations and harp music, might be described as Estonia's Enya. Peeter Vähi's music has been influenced by Tibetan, Siberian, Turkish and Asian themes. Veljo Tormis, a leading Estonian choral composer, writes striking music based on old runic chants. His best known works include the difficult-to-perform *Curse Upon Iron* and *The Ingrian Evenings*.

While modern US and European (but not Russian) music is popular among Estonians, local groups have a strong fan base. Rock thrives in Estonia and there are big annual festivals like Rock Summer in Tallinn and the Pühajärve Beach Festival in Otepää. Although rap and hip hop are making inroads (as evidenced in the speech, dress and attitude of Estonian youngsters) a seminal Estonian expression of these styles is yet to emerge.

### Literature

Although records indicate that there was an Estonian text from the 16th century, the history of written Estonian is little more than 150 years old. A New Testament had been published in South Estonian in 1686, and a complete Bible in North Estonian (the 'dialect' which became the Standard Estonian of today) by 1739, but texts until the mid-19th century were mainly pious tracts read only by the clergy. Baltic Germans published an Estonian grammar book, and dictionary too, but it wasn't until the national awakening movement that the publication of books, poetry and newspapers began. This elevated Estonian from a mere 'peasants' language' to one with full literary potential.

Estonian literature grew from the poems and diaries of a young graduate of Tartu University, Kristjan Jaak Peterson. Also a gifted linguist, he died when he was only 21 years old in 1822. The national epic poem *Kalevipoeg* (Son of Kalev) was written between 1857 and 1861 by Friedrich Reinhold Kreutzwald (1803–82), who was inspired by Finland's *Kalevala*, a similar epic created a few decades earlier. Kreutzwald put together hundreds of Estonian legends and folk tales to tell the adventures of the mythical hero Kalevipoeg, which ends with his death and his land's conquest by foreigners, but also hope for future freedom:

But one day an age will dawn when
A bright flame bursts forth to free
His hand from the vise of stone
Then Kalev's son will return home
To bring happiness to his children
And build Estonia's life anew.

Lydia Koidula (1843–86) was the poet of Estonia's national awakening and first lady of literature (see the boxed text 'The Dawn of Poetry' in the Southwest Estonia chapter).

Anton Hansen Tammsaare is considered the greatest Estonian novelist for his *Tõde ja Õigus* (Truth and Justice), written between 1926 and 1933. A five-volume saga of village and town life, it explores Estonian social, political and philosophical issues. Eduard Vilde (1865–1933) was an influential early-20th-century novelist and playwright who wrote *Tabamata Ime* (Unattainable Wonder). *Tabamata Ime* was to be the first play performed at the opening of the Estonia Theatre in 1913 but was substituted with *Hamlet* as his scathing critique of the current-day intelligentsia was deemed too controversial. In most of his novels and plays, Vilde looked with great irony at what he saw as Estonia's mad, blind rush to become part of Europe and constantly questioned national identity in an attempt to posit self reliance as the truest form of independence.

Oskar Luts is often revered as Estonia's Mark Twain for his school and childhood tales including *Kevade* (Spring), written in 1912–13. Paul-Eerik Rummo (born 1942) is one of Estonia's leading poets and playwrights, dubbed the 'Estonian Dylan Thomas' for his patriotic pieces which deal with contemporary problems of cultural identity. His most famous play is 1971's *Puhkatrinu mäng* (The Cinderella Game), a clever metaphor of Soviet Estonia which has been performed at New York's La Mama and throughout Europe.

More recently, Mati Unt has played an important role in concreting the place of Estonian intellectuals in the modern world, and has written, from the 1960s onwards, quite cynical novels (notably *Sügisball*, or Autumn Ball), plays and articles about contemporary life in Estonia. The novelist Jaan Kross has won great acclaim for his historical novels in which he manages to tackle Soviet-era subjects. He is possibly the Estonian author best known abroad, and his most renowned book, *The Czar's Madman*, has been translated into English. Kross' latest release *(Tahtamaa)* was a resounding bestseller with plans for an English translation. Another leading novelist is Arvo Valton who, like Kross, spent some time as an exile in Siberia. His work, *Masendus ja Lootus* (Depression and Hope), deals with that experience.

Estonia also has a number of outstanding contemporary poets. Jaan Kaplinski has had two collections, *The Same Sea in Us All* and *The Wandering Border*, published in English. His work expresses the feel of Estonian life superbly. Kross and Kaplinski both have been named as Nobel prize candidates.

Tõnu Õnnepalu's *Piiri Riik* (Borderland, published under the pseudonym Emil Tode), is about a young homosexual Estonian who travels to Europe and questions himself and his identity when he becomes a kept boy for an older, rich gentleman. It is a clever and absorbing critique of modern Estonian values, translated into German, French and English. In popular fiction Kaur Kender's *Independence Day* tells the misadventures of young and ambitious entrepreneurs in post-independence Estonia.

## Visual Arts

The undisputed national treasure here is eclectic graphic artist Eduard Wiiralt, an Estonian born near St Petersburg in 1898 who studied art in Tallinn and Tartu and who died in Paris in 1954, where he'd lived for 22 years. He is considered not only a superb local artist, but a truly international talent based on the diverse themes embodied in his progressive style, inspired by extensive travels and studies abroad. His subjects range from cabaret dancers and North African villagers to boxers and the majestic landscapes of Sami Land.

Kristjan Raud (1865–1943), who illustrated *Kalevipoeg*, was the leading national idealist figure of the 19th century in Estonia. Ants Laikmaa (1866–1942), known for his sensitive landscape paintings, was so dedicated to his craft that he walked from Estonia to Düsseldorf in Germany to study art, and later opened an art school in Tallinn. Contemporary Estonian art from the 1970s has leaned towards geometrical abstraction, and leading exponents include Raul Meel and Siim-Tanel Annus.

The artist with the most recognisable work is Navitrolla, whose bright, fanciful and beautiful inventions of other worlds in which humans play no part adorn T-shirts, coffee mugs and postcards all over Estonia's main towns. He is the most popular current artist in Estonia, and embedded in the mainstream. Jüri Arrak is often considered the greatest contemporary painter. His work is also fanciful and bright, with unusual, sometimes droll or jarring subject matter that is more evidently glum than that of Navitrolla.

Two modern, young Estonian artists to make a name for themselves on the international scene are Jaan Toomik and Raoul Kurvits. Toomik experiments with new artistic forms in his paintings and continues the never-ending quest by Estonians to define themselves as a people. Kurvits has an equally unique vision and incorporates elements of performance into his intensely emotional and confronting art.

## Cinema

The first 'moving pictures' were screened in Tallinn in 1896, and the first theatre opened in 1908. Johannes Pääsuke (1892–1918), although primarily a photographer, is considered the first Estonian film maker. Estonia's cinematographic output has not been prolific, but there are a number of standouts. The most beloved film of Estonians is Arvo Kruusement's *Kevade* (Spring, 1969), an adaptation of Oskar Luts' country saga. Its sequel, *Suvi* (Summer, 1976) was also popular though regarded as inferior. Kaljo Kiisk's *Nipernaadi* (Happy-Go-Lucky, 1983) is a much adored film, about an itinerant bohemian (an Estonian Peer Gynt) who wanders around Estonia, and the relationships he establishes with people he meets along the way.

Grigori Kromanov's *Viimne reliikvia* (The Last Relic, 1969) was a brave and unabashedly anti-Soviet film which has been screened in some 60 countries. Some excellent Estonian documentaries include Andres Sööt's *Jaanipäev* (Midsummer's Day, 1978), Mark Soosaar's *Miss Saaremaa* (1988) and Peeter Tooming's *Hetked* (Moments, 1976).

More recently, Sulev Keedus' unforgettably lyrical *Georgica* (1998), about childhood, war, and life on the western islands, and *Ristumine peataga* (Crossing the Highway, 1999), a comedy by Arko Okk, have made the international film festival rounds. Among Estonia's finest animated films in recent years is the Cabbagehead Trilogy (1997–2001) a thinly veiled critique on Estonia's transistion to independence, EU accession and Internet zeal.

## Theatre

It is telling of the role theatre has played in Estonia's cultural life that many of the country's theatre houses were built solely from donations by private citizens. The Estonian Drama Theatre in Tallinn, the Vanemuise Theatre in Tartu and the Drama Theatre in Rakvere (the last civic building erected in Estonia before the war) were all built on proceeds collected from people door to door. The very building of these venues came to symbolise cultural independence to the country.

Modern theatre is considered to have begun in Tartu. It was there that Lydia Koidula's *The Cousin from Saaremaa* was the first Estonian play to be performed in public. The Vanemuine Theatre (an outgrowth of the Vanemuine Society, an amateur troupe) launched professional theatre in 1906. The Estonia Theatre opened its doors in Tallinn in 1913 (although it was founded in 1906), and by the time many of Vanemuine's best talents left Tartu to found Tallinn's Drama Theatre three years later, Estonia already had its roster of stars and talented directors and playwrights. The first major Estonian opera, Evald Aav's *Vikerlased* (Vikings), premiered at the Estonia Theatre in 1928.

Estonian theatre emerged under the equal influences of the Stanislavsky school from the east and of German theatre. Several Estonians went there to study (including former Vanemuine director, Karl Menning, who studied under Max Reinhardt in Berlin). Paul Pinna, the Estonia Theatre's director in the early 20th century, also found his influences mainly in German theatre. However, throughout the 1920s and '30s, Stanislavskian methods started to predominate.

While some theatrical productions had to tow ideological lines throughout the Soviet period, stage life continued to flourish, and today the halls are rarely empty at the many daily performances around the country. The most original people on the current theatre scene, sometimes tackling themes never before or little seen on stage in Estonia, are Jaanus Rohumaa, Katri Kaasik-Aaslav and Elmo Nüganen, all particularly sensitive directors with strong, personal styles who often work out of Tallinn's City Theatre (Linnateater).

## SOCIETY & CONDUCT

Most travellers notice that Estonians tend to be reserved, conflict-avoiding and very well-behaved – until the party begins, that is! Indeed, loud, brash behaviour (including talking loudly in public or swearing in the home) can prompt stern looks of disapproval. They will be much less likely than their Russian neighbours to make initial contact. Women are often more outgoing than men.

## RELIGION

Only a minority of Estonians profess religious beliefs, but religion is another point of dissent between ethnic and Russian-speaking Estonians. Historically, Estonia was Lutheran

from the early 17th century. After much debate and ecclesiastical bickering about whether to register the Russian Orthodox Alexander Nevsky Church under the Moscow or Constantinople Patriarchate, the Estonian government decided to officially register it under Moscow in March 1999.

While many sects and religious organisations have set up in Estonia recently, including the Church of Latter Day Saints (whose well-dressed and clean-cut representatives can be seen daily on the streets of Tallinn), 7th Day Adventists, Jehovah's Witnesses, Hare Krishnas and even the Children of God, these have made inroads primarily with the Russian-speaking population.

# Facts for the Visitor

## SUGGESTED ITINERARIES
Your itinerary will depend on your situation but these hints may help you plan your trip.

**Three days** Tallinn and Lahemaa National Park
**One week** Tallinn and around, Tartu, Taevaskoja, Lahemaa. Or, from Tallinn, head to one of the islands
**Two weeks** Tallinn plus Lahemaa, then over to the western islands, Tartu, Taevaskoja, Setumaa, Lake Peipsi and back via the northeast
**One month** The above plus Pärnu, and longer stays in the south, around Lake Peipsi and the northeast, including canoe, biking or hiking trips

## PLANNING
For general information, see the introductory Facts for the Visitor chapter.

## Maps
E.O.Map has a series of fold-out maps for every county in Estonia including city and town centre maps, with detailed information on sites of interest (around 40 EEK each). Regio produces road atlases and maps for professional reference (around 85 EEK) and digital maps on CD-ROM.

## RESPONSIBLE TOURISM
Due both to the excessive pollution caused by Soviet-era industrialisation and a traditionally close link with nature, Estonians are quite sensitive about nature conservation. Two words: tread carefully! Estonians are determined to keep their country clean. In protected areas, follow the instructions and suggestions given for tourists, keep to the prescribed trails and don't leave rubbish for others to pick up. In Tallinn, after years of Finnish 'vodka' and 'Gin Long Drink' tourism, people are fed up with rowdy drunken behaviour, and visitors relieving themselves on streets in the city centre. You'll get better treatment if you indulge in moderation.

## TOURIST OFFICES
There are tourist information centres in many of the larger centres, national parks and reserves throughout Estonia and help is never far away. See the Information sections in each chapter and section for individual addresses. The main administrative office of the **Estonian Tourist Board** (☎ 627 9770, fax 627 9777; ⓦ www.visitestonia .com; Roosikrantsi tänav 11) is in Tallinn. The **North Estonia bureau** (☎ 038-50 130, fax 50 400; ⓔ north@visitestonia.com; Pärnu tänav 6, Paide) advises on the greater northern region.

## VISAS & DOCUMENTS
See the introductory Facts for the Visitor chapter.

## EMBASSIES & CONSULATES
### Estonian Embassies & Consulates
Estonian diplomatic representation in other countries includes:

**Australia** (☎ 02-9810 7468, fax 9818 1779, ⓔ eestikon@ozemail.com.au) 86 Louisa Rd, Birchgrove, NSW 2041
**Canada** (☎ 416-461 0764, fax 461 0353, ⓔ estconsu@ca.inter.net) 202-958 Broadview Ave, Toronto, Ontario M4K 2R6
**Finland** (☎ 9-622 0260, fax 622 02610, ⓔ embassy.helsinki@mfa.ee) Itäinen Puistotie 10, 00140 Helsinki, Suomi
**Germany** (☎ 030-25 460 600, fax 25 460 601, ⓦ www.estemb.de) Hildebrandstrasse 5, D-10785 Berlin
Honorary consulates in Hamburg, Düsseldorf, Kiel and Ludwigsburg.
**Latvia** (☎ 781 20 20, fax 781 20 29, ⓔ embassy.riga@mfa.ee) Skolas iela 13, Rīga LV 1010
**Lithuania** (☎ 5-278 0200, fax 278 0201, ⓔ embassy.vilnius@mfa.ee) Mickevičiaus gatvé 4A, Vilnius
**Russia** (☎ 095-290 5013, 095-737 3640, fax 095-737 3646, ⓦ www.estemb.ru) Malo Kislovski 5, 103009 Moscow
Consulate: (☎ 812-238 1804, fax 812-325 4246, ⓔ consulate.peterburg@mfa.ee) Bolsaja Monetnaja 14, 197101 St Petersburg
**Sweden** (☎ 08 5451 2280, fax 08 5451 2299, ⓔ info@estemb.se) Tyrgatan 3, 10041 Stockholm
**UK** (☎ 020-7589 3428, fax 7589 3430, ⓔ embassy.london@mfa.ee) 16 Hyde Park Gate, London SW7 5DG
**USA** (☎ 202-588 0101, fax 588 0108, ⓦ www.estemb.org) 2131 Massachusetts Ave, NW, Washington DC 20008. Operating out of temporary facilities until mid-2003; see website
Consulate: (☎ 212-883 0636, fax 883 0648) 660 3rd Ave, 26th floor, New York

## Embassies & Consulates in Estonia

Here is a list of some foreign embassies in Tallinn. For information on other countries and their representatives, or for visa-related information contact the **Estonian Foreign Ministry** (☎ 631 7600, fax 631 7099; W www .vm.ee; Islandi väljak 1, EE15049 Tallinn).

**Australia** (☎ 654 1333, fax 667 8444, e mati@standard.ee) Kopli tänav 25
**Canada** (☎ 627 3311, fax 627 3312, e canembt@uninet.ee) Toomkooli tänav 13
**Finland** (☎ 610 3200, fax 610 3281, W www.finemb.ee) Kohtu tänav 4
Consulate: (☎ 610 3300, fax 610 3288) Pikk jalg 14
**Germany** (☎ 627 5300, consular 627 5303, fax 627 5304, W www.germany.ee) Toom-Kuninga tänav 11
**Latvia** (☎ 646 1313, consular ☎ 646 1310, fax 646 1366, e embassy.estonia@mfa.gov.lv) Tõnismägi 10
**Lithuania** (☎ 631 4030, visas 641 2014, fax 641 2013, e amber@anet.ee) Uus tänav 15
**Russia** (☎ 646 4175, 646 4178, e vensaat@ online.ee) Pikk tänav 19
Consulate in Narva: (☎ 035-60 652, fax 035-60 654) Rüütli tänav 8
**Sweden** (☎ 640 5600, fax 640 5695, W www.sweden.ee) Pikk tänav 28
**UK** (☎ 667 4700, fax 667 4725, W www.britishembassy.ee) Wismari tänav 6
**USA** (☎ 668 8100; fax 668 8134, W www.usemb.ee) Kentmanni tänav 20

## CUSTOMS

Regulations change often, so it's wise to double-check before coming and going with the **Customs Department** (Tolliamet; ☎ 696 7435, 24hr infoline 630 8282, fax 696 7727; W www.customs.ee; Lõkke tänav 5). In general, travellers over 21 years of age are allowed to bring in or take out duty free 1L of hard alcohol, 1L of alcohol up to 21% proof, 10L of beer and 200 cigarettes.

Items made before the year 1700 may not be taken out of the country. An item made outside Estonia before 1850 or in Estonia before 1945 has to have a special permit to be taken out. These may be subject to 100% duty. Permits can be obtained from the **Division of the Export of Cultural Objects** (☎ 644 6765; Sakala tänav 14). Cash amounts exceeding 80,000 EEK must be declared upon leaving the country.

## MONEY

Estonia's currency is the kroon (pronounced 'krohn'), commonly written as EEK which stands for Eesti Kroon (Estonian Crown). It is divided into 100 sents (cents). The kroon comes in 2, 5, 10, 25, 50, 100 and 500 EEK notes, each featuring a national hero. There are coins of 10, 20 and 50 sents.

The kroon is the only legal tender in Estonia. It was the first new Baltic currency to be introduced (in June 1992), and has held its initial rate of 8 EEK to 1DM, now fixed to the euro at 15.66 EEK making it stable by any standard.

| country | unit | kroon |
| --- | --- | --- |
| Australia | A$1 | EEK 9.52 |
| Canada | C$1 | EEK 11.03 |
| euro zone | €1 | EEK 15.66 |
| Latvia | 1Ls | EEK 25.45 |
| Lithuania | 1Lt | EEK 4.53 |
| Sweden | 1 SKr | EEK 1.70 |
| UK | UK£1 | EEK 24.92 |
| USA | US$1 | EEK 17.124 |

## POST & COMMUNICATIONS
### Post

Mail service in and out of Estonia is quite reasonable; expect letters or postcards to take about one or two days within Estonia, three or four days to Western Europe or about a week to North America and other destinations outside Europe. There is a poste-restante bureau, where mail is kept for up to one month, in the basement of Tallinn's **central post office** (Narva maantee 1, Tallinn 10101).

To post a letter up to 20g within Estonia expect to pay around 5 EEK, within the Baltics 5.50 EEK and elsewhere in Europe 6.50 EEK. Post destined for Canada, Africa, Asia and Australia will cost around 8 EEK. For packages to the UK/Europe, the charge for up to 1kg is 85 EEK plus 98 EEK for each extra kilogram. For packages up to 1kg to the USA, it costs 120 EEK plus 38 EEK for each extra kilogram.

### Telephone

Estonia's telephone system has undergone some major restructuring in recent years. To call other cities or regions within Estonia, simply dial ☎ 0, followed by the area code and telephone number. Tallinn now has no area code and all Tallinn numbers have seven digits. Tartu numbers have six digits. In towns elsewhere in Estonia numbers have five digits. Mobile/cell phone numbers are the exception to these rules.

Estonia's country code when calling from abroad is ☎ 372, followed by the local city code and subscriber number. For example, to call Tartu, dial ☎ 3727 followed by the subscriber number. For Tallinn, simply dial ☎ 372 plus the seven-digit number.

To place a collect call from Estonia, dial ☎ 16116. Note that this service does not provide collect calls to all countries but may suggest alternate numbers.

**Emergency Services** The nationwide emergency phone number for police is ☎ 110 and for ambulance, fire and medical emergency ☎ 112. Call ☎ 1888 for 24-hour car assistance.

**Public Phones** Public telephones accept chip cards (50 or 100 EEK), available at post offices, hotels and most kiosks. For placing calls outside Estonia, an international telephone card with PIN number, such as *Voicenet* (available at many kiosks), is better value.

**Long-Distance Calls** To make a national call, dial 0-area code-subscriber number. There is no area code for Tallinn, just dial 0 if calling from outside the Tallinn region.

**International Calls** To make an international call dial 00-country code-area code-subscriber number. Calling Estonia from abroad, dial the country code (☎ 372) followed by the area code (ie, no area code for Tallinn, Tartu 7, and so on), then the subscriber number.

**Mobile Calls** Mobile/cell phone numbers begin with the prefix 05. To make a mobile call anywhere within Estonia, simply dial the number. To reach Estonian mobile numbers from outside Estonia, dial the country code (☎ 372) and the mobile number without the 0.

### Email & Internet Access
Every city and town, and even some rural dots on the map, boast at least one place to access the Internet, often signposted like traffic signs. Prices range from 15 to 60 EEK per hour. See individual chapters for details and further information.

## DIGITAL RESOURCES
Almost any enterprise, activity or subject uniquely Estonian now has a presence on the Web. For some background information on Estonia try the Estonia-Wide Web (W www.ee/www/welcome.html). The main search engine in Estonia is W www.neti.ee. For planning a trip to Estonia, your first site should be W www.visitestonia.com. A useful site for tourist services is W www.turismiweb.ee; also handy is W www.1182.ee, the website for the main information line/directory assistance.

For a listing of festivals and events during your stay, visit W www.kultuuriinfo.ee. With the Electronic Journal of Folklore (W www.haldjas.folklore.ee/folklore) you can find interesting articles on Estonian mythology, rituals and humour. The Eesti Institut website W www.estonica.org is an excellent source of historical and cultural information. Tallinn in Your Pocket (W www.inyourpocket.com) has a useful homepage. See individual chapters for other suggestions.

## BOOKS
The selection of foreign-language books in Estonia isn't large and English-language books can be quite costly, so it's best to read up before you get there. Still, locally published books (some in English) will only be available in Estonia. For books dealing with the Baltics in general, see Books in the regional Facts for the Visitor chapter.

### Lonely Planet
If you lose this book or want to pick up other titles such as LP phrasebooks or guides for your onward journey, try **Apollo** or **Rahva Raamat** in Tallinn. In Tartu, try **Ülikooli Raamatukauplus**. Otherwise, don't lose this book!

### Photography
Some of the most spectacular and sensitive photographs of Estonia have been taken by Ann Tenno and published in books which best capture the spirit of Estonian nature: *Pictures of Estonia, Estimaa Saared ja Rannad* (Estonia's Islands and Beaches), *Tallinna Album, Manor Houses of Estonia*, and her masterpiece *Life After* (with photos

of loss and decay from across all of the Baltic region). These books are widely available in most major Estonian bookshops. A series of photo books by Peeter Tooming is also worthwhile; the *55 Years Later* series objectively compares areas throughout Estonia as they looked in the 1930s and '90s.

## History & Politics

Toivo Raun's *Estonia and the Estonians* (1991) is worth hunting down for a sober account of a nation, its history and its people. For a detailed account of the history of the Estonian-Russian border through the ages, Edgar Mattisen's *Searching for a Dignified Compromise* (1996) explains its current zigzag shape. *War in the Woods* (1992), written by former Prime Minister Mart Laar, offers a gripping account of partisan resistance to the Soviet power in the 1940s and 1950s and the sad fate of these brave 'forest brothers'.

Former president, Lennart Meri, has authored several books on Estonian history and mythology. His *Hõbe Valge* (Silver White), available in English, has been a must-read for all Estonian intelligentsia, and masterfully incorporates historical fact with folklore to weave a unique recounting of Estonia's history and destiny.

*The Integration of Non-Estonians into Estonian Society* (1997), edited by Aksel Kirch, is a series of essays of mixed quality dealing with one of post-independence Estonia's biggest problems. Karl Aun's *The Political Refugees: A History of the Estonians in Canada* (1985) gives a very good description of what life was like for the thousands of Estonians who emigrated during wartime.

## Culture

The first book in English about the life and work of Lydia Koidula, Madli Puhvel's *Symbol of Dawn* (1995), isn't too psychologically penetrative, but is a poignant recounting of the life of Estonia's first lady of poetry, with good descriptions of the overall atmosphere of the national awakening in 19th-century Tartu. Paul Hillier's *Arvo Pärt* (1997), published by Oxford University Press, was the first book to examine the life and works of Estonia's best-known musical composer.

## Fiction

Like many writers living under repressive governments, Estonia's most celebrated novelist, Jaan Kross, who was exiled to Siberia for eight years under Stalin, has used historical tales to address contemporary themes. *The Czar's Madman*, first published in 1978, was among the first Baltic writing to become available in English when published by Harvil in 1992. One strand of the work is woven around the true story of Timotheus von Bock, an Estonian German noble whose honesty compelled him to write to Tsar Alexander I suggesting changes in the way Russia (of which Estonia was then part) was governed. Von Bock was locked away for his efforts.

## FILMS

Except for several documentaries, few international films have found a subject in Estonia. Probably the best has been Andrew Grieve's *Letters from the East* (UK, 1995), about an Estonia-born cellist in Britain who returns to her homeland to find her long-lost mother. Sasha Buravsky's *Cold* (1999) is a US/Estonian/Russian co-production partially set in Tallinn, about the years following WWII. Unfortunately, the best-known film featuring the area has been Finnish Ilkla Jarvilaturi's 1993 *Darkness in Tallinn*, a sensationalist thriller which portrayed the capital in the worst possible light.

*Names Engraved on Marble* is based on the book of the same name that was banned during Soviet times. Produced by Estonia's 28-year-old Kristian Taska, the film portrays the declaration of the first Estonian Republic and its subsequent demise. Entering production in late 2002 was a German produced English-language film *Baltic Storm*, a political thriller that suggests a conspiracy behind the 1994 sinking of the ferry Estonia.

Film buffs can find out more on the website of the **Estonian Film Foundation** (Ⓦ *www .efsa.ee*).

## NEWSPAPERS & MAGAZINES

English-language print media is plentiful in Estonia. There are the helpful guides *Tallinn In Your Pocket* (35 EEK), issued bi-monthly, and *Pärnu In Your Pocket* (25 EEK), issued annually. The weekly *Baltic Times* is worth picking up to get a grip on the recent political and cultural events which will be influencing the people you'll meet on your travels. The bi-monthly *City Paper*, also covering Latvia and Lithuania, is better for its informative, some-times quirky features than for its listings.

The glossy quarterly *Global Estonian* is an English-language magazine with a na-tionalist edge, offering up a smorgasbord of Estonian-related information for Estonians abroad.

The latest issues of foreign-language newspapers are plentiful in Tallinn. An im-pressive selection is sold in the Viru and Olümpia hotels; at the Finnish supermarket, Stockmann, close to the Olümpia at Liivalaia 53; and at the R-kiosk on Vabaduse väljak.

The most popular Estonian papers are *Postimees* (W www.postimees.ee) strongest on culture and international news; *Päevaleht* (W www.epl.ee) and *Sõnumileht*, best for regional news; and the business paper *Äripäev*, which has a few English resumes. They are published five or six times weekly with circulations of 50,000 to 90,000. *Õh-tuleht* is heavier on scandals. *Eesti Ekspress* (W www.ekspress.ee) is a colour weekly and equally popular, published every Thursday, with TV listings. The fortnightly *Luup* is the closest you'll find to *Newsweek* in Estonian. A full listing of the Estonian-language newspapers and magazines is online at W www.zzz.ee. There are also several Rus-sian dailies (the most popular is *Estonia*) and weekly magazines.

## RADIO & TV

Six TV channels can be picked up in Tallinn and along the northern coast of Estonia – state-run Eesti TV plus two other Estonian channels and three from Finland which broadcast a handful of English-language programmes. Among its mainly Estonian-language output, Eesti TV (W www.eta.ee/tv) shows a few good British programmes and some locally made Russian-language ones. A news bulletin in Estonian is at 6pm. One of the most popular shows, *Aktuaalne Kaamera*, a news magazine programme, airs at 9pm. Most hotels have satellite TV offer-ing an onslaught of European programmes.

Estonian Radio broadcasts 15 minutes of local news in English at 6pm on weekdays. Its frequencies are 103.5 FM and can be ac-cessed on the Web at W www.er.ee.

The two most popular stations among young pop and Euro-disco lovers are Sky

Plus on 95.4 FM and Radio 2 on 101.5 FM, while Radio Eva on 88.3 FM plays older, quieter pop. Both Radio Uuno on 97.2 FM and Radio Kuku on 100.7 FM are also favourite local pop stations. The most pop-ular Russian-language stations are Sky on 98.4 FM and Radio 100 on 100 FM.

## PHOTOGRAPHY & VIDEO

While film processing and printing are widely available throughout the country, black and white film and processing is harder to come by, even in the capital. Slide film and Camcorder tapes are available from photographic specialist shops and depart-ment stores. See also Photography & Video in the introductory Facts for the Visitor chapter and the Tallinn chapter.

## PUBLIC HOLIDAYS & SPECIAL EVENTS

National holidays in Estonia include:

**New Year's Day** 1 January
**Independence Day** Anniversary of 1918 declaration, 24 February
**Good Friday** Easter Monday is also taken as a holiday by many people
**May Day** 1 May
**Võidupüha Victory Day** Commemorating the anniversary of the Battle of Võnnu (1919), 23 June
**Jaanipäev St John's Day** Taken together, Victory Day and Jaanipäev are the excuse for a week-long midsummer break for many people, 24 June
**Day of Restoration of Independence** (1991) August 20
**Christmas Jõulud** 25 December
**Boxing Day** 26 December

Estonia has a long list of festivals and cul-tural events, especially during the summer months. Three major events are the national song festival, the midsummer celebrations, and the Baltika folk festival, next due in Tallinn in 2004.

The Estonian National Song Festival, which climaxes with a choir of up to 30,000 people singing traditional Estonian songs on a vast open-air stage to an audience of 100,000, is held every four years, and is next in Tallinn from 2–4 July 2004. The **Tallinn Culture Board** (☎ 640 4607, fax 640 4606) and the city tourist information cen-tre in Tallinn (see Tallinn, Information) issue information on events in and around the capital. They include:

**Tartu Ski Marathon** – mid-February
**Student Jazz Festival** – an international festival attracting musicians from the entire Baltic region; Tallinn, mid-February
**Day of the Setu Lace** – a traditional Setu folk festival; Obinitsa near Võru, 1 March
**International Harpsichord Days of Music** – Tallinn, April
**Jazzkaar** – an international jazz festival; Tallinn, April
**University Spring Days** – wild student festival; Tartu, April
**Pühajärve Beach Festival; Otepää** – local and international music; June
**Old Tallinn Days** – Tallinn Old Town festival; early or mid-June
**Memme-taadi Days** – folk dancing, songs and craft fairs; Rocca al Mare, west of Tallinn, June
**International Music & Theatre Festival FiESTa** – Pärnu, late June
**Õllesummer** Baltic-Scandinavia's largest beer festival; Tallinn; July
**Tallinn Rock Summer** – the Baltics' biggest three-day, international rock-music festival; Tallinn Song Bowl, July
**Visual Anthropology Festival** – film festival focusing on issues of cultural survival; Pärnu, July
**International Organ Music Festival** – concerts throughout Estonia; early August
**International Bagpipe Music Festival** – every two years; Lahemaa National Park, early August
**Classical Music Festival & Country Music Festival** – two separate weekend musical events; Pärnu, August
**Day of the Setu Kingdom** – a new king of the traditional Setu kingdom is appointed; Obinitsa near Võru, around 28 August
**Lillepidu** – international flower festival; Tallinn, early September
**Winter Days** – festivities through Tallinn Old Town; late December

## ACTIVITIES

See the introductory Facts for the Visitor chapter for general information on activities in Estonia.

For water sports enthusiasts, the Käsmu Maritime Museum in the Lahemaa National Park arranges sailing, rowing and diving summer camps, as well as traditional one-log canoe building camps. You can also canoe in your own hand-built canoe across the bogs of the Soomaa National Park and go bog-walking in the Endla Nature Reserve.

Near Arula outside of Otepää, **Toonus Pluss** (☎ 076 79 702 evenings only, mobile 050 55 702; W www.toonuspluss.ee) specialises in canoeing trips, mountain biking and combination canoe/hike/bike trips throughout most regions of Estonia. Routes include Võru to Räpina, Räpina to Tartu and Põlva to Värska.

You can ski and snowboard at the **Kuutsemäe Sports Centre** (☎ 076-69 007; e info@ kuutsemae.ee) and the **Tehvandi Sports Centre** (☎/fax 076-69 500; e tehvandi@tehvandi.ee), both near Otepää in southeastern Estonia.

## ACCOMMODATION

The **Estonian Youth Hostels Association** (☎ 646 1455, fax 646 1595; W www.Baltic Hostels.net; Narva maantee 16, apartment No 25, EE10120 Tallinn) runs about 30 hostels throughout Estonia, including in the capital. It is online and you can book hostel stays in neighbouring countries as well. There are also several privately run hostels.

## FOOD & DRINKS

The Estonian diet relies heavily on pork (seal-iha), red meat, chicken, sausage and potatoes. Fish appears most often as a smoked or salted starter. Suitsukala means smoked fish. Smoked trout (forell) is one good speciality. Sült, jellied meat, will likely be served as well.

Estonian sausage varieties include suitsu-vorst (salami) and viiner (frankfurter). At Christmas time, sausages are made from fresh blood and wrapped in pig's intestine – joy to the world indeed! These blood sausages (verivorst), which locals insist are delicious and healthy, are served in most traditional Estonian restaurants, and sold in shops, all year round. For the blood-thirsty, verileib (blood bread) and verikäkk (balls of blood rolled in flour and eggs with bits of pig fat thrown in for taste) will surely satisfy.

As well as the widespread Baltic kotlett, Estonia also has the schnitsel, a slice of meat – usually pork or beef – which is pounded, breaded then fried. Barley, rice and oatmeal porridges are also staples of any daily diet. Finally, no meal in Estonia would be complete without sour cream, hapukoor, which smothers everything from salads to soups, sauces, meats and vegetables.

No-one quite knows what the syrupy Vana Tallinn liquor is made from, but it is sweet and strong and has a pleasant after-taste and is an integral part of any Estonian table. It is best served in coffee, over ice with milk, over ice cream, or in champagne or dry white wine. There are several other locally made liqueurs, including the unbearably sweet, strawberry-flavoured *Metsa Maasika* and an egg-based liqueur, *Kiiu Torn*, named after the smallest fortress in Estonia in Kiiu.

The Language chapter at the back of the book includes words and phrases you will find useful when ordering food and drinks.

## ENTERTAINMENT
Though the number of Scandinavian 'vodka tourists' on Tallinn's streets may give the impression that the main entertainment in Estonia is liquid, options in the capital run the full gamut from bowling and billiards to theatre and opera, from clubs for all tastes to a range of in and outdoor recreational sports. In smaller towns, where choices are understandably fewer, sports and outdoor activities enjoy primacy.

## SPECTATOR SPORTS
Basketball is Estonia's most popular sport these days. In Tallinn, the local basketball team, Kalev, plays to capacity crowds at the **Kalevi sports hall** *(Juhkentali tänav 12)*, which also hosts occasional boxing tournaments. Ice hockey matches are played at the arena in the Linnahall. The Estonian soccer team plays at the Kadriorg stadium, 2km east of the Old Town.

Swimming competitions are held at the **Kalev pool** *(Aia tänav 18)*. There are horse races most Saturday afternoons at 1pm, at the **Hippodrome** *(Paldiski maantee 50)*.

To witness a truly unique Estonian sport, be on the lookout for **kiiking** events, where the gentle pleasure of riding a swing becomes something of an extreme sport, contested by the number of rotations a competitor can achieve based on the length of the swing. Visit ⓦ www.kiiking.ee for the kiiking story.

## SHOPPING
In Tallinn and most major centres all needs are met and some fine souvenirs and gift ideas abound. Traditional items are hand-knitted garments, lace, leatherbound books, bottles, ceramics, amber, silverware and objects carved from limestone. The syrupy sweet and surprisingly strong liqueur Vana Tallinn forms an integral part of any Estonian gift pack. Prints of Kristjan Raud's Kalevipoeg drawings would make memorable souvenirs. Markets provide a good local shopping experience and some genuine bargains. The kaibemaks is a value-added tax, set at 18% on most items. Medicines and books attract 5% tax. There is no tax refund for items bought within Estonia although duty-free shops appear at the airport and harbour. See also Shopping in the Tallinn chapter.

# Tallinn

**pop 398,434**

Tallinn is an enduring enigma, the city owes much of its appeal to the many contradictions that grant it immunity to stereotypes. Few places in Europe retain the aura of medieval times as authentically as Tallinn's Old Town, yet few capitals have driven a nation's desire for modernity and reform beyond all expectations of what could be achieved in one decade of independence. The soul of Tallinn is as modern as it is medieval.

Tallinn's port has long brought prosperity to the city and made it vulnerable to invaders. Medieval turrets and needling spires remain constants in an evolving city skyline, although a visit to one of the drab apartment block suburbs such as Lasnamäe, shows a very different side of the capital. The World Heritage listed Old Town and modern city centre correspond in time through use of the country's national stone, dolomite limestone. The two-tiered Old Town is defined by some of the world's best preserved medieval walls and towers. The energy and immediacy of the lower town, Vanalinn, contrasts with the grand old buildings and parklands on the hill of Toompea; where a Parliament surrounded by the shell of a 13th century castle aims to govern with a paperless office and should know the results of the next elections through online voting.

Those seeking a glimpse of Estonia's Soviet past are advised to look elsewhere. Tallinn's eclectic, multilingual, and E-culture-obsessed residents are so well connected with Scandinavia that their city has been dubbed 'Tallsinki'. Over 40% of Tallinners are Russians and with ethnic Estonians give a remarkable impression of peaceful co-existence. However many of Tallinn's less fortunate are Russians, now without the privileges that drew them here in Soviet times and increasingly obliged to confirm which side of the border their allegiance lies.

## HISTORY

The site of Tallinn is thought to have been settled by Finno-Ugric people in about 2500 BC. There was probably an Estonian trading settlement here from around the 9th century AD, and a wooden stronghold was built on Toompea in the 11th century. The

## Highlights

- Loose yourself wandering cobblestone streets and explore the medieval treasures of Old Tallinn
- Survey the rooftops and spires of Vanalinn after a climb to the heights of Toompea
- Eat, drink and party away long winter nights in the warmth of basement restaurant, historic pub, club or Old Town sauna
- Sail through Tallinn bay by boat or yacht, or take an island hop with a short cruise
- Witness the sunset over Kadriorg Park or by Pirita beach, especially during the White Nights
- Inspect ancient stone cyst graves and ritual sites in Jõelähtme and around Rebala Nature Reserve

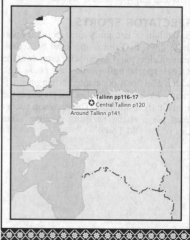

Tallinn pp116-17
Central Tallinn p120
Around Tallinn p141

Danes under King Waldemar II (who conquered northern Estonia in 1219) met tough resistance at Tallinn and were on the verge of retreat when, so the story goes, a red flag with a white cross fell from the sky into their bishop's hands. Taking this as a sign of God's support, they summoned new energy and went on to win the battle; the flag became their national flag (see the Otepää section of the Southwestern Estonia chapter for the present-day Estonian flag's origins). The Danes set their own castle on Toompea.

The origin of the name Tallinn is thought to be from *Taani linn* which is Estonian for 'Danish town'.

The Knights of the Sword took Tallinn from the Danes in 1227 and built the first stone fort on Toompea. German traders arrived from Visby on the Baltic island of Gotland and founded a colony of about 200 people beneath the fortress. In 1238 Tallinn returned to Danish control, but in 1285 it joined the German-dominated Hanseatic League as a channel for trade between Novgorod, Pskov and the west. Furs, honey, leather and seal fat moved west; salt, cloth, herring and wine went east.

By the mid-14th century, when the Danes sold northern Estonia to the Teutonic Order, Tallinn was a major Hanseatic town with about 4000 people. A conflict of interest with the knights and bishop on Toompea led the mainly German artisans and merchants in the Lower Town to build a fortified wall to separate themselves from Toompea. However, Tallinn still prospered and became one of northern Europe's biggest towns. Tallinn's German name, Reval, co-existed with the local name until 1918.

Prosperity faded in the 16th century. The Hanseatic League had weakened; and Russians, Swedes, Danes, Poles and Lithuanians fought over the Baltic region. Tallinn survived a 29-week siege by Russia's Ivan the Terrible in 1570–71. It was held by Sweden from 1561 to 1710 until, decimated by plague, Tallinn was surrendered to Russia's Peter the Great.

In 1870 a railway was completed from St Petersburg, and Tallinn became a chief port of the Russian empire. Freed peasants converged on the city from the countryside, increasing the percentage of Estonians in its population from 52% in 1867 to 89% in 1897. By WWI Tallinn had big shipyards and a large working class in its population of over 100,000.

Tallinn suffered badly in WWII, with thousands of buildings destroyed during Soviet bombing in 1944. After the war, under Soviet control, large-scale industry was developed in Tallinn – including the USSR's biggest grain-handling port – and the city expanded, its population growing to nearly 500,000 from a 1937 level of 175,000. Much of the new population came from Russia, and new high-rise suburbs were built on the outskirts to house the workers.

The 1990s saw the city transformed into a contemporary mid-sized city, with a beautifully restored Old Town and a modern business district surrounding it.

## ORIENTATION

Tallinn spreads south from the edge of Tallinn Bay (Tallinna Laht) on the southern shore of the Gulf of Finland. At the city's heart, just south of the bay, is the Old Town (Vanalinn), which divides neatly into two parts: Upper Town on Toompea (the hill dominating Tallinn), which boasts great views and is the site of the parliament buildings; and the Lower Town, which spreads out from Toompea's eastern side and features most restaurants and businesses.

The Lower Town is centred on Raekoja plats (Town Hall Square), and is still surrounded by most of its 2.5km medieval wall. Around the Old Town is a belt of green parks which follows the line of the city's old defence moat. Outside this old core, radiating outwards, is the New Town, dating from the 19th and early 20th centuries. Vabaduse väljak (Freedom Square) is today's city centre on the southern edge of the Old Town.

### Maps

E.O.Map produces a map of Tallinn (45 EEK), with detailed coverage of the Old Town and modern centre. Many sights of interest are marked and the street index provided is useful. Walking tour and basic orientation maps are available from the tourist information centre and throughout the Old Town, some free of charge.

## INFORMATION
### Tourist Offices

The **main tourist information centre** (☎ 645 7777, fax 645 7778; **w** www.tourism.tallinn.ee; Kullassepa tänav 4; open 9am-7pm Mon-Fri, 10am-5pm Sat & Sun May & June; 9am-8pm Mon-Fri, 10am-6pm Sat & Sun July & Aug; 9am-6pm Mon-Fri, 10am-5pm Sat & Sun Sept; 9am-5pm Mon-Fri, 10am-3pm Sat & Sun Oct-Apr) is on the corner of Niguliste tänav 2. Staff members keep themselves busy booking accommodation and theatre tickets, arranging sightseeing tours and city guides, and selling travel guides. It also sells the Tallinn Card (see the boxed text 'Tallinn Card').

The **port tourist office** (☎/fax 631 8321; open 8am-4.30pm daily) is in Terminal A at

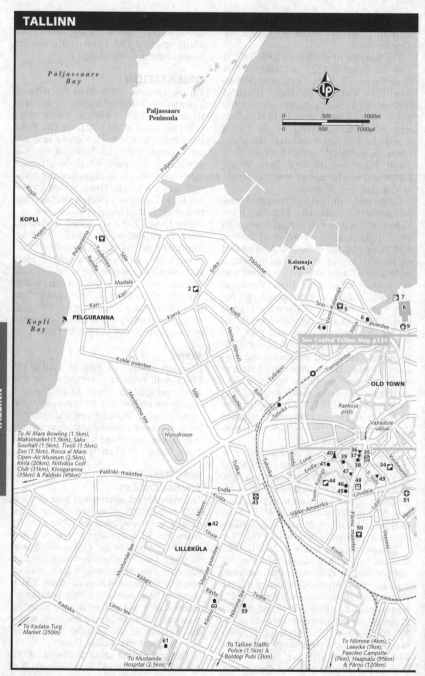

# TALLINN

*Paljassaare Bay*

**Paljassaare Peninsula**

**KOPLI**

Kopli

Vasara

Pelguranna

Tuuleman

Randla

Sõle

Madala

Kari

Kaera

Kari

**PELGURANNA**

*Kopli Bay*

Kolde puiestee

Sõle

Mennetsa tee

Rõstiku

Rohu

Heina (Kanav)

Telliskivi

Tehnika

*Hipodroom*

Paldiski maantee

To Al Mare Bowling (1.5km), Maksimarket (1.5km), Saku Suurhall (1.5km), Tivoli (1.5km), Zoo (1.5km), Rocca al Mare Open-Air Museum (2.5km), Keila (20km), Niitvälja Golf Club (31km), Kloogaranna (35km) & Paldiski (45km)

Endla

Koskla

Tuulka

Moori

**43**

Tihase

● **42**

**LILLEKÜLA**

Räägu

Mustamäe tee

Kadaka

Linnu tee

Sõprue puiestee

Rästa

Nõmme tee

Kännu

Tedre

**60**

**59**

To Kadaka Turg Market (250m)

**61**

To Mustamäe Hospital (2.5km)

To Tallinn Traffic Police (1.5km) & Buldogi Pubi (3km)

Erika

Kopli

Tööstuse

Soo

Vana-Kalamaja

Põhja

**Kalamaja Park**

**5**

**4**

**6** puiestee

**7**

**8**

**9**

**See Central Tallinn Map p120**

Toompuiestee

**OLD TOWN**

*Raekoja plats*

*Vabaduse väljak*

Koidu

Luise

Endla

Toom-Kuninga

**40**

**41**

**36**

**39**

**37**

**38**

**35**

**34**

Kentmanni

**44**

**46**

**45**

**47**

**48**

**49**

Liivalaia

S Suur

Tatari

Väike-Ameerika

Pärnu maantee

Koidu

**50**

**51**

Herne

Veereni

To Nõmme (4km), Leevike (7km), Paeoleo Campsite (7km), Haapsalu (95km) & Pärnu (120km)

0 — 500 — 1000m
0 — 500 — 1000yd

# TALLINN

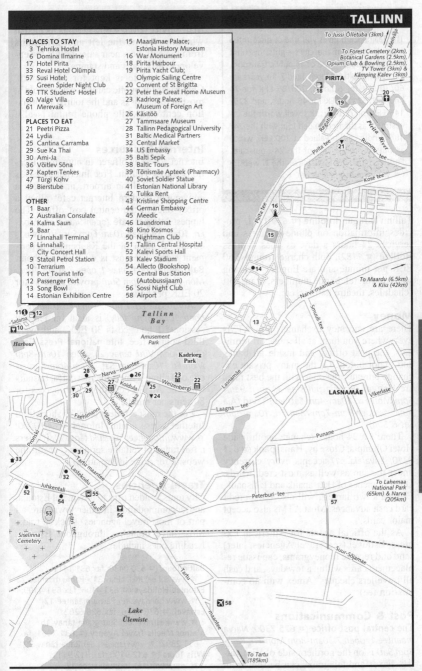

**PLACES TO STAY**
3 Tehnika Hostel
6 Domina Ilmarine
17 Hotel Pirita
33 Reval Hotel Olümpia
57 Susi Hotel;
   Green Spider Night Club
59 TTK Students' Hostel
60 Valge Villa
61 Merevaik

**PLACES TO EAT**
21 Peetri Pizza
24 Lydia
25 Cantina Carramba
29 Sue Ka Thai
30 Ami-Ja
36 Võitlev Sõna
37 Kapten Tenkes
47 Türgi Kohv
49 Bierstube

**OTHER**
1 Baar
2 Australian Consulate
4 Kalma Saun
5 Baar
7 Linnahall Terminal
8 Linnahall;
   City Concert Hall
9 Statoil Petrol Station
10 Terrarium
11 Port Tourist Info
12 Passenger Port
13 Song Bowl
14 Estonian Exhibition Centre

15 Maarjamäe Palace;
   Estonia History Museum
16 War Monument
18 Pirita Harbour
19 Pirita Yacht Club;
   Olympic Sailing Centre
20 Convent of St Brigitta
22 Peter the Great Home Museum
23 Kadriorg Palace;
   Museum of Foreign Art
26 Käsitöö
27 Tammsaare Museum
28 Tallinn Pedagogical University
31 Baltic Medical Partners
32 Central Market
34 US Embassy
35 Balti Sepik
38 Baltic Tours
39 Tõnismäe Apteek (Pharmacy)
40 Soviet Soldier Statue
41 Estonian National Library
42 Tulika Rent
43 Kristiine Shopping Centre
44 German Embassy
45 Meedic
46 Laundromat
48 Kino Kosmos
50 Nightman Club
51 Tallinn Central Hospital
52 Kalevi Sports Hall
53 Kalev Stadium
54 Allecto (Bookshop)
55 Central Bus Station
   (Autobussijaam)
56 Sossi Night Club
58 Airport

## Tallinn Card

The Tallinn Card gives you free or discounted entry to many of the city's sights, discount shopping and free use of all public transport. Prices for adults/children aged 7-14 years are 60/30 EEK for 6 hours, 205/85 EEK for 24 hours, 275/115 EEK for 48 hours, and 325/145 EEK for 72 hours. It's well worth the investment as the free guided tour with the 24/48/72 hour card is valued at 200 EEK, which all but covers the cost of the 24-hour card. Further details are available on the TI website (**W** www.tourism.tallinn.ee).

Tallinn harbour. **Infoline** (☎ 626 1111) provides information on phone numbers and services 24 hours a day, as does **Express Hotline** (☎ 1182); both charge around 2.50 EEK per minute and are English-speaking sources for telephone numbers, transport schedules, theatre listings, etc.

## Money

There are currency exchanges and ATMs everywhere you turn: at all transport terminals, the post office, and inside all banks and major hotels. Of the many private exchange bureaus, the ones with the best rates are **Haggai** (Estonia puiestee 3; open 9am-6pm Mon-Fri, 10am-4pm Sat) and **Tavid** (Aia tänav 5; open 9am-7pm Mon-Fri, 10am-5pm Sat & Sun).

There's a 24-hour exchange booth inside Hotel Olümpia. Close by, **Hansapank** (☎ 631 0310; Liivalaia 51) accepts every currency under the sun as well as most credit cards. Other branches of Hansapank and Ühispank, Estonia's two largest, will also issue credit card cash advances. Most ATMs also accept major cards.

As the official agents for American Express, Estravel (see Travel Agencies, later) send and receive moneygrams, can issue replacement cards within a few days, and cash all travellers cheques (Amex with no commission fee).

## Post & Communications

The **central post office** (☎ 625 7300; Narva maantee 1; open 7.30am-8pm Mon-Fri, 8am-6pm Sat) is on the northern side of Viru väljak. Faxes and telegrams can be sent from any window on the second floor. **Express Mail Service** (EMS; ☎ 605 3250) is located at windows 4–9, to the left and downstairs from the entrance, near sales points for envelopes, jiffy bags and stamps.

Poste restante is kept for one month. Chip cards for public cardphones are sold at most hotels, kiosks and the tourist information centre. Mobile phone rental is also freely available.

## Internet Resources

Internet access is offered in numerous locations across Tallinn. Free Internet access is available at Tallinn airport, and there's a convenient modern Internet café (albeit a pricey one) in the central post office. The hippest **Internet café** (open 9am-9pm Mon-Fri, 10am-8pm Sat, 10am-6pm Sun) in town is on the 5th floor of the Kaubamaja department store. The cost is 40 EEK per hour. **Balti Sepik** (Süda tänav 1; open 7.30am-10pm Mon-Sat, 9am-8pm Sun) provides access for 20 EEK per hour.

**Arvutisaal** (2nd floor, Vana-Posti tänav 2; open 10am-8pm daily) is ideal for lengthy sessions; 1 hour costs 30 EEK, and every third hour is free. **International Press Café** (2nd floor, Viru tänav 23; open 10am-8pm Mon-Fri, 10am-6pm Sat, 11am-4pm Sun) is one of Tallinn's finest Internet cafés, upstairs from the Apollo bookshop, with access for 80 sents per minute.

For the most efficient long- or short-term Internet access, contact **Infonet** (☎ 640 0000; **W** www.infonet.ee; Suurtüki tänav 8). It offers a full range of reliable services (consult the website for price information).

## Travel Agencies

City tours, guided trips to provincial Estonia, and accommodation in other towns are all part of most travel agencies' stock in trade. Most have branches throughout Estonia. Leading ones include:

**Baltic Tours** (☎ 630 0430, fax 631 1411; **W** www.bt.ee) Pikk tänav 31 • Pärnu maantee 22
**Estonian Holidays** (☎ 631 4106, fax 631 4109; **W** www.holidays.ee) Pärnu maantee 12
**Estravel** (☎ 626 6266, fax 626 6202; **W** www.estravel.ee) Suur-Karja tänav 15
**Mainor Meelis Travel Agency** (☎ 631 2061; fax 631 2397; **W** www.meelis.ee) Raua tänav 39
**Wris Tours** (☎ 612 9100, fax 612 9111; **W** www.wris.ee) Toompuiestee 17

## Bookshops

The best selection of English-language books is at **Allecto** (☎ 660 6493; Juhkentali tänav 32-5). You can order books there, too. Art books are the speciality at **Euro Publications** (☎ 661 2210; Tartu maantee 1), and it places foreign orders. It's opposite the Kaubamaja and connected to the Tallinn Art Academy. Travel books galore (with the country's largest Lonely Planet selection) are at **Apollo** (☎ 654 8485; Viru tänav 23). For guides, maps and Estonian-language books try **Rahva Raamat** (☎ 644 3682; Pärnu maantee 10). Central bookshops stock city and regional maps covering most destinations in Estonia. For used or antique books and photos, a visit to the friendly **Mr Kolk** (☎ 641 8005; Rüütli tänav 28/30) will fulfil any 'old bookshop' fantasy you may have harboured.

## Cultural Centres

There's the **British Council** (☎ 631 4010; Vana-Posti tänav 7); the excellent **French Cultural Centre** (☎ 644 9505; Kuninga tänav 4); and the **German Goethe Cultural Institute** (☎ 645 7414; Tolli tänav 4).

## Laundry

There's a central **laundromat** (Pärnu maantee 48), opposite Kino Kosmos, and the clean, **Sauberland** (Maakri tänav 23), with expensive dry-cleaning service, near Stockmann. To wash and dry a 5kg load costs around 60 EEK. Service washes will cost at least 30 EEK extra.

## Left Luggage

There's a **left-luggage room** (pakihoid; open 7am-8pm daily) in the main ferry terminal at the passenger port. Lockers are available 24 hours. Luggage lockers are also located at the central bus station (Lastekodu tänav 46; open 5am-11.30pm daily). A left-luggage service is offered at the **Merekeskus Shopping Centre** (Mere Puiestee 10; open 8am-6pm daily). At the time of writing, the one at the train station remained inconveniently closed.

## Medical Services

The **Tallinn Central Hospital** (☎ 620 7010; Ravi tänav 18), just south of Liivalaia, some 300m west of the Hotel Olümpia, has a full range of services, a polyclinic, a 24-hour emergency room, and is used to foreigners dropping in. There's also Tallinn's largest, **Mustamäe hospital** (☎ 697 1400; Sütiste tee 19, Mustamäe).

Western in price, service and attitude are Tallinn's privately run medical centres, like **Meedic** (☎ 646 3390; Pärnu maantee 48A) and **Baltic Medical Partners** (☎ 601 0550; Tartu maantee 32), an excellent dental clinic.

All pharmacies sell Western medicines. **Tõnismäe Apteek** (☎ 644 2282; Tõnismägi 5; open 8am-5pm Mon-Fri, 9am-5pm Sat & 10am-5pm Sun) also runs a night service (just ring the bell).

To call an ambulance, dial ☎ 03. Tallinn water is considered safe to drink.

## WALKING TOUR

One of the greatest pleasures of any visit to Tallinn is simply wandering through the winding streets of the **Old Town** (Vanalinn) down its many lanes, through doorways and around medieval courtyards.

The Town Hall Square (Raekoja plats) is a natural starting point for an exploration of the Old Town. From here brief passages radiate towards the streets Vene, Pikk and Lai that stretch north, providing the framework of the lower Old Town and much of its character. Follow the well preserved medieval walls and climb the winding Lühike Jalg to Toompea, taking in its monumental towers, the Riigikogu, Toomkirik and Nevsky Cathedral.

This tour will take around two hours but a full day is recommended to thoroughly explore the many museums and sites of the Old Town. For a greater appreciation of Tallinn's medieval ambience, digress to the smaller streets and outer edges as far as time and energy levels permit.

## Raekoja Plats

The only surviving Gothic town hall in northern Europe rises over the Town Hall Square (Raekoja plats) which has been at the heart of Tallinn life since markets were held here from the 11th century (the last was in 1896). The **Town Hall** (Raekoda; ☎ 645 7900; tower admission adult/student & child 25/15 EEK; open 11am-6pm Tues-Sun June-Aug), built between 1371 and 1404, was the seat of power in the medieval Lower Town. Its minaret-like tower is supposedly modelled on a sketch brought back by an explorer from the Orient. **Vana Toomas** (Old Thomas), the warrior-and-sword weather vane at its peak, has guarded

# CENTRAL TALLINN

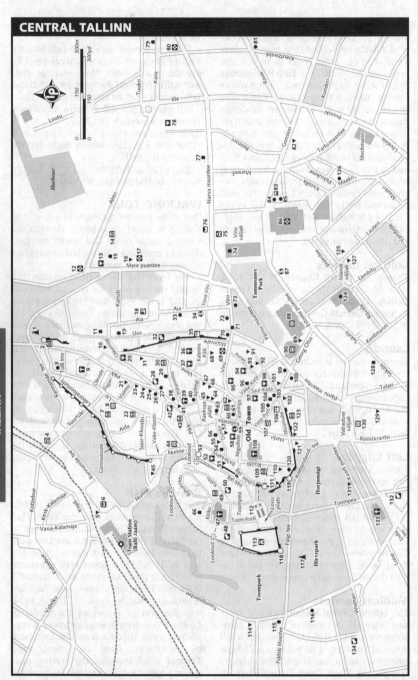

## CENTRAL TALLINN

**PLACES TO STAY**
11  Hostel UUS 26
15  Metropol
19  Old House B&B
29  Schlössle
46  Olematu Rüütel
54  St Petersbourg
56  Eeslitall Hotel; Eeslitall
    Restaurant
74  Viru Hotel
77  Reval Hotel Central
79  Dorell Hotel
96  Vana Tom
104 Domina City Hotel
115 Grand Hotel Tallinn
128 Helke

**PLACES TO EAT**
5   Nehatu
10  Siam
16  Peetri Pizza
21  Le Bonaparte Restaurant &
    Café
23  Lübeck
24  Golden Dragon
25  Pudru ja Pasta
31  Egoist
41  Maiasmokk Kohvik &
    Restaurant
45  Renessanss
51  Vanaema Juures
55  Kuldse Notsu Kõrts
57  Raeköök
62  Olde Hansa
64  Troika
65  Café Anglais
66  Elevant
67  Tanduur
68  Controvento
82  Poliina
89  Armaada Sandwicherie
91  Crêperie Sans Nom
92  Buongiorno
93  Must Lammas
101 Gateway
102 Coffik Cafeteria & Buffet
110 Mõõkala
111 Neitsitorn
    (Virgin's Tower)
114 Café Toome
121 Vana Tunnel
122 Gloria Veinikelder
125 Eesti Maja
127 Imanta

129 Peetri Pizza
131 Võiroos Café

**BARS & CLUBS**
13  Spirit
20  Levi'st Väljas
37  Kloostri Ait
52  Von Krahli Theatre Baar
58  Vinoteek
78  Decolte
94  X-Baar
95  Kõwer Kõrts
97  Nimeta Baar
98  Nimega Baar

**OTHER**
1   Estonia Ferry Disaster
    Memorial
2   Great Coast Gate; Fat
    Margaret Bastion; Maritime
    Museum
3   German Goethe Cultural
    Institute
4   Infonet
6   Bus Station
7   Natural History Museum
8   City Theatre (Linnateater)
9   St Olaf Oleviste Church &
    Tower
12  Merekeskus Shopping Centre
14  Architecture & Arts Centre of
    Estonia
17  Rotermanni Keskus; Rasastra
18  Kalev Swimming Pool
22  Applied Art Museum
26  Baltic Tours
27  Brotherhood of Blackheads;
    St Olaus' Guild
28  Swedish Embassy
30  City Museum
32  Lithuanian Embassy
33  Rimi Kaubahall
34  Tavid Exchange Bureau
35  Kino Forum
36  Dominican Monastery; St
    Catherine's Church
38  St Canutus Guild Hall
39  Holy Spirit (Pühavaimu)
    Church
40  Raeapteek
42  Russian Embassy
43  State History Museum &
    Great Guild
44  Puppet Theatre

47  Toomkirik
48  Canadian Embassy
49  National Art Museum
50  Finnish Embassy
53  Pikk Jalg Gate Tower
59  Tourist Information Centre
60  French Cultural Centre
61  Museum of Estonian
    Photography
63  Town Hall; Tristan ja Isolde
69  De La Gardie Shopping Plaza
70  Käsitöö Market
71  Viru Gate
72  Apollo (Bookshop);
    International Press Café
73  Flower Market
75  Taxi & Route-Taxi Stand
76  Central Post Office
80  Le Gallerie Passage
81  Mainor Meelis Travel Agency
83  Gonsiori Bus Stop
84  Academy of Art
    (Kunstiakadeemia)
85  Euro Publications
86  Kaubamaja Department
    Store; Internet Café
87  Haggai
88  Estonia Theatre; Estonia
    Concert Hall
90  Estonia Drama Theatre
99  Rahva Raamat (Bookshop)
100 Estonian Holidays
103 Estravel
105 British Council
106 Kino Sõprus; Hollywood Club
107 Arvutisaal
108 St Nicholas (Niguliste) Church;
    Museum of Religious Art
109 Archaeological Museum
112 Alexander Nevsky Cathedral
113 Toompea Castle
116 Wris Tours
117 Linda Monument
118 Pikk Hermann
119 Kiek-in-de-Kök Tower
120 Mr Kolk (Bookshop)
123 Theatre & Music Museum
124 Sakala Conference & Cultural
    Centre
126 Sauberland
130 Russian Drama Theatre
132 Latvian Embassy
133 Kaarli Kirik
134 British Embassy

**TALLINN**

Tallinn since 1530. The arches at ground level along the northern side of the hall were a trading place in the Middle Ages. Inside, the **Citizens' Hall** has an impressive vaulted roof, while the fine 1374 bench-ends in the **Council Hall** are Estonia's oldest wood carvings. There is a **tower** you can

climb, and occasional exhibitions are held in the Citizens' Hall.

The former **Town Jail** (Linnavangla), in a lane behind the main building, is now home to the **Museum of Estonian Photography** (Raevangla Fotomuuseum; ☎ 644 8767; Raekoja plats 4/6; adult/student 10/5 EEK;

*open 11am-5pm Thur-Tues)*. Lesser offenders were shackled to the town hall in irons that still hang there today. The **Raeapteek** *(Town Council Pharmacy)*, on the northern side of the square, is another Tallinn institution, although the present facade is 17th century, there has been a pharmacy or apothecary shop here since at least 1422, at one time passing through 10 generations of the same family. An arch beside the Raeapteek on Raekoja plats leads into the charming, narrow Saia kang (White Bread Passage), once filled with the aromas of a popular bakery. At its end is the striking 13th- century Gothic **Pühavaimu Kirik** *(Holy Spirit Church;* ☎ *646 4430)*, used by Lutherans. Its clock is the oldest in Tallinn, with carvings dating from 1684, and the tower bell (1433) is the oldest in Estonia. Inside are a fine 1483 wooden altarpiece, 16th-century carved bench-backs and a 17th-century baroque pulpit. A dramatic fire in May 2002 badly damaged the tower of the Holy Spirit Church; although restoration efforts continue, the church has now been re-opened to visitors. Check information posted outside for classical music concerts.

## Around Vene

Several 15th-century warehouses and merchant residences surround Raekoja plats, notably when heading towards Vene (the Estonian word for Russian, named for the Russian merchants who traded here centuries ago). Vene is now one of the Old Town's favourite restaurant precincts. The **City Museum** *(Linnamuuseum;* ☎ *644 6553; Vene tänav 17; adult/student 25/10 EEK; open 10.30am-5.30pm Wed-Mon Apr-Oct, 11am-4.30pm Nov-Mar)* was itself once a medieval merchant's home. This is Tallinn's most interesting museum, tracing the city's development from its very beginnings through to 1940 with displays and curious artefacts.

Further down on Vene, look for an 1844 Catholic church set back from the street with the Latin inscription 'Hic Vere Est Domus Dei' on its wall. A small door in the corner of the courtyard leads you into the **Dominican Monastery** *(Dominiiklaste klooster;* ☎ *644 4606;* e *kloostri@hot.ee; Vene tänav 16; adult/student 25/15 EEK; open 9.30am-6pm daily mid-May–mid-Sept, visits other times by arrangement)*, founded in 1246. The monastery housed Scandinavian monks who aimed

to convert Estonians to Christianity and educate the local population. Once wealthy, with its own brewery and hospital, the monastery was ruined by plunder during the Reformation in 1524–25 and by a fire in 1531; today it houses Estonia's largest collection of stone carvings. **St Catherine's Church** *(Katariina Kirik)*, on the south side of the cloister, was once the biggest in northern Europe. Unfortunately, it has not been restored and is closed to visitors. Nevertheless, the open areas contain a wealth of lovely 15th- to 17th-century stone carvings.

## Pikk

Pikk (long street) runs north from Raekoja plats towards Tallinn port and is lined with the houses of medieval German merchants and gentry. Many were built in the 15th century, usually with three or four storeys, the lower two being living and reception quarters and the upper ones used for storage.

Also on Pikk are the buildings of several old Tallinn guilds (associations of traders or artisans, nearly all German dominated). The **Great Guild** *(Pikk tänav 17)*, to which the most eminent merchants belonged, has a Gothic doorway. The building dates from 1410 and one of its fine vaulted halls retains its original appearance. Today it houses the **State History Museum** *(Ajaloomuuseum;* ☎ *641 1630; Pikk tänav 17;* w *www.eam.ee; adult/student 10/5 EEK; open 11am-6pm Thur-Tues)*, devoted to Estonian history up to the mid-19th century.

**St Canutus Guild Hall** *(Kanuti Gildi Saal; Pikk tänav 20)*, on the east side of the street, has statues of Martin Luther and St Canute on the front. Though the building only dates from the 1860s, the site had previously housed the St Canutus Guild for several centuries. Its members were master artisans. The adjoining buildings of the **Brotherhood of Blackheads** *(Mustpeade Vennaskonna hoone; Pikk tänav 24)* and the **St Olaus Guild** *(Olevi Gildi Hoone; Pikk tänav 26)* are closed to the public except for regular concerts. The Blackheads were unmarried merchants who took their name from their patron saint, Maurice. His head is between two lions on one of the stone reliefs on the building's facade (1597). The St Olaus Guild – probably the first guild in Tallinn – began in the 13th century, and developed a membership of more humble non-German artisans and traders.

At the northern end of Pikk is the **Great Coast Gate**, the medieval exit to Tallinn port. It's joined to **Fat Margaret** (Paks Margareeta), a rotund 16th-century bastion which protected this entrance to the town. Fat Margaret's walls are more than 4m thick at the base. Inside is the **Maritime Museum** (Meremuuseum; ☎ 641 1408; Pikk tänav 70; adult/student 25/10 EEK; open 10am-6pm Wed-Sun). There are great views from the platform on the roof. In the grounds stands a **white cross** in memory of the victims of the Estonia ferry disaster, Europe's worst peacetime maritime tragedy. A **monument**, entitled 'Broken Line', stands to the side of the cross and a 3m-long granite table lists the 852 people who died when the popular Estline ferry sank in September 1994, en route between Stockholm and Tallinn.

### Lai

The majestic **St Olaf Church** (Oleviste Church), at the top end of Lai (wide street) was the focal point of old Tallinn's Scandinavian population. Although dedicated to the 11th-century king Olaf II of Norway the church is linked in local lore with another Olaf, its legendary architect, who ignored the prophesies of doom for whoever would complete the church's construction, and fell to his death from the tower. It's said a toad and snake then crawled out of his mouth. The incident is shown in one of the carvings on the eastern wall of the 16th-century Chapel of Our Lady, adjoining the church, which shows a skeleton with a toad on its chest and a snake around its skull. The 124m **St Olaf tower** (Oleviste tower) is a chief Tallinn landmark and was a former surveillance centre for the KGB.

Nearby, on the corner of Pagari tänav, is the former KGB headquarters, now a police department. Notice how the lower windows of the four-storey building have been bricked up, in order to prevent the sounds of violent 'interrogations' from being heard by those passing by on the street.

Further south along Lai you'll see some fine 15th- to 17th-century facades, including No 29 near the corner of Suurtüki, and No 23 opposite Vaimu. The **Natural History Museum** (Loodusmuuseum; ☎ 641 1739; e muuseum@online.ee; Lai tänav 29; adult/student 25/10 EEK; open 10am-5pm Wed-Sun) occupies the rear of an attractive courtyard. It

has comprehensive exhibits of every bird and mammal found in Estonia. The **Applied Art Museum** (Tarberkunstimuuseum; ☎ 641 1927; Lai tänav 17; adult/student 15/5 EEK; open 11am-6pm Wed-Sun), in a 17th-century barn at the corner of Aida tänav, has a collection of excellent modern woven rugs, ceramics, glass, metal and leatherwork.

### Lower Town Walls and St Nicholas Church

The longest-standing stretch of the Old Town wall, with nine towers, spans from Väike-Kloostri tänav, along Laboratooriumi to the northern end of Lai.

At the end of Aida tänav, furthest from Lai, is a tiny passageway through the town wall; on the other side you'll find one of the most picturesque spots to photograph a line-up of four **towers** (another can be found along Kooli). Follow the walls along Gumnaasiumi tänav to the gate at the intersection of Suur-Kloostri and Väike-Kloostri tänav. From here it's possible to walk along the top of the wall for a closer inspection of the four towers. A small **ticket office** (adult/concession 7/5 EEK; open 10am-7pm Mon-Fri, 11am-4pm Sat & Sun) is situated adjacent to the gate. In all, 26 of the original 45 towers remain today. In order of proximity; the Sauna tower, the Golden Leg tower, the Back-of-the-Nuns tower and the Lowenschede tower.

From the gate follow Väike-Kloostri, Nunne and Rataskaevu, passing the **well** where in medieval times animals were sacrificed to appeal for prosperity in the year ahead. **St Nicholas Church** (Niguliste Kirik; open 10am-5pm Wed-Sun), named after St Nicholas of Bari, patron saint of sailors, has an early Gothic north doorway, but is mostly a 15th-century construction. It is now used for organ recitals and as a **museum of art** from medieval Estonian churches. It is definitely worth a visit and concerts are regularly held there, mainly weekend afternoons. Behind it is the excellent **Archaeological Museum** (☎ 644 4805; Rüütli 10; open by arrangement).

St Nicholas stands on the foot of a small slope that looks like an abandoned demolition site. In warmer months the ruins are covered with a wooden deck, a usual setting for outdoor drinks. It's the carefully exposed wreckage of the buildings that stood here before the Soviet bombing of Tallinn on 9 March 1944. A sign in English facing Harju details the damage done to the city that night. Down the street is the **Theatre & Music Museum** (☎ 644 2132; Müürivahe 12; adult/student 15/5 EEK; open 10am-5pm Wed-Sun), which highlights Estonia's musical traditions, instruments and stars.

## UPPER TOWN
### Toompea

A winding stairway connects Lühike jalg, off Rataskaevu, to Toompea ('**tom**-pe-ah'). According to Estonian legend, Toompea is the burial mound of Kalev, the heroic first leader of the Estonians, built by his widow Linda. In German times this was the preserve of the feudal nobility and bishop, looking down on the traders and lesser beings of the Lower Town.

Although the most impressive – and until the 17th century the only – approach to Toompea is through the red-roofed **Pikk jalg Gate Tower** ('Long leg', dating from 1380) at the western end of Pikk, **Lühike jalg** (Short Leg) is not without character. A number of ghostly apparitions have been reported inside the **haunted house** (Lühike jalg 70), including a crucified monk and a black dog with burning eyes. It's thought to be the most haunted house in Tallinn.

At the top of Lühike jalg is Estonia's parliament building, the Riigikogu, which meets in **Toompea Castle** at the western end of Lossi plats. The seat of the government is in the same building. Nothing remains of the 1219 Danish castle here, but three of the four corner towers of its successor, founded by the Knights of the Sword in 1227–29, still stand. The castle's mainly baroque appearance dates from the 18th century when, under Catherine the Great, it was rebuilt and had its moat filled in.

The finest of the castle towers is the 1371 **Pikk Hermann** at the southwest corner, topped by the national flag. The two other surviving towers, plus most of the northern wall of the old castle, can be seen from the yard of Toom-Kooli 13. Signposts near the 13th-century **Toomkirik** (Dome Church) give directions to Toompea's favourite lookout points.

The central location of the Russian Orthodox **Alexander Nevsky Cathedral** (Lossi plats), opposite the parliament buildings, was no accident: the church was one of many Orthodox cathedrals built (1894–1900) as part of a general wave of Russification in the Russian Baltic provinces in the last quarter of the 19th century. Impressive it is, though it looks rather out of place among its older neighbours. As a symbol of Russian dominance it is still viewed with mixed emotions by many locals.

The parklands around the old castle walls invite exploration of the towers and views. Don't miss the tall, stout **Kiek-in-de-Kök** (☎ 644 6686; Komandandi 2; admission 15 EEK; open 10.30am-6pm Tues-Fri mid-May–Sept, 11am-5pm Oct–mid-May). Its name is Low German for 'Peep into the Kitchen'; from the upper floors medieval voyeurs could see into the houses of the Lower Town. Built in about 1475, Kiek-in-de-Kök now houses a museum with several floors of maps, weapons and models of old Tallinn.

Digress with a pleasant downhill stroll from the Kiek-in-de-Kök, to the **Hirvepark** with a **statue** of Linda grieving, which has come to symbolise the tragic fate of those deported from Estonia during and after WWII.

### Around Toomkirik

Toompea is named after the Lutheran Toomkirik (Dome Church), founded in 1233, which is at the northern end of Toom-Kooli. This magnificent structure dates from the 15th and 17th centuries (it was largely rebuilt after a fire in 1684) but the tower was built in 1779. Among other things, the church was a burial ground for the rich and noble. The finest of the **carved tombs** inside are those on the right as you approach the altar, including life-size figures of the 16th- century Swedish commander, Pontus de la Gardie, and his wife. The Swedish siege of Narva, where de la Gardie died, is shown on the side of their sarcophagus. The marble Greek temple-style sarcophagus belongs to Admiral Samuel Greigh, an 18th-century Scot who joined the Russian navy and became a hero of Russo-Turkish sea battles. Admiral Adam Johann von Krusenstern, a German Estonian who was the first Russian citizen to sail around the world, has another elaborate tomb.

Estonia's **National Art Museum** (Eesti Kunstimuuseum; ☎ 644 9340; Kiriku plats 1; adult/student 20/5 EEK; open 11am-5.30pm Wed-Sun) boasts an impressive 59,000 items, many of which are on show in this 18th-century noble's house near Toomkirik. The art museum dates from 1919 and is the largest in Estonia.

From Kiriku plats, Piiskopi turns into Pikk jalg; pass through the gateway to the **Danish King's courtyard**. In this open space in summer, artists set up their easels and teens congregate. One of the towers here, **Neitsitorn** (*Virgin's Tower;* ☎ *644 0896; Lühike jalg 9a; open 11am-11pm daily*), has been turned into a popular café-bar of the same name, and has good views. Its name is ironic – it's said to have been a prison for medieval prostitutes! Both Lühike jalg and the Kings' stairs to the right lead down to the St Nicholas Church and Raekoja Plats.

## EAST OF THE CENTRE
### Kadriorg
The park Kadriorg (*Narva maantee*), 2km east of the Old Town, is pleasant and wooded, with oak, lilac and horse chestnut trees. It has long been city residents' favourite strolling grounds. Weekends are especially popular among cyclists, sun-tanners and leisure-seekers, but the park is so spacious it never feels crowded. Together with the baroque Kadriorg Palace, it was designed for the Russian tsar, Peter the Great, by the Italian Niccolo Michetti, soon after Peter's conquest of Estonia in the Great Northern War.

Kadriorg Palace now houses the **Museum of Foreign Art** (*Väliskunsti Muuseum, Kadrioru loss;* ☎ *606 6400; Weizenbergitänav 37; adult/student 35/20 EEK; open 10pm-5pm Wed-Sun Oct-May, 10am-5pm Tues-Sun June-Sept*). It was built between 1718 and 1736 with Peter himself laying an amazing three bricks! They were left bare for visitors to marvel at. In the 1930's, the palace was the private domain of the president of the independent Estonia. With new independence, part of the palace complex has again become the presidential home.

Behind the palace is the cottage Peter the Great occupied on visits to Tallinn while the palace was being built. Today it houses the **Peter the Great Home Museum** (*☎ 601 3136; Mäekalda tänav 2; admission 6 EEK; open 10.30am-6pm Wed-Sat May-Sept*) where you may examine his clothes and the boots he made.

Just west of the park, the last home of the great Estonian novelist Anton Hansen Tammsaare now contains the **Tammsaare Museum** (*☎ 601 3232; Koidula tänav 12A;*

*admission 5 EEK; open 11am-6pm Wed-Mon*) with excerpts from his works.

### Song Bowl
The Tallinn Song Bowl (*Lauluväljak; Narva maantee*), site of the main gatherings of Estonia's national song festivals, is an open- air amphitheatre said to reach capacity at 150,000 people. In September 1988 some 300,000 squeezed in for one songfest and publicly demand for independence during the Singing Revolution. Approximately half a million, including a large number of Estonian émigrés, were believed to have been present at the 21st Song Festival in 1990, the last major festival before the restoration of Independence. An Estonian repertoire was reinstated and around 29,000 performers sang under the national flag for the first time in 50 years. Heading out of town, the song bowl is on the left side of Narva maantee, a short distance past the fork where Pirita tee heads off to the left, up the side of Tallinn Bay.

### Pirita Tee
This coastal road curving northwards alongside Tallinn Bay is an ideal walk, affording a sea view that's particularly spectacular during late-night summer sunsets. It's a favourite place for couples to stroll and for others to walk in solitude and quiet reflection, a favourite Estonian pastime. There's a vast pine forest spreading east from much of Pirita tee with paths that delight joggers and cyclists.

Some 2km north of Kadriorg Park, the **Maarjamäe Palace** (*Maarjamäe loss*) contains a section of the **Estonia History Museum** (*☎ 601 4535; Pirita tee 56; adult/student 10/8 EEK; open 11am-6pm Wed-Sun*), which covers the mid-19th century onwards. The neo-Gothic limestone palace was built in the 1870s as a summer cottage for the Russian General, A Orlov-Davydov.

Further north along Pirita tee is an unmistakably Soviet **war monument** rising in its concrete glory to a sharp point on the eastern side of the street. The 'powers that were' decided to erect this monument over the graves of German soldiers who died fighting the Soviets on the Leningrad front, buried there during the German wartime occupation of Estonia. Most of the graves were bulldozed for the purpose, but some remain behind the statue.

**TALLINN**

## Pirita

Some 1.5km beyond Maarjamäe, just before Pirita tee crosses the Pirita River, a short side road leads down to **Pirita Yacht Club** and the **Olympic Sailing Centre** (see Boat in the introductory Getting Around chapter), near the mouth of the river. This was the base for the sailing events of the 1980 Moscow Olympics, and international regattas are still held here.

Usually docked in the harbour here is the **Lembit submarine**, built in Britain in 1936 and one of the few subs in the old Estonian navy. At the time of writing the Lembit was undergoing maintenance; contact the tourist information centre for a progress report and access details.

In summer you can rent rowboats beside the road-bridge over the river. North of the bridge is the city's largest and most popular **Pirita beach** (and it's only 6km from the city centre). Where Pirita tee meets Merivälja, the ruined **Convent of St Brigitta** (☎ 605 5010; *adult/student 20/10 EEK; open 10am-6pm daily*), built in the early 15th century but destroyed in the Livonian War in 1577. Though it originally housed both nuns and monks of the Swedish-based Brigittine Order it soon became a female monastery. In 1996, Brigittine nuns in Estonia were granted the right to return to the convent and reactivate the monastery. The convent's recently completed new headquarters are adjacent to the St Brigitta ruins.

## Botanical Gardens & TV Tower

About 2.5km east of Pirita are the **Botanical Gardens** (☎ 606 2666; *Kloostrimetsa tee 52; adult/student & child 40/20 EEK, family ticket 60 EEK; open 11am-4pm Tues-Sun*), a 123-hectare piece of land and series of greenhouses which boast over 8000 species of plants, and a 4km nature trail. The 314m **TV tower** (w *www.teletorn.ee; Kloostrimetsa tee 58a; admission 30 EEK; open 1pm-2am daily*) is 400m further east. You can climb it with the help of an elevator. There's a restaurant at the 170m point, not quite as tacky as other TV tower restaurants due to renovations. At the base there are still a few bullet holes from events during the August 1991 attempted Soviet takeover (it was as violent as things became in Estonia's bid for independence).

**Getting There & Away** Tram Nos 1 and 3 go to the 'Kadriorg' stop right by Kadriorg

Park. Bus Nos 1, 8, 34 and 38 all run between the city centre and Pirita, stopping on Narva maantee near Kadriorg Park, and at Maarjamäe. Bus Nos 34 and 38 go to the Botanical Gardens (Kloostrimetsa stop) and the TV Tower (Motoklubi stop).

## SOUTHWEST OF THE CENTRE

The **Estonian National Library** (☎ 630 7611; *Tõnismägi 2*), an impressive building which looks as solid as a fortress, is an example of a mini renaissance in the use of Estonia's national stone, dolomite limestone, in architecture. Built in 1982 by Raine Karp (who also designed the similar Sakala conference and cultural centre on Rävala puiestee and the enormous Linnahall concert hall by the port), it's worth seeing the cavernous interior. It also frequently holds worthwhile exhibits on the upper floors (though you may need a day pass from reception).

Some 4km due west of the centre (or a 15-minute ride on Bus No 40 or 48 from Viruväljak) is **Pelguranna**, which supposedly has the cleanest **beach** in the Tallinn area. It has a distinctly 'local' feel but is a pleasant alternative to Pirita.

## Zoo & Rocca al Mare

The **Tallinn Zoo** (☎ 694 3300; *Paldiski maantee 145;* w *www.tallinnzoo.ee; adult/student & child 34/17 EEK; open 9am-5pm daily Sept, Oct & Apr, 9am-3pm daily Nov-Mar, 9am-7pm daily May-Aug*) boasts the world's largest collection of wild goats and 334 different species of animals, birds, reptiles and fish. It's a good place for your kids to meet other kids – the entire child population of northern Estonia is there on summer weekends. Opposite the zoo is **Tivoli** (*day pass 165/55 EEK per adult/child; open 10am-9pm daily, closed winter*) a small amusement park for the kids.

One kilometre beyond the zoo, Rannamõisa tee branches right towards Rocca al Mare and its **Open Air Museum** (☎ 654 9100; *Vabaõhumuuseumi tee 12; adult/child May-Sept 28/10 EEK, Oct-Apr 12/7 EEK; open 10am-6pm daily Oct-Apr, 10am-6pm daily May-Sept*). Note that the buildings close at 6pm, but the grounds are open until 8pm. Most of Estonia's oldest wooden structures, mainly farmhouses as well as a chapel (1699) and windmill, are preserved here. There are views back to the city and you can walk in the 84-hectare woods or down to the sea. Most

## Wooden Architecture

Visitors to Tallinn will likely find the Old Town's pastel architectural delights the most memorable parts of the city. However, the charming, sometimes dilapidated wooden houses which skirt the centre tell a truer story of the city's – and country's – heart and development.

The people of a Nordic, heavily forested land like Estonia will naturally have found many functional uses for its greatest resource, wood. That it would become tied to personal living space is also no surprise, considering the close relationship the ancient dwellers had with wood and the spirits thought to inhabit it. As a living entity, wood was treated with respect – and the respect was mutual, as wood framed all aspects of people's lives, from tools and sailing vessels to houses.

The oldest wooden structures in Tallinn are the **Jaani Seegi Church** (1724) on Tartu maantee 16 (behind the concrete wall), and the **Kazan Church** (1721) at Imanta 33 (along Liivalaia tänav opposite the Hotel Olümpia), which is an odd-looking, intriguing combination of Orthodox and Lutheran baroque styles.

In the late 19th and early 20th centuries, wood provided an expedient, cheap way to house the huge influx of workers flooding the cities. Slum areas developed out of quickly erected tenements. So too, however, did villas, sports facilities, lighthouses, observation towers – buildings to nurture every facet of life. In general, the planning and design of wooden housing was approached with as much reverence and care as with more publicly esteemed stone, limestone or brick buildings.

Wood – mainly pine, spruce and oak – was the main building material in the independent, interwar period, and an attempt was made to incorporate national romantic visions highlighting peasant and country architectural elements into modernised city designs, a back-to-roots trend which recurred periodically throughout the 20th century. A typical feature of this romantic architecture is a sun motif placed atop window frames (see houses at Laulupeo tänav 6, 7, and 10).

Wooden architecture was by no means simple or uniform, and was influenced by fashions and styles. In Tallinn alone, you can see the influences of Art Deco (the lovely houses by St Petersburg architect Alexander Vladovski at Koidula tänav 10, Narva maantee 55 and Jakobsoni tänav 6); Art Nouveau (Koidula tänav 7 & 9, the gorgeous door at Kaupmehe tänav 8); neo-Renaissance (Toompuiestee 21, Roosikrantsi tänav 3) functionalism, classicism, eclecticism and Gothic revivalism.

While modern tastes have turned away from wood as a prime building material (the use of glass and metal in the city centre's 'skyscrapers' has given a completely new look to Tallinn), a few signs point to a comeback – witness the sleek incorporation of wood into the Danish embassy at Wismari tänav 5 and the De La Gardie shopping plaza at Viru tänav 13/15.

Still, the charming wooden houses in the Kadriorg, Kalamaja, Lilleküla and Veerenni areas of the city are endangered species, with natural decay, fires and encroaching business developments threatening them. Take a walk and enjoy them before it's too late!

buildings tend to close earlier than the official opening hours (call for details). On Sunday mornings there are folk song and dance shows. It also has an on-site restaurant serving traditional Estonian meals. Every June, Rocca al Mare celebrates its *Memme-taadi days*, with folk dancing, songs and craft fairs.

Bus No 21 from the train station goes straight to Rocca al Mare, and the zoo is served by trolleybuses No 6 and 7 from the centre.

## OTHER ATTRACTIONS
### Exhibitions

Many of the museums stage temporary exhibitions along with their permanent displays.

Check with the tourist information centre and local listings for exhibitions in art galleries.

In a beautifully restored salt cellar building east of the Old Town, the **Architecture & Arts Centre of Estonia** (☎ 625 7000; *Ahtri tänav 2; adult/student architecture 30/10 EEK, arts 20/5 EEK; open noon-8pm Wed-Sun*) has interesting architectural displays and temporary modern art exhibitions.

Some of the best shows are at **Shifara Galerii** (*Vana-Posti tänav 7*), mainly the works of renowned Estonian graphic artist and printmaker Eduard Wiiralt, acclaimed for his virtuosity in depicting scenes from his many travels and of life within his adopted city of Paris. There's also **City Galerii** (*Harju tänav*

TALLINN

*13)*, the most alternative it gets in Tallinn; **Vaal** *(Väike-Karja tänav 12)*, with hip and modern exhibits; the **Russian Gallery** *(Pikk tänav 19)*, with contemporary Russian paintings; and **Le Galerie Passage** *(Narva maantee 15)*, with funky, interesting exhibits and unusual themes.

Major trade fairs and exhibitions are held at the **Estonian Exhibition Centre** *(☎ 613 7337; Pirita tee 28)*. Special events and prominent exhibitions of sports and culture are regularly held at the **Saku Suurhall**, which hosted Estonia's Eurovision Song Contest in May 2002.

## BOWLING
Bowling has been popular for years. Favoured lanes are at **Al Mare** *(☎ 656 2964; Paldiski maantee 96)* in a big modern complex near the zoo, and **Bowling Club** *(☎ 630 0119; Merivälja tänav 5, Pirita Beach)*.

## SAUNAS
After independence, most public Russian-style *bahnias* were sadly remodelled into their second-cousin variety, Finnish saunas. Still, they are an essential element of any trip to Estonia. If you aren't invited to one by a friend, find your own. The most luxurious in town is on the top floor of the **Reval Hotel Olümpia** *(☎ 631 5333; Liivalaia tänav 33)*. One of the only original places left with the aura of a sweat-out, Russian-style, is the **Kalma Saun** *(☎ 627 1811; Vana-Kalamaja 9A; open 10am-11pm daily)*, in a grand building behind the train station. There are dozens of small, private saunas for rent by the hour around town.

## SWIMMING
For serious swimming in a heavenly, indoor pool of Olympic proportions, head to **Kalev** *(☎ 644 8406; Aia tänav 18)*; sauna is also available. If you just want to splash around or have a few drinks in between laps, **Top** *(☎ 639 8836; Regati puiestee 1)*, inside Hotel Pirita, is your place.

## GOLF
The Baltics' original golf course is the 18-hole **Niitvälja Golf Club** *(☎ 678 0110; open Apr-Nov)*, in Niitvälja, 34km west of Tallinn past Keila, and is accessible by electric train. Other facilities include a café, bar, restaurant and sauna.

## ORGANISED TOURS
Guided tours of Tallinn are now practically made to order. The tourist information office can advise on the range of thematic or novelty tours offered and provide multilingual guides or guides for special interest groups. **Tallinn Walking Tours** *(☎ 610 8616; ℮ incoming@reisiekspert.ee)* runs the Tallinn Official Sightseeing Tour two or three times daily, as well as tailor-made tours costing 100 EEK per person.

## PLACES TO STAY – BUDGET
### Camping
**Kämping Kalev** *(☎/fax 623 9191; Kloostrimetsa tee 56a; tent & parking/caravans 200/275 EEK, 2-/4-bed cabins 320/400 EEK; open mid-May–mid-Sept)* has a good range of budget accommodation 8km from the centre. Meals are available in the pub nearby and there's a handy shop for self-caterers. Take bus number 34 or 38 from Viru väljak in the centre to the Motoklubi stop.

**Peoleo** *(☎ 650 3965; ℗ www.peoleo.ee; Pärnu maantee 555; cabins/singles/doubles from 400/590/780 EEK, camping/beds per person 70/190 EEK; open May-Aug)*, across the street from Leevike, has limited tent space.

### Hostels
**Merevaik** *(☎ 655 3767, fax 656 1127; ℗ www.hostelmerevaik.ee; Sõpruse puiestee 182, 3rd floor; beds with/without HI card 108/120 EEK)* has a common room and self-catering kitchens. Take trolleybus No 2 or 3 from diagonally opposite the Scandic Hotel Palace to the Linnu tee stop.

**Vana Tom** *(☎ 631 3252, fax 612 0511; ℗ www.hostel.ee; Väike-Karja 1; dorm beds 230 EEK, doubles with shared bathroom from 495 EEK)* has an unbeatable location, 30 seconds' walk from Raekoja plats. Try to avoid the top rooms unless you'd like a second-hand experience of the strip club upstairs.

**Tehnika Hostel** *(☎/fax 653 3173; Tehnika 16; dorm beds 200 EEK)* is in a basic apartment block rather close to the railway, but a convenient walk to the Old Town past vintage wooden buildings.

**Hostel Uus 26** *(☎ 641 1281; Uus tänav 26; dorm beds 200 EEK, singles/doubles with shared bathroom 240/400 EEK)* has a friendly reception and convenient Old Town location, although traffic may pass a little close

Raekoja plats (Town Hall Square), Tallinn

Brotherhood of the Blackheads door, Tallinn

Pierced punks, Tallinn

St Nicholas Church (Niguliste Kirik), Tallinn

Sculpture, Tallinn

Rooftops and medieval towers, Tallinn

Pikk jalg (Long Leg), Toompea, Tallinn

to the windows. Be warned, bath and shower facilities may induce claustrophobia.

## Private Homes & Apartments

**Rasastra** (☎/fax 661 6291; W www.bedbreak fast.ee; Mere puiestee 4; singles/doubles/ triples 260/460/640 EEK, breakfast 30 EEK), in the Rotermanni Keskus shopping centre, can set you up in people's houses in central Tallinn and the Baltics.

**Old House** (☎/fax 641 1464; W www.old house.ee; Uus tänav 22; singles/doubles with breakfast 450/650 EEK), a well positioned and professional B&B, offers warm and friendly hospitality in clean surroundings. Apartment rental is also available for up to 10 people.

## Hotels

**TTK Students' Hotel** (☎ 655 2679, fax 655 2666; e ttkhotell@hot.ee; Nõmme tee 47; singles/doubles with shared bathroom 300/ 350 EEK), south of the city centre, is a jaded but budget-friendly place with two-room apartments for one or two people. Note that ISIC card holders receive discounts. Take bus No 17 or 17a to the Koolimaja stop or trolleybus No 2, 3, 4 or 9 to the Tedre stop.

**Eeslitall Hotel** (☎ 631 3755, fax 631 3210; W www.eeslitall.ee; Dunkri tänav 4; singles/ doubles without bath 450/585 EEK) has small rooms that somehow find character from heating and lighting fixtures from the old days. Below is the popular Eeslitall restaurant, giving guests the chance to pop downstairs to the courtyard for a reduced-price breakfast or live music shows. The location is superb and there's 24-hour security; book well ahead for weekends.

**Dorell Hotel** (☎ 626 1200, fax 662 3578; Karu tänav 39; doubles with private/shared bathroom from 600/415 EEK) is another good choice, with clean renovated rooms, sauna access and a bar serving inexpensive meals.

**Helke** (☎ 644 5802, fax 644 5792; Sakala 14; singles/doubles with shared bathroom 400/ 490 EEK) is a friendly place on the southern fringe of the Old Town. Rooms are comfortable and breakfast is included.

**Peoleo** (☎ 650 3965; W www.peoleo.ee; Pärnu maantee 555; cabins/singles/doubles from 400/590/780 EEK, camping/beds per person 70/190 EEK; open May-Aug), across the street from Leevike, has limited tent space and two to four bed cabins, often used for partying. Pets are welcome at 170 EEK. Take bus No 190 from Viru väljak.

## PLACES TO STAY – MID-RANGE

**Valge Villa** (☎/fax 654 2302; Kännu tänav 26/2; singles/doubles with breakfast 550/700 EEK) is a super-friendly, family-run place, a 3km ride from the centre on trolleybus No 2, 3 or 4 to the Tedre stop. It gets great reports from travellers. Each of its comfy rooms has an Internet connection and it has weekend or long-stay specials.

**Susi Hotel** (☎ 630 3300, fax 630 3400; W www.susi.ee; Peterburi tee 48; singles/ doubles with bathroom 600/800 EEK, suite with sauna from 1800 EEK), one of the wackiest, liveliest places in town, is 4km east of the centre. It has colourful and fully equipped rooms in a place that should appeal to the eccentric in everyone. Its Green Spider Night Club reveals a lighter side of Tallinn.

**Hotel Pirita** (☎ 639 8600, fax 639 8821; Regati puiestee 1, Pirita; singles/doubles with bathroom from 795/1080 EEK), a 400-bed, 2-storey hotel, is on the seafront next door to the Olympic Sailing Centre. Rooms are clean and modern, and balconies on the sea side afford views over Tallinn Bay to the city centre. Without this view rooms may seem a little charmless.

**Olematu Rüütel** (☎ 631 3827, fax 631 3826; e nonexistent@hot.ee; Kiriku põik 4a; doubles without/with bathroom 650/800 EEK, extra bed 80 EEK), a boutique guesthouse, is one of few accommodation options on Toompea. Its three spacious rooms are proving popular so early reservations are essential.

## PLACES TO STAY – TOP END

There has been an explosion of sumptuous, first-rate hotels in Tallinn. This category now suffers from an excess of riches, but the choice is yours – just have your credit card ready. Breakfast is included for all of these choices.

**Schlössle** (☎ 699 7700, fax 699 7777; e schlossle@schlossle-hotels.com; Pühavaimu 13/15; singles/doubles from 3560/4150 EEK, child 0-12 yrs free), in Old Town's centre, has sparkling rooms in a complex of buildings that have witnessed 600 years of Tallinn life. All needs are catered for under its five stars.

**St Petersbourg** (☎ 628 6500, fax 628 6565; e stpetersbourg@schlosse-hotels.com;

TALLINN

*Rataskaevu tänav 7; singles/doubles from
3150/3780 EEK)* first opened in the 1850s at
the same spot in the Old Town. The subdued, old-world splendour cannot fail to
charm, as does the Dean Martin played on
high rotation. Free Internet access is available
to guests at all hours.

**Grand Hotel Tallinn** *(☎ 667 7000, fax 667
7001; ⓦ www.grandhotel.ee; Toompuiestee 27;
singles/doubles from 1900/2100 EEK, child 0-
16 yrs free)* has redefined its 164 rooms with
a style to suit professionals. A bar, restaurant and café on-site retain a French theme.

**Domina City Hotel** *(☎ 681 3900, fax 681
3901; ⓔ city@domina.ee; Vana-Posti 11;
singles/doubles from 1800/2100 EEK)* epito-
mises modern classic. A winding marble
stairway and luxuriant foyer give an illusion
of space within the confines of the Old Town.
Promotional packages deserve consideration.

**Metropol** *(☎ 667 4500, fax 667 4600;
ⓦ www.metropol.ee; Mere puiestee 8B; doubles
with/without sauna 1700/1400 EEK)*, with all
manner of services under its roof, seems
fully self-contained; rooms with own sauna
are hard to resist.

**Domina Ilmarine** *(☎ 614 0900, fax 614
0901; ⓔ ilmarine@domina.ee; Põhja puiestee
23; singles/doubles from 1600/1900 EEK,
apartments from 1400 EEK)* reflects its proximity to Scandinavia and the port with its
airy split-level apartments and the friendliest
staff this side of Helsinki.

**Reval Hotel Central** *(☎ 669 0690, fax 669
0691; ⓔ sales@revalhotels.com; Narva maantee 7; singles/doubles from 1100/1300 EEK)*
remains the cheapest of the expensive city-
centre hotels, and has friendly service without pretence a short walk from the Old Town.
Its business centre with Internet facilities
never closes.

With interiors that reveal nothing of their
past, Tallinn's original starlets are still popular despite increasingly tough competition.

**Reval Hotel Olümpia** *(☎ 631 5333, fax 631
5325; ⓔ olympia.sales@revalhotels.com; Liivalaia tänav 33; singles/doubles from 1950/
2300 EEK)*, 700m south of the Old Town, was
built for the 1980 Moscow Olympics. It's
famed for its glass-windowed sauna and buffet breakfast.

**Viru Hotel** *(☎ 630 1311, fax 630 1303;
ⓦ www.viru.ee; Viru väljak 4; singles/doubles
from 1560/1875 EEK)* was perhaps born ugly
in the wrong part of town but has risen to

cult status, due largely to its impeccable service, attention to detail and the mini shopping centre that thrives beneath it.

## PLACES TO EAT
### Restaurants
**Estonian** While in Tallinn, don't forget to
try the meaty local cuisine. Some fine dining options exist in the capital with satisfying rewards for courageous palates and treats
for those more timid. Generally restaurants
in the Old Town offer better value for lunch
than dinner.

**Eesti Maja** *(☎ 645 5252; Lauteri tänav 1;
meals 120 EEK; open 11am-11pm daily)* offers genuine Estonian cuisine. The buffet
allows for a sampling of some exotic meat
dishes without demanding a full-plate commitment.

**Vanaema Juures** *(Grandma's Place; ☎ 626
9080; Rataskaevu tänav 12; meals 140 EEK;
open noon-10pm Mon-Sat, noon-6pm Sun)*
was one of Tallinn's most stylish restaurants
in the 1930s and offers 100% authentic Estonian dishes. It serves non-Estonian dishes
also, with a menu to suit foreign tastes.

**Kuldse Notsu Kõrts** *(☎ 628 6567; Dunkri
tänav 8; meals 110 EEK; open noon-midnight
daily)* has a meaty image and a prevalence
of pork, but this light and cheerful place can
also satisfy vegetarians who choose from
the menu cautiously. Music here is a plus,
though acoustics may distract.

**Nõmme Kõrts** *(☎ 048-58 096; off the
Tallinn-Rapla road; meals 120 EEK; open
noon-midnight Mon-Fri, noon-2pm Sat-Sun)*,
some 45km outside Tallinn, serves delicious huge portions of authentic Estonian
fare in friendly old-fashioned rural ambience, which you won't find in Tallinn. Well
worth the journey, it's an experience beyond
a meal. By car, follow Viljandi maantee for
45km until the Nõmme Kõrts sign to turn
left just before the first railway crossing. All
buses to Rapla and Viljandi stop at the
Aranküla stop, 1km past this turn-off.

**Russian & Caucasian** Options for authentic inexpensive Russian meals have diminished in recent times, although cheap
eats can still be found around the train station and north in Kopli. **Baar** *(Sõle tänav 75;
open 11am-11pm)* is a cellar bar serving
tasty inexpensive Russian meals in a cosy
atmosphere (not to be confused with the

Baar north of the station). Take tram No 1 or 2 to the Maleva stop.

**Rennessans** (☎ 646 4138; Nunne tänav 11; meals 110 EEK; open noon-midnight Mon-Sat, noon-10pm Sun) serves Ukrainian and Russian specialities in a semi-formal setting with some odd touches. Beware the salo…

**Troika** (☎ 627 6245; Raekoja plats 15; meals 140 EEK; open noon-midnight daily) leads in ambience, with evocative otherworldly decor and fine memorable meals. The bar stocks many variations on the theme of vodka.

**Must Lammas** (☎ 644 2031; Sauna tänav 2; meals 170 EEK; open noon-11pm Mon-Fri, noon-6pm Sun) shows a casual sophistication, with a wholesome Georgian menu that goes well with Georgian wine. Try an entrée of dolmas before a Caucasian kebab.

**Asian** There are a few excellent choices for Asian food lovers.

**Golden Dragon** (☎ 631 3506, Pikk tänav 37; meals 140 EEK; open noon-11pm daily) is one of the best bets for Chinese delicacies, with a wide range of excellent seafood dishes.

**Ami-Ja** (☎ 646 6096; Narva maantee 36; meals 100 EEK; open noon-11pm daily) is the only real choice for Japanese food in Tallinn and happens to be first-rate, despite a décor bordering on cafeteria kitsch. It has mouth-watering sushi, and hearty ramen soups.

**Siam** (☎ 641 2460; Olevimägi tänav 4; meals 160 EEK; open noon-11pm daily) is a place that Thai food lovers will not want to leave in a hurry; dishes are reputedly spicy and vegetarians are well catered for.

**Sue Ka Thai** (☎ 641 9347; Vilmsi tänav 6; 120 EEK; open noon-11pm Mon-Sat, noon-10pm Sun) is a rarity in Tallinn, offering inexpensive and pleasantly spiced Asian-inspired meals, best enjoyed after a stroll through nearby Kadriorg. Deliveries can be made.

**Indian** There's no lack of sophisticated restaurants in Tallinn. **Elevant** (☎ 631 3132; Vene tänav 5; meals 170 EEK; open noon-11pm daily) is no exception, with its winding staircase, East-meets-Scandinavia pastel walls and rarefied taste in music. Here, East-meets-Scandinavia decor and a rarefied taste in music. The subdued ambience and spice levels are ideal for those who like it mild.

**Tanduur** (☎ 631 3084; Vene tänav 7; meals 180 EEK; open noon-midnight daily), next door

to Elevant, also offers fine but pricey interpretations of curries, kormas and rogan josh.

**Italian** Pasta lovers won't be disappointed, with a few worthwhile Italian eateries.

**Controvento** (☎ 644 0470; Katariina käik; meals 120 EEK; open noon-11pm daily) is on Tallinn's most atmospheric alleyway (enter through the arch at Vene tänav 12). Pasta lovers could do little better than here. The lasagne is particularly tasty.

**Buongiorno** (☎ 640 6858; Müürivahe 17; meals 110 EEK; open 10am-11pm daily), the most authentic of all the Italian places, is an unprepossessing little cellar space. Its food is simple, tastes great, and reasonably priced. Try the bruschettas or paninis. It also has a full breakfast menu.

**Pudru ja Pasta** (Pikk tänav 35; small/large serves 45/70 EEK; open 11am-11pm daily) has variations on pasta dishes not quite like nonna would make. The vibrant red and cowhide patterned decor adds to the funky atmosphere.

**Other Cuisines** There are very few German restaurants in town. **Bierstube** (☎ 646 1847; Süda tänav 7; meals from 95 EEK; open 11am-midnight daily) is known more for its large selection of imported beer than its meals, but its meaty dishes are large and tasty.

**Kapten Tenkes** (☎ 644 5630; Parnu Maantee 30; meals from 110 EEK; open noon-11pm Mon-Sat, 1pm-10pm Sun) provides an interesting range of Hungarian dishes, such as Fish a la Carpathia. Pray that the wreath of 200+ garlic bulbs overhead doesn't fall on someone you love.

**Cantina Carramba** (☎ 601 3431; Weizenbergi tänav 20A, Kadriorg; mains from 90 EEK; open noon-midnight daily), Tallinn's favourite Tex-Mex place, is where to head for some well flavoured Mexican, with burritos, snacks and main meals.

**Eeslitall** (The Donkey's Stable; ☎ 631 3755; Dunkri tänav 4; meals 120 EEK; open 9am-midnight), dating from the 16th century, is a fairly calm, laid-back place with a good cellar bar and a rear courtyard which bursts into life each summer. It's below the Eeslitall Hotel just off Raekoja plats, and has a small vegetarian menu as well as an excellent salad buffet.

**Raeköök** (☎ 627 6520; Dunkri tänav 5; meals around 80 EEK), opposite Eeslitall, with a staple fare of fillets and pizzas; sauna is also available in this huge complex.

**Lübeck** (☎ 646 4082; Pikk 43; meals 70 EEK; open 11am-11pm daily) has a fierce grill that transforms your chosen raw ingredients into a meal. If fast food chains existed in the Hanseatic days they would have looked like this.

**Top End** Decadently tasteful **Lydia** (☎ 626 8990; Koidula tänav 13A; meals from 220 EEK; open noon-11pm Mon-Fri, noon-7pm Sun) has a cigar lounge, a formal dining room and summer terrace. The meals claim inspiration from poet Lydia Koidula.

**Mõõkala** (Swordfish; ☎ 631 3583; Rüütli tänav 16/18; meals from 220 EEK; open noon-midnight daily) is where seafood fans will find paradise. An exquisite array of ordinary and exotic fish is served in a cosy cellar setting in what was once the home of Tallinn's executioner, hence perhaps the name.

**Olde Hansa** (☎ 627 9020; Vanaturg tänav 1; meals from 190 EEK; open 11am-midnight daily) is the favourite of the jovial medieval-themed restaurants in Tallinn. If the costumed waiters don't pull you in, intrigue over its well crafted menu will. It's the city's most lucrative restaurant, perhaps due to its popularity with tour groups.

**Vana Tunnel** (☎ 631 0630; Harju tänav 6; meals 180 EEK; open noon-11pm Mon-Sat) offers swift service, decent grills, casual elegance and a memorable experience inside a medieval water tunnel.

**Le Bonaparte** (☎ 646 6666; Pikk tänav 46; meals 290 EEK; open noon-3pm & 7pm-midnight Mon-Sat, closed Sun) serves superior French cuisine, and you will be coddled and pampered as your wallet thins. Its café provides a similar indulgence at less cost.

**Gloria** (☎ 644 6950; Müürivahe 2; meals from 240 EEK), considered Tallinn's best and most refined restaurant, is nestled neatly in the Old Town wall. Expect a fusion of Russian- and French-inspired delicacies at top prices. It also has a formidable wine cellar (see Entertainment later in this chapter).

**Egoist** (☎ 646 4052; Vene tänav 33; meals from 300 EEK) is in a league of its own. The menu boasts classic decadent delights such as lobster and duck prepared to perfection, as you'd expect for this price. Its wine list will impress.

## Cafés

**Light Meals** If you're after a quick snack, there are plenty of excellent options in the city centre.

**Café Anglais** (☎ 644 2160; Raekoja plats 14, 2nd floor; open 11am-11pm daily), overlooking Town Hall Square, is an understated meeting place for some of the eccentric types of Tallinn, who know the value of its good coffee and home-made pastries, French-style sandwiches and salad.

**Neitsitorn** (☎ 644 0896; Lühike jalg 9A; open 11am-10pm daily) is well worth the climb to Toompea. In one of the old towers of the city wall, this café serves good hõõgvein (mulled wine), great coffee and standard meals with fine views.

**Võitlev Sõna** (☎ 627 2627; Pärnu maantee 28; meals 120 EEK) is polished industrial chic amid much talk and mobile phone calls, not to mention great curries. Downstairs has a 'mission control' feel.

**Crêperie Sans Nom** (Müürivahe 23A; meals 80 EEK) creates an elegant atmosphere; meat and dessert crêpes are its specialities, using a finer buckwheat flour than the Breton originals.

**Café Toome** (☎ 662 1875; Toompuiestee 29; meals 70 EEK) is a casual, fun, yet stylish place due to its Art Deco-revival interior and tasty, satisfying meals.

**Imanta** (☎ 645 5389; Rävala puiestee 9; open 10am-5pm Mon-Fri only; meals 50 EEK), another good bet for cheap fill-ups, is a cafeteria-style place.

**Võiroos** (☎ 641 8237; Kaarli puiestee 4; open 24hr), a friendly shack, gets smoky and rather interesting in the early hours as it attracts an unusual crowd who drift in to graze before dawn.

**Coffee & Cakes** Tallinn's tradition of fine cakes and pastries appeals to anyone seeking new depths of indulgence. Patisseries offer French favourites and unique Estonian treats.

**Maiasmokk** (Sweet-Tooth Café & Restaurant; ☎ 646 4070; Pikk tänav 16; meals 190 EEK; open noon-midnight daily) has been considered a favourite since 1865, and to this day its Art Nouveau tearoom is nearly always packed. Maiasmokk held a place of honour as the most elite café during Estonia's pre-WWII period of independence; the upstairs restaurant has popular old-world dishes.

**Tristan ja Isolde** (☎ 644 8759; Town Hall building, Raekoja plats; open 8am-11pm daily) is an essential stop for coffee connoisseurs offering a wide variety of freshly roasted brews. The good fruit cocktails, smoothies and unpasteurised Estonian beer are equally enticing alternatives.

**Poliina** (Gonsiori 10; open 9am-11pm daily) has a good selection of fine salads and meat patés (take-away possible) alongside scrumptious vegetarian offerings.

**Gateway** (☎ 644 6307; Suur-Karja tänav 17/19) is a sparkling new café with pastry treats that have already won popular support.

**Türgi Kohv** (Pärnu maantee 40) is ideal if you need a caffeine kick on the run. Turkish coffee and not much else is sold in this neat little space.

## Fast Food

**Armaada Sandwicherie** (Georg Otsa tänav; hot baguette rolls from 25 EEK; open 24hr) is a quick takeaway option around the corner from the Drama Theatre where burgers seem to have interbred with baguettes under dangerous levels of sour cream.

If you want a burger, you won't need to search far for popular fast food chains such as **Hesburgers** and **Nehatu's**, which pepper Viru tänav, Viru väljak and the train station.

**Peetri Pizza** (delivery ☎ 656 7567; pizzas from 40 EEK) has numerous outlets doling out thin-crusted and pan pizzas, including ones at Pärnu maantee 22 (takeaway only), Mere puiestee 6 and on Pirita tee across from the Hotel Pirita.

**Sbarro's** (Endla tänav 45), the NY based pizza/pasta franchise inside the Kristiine Shopping Centre, offers a real US experience.

**Coffik** (Suur tänav 18) is a relaxed bar and café with a buffet in the basement below. Cheap and filling meals are available downstairs for under 40 EEK, with every salad known to cabbage in its salad bar.

## Self-Catering

The always-bustling **Central market** (Kesk-turg; open 7am-5pm daily), off Lastekodu tänav (take tram No 2 or 4 to the Keskturg stop), is the best place for fresh meats and vegies.

The **supermarkets** inside Kaubamaja and Stockmann at Liivalaia tänav 53, as well as the **Rimi Kaubahall** (Aia tänav) in the Old Town, have excellent selections, impressive

as the US-style food emporiums out in the suburbs, like **Maksimarket** (Paldiski maantee 102), past the zoo.

## ENTERTAINMENT

Large multilingual posters listing what's on where are plastered up at every major street corner in the Old Town, including the corner of Harju and Niguliste, the corner of Vene tänav and Vana Turg, and next to the Viru Gate. The *Baltic Times* runs weekly entertainment listings, and the **free information hotline** (☎ 626 1111) can also tell you what's on where, and is in English.

### Pubs & Bars

Pubs in Tallinn, as elsewhere double as popular night spots and are usually open from around 11am to as late as 4am daily, closing earlier on Sundays.

**Nimeta Baar** (Bar with No Name; ☎ 641 1515; Suur-Karja tänav 4/6) retains its popularity with ex-pats and visitors due to its central location, flavoursome meals, popular music, sports telecasts and beers.

**Nimega Baar** (Bar with a Name; ☎ 620 9299; Suur-Karja tänav 13), Nimeta's sister pub, is equally popular and makes a good alternative.

**Kloostri Ait** (☎ 644 6887; Vene tänav 14), aside from being a focal Tallinn meeting place, is a very relaxed veteran on the scene with occasional good folk music concerts.

**Von Krahli Theatre Baar** (☎ 626 9090 Rataskaevu 10/12) is another old favourite and the experimental theatre inside is well worth a visit. It often has jazz bands, and its unique atmosphere and young, energetic crowd makes it a really good place to meet friends.

**Kõwer Kõrts** (☎ 644 8852; Viru tänav 8), on the main drag just a few metres from the Viru gate, attracts tourists and locals with its large beer selection and fun atmosphere.

**Levi'st Väljas** (Olevimägi 12), which translates roughly as 'out of range', is a true alternative which hasn't lost its blighted underground feel and remains a haven off the tourist path, especially for Tom Waits fans.

**X-Baar** (☎ 620 9166; Sauna tänav 1; open 2pm-1am daily), right in the Old Town, is the city's most popular gay and lesbian bar. Look for the rainbow flag outside.

The following places, out of the centre, are for those who want to meet local people

TALLINN

and get a feel for Tallinn life outside the protective bubble of the Old Town.

**Buldogi Pubi** (☎ 650 4123; Jaama 2), in the centre of the upmarket suburb Nõmme, is big, lively, friendly and popular with the locals.

**Jussi Õlletuba** (☎ 623 8696; Liilia tee 2), in Merivälja (north of Pirita), is a friendly, relaxed pub with billiards and live music.

**Baar** (Vana Kalamaja 30; open 9am-11pm daily) is north of the train station. If you really want cheap drinks in a happening, local setting, you'll feel like you slipped into another world here. Friday nights are especially popular, and the place attracts an eclectic mix. It's also a good spot to drop into after a trip to the nearby sauna (see Activities earlier).

## Wine Cellars

**Vinoteek** (☎ 631 3891; Niguliste tänav 6) select from the world's vineyards mapped out for your convenience. Imbibe peacefully at a table that awaits or have your wine accompany you elsewhere.

**Gloria Veinikelder** (☎ 644 6950; Müürivahe 2) offers a vast wine selection and a cosy ambience for connoisseurs who wish to inspect one of the Baltic's finest cellars.

## Nightclubs

Dance music is the pulse of Tallinn. The monthly **Vibe** (w www.vibe.ee) and **Mutant Disco** (w www.mutantdisco.com) events should not be missed for the latest offerings from a range of imported and local DJs. See the websites for dates and locations. Otherwise the mainstream clubs are the most popular.

**Spirit** (☎ 661 6080; Mere puiestee 6a; open 10pm-4am Wed-Sat, café open 11am-11pm daily) is a sophisticated Scandinavian-inspired bar with rave arena upstairs, which hosts a fluid list of guest DJs.

**Terrarium** (☎ 661 4721; w www.terrarium .ee; Sadama 6; open 10pm-5am Fri & Sat) is an increasingly popular, slightly more down-to-earth club by the port.

**Hollywood** (☎ 627 4770; w www.club -hollywood.ee; Vana-Posti tänav 8; open 10pm-5am Fri & Sat), inside the Sõprus cinema, attracts the largest crowds of Tallinn's youth and beauty to a techno beat.

**Opium** (☎ 620 0123; Merivälja 5; open 10pm-4am Fri & Sat) is another upscale disco playing relentless pop, inside the Pirita beach house, located about 6km from the city centre.

**Sossi** (☎ 601 4384; Tartu maantee 82; open 10pm-1am Wed, 10pm-3am Thur-Sat) will play the kind of nostalgia that draws a more mature crowd and those who prefer music as it was, before it went digital.

**Decolte** (☎ 666 4999; Ahtri 10a; open 10pm-5am Wed-Sat) satisfies demand for some of the tackier aspects of club culture: light shows, live dancing, overactive smoke machines and under-aged clubbers.

**Nightman** (☎ 626 1847; Vineeri tänav 4, off Pärnu maantee; open 9pm-4am Wed & Thur, 10pm-6am Fri & Sat) is Tallinn's main gay and lesbian club, and an increasingly popular hangout for a straight and alternative crowd.

## Cinemas

The worst of US blockbusters and comedies are shown here, all in original English, with subtitles. The main cinemas in Tallinn are the **Kino Sõprus** (Vana-Posti 8), slap-bang in the Old Town in a beautiful, grand Stalin-era building; and the **Kino Kosmos** (Pärnu maantee 45).

**Kino Forum** (☎ 644 8466; Uus tänav 3), close to the Viru Gate, shows foreign, cult and alternative films.

## Opera, Ballet, Dance & Theatre

Tallinn has several companies staging dramas (including translations of Western plays) in repertory from September until the end of May. Everything is in Estonian (except at the Russian Drama Theatre). A useful website is for listings is w www.concert.ee.

**Estonia Theatre** (box office ☎ 626 0215, 626 0260; Estonia puiestee 4; tickets 20-200 EEK; box office open noon-7pm daily), Tallinn's main theatre, also houses the Estonian National Opera and Ballet. Tickets for matinee performances are available one hour before the performance begins.

Other theatres include the **Russian Drama Theatre** (☎ 641 8246; Vabaduse väljak 5); the **Estonian Drama Theatre** (☎ 644 3378); and the **Puppet Theatre** (Nukuteater; ☎ 641 1617; Lai tänav 1).

**Von Krahli Theatre** (☎ 626 9090; Rataskaevu tänav 10) is known for its experimental and fringe productions. **St Canutus Guild hall** (☎ 646 4704; Pikk tanav 20) hosts classic and modern dance performances.

City Theatre (Linnateater; ☎ 665 0800; Lai tänav 23) is the most beloved theatre in town and always puts on something memorable.

## Classical Music

The Hortus Musicus Early Music Consort and the Estonia Philharmonic Chamber Orchestra and Choir are Tallinn's leading smaller musical ensembles. For information on the excellent Hortus Musicus, call its headquarters at Väravatorn (☎ 644 0719).

The Estonia Concert Hall (Kontserdisaal; ☎ 614 7761; Estonia puiestee 4), adjoining the Estonia Theatre, is where the city's major classical music events are held two or three times weekly. Tickets can be bought from the box office inside the concert hall.

Chamber, organ, solo and other smaller-scale concerts are held in the Estonia Theatre café and several halls around town, such as the Town Hall (Raekoja; ☎ 645 7900; Raekoja plats), and the Brotherhood of the Blackheads (☎ 644 1511; Pikk tänav 26), which has concerts almost nightly.

St Nicholas Church (Niguliste Kirik; ☎ 644 9911), which has incredible acoustics, holds chamber music concerts on weekends.

Pühavaimu Kirik (Holy Spirit Church; ☎ 646 4430; Pühavaimu tänav 2) offers free concerts; check information outside the Church for details.

The City Concert Hall (☎ 641 1500; Mere puiestee 20) is a 4200-seat venue in the Linnahall near the harbour. Some big events are held here.

Tickets for all these venues are also sold at the Estonia Concert Hall box office and at the tourist information centre (see Information – Tourist Offices, earlier).

## SHOPPING

Retail pleasures abound with most shops and boutiques concentrated conveniently in the Old Town. But 'mall culture' has already made inroads, with megastores in the outlying areas.

Kristiine Shopping Centre (Endla tänav 45) is an actual US-style indoor mall, authentic down to the food court, escalators, screaming babies and teens with nothing to do. Take tram number 2 or 3 from the centre.

Rotermanni Keskus (Mere puiestee 4) is the place to see what an Estonian version of a mall looks like, if only for the sake of comparison.

Kadaka Turg market (cnr Tammsaare & Mustamäe tee, Mustamäe; trolley No 1, bus No 92), a must-visit for bargain hunters, is filled with clothes and gadgets of all kinds and is a great place to watch people.

Traditional knitted sweaters, hats, gloves and socks, hand-made leather-bound books and bottles are the most popular Estonian souvenir items and can be found in dozens of shops throughout the Old Town. All sizes and styles can be found just inside the city walls on Müürivahe near the Viru Gate.

Käsitöö (Weizenbergi tänav 27, Kadriorg), opposite the last stop on tram No 1 and 3, is the best place to buy traditional folk costumes. You'll find souvenirs at cheaper prices here than in town.

Helina Tilk (Voorimehe puiestee 3) is the place to pop into if you fancy some funky porcelain and other inspired quirky objects.

Keraamika (Pikk 33), top of the class in funkiness, is a great little place where you can watch the potter at work amid a jungle of wild ceramics for sale.

Bogapott (Pikk jalk 9) is where you can sip coffee while watching the potters at work.

Some of the best antique shops in town include Antiik & Kunst (Dunkri tänav 9) and Antikvaar (Rataskaevu 20/22).

One can hardly leave Estonia without a bottle of the national liqueur, Vana Tallinn (or the gift box with mini bottles), but a more original souvenir would be a Navitrolla T-shirt, on sale at Le Galerie Passage (Narva maantee 15).

## GETTING THERE & AWAY

This section concentrates on transport between Tallinn and other places in the Baltics. See the introductory Getting There & Away chapter for details on ferry, air, train and bus links with countries outside the Baltic region. The Tallinn Information section lists some useful travel agents.

### Air

Rīga is served by airBaltic through codeshare with Estonian Air three days weekly, while Finnair flies six days weekly. To Vilnius, Finnair flies three days weekly also through code-share with Lithuanian Airlines, Estonian Air flies five days weekly. Prices fluctuate, but expect to pay around 3200 EEK for all Rīga and Vilnius fares. Pärnu-based company Air Livonia (☎ 44-75 007,

*fax 75 006;* e *info@airlivonia.ee)* flies from
Pärnu to Kuressaare (Saaremaa) weekly (200
EEK) via Ruhnu Island, with additional
flights to Ruhnu weekly. Flights from Pärnu
to Kihnu Island leave daily (120 EEK). **Avies**
(☎ *605 8022, fax 621 2951)* also flies several
times weekly to/from Tallinn and Kuressaare;
flying time is about 45 minutes (495 EEK return). Most airlines offer youth fares. Estonian airports have charter flights to destinations
within Estonia and throughout the region.

**Tallinn airport** (☎ *605 8888;* w *www.tallinn
-airport.ee)* is 3km southeast of the city centre
on Tartu maantee.

Airline offices in Tallinn include:

**Estonian Air** (☎ 640 1101; e ov@estonian-air.ee)
  Leenujaama tee 13
**Finnair** (☎ 611 0950, airport 605 8333; e finn
  air@finnair.ee) Roosikrantsi 2

A regular helicopter service (14 times daily
on weekdays) shuttles passengers between
Helsinki and Tallinn, taking 18 minutes to
complete the journey from Tallinn's Linnahall terminal roof to central Helsinki (single/
return from 1610/2130 EEK). Tickets can
be bought in Tallinn from **Copterline**
(☎ *610 1818, fax 610 1919;* e *copterline@
copterline.ee; Mere puiestee 20).* There's
also an office in Helsinki (☎ *358-9-681
1670, fax 358-9-681 16767;* e *contact@
copterline.com; Hernesaari, Hernematalankatu
2, Helsinki).*

## Bus

Buses to places within 40km or so of
Tallinn, and some buses to Pärnu, go from
the local bus station beside the train station.
Information and timetables for these services can be had 24 hours via **Harju Linnid**
(☎ *644 1801).*

For detailed bus information and advance
tickets for all other destinations, go to the
**central bus station** (*Autobussijaam;* ☎ *680
0900; Lastekodu tänav 46),* 1km along
Juhkentali from the Hotel Olümpia. It has a
large and easy-to-understand timetable, an
information desk staffed by people who
speak some English, a left-luggage room
and a café. A useful website for bus timetables throughout Estonia can be found at
w www.bussireisid.ee. Although it's in Estonian, you probably won't need to look for
an interpreter.

Eurolines tickets to Russia, Latvia, Lithuania and other international destinations are
not sold at the main ticket counters, but at
the far end of the main hall in the **Eurolines
office** (☎ *680 0909, fax 680 0901;* w *www.eu
rolines.ee; open 6.30am-11.30pm Mon-Fri).*

Services within the Baltic region to/from
Tallinn include:

**Haapsalu** 52 EEK, 1½ hours, 100km, more than
  20 buses daily
**Kärdla** 130 EEK, 4½ hours, 160km, three buses
  daily
**Kuressaare** 160 EEK, 4½ hours, 220km, nine
  buses daily
**Narva** 75 EEK, 4 hours, 210km, 15 buses daily
**Pärnu** 60 EEK, 2 hours, 130km, more than 20
  buses daily
**Rīga** 200 EEK, 5½ hours, 310km, five buses daily
**Tartu** 80 EEK, 2½-3½ hours, 190km, about 30
  buses daily
**Vilnius** 400 EEK, 12 hours, 600km, two buses
  daily
**Võru** 85 EEK, 4½ hours, 250km, seven buses daily

## Train

**Central station** (*Balti jaam; Toompuiestee 35)*
is just outside the northwest edge of the Old
Town. Tram Nos 1 and 2 go from Kopli
tänav at the back of the station and travel to
the Linnahall stop near the ferry terminals,
continuing to the Mere puiestee stop near
the Viru hotel. Tram No 1 then heads east
along Narva maantee to Kadriorg, and No 2
goes south down Tartu maantee to the Autobussijaam stop near the bus station.

The central station has two ticket areas:
one at ground level sells tickets to destinations within Estonia; and upstairs in the
main hall tickets are sold for destinations
outside Estonia. Tickets for suburban trains
(referred to as *elektrirong* or electric train)
servicing the Tallinn area, including Paldiski, are sold in a separate building situated
behind the station near the platforms.

The twice-weekly Tallinn–Minsk train
passes through Rīga and Vilnius. The *Baltic
Express* between Warsaw and Tallinn no
longer operates.

St Petersburg and Tallinn are serviced by
an overnight train on alternate evenings
(228/390 EEK 3rd/2nd class, 1st class not
available, nine hours). An overnight train
every evening runs between Moscow and
Tallinn (724/1459 EEK 2nd/1st class, around
14 hours).

The main services within Estonia include:

**Kloogaranna** 12 EEK, 1 hour, 39km, three trains
   daily
**Narva** 70 EEK, 4 hours, 210km, one train daily
**Paldiski** 12 EEK, 1¼ hours, 48km, 10 trains daily
**Pärnu** 40 EEK, 3 hours, 141km, two trains daily
**Tartu** 70 EEK, 3½ hours, 190km, two trains daily
**Valga** 115 EEK, 5 hours, 252km, one train daily

## Car & Motorcycle
There are 24-hour fuel stations run by foreign
oil companies Neste, Statoil and Shell, at
strategic spots in the city and on major roads
to/from Tallinn. They also sell a terrific range
of imported sweets, chocolates and junk-food
delights. Note that entry for cars into the Old
Town now costs 25 EEK. **Tallinn traffic
police** (☎ 612 5605; Rahumäe tee 6).

**Car Rental** Finding a car to rent in Tallinn
for less than 900 EEK is a minor miracle.
It's much cheaper to rent a car in Tartu,
Pärnu or Võru (see regional chapters for details). Some car rental agencies have offices
in each of the Baltic capitals, allowing you
to hire a car in one city and drop it off in another. Some of the major agencies include:

**Avis** (☎ 605 8222, fax 638 8221) Airport
**Hertz** (☎ 605 8923, fax 605 8953; e hertz@
   hertz.ee) Airport
   (☎ 611 6210, fax 611 6209;
   e reservation@hertz.ee) Ahtri tänav 12
**Tulika Rent** (☎ 612 0012, fax 612 0041) Tihase
   34 – bookings through Palace, Olümpia,
   Central and Peoleo hotels

## Boat
Tallinn's two main ferry terminals (sadama)
are at the eastern end of Sadama tänav about
1km northeast of the Old Town. Only Linda
Line hydrofoils to Helsinki leave from the
**Linnahall terminal** (☎ 641 2412); look for
the enormous limestone structure.

The **main Passenger Port** (☎ 631 8550;
Sadama tänav 21-29) is divided into four terminals and handles all other boat traffic. The
main terminal has a café, bar, shops and left-
luggage room. Tram Nos 1 and 2 heading
north along Mere puiestee, and bus Nos 3, 4
and 8 travelling west along Narva maantee
go to the Linnahalli stop (by the Statoil fuel
station) at the western end of Sadama, a five-
minute walk from all the terminals. A private
shuttle bus (25 EEK) runs every 15 minutes

between the main terminal and the Viru,
Palace and Olümpia hotels.

The shipping lines' main booking offices
are:

**Eckerö Line** (☎ 631 8606) Passenger Port,
   terminal B
**Linda Line** (☎ 641 2412) Linnahall Port
**Nordic Jet** (☎ 613 7000, fax 613 7222) Passenger
   Port, terminal C
**Silja Line** (☎ 611 6661, fax 611 6655) Passenger
   Port, terminals A & D
**Tallink** (☎ 640 9800; w www.tallink.ee) Passenger
   Port, terminal A

You can also buy tickets from a number of
travel agents around town.

Canoes and rowboats can be hired from
the **Pirita marina** (☎ 639 8980; Regati puiestee
1), behind the Pirita Hotel. For yachting information, yacht hire and activities contact
the **Tallinn Olympic Yachting Centre** (☎ 639
8800, fax 639 8964; w www.piritatop.ee).

## GETTING AROUND
### To/From Airport
Tallinn airport is on the Tartu road 3km
southeast of the centre. Bus No 2 runs every
30 minutes or so from outside the Art University (Kuunstakadeemia), tickets are 10
EEK purchased from kiosks or 15 EEK
from the driver. A taxi from the airport to
the city centre should cost around 80 EEK.

### Bus, Tram & Trolleybus
The Old Town is best explored on foot.
Buses, trams and trolleybuses will take you
everywhere else from 5am or 6am to about
midnight. Tickets (piletid) or day and month
passes are sold from street kiosks, single trip
tickets are 10 EEK, or individual tickets can
be purchased (at a higher price) from the driver. Visit w www.bussireisid.ee for the latest
timetables (in Estonian only).

### Train
Few of the suburban rail services from the
central station in Tallinn go to places of
much interest in the city. The one line that
may be useful heads south to Nõmme,
Pääskula and Laagri. There are about 40
daily trains along this line from 5.20am
until a little after midnight. Most continue
beyond the city bounds to Keila, Paldiski or
Kloogaranna, but some only go as far as
Pääskula.

## Islands

To understand a country and its people, just look at a map – for geography marks a nation. Estonia's most conspicuous feature is water. The coastline is 3794km long. Water indents the shores, jaggedly, gently, and seeps onto land from 420 rivers and 1400 lakes, creating vast swamplands and wild bogs.

In Estonia's waters lie 1521 islands – 4133 sq km of territory. Most are uninhabited, tiny dots. But the inhabited, accessible ones are an essential, formative part of the country; places where old traditions are kept alive, places of retreat and isolation, and places of great beauty.

Around Tallinn, the easily accessible islands will give you more of an 'Estonian experience' than extra time in the capital. Larger islands like Saaremaa and Hiiumaa, the southern islands of Kihnu and Ruhnu, and the eastern island of Piirisaar are dealt with in their respective chapters.

### Aegna

A 45-minute ferry trip from Pirita Harbour (or, if the water is low, a hop, skip and wade from Rohuneeme, at the northern point of the peninsula stretching out past Pirita), this tiny 3 sq km island is the most frequently visited and easily accessed. It has been populated for centuries by local fishers and, from 1689, postal workers who operated mail boats from there to Sweden via Finland. It was a Soviet military base, off-limits to Tallinners until 1975, and to other Estonians until 1991. However, by the 1960s bureaucrats were already building *dachas* on the island, which was a vacation retreat between the wars. Today, there are military remnants, an old church and cemetery, remains of a medieval village, a store, café and mini golf. Roads and paths through forests lead to splendid picnic spots on sandy beaches. The best ones line the north coast.

Aegna was the scene of a tragedy in 1999; schoolchildren found a WWII bomb and one girl died when it went off. Bombs are still an occasional problem in the forests and marshes from Murmansk to Odesa; however, generally this island is well-trodden and safe.

### Getting There & Away

The **Tallinn tourist information centre** (☎ 645 7777) will set you up with a place to stay in one of the small hotels on the island and provide information on chartering a boat (see also Yacht Charter in this chapter). Ferries run daily in summer from **Pirita Harbour** (☎ 639 8980) to Aegna, though schedules change from season to season. Visit the **Monica Cruise website** (W www.hot.ee/monica cruise) for details on cruises from Pirita–Aegna–Naissar.

### Naissaar

Only 8.5km from the mainland in Tallinn Bay is Naissaar, the sixth largest island in Estonia at 18.6 sq km. It has been used for the military defence of the capital since the Great Northern War. A railway was even built before WWI for a speedier build-up of armaments. Curiously, in 1917–18, tsarist troops took the island and tried to form their own government. Soviet military traces remain (the island was closed until 1995), with an old army village, gun batteries, empty mines and deep-sea mine anchors. Forest covers 85% of the island. There are dreamy stretches of unblemished beaches and two nature trails: south takes you to historical sights, such as memorials, military ruins, a wooden church, a cemetery for English sailors from the Crimean (1854–55) and Russo-Swedish (1808–09) wars; north goes through forests, mires and past large erratic boulders (one has a perimeter of 26.7m).

### Places to Stay & Eat

**Võisilma Nature Centre** (mobile ☎ 051-03 850) organises accommodation and meals on Naissaar, but usually restrict their activities to the warmer months. Call ahead for information on opening times and bookings. You could also stay down the east coast in a small village farmhouse called **Rähnipesa** (mobile ☎ 052 48 103; beds with breakfast 200 EEK). There are comfy beds in rustic surroundings, a sauna (200 EEK per hour) and a small bar. Extra meals can be ordered and boat rental is possible.

## Islands

### Getting There & Away
Visit the Monica Cruise website (**W** www.hot.ee/monicacruise) regarding ferry cruises to Naissaar. Tallinn-based **Bona Reisid** (**☎** 630 6670; **e** info@bonareisid.ee) can organise trips to the island, with or without tour guides. Rähnipesa (see Places to Stay & Eat earlier) can also arrange transport. Prices vary, but expect around 500 EEK for a round trip. For further information on the island, contact the **Naissaar Nature Park Administration** (**☎** 654 0842; koitnlp@hot.ee).

### The Pakri Islands
Across from Paldiski, 52km west of Tallinn are Väike (small) and Suur (large) Pakri, a misnomer as Väike Pakri at 12.9 sq km is 120 hectares larger than Suur Pakri, to which it is connected by a causeway. They were settled in 1345 by Swedes from the Padise monastery on the mainland. Later communities made a living from fishing and seal-hunting. Four villages were formed, two churches built, a museum founded, and the inhabitants (340 by the early 1930s) developed a Swedish dialect heavily influenced by Estonian. From 12–16 August 1944, the islands were evacuated and taken over by the Soviet army. They were off-limits for the next 50 years. Suur Pakri especially suffered, its surface blown to bits by bombing units' target practice.

The islands are open only to visitors with a permit (easy to obtain) because the Soviets left behind rusty bomb and missile shells and even unexploded ammunition. Further, water in puddles contains a bacteria that causes a nasty disease, Tularemia. But don't panic – leave pieces of metal and puddles alone and you'll have these very special islands to yourself. Shrubs, juniper groves and grasslands cover them, but the highlights are the exposed, impressive Estonian Glint's limestone cliffs. The northeast of Väike Pakri is especially beautiful – with some care, you can climb down to the beach to appreciate the cliffs up close. Dirt roads for mountain biking crisscross the islands.

### Getting There & Away
Contact the Tallinn tourist information centre regarding your plans to visit. They can advise on permits and also help find people to boat you across and back, or you can hire your own boat from **Paldiski** (**☎** 678 0402) or **Lohusalu Harbour** (**☎** 677 1640; **e** lohusalu@grupp.ee).

### Prangli
This 6 sq km island lies 18km northwest of the Leppneeme Harbour. Its history is also connected to the Swedes, who arrived in the late 13th century. Now only 150 people live there. Half of the island is forested, and several roads extend to the north and southwestern tips. The tips curl around, forming small bays and inlets, themselves dotted with islets. There's a church, cemetery, wonderfully deserted sandy beaches on the south coast, and not much else but glorious peace and quiet.

### Places to Stay & Eat
There is basic accommodation at the **Kelnase Harbour** (**☎** 654 0942). If you bring your own tent the people at the harbour will show you the permitted areas on the island. Accommodation in an old schoolhouse can be arranged through **Walter Puuström** (**☎** 654 0940). There is a convenience shop and café at the harbour.

### Getting There & Away
Boats generally leave twice a day (early morning and early evening, returning from Prangli shortly after arriving) from **Leppneeme Harbour** (**☎** 609 1319) or call **Helge boat service** (mobile **☎** 056 460 966). Bus No 115 from beside the Tallinn train station goes to Leppneeme three times a day (from the stop it's a 1.5km walk to the harbour), or there's an early morning minibus that leaves Merivälja (at the end of Bus line No 1 from central Tallinn) at 8am, in time to catch the morning boat. In winter call the Leppneeme Harbour for information on the latest weather conditions and advice on reaching Prangli, or contact Bona Reisid (see details earlier). Further information on Prangli and the Helge boat service is available through the **Viimsi Community** (**☎** 606 6805; **e** info@viimsivv.ee).

### Route-Taxi

From 7am to 12.30am-1am there are route-taxis *(liinitaksod)*, minibuses with a flat fare of 10 EEK (pay the driver). They drop passengers anywhere along their fixed routes out to the suburbs. The terminal is beside the Viru hotel.

### Taxi

Taxis are supposed to cost a minimum of 7 EEK/km, with a minimum price of 35 EEK per journey. Tallinn taxis are the best and most numerous in the Baltics; drivers use their meters and adhere to prices agreed upon beforehand for longer journeys. There are ranks at the bus and train stations, at Viru väljak and along Georg Otsa tänav. Ordering by phone will get you cheaper rates; try **Linnatakso** (☎ 644 2442).

# Around Tallinn

Countryside and unspoiled coast are not far from Tallinn and there are several places worth making time to visit. All are local telephone calls from the city.

### WEST OF TALLINN
### Beaches & Cliffs

The coast west of Tallinn is a favourite summer escape for city folk and the first long, sandy beach is at **Vääna-Jõesuu**, 24km from the city centre. From the main coast road it's about 600m down a side track to the beach. The beach continues south across the mouth of the Vääna River, where there's a stretch of 30m cliffs, one of the highest on the Estonian coast. The road runs right along the cliff top to a very popular lookout called Türisalu (45m), some 2km after the Naage bus stop (the Russian film version of *Hamlet* was filmed here). This is a traditional destination for newlyweds and for those just practising. There are more beaches further west at **Lohusalu**, and at **Laulasmaa** and **Kloogaranna** on Lahepera Bay, all 35-40km from Tallinn.

### Keila & Keila-Joa

About 30km west of Tallinn, the small village of Keila-Joa near the coast boasts a lovely little waterfall (at 6.1m the second highest in the country). There's a manor house (1883) on the banks of the falls. The large park and forest which surround it are perfect for a day's picnicking or hiking (1.7km to the sea).

Keila, a small town some 11km southeast of Keila-Joa, is the region's main centre, and has the excellent **Harjumaa Museum** (☎ 678 1668; Linnuse tänav 9; adult/student 8/5 EEK; open 11am-4pm Wed-Sun Nov-Mar, 11am-6pm Wed-Sun Apr-Oct). It features exhibits on some ancient archaeological finds as well as how life was lived on the Pakri islands.

If you'd like to stay in the area, you could try **Jaagu Farmhotel** (☎ 671 7072; beds 150 EEK), which offers basic farm accommodation 4km south of Keila.

### Paldiski
#### pop 4226

Fifty-two kilometres west of Tallinn lies a town which many older residents remember fondly as a pre-Soviet resort of clean beaches and guesthouses. Though the area was originally a Swedish port (they had settled the Pakri islands from the 13th century) Catherine the Great enlarged it and had a fortress built there, in what was then called Baltiski Port. A prestigious Maritime School was opened in 1876.

This area was the first in Estonia to be occupied by Soviet troops (in 1939) and the last to see them leave (August 1994). It became the main Soviet naval base in Estonia, and the town was a completely closed nuclear submarine station until 1994; only in 1995 were the decommissioned reactors removed. The reactors functioned continuously from the early 1970s until 1989, and in 1994 a civilian died after stumbling upon radioactive materials – allegedly stolen from the disused base – on wasteground near Tallinn.

While you'll notice that a lot of restoration and clean-up still needs to be done, remember that an enormous amount has already been achieved (with the help of US$200 million from the USA). The beaches are now safe for swimming, the army barracks have been cleaned up and the 1842 St Nicholas Lutheran Church has re-opened.

The most prominent landmark in Paldiski is the submarine training base (it's the darkly imposing concrete structure visible from anywhere in town). Locals dubbed it the 'Soviet Pentagon' owing to its monumental stature. In its day the building served as the main training facility for submariners throughout the Soviet Union. It is not open

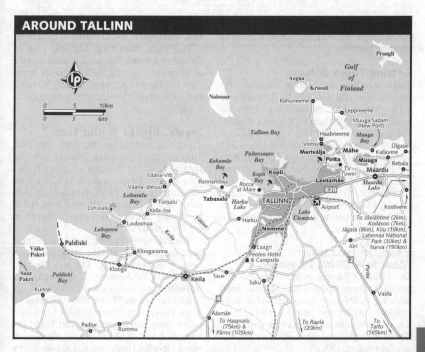

AROUND TALLINN

TALLINN

to visitors and entering the grounds is not recommended as the facility is guarded and potentially unsafe.

A trip to the lighthouse on the north-western tip, passing through destroyed army barracks and missile sheds, gives an insight into Paldiski's recent past. The former training sites are deteriorating but the odd bunker and a staircase built into the limestone, with markers showing strata of rock formation on the exposed sides of the cliff, are still visible. A number of large erratic boulders dot the peninsula and the views from the edge of the cliff are remarkable.

**Places to Stay & Eat** On the main street is **Valge Laev** (*White Boat; ☎/fax 674 2035; e valgelaev@hot.ee; Räe tänav 32; meals 80 EEK; doubles from 750 EEK*). It offers decent meals in its restaurant and has now opened a polished, clean hotel boasting a nautical theme. There are several **cafés** in town.

## Padise & Lohusala Peninsula

At Padise, about 15km south of Paldiski on a back road between Tallinn and Haapsalu, is an atmospheric Cistercian monastery from the 13th-16th centuries with a 13th-century cemetery. It was damaged in the Livonian War in the 16th century and again in a 1766 fire. Padise is 4km west of Rummu (the site of Estonia's best-known prison) located on the Haapsalu–Rummu–Keila–Tallinn bus route.

**Places to Stay** Travel Agencies in Tallinn can help arrange tours and accommodation in the area.

**Laulasmaa Training & Holiday Centre** (*☎ 671 5521, fax 671 5663; Laulasmaa; singles/doubles/triples with breakfast 250/ 350/450 EEK*), just 400m from the beach, seems more an institution than a hotel. Nevertheless, facilities are more than adequate and rooms have private bathrooms a stone's throw from the sea.

Past the Lauslasmaa Training Centre on the Laulasmaa-Lohusala road, **Metsatuka** (*☎ 671 5590, mobile 051 49 392; 2-3 bed cabins from 100 EEK per person*) has cabins with electricity, kitchen and sauna. From there it's a short walk from the Lohusalu Peninsula and harbour, where yacht rental is available. Heating is also available if booked in advance. Bus numbers 110 and 126 will stop opposite the camping grounds near the harbour.

## Getting There & Away

Buses travelling west along the coast, including Nos 108 and 126 to Rannamõisa, Vääna-Viti and Vääna-Jõesuu, go from the terminal beside Tallinn's train station (Balti Jaam). Bus Nos 108, 110, 136 and 172 go from there to Keila-Joa. Bus Nos 145 or 241 go to Paldiski. Call **Harju Linnid** (☎ *644 1801*) for timetables and the best buses for your destination. Three trains daily leave for Kloogaranna from Balti Jaam. Ten trains daily go to Paldiski, and five daily buses (leaving from beside the train station) make the trip, via Keila.

## EAST OF TALLINN
## Maardu & Rebala Reserve

On Tallinn's eastern border, the Tallinn–Narva highway crosses the Maardu area, which is partly an industrial wilderness thanks to phosphorite mining and other industries which raged unchecked here in the Soviet era. Phosphorite mining in Estonia was stopped in 1991.

As early as 1987, a 25 sq km area to the east and south of Maardu Lake (which lies beside the highway) was declared the **Rebala Reserve** (☎ *603 3097*). Within this area are 300 archaeological sites with traces of historic and prehistoric settlements and cultures (the oldest are about 5000 years old).

Within the reserve is the Maardu Manor, an 18th-century building that stands on the site where the original manor was built in 1379. There are also sites of pre-Christian cults and 'sliding rocks' said to cure infertility in women who slide down them bare-bottomed. If you want to give the rocks a try, they are just south of the **Kostivere** village, a few kilometres from the main highway.

At Jõelähtme a number of late bronze-age stone burial cysts lie beside Peterburgi maantee around 30 minutes by bus from Tallinn, on the main route to Narva. Inside the information centre adjoining the site (and posted outside for after-hours visitors)

you can find details of the graves, their origins, and objects found during excavations.

The **Wolf Piles** near Muuksi, east of Jõelähtme towards Lahemaa, is also a couple of kilometres off the Tallinn–Narva highway. It's the site of approximately 80 more burial chambers, the largest concentration in Estonia.

## Jägala, Ülgase & Kiiu Torn

There's a northbound turn-off from the Tallinn–Narva highway leading towards **Jägala**, the site of 'Estonia's Niagara Falls', the country's largest waterfall (7.2m), with the waters of the Jägala River tumbling over pretty limestone banks. On your way, you'll pass under a triple-arched stone bridge from the 19th century.

Several ruins of phosphorite mines have been preserved in **Ülgase**, near the coast, north of Rebala village. The area between Ülgase and the highway is vast industrial wasteland, with eerie mountains of soil.

**Kiiu Torn** (☎ *607 3434; Kiiu; adult/student or child 5 EEK/admission free; open 10am-8pm daily*), housed in the smallest fortress in Estonia, 6km east of Maardu on the Narva road, was built in the 16th century. The four-storey tower was restored in 1975 and is now a cute little restaurant. A popular sweet egg liqueur, Kiiu Torn, is named after this fortress.

## Getting There & Away

The Maardu area is served by city bus Nos 183, 184 and 186, which leave from the Kivisilla stop, a block east of the Gonsiori tänav bus stop. Buses also occasionally leave from the train station. To reach Ülgase, take any of these buses to Kallavere, then change to bus No 185. Call **Harju Liinid** (☎ *644 1801*) to find the best route for your destination and for information on buses headed further east.

From the bus stop next to the train station, take bus No 143 to Jägala, or bus Nos 150, 151, 152, 153 or 154 to Kiiu. Bus Nos 106, 134 or 143, departing from near the train station, will go through Jõelähtme; a small information centre building with a large information symbol along the highway marks the site of the burial cysts.

# Northeastern Estonia

Lahemaa National Park (the 'Land of Bays'), about a third of the way from Tallinn on the main route to the Russian border, provides easy access to the splendours of nature inland and along the austere, yet beautiful north coast. While the park is the highlight of this region, a journey further east towards the historic border town of Narva offers an insight into another Estonia and can lead to some unusual discoveries, as the area's exaggerated reputation as a polluted industrial wasteland has so far kept tourists away. The population is predominantly Russian-speaking in the Narva region and following the border south.

## LAHEMAA NATIONAL PARK
☎ 032

Estonia's largest national park *(rahvuspark)*, Lahemaa takes in a stretch of deeply indented coast with several peninsulas and bays. There are 480 sq km of forested hinterland including 14 lakes, rivers, waterfalls and several villages, plus 220 sq km of marine area.

The park is an alluring, unspoiled section of rural Estonia with varied coastal and inland scenery. The natural attractions of the coast, forests, lakes, rivers and bogs encompass many areas of historical, archaeological and cultural interest. About 24% of the park is human-influenced, 68% is forest or heath and 8% is bog. Roads traverse the park from the Tallinn–Narva highway to the coast, and a few parts are accessible by bus. Walking, hiking and cycling trails encourage exploration of a more active kind.

When it was founded in 1971, Lahemaa was the first national park in the Soviet Union. Though protected areas existed before that, the authorities believed that the idea of a national park would promote incendiary feelings of nationalism. Sly lobbying (including a reference to an obscure decree signed by Lenin which mentioned national parks as an acceptable form of nature protection) and years of preparation led to eventual permission. Latvia and Lithuania founded national parks in 1973 and 1974 respectively, but it wasn't until 1983 that the first one was founded in Russia.

Around 300,000 people now visit the Lahemaa National Park every year, but only a small number go out of season when the

## Highlights

- Visit one of Estonia's majestic manors or hire a National Park guide to reveal elusive wildlife havens
- Walk the trails through Lahemaa, or explore by bicycle, canoe or horse
- Travel the old Viking trade route east to Toila and gaze over the horizon from the magnificent Baltic Glint
- Time travel to an era of secrecy and stoicism in the historic centre of Sillamäe
- Visit the Narva fortress and wave to those visiting Russia's Ivangorod fortress waving at you
- Discover your own desert island in the Lahemaa National Park

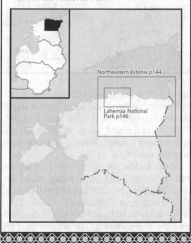

Northeastern Estonia p144

Lahemaa National Park p146

park is transformed into a magical winterland of snowy shores, frozen seas and sparkling black trees.

## Geography & Geology

The landscape is mostly flat or gently rolling, with the highest point just 115m above sea level. Geologically, much of the park is on the North Estonian limestone plateau whose northern edge, stretching east–west across the park, forms a bank up to 65m high, known as the Baltic or North Estonian Glint (see Facts about Estonia – Geography). The

NORTHEASTERN ESTONIA

143

## NORTHEASTERN ESTONIA

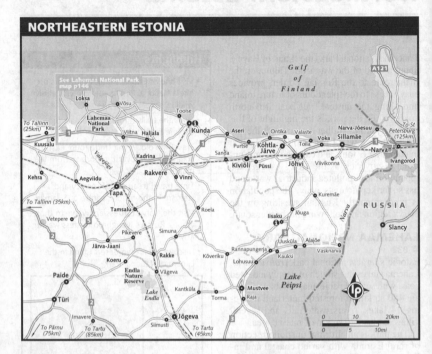

highest parts are inland and therefore barely visible. In Lahemaa, the Glint is most visible at Muuksi, where it is 47m high, but only 23m above ground level. At Nõmmeveski and Joaveski, rivers flowing over the bank become waterfalls.

Stone fields, areas of very thin topsoil called 'alvars', and large rocks called 'erratic' boulders, brought from Scandinavia by glacial action, are typically Estonian. There are as many as 50 large boulders in the country – eight in Lahemaa. The biggest one (580 cubic metres) is the Majakivi (House Boulder), while the Tammispea boulder is the highest at 7.8m. The best known stone field is on the Käsmu Peninsula.

### Flora & Fauna

Some 838 plant species have been found in the park, including 34 rare ones. There are 50 mammals, among them brown bear, lynx and American mink, none of which you're likely to see without specialist help. Then there are 222 birds (mute swan, black stork, black-throated diver and crane nest) and 24 species of fish. Salmon and trout spawn in the rivers.

### Information

**Lahemaa National Park Visitors Centre** (*Lahemaa Rahvuspark Külatuskeskus;* ☎ 95 555, fax 95 556; ⓔ info@lahemaa.ee; open 9am-7pm daily May-Aug; 9am-5pm daily Sept; 9am-5pm Mon-Fri Oct-Apr) is in a converted wagon-house and stable on the manor estate in Palmse, 8km north of Viitna in the southeastern part of the park. It has some of the most informed staff of any information centre in Estonia and it can help you tailor your stay at Lahemaa to your interests and make your visit a truly enriching experience. It's wise to contact them before you arrive, even if you wish to make independent, unguided trips within the park. The centre sells detailed maps and booklets about every facet of the park.

To reach the visitors centre from Viitna, follow the road signposted for Võsu, almost directly opposite the main bus stop. Buses from Tallinn and Narva only stop at Viitna, so your best bet is to hitch or hike the remaining 8km to Palmse. You can pre-arrange a guide to meet you at the bus stop (the visitors centre can give you contact details).

## Palmse

The restored **manor house** *(adult/student 25/15 EEK; open 10am-7pm daily May-Aug; 10am-3pm Tues-Sun Sept; visits by arrangement in winter)* and park at Palmse, 8km north of Viitna, is the showpiece of Lahemaa. In the early 13th century the Danish king gave the land to Cistercian monks from Gotland who had come to convert northeastern Estonia. It belonged to the Baltic-German von der Pahlen family from 1677 until 1923 when the property was expropriated by the state and used as a holiday resort for the Estonian Home Guard *(Kaitseliit)*. Restoration began after the founding of the national park.

The existing buildings are restored versions of those that were built in the 18th and 19th centuries. The fine baroque house, dating from the 1780s, invites an inspection of its period furniture and fittings. Out of hours you can walk around the landscaped gardens of the estate, frequented by mute swans. Behind the manor house is a park, first laid out in medieval times, when ponds were dug for fish breeding. The forest section of the park was added in the 19th century. In the Old Storage House, there's a small **museum** *(adult/student 20/10 EEK; open same hrs as manor, closed Oct-Apr)* with antique cars and motorcycles, including a rusty old Harley Davidson.

In the von der Pahlens' time, Palmse had its own brewery, distillery, smithy, orchard, granaries, limestone quarry and water mill, many of which have been restored and are once more in use. The *ait* (storage room) is a summer exhibition hall; the *viinavabrik* (distillery) is a hotel and restaurant; the *kavaleride maja* (house of Cavaliers), which once housed summer guests, is a souvenir and book shop; and the wonderful *supelmaja* (bath house) must be one of the most romantic cafés in Estonia. The old granary, facing the manor on the opposite side of Võsu maantee, is the village school's canteen.

The Lahemaa area is rich in folk music and dance traditions. A small amphitheatre, across the lake behind the manor house, is the setting for the International Bagpipe Music Festival, held every two years on the first weekend in August (next planned for 2003). Contact the manor for information regarding this and other cultural events.

## Other Destinations

The small coastal towns of **Võsu** and, to a lesser extent, **Loksa**, are popular seaside spots in summer. Võsu has a long, sandy beach, and Loksa has a ship repair yard. There are also good beaches at **Käsmu** (Captains' Village), an old sailing village across the bay from Võsu; and between Altja and Mustoja. There's a very scenic hiking/biking route east along the old road from Altja to **Vainupea**, where there's a camp site.

The former Soviet Coast Guard's barracks at Käsmu now shelters the **Käsmu Meremuuseum** *(Maritime Museum; ☎ 38 136; Merekooli tee 4; admission by donation; open 9am-7pm daily)*. In the 1920s, a third of all registered boats in Estonia belonged to this village; at one time there were 62 long-distance captains living here. From the end of WWII the entire national park's coastline was a military-controlled frontier. A 2m-high barbed wire fence was constructed to ensure villagers did not access the beach or sea, and it was not until Estonia regained its independence in 1991 that fishers could freely go out in their boats. The museum has photographs and memorabilia tracing the history of the village and exhibits on marine life from the area. Käsmu is becoming a popular artists' haven and the museum acts as a cultural centre with small exhibitions of local works. It also arranges sailing, rowing, diving and canoe-building camps, and the *Viking Days* festival in August, where Vikings of all nations congregate for a bloodless battle.

The fishing village of **Altja** was first mentioned in 1465, though today no building older than 100 years is left. The park has reconstructed traditional net sheds here and set up an open-air museum of stones along the protected coastline. Altja's *Kiitemägi* (Swing Hill), complete with traditional Estonian swings, has long been the centre of Midsummer's Eve festivities in Lahemaa. Other coastal villages with an old-fashioned flavour are **Natturi** and **Virve**.

Until 1992, **Hara Island** was a Soviet submarine base and hence a closed area. Soviet-era maps of the park did not mark the island (and also featured false roads running through the park). During the 1860s the island enjoyed a successful sprat industry and about 100 people worked there. If you're interested in a trip over, the visitor centre can help find someone to take you.

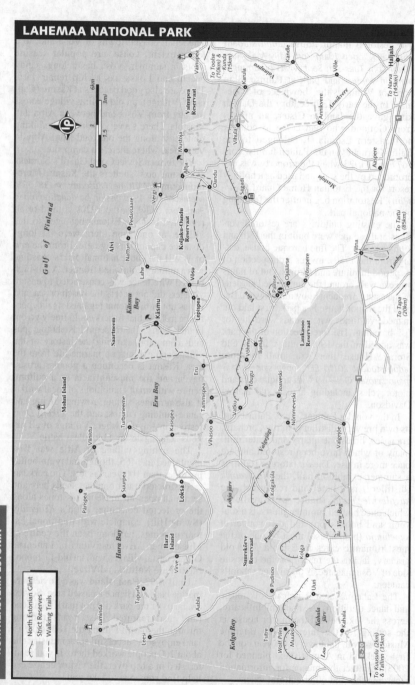

# LAHEMAA NATIONAL PARK

**Legend:**
- North Estonian Glint
- Strict Reserves
- Walking Trails

When waters are low it's also possible to walk to **Saartneem** and **Älvi**, two other small islands. But check with the centre before rolling up your trousers, as conditions apply to visits. Älvi is a strictly protected nature reserve and Saartneem is only open to visitors from mid-July, after the bird nesting season is finished.

From Viinistu it is possible to cross over to **Mohni Island** and guided tours are available (see Organised Tours later).

Inland, old farm buildings still stand in villages like **Muuksi**, **Uuri**, **Vatku**, **Tõugu** and **Võhma**. On the small hill of Tandemägi, near Võhma, four stone tombs from the 1st century AD and earlier have been reconstructed after excavation. There are more old German manors at **Kolga**, **Sagadi** and **Vihula**.

Now fully restored, Sagadi Manor houses a **Forest Museum** (☎ 58 888; adult/student 30/10 EEK, including entry to manor; open 11am-6pm Tues-Sun 15 May-30 Sept, visits by arrangement 1 Oct-May 14), with a 15m-long exhibit showing the differing characteristics of limestone according to depth. The manor's former grain drier is now a shop.

The classical-style manor house at Kolga dates from the end of the 17th century but was largely rebuilt in 1768 and 1820, and is now undergoing extensive restoration. It currently houses a restaurant, with a small hotel on the grounds.

## Walking Trails

The park has several marked nature trails including:

**Altja** – 3.5km circular trail beginning at 'Swing Hill' on the coast at Altja, taking traditional net sheds and fishing cottages, and the open-air museum of stones

**Beaver Trail** – 1.7km trail, 900m north of Oandu; a beautiful trek past beaver dams, although you're unlikely to see the shy creatures

**Käsmu** – 3.5km circuit from Käsmu village, taking in coast, pine forest, 'erratic' boulders and the lake Käsmu järv; a longer route takes you to Eru

**Majakivi** – 3.5km trail on the Juminda Peninsula taking in the 7m-high Majakivi boulder

**Oandu** – 4.7km circular trail, 3km north of Sagadi, is perhaps the park's most interesting. Note the trees which wild boars and bears have scratched, and don't forget to sign the guestbook at the start of the trail.

**Viitna** – 2.5km path starting at the Holiday Centre and taking in lakes and forest shaped by glacier

**Viru Rapa** – 3.5km trail across the Viru Bog, starting at the first kilometre off the road to Loksa off the Tallinn–Narva road; look for the insectivorous Sundew (Venus Fly-Trap, Charles Darwin's favourite plant)

## Organised Tours

Several Tallinn travel agencies (see Tallinn chapter) offer tours to the park. The visitors centre provides information on guides for tours of the park in several languages for up to 50 people at a time. For information on guided tours around the islands of Hara, Saartneem and Älvi, contact the visitors centre too. **Anne Kurepalu** (e anne@phpalmse.ee) arranges tours through the fragile ecosystem of Mohni Island for individuals and groups.

**Pallase Tallid** (☎ 52 985; e pallase@estpak .ee), near Viitna, offers riding tours, camps and sleigh rides. **Kuusekännu Ratsatalu** (☎ 52 942; e kusekannu@btg.ee), 500m south of the Tallinn–Narva road, arranges horse riding for all levels and trail rides through Lahemaa. Both allow camping provided guests bring their own tents and book ahead for catering.

Canoe trips can be arranged for the Lahemaa region and for exploring other Estonian rivers. Visit w www.kanuu.ee for more information (in Estonian only). The Valgejõgi makes for an especially scenic trip.

## Places to Stay

The **Lahemaa National Park Visitor Centre** (see Information earlier) at Palmse can help you organise accommodation options at local tourist farms; camping facilities start from 25 EEK a night and cabin accommodation from 140 EEK. Ask about discounts for longer stays.

There is a **camp site**, free to use, 300m south of the Oandu trail. **Eesti Karavan** (☎ 44 665, mobile 050 52 053; open May-Aug), in Lepispea 1km from Võsu, has places for caravans only.

**Viitna Holiday Centre** (☎ 93 651; dorm beds/singles/doubles/cabins 60/110/150/300 EEK), in Viitna, 600m east of the bus stop on the Tallinn–Narva road, lies in a wooded area beside a clean lake. There are beds for 148 people in rooms for one to six. Cabins have shower and toilet, and there's a sauna available for rent.

**Ojaäärse Hostel** (☎ 34 108; e sagadi .hotell@rmk.ee; bunk beds 150 EEK; open *year-round)*, 1.5km southeast of Palmse, has recently passed into the care of the Sagadi manor. The 42-bed hostel, in a restored farm dating from 1855, overlooks a lake and has shared rooms with two to six bunk beds. There is a sauna for hire, a private kitchen and breathtaking views. To reach it, start following the road from Palmse to Sagadi and turn right down a wooded trail signposted Ojaäärse. If you prefer to go on foot, cut through the park from Palmse manor by following the river.

**Merekalda Boarding House** (☎ 38 451; w www.merekalda.ee; Neeme tee 2, Käsmu; *doubles with/without shower low season 600/ 400 EEK, high season 600/500 EEK, 2-person cabin 200 EEK, tent pitch 25 EEK)* is a lovely place overlooking the sea with elegant rooms; ask for one with a sea view and indulge in it! Cabins have shared toilet and a sauna by the shore. You can rent boats, waterbikes and sailboards, and there's a small café on the premises. Note that camping and the cabins are only available from mid-May to mid-September.

Käsmu's thriving local B&B industry means that there are several good options available.

**Sireli B&B** (☎ 38 422; Neeme tee 19; *singles/doubles 300/500 EEK, 2-person cottage 750 EEK)* has neat rooms with living area, kitchen access and a large garden. Food and necessities are available a short walk down the street.

**Rannaliiv** (☎/fax 38 456; e rannaliiv@hot .ee; Aia tänav 9; *singles/doubles from 350/570 EEK)*, in Võsu, has newly renovated rooms and an innovative construction. It was originally built as a holiday home for builders, and a sauna and new spa await.

**Park Hotel Palmse** (☎/fax 34 167; *singles/ doubles with breakfast mid-Apr–mid-Oct 690/890 EEK, mid-Oct–mid-Apr 590/790 EEK)* offers pristine and pine-fresh rooms inside the Palmse Manor distillery; book well ahead as it is favoured by groups.

**Sagadi Manor** (☎ 98 647; e sagadihotell@ rmk.ee; *hostel dorm beds from 200 EEK, hotel singles/doubles 700/900 EEK)*, in Sagadi, is a restored governor's house with combined hotel and hostel accommodation. Spotless triples or six-/eight-bed dorms are available amid some of the grandest surroundings in Estonia. It's an experience you won't soon forget.

## Places to Eat

**Viitna Kõrts** (☎ 58 681; *shop & bistro open 7.30am-8pm daily, restaurant open noon-11pm Sun-Thur, noon-2am Fri-Sat)*, almost opposite the eastbound bus stop at Viitna, is a reconstruction of an 18th-century tavern with a rustic-style restaurant as well as a shop and bistro, serving great early morning breakfasts.

**Altja Kõrts**, in Altja, is the place to try for traditional Estonian dishes, revitalising mugs of Viru Õlu (beer) and bread with honey and other 'plain coast dwellers' food which it serves in the tavern room, originally reserved for the village gentry. Ask at sister pub Viitna Kõrts for directions and hours.

**Võsu Grill** (Mere 49, Võsu; *open noon-1am daily)* serves good food for hearty appetites, and there are also some vegetarian dishes.

There are two eating options at Sagadi Manor, and **Merekalda** in Käsmu has its own café. There's a **tavern** in Vergi. The **Park Hotel Palmse** serves meals both in its restaurant and bar.

If you are staying at a tourist farm, don't miss the opportunity to sample some traditional home cooking. Just ask your host in advance.

## Getting There & Away

Vergi is the only coastal port in Lahemaa which has a customs services for those that arrive by sea.

**Viitna** To reach Viitna from Tallinn by public transport, take one of the 19 daily buses that head for Rakvere, 25km beyond Viitna (30 EEK, one hour). The Tallinn–Narva and Tallinn–St Petersburg buses don't stop at Viitna. To go from Narva to Viitna take a bus to Rakvere (75 EEK, about seven of each daily) and then a bus to Viitna (15 EEK, 18 daily). From Tartu there's a bus to Võsu, stopping at both Viitna and Palmse (80 EEK, 2½ hours).

**Other Destinations** There are two buses daily from Tallinn to Võsu, one of which goes on to Käsmu (40 EEK, 1¼-1½ hours). A bus also connects Viitna and Käsmu, but runs only once daily, four days per week. Visit w www.bussireisid.ee for the latest timetables (in Estonian only).

## Getting Around

A car is handy to get from village to village if pressed for time, but biking is the ideal way to take everything in properly. Do beware of bike theft, though – as peaceful as the place is, this is not a rare occurrence. Hiking and cycling routes have been upgraded in recent years (marked blue and red respectively); maps and trail information are available from the visitors centre.

You can also use the buses running to the coastal villages to get around the park, though these are quite infrequent (see Getting There & Away earlier).

The hotels in Palmse and Sagadi rent out bicycles for 50 to 100 EEK a day, as do most of the tourist farms in the park. You can also rent a bike in Tallinn and take it on the bus to Viitna as cargo. Car rental costs less from Rakvere than in larger centres. Fuel stations that are open 24 hours are at Vihasoo, Loksa, Palmse and Viitna.

## EAST OF LAHEMAA

The territory from Lahemaa to the Russian border at Narva has for decades been Estonia's main industrial area. Oil shale, a combustible stone used in power generation, is primarily derived from the region and is the country's biggest industry, but like every other industry here output has been reduced sharply. The low potency and high levels of sulphur dioxide generated in deriving power from oil shale have long been a source of concern, with initiatives underway to replace oil shale with natural gas, peat or other energy sources. This has made the area less polluted than it has been in decades. By 2005 dust and ash emissions should be reduced to 75% of 1995 levels following the Environment ministry's strategy to reduce emissions from electricity production, in keeping with EU standards.

This has made the area less polluted than it has been in decades (though the cities in this region still have significantly higher levels of air pollution than Tallinn). Visitors are predominantly Russians who use the sanatoriums in Narva-Jõesuu and along the northern shores of Lake Peipsi. Many Estonians are wary of this predominantly Russian-speaking area but the tourism industry is making inroads with its efforts to promote the region's attractions. Given some time and open-minded exploration, east Estonia will reveal significant historic and natural wonders and even some beautiful scenery.

## Lahemaa to Sillamäe

**Kunda & Around** Home to a mammoth cement plant, Kunda (pop 3843) was once covered in a lovely grey dust blanket – day and night. Special filters on the chimneys have now eliminated this. Today, the **Kunda Museum** (☎ 032-21 594; Jaama tänav 9; open noon-5pm Thur & Fri, 10am-3pm Sat) stands in the main building of the original factory, on the north side of town. The Kunda **tourist office** (☎ 032-22 170, fax 55 697; Kasemäe tänav 7; open 10am-4pm Mon-Fri) answers cement- and Kunda-related questions.

On a headland at **Toolse**, 8km west, are the evocative ruins of a castle built in 1471 by the Livonian Order as defence against pirates. At **Purtse**, 10km north of Kiviõli, there's a picturesque, restored, 16th-century **castle** (☎ 033-59 388; open 10am-6pm Apr-Sept, visits by arrangement). The coast between Aa and Toila is lined by cliffs where it coincides with the edge of the Baltic Glint. At **Ontika**, north of Kohtla-Järve, these cliffs reach their greatest height of 56m. The views out to sea are spectacular, though getting a good look at the cliffs is near-impossible as they're obscured by trees, and climbing down can be a deadly affair. To save lives, a 2-million EEK metal staircase was built in 1999, 5km east at **Valaste**, facing Estonia's highest waterfalls (25.6m), which, depending on the month, may be a meek trickle.

**Kohtla-Järve** As the centre of the region's oil-shale extraction Kohtla-Järve (pop 47,106) is worth a trip if you want to see a typical Russian industrial town. Its aggressive feel is intensified with its harshly artificial landscape, evidence of the hard labour in progress below. For an idealised view of life underground, visit **The Oil Shale Museum** (☎ 033-24 017; adult/student 50/25 EEK; visits by arrangement).

**Jõhvi** As the region's administrative centre, Jõhvi (pop 11,882) has few sights, but there's a number of services including a busy and very helpful little **tourist information centre** (☎/fax 033-70 568; ℮ johvi@visitestonia.com; Rakvere maantee 13a; open 10am-6pm Mon-Fri, 10am-2pm Sat May-Sept; 10am-5pm Mon-Fri Oct-Apr).

**Toila** Along a former trade route of the Vikings, Toila (pop 2321), a lovely village on the coast 12 km northeast of Jõhvi, is famous for its parklands. Here stood the majestic Oru Castle, built by famous St Petersburg businessman Yeliseev in the 19th century, which was later used as President Konstantin Päts' summer residence between the wars and subsequently destroyed. Parts of the park are being reconstructed, including the old terrace, making it very pleasant to stroll or picnic in. The views from the Baltic Glint in the Toila region are spectacular, and here the glint forms part of the Saka-Ontika-Toila landscape reserve. There are seven buses daily to Toila from Jõhvi, and two to Ontika (none on Sundays).

## Organised Tours
The tourist information centre in Jõhvi (see earlier) books guides and accommodation in farmhouses. Also in Jõhvi, the **Ida-Viru information centre** (*☎ 052 23 700 mobile; e kaldur@ida-viru.ee*) offers a range of tours tailor-made to suit the interests of individuals and groups, throughout the Ida-Virumaa region and around Lake Peipsi.

In Iisaku, some 20km south of Jõhvi, there is also a small **information centre** (*☎/fax 033 93 006; e iisakuinfo@hot.ee; Tartu Maantee 49*).

**Alutaguse Hiking Club** (*Alutaguse Matkaklubi; mobile ☎ 051 41692, fax 023-70 568*) organises great biking and hiking tours of the area, from one to four days, down the northern sea coast and/or through the villages and along the north coast of Lake Peipsi.

## Places to Stay & Eat
**Ontika Manor** (*☎ 033-73 738, fax 73 679; singles/doubles with breakfast 290/490 EEK*), near Ontika, offers sauna, breakfast and lunch options with accommodation.

**Sanatoorium Toila** (*☎ 033-25 233; e info@ toilasanatoorium@hot.ee; Ranna tänav 12; camp sites/caravans 25/200 EEK, singles/ doubles from 500/620 EEK*), in Toila, is a large institution-like centre where a range of treatments are available.

**Fregatt** (*☎ 033-69 647; Pikk tänav 18; open noon-10pm daily*), a restaurant in Toila, comes well recommended by locals.

**Jõhvi Kelder** (*☎ 033-70 343; Tartu tänav 2; open 11am-11pm Sun-Thur, 11am-1am Fri & Sat*, about 300m from the tourist information

centre in Jõhvi, is a down-to-earth place for some social drinks.

## SILLAMÄE
☎ 039 • pop 17,200
Sillamäe, situated on the coast between Kohtla-Järve and Narva, is one of the region's pleasant surprises, though you'll find scant information about it, even from tourist bureaus. This town, 94% Russian-speaking, gets few visitors. However, its look, feel and history are unique in Estonia.

A settlement has existed here since at least the 16th century, but the area's potential as an industrial centre was explored only after WWI by Estonians who built a small port and an unsuccessful oil-shale mine nearby – later bolstered by Swedish investment. This was trashed by the Soviets during their 1941 retreat but started up with fervour after their return in 1944 when it was discovered that small amounts of uranium can be extracted from oil shale. The area became strictly off-limits after 1946, and was known as Moscow 400, Leningrad 1 and Narva 1 before being named Sillamäe in 1957 (the town was often omitted from Soviet-era maps).

The infamous uranium processing and nuclear chemicals factory was quickly built by 5000 Russian political prisoners, and the town centre by 3800 Baltic prisoners of war who had previously served in the German army. Only unfinished uranium was processed at the plant, in which only Russians were allowed to work, though the eerily abandoned huge buildings on the city's western border are testament to Soviet plans to process pure, nuclear reactor-ready uranium; only the disbanding of the USSR saved Estonian ecology from this. The plant was closed in 1991 and today the radioactive waste is buried under concrete by the sea; fears of leakage have alarmed environmentalists.

Some of the Soviet Union's top scientists also worked here to develop and invent rare and precious metals (such as Neobi, in 1978), some of which are still made and exported around the world.

Today, the lovely, pleasant town centre is a living museum of Stalinist-era architecture and town planning; any town of this size, built in the late 1940s in Russia would be in a much greater state of decay. Sillamäe, planned by Leningrad architects, features grand, solid buildings with gargoyles and a cascading staircase ornamented by large urns. Around the central square, there's a **town hall** specially designed to resemble a Lutheran church, a **cultural centre** (1949) which still has reliefs of Marx and Lenin on the walls inside, and a very Soviet-style monument erected in 1987 to commemorate the 70th anniversary of the October Revolution. This is one of few places in Estonia where the aura of the USSR still lives on, and it feels caught between two worlds. The **Sillamäe Museum** (☎ 72 425; Mayakovsky tänav 18A) details the history of the area.

## Places to Stay & Eat
**Krunk** (☎ 24 076; Kesk tänav 23; singles/ doubles 300/600 EEK; restaurant open noon-6pm Mon-Fri) is the one hotel in town and has a restaurant/café.

**Kalevi Sports Complex** (☎ 74 077; Kesk tänav 30), at the eastern end of Kesk tänav, has been known to offer cheap accommodation with bar and Internet café. There's a **cafeteria** (Kesk tänav 12) down the road from the centre.

## Getting There & Away
Many of the 15 daily Tallinn–Narva buses stop in Sillamäe (and Kohtla-Järve), plus there are 15 daily buses from Narva (as well as regular taxi-buses), and seven buses daily from Jõhvi.

## NARVA
☎ 035 ● pop 68,117
Narva, on Estonia's easternmost border, 210km from Tallinn and 130km from St Petersburg, has the busiest border crossing in Estonia. Only the thin Narva River separates Narva from Ivangorod (Estonian: Jaanilinn) in Russia. With an industrial base that has suffered from Estonia's economic problems, Narva had some of the highest unemployment in the country and was a centre of Russian political discontent for a few years following independence. Over 90% of the town's predominantly Russian-speaking population (only 4% of the population is Estonian) was not eligible for automatic Estonian citizenship after independence.

A set of problems arose in the area that no-one seemed to want to address; talks of a 'special status' – even secession for Narva – surfaced from time to time in the early years of Estonian independence, but by the same token, there were also occasional calls from Ivangorod residents for annexation into Estonia. Even today, the area raises controversy. Many state officials and policemen still do not speak Estonian. Now the government is trying to stimulate the local economy and has finally begun, with foreign collaboration, a more realistic education policy for Russian-speaking children with the goal of eventual assimilation (see Education in the Facts about Estonia chapter). Strategically sited on a system of inland waterways, the region has been populated since the Stone Age, and was mentioned as a fortified trading point in 1172. It was embroiled in border disputes between the German knights and Russia; Ivan III of Muscovy built a fort at Ivangorod in 1492. In the 16th and 17th centuries, Narva changed hands often from Russian to Swede, until falling to Russia in 1704.

Narva was almost completely destroyed in 1944 during its recapture by the Red Army. Afterwards it became part of the northeastern Estonian industrial zone and one of Europe's most polluted towns, with two big power stations around it emitting an estimated 380,000 tonnes of sulphur dioxide and 200,000 tonnes of toxic ash a year by 1990. These emissions have been cut greatly in recent years and Estonia has set targets to reduce sulphur dioxide emissions by 80% of the 1985 levels before 2005.

About 12km north of Narva is the holiday resort, Narva-Jõesuu, a pretty but dilapidated town, which has been popular since the 19th century for its long white sandy beach backed by pine forests. There are many unique, impressive early-20th-century wooden houses and villas throughout the town.

## Orientation & Information
The main landmark, the castle, is by the river, just south of the bridge. The train and bus stations are next to each other on Vaksali tänav; from there it's a 500m walk north along Puskini tänav to the castle. You'll pass the **tourist information centre** (☎ 60 184, fax 60 186; e narva@visitestonia .com; Puskini tänav 13; open 10am-5pm Mon-Fri mid-Sept–mid-May; 10am-6pm Mon-Fri, 10am-2pm Sat & Sun mid-May–mid-Sept), where maps and a leaflet for a self-guided walking tour of Narva are available.

NORTHEASTERN ESTONIA

## Things to See

Few of Narva's fine Gothic and baroque buildings survived its 'liberation' by the Red Army in 1944. The imposing **Narva Castle** was built by the Danes at the end of the 13th century. Across the waters, on the Russian side of the river, stands the matching Ivangorod Fortress, forming an architectural ensemble unique in northern Europe. Restored after damage in WWII, Narva Castle houses the **Town Museum** (☎ 99 247; adult/student 50/10 EEK; open 10am-6pm Wed-Sun). North of the castle, the baroque **Old Town Hall** (Raekoja väljak), built 1668–71, is impressive; as is the 19th-century **home of Baron von Velio** (cnr Sepa & Hariduse tänav), two blocks north. The Russian Orthodox **Voskresensky Cathedral** (Bastrakovi), built 1898, is situated north of the train station. On the square in front of the train station is a monument to the Estonians who were loaded into cattle wagons here and deported to Siberia in 1941.

## Organised Tours

**Reiviis Travel Agency** (☎ 33 510, fax 24 601; Lavretsov tänav 8) offers city and regional tours at reasonable prices.

## Places to Stay & Eat

**Hostel Lell** (☎ 49 009; e lell77@hot.ee; Partisani tänav 4; singles/doubles/deluxe doubles with private bath 150/300/500 EEK) has neat but basic rooms and a restaurant serving good Russian cuisine.

**Hotel Vanalinn** (☎ 73 253; Koidula tänav 6; singles/doubles 490/750 EEK), just north of the castle in a renovated 17th-century building, is one of the best things about Narva. There are 28 rooms, all with private bathroom and generous discounts for kids.

There are a few restaurants and cafés along Puskini tänav and Lavretsov tänav.

**German Pub** (☎ 91 548; Puskini tänav 10; meals 70 EEK) is a good choice for a light meal or sundae treat in comfortable pub surroundings.

**Gulliver Pub** (☎ 91 551; Lavretsov tänav 7; meals 60 EEK) gives a warm welcome with decent meals and fine service.

**Rossan Baar** (☎ 94 482; Puskini tänav 12) is popular with locals and gives a fair insight into life across the border.

In Narva-Jõesuu, there are about a dozen hotels and spas to choose from, all near the beach.

**Narva-Jõesuu Sanatoorium** (☎ 77 000, fax 77 535; e sanatoor@hot.ee; Aia 3; singles/doubles/deluxe from 430/780/880 EEK) understands the health trade in an institutionalised kind of way, offering an array of herbal and mud baths and other curative thrills.

## Getting There & Away

There are 15 daily buses from Tallinn to/from Narva (75 EEK, four hours), seven passing through Rakvere, some continuing to Narva-Jõesuu. Tallinn–St Petersburg buses also stop at Narva. There are 10 buses daily to/from Tartu (90 EEK, 3½ hours).

One train daily runs from Tallinn to Narva and vice versa (70 EEK, four hours), stopping at Rakvere on the way.

## KUREMÄE
☎ 033

Originally the site of ancient pagan worship, the village of Kuremäe, 20km southeast of Jõhvi, is home to the stunning Russian Orthodox **Pühtitsa Convent** (☎ 92 124; admission free; open noon-6pm Mon-Fri). Built between 1885 and 1895, the magnificent nunnery has five towers topped with green onion domes and is a place of annual pilgrimage for Russian Orthodox believers, operating a fully self-sufficient entity. Murals by the convent gate depict the Virgin Mary who, it is said, appeared to a 16th-century shepherd by an oak tree. An icon was later found in the area and it is still in the main church of the convent. There is also a revered holy spring which never freezes.

Today, about 160 nuns and novices live in the convent and visitors can stay overnight in one of the dormitories, but only if they are Orthodox themselves or serious students of religion. One bus daily runs from Tallinn to Kuremäe, and between two and six a day run from Jõhvi.

## LAKE PEIPSI (NORTH)
☎ 033

Estonia's finest – and least crowded – beaches are found on the northern coast of Lake Peipsi; 42km of clean, sandy dunes hug the shoreline of what appears to be a sea rather than a lake. The area had popular resorts during Soviet times but many of them have been left to crumble. Development has been slowly arriving to this beautiful area with enormous tourism potential.

On the far northeastern corner of the lake, at the foot of the Narva River, is the isolated fishing village of **Vasknarva**, with about 100 residents. There is an evocative Orthodox church here, which was believed to have hosted a KGB radio surveillance centre in Soviet times. Scant ruins of a 1349 Teutonic Order castle stand by the shore of Lake Peipsi. At **Alajõe**, you'll find the area's main Orthodox church and a few shops. **Kauksi**, where the Narva–Jõhvi–Tartu road reaches the lake, is the area's most popular beach.

From **Lohusuu** extending southwards is Old Believers' territory (see Lake Peipsi, South in the Southeastern Estonia chapter for more details). Further south, towards Jõgeva, are the lakeside towns of **Mustvee** and **Raja**. Mustvee, a town of just 2000, has four **churches** (there used to be seven): Orthodox, Baptist, Lutheran and Old Believer. There is also a forlorn WWII war memorial by the sea, the **Mourning Lady**, a young woman with her head hung low. Some 8km south is the charming, one-street village of Raja, where a wooden church contains some rare icons dating from the 19th century when a well-known school of icon painting was founded there.

Locally caught and smoked fish is a speciality of the area; if you're lucky you'll see them on sale by the side of the road. If not, ask where you can buy *suitsukala*.

## Places to Stay & Eat

There are a number of resorts around Alajõe, but many are in dire need of repair.

**Uusküla Holiday Centre** (☎ 93 249; e tasandik@hot.ee; singles/doubles from 300/ 400 EEK), near Kamping Karu Urgas, is a sprawling, well-kept complex of cottages and lodges, including a **restaurant**.

**Kauksi Beach** (☎ 93 835; e kauksirand@ hot.ee; tent sites 25 EEK, beds per person from 120 EEK), a popular and sometimes crowded camp site, has small cottages, a **café** and entertainment centre on the grounds.

## Getting There & Away

Buses leave from Kohtla-Järve to Vasknarva once or twice daily most days. To Kauksi and Alajõe, two buses a day leave from Kohtla-Järve and Jõhvi. There are also about 10 Tartu-bound buses a day from Narva, many of which will stop in Kauksi.

## ENDLA NATURE RESERVE

Endla Nature Reserve (Endla Looduskaitseala), covering a boggy area inhabited by beavers, begins south of Koeru, some 10km north of Jõgeva, and includes Lake Endla and the 5m-deep spring (Estonia's deepest) from which the Oostungu River flows. The reserve, established in 1981, covers a total area of 8162 hectares.

The reserve **headquarters** (☎ 077-63 133, fax 077-45 339; e kkimel@hot.ee) is in Torma. You can visit the reserve and follow a 1.5km nature trail on boards across the bog, taking in two watchtowers along the way. Guided tours are also available. Visits have to be arranged in advance through the headquarters.

# Southeast Estonia

The focus of southeast Estonia is the historic university town of Tartu, Estonia's second largest city, 186km southeast of Tallinn. Beyond Tartu is an attractive region of gentle hills and lakes including the highest point in the Baltic region and some of Estonia's prettiest countryside. The southeast is also Estonia's prime skiing and winter sports destination. To the far east lies exotic, unexplored lands, where Orthodox Old Believers live in cluster villages by the shores of Lake Peipsi, and where the Setus, an ethnic group whose ancient lands are now split by the border with Russia, struggle to preserve their culture. The southeast gets relatively few tourists – visitors can still feel a sense of discovery here – though its potential for nature exploration is vast.

## TARTU
☎ 07 • pop 101,140
Tartu, with its large number of students, rich cultural life and ambitious sports agenda, is a small but busy place. Parks in the hilly city centre as well as the Emajõgi River, flowing through on its way from Võrtsjärv to Lake Peipsi, give the town a pleasant, comfortable and spacious feel. For a balanced Estonian experience, visit Tartu. The city cultivates its image as Estonia's spiritual capital, often considered to be more 'Estonian' than the real capital, and a measure of its importance is that the Estonian Song Festivals often begin here.

Tartu was the cradle of Estonia's 19th-century national revival and is the site of the country's original and premier university. The town escaped Sovietisation to a greater degree than Tallinn and retains a sleepy, pastoral air. It is notable for its classical architecture stemming from a comprehensive rebuilding after most of the town burnt down in 1775. This monumental timelessness infused with a youthful idealism from the city's vibrant student population makes Tartu one of the country's most interesting places. The free thinking crowds evident in the city's bars and clubs give a positive and self-assured view of the future Estonia.

Two big social/sporting events in the local calendar are the **Tartu Ski Marathon**, 60km cross-country from Otepää, which is raced

- Enlighten yourself to Estonian folklore and rich cultural heritage at Tartu's National Museum
- Get caught up in the revelry and antics of Tartu's spirited student population
- Experience the sanctity of Pühajärv and re-energise in the region recommended by psychics
- Ski cross-country or summer ski through Otepää and Haanja
- Stand at a makeshift altar but beware of a supernatural presence in the sand caves of Piusa
- Witness a different way of life in a Setu village or farm, at a festival or feast

Southeast Estonia p155
Tartu p157
Otepää & Around p165
Võru p168

by hundreds in mid-February; and the **Tartu Bicycle Marathon** (ⓦ www.tartumaraton.ee), a 136km race held at the end of May with a second race in mid-September.

## History
There was an early Estonian stronghold on Toomemägi Hill around the 6th century AD. In 1030 Yaroslav the Wise of Kyiv, ruler of the Russian ancestor-state Kyivan Rus, is said to have defeated the Estonians and founded a fort here called Yuriev. The Estonians regained control, but in 1224 were

# SOUTHEAST ESTONIA

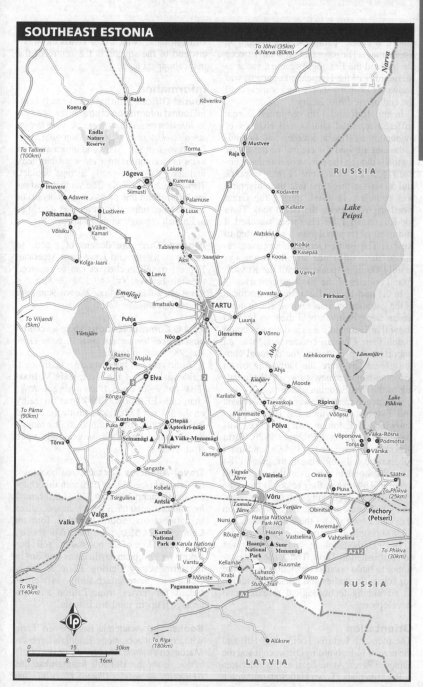

To Jõhvi (35km) & Narva (80km)

*Narva*

Koeru

Rakke

Köveriku

RUSSIA

To Tallinn (100km)

Endla Nature Reserve

Torma

Raja

Mustvee

Jõgeva

Laiuse

Kuremaa

Siimusti

Palamuse

Luua

Kodavere

Kallaste

*Lake Peipsi*

Imavere

Adavere

Põltsamaa

Lustivere

Võisiku

Väike-Kamari

Alatskivi

Tabivere

Aksi

*Saadjärv*

Kolkja

Kasepää

Koosa

Kolga-Jaani

Laeva

Varnja

*Emajõgi*

Ilmatsalu

**TARTU**

Kavastu

*Piirisaar*

To Viljandi (5km)

Puhja

Luunja

*Võrtsjärv*

Nõo

Ülenurme

Võnnu

*Ahja*

Mehikoorma

*Lämmijärv*

Rannu

Majala

Vehendi

Elva

Ahja

Mooste

*Kiidjärv*

Karilatsi

Taevaskoja

Rõngu

Mammaste

Räpina

Võõpsu

*Lake Pihkva*

To Pärnu (90km)

Kuutsemägi ▲

Puka

Otepää ▲

▲ Apteekri-mägi

Seinamägi ▲

▲ Väike-Munamägi

Põlva

Võporsova

Väika-Rõsna

Podmotsa

Tonja

Värska

Tõrva

*Pühajärv*

Kanepi

*Vagula Järve*

Väimela

Orava

Piusa

Säätse

To Pihkva (25km)

Sangaste

Kobela

Antsla

*Tamula Järve*

Võru

*Verijärv*

Obinitsa

Pechory (Petseri)

Valka

Tsirgulliina

Valga

**Karula National Park**

Karula National Park HQ

Nursi

Haanja National Park HQ

Meremäe

Vahtseliina

A212

To Pihkva (30km)

Varstu

Rõuge

Haanja

**Haanja National Park**

▲ Suur Munamägi

Vastseliina

Kellamäe

Ruusmäe

Mõniste

Krabi

*Luhasoo Nature Study Trail*

Misso

RUSSIA

Paganamaa

A2

To Rīga (140km)

To Rīga (180km)

Alūksne

LATVIA

0        15        30km

0      8      16mi

defeated by the Knights of the Sword who placed a castle, cathedral and bishop on Toomemägi. The town that grew up between the hill and the Emajõgi became a successful member of the Hanseatic League. It was known as Dorpat – its German name – until the end of the 19th century.

In the 16th and 17th centuries, Dorpat suffered repeated attacks and changes of ownership as Russia, Sweden and Poland-Lithuania all vied for control of the Baltic region – though the period of Swedish control (1625–1704) was one of relative peace and it was at this time that the university was founded. In 1704, during the Great Northern War, Peter the Great took Tartu for Russia. In 1708 his forces wrecked it and most of its population was deported to Russia. The Baltic Germans, however, retained their influence and the town was mainly German-speaking until the Russification policies of the late 19th century.

In the mid-1800s, Tartu became the focus of the Estonian national revival. The first Estonian Song Festival, held there in 1869 to show that Estonian songs and singers could match their German counterparts, was an important step in raising the national consciousness, as were the launching of an Estonian-language newspaper and the founding of the first Estonian societies.

The peace treaty between Soviet Russia and Estonia, by which the Russians acknowledged Estonian independence, was signed in Tartu on 2 February 1920. Tartu was severely damaged in 1941 when Soviet forces retreated – blowing up the grand 1784 Kivisild stone bridge over the river, and again in 1944 when they retook it from the Nazis. Both occupying forces committed many atrocities. A monument now stands on the Vlaga road where the Nazis massacred 12,000 people at Lemmatsi.

In 1993, the Estonian Supreme Court was re-established in Tartu. Today the city continues to build upon its reputation as a centre for scientific studies and it leads the nation in advancing technological research and development.

## Orientation

The focus of Tartu is Toomemägi Hill and the area of older buildings between it and the Emajõgi River. At the heart of this older area is Raekoja plats (Town Hall Square), with a footbridge at its eastern end over the river. Ülikooli tänav, which runs across the western end of the square, is the centre of the main shopping area.

## Information

**Tourist Offices** Tartu has an extremely helpful **tourist information centre** (☎/fax 442 111; e info@tourism.tartumaa.ee, w www.tartumaa.ee; Raekoja plats 14; open 10am-6pm Mon-Fri, 10am-3pm Sat). Maps and information on tours or accommodation are available here, including the twice-yearly listings booklet, *Tartu Today* (15 EEK). The southern Estonian **information line** (☎ 1188) gives details of events, entertainment and transport schedules in English, throughout the southeast.

**Money** There are dozens of places to change cash in the Old Town. Lost American Express travellers cheques can be replaced through **Estravel** (☎ 440 300; e tartu@estravel.ee; Vallikraavi tänav 2; open 9am-6pm Mon-Fri, 10am-3pm Sat).

**Post & Communications** There's a **central post office** (Vanemuise tänav 7; open 8am-7pm Mon-Sat) in town.

Tartu's coolest Internet café is on the east, residential side of the river; **Café Virtuaal** (Pikk tänav 40; open 11am-midnight daily) charges 30 EEK/hour. **13th Korrus** (in reality on the 3rd, not 13th, floor), inside the central **Rüütli Keskus** (cnr Rüütli & Küütri tänav), keeps casual hours but is generally open from 10am.

**Travel Agencies** For tours and bookings, try **Estravel** (see Money earlier in this chapter) or **Hermann Travel** (☎ 301 444; e tartu@hermann.ee; Lossi tänav 3), which specialises in nature tours. **South Estonian Tourism Centre** (☎ 474 553; e lets.travel@kiirtee.ee), on the 2nd floor of the bus station, sells bus tickets for European destinations (see Bus in the introductory Getting There & Away chapter for more information), as well as tickets for ferries from Tallinn and can arrange tours in southern Estonia.

**Bookshops** Academia has blessed Tartu with excellent bookshops. Estonia's largest is **Mattiesen** (Vallikraavi tänav 4), next to Café Wilde. Both the **Ülikooli Raamatukauplus** (University Bookshop; Ülikooli tänav 11) and

# TARTU

**PLACES TO STAY**
5 Oru Villa
11 London Hotel
14 Draakon Hotel
30 Park Hotel
33 Barclay Hotel
41 Tartu Hostel
45 Pallas Hotel;
   Entri Restaurant
48 TU Student Village

**PLACES TO EAT**
6 Old Student Café
10 Tsink Plekk Pang
12 Pronto Pizza;
   Internet 13th Korrus
18 Taverna
24 Babylon Kebab House

26 Püssirohukelder
34 Café Wilde;
   Wilde Irish Pub;
   Mattiesen Bookshop
47 Pizza Opera
50 Student Canteen

**OTHER**
1 Zavood
2 Estonian Sports Museum
3 St Johns Church (Jaani Kirik)
4 Gildi Antique
7 University; Art Museum
   of Tartu University;
   Student Lock-Up
8 Hermann Travel
9 University Bookshop
13 Rüütli Pub

15 Obu Gallery
16 Tourist Information Centre
17 Kivisilla Art Gallery;
   Postimehe Raamatuäri
19 Manhattan Club
20 City Museum
21 Café Virtual
22 Atlantis Nightclub
23 Illegaard
25 Town Hall; 24 hr Pharmacy
27 Museum of University History
28 Observatory/AHHAA Centre
29 Old Anatomical Theatre
31 Estonian National Museum
32 University Library;
   Museum of Books
35 Estravel
36 Kaubahall Shopping Centre

37 Central Post Office
38 Central Bus Stop
39 Central Market
40 River Port
42 Bus Station;
   South Estonian
   Tourist Centre
43 Tirol Pub
44 Kaubamaja Department Store
46 Vanemuine Theatre
49 Weeping Cornflower
   Monument
51 KGB Cells Exposition
52 Literature Museum
53 Museum of Zoology;
   Museum of Geology
54 Vanemuine Theatre
55 XS Club & Bowling

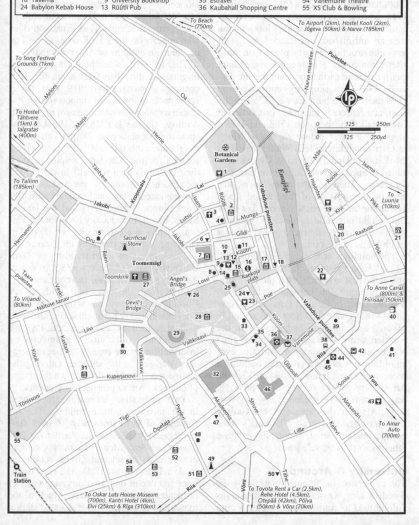

**Postimehe Raamatuäri** (Raekoja plats 16) have wider selections than you'll find in Tallinn. All stock maps, guides and some English-language books. **Gildi Antique** (Rüütli tänav 12) has shelves of vintage Estonian and German books, magazines, medallions and objects of a religious or political persuasion.

## Raekoja Plats

Many of Tartu's shops, restaurants and offices are on or near the square. The older streets are to its north, while the area to its south has been meagrely redeveloped since 1944, when it was flattened by Soviet bombardment. The vast, still-empty lots lend the area an unfinished, unbalanced feel with new construction efforts placed on hold after remnants of a 14th-century merchant quarter were unearthed beneath the site earmarked for a new shopping centre. Raekoja Plats itself was rebuilt after a 1775 fire. Its dominant feature is the finely proportioned **Town Hall** (built between 1782 and 1789), topped by a tower and weather vane, which its German architect, JHB Walter, based on the design of Dutch town halls. Clocks were added to encourage students to be punctual for classes. There's a **pharmacy** (open 24hr) now occupying part of the ground floor. The statue out the front was erected in 1999 and delightfully reflects the city's youthful spirit – two lovers embraced in a kiss under an umbrella in the rain.

The buildings at Raekoja plats Nos 6, 8, 12 and 16 are also neoclassical, but No 2, one of the first to be built after the 1775 fire, is in an earlier, late-baroque style. No 18 was the home of Colonel Barclay de Tolly (1761–1818), an exiled Scot who settled in Livonia and distinguished himself in the Russian army's 1812 campaign against Napoleon. Foundations laid partially over an old town wall have given the building a pronounced lean. It now houses the **Kivisilla Art Gallery** (☎ 441 080; Raekoja plats 18; adult/student 10/5 EEK; open 11am-6pm Wed-Sun). Also in the square, **Obu Gallery** (Raekoja plats 8) is run by Estonia's most popular modern artist, Navitrolla – whose fanciful work is on sale here.

### University & Around

The university was founded in 1632 by the Swedish king, Gustaf II Adolf (Gustavus Adolphus), to train Lutheran clergy and

government officials. It was modelled on Uppsala University. A restored statue of Gustaf Adolf, unveiled by Carl XVI Gustaf of Sweden during his 1992 visit to Estonia, stands at the rear of the main university building. The university closed during the Great Northern War around 1700 but re-opened in 1802 developing into one of the Russian empire's foremost centres of learning, with an emphasis on science that continues today. Those who worked here in the 19th century included physical chemistry pioneer W Ostwald, physicists HFE Lenz and MH Jakobi, and the founder of embryology, natural scientist Karl Ernst von Baer who appears on the 2 EEK note, as well as on the main building on Ülikooli tänav.

The university's teaching language was originally Latin, then German in the 19th century and Russian until 1919. This proved no obstacle in the rise of support for the Estonian national revival movement in the 19th century. (In the late 1850s, the Latvian-speaking population in Dorpat/Tartu were caught up in this tide and called themselves, for the first time, 'Latvians', helping to spark their country's own revival.) In early 2002 the student body stood at about 15,000, 370 of whom are international students primarily from Europe, Scandinavia and the United States. See the introductory Facts for the Visitor chapter for information on Estonian language courses offered by the University.

The impressive main building of **Tartu University** (Tartu Ülikooli; ☎ 375 300; e prof fice@ut.ee, w www.ut.ee; Ülikooli tänav 18), a block from the town hall, with its six Corinthian columns, dates from 1803–09. The university departments, the korps or student residences, and other buildings are scattered around the city. The university's **information centre** (☎ 375 100; open 8am-4pm Mon-Fri), to the left after entering the main doors, provides details on a full range of courses open to prospective students.

Two interesting museums are housed in the university's main building. The **Art Museum of Tartu University** (Ülikooli Kunstimuuseum; ☎ 375 384; adult/child 7/4 EEK; open 11am-5pm Mon-Fri) contains mainly plaster casts of ancient Greek sculptures made in Europe in the 1860–70s, a few mummies and one of only two surviving casts of Immanuel Kant's death mask. Much of the museum's collection was evacuated during

WWI, and hundreds of its antique ceramics, sculptures, coins and paintings still remain in the Art Museum in Voronezh, Russia.

In the 19th century, student rebels were placed in solitary confinement inside 'lock-up' rooms in the attic. Being noisy after hours or failing to return library books on time could net you two days; insulting a lady, four days; insulting a (more sensitive?) cloakroom attendant, five days; duelling, up to three weeks. Today, one of these rather comfy rooms, with walls covered in original graffiti, is open as the **Student's Lock-Up** (adult/child 5/2 EEK; open 11am-5pm Mon-Fri), and can be visited with permission from the Art Museum. Other lock-ups were destroyed in a 1905 fire.

You can catch a glimpse of modern-day student misdeeds at the **University Spring Days festival** at the end of April. Students take to the streets to celebrate winter's end in every way imaginable. Raucous fun, parades and boat rallies are the order of the five sleepless days.

North of the university on the continuation of Ülikooli, the Gothic brick **St John's Church** (Jaani Kirik), founded in 1330 but ruined by Soviet bombing in 1944, has been under restoration for years. It has rare terracotta sculptures in niches around the main portal.

The nearby **Botanical Gardens** (Bota-anikaaed; Lai tänav 40; greenhouse admission adult/child 18/5 EEK; open 9am-5pm daily), founded in 1803, nurtures 6500 species of plants and a large collection of palm trees in its giant greenhouse. A wander through the grounds is both pleasant and free.

## Toomemägi

Toomemägi (Cathedral Hill), rising behind the Town Hall, was the original reason for Tartu's existence, functioning on and off as a stronghold from around the 5th or 6th century. It's the site of several university buildings, and a peaceful, tree-shaded park that makes for scenic strolling year-round. The approach to the hill from Raekoja plats is along Lossi tänav, which passes beneath the 1836–38 **Inglisild** (Angel's Bridge), which encourages lingerers with its Latin inscription 'Otium reficit vires' (Rest restores strength). On weekdays you can catch a free jazz or operatic performance by eavesdropping on rehearsals in the nearby Music School.

Toomemägi's most imposing structure is the ruined Gothic **Toomkirik** (dome-church)

at the top. Built by German knights in the 13th century, it was rebuilt in the 15th century, despoiled during the Reformation in 1525, used as a barn, and partly rebuilt in 1804–07 when the university library was installed in the choir at its east end. The library and its **Museum of Books** (Struve tänav 1) are now at modern premises in town and in the library's former place is the **Museum of University History** (☎ 375 677; adult/student 20/5 EEK; open 11am-5pm Wed-Sun). Inside is a reconstructed autopsy chamber.

North of the cathedral, on the top of the hill, are a couple of small 17th-century Swedish cannons and a **sacrificial stone** of the ancient Estonians. They stand by a small bridge in front of a rocky mound thought to have been part of a defensive bastion but now known as Musumägi (Hill of Kisses). Nowadays students burn notes on the sacrificial stone after exams.

Also on top of the hill are **monuments** to the Rīga-born poet Kristjan Jaak Peterson and Baltic-German Karl Ernst von Baer, both of whom studied at Tartu University in the 19th century; and to Johann Morgenstern, founder of the library and museum.

On the eastern side of the hill, on the site of the old castle, there is an **observatory** (tähetorn; ☎ 372 932; visits by arrangement). Science-based exhibitions are regularly held in the observatory's AHHAA centre; contact the observatory for details on these. A sculpture out the front commemorates the 19th-century astronomer Georg Struve. The **Old Anatomical Theatre** which functioned until 1999, stands to the southwest. It now houses a modern science centre not open to the public, however an Anatomical Museum is in the planning stages for these premises. There is also a monument to Friedrich Robert Faehlmann, a 19th-century physicist whose collection of Estonian folklore and legends inspired Kreuztwald to complete his Kale-vipoeg epic. The 1913 **Kuradisild** (Devil's Bridge) crosses the road on the south side of the hill, around which Vallikraavi tänav follows the line of the old castle moat.

## Beaches

There's a beach area at the Anne Canal, across the main traffic bridge by the bus station then 1km southeast (veer to the right). The water is much cleaner at the small but pleasant beach on the Emajõgi banks, a 1km walk northwest after crossing the traffic bridge at the foot of Kroonuaia tänav (cross and turn left along Ranna tee).

## Other Attractions

The **Estonian National Museum** (*Eesti Rahvamuuseum*; ☎ 421 311; W www.erm.ee; Kuperjanovi tänav 9; temporary exhibitions adult/student 12/5 EEK, permanent & temporary exhibitions 20/14 EEK; open 11am-6pm Wed-Sun) traces the history and cultural traditions of the Estonian people. It's Estonia's finest museum, and the best place to learn about native customs and life in Estonia through to the present. The regional displays of folk costume and large exhibit of uniquely handcrafted tankards should not be missed.

The **City Museum** (*Linnamuuseum*; ☎ 461 911; Narva mantaa 23; adult/student 20/5 EEK; open 11am-6pm Tues-Sun) covers Tartu's history up to the 19th century. The **Estonian Sports Museum** (*Spordimuuseum*; ☎ 300 750; Rüütli tänav 15; adult/student 10/5 EEK; open 11am-6pm Mon-Fri) chronicles the history of Estonia's Olympic performance (quite distinguished if you recall Estonia's achievements in Salt Lake City).

The **Museum of Zoology** (*Zooloogiamuuseum*; ☎ 375 833; Vanemuise tänav 46; adult/student 15/7 EEK; open 10am-4pm Wed-Sun), which has displays on everything from protozoa to the Kamchatka snowsheep, and the **Museum of Geology** (*Geoloogiamuuseum*; ☎ 375 839; Vanemuise tänav 46; adult/student 8/4 EEK; open 10am-4pm Wed-Sun) are at the same address. The nearby **Literature Museum** (*Kirjandusmuuseum*; ☎ 420 155; Vanemuise tänav 42; admission free; open 9am-5pm Mon-Fri) specialises in Finno-Ugric studies and houses collections of the works of Kreutzwald and Lydia Koidula.

The **Oskar Luts House Museum** (*Oskar Lutsu Majamuuseum*; ☎ 461 030; Riia maantee 38; adult/student 5/3 EEK; open 11am-5pm Wed-Sun) is the home of one of Estonia's most beloved novelists. Luts wrote *Kevade* (*Spring*), which became the country's most popular film.

The former KGB headquarters on Riia maantee, at the corner of Pepleri tänav, now house the sombre museum **KGB Cells** (*KGB Kongide Ekspositsioonid*; ☎ 461 717; Riia maantee 15b; adult/student 5/3 EEK; open 11am-4pm Tues-Sat). In 1990 a **weeping cornflower monument** was erected in front of The KGB buildings in memory victims of Estonian deportation and repression. The blue cornflower is Estonia's national flower.

The Song Festival Grounds (*Laululava*) are in **Tähtvere Park** at the northern end of Tähtvere tänav, 2km north of the centre. Note how the stage's semi-dome is perfectly framed by an archway as you approach the main entrance (click here for fail-proof photography). It is also a site for midsummer bonfires on the night of 23 June.

On the eastern side of the Emajõgi River, on the southwestern corner of Narva maantee and Peetri tänav is a **stone monument** where the fire was lit for the first Estonian Song Festival in 1869.

Aside from the elegance of the Old Town architecture, Tartu is also rich in lovely wooden houses. Some buildings exhibit an eclectic array of styles which appear in later features. Art Nouveau doors add charm to Kastani tänav 23, Tolstoy tänav 3 and Kesk tänav 16. The houses at Veski tänav 11, Kalevi tänav 31 and along Vene tänav are also worthy diversions.

## Bowling

Estonia's original bowling alley, now the **XS Bowling Club** (☎ 427 410; Vaksali tänav 21), is a freshly renovated four-lane operation now enjoying better days (legend tells of balls once used as target practice by a rifle club). Prices start from 90 EEK/hour. The polished lanes at nightclub/sports bar **Manhattan** (☎ 403 136; Narva maantee 25; open 7.30am-3am Mon-Fri, 10am-3am Sat & Sun) are similarly priced.

## River Cruises

Throughout the summer months, **Laevatöö** (☎ 340 026) runs a motor ship, *Pegasus*, which leaves from the River Port four times daily (from 11am) on hour-long cruises along the Emajõgi. A hydrofoil, *Polaris*, also sails three times a week to Piirissaare (see Lake Peipsi (South) later in this chapter for more information).

## Places to Stay – Budget

**TU Student Village** (☎ 420 337; Pepleri tänav 14; e telts@ut.ee; dorm beds around 70 EEK, apartments per person 150 EEK) is one place where you should reserve ahead, but in summer it's usually possible to just show up and ask nicely for a place. Three rooms offer

Central Square (Kesk väljak), Kuressaare, Saaremaa

Forest Fairy, Metsamoor Park

Piusa sand caves

Medieval Kuressaare Castle

Colourful house, Pärnu

Eemu Tuulik (windmill), Muhu

Karja Church, Saaremaa

Suur Tõll, Saaremaa

disabled facilities and a laundry is situated onsite. Freshly renovated apartments with one- to three-bed apartments are also available at Purde tänav 27 about 2km southwest of the centre. To get there take bus 12 or 13 to the E-Kaubamaja stop.

**Tähtvere Hostel** (☎/fax 421 708; Laulupeo tänav 19; singles/doubles/luxury doubles/ quads from 200/350/450/700 EEK) is located about a 1km walk west of the centre. It offers perfectly comfy rooms with bathroom, TV, fridge and telephone and luxury double rooms with fireplace. There's a sauna, tennis court, swimming pool and sports complex on this green, quiet premises.

**Kooli Hostel** (☎ 461 471; Põllu tänav 11; singles 356 EEK, 2/3-bed rooms per person 120/100 EEK) on the 5th floor in a residential area north of the city, specialises in student accommodation and lets you into the Tartu student experience with shared bathrooms and communal mingling areas. Take bus numbers 4, 9 or 34 to Põllu tänav.

**Tartu Hostel** (☎ 314 300; e info@tartu hotell.ee; Soola tänav 3; hostel rooms per person 200 EEK, hotel singles/doubles 375/640 EEK, with shower 695/995 EEK) does have the location and reasonable rooms but, beware, this charm-free old Soviet building is undergoing large scale and lengthy renovations.

## Places to Stay – Mid-Range

**Oru Villa** (☎/fax 422 894; w www.oruvilla.ee; Oru tänav 1; singles/doubles from 450/880 EEK) is an historic 1920s cottage with warm homelike ambience that suggests a colourful history in this former residence of dignitaries. Rates include breakfast and morning sauna.

**Rehe Hotel** (☎ 307 287, fax 412 355; e rehehotell@rehehotell.ee; Võru tänav 235; singles/doubles from 400/600 EEK) offers comfortable rooms and security parking, with signage, inspired by Hollywood, no-one could miss 5km from the centre on the road to Võru.

**Kantri Hotel** (☎ 383 044, fax 477 213; e info@kantri.ee; Riia maantee 195; singles/ doubles 610/850 EEK) is a 10-minute ride on bus No 2, 6 or 7 from the centre of town, but this mansion-like building in a country setting on the outskirts of Tartu is worth every one of those minutes.

**Park Hotel** (☎ 427 000, fax 427 655; e info@parkhotell.ee; Vallikraavi tänav 23; basic singles 460 EEK, singles/doubles/suites from 800/1080/1300 EEK), nestled to the side

of Toompea, is a little plain and overpriced, but its parkland setting provides a haven close to the centre.

## Places to Stay – Top End

**Pallas Hotel** (☎ 301 200, fax 301 201; e pal las@pallas.ee; Riia maantee 4; singles/doubles from 950/1200 EEK), on the top two floors of a renovated building that used to house a famous art school, has some of the most uniquely decorated rooms in Estonia, with original canvases from the 1920s which modern-day artists have 'extended' to cover the walls of the deluxe suites. Views of the city from the deluxe rooms are magnificent and many of the regular rooms also have panoramic views of the city.

**Barclay Hotel** (☎ 447 100, fax 447 101; e barclay@barclay.ee; Ülikooli tänav 8; singles/ doubles/suites/suites with sauna 990/1480/ 1800/2300 EEK) has witnessed some drama with history unfolding within its walls. Dating from 1912, it functioned as the Soviet army's headquarters until 1992; Chechen rebel leader Dzhokhar Dudayev kept a room here as his office, and even more recently the hotel played host to a siege! Today's luxuriously appointed establishment has a reputation in its own right for top-rate facilities and impeccable service.

**Draakon Hotel** (☎ 442 045, fax 423 000; Raekoja plats 2; singles/doubles 975/1500 EEK, doubles with sauna 2200 EEK) has stylish and simple rooms. Old town square enthusiasts need look no further. Doubles with private sauna are well worth the upgrade.

**London Hotel** (☎ 305 555, fax 305 565; e london@londonhotel.ee; Rüütli tänav 9; singles/doubles from 1100/1500 EEK) is an eclectic new establishment that shows khaki can be creative. Rooms are modern and functional, while the restaurant could be Babylonian, perhaps.

## Places to Eat

**Entri** (☎ 306 812; 2nd floor, Riia maantee 4; meals from 70 EEK; open 7am-11pm Mon-Thur, 7am-1am Fri & Sat, 8am-11pm Sun), an ultra-modern restaurant with an airy, bright decor, serves delicious meals in its room with a view.

**Taverna** (☎ 423 001, Raekoja plats 20; meals 80 EEK; open 11am-midnight Sun-Thur, 11am-1am Fri & Sat), a friendly, moderately formal place, serves predominantly Italian food.

Vegetarian dishes are also included on its wide menu.

**Püssirohukelder** *(☎ 303 555; Lossi tänav 28; meals 160 EEK; open 11am-2am Mon-Thur, 11am-3am Sat, 12pm-midnight Sun)*, in a split levelled gun-powder cellar, is the place to try for a very substantial meal. The formality enhanced by the high ceilings is periodically dispelled by karaoke nights.

**Tsink Plekk Pang** *(☎ 441 789; Küütri tänav 6; meals 80 EEK)* is possibly the only Chinese pub in Estonia and the only one in the world named after zinc buckets, which are suspended from the ceiling as lampshades. Inexpensive Chinese meals and a central location makes it a popular choice.

**Babylon Kebab House** *(☎ 441 159; Raekoja Plats 3; meals 90 EEK; open 11am-9pm Sun-Tues, 11am-midnight Wed-Sat)* lays claim to being the first kebab house in Estonia. With courtyard dining and a downstairs restaurant, there's a setting for any Arabian day or night. The traditional hookahs are quite a novelty.

**Cafés & Fast Food** A sublimely decorated place, **Café Wilde** *(☎ 309 764; Vallikraavi tänav 4; open 9am-9pm Sun-Thur, 9am-10pm Fri & Sat)* is the top café in town. It serves a very fine cappuccino, delicious home-made 'grandma' cakes and sandwiches. Internet access is also provided. Its namesake is Peter Ernst Wilde, who opened a publishing house on the premises in the 18th century.

**Café Virtuaal** *(☎ 402 509; Pikk tänav 40)* has some imaginative concoctions served in a comfy interior or outdoor patio which makes it a cool place to just hang out or get online (see Post & Communications earlier in this chapter for details).

For dirt-cheap fill-ups try the **student canteen** *(Tähe tänav 4; open 9am-3pm daily)* in the basement of the university building. It may not pay to study your meal here but it should keep you going.

**Old Student Café** *(2nd floor, Ülikooli tänav 20)* is still cheap but far superior to the student canteens. This old-world café with beautiful wooden floors is a must for a light lunch or afternoon tea. It's in the original part of the university (dating from 1632). A **cafeteria** on the 1st floor has filling daily specials for under 50 EEK.

There are plenty of bistros in the Old Town serving Estonian fast food low both in price and nutritional value.

**Pronto Pizza** *(☎ 442 085; Küütri tänav 3)* spins out pizzas in many forms, with a generous salad bar that more than compensates for its sometimes improvised toppings.

**Pizza Opera** *(☎ 420 795; Vanemuise tänav 26)* has a decent range of pizzas for a quick and filling meal before or after an evening of culture.

The **central market** *(open daily)*, across Riia tänav from the bus station, is a vast indoor space with local fresh produce available.

## Entertainment

Check posters in the entrance of the main university building for what's on in the way of music and student theatre.

**Bars & Nightclubs** Upstairs from Café Wilde, **Wilde Irish Pub** *(☎ 309 765; Vallikraavi tänav 4; meals 120 EEK; open noon-1am Mon-Thur, noon-2am Fri & Sat, noon-midnight Sun)* celebrates Oscar Wilde with great food, live music, a popular terrace and a large beer selection; though how well their caramel or strawberry-flavoured beer goes down is a question of taste. Both Peter Ernst (namesake of the café) and Oscar are seen enjoying a time-defying moment in a smart bronze monument out the front.

**Illegaard** *(☎ 434 424; Ülikooli tänav 5; open 5pm-2am daily)*, a new wave inspired jazz vault, attracts an artsy crowd who cluster around tables for lively conversations. Check posters around town for live sessions.

**Zavood** *(Factory; ☎ 441 321; Lai tänav 30; open 4pm-2am daily)* is a popular late-night place to hang out. It has an alternative feel, offering your best chance to see a student band.

**Tirol Pub** *(☎ 203 403; Turu tänav 21)*, where Tirol meets Tartu, is a victory for all things kitsch. The drunkenness test involving nails and hammer is recommended on exit.

**Rüütli Pub** *(Rüütli tänav 2)* serves filling meals and drinks in laid-back style. The real Estonian beer snacks must be sampled here.

**Atlantis** *(☎ 385 485; Narva maantee 2; open 10pm-3am Sun-Thur, 10pm-4am Fri & Sat)*, overlooking the Emajõgi River, makes up in popularity what it lacks in taste, hosting some good retro music nights.

**XS Bowling Club** *(☎ 427 410; Vaksali tänav 21; open 11pm-3am Tues-Thur, 10pm-4pm Fri & Sat)*, near the train station, is a popular dance club, attracting a friendly and very mixed crowd. You can bowl under the same roof until it's time to club.

**Theatre** Named after the ancient Estonian song god, **Vanemuine Theatre** (☎ 442 272; *Vanemuise tänav 6)* was the first Estonian-language theatre troupe when founded in 1870 (the professional theatre, however, began in 1906). Today it's housed in a modern building which also has a concert hall.

### Getting There & Away
**Air** Regular charter flights to Helsinki are dispatched by **Tartu airport** (☎ 309 210); charters are also available to most places in Estonia or to European destinations.

**Bus** There is a **left-luggage room** *(pakihoid; open 6am-10pm)*, off the ticket hall on the ground floor of the **Tartu bus station** (☎ 477 227; *Turu tänav 2)*.

Some 50 buses a day run to/from Tallinn (80 EEK, 2½ to 3½ hours). The last bus to Tallinn leaves at 11pm. Visit ⓦ www.bussireisid.ee for a full listing of services to/from Tartu. Other daily services to/from Tartu include:

**Haapsalu** 95 EEK, 4½ hours, one bus
**Kuressaare** 150 EEK, 5½-6½ hours, four buses
**Narva** 90 EEK, 2¼-3½ hours, 10 buses
**Pärnu** 95 EEK, 3-4½ hours, 16 buses
**Rīga** 190 EEK, 4 hours, one morning bus
**St Petersburg** 160 EEK, 7¾ hours, one bus
**Valga** 60 EEK, 1½-2½ hours, eight buses
**Viljandi** 45 EEK, 1½-2½ hours, 16 buses
**Võru** 45 EEK, 1½ hours, 26 buses

**Train** The seemingly abandoned **train station** (☎ 373 200; *Vaksali tänav 6)* is 750m west of Toomemägi. Timetables are posted outside, tickets are sold on the train. Call ☎ 373 220 or ☎ 1188 for train schedules.

Two trains make the unforgivably long ride to Tallinn (70 EEK, 3½ hours) daily. Four trains run from Tartu to Elva; two to Valga also stop at Elva. There is one to/from Põlva.

### Getting Around
The central stop for city buses is on Riia maantee, opposite the Kaubamaja department store.

You can rent cars, with reduced prices for longer rentals, from **Ainar Auto** (☎/fax 366 550; ⓔ ainaerauto@hot.ee; *Turu tänav 28)* or

**Toyota Rent A Car** (☎ 362 202; ⓔ *toyota@ valoor.ee; Aardla tänav 23a)*. Bikes can be rented from **Jalgratas** (☎ 421 731; *Laulupeo 19),* adjoining the Hotel Tähtvere.

## AROUND TARTU
There are many scenic places within 35km of Tartu which are all fine day-trip options.

### Elva
☎ 07 • pop 5980
A small town, 27km from Tartu in a hilly, forested landscape on the Tartu-Valga road, Elva has two pretty lakes, Verevi and Arbi, in the middle of the town. In the depths of winter Lake Arbi becomes a skating rink. About six trains and buses go there daily from Tartu.

Yet if you've made it this far, why not consider heading to the eastern shore of **Võrtsjärv**, Estonia's second biggest lake (266 sq km), 15km west of Elva.

**Vehendi**, 6km west of Rannu, is another good place to visit. Pine woods surround this quiet village, which has excellent fishing, swimming and boating opportunities.

**Places to Stay Verevi Guesthouse** (☎/fax 457 084; *Raudsepa tänav 2; singles/doubles 350/550 EEK),* overlooking Lake Verevi in Elva, is your best bet.

**Waide Motel** (☎ 306 606, fax 303 605; ⓔ *info@waide.ee; singles/doubles 380/595 EEK),* some 2km from Elva towards Rannu, is a two-storey cottage-like house, 600m from a swimming beach, with ample facilities for those who can't stand still: fishing, rowing and pedal-boat rental, bicycle rental, tennis, volleyball, mini-golf and ski hire.

**Vehendi Motel** (☎/fax 460 580; *beds for 1/2/4 people 300/500/800 EEK)* in nearby Vehendi, is a wonderful place with a sauna, pool and tennis court. Horse riding and boating activities are also available.

There's also a **campsite** by the beach at Trepimäe, to the north of Vehendi village.

### Activities
In Luunja, some 10km east of Tartu on the road to Räpina, **Saksa Talu** (☎ 351 087; ⓔ *saksahobused@hot.ee)* tailors horse riding and accommodation packages and invites participants for winter sled expeditions. There are two afternoon buses that leave gate No 8 daily from Tartu bus station (to the Sirgu stop).

Five kilometres west of Elva in Majala, **Sillu Tall** (☎ *052 65 414)* offers horseback tours of the environs for 100 EEK per hour in English, Finnish and German. No formal accommodation is offered but camping is welcome.

## OTEPÄÄ
☎ 076 • pop 2200

The serene hilltop town of Otepää, 44km south of Tartu, is the centre of a picturesque rural area with many small hills and lakes. The district is a favourite among Estonians for country breaks and, in winter, is Estonia's prime ski resort.

### Orientation & Information

The centre of town is the triangular main 'square', Lipuväljak, with the bus station just off its east corner. The post office is beside the bus station.

On Lipuväljak you'll find the classical Town Hall. Inside the hall is Otepää **tourist information centre** (☎ *55 364, fax 61 246;* e *otepaa@visitestonia.com; Lipuväljak 11; open 9am-6pm Mon-Fri, 9am-3pm Sat-Sun).* Luggage can be discreetly left at the tourist information centre free of charge.

There's also the headquarters of the **Otepää Nature Park** (☎ *55 876;* e *otepaa .looduspark@mail.ee; Kolga tee 28)* which oversees the 23,000 ha park that comprises forests and some 65 lakes, including Pühajärv.

The folks at the **Otepää Travel Agency** (☎ *54 060;* e *otepaarb@hot.ee; Lipuväljak 11)* are friendly and helpful and can assist with planning your visit to the region.

**Ühispank** *(Lipuväljak 11)* has currency exchange facilities and also gives cash advances on credit cards.

### Church

Otepää's pretty little 17th-century church is on a small hilltop across the fields about 100m northeast of the bus station. It was in this church on 23 May 1884 that the Estonian Students' Society consecrated its new blue, black and white flag – which in turn became the flag of independent Estonia. Facing the church's west door is a small mound with a monument to those who died in the 1918–20 independence war. The former vicar's residence now houses two museums – **Flag Museum** *(Eesti Lipu Muuseum;* ☎ *55 075)* and **Ski Museum** *(Suusamuuseum;* ☎ *63 670;*

e *suusamuuseum@hot.ee)* – both museums can be viewed by appointment.

### Linnamägi

The tree-covered hill south of the church is Linnamägi (Castle Hill), a major stronghold from the 10th to 12th centuries. There are traces of old fortifications on top, and good views of the surrounding country. Archaeological finds indicate that the area around the hill was inhabited as early as the 1st century.

### Pühajärv

The islets and indented shore of 3.5km long Pühajärv (Holy Lake) on the southwest edge of Otepää, provide some of the area's loveliest views. The lake is circled by tracks and walkable roads. Its northern tip is just over 2km away, along the Kääriku road, from Otepää centre. The lake's mystical aura no doubt accounts for its name, and the area was blessed by the Dalai Lama when he came to Tartu in 1992 for a conference of unrepresented nations. A **monument** to him stands to the east of the lake. Pühajärv, legend has it, was formed from the tears of mothers whose sons died in a battle of the Kalevipoeg epic, its islands are their burial mounds. Major midsummer Jaanipäev festivities take place here every year. If energy levels are low after the walk to the lake, recharge at the **energy column** down Mäe tänav. The column was erected in 1992 to mark the long held belief of psychics that this area resounds with positive energy.

### Activities

Otepää is Estonia's favourite ski destination and the breeding ground of many of its champions. Most skiing is cross-country but a ski jump looms out of the forest 1km south of the town at **Apteekri-mägi**, and there's downhill skiing available on **Kuutsemägi**, 12km west, **Ansomägi** 2km south, **Meegaste mägi** 10km west, and **Seinmägi** 10km to the southwest. The 63km Tartu **Ski Marathon** begins in Otepää every February.

Among the top ski centres is the **Kuutsemäe Sports Centre** (see Places to Stay – Out of Town later in this section) overlooking Kuutsemägi. It sells one-day hill tickets from 120 EEK for weekends, with reduced ticket prices Monday to Thursday. Full ski equipment is also available for hire. The centre also rents motor sledges and arranges ski tuition.

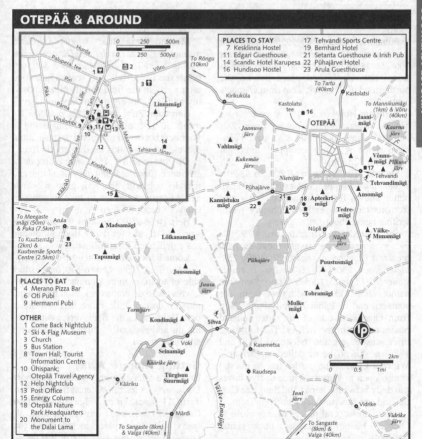

## OTEPÄÄ & AROUND

PLACES TO STAY
7 Kesklinna Hostel
11 Edgari Guesthouse
14 Scandic Hotel Karupesa
16 Hundisoo Hostel
17 Tehvandi Sports Centre
19 Bernhard Hotel
21 Setanta Guesthouse & Irish Pub
22 Pühajärve Hotel
23 Arula Guesthouse

PLACES TO EAT
4 Merano Pizza Bar
6 Oti Pubi
9 Hermanni Pubi

OTHER
1 Come Back Nightclub
2 Ski & Flag Museum
3 Church
5 Bus Station
8 Town Hall; Tourist Information Centre
10 Ühispank; Otepää Travel Agency
12 Help Nightclub
13 Post Office
15 Energy Column
18 Otepää Nature Park Headquarters
20 Monument to the Dalai Lama

---

The **Tehvandi Sports Centre** (see Places to Stay – Out of Town later in this section) rents ski equipment, skates and snowboards and in the warmer months water bikes, rollerblades and for something a little different, roller skis. Packages for canoeing and horseback riding are also offered.

### Places to Stay
**In Town** In the centre of town, **Kesklinna Hostel** (☎ 55 095; Lipuväljak 11; dorms beds 120-180 EEK, singles 250 EEK) has bare one- to four-bed rooms.

**Edgari Guesthouse** (☎ 54 275; Lipuväljak 3; singles/doubles 200/300 EEK), in the heart of town, has clean, freshly renovated rooms, dining and kitchenette, with a TV in the communal lounge.

**Scandic Hotel Karupesa** (☎ 61 500; e karupesa@scandic-hotels.ee; Tehvandi tänav 1a; singles/doubles/triples with breakfast 700/800/1000 EEK, suites with breakfast 1400-2200 EEK), has luxurious rooms. Its à la carte restaurant is definitely the finest – and most expensive – place to eat for miles around.

**Out of Town** About 1.5km from Otepää centre, **Hundisoo Hostel** (☎ 55 227, mobile 050 87 332; Kastolatsi tee 3; dorm beds 80-150 EEK; open year-round) is a very comfortable youth hostel with beds in standard or renovated rooms. All rooms come with shared bathroom.

**Tehvandi Sports Centre** (☎/fax 69 500; e tehvandi@tehvandi.ee; off Tehvandi tänav; singles/doubles/triples 380/490/690 EEK), just outside of Otepää, has neat and functional rooms.

**Pühajärve Hotel** (☎ 65 500; e pjpk@pjpk .ee; singles/doubles/suites/suites with sauna 600/750/1190/1390 EEK) is a large, institutional but refurbished place out on the northern tip of Pühajärv, 2km from Otepää's centre.

**Bernhard Hotel** (☎ 69 600; e hotell@bern hard.ee; Kolga tee 22a; doubles/triples 800/ 950 EEK, suites 1600-2500 EEK), near Pühajärve Hotel, is a fully equipped, three-star hotel with 32 rooms.

**Setanta Guesthouse** (☎ 68 200, fax 68 201; e setanta@estpak.ee; doubles from 650 EEK), better known for its Irish Pub, has views from its terrace over lake Pühajärv worth writing home about.

**Sangaste Castle** (Sangaste Loss; ☎ 79 300/ 01; e sloss@hot.ee; singles/doubles with breakfast & sauna low season 200/400 EEK, high season 250/500 EEK; museum adult/ student/6-12 yrs 15/10/5 EEK; open 9am-6pm daily), about 15km southwest from the southern end of Pühajärv and about 25km from Otepää, is one of the most unusual places to stay in the Baltics. The fairy-tale brick castle, erected between 1874 and 1881, is said to be modelled on Britain's Windsor Castle. The castle (free to guests) is also open to visitors. Three to five buses run daily between Otepää and Sangaste Castle, and one bus runs daily to/from Tartu.

There are several places to stay close to Otepää's slalom and cross-country skiing hot spots.

**Kuutsemäe Sports Centre** (☎ 69 007; e info@kuutsemae.ee; doubles/triples/quads 550/600/800 EEK, cottage 1900 EEK), right at the slalom course and downhill slopes, has a wide range of accommodation. Prices drop on weekdays and in summer, and a three-bedroom cottage with sauna can be rented.

**Arula Guesthouse** (☎ 70 690, fax 71 589; e arula@arula.ee; Arula village; bed in 1–5-bed dorm 300 EEK) is just 1km east of Kuutsemäe Sports Centre. Rooms have showers and breakfast is included in the price as well as use of the sauna and swimming pool. Ask about row- and paddle-boat rental in summer.

### Places to Eat & Drink
Most out-of-town hotels have their own restaurants, the **Setanta Irish Pub** (☎ 68 200,

fax 68 201; e setanta@estpak.ee) being one of the most popular.

**Merano Pizza Baar** (☎ 79 444; Tartu maantee 1a; pizzas under 60 EEK; open 9am-midnight Sun-Thur, until 4am Fri & Sat), opposite the Town Hall, may seem a little loud after a day in the field and its pizzas possibly a little lightweight, but they are tasty.

**Hermanni Pubi** (☎ 79 241; Lipuväljak 10; meals 60 EEK; open 11am-11pm daily) is your best bet for an inexpensive meal, amid recycled wooden skis used to good effect.

**Oti Pubi** (☎ 69 840, Lipuväljak 26, meals 70 EEK; open 10am-midnight daily) is a large and friendly pub with generous glass windows and an upstairs terrace to take in some of Otepää's beautiful scenery.

**Help** (☎ 55 267; Lipuväljak 4; open 10pm-4am Fri-Sat) calls for dance floor action and has a dedicated local following.

**Come Back** (Tartu maantee 16; open 10pm-3am Sun-Thur, 10pm-4am Fri-Sat), on the other side of town, is more popular with out-of-towners who do come back even though admission costs a little more here! Music at both Help and Come Back varies with visiting djs and is usually a blend of innovative and mainstream.

### Getting There & Away
Buses are Otepää's only public transport. Daily services to/from Otepää include: from Tartu 11 buses; from Valga, via Sangaste Castle, six buses; and from Tallinn three (3½ hours) buses. Other places include Põlva, two buses; Võru, one bus daily. For further details on bus timetables visit w www.bussireisid.ee.

## PÕLVA & TAEVASKOJA
☎ 079 • pop 7200
Põlva lies in an attractive valley 48km southeast of Tartu, and is well worth a stop on the way to Võru, 25km to its south. The town itself has little to entice tourists – although its typical country church dates from 1452 and there are two war monuments. It's a good springboard for exploring the surrounding countryside. The **tourist information office** (☎/fax 94 089; e polva@visitestonia.com, w www.polvamaale.ee; Kesk tänav 16; open 10am-6pm Mon-Fri, 10am-2pm Sat & Sun) and **Kagureis travel agency** (☎ 98 530, fax 98 531; w www.kagureis.ee; Uus tänav 5) can help organise hiking, biking, canoeing, riding and skiing trips. This agency also organises

accommodation at Pesa Hotel and Timmo Riding Centre (see Places to Stay & Eat for details).

Taevaskoja, 7km north of Põlva, is in the valley of the Ahja River and an idyllic base for expeditions of all kinds, or just for a picnic. The area is noted for two large caves, Väike and Suur Taevaskoja, which are about 2km past the train tracks coming from the Tartu–Põlva road. There are strikingly beautiful red sandstone embankments above the caves, up to 24m high and 190m long, pockmarked by swallows and kingfishers which nest in them. Signposted multilingual commentaries detail the myths that surround these formations. There are paths and biking trails in the surrounding woods, and you can also walk up the river to Kiidjärv, 6km north, where you can take to a canoe.

### Places to Stay & Eat

**Pesa Hotel** (☎ 98 530, fax 98 531; Uus tänav 5; singles/doubles 500/660 EEK), in Põlva, is a modern, though pricey, hotel with comfortable rooms. There is also a restaurant and many activities on offer here, such as cycling and canoeing trips, plus snowboarding and snowmobiles for hire.

**Timmo Riding Centre** (bookings taken through Kagureis at the Pesa Hotel; beds 150-200 EEK), just 3km north of Põlva, can put you up for the night or put you up on a horse for a ride. Camping equipment and bikes can also be hired here. The stables have a small pub on the premises.

**Taevaskoja Tourism & Holiday Centre** (☎ 92 067, mobile 051 49 822; beds per person from 150 EEK), in Taevaskoja, will see to it that you'll enjoy yourself, year-round. There are 17km canoe trips on the narrow but pretty Ahja River (which has some rapids), bike tours, bird observation tours in spring, and winter sled picnics and skiing. They can also organise basic cabin-style accommodation.

**Restaurant Põlva** (☎ 94 110; Kesk tänav 10; meals 80 EEK) is your best bet for a decent meal in town.

### Getting There & Away

From Tartu you can reach Põlva either by bus (one hour, 12 daily) or by the daily train (one hour).

Taevaskoja is 2km east of the Tartu-Põlva road, which is the nearest a bus will take you. There are 11 buses daily between Põlva

and Võru, two between Põlva and Otepää and eight between Põlva and Tallinn.

A daily train from Tartu stops at Taevaskoja, which is a 1km walk from the Tourism and Holiday Centre and 2km from the caves, but this does not allow for a convenient day trip.

## VÕRU
☎ 078 • pop 14,800
Võru, 64km south of Tartu on the eastern shore of Lake Tamula, is a provincial town. It has the headquarters for many organisations which promote regional tourism and aim to protect the local culture, language and tradition, unique to Estonia.

The **Võro Institute** (☎ 21 960; e wi@wi.ee; w www.wi.ee) declared Võro-Seto a separate language in 1998, rather than a dialect of Estonian as it had previously been considered. The north- and south-Estonian languages developed quite separately until the end of the 19th century when, in the interests of nationalism, a one-country, one-language policy was adopted, with the dominant north Estonian becoming the country's main language. Today, many (mostly older) people in Võrumaa and Setumaa can be heard conversing in Võro-Seto, which sounds choppier than Estonian.

### Information

Võru has a **tourist information centre** (☎/fax 21 881; e info@visitestonia.com, w www.vorulinn.ee; Tartu maantee 31; open 10am-6pm Mon-Fri, 10am-2pm Sat & Sun May-Sept, 9am-5pm Mon-Fri Oct-Feb).

### Things to See & Do

Võru, founded in 1784 by a special decree from Catherine the Great, was the home of Friedrich Reinhold Kreutzwald (1803–82) who was named the father of Estonian literature for his folk epic Kalevipoeg and who worked as a doctor here. His former home is now the **Kreutzwald Memorial Museum** (Kreutzwaldi tänav 31; adult/student 10/5 EEK; open 10am-5pm Wed-Sun).

In front of the 18th-century **Lutheran Church** overlooking the central square is a granite **monument** to 17 local town council officials who lost their lives in the 1994 Estonia ferry disaster.

There's a cinema inside the **Cultural Centre** (Liiva tänav 11). **Võrumaa Regional**

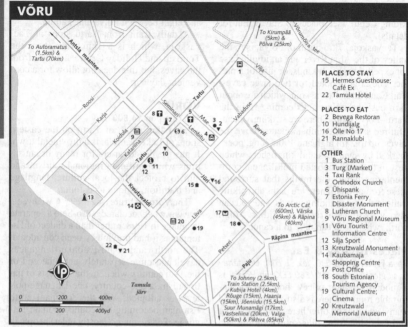

**VÕRU**

PLACES TO STAY
15 Hermes Guesthouse;
 Café Ex
22 Tamula Hotel

PLACES TO EAT
2 Bevega Restoran
10 Hundijalg
16 Õlle No 17
21 Rannaklubi

OTHER
1 Bus Station
3 Turg (Market)
4 Taxi Rank
5 Orthodox Church
6 Ühispank
7 Estonia Ferry
 Disaster Monument
8 Lutheran Church
9 Võru Regional Museum
11 Võru Tourist
 Information Centre
12 Silja Sport
13 Kreutzwald Monument
14 Kaubamaja
 Shopping Centre
17 Post Office
18 South Estonian
 Tourism Agency
19 Cultural Centre;
 Cinema
20 Kreutzwald
 Memorial Museum

**Museum** (Katariina tänav 11; adult/student 8/3 EEK; open 11am-4pm Wed-Sun) is a local history museum.

**Silja Sport** (☎ 21 916; e siljasport@hot.ee; Tartu tänav 31) rents bikes, snowboards and ski equipment. Ask the tourist information centre (see Information earlier in this section) about December snow-safari tours.

There's **Ühispank** (Tartu maantee 25) and a conveniently located **Kaubamaja** department store (Kreutzwaldi tänav 30) here too. Car rental is available through **Autoramatus** (☎ 23 505; Antsla tee 46c).

## Organised Tours
The **South Estonian Tourism Agency** (☎ 68 680, fax 68 681; e tourism@wk.ee; w www .tourism.wk.ee; Jüri tänav 22a) knows the attractions of Võrumaa well – they can arrange all kinds of tours, including excursions to Haanja Nature Reserve and Setumaa both sides of the border, Setu song performances and day trips to Russia. Some innovative health packages are also offered.

**Toonus Plus** (☎ 076-79 702 evenings only, mobile 050 55 702; w www.toonuspluss.ee), near Arula and about 10km from Otepää,

specialises in canoeing trips, which include combined hiking and mountain biking tours for all ages and abilities. Routes include Võru to Räpina, Räpina to Tartu and Põlva to Värska.

## Places to Stay & Eat
The tourist information centre can arrange accommodation in and around Võru, as does the South Estonian Tourism agency.

**Hermes Guesthouse** (☎ 21 326, fax 23 231; e hermes@hot.ee; Jüri tänav 32A; singles/ doubles without bathroom from 200/300 EEK, with bathroom from 410/520 EEK) has nice rooms despite the characterless exterior, though better options exist out of town.

**Kubija Hotel** (☎ 22 341, fax 22 342; e infor@kubija.ee; Männiku tänav 43; singles/ doubles/twin 650/750/850 EEK), out of town and 4km south of the centre, offers rooms with bathroom, balcony and breakfast.

**Tamula Hotel** (☎ 30 430, fax 30 431; e hotell@tamula.ee; Vee tänav 4; singles/ doubles 500/800 EEK) is a pristine new complex on the 'beach', with a tennis court.

**Jõeniidu** (☎ 78 816; beds Mon-Fri 180 EEK, Sat & Sun 200 EEK), 16km from Võru, offers farmhouse accommodation a 2km walk from the Haanja Nature Reserve and Lake Vaskna. Boating and sauna facilities are available and discounts are offered for kids.

**Õlle no 17** (☎ 28 461; Jüri tänav 17; meals 70 EEK) is still a popular choice for pub meals, omelettes and drinks.

**Hundijalg** (☎ 24 073; Jüri tänav 18B; meals 75 EEK) is a local favourite for lunches, its open grill behind the bar makes a very tasty meal.

**Bevega Restoran** (☎ 25 960; Mäe tänav 11; meals 100 EEK; open 11am-1am Mon-Wed, 11am-6am Thur-Sat) is a fine semi-formal restaurant with a wide menu selection and well-stocked bar.

**Café Ex** (Jüri tänav 32A; open 7am-11pm daily) is the best spot for breakfast.

**Johnny** (☎ 30 192; open 11am-midnight Sun-Thur, 11am-2am Fri & Sat) is a combo shop, fuel station and restaurant, located 3km out of town towards Haanja. If you have a car, the food is worth the trip.

**Rannaklubi** (☎ 21 777; Vee tänav 6; open 10pm-4am Fri & Sat) sits in a prime position by the shore of Lake Tamula. A magnet for locals and visitors, the outdoor seating facilitates long summer evening drinks or a walk by the lake between rounds.

### Getting There & Away

There are about 28 buses to/from Tartu daily (35 EEK, 1½ hours), 12 buses run to/ from Tallinn (85 EEK, 4½ hours), ten to/ from Põlva (15 EEK, 1½ hours), about four to Rõuge, Haanja or Krabi, and a bus once a week direct to Pskov and Kiev. The **bus station** (☎ 21 018) can provide the latest schedules. Take the bus to Tartu for a connection to/from Rīga and St Petersburg.

## HAANJA NATURE PARK
☎ 078

This 20,000-hectare protected area south of Võru includes some of the nicest scenery in the country and is where several of the best tourist farms are located. The **nature park headquarters** (☎ 29 090; w www.haanjapark .ee) in the village of Haanja can provide detailed information about the area and its skiing opportunities.

### Suur Munamägi & Haanja

Suur Munamägi (Great Egg Hill!) is 17km south of Võru. It's the highest hill in the

Baltics at just over 318m, though it's still easy to miss if you're not looking out for it. (Vällämägi, 4km north of Haanja, is 304m above sea level but has a higher relative height.) Suur Munamägi is part of the Haanja Upland, between Võru and the Latvian border, which has three other hills over 290m. It is covered in trees, which mask the 29m observation tower which looks out of place here, plonked on its summit in 1939.

The summit and **observation tower** (☎ 78 847; adult/child 15/7 EEK; open 10am-8pm daily May-Aug, 10am-5pm daily Sept, 10am-8pm Sat & Sun Oct) are a 10-minute climb from the Võru–Ruusmäe road, starting about 1km south of Haanja. On a clear day you might be able to see Tartu's TV towers and church spires in Pskov. Near the start of the path is a monument to the dead of the Battle of Munamägi in Estonia's 1918–20 independence war.

**Hurda Farm** (☎ 72 297) can enlighten you to the mysteries of the Druids' horoscope and traditional uses of local herbs. There are also options to keep the kids busy, camping and tent rental is also available.

## Rõuge
pop 2140

Ten kilometres west of Suur Munamägi by dirt road, or by paved road from Võru, the very special village of Rõuge stands on the edge of Ööbikuorg (Nightingale Valley). The valley is named for its nightingales which gather in spring (the natural acoustics carry their song). Rõuge is strung with a chain of seven small lakes – Suurjärv, in the middle of the village, is Estonia's deepest lake (38m) and is said to have healing properties. After centuries of tales of the water's powers and the area's special energy fields, the lake was dubbed 'Witches Lake' by Christians.

This is Estonia's prettiest village, with a quiet landscape of gentle, rolling hills and delicate, sheltered valleys reminiscent of an English countryside. There are numerous hiking, biking and cross-country skiing trails in and around the village and forests.

Rõuge's Linnamägi (Castle Hill), by the lake Linnjärv, was an ancient Estonian stronghold in the 8th to the 11th centuries. In the 13th century, Rougetaja lived here, a man who healed people with his hands, and to whom the ailing travelled from afar to see. There's a good view here, across the valley.

Opposite Rõuge's simple village church, dating from 1730, there's a monument to the local dead of the 1918–20 independence war. It was buried in one local's backyard through the Soviet period to save it from destruction.

Nearby are some natural water springs which bubble and spurt (follow the wooden stairs down from Ööbikuorg).

There's a **tourist information centre** (☎/fax 59 245; e raugeinfo@hot.ee) in Rõuge, 30m from the bus stop.

For a unique tour of the area and historical explanations of local sites and lore, call **Padimees** (☎ 59 271), who works out of the Saarsilla café. Padimees can guide you through nearby places to assess whether you are sensitive to the area's energy fields.

### Places to Stay & Eat

**Vaskna Talu** (☎ 29 173; e info@vaskna.ee; singles/twins per person/doubles 300/250/500 EEK), just south of Haanja by lake Vaskna, is a farmhouse in a particularly pretty spot. Swimming, boating and water-biking are possible here.

**Rohtlätte Talu** (☎ 79 315; camping/rooms per person 30/200 EEK), near the village of Nursi, 12km from Võru on the Valga road, is a comfortable place offering boating trips on lake Kahrila.

**Mäe Talu** (☎ 59 150; e kalmer.kobak@ mail.ee; rooms per person from 140 EEK) is near the village centre on a peaceful hill, a good starting point for many hiking trails, and a sauna is available.

**Saarsilla Café** (☎ 59 271; Haanja maantee 2; open 10am-11pm daily), just outside of Rõuge, boasts a lovely terrace by lake Suurjärv. Several shops, a few cafés, a restaurant and a post office lie 1km out of town on the road to Nursi.

### LUHASOO, PAGANAMAA & KARULA NATIONAL PARKS
☎ 078

Some 15km south of Rõuge, hugging the Latvian border, is the Luhasoo Nature Study Trail located in wild swampland. While a walk through a swamp may not be what you had in mind, this 4.5km well-marked trail through a landscape very typical of Estonia will deepen your understanding of the land and the myths it has given birth to as well as acquaint you with some resilient yet delicate

### Devil's Run

Along the Latvian border just south of the village of Krabi lies **Paganamaa** (Devil's Land), another scenic area with four lakes strung out along the Estonian side of the border in the Piiriorg Valley. Legend has it that this was the home of Vanapagan (Old Heathen), a devil who set about building a bridge across Lake Kikkajärv to his friends in Latvia. As he was collecting boulders, a thunderstorm frightened him (thunder was the god of heaven to ancient Estonians) and he ran, creating the craters and sharp valleys that are characteristic of the area (glacier-formed, to us modern heathens). The small island in Kikkajärv is supposed to be one of the boulders he dropped on the run. There's an observation tower and bathing spot at Liivajärv, a lake which lies half in Estonia, half in Latvia.

nature. Venus flytraps (an insectivorous plant) grow here, as do water lilies and many types of berries.

To get there, take the Krabi road from Rõuge and, after the Pärlijõe bus stop turn right towards Kellamäe, then continue another 5km. Bring rubber boots, and stick to the boarded trails to protect the land.

Farther along the main road bordering Paganamaa, and 12km along dirt roads north of the village of Mõniste, is an area of round, wooded hills dotted with many small lakes and ancient stone burial mounds which forms the Karula National Park. The **National Park Visitors Centre** (☎ 52 456; e kiri@karularahvuspark.ee) in Ahijärve past Lüllemäe, 25km east of Valga. The highlight is Ähijärv, a 3km long lake with several bays, inlets and promontories. This area can also be reached via Antsla to the north. In addition to information available at the visitor centre, boards are posted at other sites around the park. There are four marked trails in the park, the longest beginning in Lüllemäe.

**Veetka Farm** (☎ 67 633; e irjekarjus@ hot.ee) can acquaint you with the charms of the region through winter sleigh rides, or the charms of your travelling companion with a romantic raft ride for two. Enter the realm of the Forest Fairy with trips to **Metsamoor** park and learn about local herbs or try cooking as the woodsfolk do.

## Places to Stay

In Vastse-Roosa, near Mõniste **Metsavenna Talu** (☎ 91 280; e metsavenna.talu@mail.ee; camping Metsavanna/regular camping/chalet beds 20/30/200 EEK), 8km west of Paganamaa, has an authentic reconstruction of typical living quarters used by the Forest Brothers resistance (Metsavendlus). Being the initiative of one of the original brothers, authenticity is assured. It is also possible to camp overnight in the quarters, or opt for regular camping or chalet beds. Sauna or guided nature tour is also available.

## VALGA

☎ 076 • pop 14,200

The border town of Valga, contiguous with Valka in Latvia, is where the Rīga–Tartu road, and the main railway from Rīga and the south, enter Estonia. This region was the only one in serious contention between Estonia and Latvia after WWI as they defined their borders. A British mediator had to be called in to settle the dispute and suggested the current border line, effectively splitting the town in two.

Sites of interest include the 19th-century **St John's Church** (Jaani Kirik), and a local history **museum** (Valga Koduloomuuseum).

An estimated 30,000 people were murdered at the Nazi death camp Stalag-351, located in converted stables at Priimetsa on Valga's outskirts.

The train station, doubling as a bus station where there's a map of the town on an outside billboard, was built after the war by German prisoners. Non-Estonian and non-Latvian passport holders cannot cross at any of the city borders, but only at the international crossing out of town.

Between two and five daily buses run between Tartu and Valga (1¾ hours). Trains run from Tallinn to Valga twice per week. Twice daily trains go from Tartu to Valga via Sangaste Castle. There are also eight buses daily to Sangaste Castle. For bus schedules call ☎ 41 513; train schedules ☎ 64 207.

If stuck in Valga, a far better fate than being stuck in Valka, the **Hotel Söde** (☎ 41 650; Jaama tänav 1; singles/doubles from 290/490 EEK) has basic rooms but friendly service.

## VASTSELIINA CASTLE

Vastseliina Castle (Vastseliina linnus) was founded by the Germans on their border with Russia in the 14th century. The evocative ruins stand on a high bluff above the Piusa River on the eastern edge of the village of Vahtseliina, 4km east of the small town of Vastseliina, itself 12km southeast of Võru along the road to Pskov (Pihkva). The area prospered from its position on the Pskov–Rīga trade route until the mid-19th century and was also the scene of many battles.

The castle stands on the Meremäe road out of Vahtseliina. In the valley, down to the left as you walk from the former inn to the castle, is the park of the old Vastseliina manor, where a pretty 15km hiking trail (Piusa Matkarada) along the river begins a circuit north to Suuremetsa. A map near the ruins details the region's hiking and mountain biking routes.

To reach Vahtseliina turn east off the Võru–Pskov (Pihkva) road 1km south of the southernmost turning to Vastseliina (which is just west of the road) and go 2km. Several buses from Võru go to Vastseliina daily and some, including most of those to Misso, continue along the Pskov road to the Vahtseliina turning and beyond.

## SETUMAA

In the far southeast of Estonia lies the (politically unrecognised) area of Setumaa, stretching over into Russia. It's one of the most interesting and tragic areas of the country, politically and culturally. Its native people, the Setus, have a mixed Estonian-Russian culture. They are originally Finno-Ugric but the people became Orthodox, not Lutheran, because this part of the country fell under Novgorod and later Pskov's subjugation and was not controlled by Teutonic and German tribes and barons, as was the rest of Estonia. They never fully assimilated into Russian culture and throughout the centuries retained their language (today known as Võro-Seto; see Võru earlier in this chapter), many features of which are actually closer in structure to Old Estonian than the modern Estonian language. The same goes for certain cultural traditions, for instance leaving food on a relative's grave; this was practised by Estonian tribes before Lutheranism.

All of Setumaa was in independent Estonia between 1920 and 1940, but the greater part of it is now in Russia. The town of **Pechory** (Estonian: Petseri), 2km across the border in Russia and regarded as the 'capital' of Setumaa, is famed for its fabulous 15th-century monastery, considered the most breathtaking in Russia (it looks more like an Italian villa than a monastery).

Today, the Setu culture is in the sad, slow process of disappearing. There are approximately 4000 Setus in Estonia (another 3000 in Russia), half the early 20th century population. While efforts are made to teach and preserve the language, and promote customs through organised feasts, the younger generation are being quickly assimilated into the Estonian mainstream. The impenetrable border with Russia that has split their community since 1991 has further crippled it.

A rough look at the Setu landscape illustrates how unique it is in the Estonian context. Notably, their villages are structured like castles, with houses facing each other in clusters, often surrounded by a fence. This is in stark contrast to the typical Estonian village where open farmhouses are separated from each other as far as possible. Here, the Orthodox tradition has fostered a tighter sense of community and sociability.

Setumaa is particularly known for its women folk singers who improvise new words each time they chant their verses. Setu songs, known as the *leelo* are polyphonic and characterised by solo, spoken verses followed by a refrain chanted by a group.

## Obinitsa & Piusa
☎ 078

In Obinitsa, there is a **tourist information centre** (☎ 54 190; e *srtour@hot.ee*) with handicrafts for sale, and the worthwhile and interesting **Setu House Museum** (*Setu Tare Muuseum; adult/student 10/5 EEK, guided tour 25 EEK; open 11am-5pm Tues-Sun May-Oct, other times by arrangement*) doubles as an archive of Setu culture. With advance notice it can provide meals from the Setu kitchen. Also in town is a church (1897), a cemetery and a sculpture to the Setu 'Song Mother', which stares solemnly over lake Obinitsa. This is the site of many Setu celebrations and feast days.

The road north from Obinitsa passes under a railway bridge after some 5km. The first dirt road east, following the sign for the Piusa Pood (shop), will take you to one of the most unique sights in Estonia, the **Piusa sand caves**. The Piusa Koopad are what's left from a sand mining industry begun in

the area in 1922. Sand is still mined for glass production 1km north of this spot. You can visit the smaller of the two unused caves; the larger one is plunged in darkness and home to 2000 bats (one of Europe's largest bat counts, so you probably wouldn't want to intrude), just behind the friendly shop/café.

Wander through a maze of cathedral-like caves – bring a flashlight! – inspect the would-be works of art carved into the walls or look for the sand altar, made by some well known modern-day Estonian witches in the early 1990s. If you place your palms on the altar top and they feel warm, your spiritual energy is derived from the land, if they feel cold, your energy comes from the sky.

## Värska & Around
☎ 079

The pretty town of Värska is known for its mineral water, drunk throughout Estonia, and its healing mud baths. There's also the **Setu Farm Museum** (*Setu Talu Muuseum;* ☎ *64 359; adult/student 10/5 EEK*) on the south edge of town, presided over by a large wooden effigy of Peko (See the boxed text 'Day of the Setus'). The museum comprises a recreated 19th-century farmhouse and outbuildings, it also displays modern Setu-inspired handcrafts with books and recordings of traditional Setu music available.

**Võporzova** and **Tonja**, a few kilometres north of Värska on the west side of Värska Bay, are classic Setu villages. In Võporzova there's a monument to folk singer Anne Vabarna who knew 100,000 verses by heart. Võporzova homesteads typically consist of a ring of outer buildings around an inner yard, while Tonja's houses face the lake from which its people get their livelihood.

Traditional Setu holidays are still celebrated. The biggest feast of the year, **Lady Day**, falls on 28 August (though it is celebrated only in Pechory) close to which the **Day of the Setu Kingdom** is held. The **Day of the Setu Lace** is 1 March and **midsummer** celebrations are held on 6 July in accordance with the Julian calendar (see the boxed text 'Day of the Setus').

Other exotic features of this area are the borders. There are only a few official border crossing points with Russia, the rest are abandoned control points, or seemingly unguarded wooden fences, creepy dead ends or lonely plastic signs. One road, from Värska

## Day of the Setus

Peko, the pagan god of fertility, is as important to the Setus as the Orthodox religion they follow. The 8000-line Setu epic *Pekolanõ* tells the tale of this macho god, the rites of whom are known only to men. The epic dates back to 1927 when the Setus' most celebrated folk singer, Anne Vabarna, was told the plot and spontaneously burst into song, barely pausing to draw breath until she had sung the last (8000th) line.

The Setus don't have a proper king. He sleeps night and day in his cave of sand, according to traditional Setu folklore. So, on the Day of the Setu Kingdom – proclaimed around 20 August each year – a *ülemtsootska* (representative) for the king has to be found. The Setus then gather around the statue of their 'song mother' in search of a singer worthy of being crowned the sleeping king's royal singer. Competitions of a less aesthetically pleasing nature are later held to find a strongman for the king.

The Setu king's dress, and the bread, cheese, wine and beer he eats and drinks are important too. On the same day that his kingdom is declared for another year, people from the Setu stronghold are selected to serve the king as his mitten and belt knitters, and bread, beer, wine and cheese makers.

And so completes the royal throne. Amid the day's glorious celebrations, traditional Setu songs and dances are performed and customary good wishes exchanged. The women are adorned with traditional Setu lace and large silver breast plates and necklaces, said to weigh as much as 2kg or 3kg each. Later in the day respects are paid to the dead.

In 1996, the Setu community made steps to join the Unrepresented Nations & Peoples Organisation (UNPO), a worldwide organisation serving to unite unrepresented peoples such as Chechens, Kurds and Setus.

to Saatse even crosses the zigzagging border line (agreements on which to this day have not been finalised) into Russian territory for 2km. You're not allowed to stop on this stretch.

Near the tiny, ancient village of **Podmotsa**, northeast of Värska, a beautiful Orthodox church in the Russian village of Kulje is visible across the inlet – as is the border guard watchtower. Where the road ends at the border is a clearing that would make an ideal camp site for the eccentric tourist. But be aware that crossing the border at any nonofficial point (even if you have a Russian visa) is illegal and can lead to your arrest.

### Places to Stay

The Obinitsa tourist information centre has the names of several inexpensive and comfortable farm-stay possibilities in Obinitsa and Meremäe. The South Estonian Tourism Agency in Võru (see Võru earlier in this chapter) organises farm stays in Setumaa, including the Setu communities in Russia.

**Värska Hotel** (☎ 64 635; Silla tänav 1b; e värska.hotell@mail.ee; singles/doubles with breakfast 250/490 EEK) is nicer inside than it looks from the outside and has decent rooms.

**Värska Sanatoorium** (☎ 64 793; rooms per person 170-240 EEK), 3km north of Värska in

the village of Väike-Rõsna, has a sickly, medicinal odour, but its rooms are cheap, as are its mud baths, water massages and meals.

### Getting There & Away

There are four buses a day each way between Tartu and Värska, via Räpina. The same bus can continue on to Koidula, 2km across the border from Pechory. From Võru, at least three buses a day go to Meremäe-Obinitsa. There are no buses running between Võru and Värska.

### LAKE PEIPSI (SOUTH)
☎ 07

In the 18th and 19th centuries, Russian Old Believers, a sect of the Orthodox Church persecuted for refusing to accept liturgical reforms carried out by Patriarch Nikon in 1666, took refuge on the western shores of Lake Peipsi (Chudkoye Ozero in Russian), particularly in Kallaste. They founded several coastal villages, namely Kolkja, Kasepää, and Varnja, and settled the island of Piirisaar.

Four kilometres south of **Alatskivi** and 38km from Tartu, in the hamlet of Rupsi, is the **Liiv Museum** (☎ 453 846; e lm@kiirtee .ee), well worth a stop on your way into the region. It houses exhibitions on both Juhan Liiv, a celebrated writer and poet who died in

1913, and Eduard Tubin, a composer of some of Estonia's best known songs and symphonies (No 5 is highly regarded). Both were born in the area. Occasional concerts and poetry competitions are held at the museum, which also doubles as the region's tourist information centre. Visitors are welcome at any time of the day or night.

From Alatskivi, it's a worthwhile 6km ride or drive southeast to **Kolkja**, a village of Russian Old Believers with a dainty, green wooden Orthodox church, an **Old Believers' Museum** (*☎ 453 445, mobile 050 49 908; open only by arrangement*) in the new schoolhouse, and some of the most charming village architecture in the country. Unlike most of Estonia's Russian population, the people and their descendants have been living here for centuries, and most also speak Estonian. Few tourists make it out here, and even the dogs stop and stare at strangers; this is true Estonian exotica.

**Kallaste** (pop 1285), 8km north of Alatskivi, is where a settlement of Old Believers has existed since 1720, when the area was known as Krasniye Gori (Red Mountains) because of the red sandstone cliffs up to 11m high that surround this town. Nearly all the villagers are Russian-speaking. There's a large Old Believers' cemetery at the southern end of town, a sandy beach with small caves, and a **lakeside café** (*open until 1am daily*).

The northern half of Lake Peipsi is covered in the Northeast Estonia chapter.

## Places to Stay & Eat

The best places to stay in the area are just north of Kallaste.

**Hansu Farm** (*☎/fax 452 518; ⓔ hans.turism@mail.ee; beds 220 EEK*) is about 3km north of Kallaste at the village of Kodavere, and 50m west of the main road. This pleasant farmhouse has a sauna, home-cooking, and a programme for 'health tourism'.

**Pootsman** (*☎ 734 411, mobile 07 73 411, ⓔ pootsman@pootsman.ee; tent sites 30 EEK, beds 300 EEK*), also near Kodavere, on the main road is about 2km from the shore of Lake Peipsi. In addition to accommodation, it organises boat and pedal boat rental and has a sauna, shop and café.

## Getting There & Away

Though a car is the handiest way of getting around this area, biking is an excellent option (though outside Tartu, official bike rental is next to impossible to find). At least eight buses a day go to/from Tartu to Kallaste, some of which stop in Alatskivi, about five of them stop in Kolkja (two on weekends).

## Piirisaar

An island on the border with Russia, 50km due east of Tartu, Piirisaar marks the southern end of Lake Peipsi. It used to be a refuge for young men fleeing from conscription into tsarist armies. In its heyday at the end of the 1920s, the island had 700 inhabitants. Now 97 Russian Old Believers live there and their average age is 64. There's a working church with services every Sunday morning, a border guard station (climb the observation tower for a great view), a general store, a few villages, marshland and not much else. A visit on the two biggest feast days in the Orthodox Old Believers' calendar could prove interesting: 12 July is **Peter and Paul Day**, and 28 August is **Uspeniya** (Lady Day).

Hydrofoils make the 90-minute trip Friday and Sunday all summer from the River Port in Tartu. Only on Sunday morning can you make a stopover (3 hours). Accommodation on the island can be arranged by the general store (*☎ 434 160*).

# West Estonia & the Islands

West Estonia is the most intriguing part of provincial Estonia. The large islands of Hiiumaa and Saaremaa, with their trademark windmills, juniper groves, old-fashioned rural pace and coastal vistas stretching gently into infinity, are close to an Estonian idea of earthly paradise. The region claims more sunshine and less snow than the mainland. Less visited, smaller islands, the Vilsandi National Park and much of the mainland coast, including the historic town of Haapsalu and the Matsalu Nature Reserve – a water bird sanctuary – are also integral parts of the 'Estonian experience'.

The Biosphere Reserve of the West Estonian Archipelago was set up in 1989 to protect the natural wonders of Saaremaa, Hiiumaa, Muhu, Vormsi and the hundreds of islands in the vicinity. The Läänemaa region around Haapsalu is now part of the Silma Nature Reserve (see under Vormsi later in this chapter and the Facts about Estonia chapter for more information).

Camping in Saaremaa is an option best considered from mid-May to early September as many sites at other times are closed or without heating. Camp sites can book out very early on, so do call ahead.

Several travel agencies in Tallinn and the larger towns on the islands arrange tours to the west Estonian islands (see under Travel Agencies in the Tallinn chapter and Information in the Kärdla and Kuressaare sections of this chapter for details). The Estonian Ecotourism Association website (W www .ecotourism.ee) is a useful source of ecotourism information.

## HAAPSALU
☎ 047 • pop 12,000
Haapsalu stands on a peninsula jutting out into Haapsalu Bay, a 15km inlet on Estonia's west coast. It is a pleasant place to stroll through for a few hours or for a stop overnight on the way to or from Hiiumaa. It's also a good base for visiting Vormsi Island, Noarootsi or Matsalu Nature Reserve.

### History
Following conquest of this region by the German Knights of the Sword in 1224, the Ösel-Wiek (Estonian: Saare-Lääne) bishopric,

## Highlights

- Follow the path of Russia's 18th century elite, along the promenade beside Haapsalu's Africa beach
- Discover Estonia's Swedish history on the nature-rich island of Vormsi or Orissaar, Oden's island grave
- Take the Lighthouse Tour of Hiiumaa and share in some Hiiumite humour over a Hiiu brew
- Go seal-spotting or study rare orchids in the remote Vilsandi National Park
- Witness the impact of Soviet military installations and a meteorite crater on the island of Saaremaa
- Feed a gothic fantasy or reflect on a medieval mystery at Kuressaare's castle

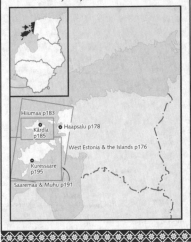

Hiiumaa p183
Kärdla p185
Haapsalu p178
West Estonia & the Islands p176
Kuressaare p195
Saaremaa & Muhu p191

covering west Estonia and its offshore islands, was formed in 1228. For over 300 years the bishops ruled most parts of the region from Rīga.

Haapsalu became the bishop's residence in the 1260s and a fortress and cathedral were built soon afterwards. In 1559, early in the Livonian War, the territory fell into the hands of Danish Duke Magnus. Swedes gained control in the 17th century but Russia wrested the region from them during the Great Northern War.

# WEST ESTONIA & THE ISLANDS

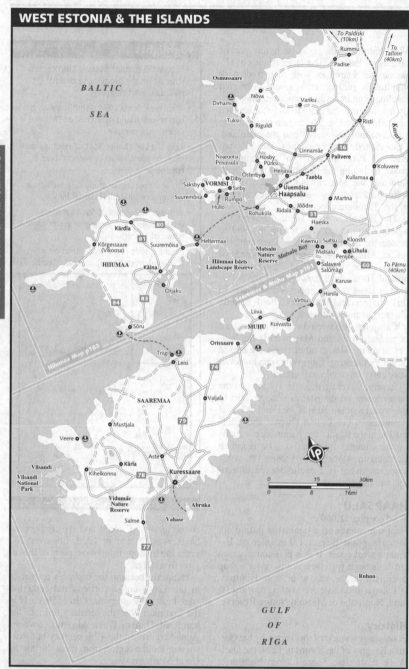

To Paldiski (10km)
Rummu
To Tallinn (40km)
Padise

BALTIC SEA

Osmussaare

Nõva
Variku
Dirhami
Risti
Tuksi
Riguldi
17
16
Linnamäe
Palivere
Koluvere
Noarootsi Peninsula
Hosby
Pürksi
Herjava
Kullamaa
Österby
Diby
Taebla
Martna
Säksby
VORMSI
Sviby
Üuemõisa
Suuremõisa
Rumpo
Haapsalu
Hüllo
Rohuküla
Ridala
Jõõdre
31
Haeska

Kärdla
80
Suuremõisa
Keemu
Suitsu
Kloostri
81
Heltermaa
Matsalu
Lihula
Körgessaare (Vikoosa)
Matsalu Nature Reserve
Matsalu Bay
Penijõe
HIIUMAA
Käina
Salavere
60
To Pärnu (40km)
Hiiumaa Islets Landscape Reserve
Salümägi
Orjaku
Karuse
84
83
Virtsu
Hanila
Sõru
Liiva
MUHU
Kuivastu
Trigi
Orissaare
Leisi
74

SAAREMAA
Valjala
Mustjala
79
Veere
Aste
Vilsandi
Kärla
Vilsandi National Park
Kihelkonna
78
Kuressaare
Vidumäe Nature Reserve
Abruka
Salme
Vahase
77
Ruhnu

0    15    30km
0    8    16mi

GULF OF RĪGA

In the 19th century Haapsalu became a spa centre when the curative properties of its shoreline mud were discovered. The Russian composer Tchaikovsky and members of the Russian imperial family would visit the city for mud baths. A railway from Tallinn and St Petersburg was built between 1904 and 1907 and a 214m-long covered platform, said to be the longest in the former Russian empire, was built at Haapsalu station to shelter eminent arrivals. The imposing covered platform with its wooden lace ornaments and grand colonnade now has state protection as an architectural monument. In the Soviet era, a military air base nearby ensured that Haapsalu would be off limits for foreign tourists until 1992.

People looking for spas and sanatoriums might opt for Haapsalu over Pärnu for extra peace and the ultimate mud treatment. Haapsalu lays claim to superior mud, the most researched in the country; its mud is used by the many health centres throughout Estonia.

## Orientation

The tourist information centre is situated in the town centre at Posti tänav 37,750m northeast of the bus/train station. The castle and the heart of the Old Town are around 500m further north of the information centre along Posti tänav.

## Information

The **tourist information centre** (π 33 248, fax 33 464; w www.haapsalu.ee; Posti tänav 37; open 9am-6pm Mon-Fri, 10am-3pm Sat & Sun mid-May–mid-Sept, 9am-5pm Mon-Fri mid-Sep–mid-May) can advise on local events, give information on the region's sites and anything else required to enjoy your stay.

The friendly and obliging **Haapsalu Travel Service** (π 24 180, fax 24 181; e haapsalu travel@hot.ee; Karja tänav 5) caters for tour groups of all sizes and specialisations, with tours throughout the region, including to the Matsalu Nature Reserve and the Tahkuna peninsula in Hiiumaa.

Several ATMs can be found down Posti tänav. The **post office** (cnr Niine & Nurme tänav) is a block east of Posti tänav. Internet access (20 EEK/hour) is available on the 2nd floor of the **main library** (Posti tänav 3; open 10am-7pm Mon-Fri, 11am-4pm Sat); membership of the library is not a prerequisite and Internet use if often free at off-peak times.

### Glorious Mud

The Pharaohs of ancient Egypt and European elite for centuries have turned to mud in the quest for health and vitality. In Estonia, mud is a serious business – local, general, electric, galvanic or aromatic mud treatments have sustained their popularity throughout two centuries of tumultuous history. It's clear this mud is special mud – the compound applied must contain the right kind of minerals which can include sodium, calcium, carbon, fluoride, iodine, sulphate and a special blend of bacteria. It may not look pretty or smell pleasant, but among the benefits of treatment are increased metabolism and improved blood circulation. Sufferers of arthritis, soft tissue inflammations and skin conditions such as eczema are all encouraged to submit to mud. Most mud baths and sanatoriums also offer a range of complementary therapies, but be warned not everyone is made for mud treatments and a doctor's advice is recommended before getting down and dirty.

## Castle & Cathedral

The focus of the Old Town and Haapsalu's main site is the Bishop's Castle (1279) and surrounding circular wall, 803m long and 10m high. Today it stands in partial but very picturesque ruins; a turreted tower, most of the outer wall and some of the moat remain. A modern song stage and a worthwhile city history **museum** (admission free; open 10am-6pm Tues-Sun mid-May–mid-Sept) also grace the area, which has the aura of a sanctuary for visitors on quiet days.

In the castle grounds stands a Roman-Gothic cathedral, with three inner domes, the largest such structure in the Baltics. Its acoustics are quite rightly praised as phenomenal. The cathedral was not strictly Roman Catholic from the start, due to the lukewarm welcome Christianity received in these parts. It was assimilated into the Episcopal stronghold in the second half of the 13th century. The cathedral is open to visitors at weekends from noon to 4pm and concerts are regularly held here.

On the southwestern side of the cathedral is Haapsalu's most famous window. (See Special Events later in the Haapsalu section).

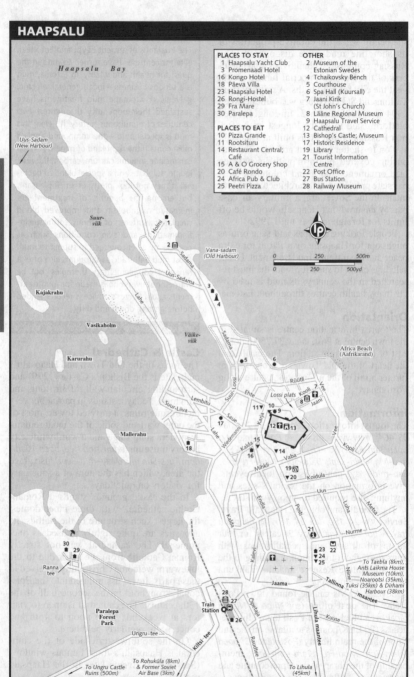

# HAAPSALU

**PLACES TO STAY**
1 Haapsalu Yacht Club
3 Promenaadi Hotel
16 Kongo Hotel
18 Päeva Villa
23 Haapsalu Hotel
26 Rongi-Hostel
29 Fra Mare
30 Paralepa

**PLACES TO EAT**
10 Pizza Grande
11 Rootsituru
14 Restaurant Central;
   Café
15 A & O Grocery Shop
20 Café Rondo
24 Africa Pub & Club
25 Peetri Pizza

**OTHER**
2 Museum of the
  Estonian Swedes
4 Tchaikovsky Bench
5 Courthouse
6 Spa Hall (Kuursall)
7 Jaani Kirik
  (St John's Church)
8 Lääne Regional Museum
9 Haapsalu Travel Service
12 Cathedral
13 Bishop's Castle; Museum
17 Historic Residence
19 Library
21 Tourist Information
   Centre
22 Post Office
27 Bus Station
28 Railway Museum

Haapsalu Bay

Uus-Sadam
(New Harbour)

WEST ESTONIA & THE ISLANDS

Suur-
viik

Kajakrahu

Vasikaholm

Karurahu

Mallerahu

Holmi

Vana-sadam
(Old Harbour)

Sadama

Uus-Sadama

Lahe

Väike-
viik

Africa Beach
(Aafrikarand)

Rüütli

Vee

Lossi plats
Kooli

Jaani

Lembitu

Ehte

Suur-Lossi

Karja

Suur-Liiva

Saue

Wiedemanni

Lahe

Kalda

Mihkli

Vaba

Kopli

Vee

Koidula

Uus

Luha

Metsa

Endla

Posti

Nurme

Kalda

Kaleri

Jaama

Jaama

Opetaja

Rautere

Kuuse

Lihula maantee

To Taebla (8km),
Ants Laikma House
Museum (10km),
Noarootsi (35km),
Tuksi (35km) & Dirhami
Harbour (38km)

Tallinna maantee

Ranna
tee

Paralepa
Forest
Park

Ungru-tee

Train
Station

Kiltsi tee

To Ungru Castle
Ruins (500m)

To Rohuküla (8km)
& Former Soviet
Air Base (3km)

To Lihula
(45km)

0        250        500m
0        250        500yd

## Museums
The **Lääne Regional Museum** (☎ 36 065; Kooli tänav 2; adult/student/family 10/5/15 EEK; open 10am-6pm Wed-Sun mid-May–mid-Sep, 11am-4pm Wed-Sun mid-Sep–mid-May), at the eastern end of Lossi plats in the former town hall, was built in 1775 and now houses exhibits on the region's history. The **Museum of Estonian Swedes** (Rannarootsi Muuseum; ☎ 37 165; Sadama tänav 32; adult/student 25/15 EEK; open 11am-5pm Tues-Sun 15 May-14 Sep, Wed-Sun 11am-4pm 15 Sep-14 May) shows the Estonian-Swedish culture over the centuries and its legacy. The **Railway Museum** (Raudteemuuseum; ☎ 34 574; train station building; adult/student 15/5 EEK; open 10am-6pm Wed-Sun) records the golden years of train travel from Haapsalu station.

## Other Attractions
The streets in the area around the castle are the hub of the historic centre; worth checking out is the **residence** (Saue tänav 11), dating from 1782. Between Kooli tänav and Jaani tänav, east off Lossi plats, is the 16th-century **St John's Church** (Jaani Kirik).

On the shore north of here is a park with **Africa Beach** (Aafrikarand) at its eastern end – with cafés and clubs but no actual beach – the 1905 **Spa Hall** (Kuursaal) at its western end, and a **promenade** that once led as far north as the yacht club. Sculptures dating from Haapsalu's fashionable era can be found along the promenade, including a sundial commemorating mud-cure pioneer Dr Carl Abraham Hunnius and the **Tchaikovsky Bench**, erected in 1940. Sculptures of exotic wild animals that were once set in the water here left the beach its name.

On the western edge of town, beyond the train station, is the **Paralepa Forest Park** with a serene, moody beachfront ideal for atmospheric walks. Also this way, near a former Soviet air base off Kiltsi tee, are the ruins of **Ungru Castle** which, according to legend, had such fine gardens that even Peter the Great travelled to see them. The ruins have recently passed into private ownership, check with the tourist information centre as access may be restricted once development begins.

## Special Events
Haapsalu boasts a full calendar of events year round, although most are held between June and August. Men from the Baltics, Russia

and Finland contest the 'Strongman Haapsalu' title in June. A summer music festival and 'Medieval Haapsalu', a three-day music, arts and crafts festival, a blues festival and the women-only Baltic/Nordic Female Jazzfest are among the listings each year. The biggest annual event is Valge Daami Päevad (Days of the White Lady), for further information see the boxed text 'Days of the White Lady'.

Visit ⓦ www.haapsalu.ee for details of all events and ticket information, or ask at the information centre.

## Places to Stay
Contact the tourist information centre about B&B placements in town.

**Haapsalu Yacht Club** (☎ 35 632; Holmi tänav 5a) plans to offer accommodation once renovations are complete in 2002.

**Rongi-Hostel** (☎ 34 664; beds in 4-bed/2-bed cabins 99/150 EEK; open June-Sept), set-up in the wagons of a stationary train at the Haapsalu station, offers some unique lodgings. It feels pricey when you think that you could almost travel to another country for the same price on a moving train. The atmosphere is fun, and you can see the luxurious, communist party boss's sleeping compartment. The solar heated shower carriage is a more recent addition.

**Paralepa** (☎ 051 06 735 mobile; ⓔ para lepa@hot.ee; Ranna tee 4; tents/caravans/beds 35/100/140 EEK; open June-Aug) is the best budget option on the edge of town. The hostel may have basic rooms but its splendid beachside position certainly compensates. There are discounts for children's beds, a small café, and campers are welcome.

**Haapsalu Hotel** (☎ 33 347, fax 33 191; e exotrade@hot.ee; Posti tänav 43; singles/ doubles 550/800 EEK) may resemble an ageing office block but inside has bright modern facilities and spacious rooms.

**Fra Mare** (☎ 24 600, fax 24 604; e admin@ framare.ee; Ranna tee 2; singles/doubles 620/ 880 EEK), one of Haapsalu's newest spa centres has rooms with a range of health packages on offer, including mud baths, laser or herbal treatments.

**Promenaadi Hotel** (☎/fax 37 250; e prom enad@estpak.ee; Sadama tänav 22; singles/ doubles 750/970 EEK) maximises its beachfront position with extensions of all kinds and a glass-walled dining area.

**Kongo Hotel** (☎ 24 800; e kongohotel@ hot.ee; Kalda tänav 19; singles/doubles/with kitchen 700/850/1000 EEK Sept-Apr, 950/ 1150/1350 EEK June-Aug) is airy, upbeat and welcomes a younger crowd and those inclined to self-cater. It has kitchenette facilities.

**Päeva Villa** (☎/fax 33 672; e paevavilla@ hot.ee; Lai tänav 7; singles/doubles/twins/ suites 400/700/800/1200 EEK) seems a little stark and a bit short on landscaping but otherwise has its fair share of comforts. Prices fall sharply off season.

## Places to Eat

**Africa** (☎ 33 969; Tallinna mantee 1; meals 35-80 EEK; bar open 11am-midnight Sun-Thur, 11am-2am Fri & Sat, club open 10pm-5am Fri & Sat), right next door to the Haapsalu Hotel, is a western-style bar/restaurant complex with a disco on Friday and Saturday. It has decent food, friendly service and is Haapsalu's best spot for a fun night out.

**Peetri Pizza** (☎ 33 003), next to Africa, is handy for pizza to go.

**Pizza Grande** (☎ 37 200; Karja tänav 6; meals from 100 EEK; open 11am-midnight daily), closer to the castle, is a step up, serving Italian dishes in a comfy atmosphere.

**Rootsituru** (☎ 37 072; Karja tänav 3; meals from 110 EEK; open 11am-1am daily), opposite Pizza Grande alongside the castle walls, has fine food and atmosphere with occasional live jazz.

**Café Rondo** (☎ 44 592; Posti tänav 7; open 7.30am-5.30pm Mon-Fri, 9am-6pm Sat & Sun)

is a practical place for breakfast, serving freshly baked apple cakes and cinnamon buns.

**Restaurant Central** (☎ 35 595; Karja tänav 21; meals 180 EEK; open noon-midnight Mon-Thur, until 2am Fri-Sat), the most formal choice in town, is a bit stiff but has good meals. It also runs a café with much cheaper meals on the terrace outside.

The **A&O grocery shop** (Karja tänav), opposite the castle, is open 9am to 9pm daily for self-catering and snacks.

## Getting There & Away

Haapsalu is an easy, bumpy 100km drive (about 1½ hours) from Tallinn. More than 20 buses a day go to/from Tallinn (60 EEK, 1½ hours). There's also one daily bus to/from Tartu (95 EEK, 4½ hours). The **bus station** (Jaama tänav 1) is inside the train station from which passenger trains no longer run; the ticket office is inside the main building of the Emperor's Pavilion. From Haapsalu, there's daily buses to Pärnu, Kärdla and Virtsu.

Ferries to Hiiumaa and Vormsi leave from Rohuküla, 9km west of Haapsalu. More information is given in the Hiiumaa and Vormsi sections of this chapter.

## Getting Around

Bus No 1 runs almost hourly between Lossi plats, the train station and Rohuküla; timetables are posted at Lossi plats and the bus station. Bus No 2 goes about hourly between the bus station and the Yacht Club. For taxi service, call ESRA Taxi (☎ 34 555). The Haapsalu tourist information centre can advise on the best options for car rental for around Haapsalu and the islands.

## AROUND HAAPSALU
### Taebla
**pop 2930**

About 10km east of Haapsalu and 2km beyond Taebla is **Ants Laikmaa House Museum** (Ants Laikmaa majamuuseum; ☎ 96 688; adult/ student 10/5 EEK; open 10am-6pm Wed-Sun mid-May–mid-Sept, 10am-4pm Wed-Sun mid-Sep–mid-Apr), in the eclectic house of inexhaustible artist Ants Laikmaa (1866–1942) who walked more than 2600km from Rīga to Düsseldorf in Germany (in six weeks apparently) to study art there. His efforts extended to designing and building the house itself. Buses along the Tallinn-Haapsalu road will drop you at Taebla.

The tourist information centre and Haapsalu Travel Service both arrange accommodation in Taebla and surrounds, with rooms from 150 EEK per person.

**Kiige Farm** (*☎/fax 95 492, 050-94 207; Linnamäe, Oru district;* e *kiigefarm@hot.ee; summerhouse singles/doubles in main house, with shared bath 150/280 EEK),* 10km north of Taebla at Linnamäe, is a small family homestead with beds in a pretty wooden summerhouse or in the main house with shared bath. It arranges mushroom- or berry-picking treks in the forest, yachting and fishing trips and proudly boasts a giant swing.

## Tuksi

**Roosta Holiday Village** (*☎ 97 230; Tuksi;* e *roosta@estpak.ee; 1-3 bedroom cottages 1100-1900 EEK; open year-round)* is an attractive, Swedish-built, holiday cottage complex in a pine forest beside a relatively deserted stretch of open coastline. The 31 wooden cottages accommodate four to 10 people and come with a choice of one to three rooms. Each is equipped with a kitchenette, living room, shower and veranda. Some cottages have disabled facilities and there's a limited amount of caravan space. On site is a restaurant, bar, sauna, tennis courts and minigolf course. Car, bicycle, sailboard or rowboat rentals are also available.

**Roosi Farm** (*☎/fax 93 347; doubles per person 240 EEK),* not to be confused with Roosta, is a little farther north at Nõva. Accommodation is provided in this private home within a stone's throw of the sea and forest, for those who book well ahead. Yachting and fishing trips are arranged, as are organised excursions to the island of Osmussaare.

To get to Tuksi from Haapsalu, turn north off the main Tallinn–Haapsalu road 2km east of Herjava and continue about 30km through Linnamäe and Riguldi. It's well off the beaten track and the only buses that go there are Haapsalu–Variku–Nõva–Dirhami buses, which go once each way daily except Monday and Thursday. It can take a painful 2¼ hours depending on whether the bus goes direct or via Nõva and Variku.

There's a **harbour** (*☎ 97 221)* at Dirhami, a few kilometres north of Tuksi, where boats can be chartered for **Osmussaare**. Osmussaare is a small island 7.5km from the mainland that was once inhabited by Estonian Swedes and known to them as

Odensholm, the legendary burial place of the Viking god Oden. The island's **cemetery** and **chapel ruins** bear witness to the Swedish community that populated the island before being driven out to make way for a Soviet army base in the early 1940s.

## Noarootsi
**pop 750**

The Noarootsi Peninsula is 2km across the bay from Haapsalu but about 35km by road. Until their exodus in 1944, it was populated for several centuries by Estonian Swedes. There's an old church from the Swedish era at **Hosby,** a fine manorial park at **Pürksi** and views over to Haapsalu from the old Swedish village of **Österby.**

One daily bus goes between Haapsalu and Österby via Pürksi, taking 1¼ hours.

## VORMSI
**☎ 047 • pop 250**

Vormsi, Estonia's fourth biggest island at 93 sq km, lies 3km off the Noarootsi Peninsula. Ferries, however, make a 10km crossing to **Sviby** on Vormsi's south coast from Rohuküla, 9km west of Haapsalu. Vormsi had a mainly Swedish population (of up to 2500 people) until 1944. Nature remains largely undisturbed, and the peninsula sprawling to the south and the 30 islets embraced by Hullo Bay are protected under the Silma Nature Reserve (*☎ 29 431).* Further information is available through the Haapsalu tourist information centre or by contacting the headquarters of the Hiiumaa Protected Areas Administration in Kärdla (see under Information in the Kärdla section later in this chapter). The peninsula, 'Rumpo's Nose', is the only place where Arctic lichen grows south of the Arctic Circle.

### Things to See
Vormsi – 16km from east to west and averaging 6km from north to south – is a good place to tour by bicycle, but you could also take a car or walk. There are about 10km of paved road. **Hullo,** Vormsi's largest village, lies about 3km west of Sviby. A farther 7km by paved and dirt road will bring you to **Saksby,** the westernmost village, from where it's a short walk to a lighthouse. **Rumpo** is due south of the stretch between Sviby and Hullo.

Other highlights include: the 14th century church at Hullo, which has a fine baroque pulpit and a collection of old Swedish-style, wheel-shaped crosses in the graveyard; the southern **Rumpo Peninsula** dotted with juniper stands; and the 5.8m high boulder, Kirikukivi (Church Rock), near **Diby** in the northeast.

### Places to Stay

The following places to stay can be booked through the tourist information centre in Haapsalu. Both accommodation options rent out bicycles and boats, have saunas, can meet guests arriving at Sviby Port, and include breakfast in the price.

**Mäe Farm** (☎ 26 106; ℮ streng@hot.ee; rooms 200 EEK; open Apr-Nov), near Rumpo, is the best place to stay. It's just a few steps away from the coast and has rooms in an authentic, old-style, working farmhouse.

**Elle-Malle Boarding House** (☎/fax 32 072; double/quads in cottage with breakfast 480/ 960 EEK, windmill room with breakfast 310 EEK) is in a windmill in Hullo. If you need more creature comforts, check out this place. There's a romantic double room inside the windmill (only available in summer) or rooms inside a separate wooden cottage (available year round).

### Getting There & Away

A ferry leaves Rohuküla for Sviby twice daily, with an extra run Monday, Wednesday and Friday. The journey takes 45 minutes. The ferry carries cars, bicycles and passengers. If you're taking a vehicle in summer or at a weekend, buy your outward ticket or reserve a place in advance (☎ 33 666) from the Rohuküla terminal. For the latest timetable and fares visit ⓦ www.slk.saaremaa.ee.

Haapsalu town bus No 1 runs hourly to Rohuküla from Lossi plats and the bus station, where timetables are posted. All the Vormsi ferries wait for this bus except on Sunday morning. There are also daily buses to/from Tallinn.

### MATSALU NATURE RESERVE

When birds die and go to heaven, they land in Matsalu; or at least that is how the Estonian Ecotourism Association speaks of the bird (and bird-watchers') paradise of Matsalu Bay. The deepest inlet in the west Estonian Coast and over 20km long, it is an important water bird habitat protected as the Matsalu Nature Reserve (Matsalu Looduskaitseala).

The Reserve is a prime bird migration and breeding ground both in the Baltics and Europe, and has been a site of major research since 1970 when the Matsalu Ringing Centre was set up here, from which all bird ringing activities in Estonia are coordinated.

Spring migration peaks in April/May, but some species arrive as early as March. Autumn migration begins in July and can last until November.

**Bird-watching towers**, with extensive views of resting sites over various terrain, have been built at Penijõe, Kloostri, Haeska, Suitsu and Keemu. There are two marked **nature trails**, one at Penijõe (5km), another at Salevere Salumägi (1.5km). Bring your rubber boots as the ground is wet and muddy. The reserve's headquarters is 3km north of the Tallinn-Virtsu road at Penijõe near Lihula. There is a small **visitors' centre** (☎ 24 223; ⓦ www.matsalu.ee) and a permanent **exhibition** (open 8am-5pm Mon-Thurs, 8am-4pm Fri & Sat) with slide show. It arranges tours of the reserve, from two-hour boat trips around the reed banks to several days of bird-watching.

The Matsalu Nature Reserve visitors' centre arranges accommodation in guesthouses at Haeska, Matsalu and Penijõe for about 150 EEK per person. There are several eating options in Lihula, east of the reserve.

# Hiiumaa

☎ 046 • pop 10,390

Hiiumaa, Estonia's second biggest island (1023 sq km) is quiet and sparsely populated. It boasts delightful stretches of coast and inland areas. The first thing to strike visitors is the sweet freshness of the air – pine mingled with sea breeze. Pollution levels here are among the lowest in Estonia and crime is virtually nonexistent. Like Saaremaa, Hiiumaa retains some of the atmosphere of pre-Soviet Estonia, having been touched little by industry or Russian immigration. Hiiumaa is not quite visible from the mainland, 22km away.

Hiiumites retain a unique sense of humour and folklore, proof of just how self-contained is the world of Hiiumaa. People who move onto the island must carry the name ise-hakanud hiidlane (would-be islanders) for 10 years before being considered true residents. Hiiumaa is also said to be a haven for fairies

# HIIUMAA

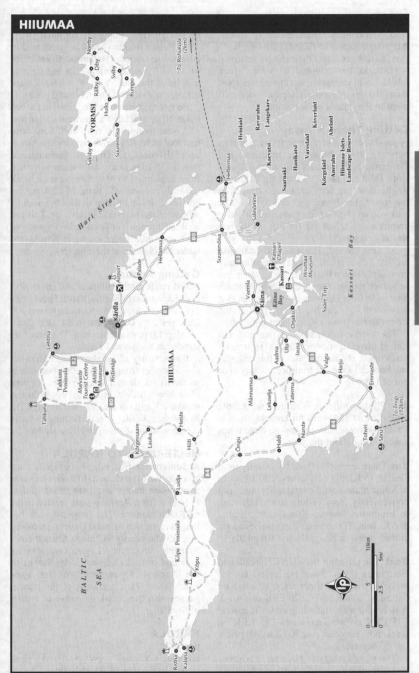

and elves, ancestors of those born on the island. Modern-day Hiiumites rarely discuss
this unique aspect of their family tree, however, as this can anger their elusive relatives.

Hiiumaa has adopted its own 'green
label'. Local tourism based businesses sport
a small logo to demonstrate their commitment to Hiiumaa's conservation.

## Getting There & Away

A passenger and vehicle ferry service runs
between Rohuküla on the mainland and
Heltermaa at Hiiumaa's eastern end. Buses
from Tallinn via Haapsalu run right through
to Hiiumaa, the ferry crossing included in
the trip. Other buses will drop you off or
pick you up at either ferry terminal. It's also
common to hitch or ask for lifts off the ferries at either end.

At their closest, Hiiumaa and Saaremaa
are just 5.5km apart. There is a regular ferry
crossing between the two in the summer, but
in winter months the quickest way to reach
Saaremaa from Hiiumaa is – ridiculous as it
may seem – to catch a bus to Tallinn and
from there hop on a Kuressaare-bound bus.

The tourist information office and Tiit
Reisid travel agency in Kärdla (Hiiumaa's
main town; see Kärdla later in this chapter)
can book all kinds of transport tickets in or
out of Estonia.

**Air** Flights to/from Tallinn and **Kärdla
airport** (☎ 31 381) with **Air Livonia** (☎ 044-
75 007; ⓦ www.airlivonia.ee) go three times
a week throughout the year.

**Bus** There are two to three buses daily from
Tallinn to Kärdla (4½ hours; 130 EEK) or
to Käina in the east. Several other buses run
conveniently from Tallinn straight through
to Emmaste, Nurste, Kõrgessaare, Luidja
and Kalana. These buses can also be caught
at their stops in Haapsalu and Rohuküla.

**Boat** The crossing between Rohuküla and
Heltermaa takes about 1½ hours. Ferries
make the trip seven times daily (six times on
Saturday; adult/child 45/20 EEK one way).
A ticket for a car including driver is around
145 EEK on weekdays and 115 EEK on
weekends. Bicycles cost 30 EEK. All prices
fall off season.

You should reserve a place far in advance
if you're taking a vehicle, particularly during

summer or at weekends. Outward tickets can
be bought from **Rohuküla terminal** (☎ 91
139). Return tickets should be purchased in
advance, or from the **Heltermaa ticket office**
(☎ 31 630) a small building on the right as
you leave the pier. Visit ⓦ www.slk.saare
maa.ee for the latest timetable and prices.

Ferry departure times are posted in the bus
ticket office at Haapsalu bus/train station too.

A year-round ferry runs from **Sõru ferry
terminal** (☎ 95 408), on the southwesternmost
tip of Hiiumaa, to Triigi on Saaremaa. In
summer it runs twice daily each way, and
from September to May three times a week
(20 EEK per person, 1 hour, 75 EEK per car
one way). It is advisable to double-check its
schedules and to reserve in advance. This can
be done through Tiit Reisid travel agency or
the tourist information centre in Kärdla (see
under Kärdla later in this chapter).

## Getting Around

Paved roads circle Hiiumaa and cover several side routes. In Kärdla, **Kerttu Sport** (☎ 31
577; Vabrikuväljak 1) rents out cars from 300
EEK per day. **Dagotrans** (☎ 31 183; tänav,
Sõnajala 11) rents out bicycles. There are fuel
stations at Kärdla and Käina.

Buses, nearly all radiating from Kärdla but
also a number from Käina, get to most places
on the island, though in some cases not very
often. Bus schedules are posted inside the bus
station in Kärdla or are available through Tiit
Reisid (see Kärdla later). Hitching is fairly
common on the roads to and from Heltermaa.

## HELTERMAA TO KÄRDLA

At **Suuremõisa**, 6km inland from Heltermaa,
you can visit the chateau-like, late-baroque
**Suuremõisa manor and park** (adult/student
8/4; open 10am-4pm Jun-Sep), created in the
mid-18th century. The property once belonged to the rich baronial Ungern-Sternberg
family. The nearby **Pühalepa Church** dates
from the 13th century. Legends surrounding
a mound of rocks known as the **Stones of
the Ancient Agreement** (Põhilise leppe
kivid), about 1km northeast of the manor,
suggest that they mark the grave of a ruler
of Sweden.

## KÄRDLA

**pop 3770**

Hiiumaa's 'capital' grew up around a cloth
factory founded in 1829 and destroyed during

WWII. It's a green town full of gardens and trees, with a sleepy atmosphere and few diversions except that it's Hiiumaa's centre for services of all kinds.

## Orientation

The town's main focus is Keskväljak (central square), a long plaza 500m north of the main Heltermaa-Kõrgessaare road. The bus station lies 200m north of its northern end. Another 200m north along Sadama tänav is Vabrikuväljak, where the cloth factory used to stand. To the west is Rannapark, which runs down to the sea.

## Information

Kärdla **tourist information centre** (☎ 22 233, fax 22 334; W www.hiiumaa.ee; Hiiu tänav 1; open 9am-6pm Mon-Fri mid-May–mid-Sep, 10am-4pm Sat & Sun, 10am-4pm Mon-Fri mid-Sep–mid-May) takes pride in its island and can provide a wealth of information and practical help. It arranges accommodation and takes bookings for the Hiiumaa Guides Association, which charges from 100 EEK/hour for illuminating local tours. It also produces a number of refreshingly well written guides to the area, like **The Lighthouse Tour** (20 EEK), a 40-page driving tour of the island published in English, Swedish, Finnish, German and Estonian.

The **Cultural Centre** (☎ 32 192; Rookopli tänav 18) is also a good place to check out what's going on in town. For local arts and crafts, visit the **Liisa Souvenir Shop** on the corner of Vabaduse and Kalda tänav.

There are three ATMs along Keskväljak providing cash advances on credit cards, and you can change money at **Ühispank** (Keskväljak 7).

There's a **post office** (Keskväljak 4; open 8am-4.30pm Mon-Fri, 9am-1pm Sat) in town, as well.

Staff at **Tiit Reisid** (☎ 32 077; W www.tiit reisid.ee; Sadama tänav 13), inside the bus station, are Hiiumaa experts and can help with every aspect of travel to/from and on the island. It arranges accommodation and tours (details are available on the website), as well as ferry tickets.

## Things to See & Do

You can visit the small **Hiiumaa Museum** (☎ 32 091; Vabrikuväljak tänav 8; adult/student 10/5 EEK; open Mon-Fri 10am-5pm

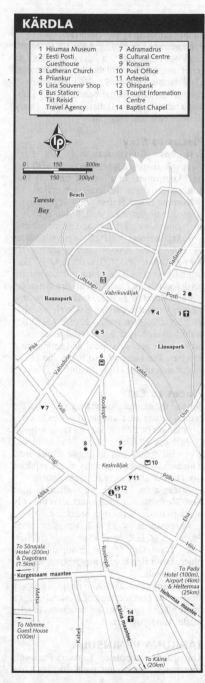

**KÄRDLA**

| 1 Hiiumaa Museum | 7 Adramadrus |
| 2 Eesti Posti Guesthouse | 8 Cultural Centre |
| | 9 Konsum |
| 3 Lutheran Church | 10 Post Office |
| 4 Priiankur | 11 Arteesia |
| 5 Liisa Souvenir Shop | 12 Ühispank |
| 6 Bus Station; Tiit Reisid Travel Agency | 13 Tourist Information Centre |
| | 14 Baptist Chapel |

WEST ESTONIA & THE ISLANDS

*daily May-June, Mon-Fri 10am-5pm July-Apr),* mainly concerning the cloth factory.

**Dagotrans** *(☎ 31 183; Sõnajala tänav 14)* rents out bikes and can advise on where to pedal from Kärdla. Call the Hiiumaa Tenniseklubi **tennis club** *(☎ 33 010; Turu tänav 2)* about court hire. At the **beach** (follow Lubjaagu tänav to the end) there's a clean, sandy shore, a café and minigolf.

## Places to Stay

**Eesti Posti Guesthouse***(☎ 91 871; Posti tänav 13; singles/doubles 150/300 EEK)* has well-kept rooms in a homely building that until recently was the local post office.

**Nõmme Guest House** *(☎ 31 338; Nõmme tänav 30; singles/doubles 220/440 EEK)* is a cosy house with kitchen and sauna access.

**Sõnajala Hotel** *(☎ 32 220; e sonajala@hot .ee; Leigri väljak 3; single/double/junior suites with breakfast 250/400/1700 EEK)* is 2km from the centre. The sauna with adjoining party room is for hire and tents are available.

**Padu Hotel** *(☎ 33 037; Heltermaa maantee 22; singles/doubles with breakfast low season 310/500 EEK, high season 390/650 EEK)* is a sound choice if a little indulgence is in order, with access to pool and sauna, café and bar. The balcony will bring you closer to that wonderful Hiiumaa air.

## Places to Eat

Around the market area on the east side of the central square are a couple of places to eat.

**Priiankur** *(☎ 22 585; Sadama tänav 4; meals 70 EEK; open 11.30am-10pm Mon-Fri, noon-10pm Sat & Sun)* has an ample dining area, with a wide choice of healthy meals, separate from its bar and hearty meals to match.

**Arteesia** *(☎ 32 173; Keskväljak 5; open 9am-10pm daily),* a pleasant café, is the only place in town that serves breakfast.

**Adramadrus** *(☎ 32 082; Vabaduse tänav 15; meals 60 EEK; open 11am-midnight Sun-Thur, 11am-1am Fri-Sat),* a super-friendly place, has a fine tavern atmosphere and excellent meals.

**Konsum** *(open 9am-9pm daily),* a grocery store at the northern end of Keskväljak, is a good place to pick up the delicious, locally made Anno yoghurt.

## TAHKUNA PENINSULA

The sparsely populated Tahkuna Peninsula stretches 8km north into the Baltic Sea a few

kilometres west of Kärdla. Northern Hiiumaa had a population of free Swedish farmers until the late 18th century, when they were forced to leave, many ending up in Ukraine on the false promise of a better life. At Ristimägi, 7km west of Kärdla, there is a **Hill of Crosses**, a small dune decked with handmade crosses just off the main road. These mark the spot where the last 1200 Swedish people living on Hiiumaa performed their final act of worship before leaving the island in 1781. Since then it has become a tradition for first-time visitors to Hiiumaa to lay a cross there.

At Tahkuna, the peninsula's northwest tip and Hiiumaa's northern extremity, there's a **lighthouse** dating from 1875. If it's open, ask the keeper for the key and climb its 42.6m for a spectacular sea view. This area was the scene of a battle between German and Russian troops in WWII, the official Soviet story being that the Soviets bravely fought to the bitter end, the last man climbing to the top of the lighthouse and flinging himself off while still firing at the Germans. Behind it stands an eerie **memorial** to the victims of the *Estonia* ferry disaster. Facing out to sea, the 12m-tall metal frame encases a huge cross, from the bottom of which a bell with carved, sculpted faces are suspended; it only rings when the wind blows with the same speed and in the same direction as that fatal night in September 1994, which saw the *Estonia* go down.

The **stone labyrinths** near the shore are new and were placed there by enthusiastic locals encouraged by scant evidence that there may have been one there 2000 years ago.

On the road south of Tahkuna, and especially on the winding dirt road eastwards towards Lehtma, you'll see deserted **Soviet army bases**, including a complete underground bunker to wander through – bring a torch (flashlight)!

At Malvaste, 2km north of the Kärdla-Kõrgessaare road from a turning 10km west of Kärdla, there's the open-air **Mihkli Farm Museum** *(☎ 046-32 091; adult/student 10/5 EEK; open 11am-6pm mid-May–mid Sept).* It has an amazing working smoke sauna (1915) to rent for up to 10 people (100 EEK per hour). It's a completely unique, old fashioned experience – but not recommended for sensitive eyes. See also the boxed text 'Some Like it Hot' in the introductory Facts for the Visitor.

## M/S *Estonia*: Consigned to Mystery

About 30 nautical miles northwest of Hiiumaa's Tahkuna Peninsula lies the wreck of the ferry *Estonia*, which sank during a storm just after midnight on 28 September 1994. Only 137 survived the tragedy, which claimed 852 lives in one of Europe's worst maritime disasters.

In 1993 the Swedish-Estonian joint venture Estline launched the *Estonia* to service the increasingly popular route between Tallinn and Stockholm. The 15,000-tonne roll-on/roll-off ferry was already a veteran of Scandinavian seas, having sailed between Sweden and Finland for 14 years. The ferry was a source of pride and a symbol of freedom to the newly independent Estonians, even for those whose only experience of it would be seeing the huge white vessel dock at Tallinn's port.

The cause of the tragedy remains the subject of contention and burgeoning conspiracy theory. In 1997 the final report of the Joint Accident Investigation Commission (JAIC), an official inquiry by the Estonian, Swedish and Finnish governments, concluded that the ferry's design was at fault and the crew were probably under skilled in safety and emergency procedures. The report claimed the bow gate, or visor, was engineered inadequately for rough sailing conditions and that during the storm the visor was torn from the bow and in the process breached the watertight seal of the loading ramp. This exposed the car deck to tonnes of seawater that sank the *Estonia* completely within one hour. Escape time for the 989 people onboard was estimated at only 15 minutes and they were denied access to lifeboats due to the sudden list and sinking of the ferry. For those who did escape, the freezing conditions of the water that night reduced survival time to minutes.

The integrity of the report was questioned after dissent within the JAIC became public. Allegations followed that vital information had been withheld and that the Commission did not act impartially. The report also met with criticism from relatives of the victims, the majority of whom were Swedes. In 2000, a Swedish newspaper survey claimed over 70% of victims' families still called for a new investigation. Subsequent reports from Sweden and an inquiry commissioned by the ferry's German manufacturers argued that, contrary to the JAIC findings, the *Estonia* was not seaworthy, it had been poorly serviced and the visor-securing mechanisms were in need of repair.

In 2000, a joint US-German diving expedition and new analyses of the *Estonia's* recovered visor prompted theories of an explosion onboard, which explosive experts believe would be the most feasible explanation for the damage sustained and the ferry's rapid sinking. Estline suspected an underwater mine while it has also been suggested that the ferry collided with another vessel. Conspiracy theorists claim that the *Estonia* was transporting unregistered munitions cargo, as an illicit trade in weapons was to be curtailed with new export laws about to come into effect. Claims of a cover-up have been bolstered by the alleged disappearance of eight crew members, initially listed as survivors.

Unexplained interference with the wreck, together with the Swedish government's dumping of sand to stabilise it in 2000, have further fuelled conspiracy claims and calls for a new inquiry. The governments of Estonia, Finland and Sweden are resolute that the ferry will remain where it sank as a memorial to the dead – an estimated 700 people are still thought to be inside. To date no-one has been found liable and no compensation has been paid to the victims or their families.

## Places to Stay

**Malvaste Tourist Centre** (☎ 91 901; singles/ doubles/suites 180/300/600-800 EEK/suites from 690 EEK), just west of the Mihkli Farm Museum, has a large variety of accommodation. It's in the forest, a 15-minute walk from a sandy beach.

## Getting There & Away

Several buses a day go along the main road from Kärdla to the Malvaste turning, a 15-minute ride. Buses heading for Kõrgessaare,

Luidja or Kalana are the ones to look for. No scheduled buses go to Tahkuna.

## WESTERN HIIUMAA

The harbour village of **Kõrgessaare**, 20km west of Kärdla, offers little by way of distractions except an excellent restaurant (see Places to Stay & Eat later in this section) on your way westward.

At **Kõpu**, just over halfway along the Kõpu Peninsula, is Hiiumaa's best known landmark – the inland **Kõpu lighthouse**

(☎ 93 414; adult/student 20/10 EEK), the third oldest, continuously operational lighthouse in the world. A lighthouse has stood on this raised bit of land since 1531 to warn ships away from the offshore Hiiumaadal sandbank. The present white limestone tower, built in 1845, is 37m high (up 115 narrow steps) and can be seen 55km away. East of here, near the 61km highway mark, is the 1.5km Rebastemäe **nature trail**, which takes in forest paths along the highest (therefore oldest) parts of the island.

A second lighthouse stands at the western end of the peninsula near **Ristna** (Stockholm is just over 200km west of here). It was brought to Hiiumaa by freighter from Paris where it was made, together with the lighthouse at Tahkuna.

## Places to Stay & Eat
The tourist information centre and Tiit Reisid travel agency in Kärdla can arrange accommodation on the Kõpu Peninsula.

**Viinaköök** (☎ 93 337; Kõrgessaare; meals from 60 EEK), in the village centre opposite the bus stop, serves great dishes in a rustic setting and has a well-stocked bar.

## Getting There & Away
Kärdla buses run several times most days to/from Kõrgessaare and Luidja at the start of the Kõpu peninsula, and two or three times a day to/from Kalana near the end of the peninsula. Two or three buses run daily between Kärdla and Kalana near the end of the Kõpu peninsula, the journey takes about 1½ hours.

## KÄINA & KÄINA BAY BIRD RESERVE
☎ 046 • pop 2230

Hiiumaa's second largest settlement – not quite big enough to merit the label 'town' – is a fairly nondescript place, apart from the ruins of a fine, 15th-century, stone church, which was wrecked by a WWII bomb, near the main road in the middle of the village. During the Soviet regime the authorities built a grey, faceless building on top of the church cemetery, sparing the headstones of just two graves. On the western edge of Käina is the **Tobias Museum** (☎ 32 091; adult/student 5/3 EEK; open 10am-5pm daily mid-May–mid Sep) of Rudolf Tobias (1873–1918), composer of some of the first Estonian orchestral works. Visits after hours can be arranged in advance.

The main appeal of the town is its idyllic location in the south of the island near the shore of **Käina Bay**, an important bird reserve that is virtually cut off from the open sea by the twin causeways to **Kassari Island**. During the hot summer months a large part of the bay dries up and becomes nothing more than a mud field. About 70 different species breed at Käina Bay. The headquarters of the Hiiumaa Protected Areas Administration (see information under Kärdla earlier) publishes a variety of leaflets to take you through nature trails within the reserve.

Four kilometres from Käina, at Vaemla on the road to Kassari, is a small **wool factory** (Hiiu Vill; ☎ 36 121; admission free; open 10am-6pm daily), which still uses original 19th-century weaving and spinning machines to produce some fine traditional knitwear.

## Places to Stay & Eat
Two of the best hotels on the island are in Käina.

**Anno Farm** (☎ 29 120; B&B 100-250 EEK) is a very comfortable farmhouse southwest of Käina in the village of Utu, 2km south of the turn-off to Orjaku. Breakfast is delicious yoghurt, made on the farm – and you'll be happily shown the works!

**Tondilossi** (☎ 36 337, fax 36 470; Hiiu maantee 11; adult/child to age 12 180/100 EEK) is a very comfortable, wooden lodge with an **on-site café** (open 11am-6pm Mon-Sat). Ask about boat and car rental here.

**Heido** (☎ 36 485; Luige tänav 8; B&B 250 EEK; open 24 hrs), a small, six-bed hostel, also offers horse riding.

**Liilia Hotel** (☎ 36 146, fax 36 546; e liilia hotell@hot.ee; Hiiu maantee 22; singles/doubles 490/690 EEK) has 13 rooms, all with private bathroom and satellite TV. There's a restaurant with an Estonian and international menu including fish and vegetarian options.

**Lõokese Hotel** (☎ 36 107, fax 36 269; e lookeehot.ee; Lõokese tänav 14; singles/doubles from 550/690 EEK) is large and modern with a pool and children's playground.

## Getting There & Away
A good paved road runs 20km across the island from Käina to Kärdla. There are five or six buses between Kärdla and Käina on weekdays, a few less on weekends. Some are heading south or west to Aadma, Valgu, Tohvri, Nurste or Õngu. Buses also run to Kassari.

## KASSARI
pop 90

The eastern half of the 8km-long island of
Kassari is thickly covered with mixed woodland. At each end it's linked to Hiiumaa by
causeways, which support paved roads.

Southern Kassari narrows to a promontory with some unusual vegetation and ends
in a thin, 3km spit of land whose tip, **Sääre
Tirp**, is 5km from Kassari's single main
road. It's well worth making the trip to Sääre
Tirp and allowing enough time to savour the
unusual environment. On the way you'll notice a **statue** of the local hero Leiger carry-
ing a boulder on his shoulder. He was a
relative of Suur Tõll, Saaremaa's hero (neither of which are in any way related to Kalevipoeg, the Estonian national hero). Legend
has it that the Sääre Tirp is the result of an
aborted bridge he'd started to build to Saaremaa to make it easier for Suur Tõll to visit
and join in various heroic acts.

Just inland of the main road, a short distance west of the Sääre Tirp turning, is the
single-storey **Hiiumaa Museum** (☎ 97 121;
adult/student 5/3 EEK; open 10am-5.30pm
daily mid-May–mid-Sep, 10am-5pm Mon-Fri
Oct-Apr), formerly servants' quarters on the
Kassari estate. It has a large collection of
artefacts and exhibits on Hiiumaa's history,
nature and ethnography.

Another enjoyable walk, ride or drive is to
a pretty, whitewashed, 18th-century **chapel**
at the east end of Kassari. A sign 'Kassari
Kabel 2' directs you down a dirt road from
the easternmost point of the island's paved
road. A path continues nearly 2km to a small
bay in Kassari's northeastern corner.

### Places to Stay & Eat
**Vetsi Tall** (☎ 97 219; e info@vetsitall.ee;
beds from 150 EEK), on the main road between
the sea and Kassari, rolls out hospitality in
barrels, literally, with beds inside one in
three giant kegs; tent sites are also available
The on-site tavern offers some vegetarian
dishes and there are fish-smoking facilities.

### Getting There & Away
Only a few buses go to Kassari. By changing
buses in Käina (maybe with a bit of a wait)
you can get from Kärdla to Kassari and back
most days, but the times certainly aren't convenient. Alternatively it's a 6km to 7km
walk (or hitch) to the middle of Kassari

across either causeway from the main Valgu-
Käina-Heltermaa road (which is used by
buses).

## SOUTHERN HIIUMAA
The main paved road from Käina runs
southwest through Valgu and Harju, villages
separated from the coast by a 3km-wide
marshy strip. **Harju** has two restored windmills. At Emmaste the main road turns northwest to end at Haldi just past Nurste.
Hamlets and isolated farmsteads dot the
west-facing stretch of coast and its hinterland. The southern tip of Hiiumaa around the
harbour of Sõru (where ferries to Saaremaa
depart) is bleaker with few trees. North of
Haldi, dirt roads continue through Õngu to
the western Kõpu Peninsula and to Luidja,
the end of the paved road west from Kärdla.

There are buses from Kärdla and Käina to
Valgu, Harju, Emmaste, Tohvri (in the south
near Sõru), Nurste and Õngu every day.

### Hiiumaa Islets Landscape Reserve
Saarnaki, Hanikatsi, Vareslaid, Kõrgelaid
and other islets off southeastern Hiiumaa
form the Hiiumaa Islets Landscape Reserve,
now incorporated into the Hiiumaa Protected
Areas Administration with its **headquarters**
(☎ 046-22 101; e bktiit@hot.ee; Vabrikuväljak 1) in Kärdla. This is a breeding place
for some 110 bird species, including avo-
cets, eider ducks, goosanders and greylag
geese, as well as a migration halt for swans,
barnacle geese and other species. Over 600
plant species – almost half Estonia's total –
grow here including the rare red helleborine,
wild apple and shining geranium.

**Saarnaki** and **Hanikatsi**, the two largest islands at 137 and 83 hectares, were inhabited
until the 1960s or 70s. They were depopu-
lated, like many other Estonian coastal villages, because of Soviet bans on sea-going
boats that meant people could no longer earn
a living from fishing.

Birds on the islands has been carefully
monitored since 1974. A number of observation towers have been built within the
reserve, including one near the **Centre of
Hiiumaa Islets Reserve** (☎ 46-94 299;
w www.hiiulaiud.ee) at Salinõmme on Hiiumaa. It is possible to spend a night on the deserted and peaceful Saarnaki or Hanikatsi
islands but you have to get permission from
the reserve centre first. It can arrange for a

guide to take you by boat to the islands. Note some of the smaller islands are off limits until the beginning of July, after the nesting season has ended.

# Saaremaa & Muhu

☎ 045 • pop 35,950

Mainland Estonians say Saaremaa, the country's biggest island at 2668 sq km, is 'like the old Estonia'; Soviet industry and immigration barely touched the place. Although military facilities were scattered around the island, it retains the appearance and old-fashioned pace of agricultural pre-WWII Estonia, even though its famous windmills (which numbered 800 in the 19th century) no longer work and its 'typical' reed-thatched roofs aren't so typical any more.

In recent years Saaremaa has become an almost painfully popular tourist resort between May and September, especially with Finns who flock here for a cheap break. This trend sharply contrasts with 50 years of practical isolation from the mainland and has not been greeted with equal enthusiasm by all islanders.

Saaremaa (in Swedish times known as Ösel, or 'island sieve') has always had an independent streak and was usually the last part of Estonia to fall to invaders. Its people have their own customs, songs and costumes, speak Estonian with a strong accent and never spoke Russian at all. They don't revere mainland Estonia's Kalevipoeg legend, for Saaremaa has its own hero, Suur Tõll, who fought many battles around the island against devils and fiends.

Though Saaremaa has long been a popular Estonian summer holiday retreat, during the Soviet era it was closed to foreigners. Even mainland Estonians needed an invitation to visit because of its early warning radar system and rocket base. The island today is a thinly populated place of unspoiled rural landscapes with wooden farmsteads dotted among the forests that still cover nearly half the land. Saaremaa is flat but has a deeply indented 1300km coast of bays and peninsulas (and some sandy beaches). There are many remains from its intriguing past including pre-German strongholds, fine fortress-like early churches, manor houses, windmills and, not least, the attractive old

capital, Kuressaare, which has a mighty castle. Though known for its juniper groves, Saaremaa is also home to 80% of Estonia's roughly 1400 other plant species, many of which are contained in the Vilsandi National Park and other nature reserves.

Saaremaa is joined by a causeway to the neighbouring island, Muhu, to which ferries run from Virtsu on the mainland.

## History

Settlement on Saaremaa dates from the 4th millennium BC. The early coastal settlements now lie some way inland because the land has risen about 15m over the last 5000 years. In the 10th to 13th centuries Saaremaa and Muhu were the most densely populated parts of Estonia. Denmark tried to conquer Saaremaa in the early 13th century but failed, and it wasn't until 1227 that the German Knights of the Sword subjugated it. The knights took Muhu and eastern and northwestern parts of Saaremaa, setting up their headquarters at Pöide in eastern Saaremaa. The rest of Saaremaa went to Haapsalu-based bishop of Ösel-Wiek, who made Kuressaare his stronghold on the island.

Saaremaa rebelled against German rule from 1236 to 41, from 1260 to 61, and again in 1343 when the Germans were thrown off the island and the knights' castle at Pöide destroyed. In 1345 the Germans returned and forced the islanders to surrender.

All of Saaremaa became a Danish possession in 1573 during the Livonian War, and in 1645 it was transferred to Sweden by the Treaty of Brömsebro. It was taken by Russia in 1710 during the Great Northern War and made part of the Russian province of Livonia, governed from Rīga.

## Getting There & Away

**Air** Air Livonia (☎ 044-75 007; W www.air livonia.ee) flies between Kuressaare and Pärnu two to three times weekly (200 EEK). Avies (☎ 605 8022; W www.avies.ee) flies several times weekly between Tallinn and Kuressaare (495 EEK).

**Bus** At least nine direct buses daily travel each way between Tallinn and Kuressaare (160 EEK, 4½ hours). There are four buses daily to/from Tartu (190 EEK, 5½-6½ hours) and two buses daily to/from Pärnu (120 EEK, 3½ hours).

# SAAREMAA & MUHU

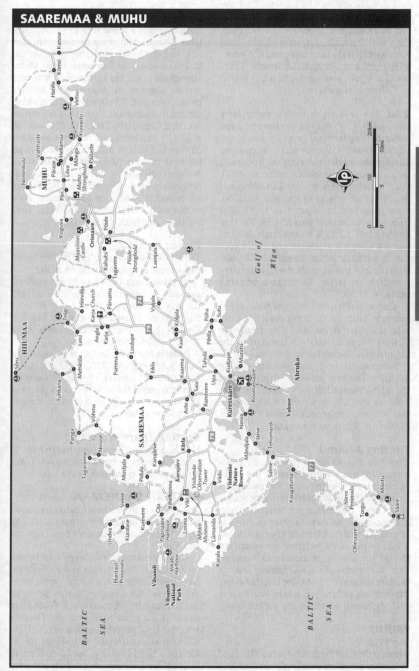

There are five buses daily between Virtsu and Saaremaa, and another five buses daily each way between Kuivastu (Muhu) and Kuressaare – a 1½-hour trip timed to connect with ferry arrivals and departures. Likewise, at Virtsu you can board a bus bound to Tallinn or elsewhere.

**Boat** The crossing between **Virtsu ferry terminal** (☎ 47-75 020) on the mainland and **Kuivastu ferry terminal** (☎ 45 350) on Muhu takes 25 minutes. Ferries make the crossing 12 times daily (10 times daily on weekends, with increased services in summer months). For timetables check **w** www.laevakompanii .ee. Prices are subject to seasonal variation, a one-way fare in summer is 35 EEK/10 EEK for adult/student plus 55 EEK for a car on weekdays, 82 EEK on weekends. In summer it is essential to reserve a place for your car in advance as far ahead as possible. Reservations can be made through the ferry terminals or at the **Kuressaare booking office** (☎ 24 350).

Year-round ferries run from Sõru on Hiiumaa to Triigi on the north coast of Saaremaa at varying frequencies (for details see Getting There & Away at the start of the Hiiumaa section earlier in this chapter).

Saaremaa is very popular with visiting yachties. The best harbour facilities are at the **Nasva Yacht Club** (Nasva Jahtklubi; ☎ 75 140, fax 55 257), 9km west of Kuressaare. See **w** www.tt.ee/renza/sadamad for details of other harbours on the island.

## Getting Around
There are over 400km of paved roads on Saaremaa and many more reasonable dirt roads. Hitching is not uncommon on the main routes (but there's not much traffic on minor roads). Buses from Kuressaare get to many places and you could use them to make day trips to several parts of the island. It's possible to put a bike or two in the baggage compartments, though you have to ask the driver for permission. It's worth calling the friendly folks at the **bus station** (☎ 31 661) for help in finding the best bus to take you where you want to go – the posted schedules can get confusing.

## MUHU
**pop 1905**
Muhu is the third biggest Estonian island and is known for its painstakingly worked folk costumes. Near the main road about halfway across the island is the 13th to 14th century **Liiva Church**, with some unusual ship murals. Just east of the road, shortly before the 2.5km causeway to Saaremaa, is the **Muhu stronghold** of the old Estonians. It was here that the islanders surrendered to the Knights of the Sword on 3 February 1227, marking the end of Estonian resistance to the German invasion. The nearby **Eemu Tuulik** (windmill; ☎ 28 130; admission free) houses a small exhibition and sells its milled flour. **Koguva** on the western tip of Muhu, 6km off the road, is an exceptionally well-preserved, old-fashioned island village: All its 105 houses are protected as an open-air museum. They were mostly built between 1880 and 1930 but some date from the mid-18th century.

## Places to Stay
The tourist information centre in Kuressaare can arrange accommodation on Muhu.

**Vanatoa Farm** (☎ 48 884; **e** vanatoa@ saaremaa.ee; rooms per person 150-500 EEK) has down to earth rooms in an idyllic location near the open-air museum of Koguva. Contact the museum's **headquarters** (☎ 94 701, 98 616) for arrangements.

**Pädaste Manor** (☎ 48 800; **w** www.padaste .com; singles/doubles 1200/1600 EEK, suites from 2200 EEK), a grand, bayside, 19th-century manor, is one of the most luxurious places in Estonia, and one of few that offers cinema hire with your bed.

## Getting There & Away
Use the Kuivastu-Kuressaare bus or hitch to reach the points along the main road. There are occasional buses to Koguva too.

## EASTERN SAAREMAA
The causeway from Muhu reaches Saaremaa near Orissaare on the northeastern coast. The main road to Kuressaare goes past Tagavere and Valjala.

**Orissaare** is the second biggest settlement on Saaremaa. The German knights built the Maasilinn Castle just north of Orissaare in the 14th to 16th centuries. It was blown up in 1576 but there are ruins to see. **Pöide**, 3km south of the main road, was the German knights' headquarters on Saaremaa. Their fortress was destroyed in 1343 in the St George's Night Uprising, but Pöide Church, built by the Germans in the 13th and 14th centuries a short distance east of the road, remains a starkly imposing reminder of their influence. Kuressaare tourist information centre (see Kuressaare section later) can put you in touch with a guide to the area.

## Kaali

The **meteorite crater** at Kaali (2.5km north of the Valjala-Kuressaare road from a turning 10km from Valjala) is a 100m wide, water-filled crater blasted into existence by a meteorite about 2700 years ago. In Scandinavian mythology, the site was known as 'the sun's grave'. As the sun had chosen to be buried there, so the Estonians became considered blessed folk. Though small, it is among the largest meteorite crater in Europe and one of few in the northern hemisphere so easily accessible to the public.

## Angla, Karja, Triigi & Tuhkana

This group of places in the northern part of eastern Saaremaa can be reached from Kuressaare or from other places in the east by several paved roads. If you are arriving on the ferry from Hiiumaa, this is the perfect spot to explore immediately.

Angla, 40km from Kuressaare on the main road to the north coast, is the site of the biggest and most photogenic grouping of **windmills** on Saaremaa – five of them of various sizes, none now in use, lined up together on the roadside. Opposite the windmills is the turn-off to **Karja Church**, 2km east, which, with the blank, fortress-like gaze of its façade, is one of the most evocative of Saaremaa's 13th- to 14th- century German churches. There's a fine crucifixion carving on one of its walls.

North of Angla, the road continues 5.5km to Leisi, the venue for **Õlletoober**, a beer festival each July showcasing both sophisticated and feral brews. For information visit **w** www.olletoober.ee From Leisi it's 3.5km to the harbour of Triigi, a picturesque bay on Saaremaa's north coast with views across to Hiiumaa.

There's a sandy beach at Tuhkana, 3km north of Metsküla, which is 10km west of Leisi, mostly by unpaved roads.

## Places to Stay

Kuressaare tourist information centre and the Mere travel agency (see under Information in the Kuressaare section later in this chapter)

arranges accommodation in Orissaare, Põide, Valjala, Angla, Karja, Triigi and Tuhkana.

**Püharisti Hostel** (☎ 45 149; **e** orissaare@ eelk.ee; Ranna puiestee 11, Orissaare; beds from 200 EEK) offers hostel-like accommodation in a warm, super-friendly environment. It can also find you some cheap tent space nearby.

**Välja Guest House** (☎/fax 29 050; B&B 250 EEK) is located at Hiieväjla, southeast of Leisi, and west of the Angla windmills. They also arrange bike rental and boating trips. Take the first right turn towards Hiieväjla and travel for 2km.

## Getting There & Away

Buses between Kuressaare and the mainland usually take the main road passing within 1km of Valjala, while the local Kuressaare-Kuivastu service takes the more southerly road through Laimjala and within 1km of Põide. There are several buses daily between Kuressaare and Orissaare (30 EEK, 1¼ hours) and several between Orissaare and Kuivastu (30 EEK) mostly in the morning.

Up to 14 buses daily run between Kuressaare and Leisi, a trip of about an hour, passing right by the Angla windmills and close to Karja Church. Those via Pärsama go right by Karja Church. Kaali is halfway between the Kuressaare–Valjala and Kuressaare–Leisi roads, about 3km from each, so you could use a bus along either road to get within walking distance.

## KURESSAARE

☎ 045 • pop 14,970

A castle was founded at Kuressaare (originally named Arensburg) in the 13th century as the Haapsalu-based Bishop of Ösel-Wiek's stronghold in the island part of his diocese. Kuressaare became Saaremaa's main trading centre, developing quickly after passing into Swedish hands in 1645. In the 19th century numerous health spas opened on the strength of the curative properties of the area's coastal mud. In the Soviet era Kuressaare was named Kingisseppa, after Viktor Kingissepp, an Estonian communist of the 1920s. Today it is a charming, leafy-green town with a busy centre and monumental castle.

## Orientation

The road from Kuivastu and the mainland enters Kuressaare as Tallinna tänav, passing southwest through modern suburbs to the central square Keskväljak. Kuressaare Castle and its surrounding park, which reaches down to the coast, are 750m beyond Keskväljak, along Lossi tänav. The bus station at Pihtla tee 25 is just over 1km from the castle and Keskväljak.

## Information

Kuressaare's **tourist information centre** (☎/fax 33 120; Tallinna tänav 2; open 9am-7pm Mon-Fri, 9am-5pm Sat, 9am-3pm Sun May-Sept, 9am-5pm Mon-Fri Oct-Apr) is inside the old town hall. It sells maps and guides, arranges accommodation, books boat trips and island tours, and sorts out car and bicycle rental.

There are several banks, ATMs and exchange bureaus on Keskväljak, including **Hansapank** (Kohtu tänav 2).

There's a **post office** (Torni tänav 1). Public card telephones are in and around the post office and at strategic points around the town.

Free Internet access at the **public library** should continue with the relocation of the library to a new complex off Tallinna maantee. During afternoons, after hours and on weekends, a convenient place for Internet access is in the Billiards Hall (see under Entertainment later in this section.) costing 15 EEK for 30 minutes. The Saaremaa School Hostel also offers Internet access (see Places to Stay later).

**Arensburg travel agency** (☎ 33 360; e abr@tt.ee; Tallinna maantee 25) is extremely knowledgeable about the island and specialises in arranged boat trips to Abruka and Vilsandi as well as personalised biking and fishing trips.

**Mere travel agency** (☎ 33 610, fax 33 609; e lii@tt.ee; Tallinna maantee 27), specialises in countryside tourism on the island and arranges accommodation in a variety of idyllic farmhouses off the beaten track. It is also an official agent for the Estonian Ecotourism Association. It caters for the disabled as well as people on special diets.

## The Castle

Kuressaare Castle stands at the southern end of the town, on an artificial island with four pointed bastion corners, ringed by a partly filled moat and surrounded by a park. It's the best preserved castle in the Baltics, the only medieval stone castle in the region that has remained intact.

A castle was founded on this site as the bishop of Ösel-Wiek's island base in the 1260s, but the mighty square fortress of locally quarried dolomite that stands today at the centre of several rings of fortification was not built until 1338 to 80. Sections of the protective walls and bastions were erected in the 15th to 18th centuries. It was designed as an administrative centre as well as a stronghold. The more slender of its two tall corner towers, Pikk Hermann to the east, is separated from the rest of the castle by a shaft crossed only by a drawbridge, so it could function as a last refuge in time of attack.

**Interior** The inside of the castle is a warren of chambers, halls, passages and stairways that will feed anyone's fantasies about Gothic fortresses. It houses the **Saaremaa Regional Museum** (Saaremaa Koduloomuuseum; adult/child 30/15 EEK; open 10am-7pm Wed-Sun) On the ground floor look for the hypocaust (hüpokaust) on the southwestern side – a furnace that fuelled a medieval central heating system. According to legend, condemned prisoners were dispatched through a small room without a floor near the Bishop's chamber, to be received by hungry lions. Legends also tell of the body of a knight found when a room previously sealed with bricks was uncovered in the 18th century. It is said that, upon discovery, the knight's body dissolved into dust, which has fuelled intrigue and given rise to several differing accounts of how the unfortunate captive met with his tragic fate.

**Exterior** The wall around the outer edge of the castle island was built at the end of the 14th century, and the cannon towers added later. The greatest of the cannon towers, completed in 1470, is at the island's northern corner. The bastions and moat were created by the Danes in the 17th century.

**Park** The shady park around the castle moat and running down to Kuressaare Bay was laid out in 1861 and there are some fine wooden resort buildings in and around it, notably the 1889 Kuursaal (Spa Hall). There's also a **Citizens' Museum** (Linnakodaniku Muuseum; Pargi tänav 5; adult/child 5/3 EEK; open 11am-6pm Wed-Sun).

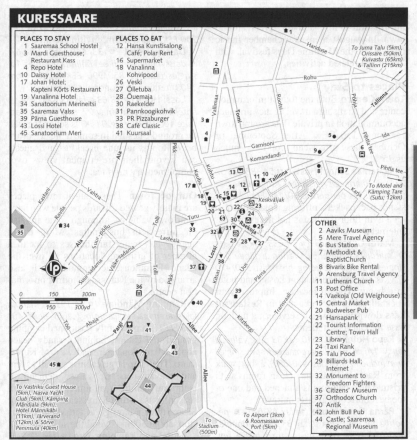

## KURESSAARE

**PLACES TO STAY**
1 Saaremaa School Hostel
3 Mardi Guesthouse;
  Restaurant Kass
4 Repo Hotel
10 Daissy Hotel
17 Johan Hotel;
  Kapteni Körts Restaurant
19 Vanalinna Hotel
34 Sanatoorium Merineitsi
35 Saaremaa Valss
39 Pärna Guesthouse
43 Lossi Hotel
45 Sanatoorium Meri

**PLACES TO EAT**
12 Hansa Kunstisalong
  Café; Polar Rent
16 Supermarket
18 Vanalinna
  Kohvipood
26 Veski
27 Ölletuba
28 Öuemaja
30 Raekelder
31 Pannkoogikohvik
33 PR Pizzaburger
38 Café Classic
41 Kuursaal

**OTHER**
2 Aaviks Museum
5 Mere Travel Agency
6 Bus Station
7 Methodist &
  BaptistChurch
8 Bivarix Bike Rental
9 Arensburg Travel Agency
11 Lutheran Church
13 Post Office
14 Vaekoja (Old Weighouse)
15 Central Market
20 Budweiser Pub
21 Hansapank
22 Tourist Information
  Centre; Town Hall
23 Library
24 Taxi Rank
25 Talu Pood
29 Billiards Hall;
  Internet
32 Monument to
  Freedom Fighters
36 Citizens' Museum
37 Orthodox Church
40 Antik
42 John Bull Pub
44 Castle; Saaremaa
  Regional Museum

To Juma Talu (5km),
Orissare (50km),
Kuivastu (65km)
& Tallinn (215km)

To Motel &
Kämping Tare
(Sutu; 12km)

0   150   300m
0   150   300yd

To Vastriku Guest House
(5km), Nasva Yacht
Club (5km), Kämping
Mändjala (9km),
Hotel Männikäbi
(11km), Järverand
(12km) & Sörve
Peninsula (40km)

To
Stadium
(500m)

To Airport (3km)
& Roomassaare
Port (5km)

WEST ESTONIA & THE ISLANDS

## Other Attractions

The best of Kuressaare's other old buildings
are grouped around the central square
Keskväljak, notably the **town hall** (1670),
on the eastern side, with a pair of fine stone
lions at the door, and the **weigh-house** (now
Vaekoja pub) across from it, both 17th-century
baroque. There's a handsome **Lutheran
Church** at the northeast end of Keskväljak
and an **Orthodox Church** (Lossi tänav 8).

**Aaviks Museum** (☎ 57 553; Vallimaa
tänav 7; adult/child 5/3 EEK; open 11am-6pm
Wed-Sun) is dedicated to the life and works
of linguist Johannes Aavik (1880–1973),
who introduced major reforms to the Estonian language, and his musically talented
cousin, Joosep Aavik (1899–1989). In the
small square on the corner of Lossi tänav

and Kauba tänav is a **monument** dating
from 1928 erected in honour of the
islanders who died during their fight for independence.

**Beaches** The best beach in the Kuressaare
area is Järverand at Järve, about 14km west,
some 2km past Mändjala. On the way – at
Nasva – there's a yacht harbour with a few
yachts for charter. There's also a beach at
Sutu, 12km east. Salme, Torgu or Sääre buses
from Kuressaare go to Järverand.

## Special Events

In March Kuressaare hosts its annual theatre
days. In summer classical and folk music
concerts are held at the open-air stage in the
grounds of the castle and inside the Kuursaal.

Fortnightly schedules are listed at the tourist information centre and on flyers around town. In August there is a chamber music festival and the Maritime Days festival, with lots of sea-related activities.

## Places to Stay

**Town Centre** Both the tourist information centre and Arensburg travel agency arranges accommodation in private flats around town for about 150 EEK. After September or October, these prices can drop by as much as 35%.

**Saaremaa School Hostel** (☎ 54 388, fax 57 226; e marika@syg.edu.ee; Kingu tänav 6; floor/doubles per person 50/145 EEK) understands backpackers, offering a place to crash on a gym floor if a bed is not necessary but Internet access is.

**Mardi Guesthouse** (☎ 24 633, fax 24 636, e mardi@kak.oesel.ee; Vallimaa tänav 5A; singles/doubles including breakfast 370/470 EEK) is a combined student hostel and hotel in a handy, central location. Improve your cocktail skills over breakfast in **Restaurant Kass** downstairs, which serves as a training base for catering students.

**Repo Hotel** (☎ 33 510, fax 33 520; Valimaa tänav 1A; w www.saaremaa.ee/repo; single/twin including breakfast 400/890), a short walk from Raekoja Plats, has clean rooms with pristine new bathrooms attached and one of the best buffet breakfasts in town.

**Pärna Guesthouse** (☎/fax 57 521, e per hoht@hot.ee; Pärna tänav 3; singles/doubles 400/550 EEK), on a quiet street just a few minutes walk from the centre, is a family-run house with a kitchenette at hand.

**Saaremaa Valss** (☎ 27 100, fax 27 145; e sanatoorium@sanatoorium.ee; Kastani tänav 20; singles/doubles 550/650 EEK) offers a decent deal if you're considering a treatment, with an indulgent range of mud baths and therapeutic packages. The shared email address and fax number also accesses the vast resources of **Meri** (☎ 22 100; Pargi 16) and **Merineitsi** (☎ 27 200; Ravila 2a), offering various accommodation and treatment packages for similar prices. Asthma sufferers or the stress-prone are invited to visit the salt chamber.

**Vanalinna Hotel** (☎/fax 55 309; Kauba tänav 8; singles/doubles 580/800 EEK) has decent rooms with wheelchair access and good coffee within reach.

**Johan Hotel** (☎/fax 33 036; Kauba tänav 13; singles/doubles 750/900 EEK, extra bed 200 EEK) has a warm, inviting rooms.

**Daissy Hotel** (☎ 33 669, fax 33 667; e daissyhotell@mail.ee; Tallinna maantee 15; singles/doubles 850/990 EEK, suites from 1400) retains its monopoly on class.

**Lossi Hotel** (☎ 33 633, fax 33 623; e lossi hotel@tt.ee; Lossi tänav 27; singles/doubles/suite 1000/1200/1800 EEK) is set on the castle grounds, nestled in some delicate shrubbery. Rooms include breakfast and guests can savour their pre-eminent views over complimentary high tea.

**Out of Town** These out-of-town places are mainly geared towards people who have their own vehicles, although some are also on infrequent bus routes. Mere travel agency has many farmhouses to let in a number of inspiring locations all over the island. Farmhouse accommodation is also arranged by the Kuressaare tourist information centre.

**Kämping Mändjala** (☎ 44 193; e mandja la@saaremma.ee; camping/cabin beds 40/180 EEK) is a pleasantly positioned camping ground and cabins, behind a sandy beach about 10km along the road west of Kuressaare. There are large cabins, as well as tent and caravan space. Be warned, demand for bathroom facilities may limit supply in high season! Buses from Kuressaare to Torgu or Sääre (three a day) go to the Mändjala bus stop, about 500m beyond the site.

**Motel and Kämping Tare** (☎/fax 37 245; e rb@kuressaare.ee; tent sites 20 EEK, camper vans 110 EEK, cabin doubles 190 EEK, room doubles 270 EEK), near the beach, 13km east of Kuressaare at Sutu, takes 25 people in sizeable rooms. There are also unheated wooden cabins and a field shower and kitchen.

**Jurna Talu** (☎ 21 919, fax 21 920; e jurna@neti.ee; singles/doubles 500/690 EEK) in Upa village, 6km from Kuressaare on the Kuivastu and Tallinn road, is a beautifully renovated farmhouse. You will have to share the bathroom with your neighbours but the wholesome breakfast more than compensates. Use of the sauna costs 200 EEK per hour and guests can ride horses at the neighbouring farm for 120 EEK an hour.

**Vastriku Guest House** (☎ 44 180, vastriku@ saaremaa.ee; doubles 500 EEK), in the village of Nasva, is a large, rustic country house with an outdoor entertainment area. Boat and canoe trips can also be arranged.

**Nasva Yacht Club** (☎ 44 044, @ nasva hotel@tt.ee; singles/doubles 630/780 EEK, suites 1100 EEK) is an elite choice surrounded by the sun, sea, sand and yachts.

**Hotel Männikäbi** (☎ 44 100, fax 44 106; doubles only with breakfast 990 EEK) is 600m past the Mändjala camping grounds. It has spacious doubles with private bath and TV. It's 300m off the road; the turn-off is just past the Mändjala bus stop.

## Places to Eat

Find late-night groceries at the **supermarket** (Lossi tänav 3; open 8am-midnight Mon-Fri, to 1am Sat & Sun), in the town square, and there are good cafés in central Kuressaare.

**Hansa Kunstisalong Cafe** (☎ 54 321; Tallinna Maantee 9) is one of Kuressaare's finest cafés, with old-world Bohemian ambience and memorable home-made pastries.

**Classic Café** (Lossi tänav 9; meals 40 EEK) offers sandwiches, pastries and daily lunch specials.

**Pannkoogikohvik** (☎ 33 575; Kohtu tänav 1; meals 50 EEK open 10am-11pm daily) serves filled pancakes for all tastes and appetites, vegetarians included.

**Vanalinna Kohvipood** (☎ 53 214; Kauba tänav 10; Meals 70 EEK; open 8am-7pm daily), always crowded, is a place to try for breakfast. Just follow the scent of fresh coffee.

**Kapteni Kõrts** (☎ 33 406; Kauba tänav 13; meals 70 EEK; open 9am-late) has a relaxed summer terrace. A questionable taste in music won't ruin the tasty, inexpensive meals served, although rowdy dance antics of fellow diners may not aid digestion.

Two good places to eat and drink are conveniently beside each other on Uus tänav.

**Õuemaja** (☎ 33 423; Uus tänav No 20A; meals under 60 EEK; open 10am-10pm daily), a no-frills restaurant with outdoor tables, is where noted writer and linguist Johannes Aavik and his musician cousin Joosep Aavik once lived. You can get very decent meat and fish meals here (faster food too).

**Õlletuba** (☎ 33 186; Uus tänav 20; meals 70 EEK; open from 8am-late daily) is probably the most relaxed pub in town, with some food but lots of beer. It welcomes those who enjoy a good drink over breakfast.

**JR Pizzaburger** (☎ 92 634; Turu tänav 4; meals 70 EEK) won't disappoint pizza lovers.

**Raekelder** (☎ 33 368; town hall basement, Rakoeja Plats; meals from 120 EEK; open noon-midnight daily) is where you can lose track of time over a luscious meal, beef is served here very well.

**Kuursaal** (☎ 39 749; Pärgi tänav 1; meals 70-120 EEK; open noon-midnight Tues-Sat, noon-10pm Sun & Mon), inside a former early 20th-century spa hall, is well worth a look-in for a coffee or light meal, but time your visit well to avoid old-time dance concerts and tour bus troops.

**Veski** (☎ 33 776; Pärna tänav 19; meals from 120 EEK; open noon-midnight Sun-Thur, noon-2am Fri & Sat), inside a windmill, is a bit hit-and-miss; it has a traditional menu and some wholesome choices.

## Entertainment

For nightlife, Kuressaare has limitations.

**Vaekoja** (☎ 33 532; Tallinna maantee 3) has the strong support of locals who linger here into the small hours.

**John Bull Pub** (☎ 39 988; Pärgi tänav 4) is a friendly place, and drinks on the outdoor deck in the park are essential on long light summer evenings.

**Budweiser Pub** (☎ 53 240; Kauba tänav 6), formerly the 'Lonkav Konn' (Limping Frog), is now the place to lunge for your Budweiser; patrons can still be seen hobbling out.

**Billiards Hall** (Raekoja tänav 1; open noon-2am daily) is for those fond of a game of pool over drinks; this perpetually dark and serious place also offers Internet access behind masked windows for 15 EEK per 30 minutes.

## Shopping

**Talu Pood** (Reakoja tänav 4) is where you can find top-quality, hand-woven crafts and lots of home-grown spices and herbs.

**Antik** (Lossi tänav 19) sells all sorts of antiques, from 19th-century farm tools to Soviet memorabilia.

The **central market** (Raekoja Plats) sells all manner of necessary and unnecessary items, including moderately priced gifts crafted from limestone.

## Getting There & Away

Direct bus/ferry connections between Kuressaare, the mainland and Hiiumaa are covered in the earlier Saaremaa Getting There & Away section. Kuressaare's **bus station**

*(☎ 31 661; Pihtla tee 25)* is the terminus for most buses on the island and schedules are posted inside.

## Getting Around

Kuressaare airport is at Roomassaare, 3km southeast of the town centre. Bus Nos 2 and 3 run throughout the day to/from the central Keskväljak. There's a **taxi rank** *(Raekoja tänav)* just off Keskväljak.

For car and scooter rental, try **Polar Rent** *(☎ 33 660; Tallinna maantee 9)*, and for bike rental, **Bivarix** *(☎/fax 57 118; Tallinna maantee 22)*. It's wise to book well ahead in summer.

## WESTERN SAAREMAA
## Sõrve Peninsula

Small cliffs, such as the Kaugatuma pank (bank) and Ohessaare pank, rear up along the west coast of the 32km southwestern Sõrve Peninsula. Legend has it that the cliffs were formed when the Devil tried in vain to wrench this spit of land from the mainland to separate Suur Tõll, who was vacationing on Sõrve, from Saaremaa. This is where the island's magic can really be felt. A bike or car trip along the coastline will expose you to some fabulous views.

This sparsely populated strip of land saw some of the heaviest fighting of WWII, and the battle scars remain; by the lighthouse at Sääre on the southern tip, you can walk around the ruins of an old Soviet army base. Other bases and the remnants of the Lõme-Kaimri antitank defence lines still stand. There's a large monument at Tehumardi, south of the beach at Järve, which was the site of a gruesome night battle in October 1944 between retreating German troops and an Estonian-Russian Rifle Division. The horror defies belief: Both armies fought blindly, firing on intuition or finding the enemy by touch. Russian-Estonian dead lie buried in double graves in the cemetery nearby.

**Mati Velandi** *(☎ 39 238)* conducts Estonian language tours through the abandoned radar base at Tehumardi and nearby Soviet military facilities at Karujarve village, called Dejevo in Soviet times. Stroll through the grounds, catch sight of an abandoned searchlight or explore cavernous multichambered bunkers, but watch your step as these sites are deteriorating.

## Viidumäe Nature Reserve

Founded in 1957, Viidumäe Nature Reserve covers an area of 1873 hectares, with a 22m observation tower on Saaremaa's highest point (54m) at Viidumäe, about 25km west of Kuressaare. The tower, about 2km along a dirt road off the Kuressaare-Lümanda road at Viidu, offers a panoramic view of the reserve and the forested and coastal wonders of the island itself. The view is particularly memorable at sunset. There are two nature trails (2.2km and 1.5km), marked to highlight the different habitats of the area. Viidumäe is a botanical reserve, its favourable climate and conditions making it home to rare plant species such as the blunt-flowered rush, the Saaremaa yellow rattle and the white-beam. Some plants are indigenous to the island.

At the reserve's **headquarters** *(☎ 76 321, 76 442; e mari.r@tt.ee; open 10am-6pm Wed-Sun June-Aug)* in Viidu there's a small permanent exhibition. Guided tours of the reserve are available, including tours for special interest groups.

## Viki & Kihelkonna

At Viki on the road to Kihelkonna, about 30km from Kuressaare, an old farm has been preserved as the **Mihkli Farm Museum** *(Talumuuseum)*. Kihelkonna, 3km beyond, has a tall, austere, early German church. There's a fishing harbour, used by yachts, at Veere on the eastern side of the Tagamõisa Peninsula north of Kihelkonna. The western side of the same peninsula, towards Harilaid, boasts some impressive, desolate coastal scenery.

## North Coast

The 22m cliff known as Panga pank, near Panga on the north coast is Saaremaa's highest cliff. Until the 16th century this was a sacrificial site from where children and animals were thrown in an appeal to the sea gods for abundant fish catches.

## Places to Stay

**Kämping Karujärve** *(☎/fax 42 034; cabins per person 125 EEK; open May-Sept)*, among the trees on the east side of Karujärv lake, some 9km east of Kihelkonna, offers basic facilities. There is a small outside song stage, a minigolf course and horse riding at weekends. Boat rental is also possible.

**Süla Talu** *(☎ 46 927; cabins per person 240 EEK)*, in an isolated patch of woods in Oja, a tiny village 4km northwest of Kihelkonna, is a great option. Not only does it have comfortable wood cabins, sauna and home-cooked meals, but it can also boat up to four people to Vilsandi or around the Tagamõisa Peninsula. Staff can offer advice, arrange horse riding and assist with a range of other activities.

**Sõrve Holiday House** (☎ 23 061; doubles/family room 360/650 EEK), near the village of Torgu on the Sõrve peninsula in rugged windswept surrounds, is a 20-minute walk to the coast.

**Ninase Puhkeküla** (☎/fax 79 743; doubles 420 EEK) at Ninase, 8km north of Mustjala, is a pleasant place with wooden cabins, from which you can explore the fishing villages and cliffs by the coast. If travelling with kids or with no immunity to kitsch, you can't miss the nearby clunky wooden male and female **folk windmills**, traditional wooden windmill-type constructions built to resemble giants in traditional costume, apparently having an argument.

## Getting There & Away

There are at least three buses daily from Kuressaare down the Sõrve peninsula to Sääre or Torgu, and six daily to Kihelkonna along different routes. A good combination bus/bike trip is bussing from Kuressaare to Viidu (bikes in the baggage compartment), then cycling north through Viidumäe Nature Reserve towards Kihelkonna or farther on to the Tagamõisa peninsula. Be sure to arrive early for your return trip as buses in these remote parts can deviate from their schedules.

## VILSANDI & VILSANDI NATIONAL PARK

Vilsandi, west of Kihelkonna, is the largest of 161 islands and islets off Saaremaa's western coast protected under the Vilsandi National Park (about 10% of all of Estonia's islands). The park covers an area of 18,155 hectares (including 161 tiny islands) and is an area of extensive ecological study. The breeding patterns of the common eider and the migration of the barnacle goose have been monitored very closely here. Ringed seals can also be seen here in their breeding season and some 32 species of orchid thrive in the park.

Vilsandi, 6km long and in places up to 3km wide, is a low, wooded island. The small islets surrounding it are abundant with currant and juniper bushes. Up to 247 bird species are observed here, and in spring and autumn there is a remarkable migration of waterfowl – up to 10,000 barnacle geese stop over on Vilsandi in mid-May and the white-tailed eagle and osprey have even been known to drop by.

A highlight on the island is a working **ostrich farm** (the birds were imported here from Africa via Finland), which provides a truly surreal sight. For a nominal fee, you can get up close to these odd-looking creatures and watch them stare at you.

The best time to visit the island is from the beginning of May to mid-June. In summer a small boat runs twice daily on Tuesday and Friday from Papisaare on Saaremaa to Vikati on Vilsandi. The one-way fare is 30 EEK. In July, if the waters are shallow enough, an old bus ploughs its way across from Papisaare to Vikati instead, a one-way journey taking about 20 minutes.

The **Vilsandi National Park headquarters** (☎/fax 46 554), at Loona, can arrange accommodation and wildlife watching tours given advance notice, as can the Mere and Arensburg travel agencies in Kuressaare.

## ABRUKA & VAHASE

Known as a 'Mecca for naturalists' by Estonians, the 10.6 sq km island of Abruka and neighbouring Vahase lie 6km from Roomassaare, off Saaremaa's south coast. Part of the island is a botanical-zoological reservation, and deer, although now endangered, also inhabit the island. Today about 40 people live on Abruka, but this population trebles with summertime residents. In summer both a mail and a **private boat** (☎ 051 36 961 mobile) provide the only regular links between the island and Saaremaa. In the depths of winter it's possible to walk across the ice to Saaremaa, but not recommended without local advice.

**Innu Farm** (☎ 26 633; beds per person 150 EEK; open mid-May–mid-Sept), on the island, provides accommodation with kitchen facilities, tents can also be pitched. The family running the centre rents out bicycles and can pick you up by boat from Roomassaare Port for 50 EEK. Horse riding tours of the island can be arranged.

The Arensburg travel agency (see Information under Kuressaare earlier in this chapter) arranges trips and walking tours of Abruka and Vahase.

# Southwest Estonia

The main city in southwest Estonia, the quiet, park-lined, coastal resort Pärnu, attracts legions of holiday-makers and those seeking better health each year. It's an amiable place where everyone seems to walk slightly off-kilter: A majority of its summer populace are either ailing elderly Finns going to and from their sanatoriums or party-hungry young Estonians stumbling from bar to disco. Elsewhere in the region you might explore the isolated coast west of Pärnu, canoe on the wild bogs of the Soomaa National Park, trail the Nigula bogs, or venture to the remote islands of Kihnu or Ruhnu.

## PÄRNU
### ☎ 044 • pop 45,500
Pärnu is 130km south of Tallinn on the main road to Rīga and a favourite summertime resort for much of Estonia and a good portion of Scandinavia. It is also where most of the country's sanatoriums are located; each year thousands partake in a wide range of therapies. In the Soviet era the pleasures of the long, sandy beach were greatly reduced by pollution, which rendered swimming inadvisable. New water filtration equipment removed any health risk by 1993 and in 2001 the beach was awarded the Blue Flag, an international designation for clean, safe water. Meanwhile, Pärnu has carved another niche for itself: Counterbalancing its party-town reputation, it has also become a kind of alternative cultural capital in Estonia. Several galleries and museums here have made admirable steps to introduce truly world-class art, the likes of which sometimes bypass even Tallinn, which in some ways is more conservative than Pärnu.

### History
Stone Age objects from around 7500 BC found at Pulli, near Sindi on the Pärnu River about 12km inland, are among the oldest human artefacts found in Estonia. At that time the mouth of the river was at Pulli and the site of Pärnu was still sea bed.

There was a trading settlement at Pärnu before the German crusaders arrived, but the place entered recorded history when the Pärnu River was fixed as the border between the territories of the Ösel-Wiek bishop (west

## Highlights

• Take to the beach, sand and sun in Pärnu, and mix it with a little mud treatment

• See the Swedish legacy on Ruhnu or the living museum of Kihnu for a real island getaway

• Bird-watch and board-walk with a difference in Nigula Nature Reserve

• Wander the vestiges of Viljandi Order castle, traverse the old moat and trenches

• Board a canoe or build your own and explore the bogs of Soomaa National Park

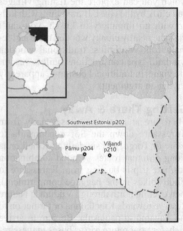

Southwest Estonia p202

Pärnu p204    Viljandi p210

and north) and the Livonian knights (east and south) in 1234. The town that grew around the knights' fort, joined by rivers to Viljandi, Tartu and Lake Peipsi, became the Hanseatic port of Pernau in the 14th century. (Sinking water levels have since cut this link.) Pernau/Pärnu had a population of Lübeck origin till at least the 18th century. It withstood wars, fires, plagues, and switches between German, Polish, Swedish and Russian rule down the centuries and prospered in the 17th century under Swedish rule until having its trade devastated by the Europe-wide blockades during the Napoleonic wars.

From 1838 the town gradually found new life as a popular resort, mud baths proving a draw as well as the beach. Only the resort area was spared severe damage in 1944 as the Soviet army drove out the Nazi occupiers, but many parts of the Old Town have since been restored.

## Orientation

Pärnu lies either side of the Pärnu River estuary, which empties into the north-eastern corner of the Gulf of Rīga, known as Pärnu Bay. The southern half of the town, a 1.5km-wide neck of land between the river and the bay, is the centre of activity. The central square is on the corner of Ringi and Rüütli tänav, with the bus station half a block to the north on Pikk tänav. The Old Town with its narrow streets stretches to the west. Rüütli is the main shopping street. Running south the streets get wider and greener before ending at the park-backed beach.

## Information

The **tourist information centre** (☎ 73 000; W www.parnu.ee; Rüütli tänav 16; open 9am-6pm Mon-Fri, 9am-4pm Sat, 10am-3pm Sun June-Aug, 9am-5pm Mon-Fri Sept-May) is where you can pick up maps, brochures and the helpful *Pärnu in Your Pocket*, published annually (25 EEK). Books, maps and other local literature can also be found at **Apollo** (Rüütli 41). The **Best Western Hotell Pärnu** (see Places to Stay later in the Pärnu section) provides tourist information services, handy should the official centre be closed.

The Pärnu Hotel has a 24-hour currency exchange. **Ühispank** (Rüütli tänav 40a), on the far side of the building behind the bus station, cashes travellers cheques and gives cash advances on credit cards; there's also an ATM.

There's a central post office (Akadeemia 7; open 8am-6pm Mon-Fri, 9am-3pm Sat & Sun).

You can access the Internet at the **Pärnu New Art Museum** (Esplanaadi tänav 10; open 2pm-7pm Tues-Fri, 10am-2pm Sat). It charges 30 EEK an hour, with a five-hour maximum. Conveniently central is **Rüütli Internetipunkt** (Rüütli tänav 25; open 11am-9pm Mon-Fri, 10am-6pm Sat & Sun), which charges 20 EEK an hour for Internet access.

**Hermann Travel** (☎ 31 034; W www.hermann.ee; Rüütli tänav 51) handles ferry, air and bus reservations in and out of Pärnu and Tallinn, and offers organised tours of the region. Nature-related tours are the speciality of **Reiser Travel Agency** (☎ 71 480; e reiser@reiser.ee; Kuuse tänav 4).

There's a **left-luggage office** (pakihoid; open 8am-1pm & 1.45pm-7pm Mon-Fri, 8am-1pm Sat) in the bus station opposite the bus parking lot, in a white wooden cabin.

## Things to See

The historic centre stretches about 700m west of the central square. The oldest building, dating from the early 15th century, is the actually white and originally bigger **Red Tower** (Punane Torn; Hommiku tänav 11). Originally bigger, this was the southeast corner tower of the medieval town wall, of which nothing more remains. At one stage the tower was used as a prison.

Two blocks west, on Pühavaimu tänav is a fine pair of large **17th-century conjoined houses**, a fascinating example of ambitious early home-renovation efforts. Originally separate residences belonging to a chemist and an eminent city councillor, the buildings date from 1640–70 but they received a neo-classicist facelift in the 1840s before merging under the banner of a department store in 1877. One block farther west is the former **Town Hall** (Raekoja Hoon; cnr Nikolai tänav & Uus tänav), a yellow and white classical edifice originally built in 1797 as the home of a rich merchant. The grey and white Jugendstil north wing with its little spire, was added in 1911.

Across Nikolai from the main town hall building there's a half-timbered house dating from 1740, and a block down the street on the corner of Rüütli tänav is the Baroque Lutheran **Elisabeth Church**, also from the 1740s, named after the Russian empress of the time. The Russian Orthodox **Catherine Church** (Ekatarina Kirik; cnr Uus & Vee tänav), from the 1760s, is named after another Russian empress, Catherine the Great.

At the far western end of Rüütli tänav is a stretch of Pärnu's **Swedish ramparts** overlooking the **moat**, from where the west side of the Old Town was defended. Where the rampart meets the western end of Kuninga tänav it's pierced by the tunnel-like **Tallinn Gate** (Tallinna Värav), which once marked the main road to Tallinn. It was one of three gates in the ramparts that the Swedes built as part of their 17th century strengthening of Pärnu's defences.

Heading back east along Kuninga tänav, there's a **17th-century house** (Kuninga tänav 21), which has a shoe hanging from its eaves,

# SOUTHWEST ESTONIA

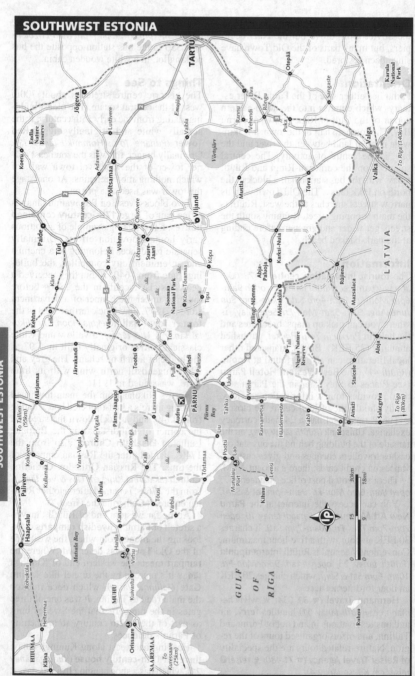

said to have been lost by Sweden's King Carl XII on this street in 1700. The **Victoria Hotel** *(Kuninga tänav 25)*, a fine 1930 Art Nouveau inspired building, stands on the site of the old Swedish Rīga Gate. In Koidula väljak, the park opposite the hotel, is the **statue of Lydia Koidula**, the poet of Estonia's national revival (see the boxed text 'Dawn of Poetry' in this chapter). There's also the charming **Lydia Koidula Memorial Museum** *(☎ 41 663; Jannseni tänav 37, Ülejõe; adult/student 10/5; open 10am-6pm Wed-Sun)* on the north side of the river.

**Pärnu Museum** *(☎ 33 231; Rüütli tänav 53; adult/student 35/20 EEK; open 10am-6pm Wed-Sun)*, on the corner of the central square, is entrenched in regional history. A slightly eccentric collection of reptiles, cute or colourful like the gecko, and the odd sleepy python, has been turned into a small but interesting **Mini Zoo** *(☎ 055 16 033 mobile; Akadeemia tee 1; adult/child 35/20 EEK; open 10am-6pm Mon-Fri, 10am-4pm Sat & Sun)*, which should silence the kids.

The **Pärnu New Art Museum** *(☎ 30 772; e aip@chaplin.ee; Esplanaadi tänav 10; adult/student 15/10 EEK; open 9am-9pm daily)*, southwest of the centre, is among the cultural bright spots in Estonia. It's a large complex that incorporates a café, which curiously sells what could be the largest collection of spices in the country, an art bookshop and several galleries with regular, daring and almost always interesting exhibitions. Founded by film maker Mark Soosaar, the centre also hosts international conferences on many facets of the art world, as well as an annual Documentary Film Festival. Pärnu's decapitated Lenin statue parked outside makes the centre easy to find.

## Mud Baths
No trip to Pärnu is complete without a mud bath. A grand neoclassical structure (1927) houses one of the town's most popular baths, **Pärnu Mudaravila** *(☎ 25 520; Ranna puiestee 1)*. It offers treatments with or without accommodation. Bathers can choose from a large selection of mud to wallow in, be it 'local' or 'electric' costing from 150 EEK. These are not just frivolous romps, however, and you are encouraged to book ahead, arrive early and consult a physician before submerging. Bus No 1 comes to the Kuursaal stop from Pärnu's post office.

## Bowling
A healthier time can probably be had at the buzzing complex just behind the Port Artur shopping centre across from the bus station. On the first floor is a **Bowling Club** *(☎ 71 222; Aida tänav 5; open 1pm-midnight Mon-Fri, 1pm-1am Sat, Sun 11am- midnight)* with six lanes. If you're a novice, lessons await.

## Places to Stay – Budget
There are three camping grounds around the city open from June to August. All have cabins and possibly tent space too.

**Kämping Valgerand** *(☎ 44 004, fax 40 135; tent/caravan 50/100 EEK, /2-/4-bed cabins 300/400 EEK)* is 6.5km west of Pärnu in a lovely wooded strip beside the sea. It's best accessed by private transport; buses to Lihula stop on the main road at Valgerand, and from there it's a 3km walk.

**Kämping Jõekääru** *(☎ 30 034, 30 031; 4-/5-bed cabins 130/110 EEK per person, tent/caravan sites 60/130 EEK)* is in Sauga, 5km north of Pärnu. Campers can use the tennis, volleyball and basketball courts.

**Linnakämping Green** *(☎ 38 776; Suure-Jõe 50b; cabin per person 95 EEK)*, 2km from Pärnu at the rowing centre on the river, offers boat and bike rentals.

Both the tourist information centre and the **Tanni-Vakoma Majutüsburoo** *(☎ 31 070; e tanni@online.ee; Hommiku tänav 5)* can help with private accommodation (from 250 EEK).

**Kalevi Pension** *(☎ 43 008, fax 59 683; Ranna puiestee 2; dorm bed/doubles/triples/family 200/400/600/800 EEK)* isn't pretty but is well positioned beside the beach. Larger rooms with their own facilities are a good choice if travelling in numbers.

**Lõuna Hostel** *(☎ 30 943, fax 30 944; e hostel louna@hot.ee; Lõuna tänav 2; dorm beds/doubles 200-250/400 EEK)* is a fresh, new hostel in a grand building overlooking a park. It offers quality budget accommodation; the gleaming new bathrooms will inspire.

## Places to Stay – Mid-Range
The string of ugly, concrete, hotel-block buildings 500m from the beach north of the Mudaravila mud baths are lacking in atmosphere, but are more comfortable than they appear.

**Mudaravila** *(☎/fax 25 525, e info@mudar avila; Sääse tänav 7; singles/doubles 380/500 EEK, accommodation with treatments from 460*

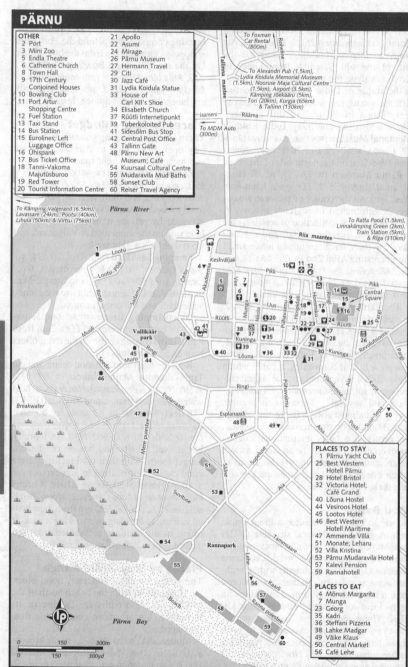

# PÄRNU

**OTHER**
2 Port
3 Mini Zoo
5 Endla Theatre
6 Catherine Church
8 Town Hall
9 17th Century
   Conjoined Houses
10 Bowling Club
11 Port Artur
   Shopping Centre
12 Fuel Station
13 Taxi Stand
14 Bus Station
15 Eurolines; Left
   Luggage Office
16 Ühispank
17 Bus Ticket Office
18 Tanni-Vakoma
   Majutüsburoo
19 Red Tower
20 Tourist Information Centre

21 Apollo
22 Asumi
24 Mirage
26 Pärnu Museum
27 Hermann Travel
29 Citi
30 Jazz Café
31 Lydia Koidula Statue
33 House of
   Carl XII's Shoe
34 Elisabeth Church
37 Rüütli Internetipunkt
39 Tuberkoloited Pub
41 Sidesõlm Bus Stop
42 Central Post Office
43 Tallinn Gate
48 Pärnu New Art
   Museum; Café
54 Kuursaal Cultural Centre
55 Mudaravila Mud Baths
58 Sunset Club
60 Reiser Travel Agency

**PLACES TO STAY**
1 Pärnu Yacht Club
25 Best Western
   Hotell Pärnu
28 Hotel Bristol
32 Victoria Hotel;
   Café Grand
40 Lõuna Hostel
44 Vesiroos Hotel
45 Lootos Hotel
46 Best Western
   Hotell Maritime
47 Ammende Villa
51 Monate; Leharu
52 Villa Kristina
53 Pärnu Mudaravila Hotel
57 Kalevi Pension
59 Rannahotell

**PLACES TO EAT**
4 Mõnus Margarita
7 Munga
23 Georg
35 Kadri
36 Steffani Pizzeria
38 Lahke Madgar
49 Väike Klaus
50 Central Market
56 Café Lehe

To Foxman
Car Rental
(800m)

To Alexandri Pub (1.5km),
Lydia Koidula Memorial Museum
(1.5km), Nooruse Maja Cultural Centre
(1.5km), Airport (3.5km),
Kämping Jõekääru (5km),
Tori (20km), Kurgja (65km)
& Tallinn (130km)

To MDM Auto
(300m)

To Kämping Valgerand (6.5km),
Lavassare (24km), Pootsi (40km),
Lihula (50km) & Virtsu (75km)

**Pärnu River**

To Ratta Pood (1.5km),
Linnakämping Green (2km),
Train Station (5km),
& Rīga (310km)

SOUTHWEST ESTONIA

Breakwater

Vallikäär
park

Rannapark

**Pärnu Bay**

Beach

0        150        300m
0        150        300yd

EEK), the accommodation arm of the baths (see under Mud Baths earlier in the Pärnu section), knows it's trade well and its health packages are tempting.

**Monate** (☎ 25 800; *Pärna tänav 12, 5th floor; singles/doubles/suites 430/600/800 EEK),* near Pärnu Mudaravila, is also popular with groups.

**Leharu** (☎ 25 700, 25 701; *Pärna tänav 12, 4th floor; singles/doubles/triples 430/600/720 EEK),* below, is virtually identical to Monate.

**Pärnu Yacht Club** (☎ 71 740; *Lootsi tänav 6; singles/doubles with breakfast low season 400/700 EEK, high season 550/850 EEK)* has small rooms with bathrooms overlooking the harbour. Friendly staff can organise car, yacht or boat rental.

A flying leap up in ambience are the twin hotels **Lootos Hotel** (☎/fax 31 030; *Muru tänav 1; singles/doubles 600/800 EEK),* and, across the street, **Vesiroos Hotel** (☎ 30 940, fax 30 942; *Esplanaadi tänav 42A; doubles/triples 900/1100 EEK).* Both establishments are under the same management and hygienically clean, guests at either can access the swimming pool.

**Best Western Hotell Maritime** (☎ 78 910, fax 78 904; e *maritime@www.ee; Seedri tänav 4; singles/doubles 790/990 EEK)* has great location and décor, though the rooms are lacking charm.

**Villa Kristina** (☎/fax 29 803; e *villa kristina@mail.ee; Suvituse tänav 1; doubles/ suites 680/1200 EEK)* is a prime choice for intimate surroundings. The owner, a doctor, has made the place hypoallergenic and can suggest the right treatment for your ills.

## Places to Stay – Top End

**Ammende Villa** (☎ 73 888, fax 73 887; e *am mende@transcom.ee; Mere puiestee 7; cottage singles/doubles 1100/1450 EEK, suites from 2850 EEK)* is a splendid Jugendstil-era building set in sprawling parklands. Rooms exhibit period furnishings and the obligatory fine taste, with singles/doubles relegated to the rear gardener's cottage.

**Rannahotell** (☎ 38 950, fax 32 918; *Ranna puiestee 5; singles/doubles from 1130/1430 EEK)* is a stunning functionalist mansion reposing quietly on the seafront. Expect all sorts of comforts.

Both the **Victoria Hotel** (☎ 43 412, fax 43 415; e *victoria@hot.ee; Kuninga tänav 25; singles/doubles from 690/990 EEK)* in the town centre, and the **Hotel Bristol** (☎ 31 450, fax 43

415; *Rüütli tänav 45; singles/doubles 860/ 1150 EEK),* run by the same team, have exquisite rooms. Victoria is the more elegant.

**Best Western Hotell Pärnu** (☎ 78 911, fax 78 905; e *hotparnu@www.ee; Rüütli tänav 44; singles/doubles from 1100/1300 EEK),* a stone's throw from the bus station, is drab on the outside, modern and comfortable within.

## Places to Eat

**Munga** (☎ 31 099; *Munga tänav 9; meals 50 EEK; open 10am-midnight daily),* in an old home tucked into a charming side street, is a must-visit. The small café has a warm welcoming ambience with some vegetarian delights.

**Café Lehe** (☎ 25 788; *Lehe tänav 5; meals 60 EEK; open 11am-10pm)* is a decent, affordable option for a light meal a short walk from the beach. The vibrant interior shows a tastefully minimalist use of the prancing cricket motif.

**Alexandri Pub** (☎ 32 184; *Vana Rääma tänav 8; meals under 70 EEK; open noon-11pm daily),* north of the river, may look like a biker bar but it's a friendly and popular place, and the range and number of locals here attests to this. Try the fried chicken (you're in the south here after all). Go north across the bridge and turn right on the first street past the traffic lights and, if your steel chariot needs a service, you'll pass a bike mechanic on the way.

**Steffani Pizzeria** (☎ 31 170; *Nikolai tänav 24; 70-90 EEK; open 11am-midnight daily)* has Pärnu's best done pizza and pasta.

**Mõnus Margarita** (☎ 30 929; *Akadeemia 5; meals 70 EEK; open 11am-midnight Mon-Fri, 11am-1am Sat & Sun)* has a colourful and kitschy Mexicana interior, but the meals could be better acquainted with chilli.

**Väike Klaus** (☎ 72 207; *Supeluse tänav 3; meals 80 EEK; open 11am-midnight Mon-Fri, 11am-2am Sat & Sun),* a hearty, German-inspired pub, is a great place for a meaty lunch, a game of billiards upstairs, or a leisurely beer to counterbalance the healthy effects of those mud treatments.

**Lahke Madgar** (☎ 40 104; *Kuninga tänav 18; meals 120 EEK; open 11am-11pm daily)* boasts a colourful, cottage-like ambience, warm service and a diverse menu. Savour the misfortune of the 'farmer's wicked turkey'.

**Café Grand** (☎ 43 412; *Kuninga tänav 25; meals 230 EEK; open noon-10pm Mon-Fri, 11am-midnight Sat)* has fine meals that won't disappoint connoisseurs. The 'Titanic chicken' will certainly go down well.

**Georg** (☎ 31 110; Rüütli tänav 43; meals 45 EEK; open 7.30am-7.30pm Mon-Fri, 9am-7.30pm Sat & Sun), a clean, stylish café with good soups, salads and meals, is a stylish but cheap fill-up option.

A great place to hang out is the **Pärnu New Art Museum café** (☎ 30 772; Esplanaadi tänav 10, open 11am-5pm daily).

**Kadri** (☎ 45 334; Nikolai tänav 12; meals 70 EEK; open 7.30am-7.30pm Mon-Fri, 9am-7.30pm Sat & Sun) is an excellent spot for tasty, inexpensive, home-cooked meals; it opens bright and early.

If you are wanting to self-cater there is the **Central market** (Suur-Sepa 18; open 8am-3pm, except Mon) and plenty of choice within the **Port Artur shopping centre** (Riia Maantee 1; open 9am-10pm daily).

The beachfront is lined with café-kiosks serving fast food to replace the calories you burn sitting in the sun.

## Entertainment

The tourist information centre distributes the annual *Pärnu Cultural Calendar* which lists details of the many events in Pärnu. It sells tickets for most cultural events too.

**Nooruse Maja Cultural Centre** (☎ 41 768; Roheline tänav 1B) is tuned into the cultural pulse of the town and puts on occasional folk shows and concerts.

**Kuursaal** (☎ 20 368; Mere Puiestee 22), a newly refurbished old spa building near the beach, hosts a range of classic and contemporary musical events and cinema.

**Jazz Café** (☎ 27 546; Ringi 11; open 10am-midnight daily) is a place where jazz, sand and mud make quite an ensemble. Spontaneous live performances here may surprise.

**Bars & Nightclubs** Aside from fine choices for food, **Alexandri Pub** and **Väike Klaus** (see Places to Eat earlier) also rake in the crowds until late every evening.

**Citi** (Hommiku tänav 8; open 9am-midnight daily) with eclectic decor and fine-weather outdoor tables, is a good choice if you have high tolerance levels for Europop.

**Tuberkuloited Pub** (☎ 27 998; Kuninga 11; open 11am-midnight Mon-Fri, 11am-2am Sat) may sound like a sick potato but it's a fine place for catching local live music. Its namesake is one of Estonia's favourite bands.

**Mirage** (Rüütli tänav 40; open 10pm-3am Fri, 10pm-3am Sat) retains its popularity despite the dazzling Vegas foyer lights and a few shady types in its casino.

**Sunset Club** (☎ 30 670; Ranna puiestee 3; open 10pm-4am Thur-Sat), in a grandiose building dating from 1939, brings in the numbers as a club or concert hall for musicians.

**Theatre & Classical Music** Pärnu Town Orchestra holds classical concerts every weekend in summer. Check with the tourist information centre or posters down Rüütli tänav. The **Pärnu Opera** (☎ 44 993) is a troupe with occasional performances around town. The **Endla Theatre** (☎ 30 691; Keskväljak 1) also puts on performances.

## Getting There & Away

**Air** Pärnu has an **airport** (☎ 75 001) on the northern edge of town, west off the Tallinn road. **Air Livonia** (☎ 75 007, fax 75 006; e info@airlivonia.ee) operates two flights a week from Pärnu to Ruhnu island, and from there to Kuressaare on Saaremaa, once a week from September to May only. Air Livonia also has daily flights year-round from Pärnu to Kihnu Island. It also operates two extra direct flights to Kuressaare per month. Tickets can be quite difficult to get as locals book far in advance.

**Bus** The **terminal** (☎ 71 002) for overland buses is at the north end of Ringi tänav, just off Pikk. **Cargobus** (☎ 27 845) sells Eurolines tickets to Riga and beyond, alternatively tickets may be bought from the driver. For destinations throughout Estonia, the **ticket office** (open 5am-8.30pm), a red-brick building, is 100m south on the opposite side of Ringi tänav. More than 20 buses daily make the 130km trip to/from Tallinn (60 EEK, two hours). See the introductory Getting There & Away chapter for Eurolines routes from Pärnu to Western Europe and Russia. Other buses to/from Pärnu include:

| | |
|---|---|
| Haapsalu | 76 EEK, 3 hours, one or two buses daily |
| Kuressaare | 120 EEK, 3½ hours, two buses daily |
| Riga | 85 EEK, 3¾ hours, six buses daily |
| Tartu | 95 EEK, 3–4½ hours, 16 buses daily |
| Viljandi | 50 EEK, 2–2½ hours, 12 buses daily |
| Vilnius | 250 EEK, 7½–8 hours, one overnight bus each way daily |
| Virtsu | 42 EEK, 1½–2 hours, two buses daily |

## Dawn of Poetry

Lydia Koidula embodied Estonia's nationalist awakening in the late 1880s. Acclaimed as Estonia's first lady of poetry and the first Estonian-language playwright, she was one of few to use what was then the mainly spoken language in poetic expression. A much-revered figure, her name adorns street plaques in every main town, her face fronts the 100 EEK note and her figure is immortalised in sculpture.

Born Lydia Jannsen in Vändra in 1843, she went on to edit and write much of her father's newspaper, *Estonian Courier*, which was then the sole Estonian-language paper and one that called on people to become aware of their culture and heritage as separate from that of the dominant Baltic Germans. Her book of poetry, *The Emajõe Nightingale*, published anonymously (authoring was not at the time considered a decent career for a lady), contained many passionate poems about her love for her homeland. Another author, Karl Jakobson, coined her pen name, Koidula, which loosely translates to 'maiden of the dawn'.

At Estonia's first National Song Festival in Tartu in 1869, two of her poems, set to music, were the highlights of this pivotal event in the cultural history of Estonia. During the Soviet time, when Estonia's official national anthem *My Fatherland, My Fate, My Joy* was banned, Koidula's poem *My Fatherland is My Beloved* (set to music by Gustav Ernesaks) became the country's unofficial anthem (sung with great emotion at Song Festivals) and to this day is cherished. Her play *The Cousin from Saaremaa* was the first Estonian play to be performed in public, in 1870.

Her close but ill-fated friendship with Friedrich Kreutzwald, already famous for his *Kalevipoeg*, gave rise to 94 letters that are regarded today as literary classics.

After marriage to a Baltic German doctor, Eduard Michelson, from Rīga she left her beloved homeland and moved with him to Kronstadt, an island outside of St Petersburg. She continued to write poetry and articles, but her separation from the national awakening she had inspired was something she felt profoundly. Fragile health, recurring depression and a series of strenuous childbirths all took their toll, with her premature death in Kronstadt in 1886. She would never know of the cultural significance she would hold posthumously.

Shortly before dying, she wrote her last poem, *Thine Unto Death*:

> To the last hour of my life
> I will cherish thee, my land
> My Estonia in its bloom
> Dear and fragrant fatherland
> The praise of mead and stream
> And thy soothing tongue
> To the last hour of my life
> Shall be spoken, shall be sung

**Train** Two painfully slow trains a day run between Tallinn and Pärnu (40 EEK, three hours). **Pärnu station** (*Riia maantee 116*) is 5km east of the town centre along the Rīga road.

**Boat** It's possible to take a ferry or private boat trip from Pärnu to Kihnu (see under Kihnu later in this chapter). **Pärnu Yacht Club** (*Pärnu Jahtklubi*; ☎ 71 740; Lootsi tänav 6) has a harbour with a customs point and passport control, making it suitable for visiting yachts.

## Getting Around

A main local bus stop in the town centre is the Sidesõlm stop on Akadeemia tee in front of the main post office. There's a **taxi stand** (*cnr Pikk & Ringi tänav*), to the side of the bus station. You can order a taxi through **E-Takso** (☎ 31 111) or through **Pärnu Takso** (☎ 41 240).

**Car & Motorcycle** The Neste, Shell and Statoil stations along Riia maantee are all open 24 hours. There's a **fuel station** next to the Port Artur Shopping Centre. **M.D.M. Auto** (☎/fax 32 113; Jannseni 36B) rents out cars for honest prices, but the best prices are with **Foxman** (☎ 76 100; Roheline tänav 64), which can set you up from 350 EEK a day.

**Bicycle** You can rent bicycles from **Ratta Pood** (☎ 32 440) but book ahead in summer.

## AROUND PÄRNU
### Lavassaare
pop 554

Railways are used in the peat-extraction industry at Lavassaare, in an area of bogs 25km northwest of Pärnu, and there's a **railway museum** (☎ 052 72 584; open 11am-6pm Sat, 10am-3pm Sun) close to the peat fields that offers rides on its little old steam engines and narrow-gauge tracks. To reach Lavassaare turn north off the Lihula road 13km west of central Pärnu, then go 12km or so north.

### Tori
☎ 044 • pop 537

There has been a **stud farm** (☎ 66 080; visits by arrangement) at Tori, 20km northeast of Pärnu on the Pärnu River, since 1856, when attempts began to breed bigger, stronger Estonian farm and cart horses. Learn more about the development of Estonia's finest breeds and other equine achievements at the **horse-breeding museum** here too. Nearby, just off the main bridge, you'll find probably the only devil statue in Estonia, the **Tori Devil**, which sits near a sandstone cave called **Tori Hell**, naturally.

### Kurgja
☎ 044 • pop 34

At Kurgja, on the Pärnu River 15km east of Vändra and 65km northeast of Pärnu, there's a **farm** (☎ 58 171; admission/guided tour 15/ 200 EEK by appointment only) still operated by 19th-century methods and machinery. It was founded in 1874 by Carl Robert Jakobson – a much revered leader of the Estonian nationalist movement – as a model farm for the latest ideas in crop rotation and cattle feeding and so on. Here too is the **Jakobson Talu museum** (☎ 58 171; open 10am-5pm daily) dedicated to Jakobson, who was also an educationalist and edited the radical newspaper Sakala in Viljandi. He appears on the 500 EEK banknote.

### Pärnu to the Latvian Border

The Highway 4 from Pärnu to the Latvian border, a 65km stretch, runs through forest much of the way, usually 2km to 3km inland. The border on the older, coastal road, from Häädemeeste (a much more pleasant drive than along the main road), is 40km south of Pärnu, but is no longer operational.

### Things to See & Do

Konstantin Päts, the semidictatorial president of independent Estonia before WWII, was born at **Tahku**, 20km down the coast from Pärnu. His statue here was the first **political monument** to be restored in post-Soviet Estonia. Estonia's biggest dunes are off the highway at **Rannametsa**, about 3km north of Häädemeeste, but they are forested and inland, so there's little to see.

The **Nigula bog** (Nigula raba), just north of the Latvian border about 10km east of the Highway 4, is protected by the Nigula Nature Reserve. The bog is a treeless peat bog filled with pools and hollows, in the western part of which there are five 'bog islands'. It is also an important bird-breeding area: Golden eagles and black-throated divers are occasional visitors to the bog, which is home to 144 bird species.

The **Nigula Nature Reserve office** (☎ 044-56 668; Pärnu tänav 2) in Kilingi-Nõmme, arranges visits to the bog, where you can follow a 3.2km-long trail along wooden planks.

### Places to Stay

The Nigula Nature Reserve office arranges accommodation. The Estonian Ecotourism Association (ⓦ www.ecotourism.ee) can also offer assistance.

**Lepanina Hotell** (☎/fax 044-65 024; ⓔ lepanina@lepanina.ee; camping/singles/doubles 50/450/700 EEK) is a sprawling, modern complex near Kabli and the coast, following the old border road. Rates include morning sauna and camping facilities are available.

**Lemme Kämping** (☎ 044-98 458; tent sites 50 EEK, 2-/4-person cabins 300/750 EEK), south of Kabli, is in a beautiful location, in woods along a sandy beach.

## KIHNU
☎ 044 • pop 500

Kihnu Island, in the Gulf of Rīga 40km south-west of Pärnu, is one of the most traditional places in Estonia, with colourful striped skirts still worn every day by most of the women, that indicate the wearer's status in the community. There are three main villages on the 7km-long island, plus a school, church, and combined village hall and bar in the centre of the island. Long, quiet beaches line the western coast. Kihnu people are among the few non-Setu Estonians who follow the Russian Orthodox religion.

Many of the island's first inhabitants, centuries ago, were criminals and others exiled from the mainland. Kihnu men made a living from fishing and seal hunting, while women effectively governed the island in their absence. The most famous of them was the sea captain, Enn Uuetoa (better known as Kihnu Jõnn), who became a symbol of lost freedom for Estonians during the Soviet period when they were virtually banned from the sea. Kihnu Jõnn, said to have sailed on all the world's oceans, drowned in 1913 when his ship sank off Denmark on what was to have been his last voyage before retirement. He was buried in the Danish town of Oksby but in 1992 his remains were brought home to Kihnu and reburied in the island's church.

There's a museum near the church, and in the south a lighthouse, shipped over from Britain, with good views of the whole island from its top. After WWII a fishery collective was established. Fishing and cattle herding continue to be the mainstay of employment for Kihnu's inhabitants.

### Getting There & Away

The Reiser Travel Agency (see under Information in the Pärnu section) arranges trips to the islands of Ruhnu and Kihnu. There are regular ferries (75 EEK round trip) from the **Munalaiu Port** (☎ 58 145) in the village of Pootsi, 40km southwest of Pärnu. The journey takes about 1½ hours.

The **Kihnurand Travel Agency** (☎/fax 69 924) on Kihnu is your best bet for information on the island, though, and it also arranges boat trips to the island from the mainland. Its offerings also include unique day excursions on the island, farmhouse or camp-site accommodation on Kihnu, bike rental, boat rental and fishing trips. Folk concerts for groups can also be arranged.

The **Tolli Tourist Farm** (☎ 69 908) can bring you over from Munalaiu by private fishing boat and/or put you up in a very comfortable, very rustic farmhouse from 150 EEK per person. Tent space and a sauna are available.

From mid-December through to April, **Air Livonia** (☎ 75 007) makes weekly flights to Kihnu from Pärnu, daily.

### RUHNU
☎ 045 • pop 70
Ruhnu Island, smaller than Kihnu at just 11.2 sq km, is 100km southwest of Pärnu and

nearer to Latvia than it is to the Estonian mainland. For several centuries Ruhnu had a mainly Swedish population of about 300, but they all left on 6 August 1944, abandoning homes and animals, to avoid the advancing Red Army. Ruhnu has some sandy beaches, but the highlight is a very impressive **wooden church** (1644), making it the oldest surviving wooden structure in Estonia. It has a wooden altar and pulpit dating from 1755 in its atmospheric, even poignant, interior. Next to it stands a second church (1912), looking even more aged than the old one. The island is flat but there's a forest of 200- to 300-year-old pines on its eastern dunes.

For organised trips to the island, see Kihnu's Getting There & Away section. Air Livonia runs twice weekly flights from Pärnu to Ruhnu. See the Pärnu Getting There & Away section for details.

### VILJANDI
☎ 043 • pop 20,610
Viljandi is a quiet country town 160km south of Tallinn en route to Valga on the Latvian border. It's a green, hilly and pretty place on the north shore of the 4km-long lake Viljandi järv, over which there are good views. Many houses here are decorated with small turrets, windmills or bay windows.

The Knights of the Sword founded a castle at Viljandi (known in German times as Fellin) when they conquered this area in the 13th century. The town around it later joined the Hanseatic League, then was subject to the usual comings and goings of Swedes, Poles and Russians. Today it has a young population, which gives the town its lively energy. Local events emphasise sports and theatre and Viljandi hosts many competitions and performances.

### Orientation & Information
The centre of town is about 500m back from the lake shore. The central square is Keskväljak, where Tartu tänav meets Lossi tänav. Lossi tänav leads south to the castle park on the edge of the centre. The **bus station** (Tallinna maantee) is 500m north of the centre, past the **main post office** (Tallinna maantee 22). The market is at the western end of Turu tänav. The **train station** (Metalli tänav 1) is 1km west of the centre along Vaksali.

The **Viljandi tourist information centre** (☎ 33 755; w www.viljandi.ee; Tallinna maantee

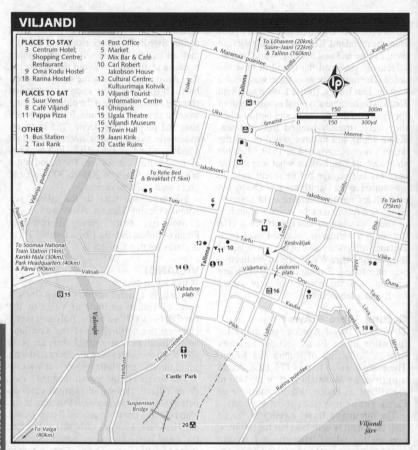

## VILJANDI

**PLACES TO STAY**
3  Centrum Hotel;
   Shopping Centre;
   Restaurant
9  Oma Kodu Hostel
18 Ranna Hostel

**PLACES TO EAT**
6  Suur Vend
8  Café Viljandi
11 Pappa Pizza

**OTHER**
1  Bus Station
2  Taxi Rank
4  Post Office
5  Market
7  Mix Bar & Café
10 Carl Robert
   Jakobson House
12 Cultural Centre;
   Kultuurimaja Kohvik
13 Viljandi Tourist
   Information Centre
14 Ühispank
15 Ugala Theatre
16 Viljandi Museum
17 Town Hall
19 Jaani Kirik
20 Castle Ruins

*2B; open 9am-6pm Mon-Fri, 9am-3pm Sat & Sun May-Aug, 10am-5pm Mon-Fri, 10am-2pm Sat Sep-Apr)* has lots information on the region. The shopping complex **Centrum**, south of the bus station square, can change money. **Ühispank** *(Vaksali tänav 2)*, gives cash advances on credit cards and has a 24-hour ATM.

### Things to See
The ruins of **Viljandi Order Castle** overlook the lake from a hill in the castle park, just south of the town centre. The view is so picturesque, it's worth coming to the town for that alone. The corner tower known as Villu Kelder is named after the leader of a 14th-century Estonian rebellion, in which he died. Also in the castle park are the medieval **Jaani Kirik** (St John's Church) and a

**suspension footbridge** built in 1931. The ravines surrounding the castle ruins are what remain of the castle moat; trenches from WWII came later. A small cemetery to the rear of the castle area is the final resting place of the Germans killed in the fighting.

There are few other pre-19th century buildings. An exception is the 18th century **Town Hall** *(Raekoja)* in the centre. The **wooden house** *(Tartu maantee 4)* was where Carl Robert Jakobson edited his influential newspaper *Sakala* from 1878 to 79. There's a statue of him reading on Keskväljak. The **Viljandi Museum** *(Laidoneri plats)* is in a classical building on the old market square. The surprisingly large **Ugala Theatre** *(☎ 33 718; Vaksali tänav 7)*, near the little Valuoja River, is one of Estonia's most modern theatres.

## Places to Stay

The tourist information centre arranges accommodation in the region, and with the closure of some of the few accommodation options in town, this is a valuable service.

**Ranna Hostel** (☎ 47 370; Ranna tee 6; beds from 100 EEK), a 40-bed hostel beside the lake, is ideal for active types or those with good intentions. The dorms are rather basic but the lake and nearby sports oval are good spots for burning energy.

**Rehe Bed & Breakfast** (☎ 45 575; Rehe tänav 18; singles/doubles 240/500 EEK) a brisk walk or drive 1.5km west over the river from the town centre offers comfortable rooms in a pleasant residential neighbourhood.

**Oma Kodu Hostel** (☎ 55 755, fax 55 750; Väike 6; singles/doubles/triples 480/680/800 EEK) is beyond a hostel in price and comforts (including en suite and TV) and retains the feel of a dormitory, but reception is friendly and can advise on the region's attractions.

**Centrum Hotel** (☎ 51 100; fax 51 101 Tallinna maantee 24; singles/doubles 700/900 EEK), near the bus station, has modern rooms with all facilities and sauna access. An à la carte restaurant is situated upstairs.

## Places to Eat

**Suur Vend** (☎ 33 644; Turu tänav 4) is a wood-panelled pub with inexpensive, ample but sometimes improvised meals. Watch out for 'Big Brother in wine sauce'.

**Pappa Pizza** (☎ 33 906), across the street from the Cultural Centre, satisfies fast-food cravings.

**Café Viljandi** (☎ 33 021; Lossi tänav 31) has a sophisticated charm, which encourages lingering over some of the region's finest cakes.

**Longford** (Lossi tänav 24), a popular, laid-back bar, is the place to relax for the evening and maybe tune into some Estonian karaoke.

## Entertainment

**Mix** (☎ 33 717; Tartu maantee 7c) is a popular bar, café and nightspot – a happening place for Vijlandi's energetically cool young crowd.

**Kultuurimaja kohvik** (Tallinna maantee 5) doubles as an art gallery. It's inside the main cultural centre and has a pleasant, summertime terrace.

## Getting There & Away

There are over 15 buses a day to/from Tallinn (70 EEK, two hours). Other services include 12 buses daily to/from Pärnu (50 EEK, two to 2½ hours) and around 16 daily to/from Tartu (45 EEK 1½-2½ hours) by various routes. There are one or two buses to/from Valga, Kuressaare and Haapsalu. Three trains run daily to/from Tallinn (56 EEK, 2½-3¼ hours). For bus schedules, call ☎ 33 680; for train schedules ☎ 49 425.

## AROUND VILJANDI

At **Lõhavere**, just east of the lovely town of **Suure-Jaani** on the Viljandi–Vändra–Pärnu road, is the site of the fortress of Lembitu, the 13th-century Estonian leader who put up the most resistance to the invading Knights of the Sword. There's a large granite monument near a hill but little more. A few kilometres east is **Olustvere Manor**, a 1730s manor house with a watermill, distillery and English-style gardens housing the **Olustvere tourist centre** (☎ 043-74 280) and a riding centre. You can also camp here. Three buses daily run between Viljandi and Olustvere.

**Vaibla** is a beach with camping facilities at the northern end of Võrtsjärv, just off the Viljandi-Tartu road. Nearby hamlets of Paissu, Kaalgu-Jaani, Leie and Paistu lay claim to scenes from the Kalevipoeg epic and sacrificial stones from pre-Christian times. A detailed map is available from the Viljandi tourist information centre.

### Soomaa National Park

Embracing Estonia's largest area of swamps, flat meadows and waterside forests, Soomaa National Park (Soomaa: literally 'land of wetlands'), covering an area of 370 sq km northeast of Viljandi, is primarily made up of four bogs – Valgeraba, Öördi, Kikepera and Kuresoo – the peat layer of which measures 7m in places. The bogs are split by tributaries of the Pärnu River, the spring flooding creating a fifth season for the inhabitants of this boggy land, where the waters can rise to 5m in March and April.

Up to 36 different mammal species inhabit the surrounding forests, among them the wolf, lynx, brown bear, elk, wild boar and otter. Thousands of birds migrate to Soomaa every year.

The best way to explore the national park, ridden with small waterways, is by canoe or by *haabja*, a traditional Finno-Ugric single-tree boat carved from aspen and used for centuries as the only means of fishing, hunting,

SOUTHWEST ESTONIA

## The Forest Brothers' Resistance and the Underground War

Today the sleepy marshes and quiet woodlands of Estonia are a haven only for wildlife, but between 1944 and 1956 much of what is now national park and nature reserve was a stronghold of the Metsavendlus pro-independence movement. The Metsavennad (Forest Brothers) fiercely resisted the Soviet occupation. Many resorted to an underground existence in the woods and some remained there for years. They knew their terrain well and used this knowledge to their advantage both for their own survival and in the fight to restore the republic.

The Soviets claimed Estonia in the Molotov-Ribbentrop pact of 1939 and, after the Germans retreated from a difficult three-year occupation, secured this claim by advancing on Tallinn in 1944. The early resistance, believing this latest occupation would not be recognised in accordance with the British-US Atlantic treaty of 1941 (which states that sovereignty and self-governance should be restored when forcibly removed), rallied support for what some thought would be a new war. As international assistance did not eventuate, the independence cause remained Estonia's own.

Resistance action began with isolated attacks on Red Army units that claimed the lives of around 3000 soldiers. Tactical expertise and secure intelligence networks resulted in damaging offensives on Soviet targets. At the height of the resistance there were over 30,000 Metsavennad and their supporters, which included women, the elderly, young people and a network of 'Urban Brothers'. The impact of resistance activity is found in Soviet records from the time, which detail incidents of sabotage on infrastructure such as railways and roads that hindered early attempts at moulding Estonia into a new Soviet state.

In the years that followed the Metsavendlus suffered high casualties, with varied and increasing opposition. The NKVD (Soviet secret police) provided incentives to some of the local population who were able to infiltrate the resistance. The Soviets coordinated mass deportations of those suspected to be sympathetic to the resistance cause and some Metsavennad supporters were coerced into acting against the resistance. By 1947, 15,000 resistance fighters had been arrested or killed. The greatest blow to the Metsavendlus came in 1949; with the deportation of 20,000 people – mainly women, children and the elderly – many of whom had provided the support base and cover for resistance activities.

The movement continued for some years but was greatly impeded by the strength of the Soviets and loss of local support due to ongoing deportations and the clearing of farmhouses for collectivisation. Some of the Metsavennad who were not killed or imprisoned escaped to Scandinavia and Canada.

There are many heroes of the Metsavendlus; most came to a tragic end. Kalev Arro and Ants Kaljurand (hirmus, or horrible Ants to the Soviets) were famous for their deft disguises and the humour and tact with which they persistently eluded the Soviets. It was only in 1978 that the final active forest brother, August Sabe, was found but, when pursued across a river by the KGB, drowned himself before capture.

Much work has been done to compile a history of the movement by recording the accounts of local witnesses. Enemies of Metsavennad are still finding themselves in court while surviving members are regarded as national heroes and are awarded some of the country's highest honours.

---

hauling hay and travel. It's a unique tour through a unique landscape, and one that's an important natural resource in Estonia.

Bogs, as forest, have historically provided isolation and protection to Estonians. Witches were said to live there to be alone. According to Estonian folklore, it is the evil will-o'-the-wisp who leads people to the bog, where they are forced to stay until the bog gas catches fire, driving the grotesque bog inhabitants out for all to see. Closer to reality, bogs were also quite handy hiding places for partisans and anyone seeking to escape military invaders, who could not penetrate them as easily as forests.

Information on the park is available from the Soomaa National Park **Visitor Centre** (☎ 043-58 685, fax 57 164; **w** www.soomaa .ee) in Kõrsti-Tõramaa in the Tipu district.

**Saarisoo Kanuukeskus** (☎ 050 61 896 mobile; **w** www.soomaa.com) offers haabja building workshops each June. If you prefer to drift than paddle, ask the information centre in Viljandi about **balloon trips** over Soomaa, and the Soomaa visitor centre can advise on where to catch the **floating sauna**.

JANE SWEENEY

## HIGHLIGHTS

- Gaze in awe at Rastrelli's remarkable Rundāle Palace

- Get stuck into Europe's finest Art-Nouveau architecture and colourful but chaotic markets in Rīga

- Join the rest of Rīga on Jūrmala beach

- Canoe down the Gauja River, bungee jump from a cable car, or hike away the day in the 'Switzerland of Latvia'

- Take a walk off the beaten track in the land of the Livs, where the seas meet at Cape Kolka

# Facts about Latvia

Latvia (Latvija) is sandwiched between Estonia and Lithuania. Rīga, its capital, is on the Baltic Coast and is Latvia's chief visitor magnet. It is the biggest, most vibrant city in the Baltics. Several other attractive destinations lie within day-trip distance of Rīga – including the coastal resort Jūrmala, the Sigulda castles overlooking the scenic Gauja River Valley, and the Rastrelli Palace at Rundāle. The less travelled parts of the country are equally rewarding to the visitor, from the dune-lined coast and historic towns of Kurzeme (western Latvia) to the remote uplands of the eastern side of the country.

This chapter contains information specific to Latvia. For a more general introduction to the history, geography, people and culture of the Baltic region, see the introductory Facts about the Region.

## HISTORY

The Latvians and Lithuanians are the two surviving peoples of the Balt branch of the Indo-European ethno-linguistic group. The Balts are thought to have spread into the southeastern Baltic area around 2000 BC from the region which is now Belarus and neighbouring parts of Russia. (The term *Balt*, which was derived from the Baltic Sea, was first used in the 19th century.) Those people who stayed behind were assimilated, much later, by Belarusian or Russian Slavs (who are ethnically the Balts' nearest relatives). By the 13th century the Balts were divided into a number of tribal kingdoms.

The Latvians are descended from those tribes who settled on the territory of modern Latvia, such as the Letts (or Latgals), the Selonians, the Semigallians and the Cours. The Latgals, Semigallians and Cours gave their names to Latvian regions: Latgale, Zemgale and Kurzeme.

The Selonians settled between the Daugava River and northern Lithuania. During succeeding centuries of foreign rule these tribes (and to a large extent the Finno–Ugric Livs who inhabited the northern coastal regions of Latvia) lost their separate identities and became merged in one Lettish, or Latvian, identity.

## Modern Times

Elections to Latvia's first post-independence parliament were held in June 1993. The centre-right moderate nationalist party Latvijas Ceļš (LC; Latvian Way), led by Valdis Birkavs, formed a governing coalition with the Latvijas Zemnieku Savieniba (Latvian Farmers' Union) and Birkavs became the country's first post-independence prime minister. Guntis Ulmanis of Latvijas Zemnieku Savieniba, a great-nephew of the pre-WWII leader Kārlis Ulmanis, was elected president – an office he held for two terms.

In August 1994 the last Soviet troops withdrew but Latvia's road to capitalism was by no means smooth. Ambitions to become the 'Switzerland of the Baltics' took an almighty knock when Latvia's biggest commercial bank, Banka Baltija, went spectacularly bust, taking the investments of 200,000 depositors with it. The banking crisis spread, and by the time the blood-letting was over 40% of Latvia's banking system had disappeared.

Much to Moscow's annoyance, Latvia celebrated the fifth anniversary of its declaration of independence in 1995 by blowing up an unused 19-storey radar tower block at the Skrunda radar station, a former Soviet base, in southern Kurzeme. Nevertheless, Moscow kept part of the station's tracking facilities in operation until August 1998, paying rent to Latvia for the privilege. Russia did not officially pass control of the area to Latvia until 21 October 1999.

Formal Russian recognition of Latvian independence was achieved in 1996 in exchange for Latvia reluctantly ceding the Abrene (Russian: Pytalovo) region – a 15km-wide, 85km-long sliver of territory down its northeastern border, immediately south of the Pechory region, which was incorporated into Russia in 1944.

## Towards Europe

Presidential elections in 1999 saw Guntis Ulmanis defeated by Latvia's current president, Vaira Vīķe-Freiberga – the first woman president of an ex-USSR country. The same year Latvia was invited to start accession talks with the European Union (EU); see the boxed text 'Joining Europe' in the introductory Facts about the Region chapter.

Merriment spilled across Rīga's streets in 2001 as the capital celebrated its 800th birthday. To herald the event the city council raised old Rīga's 14th-century House of Blackheads from the ashes and built itself a new town hall too – allegedly based on the city's original town hall but in fact a complete fabrication on the part of architects. This, coupled with the heady rash of commercial development enveloping the old city, prompted a subtle warning from Unesco that it was not unheard of for cities to be struck off the World Heritage List (a status Latvia's capital was awarded in 1997).

Latvia's determination to join Europe saw it heed the advice of NATO in 2002 to scrap a law requiring those in political office to speak Latvian. Trite as it might seem, its role as host to the 2003 Eurovision Song Contest further contributed to placing the small country firmly on the European map.

## GEOGRAPHY

Latvia is 64,589 sq km in area – a little smaller than Ireland. Unlike its relatively compact Baltic neighbours, Latvia is a lot wider from east to west than from north to south. A good half of its 494km-long, sweeping coast faces the Gulf of Rīga, a deep inlet of the Baltic Sea shielded from the open sea by the Estonian island of Saaremaa.

Latvia's borders include Estonia to the north, Russia and Belarus to the east and Lithuania to the south. Rīga lies on the Daugava River, just inland from the Gulf of Rīga. The country has four regions: Vidzeme, the northeast; Latgale, the southeast; Zemgale, the centre; and Kurzeme, the west.

The Vidzeme Upland in eastern Latvia is the largest expanse of land with elevation over 200m in the Baltics; it is topped by Latvia's highest point, Gaiziņkalns (312m).

## ECOLOGY & ENVIRONMENT

Latvia's pollution problems are being addressed. Ironically, some areas are threatened more today than during Soviet times: The Livonian coastline in northern Kurzeme – a former Soviet border-control post off-limits to local people, and threatened by forestry and property development today – is a classic example.

Financial assistance from Scandinavia and Germany has helped reduce the pollution generated by industrial centres such as Daugavpils and Liepāja. Ventspils, smothered in potash dust at the end of the 1980s, has witnessed a huge clean-up: A new water supply system aimed at reducing the amount of sewage dumped in the Baltic Sea, air monitoring and the construction of a new heating system to decrease sulphur dioxide and nitrogen dioxide omissions, are all part of the city's long-term environment plan, drawn up until 2010 and estimated to cost 16 million Ls.

Rīga's sewage treatment facilities have been upgraded, thus reducing the flow of sewage into the Daugava River and making swimming in the Gulf of Rīga less of a health hazard than before. The quality of bathing water is not the best though. In 2001 just three beaches in Latvia were awarded the European blue flag; see the boxed text 'Clean Beaches' under Ecology & Environment in the introductory Facts about the Region chapter.

State expenditure on environmental protection has more than doubled in the past five years – rising from 13.7 million Ls in 1996 to 29.6 million Ls in 2000 (86% of which was spent on water protection).

## NATIONAL PARKS & RESERVES

An increasingly large area of the country is becoming protected as new nature parks and reserves are established. **WWF Latvia** (☎ 750 56 40, fax 750 56 51; ⓦ www.wwf.lv; Elizabetes iela 8-4, Rīga LV-1010) is involved in several nature protection projects around the country, aimed at restoring natural ecosystems. The most noteworthy national parks and reserves are the following.

**Abava Valley Nature Park** The small towns of Kandava and Sabile lie within the realms of this 14,933-hectare large reserve, set up in 1999 to protect the Abava Valley

**Gauja National Park** Latvia's first and largest park, with 91,745 hectares straddling the Gauja Valley east of Rīga – castles, lovely valley scenery and walking trails; visitors centre in Sigulda

**Grīņi Nature Reserve** South of Pāvilosta in Kurzeme, this tiny reserve is a bog interspersed between dunes and woodlands

**Ķemeri National Park** Established in 1997 to protect 42,790 hectares near Jūrmala, with Latvia's oldest forest, wetlands, many bird species, nature trails and boardwalks across bogs; visitors centre in Ķemeri

**Krustkalni Nature Reserve** South of Madona in eastern Latvia

**Lake Engure Nature Reserve** Created in 1998 in northern Kurzeme, this reserve protects 18,000 hectares around Latvia's third largest lake; it's among Latvia's most significant bird reservations

**Lake Pape Nature Reserve** Close to Latvia's coastal border with Lithuania in southern Kurzeme, Lake Pape is an important wetland, home to 43 threatened plant species and 15 endangered bird species; the WWF has reintroduced wild horses here

**Moricsala Nature Reserve** Midway between Ventspils and Talsi in Kurzeme, it covers part of the Lake Usma and its shores

**Slītere National Park** This nature reserve – 16,360 hectares of coast and hinterland on Kurzeme's northern tip – became a national park in 2000; visitors centre in Slītere lighthouse

**Teiči Nature Reserve** Southeast of Madona, this large bog area covers 19,047 hectares and serves as an important feeding and nesting ground for many bird species

## GOVERNMENT & POLITICS

The Latvian political scene is a complex mosaic. More than 30 parties jostle for power (the old Communist Party is banned, but there are several post-communist groups) and government by coalition is the norm. Latvia's 100-seat parliament, the Saeima (ⓦ www.saeima.lv) is elected every four years by proportional representation; parties must win at least 5% of votes to be represented in the Saeima.

The first post-independence coalition formed in 1993 lurched from crisis to crisis, and a game of prime-minister roulette followed the Baltija Bank crash in 1995 which left the bank with a staggering 204 million Ls in liabilities – and thousands of Latvians deprived of their life savings. Elections that year saw Latvia's original four main parties mutate into 19. Nine parties cleared the 5% hurdle to enter parliament and Andris Šķēle emerged as prime minister after three rounds of voting. He led a cross-spectrum alliance of six parties. By 2002 Latvia's 19 parties had further mutated to 40-odd.

Latvia's president is elected every four years by parliament. In 1995 Latvia's first post-Soviet president, Guntis Ulmanis, won a second term in office. By 1999 however, Latvia was itching for change and, in a move that surprised the nation, parliament elected Vaira Vīke-Freiberga as president. The fact that Vīke-Freiberga was not among the five presidential candidates – all voted out in the first round of voting – made her final election all the more unusual. With 53 MP votes, the three-party coalition that brought Vīke-Freiberga to power represented a rebuff for Latvian Way (LC), the centre-right party which had long dominated Latvia's politics. Vīke-Freiberga is expected to be elected for a second in summer 2003.

The election of Vīke-Freiberga was a major step forward for Latvia. As a long-time

Canadian resident, she brought experience in a multiethnic democracy to Latvia and assumed office unburdened by petty political connections. On the other hand, she only took Latvian citizenship the year before her election, prompting critics to claim she was less 'in tune' with the real Latvia than someone who had spent all their life living in the country.

Vīke-Freiberga faced a tough challenge during her first days in office. On 5 July 1999 Prime Minister Vilis Kristopans resigned, prompting Andris Skēle's appointment as PM at the head of a conservative government formed by Skēle's People's Party, the LC and For Fatherland and Freedom. Three days later the Latvian parliament approved a controversial language law that invited criticism from the EU and made international headlines. Among the law's requirements, employees of private enterprises and self-employed people had to use Latvian at public functions. Latvian was also made obligatory at major public events, and was the language for all publicly displayed signs, banners and notices. Heeding massive international pressure, Vīke-Freiberga vetoed the bill and sent it back to parliament. The law was amended in December 1999.

But the language issue remained hot. Another amendment to the language law in late 2000 stipulated that lawyers, taxi drivers, telephone operators and a host of other professions in the private sector had to speak a certain level of Latvian. Throughout 2001 debate raged as to whether those standing for political office should speak the official state language, climaxing in mid-2002 with parliament decreeing that they don't. A couple of months previously all hell had broken loose after an OSCE official in Rīga had suggested to Vīke-Freiberga that Russian be made an official state language alongside Latvian. The response was an immediate amendment to the constitution by parliament declaring Latvian to be its only working language, and a statement of support from the EU saying that it was up to Latvia alone to decide its state language. By 2004 the primary language school pupils will be taught in, will be Latvian.

Latvia and Lithuania were invited to start accession talks with the EU in December 1999. In October 2002 all three Baltic countries were formally invited to join the EU, providing certain stringent criteria were met.

For details see the boxed text 'Joining Europe' in the introductory Facts about the Region chapter.

In April 2000 amid allegations of being involved in a paedophilia scandal along with two other government officials, Skēle lost the backing of junior coalition partners For Fatherland and Freedom and Latvian Way. He was replaced as prime minister by Rīga mayor Andris Berzins of the LC. The aptly named New Party (of centre-left leaning) joined the centre-right government to form a 69-seat majority, four-party coalition whose goals included the preservation of national identity, the creation of 'an information society' and the modernisation of the Latvian constitution to make it EU-compatible.

Parliamentary elections in October 2002 threw up no surprises. As predicted, the recently-formed centrist-right party Jaunais Laiks (New Era) secured 26 seats (with 23.9% of the votes) and its party chairman, Einārs Repše, became prime minister. Most know Repše as the young hotshot who steered the country's central bank through economic crisis in the immediate post-USSR years.

Of the 100 new MPs elected, 25 represent the left-wing bloc For Human Rights in a United Latvia and 20 belong to the conservative-reformist People's Party (which held the most seats in the previous parliament). Just 18 of the 100 MPs are women.

## ECONOMY

An economic snapshot of Latvia today is a far cry from the bleak picture painted in the 1990s. The economy is on target for Latvia to join the EU in 2004. Its record 7.6% growth in GDP in 2001 made it one of Eastern Europe's fastest growing economies, and inflation is low at 3.3%.

It is young technocrats and entrepreneurs who have reaped the rewards of this economic revolution however – for most Latvians, life is still painfully tight. The gross monthly average wage in April 2002 was 162 Ls and pensioners struggle to make ends meet with their average monthly pension of 58 Ls.

The former Soviet republic dumped the Soviet rouble in favour of its own Latvian rouble in 1992, followed by the Latvian lats in 1993. It has held its value against major currencies since, and is now bracing itself for a pegging to the euro once Latvia joins the EU. Only after it has met strict economic

## Citizenship

On 21 August 1991 Latvia proudly and firmly declared itself an independent state. But who exactly were its citizens?

Citizenship has been one of Latvia's most contentious – and complicated – issues. Upon gaining independence, the new state proclaimed that residents of the pre-1940 Latvian Republic and their descendants – including about 300,000 nonethnic Latvians (mainly Russians) – automatically became citizens of modern Latvia. Former Soviet soldiers, settled in Latvia after demobilisation, were understandably barred from citizenship, as were former Soviet secret service employees.

But other residents – roughly 35% of the population and the vast majority of native Russian speakers – were not allowed to vote in the 1993 elections because they were not citizens. This was widely seen as unjust.

Citizenship rules passed in 1994 stated that would-be citizens must have lived in Latvia for at least five years, must pass a test on Latvia's language, history and constitution, and also take a loyalty oath. Additionally, only those of certain ages could apply at certain times (only Latvian-born residents ages 16 to 20 could apply in 1996, those up to 25 in 1997, and so on), provoking an immediate outcry from Latvia's large Russian community.

Finally in 1998 the Latvian parliament repealed the harsh 'windows' restriction on who could apply, meaning all noncitizens irrespective of age could apply for citizenship through naturalisation. The law also granted automatic citizenship to children born in Latvia after 1991 whose parents were noncitizens.

Fierce opposition to the changes raised sufficient public support for a referendum to be twinned with parliamentary elections. Latvian voters narrowly approved the repeal, and European human rights groups breathed a sigh of relief. So too did those waiting for citizenship. After the referendum was passed, applications tripled to around 1000 a month. The law was finally ratified by parliament in January 1999.

As of 1 October 2002 Latvia had naturalised 56,347 noncitizens (66.7% being ethnic Russians). Some 76.6% of Latvia's total population were Latvian citizens, and 46.6% of the country's 680,196-strong Russian population were Latvian citizens.

criteria set by the Maastricht treaty, however, can it trade in the lats for the euro. See the boxed text 'Joining Europe' in the introductory Facts about the Region chapter.

The entire thrust of Latvia's economy has changed dramatically since independence, with manufacturing and agriculture dwindling and the service sector expanding – in 2001 the hotel and restaurant sector witnessed 13.6% growth, compared to 9.7% in manufacturing. Agricultural output in 2000 was 20% less than in 1995.

Following the Russian financial crisis in 1998, the young economy took a nasty tumble. But despite the setback, it clawed its way back from recession to notch up a 6.6% increase in GDP in 2000. The national bank, Latvijas Bankas, predicts 5% growth in 2002 and an annual inflation rate of 2.5%, placing Latvia firmly on a par with current EU member states. (Compare this to an annual inflation rate of 951% in 1992, 109.2% in 1993 and 35.9% in 1994!)

Western European trading partners quickly replaced the defunct Soviet Union in the

1990s, and foreign trade continues to increase steadily. The EU is Latvia's primary trading partner today; trade with Germany, the UK and Sweden accounts for some 17%, 7.5% and 7.5% respectively of foreign trade turnover. In January 2002 cargo turnover at Latvia's three key ports – Ventspils, Liepāja and Rīga – was 9.2% more than in January 2001. Latvia was the first of the Baltic countries to join the World Trade Organisation (WTO) in 1999.

Foreign investment totalled €1050 per capita in the third quarter of 2001. Estonia, Norway, Sweden, the USA and Germany remain Latvia's largest foreign investors.

Privatisation remains a thorn in the government's side. By 2001 the private sector accounted for 68% of the country's total added value (compared to 53% in 1995), but a handful of large state enterprises such as the oil shipping company Ventspils Nafta and electricity company Latvenergo continue remain in state hands. Internal bickering within the cabinet over this issue prompted Prime Minister Skēle to resign in 2000 and parliament to strike Latvenergo off its privatisation list.

## POPULATION & PEOPLE

Of Latvia's population of 2.33 million, just 58.3% are ethnically Latvian. Russians account for 29.1% of the total population (compared to 32.8% in 1995), Belarusians 4%, Ukrainians 2.6% and Poles 2.5%. There is a small Jewish community (0.4%). Latvians make up less than 50% of the population in Daugavpils, Jūrmala, Liepāja, Rēzekne, Ventspils and the capital, Rīga, where 43.7% are Russian and 41.2% Latvian.

Of particular concern is the country's declining population which dropped 13.8% between 1999 and 2000, ranking it fourth in the world as far as slow-growing populations go. Some of this is due to the migration of ethnic Russians back to Russia, but the main factor is an extremely low birthrate – at 20.3 births per 1000 people (compared to 32.2 deaths), Latvia is reckoned to have the world's lowest crude birth rate.

The divorce rate in Latvia remains among the highest in Europe – more than 60% of marriages end in divorce, while almost 40% of children are born into one-parent families.

Up to 200,000 Latvians live in Western countries as a result of emigration around the turn of the 20th century, and during and after WWII. Most live in the USA, followed by Australia, Canada, Germany and Britain.

## EDUCATION

With fluent Latvian needed for citizenship, providing facilities for Russian-speaking adults as well as school-age children is a vital tool in integrating Latvia's substantial Russian community. Since 1998 schools with a language of instruction other than Latvian have had to introduce bilingual teaching.

Despite a substantial increase in state spending on education (7.2% of GDP in 1999, compared to 4.5% in 1990), many schools remain in financial dire straits: teacher salaries are extraordinarily low and funds for essential equipment insufficient. While the privatisation of higher education has created better-equipped schools and universities, it has also made higher education unaffordable for poorer families. In 2000 just 13.9% of students aged 15 and over went on to higher education.

## SCIENCE & PHILOSOPHY

Latvia's scientific research has always been of high quality. In the early 20th century Rīga's polytechnic university produced a number of notable scientific scholars, particularly chemists; much of this top talent, however, fled to the USA and Canada in advance of the German Army or the Red Army during WWII. Today, as in Soviet times, the state still underwrites much of Latvia's scientific research through such institutions as Latvia's Academy of Science, which the Soviets founded in 1946. Currently science and education together comprise about 20% of Latvia's national budget.

Latvia's philosophical roots lie in the National Awakening movement of the late 19th century, in which university-educated 'Young Latvians' began to counter heavy German and Russian influences by emphasising Latvian culture; this was the first real exploration, for example, of Latvian folklore. Among the most prominent of these National Awakening intellectuals were Krisjānis Barons and Krisjānis Valdemārs, whose names adorn some of Rīga's largest streets.

The National Awakening gave way to another movement, called the New Current (Jaunā Strāva), in the 1890s. While not explicitly socialist, the movement attracted many intellectuals who were so inclined. The keystone book for the movement was the multivolume *Pūrs* (The Dowry), which was a compilation of essays on topical subjects like social Darwinism and historical materialism. Today, most Latvian intellectuals are again engaged in an Awakening-type movement, as post-independence Latvia reaffirms its culture.

## ARTS
### Music & Dance

Rock music is popular and, like Estonia, there are big annual festivals (see Public Holidays & Special Events in Facts for the Visitor – Latvia). Perkons (meaning Thunder) and award-winning mainstream rockers Rebel (formed out of Dr Blues, a band which had been on the scene since the late 1980s) were among the first bands to make it big in rock. Rebel notably sings in English and Russian on its album *Sarovaja Molnija* (1999). Acoustic blues is represented by Hot Acoustic, formed in 1994, while the eccentric Karl and Cuckoo-Bite contribute a new wave

## Latvian Inventions

Latvians invented, among other things, ripor (a hard-to-burn type of insulating plastic), ftorafur (an antimetabolite used in cancer treatments) and the Latvian brown cow breed. Its greatest claim to fame however, is the world's first miniature camera, sufficiently small to make 007's hair curl.

The VEF Minox was invented in 1937 by Walter Zapp (born 1905), a Latvian Jew living in Rīga, and produced by Latvia's State Electrotechnical Plant (VEF). The precision camera weighed 125g and was 8cm wide, 2.7cm tall and a nifty 1.7cm thick. During WWII secret agents used it to photograph documents.

The Minox camera produced during the Soviet occupation in 1940–41 bore the production stamp 'Made in the USSR' and is a collector's item today. From 1948 the Minox was made in West Germany.

sound to the Rīga club scene. A more recent female vocalist to listen out for is Linda Leen with her mix of rhythm and blues.

Patra Vetra, otherwise called Brainstorm, is the best-known band outside Latvia, breaking the European market with its first album in English (*Among the Suns*) in 1999, finishing third place in the Eurovision Song Contest in 2000, and going on tour with the Cranberries in 2002. The lead singer Renars Kaupers, who wrote one of the band's best-known hits songs *My Star*, has also indulged in a brief but successful film career – see Films in the subsequent Facts for the Visitor chapter. The surprise win of sexy Russian Rīgan Marija Naumova (Marija N) in the 2002 Eurovision Song Contest served to tell the world that Brainstorm's third-place ranking was not a fluke and that Latvia really could sing.

Very much the godfather of Latvian rock is the eclectic composer Imants Kalniņš, founder of the country's first rock band, Menuets, in the mid-'70s. A graduate of the Latvian State Conservatory, Kalniņš has written everything from film scores to symphonies and operas. His son, Mart Kristiāns Kalniņš, lead singer of the 'art rock' band Autobuss debesīs which released its debut album in 2001, is another name to look out for.

The National Opera House, reopened in 1996 after renovation, is the home of the Rīga Ballet, which produced Mikhail Baryshnikov and Aleksander Godunov during the Soviet years. The Latvia National Symphonic Orchestra is highly regarded. Song composers Joseph Wihtol (Jāzeps Vītols) and Alfrēds Kalniņš are important early-20th-century figures in classical music. Inga Kalna is among Latvia's leading female soloists.

Contemporary classicists include internationally renowned conductor Mariss Jansons, winner of the Latvian 1995 Grand Prix in music. Another major figure in the Latvian music scene is Raimonds Pauls, light music orchestra conductor for the Latvian State Philharmonic in the late 1960s. He later rose to become minister of culture (1988–93).

### Literature

Latvia's national epic – *Lāčplēsis* (The Bear Slayer), written by Andrējs Pumpurs in the mid-19th century – is based on traditional Latvian folk stories. The hero struggles against his enemy, a German Black Knight, only to drown in the Daugava River at the moment of final triumph. The anticipated rebirth of *Lāčplēsis*, however, leaves hope for new freedom. The first Latvian novel, *Mērnieku Laiki* (The Time of the Land Surveyors), written in the 1860s and 1870s by the brothers Reinis and Matiss Kaudzīte, has become a classic for its humorous portrayal of Latvian characters.

Rūdolfs Blaumanis (1863–1908) wrote psychologically penetrating novelettes and comic and tragic plays; among them, *Skroderdienas Silmačos* (Tailor's Days in Silmači) is still one of Latvia's most popular plays. Anna Brigadere (1861–1933) wrote much loved tales of rural life and fairy-tale dramas. Kārlis Skalbe (1879–1945) was another major writer of fairy tales.

### Visual Arts

Jānis Rozentāls was really the first major Latvian painter. At the turn of the 20th century he painted scenes of peasant life and portraits, with some influence from impressionism and Art Nouveau. Vilhelms Purvītis and Jānis Valters were the outstanding landscape artists of the time. Both – especially Purvītis – were influenced by impressionism. Olegs Tillbergs is one of the most interesting modern Latvian artists. He collects and assembles garbage and other unwanted

## Jānis Rainis

The towering figure in Latvian literature is Jānis Rainis (1865–1929), whom Latvians say might have the acclaim of a Shakespeare or Goethe had he written in a less obscure language. Rainis' criticisms of social and political oppression led to him spending much of his life in exile in Siberia and Switzerland. His leading works, all written in the first quarter of the 20th century, include the plays *Uguns un nakts* (Fire and Night) on the Lāčplēsis theme and *Jāzeps un viņa brāļi* (Joseph and his Brothers), and the poetry volumes *Gals un sākums* (The End and the Beginning) and *Piecas Dagdas skiču burtnīcas* (Dagda's Five Notebooks). Rainis' wife, Aspazija, was also a leading poet, playwright and social critic.

materials. Ivars Poikans is another contemporary artist to watch for. Karlis Rudēvics is known for his translations of Roma poetry and for his striking paintings inspired by Gypsy legends.

## SOCIETY & CONDUCT

Latvians like flowers; if you go to a birthday party or some other special event, it's nice to bring a bouquet – but make sure it's an odd number of flowers! Latvian women are a tad less emancipated than in the West, so female drivers, for instance, might provoke some mildly sexist but harmless commentary.

## RELIGION

Christianity long ago superseded Latvia's ancient religion, which was based on a belief in natural deities, though a movement in the 1920s tried to revive and preserve these ancient traditions.

Christianity first came to Latvia in the 12th century, and the crusades of the following century firmly entrenched it as the dominant religion. The type of Christianity practised today largely follows a historical pattern; eastern Latvia, which was under the Polish empire, tends to be Roman Catholic, while other areas are Lutheran.

The first Latvian Bible was published in 1689. Its translator was the Reverend Ernest Glück, and a memorial museum to him stands in the town of Alūksne. Despite attempts to quash religion during the Soviet occupation, independence has seen a rejuvenation of belief. Today the Roman Catholic Church has the largest following with roughly 500,000 adherents, followed by Lutheran (300,000), Russian Orthodox (100,000) and Old Believers (70,000).

In mid-2002 parliament was debating whether or not to make Orthodox Christmas on 7 January a national holiday.

FACTS ABOUT LATVIA

# Facts for the Visitor

For general information on travelling in the Baltic region see the introductory Facts for the Visitor chapter.

## SUGGESTED ITINERARIES

Depending on the length of your stay, you might want to do the following.

**Two to five days** Visit Rīga with a choice of day trips to Sigulda and the Gauja Valley, Jūrmala, the Ķemeri National Park, Rūndale Palace, the Pedvāle Open-Air Art Museum and nearby Kuldīga or Tukums.

**One week** Do Rīga and some day-trip destinations, then take the Rīga–Kolka coastal road with leisurely stops in Jūrmala, Ķemeri and some of the fishing villages around Roja. See where the Gulf of Rīga and the Baltic Sea meet at Cape Kolka, then nose-dive into the Slītere National Park and its Livonian villages. Return to the capital via Ventspils and Talsi, or continue south to Lithuania via Liēpaja.

**Two weeks** Explore western Latvia at a more leisurely pace, allowing time to scale Slītere Lighthouse, follow a few nature trails in the national parks and enjoy some boating, birdwatching or other activity. Or split the fortnight in two and spend a week exploring eastern Latvia – include the Gauja Valley and Alūksne's narrow-gauge railway.

## PLANNING

For general information on planning your trip see the introductory Facts for the Visitor chapter.

### Maps

Country, city and town maps of Latvia are available from Rīga-based **Jāņa sēta** (☎ 731 75 40; Ⓦ www.kartes.lv; Stabu iela 119, LV-1009 Rīga), which runs an excellent map shop in the capital. Its town plan series covers practically every town in Latvia; individual maps range in scale from 1:15,000 to 1:20,000 and cost 0.70-1.50 Ls.

With the exception of Jāņa sēta's detailed *Gaujas Nacionālais parks* (Gauja National Park, 1;100,000, 1.35 Ls), hiking maps don't exist. But Jāņa sēta does stock topographical map sheets (1:50,000, 1.98 Ls) of Latvia published by **Kartogrāfijas Pārvalde** (☎ 703 86 10; Ⓦ www.vzd.gov.lv; 11 Novembre krastmala 31, LV-1050 Rīga) covering western Latvia. The satellite-generated sheets

(1,50:000, 0.98 Ls) by the same cartographer and available on CD (13.90 Ls) are less accurate.

See CD-ROMs later in this chapter for digital maps.

## RESPONSIBLE TOURISM

Touring Latvia, as elsewhere, is an opportunity to show respect for the local culture. In Livonia, for example, this means not venturing off the beaten path without permission, as the land is a preservation area dedicated to Latvia's ancient peoples. In national parks such as the Gauja, only pitch your tent at designated camp sites.

## TOURIST OFFICES

A small network of tourist offices overseas represents the **Latvian Tourism Development Agency** (☎ 72 29 945, fax 70 85 393; Ⓦ www.latviatourism.lv; Pils laukums 4, LV-1050 Rīga). In Latvia practically every town and city has a tourist office, listed both on the Latvian Tourism Development Agency's excellent website (see Digital Resources later) and under Information in the respective regional chapters of this guide.

Some tourist offices are substantially more efficient than others, although practically all have an English-speaking staff and distribute printed information in English on its respective town and region.

## VISAS & DOCUMENTS

See the introductory Facts for the Visitor chapter.

## EMBASSIES & CONSULATES
### Latvian Embassies & Consulates

A complete list of Latvian diplomatic missions abroad is posted on the website of Latvia's Ministry of Foreign Affairs (Ⓦ www.am.gov.lv). They include:

**Australia** (☎ 02-9744 5981) 32 Parnell St, Strathfield NSW 2135
**Belarus** (☎ 0172-84 93 93, consular 84 74 75, fax 84 73 34; ⓔ daile@anitex.by) 6a Doroshevica Str, BY-220013 Minsk
**Canada** (☎ 613-238 6014, consular 238 6868, fax 238 7044; Ⓦ www.magma.ca/~latemb) 208 Albert St, Suite 300, Ottawa, K1P 5G8 Ontario

**Estonia** (☎ 646 13 13, consular 646 13 10, fax 646 13 66; e embassy.estonia@mfa.gov.lv) Tõnismägi 10, EE10119 Tallinn

**Finland** (☎ 09-476 472 44, consular 476 472 33, fax 476 472 88; e consulate.finland@mfa.lv) Armfeltintie 10, SF-00150 Helsinki

**France** (☎ 01 53 64 58 10, consular 01 53 64 58 16, fax 01 53 64 58 19; e embassy.france@mfa.gov.lv) 6 Villa Said, F-75116 Paris

**Germany** (☎ 030-826 002 22, fax 826 002 33; w www.botschaft-lettland.de) Reinerzstrasse 40-41, D-14193 Berlin

**Lithuania** (☎ 5-213 1260, fax 213 1130, e lietuva@latvia.balt.net; w http://latvia.balt .net) Čiurlionio gatvė 76, LT-2600 Vilnius

**Russia** (☎ 095-925 27 03, consular 923 87 72, fax 923 92 95; e embassy.russia@mfa.gov.lv) ulitsa Chapligina 3, RUS-103062 Moscow

**Sweden** (☎ 08-700 63 00, fax 140 01 51; e lettlands.ambassad@swipnet.se) Odengatan 5, Box 19167, S-10432 Stockholm

**UK** (☎ 020-731 20 040, fax 020-731 20 042; e embassy@embassyoflatvia.co.uk) 45 Nottingham Place, London W1U 5LR

**USA** (☎ 202-726 82 13, fax 726 67 85; w www.latvia-usa.org) 4325 17th Street NW, Washington, DC 20011

## Embassies & Consulates in Latvia

The following embassies are in Rīga:

**Canada** (☎ 722 63 15; e canembr@bkc.lv) Doma laukums 4

**Estonia** (☎ 781 20 20; e riga@mfa.ee) Skolas iela 13

**Finland** (☎ 707 88 00; w www.finland.lv) Kalpaka bulvāris 1

**France** (☎ 703 66 00; w www.ambafrance-lv.org) Raiņa bulvāris 9

**Germany** (☎ 722 90 96; w www.deutsche botschaft-riga.lv) Raiņa bulvāris 13

**Lithuania** (☎ 732 15 19) Rūpniecības iela 24

**Netherlands** (☎ 732 61 47; w www.netherlandsembassy.lv) Torņa iela 4

**Russia** (☎ 733 21 51; e rusembas@mail.junk.lv) Antonijas iela 2

**Sweden** (☎ 733 87 70; w www.swedenemb.lv) Andreja Pumpura iela 8

**UK** (☎ 777 47 00; w www.britain.lv) Alunāna iela 5

**USA** (☎ 703 62 00; w www.usembassy.lv) Raiņa bulvāris 7

## CUSTOMS

Customs rules vary within the Baltic region and are subject to change. Some general points are given in the introductory Facts for the Visitor. The Latvian Tourism Development Agency posts the latest rules on its website (see Digital Resources later in this chapter).

People over 18 can bring in and take out 1L of alcohol and 200 cigarettes, 20 cigars or 200g of tobacco without paying duty. You can import and export duty-free any amount of hard currency.

Works of art or of cultural significance (including antique books) that date from before 1945, but are less than 100 years old, are subject to a 50% customs duty; those older than 100 years attract 100% duty. They may only be taken out of the country with a licence issued by the **State Inspection for Heritage Protection** (☎ 72 29 272), inside the **Ministry of Culture** (☎ 70 47 400, fax 73 22 440; Valdemāra iela; LV-1050 Rīga).

## MONEY

Latvia's currency, the *lats* (plural: *lati*), was introduced in March 1993 and has remained stable ever since. The lats (Ls) is divided into 100 *santīmi* (singular: *santīms*). Lati come in 1 and 2 lats coins, and 5, 10, 20, 50, 100 and 500 lats notes; and santīmi come in coins of 1, 2, 5, 10, 20 and 50. The 100 Ls gold coin, minted in 1998, is a rarity.

The national bank **Latvijas Bankas** (*Latvian Bank*; w www.bank.lv) posts the lats' daily exchange rate on its website. In mid-2002 exchange rates in included:

| country | unit | lati (Ls) |
| --- | --- | --- |
| Australia | A$1 | Ls 0.33 |
| Canada | C$1 | Ls 0.37 |
| Estonia | 1EEK | Ls 0.04 |
| Lithuania | 1Lt | Ls 0.18 |
| euro zone | €1 | Ls 0.60 |
| Sweden | 1 SKr | Ls 0.07 |
| UK | UK£1 | Ls 0.94 |
| USA | US$1 | Ls 0.60 |

## POST & COMMUNICATIONS
### Post

Latvia's postal system is almost completely reliable. It costs 0.15/0.30/0.30 Ls to send a postcard letter under 20g to Latvia/Europe/elsewhere; a letter weighing 20-100g costs 0.50 Ls to send within Latvia or Europe and 0.80 Ls to the US. Mail to North America takes about 10 days, and to Europe about a week. Stamps are sold at a post office (*pasts*).

## Telephone

Public cardphones are widespread throughout Latvia, but coin-operated phones are a rarity. Calls can be made from cardphones using a *telekarte*, worth 2, 3 or 5 Ls and sold at kiosks and post offices, or with a major credit card; instructions in English are included in every booth.

Latvian telephone numbers have seven digits and need no city or area code. To make a local or national call, simply dial the seven-digit number. To make an international call, dial the international access code (00), followed by the appropriate country code, city code if applicable and subscriber's number. To call a Latvian telephone number from abroad, simply dial the country code for Latvia (371) followed by the subscriber's seven-digit number. Telephone rates are posted on the website of the partly state-owned **Lattelekom** (w *www.lattelekom.lv*) which enjoys a monopoly on fixed-line telephone communications in Latvia.

Telephone numbers kicking off with 900 or 999 are pricier than normal calls; those starting with 800 are free. To contact directory inquiries, try e 118@118.lv, dial ☎ 118 or ☎ 722 22 22 – English is spoken.

Mobile telephones likewise have seven digits and need no area code; they generally start with the digit 9. Mobile phones are difficult to rent but, providing your phone is GSM900/1800-compatible, you can buy a SIM-card package from one of Latvia's two mobile telephone operators, **Latvijas Mobilais Telfons** *(LMT;* w *www.lmt.lv)* or **Tele2** *(*w *www.tele2.lv).* Tele2's Zelta zivtiņa (literally 'gold fish') start-up kit costs 8.50 Ls (SIM plus 7 Ls credit) and local calls cost 0.168-0.234 Ls per minute. LMT's OKarte package costs 9.70 Ls (SIM plus 7 Ls credit) and calls cost 0.036-0.216 Ls per minute. The LMT network extends further than Tele2, but coverage in the countryside can be patchy with either network.

### Emergency Services
The nationwide emergency phone number for police is ☎ 02 and for ambulance ☎ 03.

### Email & Internet Access
Internet cafés – many open 24 hours – are abundant in Rīga and most large towns and seaside resorts. Online access generally costs 0.50 Ls.

In provincial Latvia an Internet café tends to translate as a *datorsalons*, crammed with square-eyed kids playing killer computer games. Make it clear you want to access the Net (rather than tangle with Lara Croft) and a kid will be kicked off to make way for you.

## DIGITAL RESOURCES

The official website of the Latvian Tourism Development Agency (see Tourist Offices earlier; w www.latviatourism.lv) is packed with oodles of intelligently written cultural, historical and practical information about Latvia, as well as some excellent links to other Latvia-related sites.

The other indispensable site for serious background information and up-to-date cultural listings is Latvians Online (w www.latviansonline.com). Its section on Latvian music reviews all the latest releases and is particularly useful, as are its links to other sites on Latvia. Music in Latvia (w www.music.lv) is another inspiring site for those keen to tune in to Latvian jazz, opera, folk and other classical genres.

World Hot.Com (w www.eurohot100.com/latvia/) throws up some interesting finds in its list of Latvia's 100 hottest websites. Sports fans can follow the highs and lows of Latvia's football, basketball and ice-hockey clubs with Sports News (w www.sportsnews.lv). Those interested in what the president has to say can click on w www.president.lv.

Numerous Latvia-focused Internet addresses are embedded in the destination chapters. For resources covering the region, see the introductory Facts for the Visitor chapter.

## BOOKS

Many of the best books about Latvia cover the whole Baltic region; see the introductory Facts for the Visitor.

*The Holocaust in Latvia 1941–1944: The Missing Centre* by Andrew Ezergailis gives a comprehensive and balanced account of this provocative subject in 465 pages, addressing among other things the sensitive issue of Latvian participation in the holocaust. *The Murder of the Jews in Latvia: 1941-1945* by Bernhard Press (translated by Laimdota Mazzarins) discusses the same terrible subject.

*The Historical Dictionary of Latvia*, compiled by Andrejs Plakans, is another

Riflemen statue, Rīga

Tram, K Barona ielā, Rīga

Art Nouveau architecture, Rīga

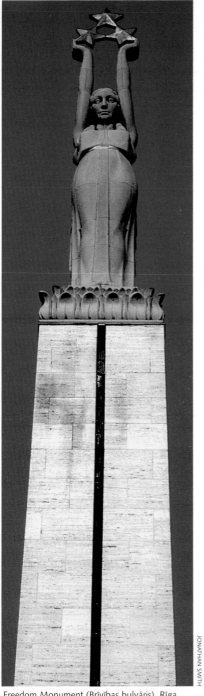

Freedom Monument (Brīvības bulvāris), Rīga

Majori beach, Jūrmala, Rīga

St Peter's Church (Pētera Baznīca), Rīga

Old Rīga from St Peter's Church

extremely useful reference tool for history fiends.

Andris Kolbergs' *The Story of Rīga*, published by Jāņa sēta, gives a good introduction to the history and culture of Latvia's capital city. The same Rīga-based publisher is also behind the appealing and informative, coffee-table picture books, *Latvian National Costumes* and *The Wooden Heritage of Latvia*, edited by Laima Slava. The latter focuses on Riga's unusual architecture and seaside summerhouses.

For an exploration of contemporary literary themes, Vieda Skultan's *The Testimony of Lives: Narrative and Memory in Post-Soviet Latvia* is well worth a look; the book takes selections from Latvian literature and comments on how they grapple with concepts of belonging and independence.

*Letters from Latvia* is the compelling journal of 79-year-old Lucy Addison who, at the outbreak of WWII, refused to leave Latvia, but instead stayed in her country of birth to endure the Soviet, German, then Soviet again, occupations. She wrote the journal in the form of letters which could never be sent to her grandchildren in England.

*To Forgive, But Not Forget* by Maja Abramovitch is a moving autobiographical account of the author's deportation as a child from her native Daugavpils on 6 August 1944 to a death camp in Germany.

*Latvian National Kitchen* by Ņina Masiļūne tells you exactly when to boil up those pigs' trotters to make *pirāgi*. Lots more tasty nuggets are stirred up in Siri Lise Doub's *A Taste of Latvia* (Hippocrene).

## FILMS

Since Latvia's first full-length sound film, *Zvejnieka dēls* (The Fisherman's Son), came out in 1940 Latvian film-making has taken off, with occasional international recognition. The state-owned Rīga Film Studio (w www.rigafilmstudios.com), prominent for its feature films during Soviet times, is less successful today – in part due to the dozen or so other film studios that have stepped up since independence.

Production studio Dauka, founded in 1969, is Latvia's leader in animation; its film *Kaķīsa dzirnavas* (The Cat's Mill) received second prize at the Chicago International Film Festival in 1994. Other contemporary film-makers of note include Laila Pakalnina,

whose 1998 feature film *The Shoe*, about occupied Latvia, was an official selection at the Cannes 1998 film festival. Pakalnina's film *Pasts* (The Mail) shows the isolation of Latvia, as symbolised by the lonely delivery of the morning mail.

Latvian director Jānis Streičs (1936–) has produced a number of films pertinent to Latvia's turbulent past. *Limousine in the Colour of Summer Solstice Night* (1981) and *The Child of Man* (1991) remain popular for their blend of irony and comedy. The latter, about a boy growing up and falling in love in Soviet-occupied Latvia, won the Grand Prix at San Remo in 1992 and was nominated for an Academy Award for best foreign film in 1994. Streičs' more recent film, *The Mystery of the Old Parish Church* (2000), addresses the prickly issue of local collaboration with Nazi and Soviet occupiers during WWII, as the victims of a former KGB agent set out to haunt their killer. The film, partly set during summer solstice, stars lead singer of Latvian band Brainstorm, Renars Kaupers.

The website w www.latfilma.lv has a wealth of information on Latvian films, directors, festivals and more.

## CD-ROMS

New or updated CD-ROMs are appearing all the time, so it's best to check the Internet. Less serious CD-ROMs – cartoons and CDs based on Latvian fairy tales and the like – are sold online by the Baltic Shop (w www.balticshop.com). Jāņa sēta (see Maps earlier) produces a map set of Latvia on CD-ROM.

An absolute must for film buffs is the CD-ROM produced by the International Centre for Cinema Arsēnals in 2000 to celebrate what would have been the 50th birthday of filmmaker Juris Podnieks (see the boxed text). Clips from his films are featured on the CD, entitled *Juris Podnieks: The 20th Century As Seen by the Latvian Filmmaker*.

**Kompass Latvia** (☎ 732 03 34; w www.kompass.lv; Elizabetes iela 31, Rīga LV-1010) publishes various lists of Baltic businesses on CD: *Kompass Latvia 2002* (18 Ls) lists over 3000 companies in Latvia, while *Kompass Baltia 2002* (74.95 Ls) does the same for 40,000 key companies across the entire Baltic region. Both can be ordered via the Internet.

Various publications published by the Central Statistical Bureau of Latvia are also

## Juris Podnieks

Latvian film director Juris Podnieks, arguably the most influential film-maker in the former USSR, had that rare gift of being at the right place at exactly the right time. During the 1970s, '80s and early '90s, Podnieks and his film crew worked tirelessly to produce riveting documentaries that in many ways predicted the collapse of the Soviet monolith.

Born in Rīga in 1950, Podnieks worked in a Rīga studio after graduating from film school in 1975. He began first as a cameraman and rose quickly, becoming a director in 1979.

Podnieks' first production was *The Cradle* (1977), a film that pictured the troubling decline in the Latvian birthrate. His 1986 film *Is It Easy to Be Young?* broke Soviet box office records – and reached 28 million people internationally – by depicting the troubled youth of the Soviet Union. His cinematic triumph was managing to get footage of some youthful Latvians vandalising a train after a rock concert.

Another Podnieks landmark was the five-part 1989 series *Hello Do You Hear Us?*. The series, broadcast in the USA, painted a gloomy portrait of the Soviet Union, from the Baltic police to the workers' strike in a Yaroslavl factory.

Even more important were *Homeland* and *Homeland Postscript*, which captured the events of the early 1990s. The film *Homeland* was completed and due to be released in February 1991. The turbulent events of January 1991, however, clearly required an addendum. When Podnieks was in Vilnius on 11 January 1991 to present *Homeland*, he was on the scene to film the storming of the Vilnius TV tower. He and his assistant, though caught in the crossfire, escaped unharmed and slipped back to Rīga with their footage.

Nine days later a shoot-out took place in Rīga as Soviet troops stormed the Ministry of the Interior. Two of Podnieks' crew members heard the confrontation, which took place about 400m from the studio, and ran out to film it. Both were killed in the crossfire – Andris Slapiņš was shot dead, and Guido Zvaigzne died of gunshot wounds two weeks later, on 5 February 1991. They were among the five people who died in the incident, and commemorative stones remain in Bastejkalns Park, across Basteja bulevāris from the Powder Tower. Endowed with new and sombre meaning, *Homeland* and *Homeland Postscript* opened on 7 February.

Juris Podnieks himself died on 23 June 1992 in a midsummer scuba diving accident, when the oxygen supply in his equipment tragically malfunctioned. He is buried in the cemetery at Mežaparks. Despite his death, the Juris Podnieks film studio carries on under his name and continues to produce documentaries. The studio can make copies of the films, some of which have English subtitles, for €17-20 (plus (30 postage within Europe). Their contact information is: **Juris Podnieks Studio** (☎ 721 69 67; e *jps@parks.lv; Citadeles iela 2, LV-1010 Rīga*).

available on CD-ROM; a catalogue is online at w www.csb.lv.

## NEWSPAPERS & MAGAZINES

The Latvian daily newspaper *Diena* (w www.diena.lv) provides the best politically independent coverage and comes out in a separate Russian-language edition. The most popular evening newspapers are *Rīgas Balss* (Latvian and Russian), *Vakara Ziņas* (Latvian) and *Spogulis* (Latvian); while the Swedish-owned *Dienas Bizness* (Latvian, with news online at w www.db.lv) and *Bizness & Baltija* (Russian, with a website at w www.bb.lv) are two equally popular weekly business newspapers.

The English-language paper *Baltic Times* (w www.baltictimes.com) is published every Thursday in Rīga and has an entertainment guide that includes cinema listings.

Quality city guide *Rīga In Your Pocket*, sold for 1.20 Ls at news kiosks, runs listings of places to stay, where to eat, things to see, entertainment and the like. It comes out every two months.

You can buy up-to-date English- and German-language newspapers and journals, such as the *International Herald Tribune*, the *Wall Street Journal Europe*, *USA Today*, *Time* and *Newsweek* at most **Narvesen newsagencies** (*Brīvibas iela 78 • K Barona iela 11; open 7am-10pm Mon-Sat, 9am-8pm Sun*). Count on paying 2.10 Ls or 1.99 Ls for yesterday's edition of the *Financial Times* and *International Herald Tribune* respectively.

## RADIO & TV

There are two state-run TV channels, LTV1 and LTV2 (which can broadcast up to 20% of programmes in Russian), operated by **Latvian State Television** (*Latvijas Televizija;* w *www .ltv.lv*). Of the handful of private TV broadcasters, **Lavian Independent Television** (*Latvijas Neatkariga Televizija;* w *www.lnt.lv*) is the most popular. Swedish-owned TV3 is another terrestrial commercial station. In Rīga, TV5 is a city channel broadcasting programmes strictly about the capital and its inhabitants – watch it online at w www.tv5.lv. **Baltcom** is a user-pays Latvian–American cable TV network which broadcasts 40 minutes of CNN in English on Saturday at 7pm. A number of pubs, bars and hotels countrywide show MTV, Eurosport and Euronews on cable TV.

The BBC World Service can be picked up 24 hours a day on 100.5 FM. Latvian State Radio, Latvijas radio I (with an Internet hook-up at w www.radio.org.lv), transmits daily short-wave broadcasts at 5935 kHz in English. FM frequencies are listed on its website. The most popular commercial channels are Mix FM on 102.7 FM, Radio SWH at 105.2 FM and Super FM on 104.3 FM.

## PUBLIC HOLIDAYS & SPECIAL EVENTS

Latvian national holidays include:

**New Year's Day** 1 January
**Easter Day** Easter Monday is also taken as a holiday by many
**Labour Day** 1 May
**Mothers' Day** Second Sunday in May
**Ligo** (Midsummer festival) 23 June
**Jāni or Jānu Diena** (St John's Day) 24 June
**National Day** (anniversary of proclamation of Latvian Republic, 1918) 18 November
**Christmas (Ziemsvētki)** 25 December
**Second Holiday** 26 December
**New Year's Eve** 31 December

Latvia shares a number of regular cultural events with Estonia and Lithuania, the most important being the national song festival (which occurs every five years), and the Baltika International Folk Festival and midsummer celebrations (see the introductory Facts for the Visitor chapter). Information on the dozens of one-off festivals is online at w www.km.gov.lv.

Latvia's major annual festivals include the following.

**Gadatirgus** – big arts and crafts fair; Open-Air Ethnography Museum, Rīga; first weekend in June
**International Festival of Organ Music** – Rīga; end of June
**Rīga Opera Festival** – Rīga; 10 days in June
**Rīga Summer** – festival of symphonic and chamber music; Rīga; every even year in July
**Jūrmala Pop Festival** – a contest not a festival, intended for TV rather than for the public; Jūrmala; mid- or late July
**Opera Music Festival** – Sigulda; July
**Festival of Ancient Music** – Bauska Castle; July
**Liepājas Dzintars** – rock festival; Liepāja; usually mid-August
**Ascension** – Roman Catholic processions, celebratory masses; Aglona; 14–16 August
**Harvest Festival** – Otte's Mill; 2nd Saturday in September
**Arsenāls** – big international film festival; Rīga; mid- or late September, even-numbered years
**Lāčplēsis Day** (Lāčplēsu Diena) – commemoration of dead heroes, named after Latvia's mythical warrior hero, whose name means 'Bear-slayer'; 11 November

## ACTIVITIES

Sweating it out in a sauna, mushroom and berry picking, canoeing and cycling in summer, and skiing, snowshoeing and snowboarding in winter, are but some of the uplifting pursuits Latvia offers to more active visitors. When it comes to animals, horse riding is popular, as is bird- and bat-watching. All three national parks plus Latvia's many nature reserves sport some well-marked nature trails aimed at helping visitors discover the country's rich flora and fauna collection. See the Facts for the Visitor chapter at the start of the book for more information on regional activities.

## ACCOMMODATION

Latvia's only hostelling organisation is **Hostelling Latvia** (☎ 921 85 60, fax 722 40 30; w www.hostellinglatvia.com; *Ciekurkalna iela 1-7, LV-1026 Rīga*).

Rīga has a vast choice of hotels – but almost all of them veer towards the top-end price bracket. The few budget rooms that do exist here are bagged quickly, making the capital an expensive city for budget travellers seeking a cheap sleep. Outside Rīga, there are plenty of decent modern hotels touting reasonable rates, alongside a handful of cheap grey concrete Soviet dinosaurs with unrenovated rooms sporting a uniform beige colour scheme.

A homestay with a Latvian family for 5-10 Ls per night can often be the most welcoming bet for budget travellers. In Rīga several agencies organise B&B with or without a local host; elsewhere, contact the local tourist office. Alternatively, contact **Lauku Ceļotājs** (*Country Traveller Association;* ☎ *761 76 00, fax 783 00 41;* ⓦ *www.celotajs.lv; Ku-u iela 11, entrance on Uzvaras bulvāris*), Latvia's country holidays association across Akmens Bridge in Rīga. The organisation arranges rural B&B accommodation in farmhouses, manor houses, palaces and guesthouses throughout Latvia (but not in Rīga). It also points campers in the direction of wild camp sites. B&B costs 5-16 Ls per night and a wide range of outdoor activities are available for an extra fee. Advance bookings can be made through any of its offices in Estonia, Lithuania or Finland (see the introductory Facts for the Visitor chapter).

## FOOD & DRINKS

Latvians consume a lot of dairy products, eggs, potatoes, fish and grains; although you will also find plenty of meat in restaurants. *Sprotes* (sprats) crop up as a starter in many places. If they're *ar sīpoliem,* they'll be with onions. You may also find *siļķe* (herring), *līdaka* (pike), *zutis* (eel), *forele* (trout) or *lasis* (salmon). If fish is *cepts,* it's fried; if *sālīts* or *mazsālīts,* it's salted; and *kūpīnats* means it'll be smoked. Soups and sausage are also popular. *Žāvēta desa* is smoked sausage. Dill seems to be Latvia's favourite herb and is sprinkled liberally on almost all savoury dishes. (Where else in the world can you buy dill-flavoured crisps?)

The sweet toothed won't be left disappointed. In summer and autumn good use is made of berries, freshly picked from the forest. Fruit pies and tarts *(kūka)* are abundant at these times of year. Cream is *krējums,* sour cream *skābais krējums* and is served with practically everything. Throughout Latvia you will find a mouthwatering choice of freshly baked cakes, breads and pastries for under 0.10 Ls.

Latvia's leading beer is Aldaris. It comes in varying degrees of darkness and costs around 0.30 Ls in kiosks (every kiosk stocks

## Black Magic

It's as black as ink, as thick as custard, as sharp as lemon, and has been produced in Latvia – and nowhere else – since 1755.

Its recipe remains a closely guarded secret: orange peel, oak bark, wormwood and linden blossoms are among some 25 fairy-tale ingredients known to stew in the wicked witch's cooking pot.

It steels the nerves, settles the stomach and stops Jack Frost from biting. A shot a day keeps the doctor away, so say most of Latvia's pensioners. In the 18th century it was administered to Catherine the Great when she was struck down by a mystery illness in Rīga. Two sips later she made an instant recovery – and left town.

Rīga druggist Abraham Kunze created the insidious concoction. Its name originates from *balsamon,* the ancient Greek word for a sweet-smelling medicinal balm or ointment. Its opaque ceramic bottle, labelled with a black and gold Rīga skyline, is reminiscent of the clay jars the potent liquid used to be stored in during the 18th and 19th centuries to keep it safe from sunrays.

It is 45% proof and guaranteed to knock the hind legs off a donkey. Drink it with coffee or Coca-Cola. Down it with a shot of vodka if you dare.

*That's* what you call Rīga Black Balsams (*Rīgas Melnais Balzāms*).

beer) and from 0.70 Ls a litre in bars. Rīga champagne *(sampanietis)* comes in two varieties – sweet *(sausais),* which is very sweet, and semi-sweet *(pussaldais).* It is dirt cheap at 2 Ls a bottle. It may not be up to French standards, but it tastes OK. Not to be missed is Latvia's infamous Balzams, a thick, jet-black, 45% proof concoction that tastes strange, if not downright revolting. Apparently, it's best served with coffee or mixed with equal parts of vodka. The brown ceramic bottle it comes in is worth the 2 Ls it costs (see the boxed text 'Black Magic').

The Language Guide at the back of the book includes words and phrases you will find useful when ordering food and drink.

## ENTERTAINMENT

The Baltics' largest city, Rīga, is also the entertainment capital, with a well-developed nightlife spanning jazzy disco and casino joints to excellent bars that service a range of tastes. On the less wild side, theatres and cinemas abound, and Rīga's symphony orchestra and opera are highly regarded.

Outside Rīga, evening entertainment rarely extends beyond a handful of bars and cafés; a few towns such as Liepāja and Valmiera have theatres.

## SPECTATOR SPORTS

Though it has exported its top talent to the USA-based National Hockey League, Latvia's sporting forte remains ice hockey. League games throughout Latvia draw enthusiastic crowds, as does the televised games of the IIHF World Ice Hockey Championships which Latvia will host in 2006. In the next championships in 2003, Latvia is lined up in preliminary matches against Sweden, Canada and Belarus.

Bobsledding is another popular winter sport, as the bobsled track in Sigulda, one of Europe's longest, plays host to international competitions.

Basketball also draws crowds, though its following is not quite as large as in Lithuania. Latvian basketball player Uljana Semonova ranks among the best female players of all time. Of Russian origin, Semonova was born in Daugavpils in 1952 and won over 45 medals (including two Olympic golds for the USSR in 1976 and 1980) in an 18-year career that saw her team never lose an international game. At 2.1m tall, she was the tallest female player in Olympic history.

## SHOPPING

Amber, while not as ubiquitous as in Lithuania, is still among one of Latvia's top souvenirs. In fact, the Nordwear shop in Rīga, which sells hand-knitted Nordic sweaters patterned with Latvian national symbols, proudly proclaims itself as one of the few amber-free souvenir shops!

Pottery and ceramics are not as prevalent as in Lithuania or Estonia. A good place to find handicrafts is Rīga's large crafts fair, the Gadatirgus, but it's only held one weekend a year in June (arrive at 6am for quality buys).

Rīga's large central market is a catch-all for anything you might need, cheaply, from pirated CDs to meats, fruits and vegetables to clothes.

For more information, see Shopping in the Rīga chapter.

# Rīga

Rīga has always been the big boy of the Baltics – a major metropolis with a proper big-city atmosphere hard to find elsewhere in the region. Set on a flat plain divided only by the 500m-wide Daugava River, the city answers the quaintness of Tallinn and Vilnius with impressive Art Nouveau architecture of its own, a historic old quarter called Vecrīga and large, gracious parks. Coupled with this toy-town cuteness is a glitzy nightlife and thriving restaurant scene. As in its sister Baltic capitals, business is booming, with more new office blocks and multi-star hotels sprouting than mushrooms after the rain – occasionally to the peril of the city's historical integrity. The reconstruction from scratch of Rīga's 14th-century House of Blackheads and town hall, both built to look 'old' on Town Hall Square – a square dreamt up by architects to accommodate the latter two – won little praise among local residents.

Fewer than half of Rīgans are ethnic Latvians (41.2% in 2001), with Russians accounting for 43% of the population. Despite Latvians being a minority in their own capital, ethnic harmony does preside in the city, with street- and shop-talk being a natural blend of Russian and Latvian.

## HISTORY

There was a Latgal, or Liv, fishing village on the site of modern Rīga which Scandinavian and Russian traders and raiders had used as a stopover for centuries before German traders from Lübeck and Bremen first reconnoitred the mouth of the Daugava in the mid-12th century. In 1201 Bishop Albert von Buxhoevden from Bremen founded the first German fort in the Baltics here, as a bridgehead for the crusade against the northern heathens. He also founded the Knights of the Sword, who made Rīga their base for subjugating Livonia. The first German settlements were at the southern end of today's Old Town. Colonists from northern Germany followed, and Rīga became the major city in the German Baltic, thriving from trade between Russia and the West and joining the Hanseatic League in 1282. The city's coat of arms still combines the key of Bremen with the towers of Hamburg – the two cities most instrumental in its founding. Furs, hides, honey and wax were

Jūrmala p254    Rīga p232
Central Rīga p234
Old Rīga p238

among the products sold westward from Russia through Rīga.

Rīga's bishop, elevated to archbishop in 1252, became the leader of the church in the lands the Germans conquered, ruling a good slice of Livonia directly and further areas of Livonia and Estonia indirectly through his bishops. But there was always a contest for

RĪGA

power between the church, the knights (who controlled most of the remainder of Livonia and Estonia), and the German merchant-dominated city authorities, who managed to maintain a degree of independence from 1253 to 1420.

Rīga reached its early peak of prosperity around the beginning of the 16th century. Following the knights' collapse in the middle of that century, the city suffered attacks by Poles and Russians. After a brief spell of independence from 1561, it fell under Polish rule in 1582, then Sweden captured it in 1621; however, both Sweden and Poland allowed it autonomy. During the Swedish period Rīga was, effectively, the second city of Sweden, and it was at this time that it first expanded beyond its fortified walls. In 1710 Russia took it from Sweden. Throughout this entire period, however, the old German nobility and merchants remained in real control.

In the Russian era Rīga grew into an important trading and industrial city, the capital of the province of Livonia. Its population jumped to 28,000 in 1794 and 60,000 by the 1840s. While the old part of the city remained a preserve of Rīga's approximately 30,000 Germans, around it grew suburbs of wider, straighter streets with wooden houses, inhabited by the largest Russian community in the Baltic provinces as well as a growing number of Latvians.

The city walls were pulled down between 1857 and 1863 to assist the free flow of commerce. Rīga developed into the world's busiest timber port and Russia's third greatest industrial city (after Moscow and St Petersburg). Russia's first cars were built here. Rīga was also renowned for the quality of the Lithuanian and Belarusian hemp and flax which it exported to the outside world.

Also in the 19th century, Latvians freed from serfdom in the countryside moved to the city and pushed into its trades, business, civil service and intellectual circles, forming about a quarter of the population by the 1860s. The Rīga Latvian Association, formed in 1868, became the core of the Latvian national awakening, inspiring a Latvian national theatre, opera, encyclopaedia and, in 1873, the first Latvian song festival. The number of Latvians in Rīga grew until they formed about half the city's population of 500,000 on the eve of WWI. There were significant communities of Jews and Western

merchants – the city's last mayor before the war, George Armitstead, came from an English merchant family.

Rīga was badly damaged in both world wars and was left with only 181,000 people at the end of WWI after evacuations and other ravages. The Germans departed after the Latvian land reform of the 1920s and Hitler's 'come home' call in 1939. In the Latvian independence era between the wars, Rīga was the centre chosen by Western diplomats, journalists and spies to eavesdrop on Stalin's Soviet Union. Flourishing nightclubs, restaurants and intellectual life earned it the nickname 'Little Paris'.

During WWII Rīga was occupied by the Germans from 1941 to 1944, and virtually all its Jewish community (estimated variously at 45,000 to 100,000) was exterminated. Thousands of Latvians left for the West towards the end of the war to avoid Soviet rule.

After the war, the city became the industrial and commercial powerhouse of the USSR's Baltic region and many thousands migrated here to work in the new industries. Rīga became the USSR's main source of railway engines and carriages, producing half its mopeds and a third of its washing machines, as well as trams, radios, telephone exchanges, robots and computers. The city sprawled outwards as large numbers of migrants arrived, and Rīga became known as the most Western city in the USSR, with a liberal arts and music scene that attracted people from all over the union.

Today, Rīga remains a bustling centre of the arts and, as the largest city in the Baltics, has acquired a reputation for its vibrant nightlife. The success of the city's 800th birthday party in 2001 – marked by a rash of historical buildings miraculously rising from the ashes – was sealed in 2002 by a budding young Russian Rīgan singer striking gold in the Eurovision Song Contest. The city went on to host the great event in May 2003.

## ORIENTATION

Rīga straddles the Daugava River, about 15km inland from its mouth in the southeastern corner of the Gulf of Rīga. Old Rīga (Vecrīga), the historic heart of the city, stretches 1km along the eastern side of the river and 600m back from its banks.

Old Rīga's skyline is dominated by three steeples. From south to north these are: St

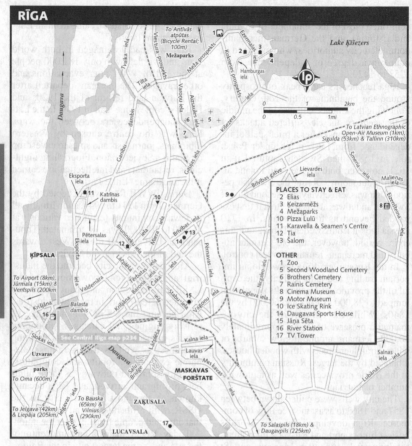

# RĪGA

**PLACES TO STAY & EAT**
2 Elias
3 Ķeizarmežs
4 Mežaparks
10 Pizza Lulū
11 Karavella & Seamen's Centre
12 Tia
13 Šalom

**OTHER**
1 Zoo
5 Second Woodland Cemetery
6 Brothers' Cemetery
7 Rainis Cemetery
8 Cinema Museum
9 Motor Museum
10 Ice Skating Rink
14 Daugavas Sports House
15 Jāṇa Sēta
16 River Station
17 TV Tower

Peter's (the tallest), the square bulk of the Dome Cathedral tower, and the simpler St Jacob's. Around most of the Old Town runs a wide band of 19th-century parks and boulevards, and beyond that is new Rīga, beginning with the areas built up in the 19th and early 20th century. Further out are the newer, mainly residential suburbs and Soviet industrial enclaves.

The boundaries between these zones are clear to see if you trace the street running northeast from Akmens Bridge (Akmens tilts) over the Daugava. First it cuts across the middle of the Old Town as a narrow, mainly pedestrian artery called Kaļķu iela. Then, gaining the name Brīvības bulvāris (Freedom Boulevard), it widens to cross the ring of boulevards and parks and passes the

Freedom Monument, a key landmark. At the towering Reval Hotel Latvija, 1.25km from the river, it enters the new town and becomes Brīvības iela.

The train and bus stations border the central market and are a five-minute walk apart on the southeastern edge of old Rīga. The ferry terminal is 600m north of old Rīga.

## Maps

Latvian, Lithuanian and Estonian maps are sold at **Jāṇa sēta** (☎ 709 22 77; *w www.kartes.lv; Elizabetes iela 83-85; open 10am-7pm Mon-Fri, 10am-5pm Sat*). The *Rīga Pilsētas plāns* (Rīga City Plan, 1:20,000, 1.50Ls), with a 1:7000 city centre inset, is one of several city maps it produces. Stock up on road and city maps for Latvia while you're here.

## INFORMATION
### Tourist Offices
The **tourist office** (☎ 703 79 00, fax 703 79 10; ⓦ www.rigatourism.com; Rātslaukums 6; open 10am-7pm daily), inside the House of Black-heads, has a small amount of information on the city and surrounds, and takes bookings for bus tours of the city (see Organised Tours).

There's another **tourist office** (☎ 722 05 55; Pragas iela 1; open 9am-6pm Mon-Fri, 10am-5pm Sat & Sun) at the bus station.

### Money
There are exchange offices at Rīga airport and dotted throughout the centre. **Bastejkubs** (Basteja bulvāris 12; open 24hr) is on the old-town fringe. ATMs accepting MasterCard, Visa, Cirrus and Plus abound in central Rīga.

Most banks change travellers cheques and Eurocheques for 2% to 3% commission. **Latvia Tours** (see Travel Agencies), the agent for American Express, cannot cash travellers cheques, but can issue them and replace lost American Express cheques and cards.

### Post & Communications
The **central post office** (☎ 701 87 38; ⓦ www.riga.post.lv; Brīvības bulvāris 19; open 7am-11pm Mon-Fri, 8am-10pm Sat) is not far from Milda (Freedom Monument). There's another **post office** (☎ 701 88 04; Stacijas laukums 1; open 8am-8pm Mon-Fri, 8am-6pm Sat) next to the train station, and an old-town **post office** (Vaļņu iela 24; open 8am-8pm Mon-Fri, 8am-6pm Sat, 8am-4pm Sun).

There is no city code for Rīga – all numbers have seven digits. For directory assistance call ☎ 701 87 38.

Rīga has reams of Internet cafés. Online access at the industrially designed **Arēna** (☎ 731 45 14; Ģertrūdes iela 46; open 24hr), in a red-brick cellar, and **Dual Net Café** (☎ 781 44 40; Peldu iela 17; open 24hr) costs 0.50 Ls an hour. **Poligons** (☎ 724 22 12; ⓦ www.poligons.lv; Dzirnavu iela 55; open 24hr) is cheaper at 0.35 Ls an hour.

### Travel Agencies
**Latvia Tours** (☎ 708 50 01; ⓦ www.latviatours.lv; Kaļķu iela 8), with branches in Ventspils and Liepāja, is one of Latvia's largest agencies and offers a bounty of services.

Other places to try for ferry and plane tickets are **World Travel Service** (☎ 733 22 33;

K Valdemāra iela 33) and **Via Rīga** (☎ 728 59 01, fax 782 81 99; ⓦ www.viariga.lv; K Barona iela 7-9). ISIC cards are handled by **Student & Youth Travel Bureau** (SJCB; ☎ 728 48 18, fax 728 30 64; ⓦ www.sjcb.lv; Lāčplēša iela 29).

### Bookshops
**Jāņa sēta** (Elizabetes iela 83-85) is the place to shop for Lonely Planet guides and other travel titles.

**Jāņa Rozes** (Elizabetes iela 85a) bookshop sells English-language novels, classical literature and Latvian-language learning cassettes. Its branch at K Barona iela 5 stocks reference books in English on Rīga and Latvia.

For dictionaries and Penguin classics, try **Globuss** (Vaļņu iela 26) which has the added bonus of an upstairs reading café.

### Libraries
The **British Council** (☎ 728 56 31, fax 728 56 66; ⓦ www.britishcouncil.lv; Blaumaņa iela 5a) runs a well-stocked library.

### Laundry
The laundrette **City Clean** (☎ 727 24 71; K Barona iela 52; open 8am-8pm Mon-Fri, 10am-5pm Sat) does dry cleaning too.

### Left Luggage
At the train station the **left-luggage room** (bagāžas glabātava; open 4.30am-midnight daily) is in the basement. It costs 0.50/1 Ls per day to leave a small/large bag.

The **left-luggage room** (open 6am-11pm daily) at the bus station charges 0.20 Ls per hour for a bag up to 10kg.

RĪGA

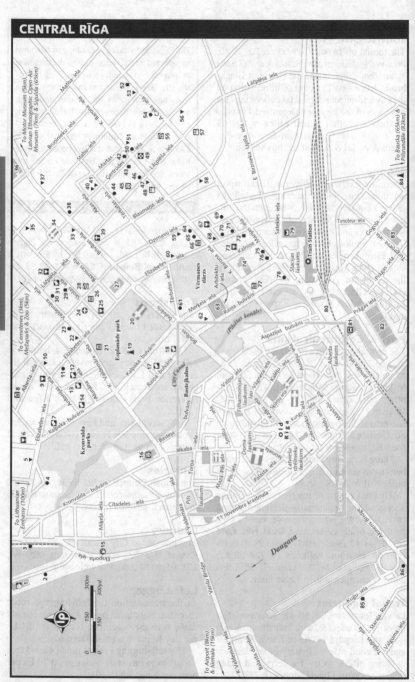

# CENTRAL RĪGA

## CENTRAL RĪGA

**PLACES TO STAY**
23 Valdemārs
27 Reval Hotel Latvija;
  Skyline
29 Laine
42 Krišjānis & Gertrude
43 ECB
52 Viktorija
72 Patricia
75 Aurora
76 Saulīte
85 Radisson-SAS Daugava

**PLACES TO EAT**
5 Vincents
10 Traktieris
22 Coffee Nation
33 Pauze
35 Zen
37 Pizza Jazz
40 Monte Kristo
41 Pizza Lulū
47 Osiris
51 Rāma
53 Staburags
56 Pelmeņi
58 Charletons
59 Dzirnavas
60 Vērmanītis
62 Pizza Jazz; German
  Embassy
68 Andalūzijas Suns;
  Kino Suns

**PUBS, BARS & CLUBS**
6 Ai Karamba!
9 Lidojoš ā
25 Hollywood Stardisco
32 M-808
67 DECO bārs
73 XXL

**OTHER**
1 Ferry Terminal
2 Hanza Maritime Agency &
  Rīgas Jūras Linija
3 Andrejosta Yacht Club
4 Word Trade Centre
7 Finnish Embassy
8 Jānis Rozentāls Memorial
  Museum
11 Mikhail Eisenstein's House
12 Swedish Embassy
13 British Embassy
14 Russian Embassy
15 Statoil (Petrol Station)
16 National Theatre
17 US Embassy
18 French Embassy
19 Jānis Rainis Monument
20 Russian Orthodox Cathedral
21 State Museum of Art
24 ARS Clinic
26 Jews in Latvia Museum
28 Poligons
30 World Travel Service
31 Estonian Consulate

34 Old Gertrude Church
36 Daile Theatre
38 Pharmacy
39 Alexandr Nevsky Church
44 Trase (Bicycle Rental)
45 New Rīga Theatre
46 Tūrinfo
48 Daile
49 Barona Centrs; Rimi Supermarket
50 City Clean
54 Norma-A (Ecolines)
55 Arēna
57 Kino-52
61 Flower Market
63 Latvia University
64 Via Rīga
65 Jāņa Rozes
66 Krisjānis Barons Memorial
  Museum;National Library
69 Latvia Tours
70 Map Shop
71 Jāņa Rozes
74 Circus
77 Latvian Nature Museum
78 Interpegro & Latvijas Balzams
79 Post Office
80 Stockmann
81 Bus Station; Tourist Office
82 Central Market
83 Science Academy
84 Jewish Memorial
86 Lauku Ceļotājs (Country
  Traveller Association)

## Medical Services

**Rīgas vecpilsētas aptieka** (☎ 721 33 40; *Audēju iela 20; open 24hr*), on the edge of the Old Town, is a 24-hour pharmacy. It charges a 0.20 Ls fee for service between 10pm and 8am. The **pharmacy** (*Brīvibas iela 68; open 8am-10pm daily*) on the corner of Ģertrūdes is another handy one to know.

**ARS Clinic** (☎ 720 10 06/7/8, fax 728 87 69; e ars@delfi.lv; *Skolas iela 5*) offers a 24-hour English-speaking service, as well as an **emergency home service** (☎ 720 10 03).

For an ambulance dial ☎ 03.

## WALKING TOUR

This walking tour takes about three hours nonstop at a leisurely pace, but you can easily make a day of it with pauses at museums, galleries and cafés. Start with a look at the northern half of old Rīga, which centres on **Doma laukums**, then head towards the riverside and walk halfway over **Akmens Bridge** for a classical view of old Rīga. Return to the southern half of old Rīga and ride the lift

up the spire of **St Peter's Church** for another rewarding view. Wander south out of old Rīga to the **central market**, a focus of the city's modern and historical life. Then head northeast for about 600m past the train station, another city hub, to the **Freedom Monument**, set in the band of boulevards and parks. From here you can stroll around the city parks, ride the lift to the 26th floor of Reval Hotel Latvija for yet another stunning city view, and – if you still have the energy – head northwest to view Rīga's sumptuous **Jugendstil** (German Art-Nouveau design) architecture.

## OLD RĪGA

Many centuries-old German buildings survive in old Rīga (Vecrīga), a protected zone of narrow, now mainly pedestrianised streets, made prettier by restoration and dotted with cafés and restaurants. Simply walking around here – not forgetting to gaze up at the playful statuettes and carvings that adorn many building facades – is one of the chief

## Art Nouveau Architecture

Rīga's architectural distinction is its Art-Nouveau style, also called Jugendstil and credited by Unesco as being the finest in Europe. Crafted in the late 19th and early 20th century, it has survived in Rīga more than in many German cities which were damaged during WWII.

The Jugendstil architectural features emphasise the ornate – monsters, flowers, masks and grotesques peer out from the upper storeys of the buildings. Different coloured tiles may be used to make the designs stand out. Often the buildings' plain interiors offer an almost comical contrast to the elaborate style of the facade.

One place that showcases the ornate Jugendstil style is along the combined residential, office and commercial streets east of Elizabetes iela, where a number of low, wooden buildings survive from the 19th century. One of the best examples, designed by Mikhail Eisenstein, father of the renowned film-maker, is the beautifully renovated, blue-and-white house at Elizabetes iela 10b, just north of the State Museum of Art.

Around the corner on **Alberta iela** – famous as a confluence of architectural schools: national romanticism, historicism, neoclassicism and rationalism – the buildings become even more fantastical. All were designed by Mikhael Eisenstein except for No 12, an Art-Nouveau apartment, formerly home to the Latvian painter Jānis Rozentāls (1866–1916) and now the **Jānis Rozentāls Memorial Museum** (☎ 733 16 41; Alberta iela 12-9; adult/child 0.60/0.30 Ls; open 11am-5pm Thur-Mon). The houses at Nos 2, 4, 6 and 8 have grandiose Art-Nouveau facades; the facade at 2a towers above the building itself.

Equally fabulous is the beautifully renovated 1905 facade of the **Stockholm School of Economics** (Strēlnieku iela 4a), considered by many to be the city's most stunning example of Art-Nouveau architecture.

---

pleasures of visiting Latvia's capital. The crumbling yet stunning golden facade of what is known as **Pie Kristapa** at Jauniela 25-29 is a classic example of but one of Rīga's dozens of different faces.

Kaļķu iela neatly divides old Rīga in half, each half focusing on a towering church – Dome Cathedral in the north, St Peter's in the south.

### Dome Cathedral

This humungous brick cathedral (Doma baznīca; ☎ 721 34 98; open 1pm-5pm Tues-Fri, 10am-2pm Sat), also known as Rīgas Doms (from the German Dom, meaning cathedral), towers beside Doma laukums, the main square within the Old Town surrounded by an unusual brew of architectural styles.

Founded in 1211 as the seat of the Rīga diocese, the church is the largest in the Baltics today. Mass is held at 8am Monday to Saturday, and at noon on Sunday. In the Soviet era, services were banned; the first service for over 30 years, in 1988, was a major event of the perestroika era.

Rīga's oldest museum, the **Museum of the History of Rīga & Navigation** (Rīgas vēstures un ku-niecības muzejs; ☎ 721 20 51; Palasta iela 4; adult/child 1/0.50 Ls; open 11am-5pm Wed-Sun), founded in 1773, is housed in the cloister of the monastery next to the cathedral. After entering the museum, turn left to descend into the **Cross Gallery**, which connects the cathedral to the cloister.

### Rīga Castle

On Pils laukums (Castle Square), **Rīga Castle** dates to 1330 when it was built as the Livonian Order's headquarters and served as the residence of the order's grand master. Today Latvia's president lives here. Painted canary yellow, the castle appears younger than it really is following various modifications through the centuries, and not very castle-like from its inland side. You get a more turreted aspect from the river or Akmens Bridge.

Part of the castle houses a **Museum of Foreign Art** (Ārzemju mākslas muzejs; ☎ 722 64 67; Pils laukums 3; adult/child 1.20/0.70 Ls; open 11am-5pm Tues-Sun), exhibiting Latvia's largest treasury of artwork dating back to the 15th century. The **History Museum of Latvia** (Latvijas vēstures muzejs; ☎ 722 13 57; ⊛ www.history-museum.lv; adult/child 0.70/ 0.40 Ls, free Wed; open 11am-6pm Mon-Sat), tracing national history, is also here.

On the opposite side of Pils laukums, there is a **Museum of Writing, Theatre & Music**

*(Rakstniecības, teātra un mūzikas muzejs; ☎ 722 19 56; Pils laukums 3; adult/child 0.40/0.20 Ls; open 11am-6pm Tues-Sun).* Looming big immediately east of the square is the **Arsenāls Museum of Art** *(Mākslas muzejs Arsenāls; ☎ 721 36 95; Torņa iela 1; adult/child 0.70/ 0.40 Ls; open 11am-5pm Tues, Wed & Fri-Sun, 11am-7pm Thur)*, the exhibition hall of the State Museum of Art (see the North of Brīvības Bulvāris section later in this chapter). Its voluminous interior magnificently frames a large collection of modern art.

## Old Rīga North

The red-brick Gothic **St Saviour's Church** *(Anglikāņu iela 2a)*, off Pils iela, was built in 1857 by a small group of British traders on 30 feet of British soil brought over as ballast in the ships transporting the building material. During Soviet times, it served as a disco for Rīga's Polytechnic Institute. It still remains the property of the Church of England. Sunday services in English are held at 10am.

Nearby are the **Three Brothers** *(Mazā Pils iela 17, 19 & 21)*, a quaint row of houses. No 17 dates from the 15th century, making it Latvia's oldest house. No 19 is the **Latvian Museum of Architecture** *(Latvijas arhitektūras muzejs; ☎ 722 07 79; Mazā Pils iela 19; admission free; open 9am-6pm Mon-Fri)*. At the end of the street is Jēkaba iela, and nearby is tall **St Jacob's Cathedral** *(Sv Jēkaba katedrāle; Mazā Pils iela)*. Its interior dates to 1225 and it's the seat of Rīga's Roman Catholic archbishopric. Next door is Latvia's **Parliament** *(Saeima; Jēkaba iela 11)*, a Florentine Renaissance building that was a focus of Latvian resistance to Soviet provocation in January 1991 and stayed barricaded for over a year.

The picturesque **Swedish Gate** *(cnr Torņa iela & Aldaru iela)* was built onto the city walls in 1698 during the Swedish period and is the only remaining old city gate. The round, peaked **Powder Tower** is a 14th-century original and the only survivor of the 18 towers in the old city wall. Nine Russian cannonballs from 17th- and 18th-century assaults are embedded in the tower's walls. In the past it has served as a gunpowder store, prison, torture chamber, museum and students' party venue. Today it is a **War Museum** *(Kara muzejs; ☎ 722 81 47; www .karamuzejs.lv; Smilšu iela 20; adult/child 0.50/0.25 Ls; open 10am-6pm Wed-Sun May-Sept, 10am-5pm Wed-Sun Oct-Apr)*.

## Rīga's Vital Organ

Architecturally, the Dome Cathedral is an amalgam of styles from the 13th to the 18th centuries: the eastern end, the oldest, has Romanesque features; the tower is 18th-century baroque; and much of the rest dates from a 15th-century Gothic rebuilding. The floor and walls of the huge interior are dotted with old stone tombs – note the curious carved symbols on some of those on the north side, denoting the rank or post of the occupant. Eminent citizens would pay to be buried as close to the altar as possible. In 1709, a cholera and typhoid outbreak, which killed a third of Rīga's population, was blamed on a flood that inundated the cathedral's tombs.

The cathedral's pulpit dates from 1641 and the huge organ (which has 6768 pipes) was built in the 1880s; today it's the world's fourth-largest organ, but it was the largest in the world when it was originally built.

The 19th-century Gothic exterior of the **Great Guild** *(Lielā gilde; Amatu iela 6)* encloses a fine 1330 merchants' meeting hall, now concert hall to the Latvian State Philharmonic Orchestra. The yellow-painted **Cat House** *(Meistaru iela 19)* is the one you see pictured on many a postcard (see the boxed text 'Cat House' later).

## Latviesu Strēlnieku laukums & Rātslaukums

The square immediately east of Akmens Bridge is known as Latviesu strēlnieku laukums *(Latvian Riflemen Square)*, once home to Rīga's central market but today dominated by the big, dark-red **Latvian Riflemen statue**. The said marksmen were eight regiments formed in WWI to fight in the Russian imperial army. When the Russian Revolution rolled around, most of them supported the Bolsheviks. They provided a palace guard for Lenin and formed key units of the Red Army during the Russian civil war – although some sided against the Bolsheviks in the concurrent Latvian independence war. During the Soviet era the riflemen were known as the Latvian Red Riflemen.

Behind the statue, in a controversial bunker – at one point slated to be razed for its ugliness – is Latvia's **Occupation Museum**

# OLD RĪGA

**PLACES TO STAY**
14 Gutenbergs
41 Hotel de Rome
55 Man-Tess
63 Konventa Sēta;
   Porcelain Museum
76 Ainavas
80 Radi un Draugi
84 Centra
93 Forums
94 Metropole

**PLACES TO EAT**
9 Ķiploka krogs
15 Ķirbis
19 Kamāla
23 Divi laši
24 Alus sēta
25 Šetpavārs Vilhelms
33 Pulvertornis
40 Kolonāde & Laima
   Clock
44 Nostalģija & Groks
45 Zivju
47 Austrumu robeža
48 Palete
56 Monte Kristo
61 Pelmeņi XL
61 1739
64 Melnie mūki

79 Habibi
83 Senais Fredis

**PUBS, BARS & CLUBS**
4 Rīgas Balzams;
   Dutch Embassy
10 Casablanca
22 Tim McShane's Irish Pub
28 Slepenais Eksperiments
30 Melnais kaķis
39 Cita Opera
43 Roxy
49 Dublin
66 Dickens
78 Pulkvedim neviens
   neraksta
81 Paddy Whelan's
88 Nautilus
89 Dizzi
92 Četri balti krekli

**OTHER**
1 Riga Castle; Museum of
   Foreign Art & History;
   Museum of Latvia
2 Museum of Writing,
   Theatre & Music
3 Arsenāls Museum of Art
5 Swedish Gate
6 Parliament

7 St Jacob's Cathedral
8 Three Brothers; Latvian
   Museum of Architecture
11 TV5 Recording Booth
12 St Saviour's Church
13 Canadian Embassy
16 Museum of the History
   of Rīga & Navigation
17 Kinogalerija
18 Dome Cathedral
20 A&E Gallery
21 Pie Kristapa
26 Cat House
27 Great Guild
29 Small Guild
31 Powder Tower;
   Museum of War
32 Memorials to Victims
   of 20 January 1991
34 Bastejkubs
35 24-Hour Marika
   Currency Exchange
36 EU Information Centre
37 Freedom Monument
38 Central Post Office
42 AirBaltic; Estonian Air
46 Wagner Hall
50 National Opera House
51 Post Office
52 Globuss

53 Rīgas vecpilsētas
   aptieka
54 Centrs Universālveikals
57 Upe
58 Russian Drama Theatre
60 Latvia Tours;
   Sievasmātes p īrādziņi
62 Museum of Decorative
   & Applied Arts
65 St John's Church
67 St Peter's Church
68 Nordwear
69 Town Hall
70 Statue of Roland
71 Tourist Office; House
   of Blackheads
72 Occupation Museum
73 Latvian Riflemen Statue
74 Mentzendorff's House
75 Dual Net Café
77 House of Dannenstern
82 Musikas salons
85 House of Johannes
   Reitern
86 Latvian Photography
   Museum
87 Protestant Church
90 Synagogue
91 Latvian People's Front
   Museum

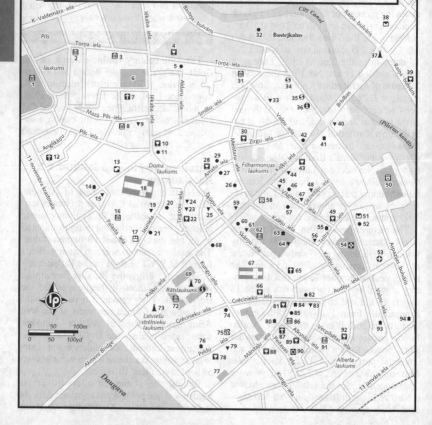

*(Latvijas okupācijas muzejs; ☎ 721 27 15; W www.occupationmuseum.lv; Latviesu Strēlnieku laukums 1; admission free; open 11am-5pm daily May-Sept, 11am-5pm Tues-Sun Oct-Apr)*. The museum gives an impressive account of the Soviet and Nazi occupations of Latvia between 1940 and 1991 – it is informative and disturbing in parts.

Providing a dramatic contrast to the forbidding concrete bunker is the **House of Blackheads**, constructed in 2001 on Rātslaukums (Town Hall Square) as an 800th birthday present to the city. An architectural gem, the ornate edifice was originally built in 1344 for the Blackheads' guild of unmarried merchants, destroyed in 1941 and flattened for good measure by the Soviets seven years later. In front of the house is a recent **statue of a sword-wielding Roland**, Roland being the medieval defender of the accused. The **town hall**, on the opposite side of the square, was built from scratch in 2002 – after chopping Rīga's former technical university in half to accommodate the latter, that is.

East of here is **Mentzendorff's House** *(Mencendorfa nams; ☎ 721 29 51; Grēcinieku iela 18; adult/child 1.20/0.40 Ls; open 10am-5pm Wed-Sun)*, a 17th-century dwelling showing how wealthy Rīgans once lived.

## St Peter's Church

Gothic **St Peter's** *(Sv Pētera baznīca; ☎ 722 94 26; spire admission 1.60/0.10 Ls, exhibition admission 0.50/0.10 Ls; open 10am-6pm Tues-Sun May-Sept, 10am-5pm Tues-Sun Oct-Apr)* is the dominant feature of the southern half of old Rīga. Don't miss the view from its famed spire, which has been built three times in the same baroque form: originally in wood in the 1660s; again in wood in the 18th century, after it burnt down from a lightning strike; and then in steel (1967–73) after it was burnt to a shell in 1941, by attacking Germans or the retreating Red Army depending on whom you consult. The spire reaches 123.25m into the sky although the lift only whisks visitors up to 72m.

## Skārņu Iela & Mārstaļu Iela

A row of particularly pretty restored buildings faces St Peter's on Skārņu iela. The former St George's Church – an original chapel of the Knights of the Swords dating to 1208 – is now the absorbing **Museum of Decorative & Applied Arts** *(Dekoratīvi lietišķās mākslas*

### Cat House

At the beginning of the 20th century, the Latvian owner of the Cat House had statuettes made of the back ends of his two black cats – backs arched and tails up. He placed them on the building's topmost pinnacles facing the Big Guild Hall across the road as a gesture of defiance against the guild that refused him entry – it was strictly reserved for rich German traders. Following a lengthy court case, he was admitted to the guild on the condition that he turn his cats around to a more elegant position.

*muzejs; ☎ 722 78 33; Skārņu iela 10-20; admission to permanent exhibition 0.50/0.40 Ls, to temporary exhibition 0.70/0.40 Ls; open 11am-5pm Tues-Sun)*. It is full of fine Latvian work; the pottery and wall hangings are particularly outstanding.

Yet more ceramics and porcelain can be viewed in the **Porcelain Museum** *(☎ 750 37 69; Kalēju iela 9-11; adult/child 0.50/0.40 Ls; open 11am-6pm Tues-Sun)*, tucked away in Konventa sēta – the restored Convent Courtyard of the **former convent** *(Skārņu iela 22)* that stood here in the 15th century. Next door, **St John's Church** *(Jāņa baznīca; Skārņu iela 24)* is a 13th- to 19th-century amalgam of Gothic, Renaissance and baroque styles. Look up to see the stone faces of two monks who, so the story goes, were bricked alive into the wall during the building's construction.

Further south, near the corner of Audēju iela, is the 17th-century **House of Johannes Reitern** *(Mārstaļu iela 2-4)*, with its elaborate stone carvings. Reitern was a rich German merchant. Just next door is the interesting **Latvian Photography Museum** *(Latvijas fotogrāfijas muzejs; ☎ 722 72 31; Mārstaļu iela 8; adult/child 1/0.50 Ls; open 10am-5pm Tues, Fri & Sat, noon-7pm Wed & Thur)*, an 18th- to 19th-century former merchant's house with unique photographs of 1920s Rīga. The baroque **House of Dannenstern** *(Mārstaļu iela 21)* also used to be home to a wealthy 17th-century merchant.

A block south, the one-room **Latvian People's Front Museum** *(Latvijas tautas frontes muzejs; ☎ 722 45 02; Vecpilsētas iela 13-15; admission free; open 2pm-7pm Tues, noon-5pm Wed-Fri, noon-4pm Sat)* remains furnished exactly as it was when it served as

RĪGA

the office of the Latvian People's Front prior to 1990. There are several tall **medieval warehouses** both on this narrow street and the parallel Alksnāja iela – at Vecpilsētas iela 10 and 11, and Alksnāja iela 5, 7, 9 and 11. Both streets lead south to **Alberta laukums**, a small square that was the site of Bishop Albert's original German settlement.

## PARKS & BOULEVARDS

East of old Rīga's confined streets, the city opens out into a perfectly contrasting band of parks and wide boulevards laid out in the 19th century. Along the boulevards are many fine 19th- and early 20th-century buildings. Some of these belong to the eclectic school of design which drew on a multitude of past styles, while others are flamboyant examples of Jugendstil (see the boxed text 'Art Nouveau Architecture' earlier) which crops up all over Rīga. The old defensive moat, known as the **City Canal** (Pilsētas kanāls), snakes through the parks and marks the line of the old city walls that were knocked down in the mid-19th century.

### Freedom Monument

The central landmark of the park ring is the Freedom Monument (Brīvības bulvāris), near the corner of Raiņa bulvāris. Paid for by public donations, the monument was erected in 1935 in the style you could describe as '30s nationalism, on a spot where a statue of Peter the Great had stood. Topped by a bronze female Liberty holding up three stars facing west, representing three regions of Latvia – Kurzeme, Vidzeme and Latgale – it bears the inscription 'Tēvzemei un Brīvībai' (For Fatherland and Freedom). During the Soviet years the Freedom Monument was off-limits, and a statue of Lenin, facing the other way down Brīvības iela, was placed two blocks east. Lenin was removed on the night of 20 August 1991, after the collapse of the Moscow coup attempt.

In the late 1980s and early '90s the Freedom Monument became a focus of the Latvian independence movement, which started on 14 June 1987, when 5000 people rallied here illegally to commemorate the victims of Stalin's deportations. Several later rallies and marches focused on the monument, which still functions as an unofficial centre for animated political debate. Since 1992 the guard of honour that stood at the monument before

WWII has been revived. If the authorities were prepared to open up Milda (as the bronze statue is called) to the public, it would be possible to walk to the top for a breathtaking view of Rīga from the small window cut at her feet.

Come here to watch the changing of the guards, who stand still as stone in front of her, every hour on the hour from 9am to 6pm daily.

### North of Freedom Monument

**Bastion Hill** (Bastejkalns), the mound beside Basteja bulvāris, is what remains of one of the bastions of Rīga's fortifications. Beside the paths either side of the canal, below Bastejkalns, stand five polished stone slabs – **memorials to the victims of 20 January 1991**. Edijs Riekstins, Sergey Kononenko, Vladimir Gomanovich, Andris Slapins and Gvido Zvaigžne were all killed or fatally wounded here when Soviet special forces stormed the Interior Ministry nearby at Raiņa bulvāris 6. Slapins and Zvaigžne were members of the film crew of the Latvian documentary maker Jūris Podnieks (see boxed text 'Jūris Podnieks' in the Facts for the Visitor chapter). No-one who has seen the films *Baltic Requiem* or *Post Scriptum*, or the documentary *Homeland*, will forget the last footage shot by Slapins that night or his gasped words 'keep filming...' as he lay dying.

**Raiņa bulvāris** was 'Embassy Row' during Latvian independence between the world wars and has assumed that status again, with the Stars and Stripes fluttering in front of No 7, France installed at No 9 and Germany at No 13. To the west, opposite the corner of Basteja bulvāris, the **National Theatre** (Nacionālais teātris; K Valdemāra iela) is an interesting baroque building (1899–1902); Latvia's independence was declared here on 18 November 1918. To the north, past the **Congress Centre** (K Valdemāra iela 5), Rīga's **World Trade Centre** (Elizabetes iela 2) is also home to some foreign embassies – Israel, Poland and Switzerland. The building used to be the Latvian Communist Party headquarters.

The **State Museum of Art** (Valsts mākslas muzejs; ☎ 732 44 61; e vmm@latent.lv; K Valdemāra iela 10a; adult/child 1.20/0.40 Ls; open 11am-5pm Wed-Mon) has collections of Russian work downstairs and Latvian

## Central Market

Whatever your heart desires – be it CDs, a pig's head, bloodied sheep carcasses or Ecuadorian bananas – Rīga's bustling, colourful central market will supply them in abundance. As well as being a fantastic place for cheap shopping, this colourful collage of people and products is a worthy attraction in itself. It is one of Europe's largest markets and also its most ancient, dating back at least to the city's founding in 1201.

Rīga's market was not always so large – nor was it always in its present location. Historians believe that a tiny market operated along the banks of the Daugava in the Dark Ages. When German crusaders, on a northward sweep, founded Rīga in 1201, this fledgling market logically relocated within the new city.

A 1330 manuscript provides the first written reference, alluding to the market near the Dome Cathedral being moved to what is now called 'Riflemen Square', east of Akmens Bridge. The market remained in Riflemen Square until 1570, when it was moved to the banks of the Daugava to facilitate trading along the river.

The market stayed on the Daugava banks for more than 350 years. Its growth corresponded to that of Rīga itself. By the mid-1600s when Rīga, then under Swedish rule, outgrew Stockholm, the market flourished with over 1000 merchants trading goods from all over the region. But in 1930 the market was moved once more, to its present location by the train and bus stations. This final move was prompted by the need to have the market closer to the railway, which had replaced the river as the principal route for trade. Confronted with the market's vast size, the city of Rīga decided to bring in five enormous Zeppelin hangars from the town of Vainode in western Latvia. At a cost of 5 million Ls, these hangars – each 35m high – were erected on the current site between 1924 and 1930. All told, the hangars provide 57,000 sq m of space for up to 1250 sellers and – crucially – central heating for Rīga's long, cold winters.

When Latvia was absorbed into the Soviet Union, the market shrank briefly, but it rebounded with produce from the southern Soviet republics. These days, it is larger than ever, seemingly bursting at the seams. If you get lost wandering through the forest of carcasses and cheese in the mammoth Zeppelin hangars, don't despair – you're not the first.

work upstairs, plus interesting temporary exhibitions. On the Kalpaka bulvāris side of the Esplanāde is the **Jānis Rainis Monument** to Latvia's national poet (see the boxed text 'Jānis Rainis' in the Facts about Latvia chapter).

The domed 19th-century **Russian Orthodox Cathedral** (*Pareizticīgo katedrāle; Brīvības bulvāris*) fronting the boulevard was a planetarium under Soviet rule but is once more used as a church.

### South of Freedom Monument
There's a colourful **flower market** (*cnr Merķeļa iela & Tērbatas iela*) south of the boulevard. The main building of the **Latvia University** (*Raiņa bulvāris 19*) dates from 1866–1906. Rīga's **National Opera House** (*Aspazijas bulvāris 3*) was built in 1860.

### NEW RĪGA
The heart of everyday Rīga life lies beyond both the Old Town and the park-boulevard

ring, in the areas built up in the 19th and early 20th centuries. The **central market** (*Centrāl tirgus*), south of the train station, always presents a lively scene and is a barometer of the city's standard of living.

Other landmarks to head for include the Russian Orthodox **Alexandr Nevsky Church** (*Brīvības iela 56*), built in the 1820s; the Gothic **Old Gertrude Church** (*Ģertrūdes iela 8*), built in 1865; or the towering Stalin-era wedding cake-like **Science Academy** (*Turgeņeva iela*).

Krišjāņis Barons, the father of Latvian folk songs, lived the last years of his life in the building which now houses the **Krišjāņis Barons Memorial Museum** (*Krišjāņis Barons memoriālais muzejs;* ☎ 728 42 65; *K Barona iela 3; adult/child 0.40/0.20 Ls; open 1pm-7pm Tues & Wed, 11am-5pm Thur-Sun*). The **Latvian Nature Museum** (*Latvijas dabas muzejs;* ☎ 722 60 78; *K Barona iela 4; admission 0.50 Ls; open 10am-5pm Wed, Fri & Sat, 10am-6pm Thur, 10am-4pm Sat*) displays dozens of fossilised fish in its somewhat fusty and furry collection.

## SUBURBS
### Motor Museum

**Rīga Motor Museum** *(Rīgas motormuzejs;* ☎ *709 71 70; Eizenšteina iela 6; adult/child 1/ 0.50 Ls; open 10am-3pm Mon, 10am-6pm Tues-Sun)* is 8km east along Brīvības iela, then 2km south to the Mežciems suburb.

The museum was opened in 1989, but its seeds were sown in 1975 when a Latvian car enthusiast, Viktors Kulbergs, saved a rare 16-cylinder 1938 German Auto Union racer from being scrapped in a Moscow factory. The racer is today shown with 100 or so other Eastern and Western cars, motorcycles and bicycles – including an 1886 Daimler Motorkutsche (a genuine horseless carriage, maximum speed 16km/h), a 1984 Cadillac Fleetwood limo and a 1942 Harley Davidson – all packed into this modern, purpose-built museum.

The stars of the collection though are cars that belonged to Soviet luminaries Gorky, Stalin, Khrushchev and Brezhnev – complete with irreverent life-size figures of the men themselves. Stalin, pockmarked cheeks and all, sits regally in the back of his seven-tonne, 6005cc armoured limousine. The car has 1.5cm-thick iron plating everywhere except on the 8cm-thick windows. It drank a litre of petrol every 2.5km. Brezhnev sits, with appropriate surprise registered on his features, at the wheel of his crumpled Rolls-Royce Silver Shadow, written off in 1980 when he strayed from the safety of an official convoy into the path of a truck.

Take bus No 21 from the Russian Orthodox Cathedral to the Pansionāts stop on Smerļa iela.

### Latvian Ethnographic Open-Air Museum

The Latvian Ethnographic Open-Air Museum *(Latvijas etnogrāfiskais brīvdabas muzejs;* ☎ *799 45 15; Brīvības gatve 440; adult/child 1/0.50 Ls; open 11am-5pm daily mid-May–mid-Oct, closed last day of each month)* sits on the shores of Lake Jugla on the city's eastern edge. Dozens of predominantly wooden buildings from rural Latvia – churches, windmills and farmhouses from Latvia's different regions – can be discovered here. Thousands of artefacts inside the

buildings provide a record of bygone country life. On summer weekends, folk dance performances are held and there's a crafts fair in early June.

Take bus No 1 from the corner of Merķeļa iela and Tērbatas iela to the Brīvdabas muzejs stop.

### Mežaparks & Cemeteries

Rīga's biggest park is Mežaparks *(Woodland Park;* ☎ *754 02 88)*, about 7km north of the centre, beside Lake Ķišezers. Here you'll find pine woods, playgrounds, lots of boats and jet skis to rent in summer, and **Rīga Zoo**, the stage for the main concerts of Latvian song festivals.

South of Mežaparks are three cemeteries: **Rainis Cemetery** *(Raiņa kapi)*, where Jānis Rainis, his wife (feminist poet Aspazija) and other Latvian cultural figures are buried; the large **Second Woodland Cemetery** *(Meža kapi II)*, which has a monument to the five dead of 20 January 1991; and the **Brothers' Cemetery** *(Brāļu kapi)*, the resting place of Latvian soldiers who died in WWI and the independence war, and notable for its many monuments and sculptures.

## ORGANISED TOURS

Most travel agencies, including the ones listed earlier in this chapter, arrange city tours and day trips to other places in Latvia including Sigulda, Cēsis, Kurzeme, Latgale and Rundāle.

**Dzintara ceļš** *(Amber Way;* ☎ *702 78 01;* @ *amber@neonoet.lv; open 9am-5pm Mon-Fri)* organises two-hour bus tours of the city, departing from in front of the House of Blackheads on Rātslaukums at noon daily. The tourist office sells tickets (6/3 Ls per adult/ child) or you can buy them direct from the bus driver.

**Liepāja** *(*☎ *953 91 84)* is a boat that takes its passengers on Daugava River tours. It departs from the boat station on 11 Novembra krastmala by Akmens Bridge (opposite the tram No 4 stop) two to five times daily. River tours last one to two hours and cost 1-2 Ls (children aged under seven free).

## SPECIAL EVENTS

Rīga hosts dozens of annual and one-off festivals. See Public Holidays & Special Events in the Latvia Facts for the Visitor chapter.

## Jews of Rīga

The history of Rīga's Jews has been tumultuous. Pre-18th century Rīga had less than 1000 Jewish residents, a consequence of social policy that granted residency only to successful Jews. Even then, laws barred them from being buried in Rīga; the Jews had to shuttle their own dead to Polish cemeteries. A more flexible policy was instituted in 1725, when clearance came through for the first Jewish cemetery to be built.

Prior to the 19th century, most Jews were concentrated in the ghetto in the Maskavas suburb, about 1km southeast of the train station. It was a 750 sq m area bounded by Lāčplēsa iela, Maskavas iela, Ebreju iela, Lauvas iela and Kalna iela. There's little trace of the area's old character now due to Nazi destruction. In the late 1800s restrictions were lifted and the Jews were able to move to other parts of Rīga.

The first **synagogue** (☎ 721 08 27, 722 45 49; Peitavas iela 6-8), built in 1905, was the only synagogue to survive the Nazi terror, because its proximity to the Old Town made them afraid to burn it. Call in advance to sample kosher food at the synagogue.

When WWII began, about 5000 Jews were among the thousands of Latvians deported to Siberia by the Soviet authorities from 1940 to 1941. The city fell to the Germans on 1 July and new atrocities began that day with hundreds of Jews executed as 'retribution' for the Germans killed in the taking of the Old Town. Others were forced to scrub the bloodstains from the site of the battle with toothbrushes. A few days later, on 4 July 1941, 300 or more Jews were taken from the streets and locked in the Big Choral synagogue. Grenades were thrown through the windows and the building was set on fire. No-one survived. The Jewish cemetery buildings were also burned that day; later the Soviets razed the old cemetery and converted it into the 'Park of the Communist Brigades'.

Several thousand more Rīga Jews were murdered before the remaining thousands were herded into the ghetto in October 1941. Half-starved, they endured forced labour until most were taken and killed in Rumbula Forest, east of Maskavas, between 30 November and 8 December. Latvian collaborators as well as Germans were responsible for the holocaust – indeed the collaborators had a reputation for greater cruelty. Other Jews transported from Germany took some of the dead victims' places in the ghetto.

After the 1943 Warsaw-ghetto uprising, the Rīga ghetto, along with others, was liquidated on Himmler's orders, but those inmates capable of work were moved to the Kaiserwald prison camp in Mežaparks. Later they were brought back to other camps with the retreating German forces.

A memorial marks the former site of the Jewish community's **Big Choral Synagogue** (Gogola iela 25). The Jewish community headquarters shares the same building as **Jews in Latvia** (Ebreji Latvijas; ☎ 728 34 84; e ebreji.latvija@apollo.lv; Skolas iela 6; admission free; open noon-5pm Sun-Thur), Rīga's small Jewish museum that recounts Latvian Jewish history from the 16th century to 1945. After renovations, the museum was due to reopen in summer 2003.

## PLACES TO STAY – BUDGET
Unfortunately, as the city is increasingly spruced up, so budget places to stay are becoming increasingly few and far between.

### Camping
In Rīga itself there is nowhere to camp. Lauku ceļotājs (see Accommodation in the earlier Facts for the Visitor chapter) can point you in the direction of out-of-town places where you can pitch a tent.

### Hostels
**Placis** (☎ 755 18 24, fax 754 13 44; e placis@ delfi.lv; Laimdotas iela 2a; singles/doubles/ triples with shared bathroom 5/7/15 Ls, doubles with shower & toilet 20 Ls) is an 80-bed place

which gives 10% discounts with an HI card. To reach the hostel, take trolleybus No 4 from the Circus stop on Merķela iela to the Teika stop.

### B&Bs
**ECB** (☎ 729 85 35, fax 729 85 25; w www.myecb.com; K Barona iela 37-18; singles/ doubles/triples 27/32/38 Ls), with its entrance opposite Ģertrūdes iela 39, is a highly efficient British-run B&B agency with spacious rooms in central Rīga. Rates include an evening meal as well as breakfast.

**Krišjānis & Gertrūde** (☎/fax 750 66 03; e kg@mail.teliamtc.lv; K Barona iela 39; singles/doubles with shared bathroom 15/25 Ls, with bathroom from 25/35 Ls), a five-room set-up with its entrance at Ģertrūdes iela 39, is named after the Latvian couple who run it.

**Patricia** (☎ 728 48 68, 923 82 67, fax 728 66 50; W www.rigalatvia.net; Elizabetes iela 22; rooms without breakfast 12.50 Ls per person, self-catering apartments from 23 Ls per person) arranges rooms in private flats all over Latvia.

## Hotels

**Aurora** (☎ 722 44 79; Marijas iela 5; singles/doubles/triples with shared bathroom 6/9/12 Ls), a cheapie by the train station, has small and noisy rooms.

**Viktorija** (☎ 701 41 11, fax 731 06 29, 701 41 40; W www.hotel-viktorija.lv; A Čaka iela 55; singles/doubles with shared bathroom 12/17 Ls, with bathroom & breakfast 30/40 Ls), 1km northeast of the train station, wins the prize hands-down for Rīga's best-value budget accommodation. Bathroom-less rooms are mostly renovated and shared showers are new, clean and pleasant to use.

**Saulīte** (☎ 722 45 46, fax 722 36 29; Merķeļa iela 12; singles/doubles with shared bathroom from 7/11 Ls, with shower & toilet 16/22 Ls) is a run-down joint around the corner from Aurora. The repainting job has long worn away here and prices reflect the degree of refurbishment.

**Mežaparks** (☎ 755 79 88, fax 755 79 64; Sakses iela 19, Mežaparks; doubles with shared bathroom 7 Ls, luxury doubles 15-30 Ls) is one of Rīga's top cheap hotels and comes complete with outstanding lake views. 'Luxury' doubles simply have a bathroom. Take trolleybus No 2 to the last stop.

**Elias** (☎ 751 81 17; Hamburgas iela 14; doubles 16 Ls), out of town close to Lake Kišezers, has seven large rooms. Take tram No 11 from K Barona iela.

## PLACES TO STAY – MID-RANGE

Prices quoted include breakfast unless mentioned otherwise. The bathroom-clad rooms at the Viktorija (see the previous section) offer excellent value mid-range accommodation too.

**Valdemārs** (☎ 733 44 62, fax 733 30 01; W www.valdemars.lv; Valdemāra iela 23; small singles/doubles without breakfast 14/22 Ls, larger singles/doubles without breakfast 20/28 Ls), with its age-old furnishings and creaky corridors, is a tad jaded. Nonetheless, its central location makes it worth a mention.

**Laine** (☎ 728 88 16, 728 98 23, fax 728 76 58; W www.laine.lv; Skolas iela 11; singles/doubles/triples with shared bathroom 15/25/30 Ls, singles/doubles with private bathroom 35/45 Ls, luxury singles/doubles with terrace and jacuzzi 60/70 Ls), tucked in a courtyard off the main street, appears run-down from the outside but isn't. Its jolly decor is green and yellow candy-striped.

**Tia** (☎ 733 39 18, fax 783 03 90; W www.tia.lv; K Valdemāra iela 63; singles/doubles/triples Oct-May from 29/36/51 Ls, June-Sept from 32/40/65 Ls) has simple but soulful rooms with unusually nice bathrooms.

**Radi un Draugi** (☎ 722 03 72, fax 724 22 39; W www.draugi.lv; Mārstaļu iela 1; singles/doubles from 33/42 Ls), in old Rīga, is owned by British-Latvians and is clean, popular and often fully booked.

**Forums** (☎ 781 46 80, fax 781 46 82; W www.hotelforums.lv; Vaļņu iela 45; doubles from 37 Ls) warrants no complaints, with comfortable rooms inside a terracotta townhouse.

**Oma** (☎ 761 33 88, fax 761 32 33; e oma@latnet.lv; Ernestīnes iela 33; singles/doubles 33/43 Ls), if you don't mind being across the river, is a pleasing hotel in a quiet neighbourhood where rooms have fresh wooden furniture.

**Karavella** (☎ 732 31 30, fax 783 01 87; W www.karavella.lv; Katrīnas dambis iela 27; singles/doubles 30/36 Ls) is a tower block in the Pētersala area, 2km north of the Old Town close to the ferry terminal. It is a fairly modern hotel run by the Latvian Shipping Company, in the Seamen's Centre. Take tram No 5 or 9, north along Aspazijas bulvāris and Kronvalda bulvāris in the city centre to the Eksporta stop on the corner of Pētersalas iela and Katrīnas dambis, 500m south of the hotel.

**Ķeizarmežs** (☎ 751 75 10, fax 755 74 61; Ezermalas iela 30; doubles from 30 Ls) is the natural choice for those seeking somewhere to sleep away from the city hustle and bustle. Ķeizarmežs is a modern block overlooking Lake Ķišezers, 7km north of the centre in Rīga's green and flowery Mežaparks.

## PLACES TO STAY – TOP END

Rīga has top hotels galore, most of which cater to a predominantly business clientele, meaning they're less than full at weekends; many offer special weekend deals as a result. Breakfast is included in the prices, unless stated otherwise.

**Ainavas** (☎ 781 43 16, fax 781 43 17; W www.ainavas.lv; Peldu iela 23; singles/doubles 60/77 Ls) markets itself as a boutique hotel and indeed, it is stylish. Each room depicts a different landscape ('Landscapes' is the name of the hotel), depicted in a painting above the bed. Heated bathroom floors and web TV are among the perks at this original spot, inside a 15th-century townhouse.

**Centra** (☎ 722 64 41, fax 750 32 81; W www.centra.lv; Audēju iela 1; singles/doubles 45/50 Ls Mar-Oct, 35/44 Ls Nov-Feb), in an old-town building dating to 1884, sports the ultimate in contemporary design.

**Konventa Sēta** (☎ 708 75 01/2/3, fax 708 75 15; Kalēju iela 9/11; singles/doubles 46/55 Ls) is a unique hotel within the restored courtyards of a 15th-century convent. The 10 medieval buildings are named after their original uses (in German and Latvian) and the rooms are exquisitely furnished.

**Gutenbergs** (☎ 781 40 90, fax 750 33 26; W www.gutenbergs.lv; Doma Laukums 1; doubles 60 Ls), a gorgeous place in the heart of the Old Town, is worth staying at, if only to dine in its stunning rooftop restaurant overlooking the spire of St Peter's Church.

**Reval Hotel Latvija** (☎ 777 22 22, fax 777 22 21; e latvija@revalhotels.com; Elizabetes iela 55; doubles from 79 Ls), once an Intourist hotel that sent shivers down the spine of many a Latvian, is a sparkling 27-storey tower of wealth and luxury today. Views from the 26th-floor bar are the best in Rīga (even better than St Peter's).

**Man-Tess** (☎ 721 60 56, fax 782 12 49; W www.mantess.lv; Teātra iela 6; singles/doubles without breakfast 55/85 Ls) is a tiny hotel in the Old Town with a stunning 18th-century facade – painted orange. Breakfast costs 4.50 Ls extra.

**Metropole** (☎ 722 54 11, fax 721 61 40; W www.metropole.lv; Aspazijas bulvāris 36-38; singles/doubles 48/54 Ls), down towards the station, was renowned as a centre of diplomatic intrigue and espionage in the 1930s.

**Radisson-SAS Daugava** (☎ 706 11 11, fax 706 11 00; W www.radisson.com/rigalv; Ku-u iela 24; doubles Mon-Fri/Sat & Sun 69/45 Ls), considered to be on the 'wrong' side of the river by many, has great views of the old-town skyline, and every imaginable facility – fitness centre, indoor swimming pool, sauna and a restaurant renowned for its Sunday brunch.

**Hotel de Rome** (☎ 708 76 00, fax 708 76 06; W www.derome.lv; Kalķu iela 28; singles/doubles from 91/100 Ls), for a long time Rīga's most prestigious hotel following its 1991 opening, remains popular with those travelling on an account other than their own.

## PLACES TO EAT

Dining out in Rīga is dizzying. The choice of cuisine – be it Korean, Caribbean or Caucasian – can be overwhelming. Thankfully, for those seeking good old-fashioned Latvian food at a price that won't break the bank, there's the self-service, cafeteria-style eateries run by the hugely successful Lido chain – all keep a comfortable country-style decor and several are listed here.

In summer, in true Mediterranean style, tables and chairs spill out onto Doma laukums and the open-air plaza along Kalķu iela, transforming the Old Town into a fun-packed plaza of cheap cafés, beer tents and late-night bars.

### Old Rīga

**Alus sēta** (☎ 722 24 31; Tirgoņu iela 6; meals 3 Ls; open 10am-1am daily), Lido's only old-town outlet, has fabulous outside seating overlooking Doma laukums and serves hearty Latvian cuisine at unbeatable prices.

**Divi laši** (☎ 721 34 70; Tirgoņu iela 8; meals 5 Ls; open 11am-1am daily), or Two Salmon as it's called in English, is Rīga's cheap fish choice with a sunny street terrace to boot. Look for the canoe moored outside.

**Ķiploka krogs** (☎ 721 14 51; Jēkaba iela 3; meals 3 Ls; open noon-midnight daily), probably not the place for a first date, dishes up garlic in all shapes, sizes and guises. The Garlic Bar also doubles as a bar (albeit a smelly-breathed one).

**Nostal-ija** (☎ 722 23 38; Kalķu iela 22; open 10am-2am daily), a retro Soviet restaurant, is the place for time travellers seeking a blast to the past. The truly mad can disco until 5am Thursday to Saturday.

**Austrumu robeža** (Eastern Border; ☎ 781 42 03; Vāgnera iela 8; meals 5 Ls; open 8.30am-midnight daily) is likewise worth a peep for its Soviet memorabilia. Eastern Border, with its entrance on Gleznotāju iela, is 1011km from Moscow.

**Lotoss** (☎ 721 26 65; Skārņu iela 7; meals 2-3 Ls; open 10am or 11am-11pm or midnight daily) lures a people-watching set with its fabulous windows and refreshing range of light lunch dishes – many meatless – on its European menu.

**Kamāla** (☎ 721 13 32; e kamala@delfi.lv; Jauniela 14; meals 5 Ls; open 8.30am-midnight daily), named after the wife of Vishnu and the daughter of the milk ocean, exudes spiritualism. Dishes are strictly vegetarian.

**Ķirbis** (The Pumpkin; Doma laukums 1; meals 5 Ls; open 9am-11pm Mon-Fri, 10am-11pm Sat & Sun), beside the cathedral, is Rīga's other vegetarian rave where heaps of colourful vegetable dishes are served buffet-style. The food is excellent, priced by weight and washes down well with freshly squeezed juices.

**1739** (☎ 721 13 98; Skārņu iela 6; meals 10 Ls; open noon-11pm daily), an upmarket Italian restaurant you pass heading towards St Peter's Church, serves authentic pastas, meat dishes and soups in a calm, refined atmosphere.

**Zivju** (☎ 721 67 13; Vāgnera iela 4; meals 15-25 Ls; open noon-midnight daily) is the expensive fish option. Its cooked tiger shrimps in fennel sauce (a mere 9.40 Ls) are sublime.

**Palete** (☎ 721 60 37; Gleznotāju iela 8; meals 10 Ls; open noon-midnight daily), a très elegante and expensive restaurant, is the place to go for fine dining; the Latvian cook spent five years cooking for Latvia's former president, and makes a tender champagne-poached sea bass or salmon teriyaki. There's piano or guitar music most nights.

## Other Areas

**Dzirnavas** (☎ 728 62 04; Dzirnavu iela 76; meals 2-3 Ls; open 8am-11pm daily), or 'The Mill' as it's called in English, is built on the site of an old mill no less. Lido is behind this authentic Latvian kitchen too.

**Vērmanītis** (☎ 728 62 89; Elizabetes iela 65; meals 2-3 Ls; open 8am-1am daily), like Dzirnavas, has the whole works – meat, potatoes, rice, salads, desserts. It overlooks a green park.

**Staburags** (A Čaka iela 57; meals 3 Ls; open noon-1am daily) is a rustic Latvian joint serving great ribs, peas and lots of beer in a cheap, farmhouse setting. The waterwheel downstairs symbolises the waterfall that used to exist at Staburags, 75km southeast of Rīga, which was flooded by a Stalin-era hydroelectric project.

**Lido atpūtas centrs** (☎ 781 21 87; Krasta iela 76; meals 2-3 Ls; open 10am-11pm daily), officially called Lido Relaxation Centre but dubbed Lido Land by those in the know, is worth the short trek. The vast eating and drinking complex is Lido at its best – there's food galore, all sorts of things to entertain the kids (animals, electric cars, a playground) and folk musicians play every evening from 7pm. You can spend a day here in fact discovering Latvia. Take bus No 107 from in front of the train station to the Lido stop.

**Russkij Dvor** (Russian Homestead; ☎ 713 49 30; Ķengaraga iela 3; meals 2-3 Ls; open 10am-11pm daily) will make you smile. Giant-sized matroshkas (Russian dolls) dot the colourful garden, and the interior is Russian kitsch at its best. A short distance from the centre, it's run by Lido.

**Traktieris** (☎ 733 24 55; Antonijas iela 8; meals 4 Ls; open 11am-11pm daily), a Russian restaurant, serves fantastic food at reasonable prices. Even the borsch is good. For dessert try the warm blinis with thick honey. Service is slack but can pick up if you speak Russian.

**Osiris** (☎ 724 30 02; K Barona iela 31; meals 5-7 Ls; open 8am-midnight Mon-Fri, 10am-midnight Sat & Sun), somewhat of a Rīga institution, remains one of the city's best spots for a leisurely breakfast or romantic evening glass of wine.

**Charlestons** (☎ 777 05 73; Blaumaņa iela 38-40; meals 6-8 Ls; open 8am-midnight daily) has a cappuccino bar, Tex-Mex grill, good-value lunchtime specials (around 2 Ls), a sumptuous display of creamy cakes and a pleasant summer terrace.

**Andalūzijas Suns** (Andalusian Dog; ☎ 728 84 18; Elizabetes iela 83/85; meals 4-8 Ls; open 11am-1am daily), a trendy bistro place in the Berga bazārs shopping mall, serves Tex Mex, pasta, burgers and karbonāde (grilled meat chop) including dozens of different Italian-, French- and other European-inspired sauces. Service is refreshingly speedy.

**Melnie mūki** (The Black Monks; ☎ 721 50 06; Jāņa sēta 1; meals 10 Ls; open noon-2am daily), just around the corner from the Andalusian Dog, serves upmarket Latvian cuisine in a beautiful setting.

**Vincents** (☎ 733 26 34; Elizabetes iela 19; meals 10-15 Ls; open 11am-midnight daily), inspired by Van Gogh, claims to have the best chef in town. Every summer the restaurant adopts a European theme – Catalonian and French have already rolled around, but future cuisines promise to be equally delicious. Also in summer, tables and chairs are put outside and the barbecued meats are cooked in front of you.

## Cafés

The city's café scene is fun, fun, fun and never more so than during Latvia's short but sweet summer when café terraces fill most of the many old-town squares and side streets. Come rain or hail, hot spots worthy of a warm-up include the following.

**Pulvertornis** (Valņu iela 3; soups/salads/meat dishes from 0.17/0.19/0.75 Ls; open 8am-8pm Mon-Fri, 9am-6pm Sat & Sun) is a dirt cheap café in the Old Town, dishing up simple cheap grub with no frills attached.

**Pauze** (Brīvības iela 3; meals 1-2 Ls; open 9am-10pm Mon-Fri, 10am-9pm Sat), featuring large windows overlooking busy Brīvības, is another cheap and cheerful spot with a canteen-style buffet.

**Senais Fredis** (☎ 722 64 63; Audēju iela 5) is one of the most unpretentious places in the Old Town to meet friends and eat lightly.

**Kolonāde** (☎ 722 35 04; Brīvības bulvāris 26), under the watchful gaze of Milda and the Laima clock, is very much a Rīga institution. Its refined terrace garden overlooks the opera house.

**Coffee Nation** (K Valdemāra iela 21; open 8am-10pm daily), a modern coffee bar, is unbeatable for sinking into a comfy armchair with a book and an extra large cappuccino, café latte or machiato. Its freshly squeezed beetroot juice is said to induce a good mood.

**Monte Kristo** (☎ 737 23 46; Ģertrūdes iela 27; open 9am-9pm Mon-Sat, noon-9pm Sun), favoured for its exotic range of coffee and cakes, has another **branch** (☎ 722 74 43; Kalēju iela 18/22) in the centre.

**Rāma** (☎ 727 24 90; K Barona iela 56; meals 1.5 Ls; open 9am-midnight Mon-Sat, 11am-7pm Sun), the café of the Society for Krishna Consciousness, lolls in a lovely pink-and-violet wooden house. Vegie fodder is dished up for no more than 1.50 Ls a tummyful.

**Zen** (☎ 731 65 21; Stabu iela 6; open noon-midnight daily) is as zen as zen can be at this oriental teahouse. Loll on floor cushions and watch your tea being prepared – the full ritual takes a very thirsty 20 minutes.

**Habibi** (☎ 722 85 51; Peldu iela 24; open noon-midnight daily), run by an English- and Russian-speaking Egyptian, has a rich and exotic interior, clad with cushions, carpets and a back room where local belly dancers shake their stuff to a water-pipe smoking clientele. Fruit-flavoured tobacco costs 5 Ls a pipe.

**Šalom** (☎ 736 49 11; Brīvības iela 158; meals 4 Ls; open noon-11pm daily) is the main hangout for Rīga's Jewish community, although kosher food has to be ordered in advance.

## Fast Food

Rīga's most popular fast food options are listed in the boxed text 'Pasties, Pancakes & Dumplings'.

**Pizza Jazz** (Raiņa bulvāris 15 • Brīvibas iela 76; open 10am-midnight Mon-Sat, 11am-midnight Sun), a Lithuanian-run chain, is said to serve the biggest and best pizza in town. Book in advance to bag a table.

**Pizza Lulū** (Ģertrūdes iela 27 • K Valdemāra iela 143-145; w www.lulu.lv; open 24hr) is run by a Canadian-Latvian team and is best for giant-sized pizza slices any time of day or night.

## Self-Catering

**Central market** (Prāgas iela; open 7.30am-6pm Tues-Sat, 7.30am-4pm Sun & Mon), Rīga's colourful market, is housed in five great zeppelin hangars behind the bus station (see the boxed text 'Central Market' earlier).

**Interpegro** (Marijas iela 1; open 7am-midnight daily) is a supermarket that's opposite the train station. Look out for the large **Stockmann** supermarket, being built by the Finns between the train and bus stations on 13 janvāra iela.

There is also the large **Rimi** (K Barona iela 46; open 8am-midnight daily) supermarket inside the Barona Centrs, a small shopping centre on three floors.

## ENTERTAINMENT

Rīga has a giddying entertainment and cultural scene. Upcoming events are listed in the Baltic Times, Rīga In Your Pocket and Rīga This Week.

## Pubs & Bars

**Rīgas Balzams** (☎ 721 44 94; Torņa iela 4; open 11am-midnight Mon-Fri, noon-midnight Sat & Sun) is a must. Ordering anything other than a black balzams is sacrilege. To discover what exactly you downed, see the

## Pasties, Pancakes & Dumplings

Latvia's answer to fast food can be found stuffed inside *pelmeņi* (meat dumplings fried, boiled or swimming in soup), *pīrāgi* (meat pasties baked in the oven) and *pankuki* (pancakes). Which is maybe why the big international fast-food chains are refreshingly few and far between in the Latvian capital.

Dozens of places dish up pasties, pancakes and dumplings. Temples devoted exclusively to the latter include **Pelmeņi** (*A Čaka iela 38a; open 8am-9pm Mon-Fri, 9am-8pm Sat*) and **Pelmeņi XL** (*Kaļķu iela 7; open 9am-4am daily*), two calorie-heavy spots where you can indulge to your heart's content – eat in or take away – for 0.55 Ls a dumpling. Pelmeņi, a cheerful polka-dotted place with its entrance on Ģertrūdes iela, cooks up soup (from 0.45 Ls) too.

The mother-in-law bakes the best pīrāgi at **Sievasmātes pīrādziņi** (*Kaļķu iela 10; open 9am-9pm Mon-Fri, 10am-9pm Sat & Sun*), quite literally called Mother-in-Law's Pīrāgi. The cute little pasties come stuffed with meat, mushrooms, fruit or cheese.

Pancakes with sweet and savoury toppings and fillings are the reason behind that long lunchtime queue that spills into the street outside **Šetpavārs Vilhelms** (*Chef William; Šķūņu iela 6; open 9am-10pm Mon-Fri, 10am-10pm Sat & Sun*), another cafeteria-style place in old Rīga.

boxed text 'Black Magic' in the Facts for the Visitor chapter.

**Ai Karamba!** (*☎ 733 46 72; Pulkveža Brieža iela 2; open 8am-midnight Mon-Sat, 9am or 10am-midnight Sun*), a laid-back and funky place reminiscent of an American diner, is a great spot for an inexpensive early breakfast, late-evening drink, and everything else in between.

**Lidojošā** (*☎ 732 11 84; Elizabetes iela 31; open 10am-midnight daily*), a cellar joint, serves lots of food and beer, much to the delight of the mainly foreign crowd which frequents Rīga's Flying Frog.

**Pulkvedim neviens neraksta** (*No-one Writes to the Colonel; ☎ 721 38 86; Peldu iela 26-28; open noon-2am Sun-Thur, noon-5am Fri & Sat*), an old favourite still going strong, is a bar and disco rolled into one where dedicated party animals continue to end the night.

**Paldies Dievam piektdiena ir klāt** (*Thank God It's Friday; ☎ 750 39 64; 11 novembra krastmala 9; open noon-2am or 4am daily*), a Caribbean bar-cum-restaurant in the Old Town, is favoured for its imaginative and exhaustive cocktail menu.

**Dickens** (*☎ 721 30 87; Grēcinieku iela 9/1; open 11am-midnight Sun-Thur, 11am-2am Fri & Sat*), a *britu krogs* (British pub), is where most anglophone expats kick off a night out. Guinness/Kilkenny costs 1.70/1.60 Ls a pint.

**Paddy Whelan's** (*☎ 721 02 49; Grēcinieku iela 4; open 10am or 11am-midnight or 1am daily*), Rīga's first Irish pub, pulls pints of Aldaris to Latvian youngsters downstairs

and older foreigners upstairs. Good pub grub and bands are other drawcards.

**Dublin** (*☎ 722 35 87; Vāgnera iela 16; open noon-2am daily*), Rīga's second Irish pub, is a tad more sedate than Paddy's.

**Tim McShane's** (*☎ 722 24 38; Tirgoņu iela 10; open 11am-1am Mon-Thur & Sun, 10am-4am Fri & Sat*), the third in the trio of Rīgan Irish pubs, attracts a mixed bag of punters.

**Melnais kaķis** (*W www.melnaiskakis.lv; Raiņa bulvāris 15 • Meistaru iela 10-12; Raiņa bulvāris open 11am-3am; Meistaru iela open 9pm-7am daily*), meaning Black Cat, is most drinkers' last port of call. Play pool here, eat or bask in the early-morning sun with a pint in hand.

**DECO bārs** (*☎ 728 92 41; Dzirnavu iela 84; open 11am-1pm Sun-Thur, 11am-5am Fri & Sat*) is known for its cocktails, slick Art Deco decor, chic pavement terrace and – come the early hours – its ultra-hip dance floor. The bar is in the Berga bazārs shopping mall.

**Skyline** (*☎ 777 22 22; Elizabetes iela 55; open 4pm-2am daily*), sky high on the 26th floor of the Reval Hotel Latvija, is a must for every first-time visitor to the capital. The crowd is glam and the city view is nothing short of stunning.

## Nightclubs

**M-808** (*☎ 724 06 33; W http://m.808.lv; Lāčplēša iela 5; open 9pm-5am Fri & Sat*), an alternative music club, lures a frantic crowd with its predominantly techno and house beats.

**Dizzi** (☎ 722 19 02; Mārstaļu iela 10; open 9pm-6am Wed-Sat), with its front door on Alksnāja iela, is Rīga's other house-music hide-out.

**Četri balti krekli** (☎ 721 38 85; w www .krekli.lv; Vecpilsētas iela 12; open noon-5am Mon-Sat, 5pm-3am Sun), literally 'Four White Shirts', is the top place to listen to Latvian rock bands. Under 21s aren't let in.

**Cita Opera** (☎ 722 07 70; w www.cita opera.lv; Raiņa bulvāris 21; open noon-last customer daily), in a cellar, plays live music from 10pm on Friday and Saturday.

**Groks** (☎ 721 63 81; Kaļķu iela 12; open noon-6am daily) is a flashback to life under communism. The modern club comes decked out as a Soviet train, complete with the cloak-room in a recreated train compartment and the DJ in the driver's cabin.

**Slepenais Eksperiments** (☎ 722 79 17; w www.slepenais.lv; Skūņu iela 15; open noon-4am daily), an industrial-designed club that has been around a long time, lures a young and energetic crowd.

**Roxy** (☎ 722 40 41; Kaļķu iela 24; open 9pm-6am daily) is a mainstream club, popular with 20-something Rīgans, bang slap in the centre of the Old Town.

**Hollywood Stardisco** (☎ 724 22 89; Skolas iela 2; open 9am-6am Thur-Sun), a large and flashy in-your-face nightclub across from the park, offers free entrance between 9pm and 11pm.

**Casablanca** (☎ 721 24 20; w www.casa blanca.lv; Smilšu iela 1-3; open 10am-1am Mon, 10am-2am Tues, 10am-3am Wed & Thur, 10am-5am Fri, noon-5am Sat, noon-midnight Sun), next to TV5, is flash, brash and full of beautiful people. Record your own two-minute TV broadcast in TV5's self-recording booth on the street outside.

**Nautilus** (☎ 781 44 77; Kungu iela 8; open 10pm-7am Wed-Sat), in the same building as a Japanese restaurant, is another hot and frantic dance floor in the Old Town.

**XXL** (☎ 728 22 76; Kalniņa iela 4; open 4pm-7am daily), Rīga's sole gay club and video bar, makes no bones about the 'face kontrole' bouncers rigorously exercise at the door.

## Classical Music
The main concert hall of the renowned Latvia National Symphonic Orchestra is the **Great Guild** (Lielā -ilde; Amatu iela 6), host to numerous other concerts too. Tickets cost

2 Ls to 7 Ls and are sold at the **box office** (☎ 721 36 43; Amatu iela 6; open noon-6pm & two hours before performances). Concerts are also held in the **Small Guild** (Mazā -ilde; Amatu iela 3-5) opposite.

Chamber and solo concerts are often held at the **Wagner Hall** (Vāgnera Zālē; ☎ 721 08 14; Vāgnera iela 4; box office open noon-3pm & 4pm-7pm daily).

The Dome Cathedral's acoustics, as well as its huge organ, are spectacular (see the old Rīga section earlier) and the twice-weekly evening organ concerts (Wednesday and Friday at 7pm) are well worth attending. Tickets (1 to 3 Ls) and concert programmes are available from the cathedral **ticket office** (☎ 721 32 13; open noon-3pm & 4pm-7pm daily), opposite the western door; from the Wagner Hall box office (see earlier); and 30 minutes before performances start.

## Cinemas
Films are generally shown in their original language – often English – with Latvian or Russian subtitles. Tickets cost about 2.50 Ls; some cinemas give 10% discounts to ISIC card holders. Call ☎ 722 22 22 or 777 07 77 (English spoken) to find out what's showing where. On the Net, see w www.filmas.lv and w www.baltcinema.lv.

Cinemas include the artsy **Kino Suns** (☎ 728 54 11; Elizabetes iela 83-85); and the mainstream **Daile** (☎ 728 38 54; K Barona iela 31) and **Kino 52** (☎ 728 87 78; Lāčplēsa iela 52-54).

**Kinogalerija** (☎ 722 90 30; Jauniela 24) hosts the British Film Club on Friday.

## Opera, Ballet & Theatre
**National Opera House** (information ☎ 707 377 77, advance bookings ☎ 707 37 45, 707 37 76, fax 707 37 82; w www.opera.lv; Aspazijas bulvāris 3; tickets 1-10 Ls; box office open 10am-7pm daily) is the home of the highly rated Rīga Ballet where Mikhail Baryshnikov made his name. Performances start most nights at 7pm.

The **Daile Theatre** (Dailes teātris; ☎ 727 02 78; Brīvības iela 75) and the **New Rīga Theatre** (Rīgas jaunais teātris; ☎ 728 07 65; w www.jrt.lv; Lāčplēsa iela 25) stage plays in Latvian. Plays in Russian take to the stage at the **Russian Drama Theatre** (Krievu drāmas teātris; ☎ 722 53 95; w www.trd.lv; Kaļķu iela 16).

Ballet, opera and theatre break for summer holidays, around June to September.

## Circus
Rīga's permanent circus (Cirks; ☎ 721 32 79; ℮ circusriga@apollo.lv; Merķeļa iela 4; tickets 1-3 Ls; shows twice daily Fri-Sun Oct-Apr) is close to the train station.

## SPECTATOR SPORTS
Football is the most popular spectator sport (posters around town announce big games), followed closely by basketball. The city's leading football clubs, PFK Daugava and FC Skonto, play at Rīga's **Daugava Sports House** (Daugavas Sporta Nams; ☎ 727 62 75, 727 20 30; K Barona iela 107), which seats 5000; and the **Skonto Stadium** (☎ 702 09 09; E Melngaila iela 1a), with a capacity of 8300. Ice hockey is played at the Daugava, although Latvia hopes to build a bigger and better multipurpose arena for the 2006 World Ice Hockey Championships, which it will host.

## SHOPPING
Street sellers peddle their wares – amber trinkets, woollen socks and mittens, paintings and Russian dolls – outside St Peter's Church on Skarnu iela and along the southern end of Vaļņu iela. Rīga's large crafts fair, the Gadatirgus, is held on the first weekend in June.

**Centrs Universālveikals** (cnr Vaļņu iela & Audēju iela), in the Old Town, is the only department store; a large branch of the newspaper and magazine shop, Narvesen, is on the ground floor.

**Berga bazārs** (Dzirnavu iela 84), literally 'Bergs Bazaar', is an upmarket mall, originally built in the late 19th century by Kristaps Bergs (1840–1907), and reconstructed in the late 1990s. The maze of courtyards is sandwiched between Elizabētes, Marijas and Dzirnavu, and has plenty of fine boutiques and galleries to browse in.

Among the mind-boggling plethora of craft and souvenir shops in Rīga, consider shopping at the **A&E Gallery** (Jauniela iela 17), off Doma laukums, for amber; **Upe** (Vāgnera iela 5) for folk music, traditional instruments and unusual toys beautifully carved from wood; **Senā Klēts** (Merķeļa iela 13) for Latvian national costumes; **Musikas salons** (Audēju iela 6) for Latvian rock, pop

### Sweetness & Light
Laima – synonymous with all things sweet in Latvia – is known as much in the capital for the city clock on which its chocolate has been advertised since 1924 as for its devilishly irresistible candies.

The country's oldest and most successful confectioner, Rīga-based Laima produces 150 different products and employs a workforce of around 800. Its chocolate-covered 'serenade', a candy sweetly stuffed with apple, apricot jam and nuts, and wrapped in shiny blue paper, is a Laima classic – as is its 'esmeralda' striped caramel. Marshmallows dipped in chocolate and flavoured with rose or vanilla, and soft caramels concocted from lemons, apples, cherries or blackcurrants are other popular suckers on its repertoire. Its slabs of dark or milk chocolate and crunchy 'Triks' chocolate bar make great trolleybus-munching material.

**Laima** (Ģertrudes iela 6 • Miera iela 22 • Smilšu iela 16 • Marijas iela 16; all open Mon-Sat) has a chain of confectionary shops in Rīga. The so-called 'Laima Clock' – a decades-old meeting spot for Rīgans – stands on the corner of Aspazijas bulvāris and Brīvības bulvāris.

and classical music; and **Sakta** (Aspazijas iela 30) for Latvian flags and wooden jewellery.

**Nordwear** (☎ 750 35 46; ₩ www.nordwear.com; Kaļķu iela 2; open 10am-7pm Mon-Fri, 10am-6pm Sat) is where Australian-born Aldis Tilēns sells Nordic wool sweaters patterned with tiny Latvian symbols and other 'amber-free' souvenirs.

**Latvijas Balzams** (☎ 722 87 15; Marijas iela 1) sells Latvian Balzams and other alcohols.

## GETTING THERE & AWAY
See the introductory Getting There & Away chapter for links with countries outside the Baltics.

### Air
Rīga airport (Lidosta Rīga; information ☎ 720 70 09; ₩ www.riga-airport.com) is at Skulte, about 8km west of the city centre. Most major European airlines have an office here, including Latvia's national carrier **AirBaltic** (☎ 720 77 77; ₩ www.airbaltic.com; airport & Kaļķu iela 15). Its Estonian counterpart,

**Estonian Air** (☎ *721 48 60;* ⓦ *www.estonian -air.ee; Kaļķu iela 15*) is in town.

AirBaltic flies twice daily Monday to Friday to/from Tallinn (code-sharing with Estonian Air) and twice a day Tuesday to Thursday to/from Vilnius. Return fares to Tallinn/Vilnius start at 76/75 Ls (three day advance purchase, maximum stay of five days).

## Bus

Buses to/from other towns and cities use Rīga's **international bus station** (*Rīgas starptautiskā autoosta;* ⓦ *www.autoosta.lv; Prāgas iela 1*), behind the railway embankment just beyond the southern edge of the Old Town. Up-to-date timetables are displayed both in the station (with final destination and departure platforms) and on the bus station's well-organised website; fares can also be checked online. Most staff in the **information office** (*izziņas;* ☎ *900 00 09; open 6am-11pm daily*) speak English.

**Ecolines** (☎ *721 45 12;* ⓦ *www.ecolines.lv; open 7am-8pm Mon-Fri, 7am-7pm Sat & Sun*) has an office at the bus station and another called **Norma-A** (☎ *727 44 44; A Čaka iela 45*) in town. It runs weekly services to/from Bremerhaven in Germany, Brussels, Kyiv, London, Moscow, Paris and Prague. See the introductory Getting There & Away chapter for details.

Weekly buses to Berlin and other cities in Germany, St Petersburg (via Jēkabpils and Rēzekne) and Kaliningrad are operated by **Eurolines** (☎ *721 40 80;* ⓦ *www.eurolines.lv; open 8am-7pm Mon-Sat, 9am-6pm Sun*), based at the bus station. Eurolines also runs daily inter-regional services to/from Valga (4.50 Ls, 3¼ hours, one daily), Tartu (8.50 Ls, 4¾ hours, one daily), Tallinn (7-8.50 Ls, 5¼ hours, five daily), Vilnius (6 Ls, five hours, four daily) and Kaunas (5.20 Ls, 3½ hours, one daily). There are also two daily buses to/from Klaipēda (5.20 Ls, six hours).

Bus services within Latvia include, among others, the following:

**Bauska** 1.20 Ls, 1½ hours, 65km, hourly between 5.30am and 5.10pm
**Cēsis** 1.30 Ls, 2 hours, 90km, hourly between 6.30am and 6.55pm
**Daugavpils** 3 Ls, 4 hours, 230km, up to seven daily
**Jelgava** 0.55-0.78 Ls, 1 hour, 40km, one or two daily
**Kolka** 2.35-2.98 Ls, 5¾ hours, 160km, three daily

**Kuldīga** 2.20 Ls, 3-4 hours, 150km, six to 10 daily
**Liepāja** 2.98 Ls, 3½ hours direct, 4-4½ hours via Kalnciems, 5-7 hours via Jelgava or Tukums, 220km, hourly between 6.40am and 4.45pm
**Rēzekne** 2.70 Ls, 4½ hours, 245km, up to six daily
**Sigulda** 0.90 Ls, 1 hour, 50km, hourly between 8.15am and 8.10pm
**Talsi** 1.65 Ls, 2½ hours, 115km, hourly between 7.55am and 8.45pm
**Tukums** 0.95 Ls, 1¼ hours, 63km, eight daily
**Valka** 1.05-2 Ls, 3¾ hours, 175km, up to four daily
**Valmiera** 1.30 Ls, 2½ hours, 120km, hourly between 6.20am and 10.20pm
**Ventspils** 2.70 Ls, 2½-4 hours, 200km, hourly between 7.05am and 10.30pm

## Train

Rīga **train station** (*centrālā stacija;* ☎ *583 30 95, advance reservations* ☎ *721 66 64; Stacijas laukums*), at the southern end of the park-and-boulevard ring, underwent a €5.8 million facelift in 2002-3.

Tickets are sold in the main departures hall: Window Nos 1-6 sell tickets for international trains (*starptavtiskie vilcieni*); window Nos 7-9 sell tickets for long-distance diesel trains (*dizeļvilcienci*); and window Nos 10-13 sell tickets for slower suburban trains (*elektrovilcienci*).

Staff at the **information desk** (*izziņas;* ☎ *583 21 34; open 8am-7.30pm daily*) don't appear to be very cooperative – a less frustrating bet for schedules is to consult the train timetable on Latvian Railways' website at ⓦ www.ldz.lv.

**Suburban** There are six suburban lines out of Rīga, served in the main by electric commuter trains (*elektrovilcienci*). Some larger suburban stations, like Valmiera, are served by speedier diesel trains en route to destinations further afield.

**Ergļi–Suntaži** Three trains daily take this line.
**Jelgava** One or two trains an hour go to Jelgava between 5.40am and 11.05pm. Some long-distance trains to Ventspils, Šiauliai, Kaunas and Vilnius stop at Jelgava too.
**Ogre–Krustpils** This line follows the Daugava River inland to Krustpils, opposite Jēkabpils. Trains terminate at all destinations between 5.10am and 11.12pm. Destinations include Ogre, Lielvārde, Aizkraukle or Krustpils. Long-distance trains heading to Daugavpils, Rēzekne, Zilupe and Moscow also take this line.
**Priedaine–Dubulti–Sloka–Ķemeri–Tukums** This is the line to take for Jūrmala. Two to five trains an

hour leave for each of Ķemeri, Sloka and Tukums II between 5.45am and 11.10pm. All call at Dubulti and most – but not all – at Majori.

**Saulkrasti–Skulte** Two to three trains an hour leave for varying destinations, including Skulte and Vecāķi, between 5.52am and 11.08pm.

**Sigulda–Cēsis–Valmiera** There are four trains daily to Sigulda, two to Cēsis and four to Valmiera. All call at Sigulda; Valmiera trains also call at Cēsis. The long-distance train to St Petersburg also takes this line. This line runs from 5.42am to 10.36pm.

**Long-Distance** The timetable for departures (*atiesanas laiks*) listing the final destination, platform number, name of train and departure time is bang opposite you when you enter the station. To check arrivals (*pienaksanas laiks*), consult on the printed timetables on the wall.

It is quicker to get to Tallinn by bus (see that section earlier). There is a slow overnight train to/from Vilnius (6/8/11 Ls for a seat/couchette/bunk in four-bed compartment, 7½ hours) via Kaunas (but again, the bus is easier to both places), and an overnight train to St Petersburg (10/20/31/50 Ls for a seat/couchette/bunk in four-bed compartment/1st class, 12¾ hours) that stops in Krustpils, Rēzekne and a handful of other towns. Other mainline services include the following.

**Daugavpils** 2.42-3 Ls, 3½-4¼ hours, 218km, four daily

**Liepāja** 2.45 Ls, 5-5¾ hours, 220km, two daily

**Valga via Sigulda, Cēsis & Valmiera** 2 Ls, 3-3½ hours, 168km, one daily

**Ventspils** 2.17 Ls, 4¾ hours, 200km, two daily

## Car & Motorcycle

Motorists have to pay 5 Ls/hour to enter the Old Town, payable with a *viedkarte* – a magnetic strip card, sold and recharged at the information desk inside the Centrs Universālveikals (see Shopping earlier) and out of town at the **Statoil** (*Eksporta iela 1C; open 24hr*) petrol station.

Major car rental firms include:

**Avis** (☎ 722 58 76; W www.avis.lv; Krasta iela 3; Airport ☎ 720 75 35)

**Budget** (Airport ☎ 720 73 27; W www.budget .com)

**Europcar** (☎ 722 26 37, 721 26 52; W www.europ car.lv; Basteja bulvāris 10; Airport ☎ 720 78 25)

**Hertz** (Airport ☎ 720 79 80; W www.hertz.com)

**Sixt** (☎ 722 40 36; W www.sixt.lv; Aspazijas bulvāris 8; Airport ☎ 720 71 31)

## Boat

Rīga's **ferry terminal** (☎ 732 98 82; W www .rop.lv; Eksporta iela 1) is about 1.5km downstream (north) of Akmens Bridge. It is served by a twice-weekly ferry to/from Kiel ferry, tickets being sold at the **Hanza Maritime Agency** (☎ 732 35 69, fax 732 57 51; W www .hanza.lv; Eksporta iela 3a). There is also a twice-weekly ferry to/from Lübeck.

Between mid-April and mid-September the *Max Mols* ferry sails every second day between Nynashamn, 60km south of Stockholm, and Rīga. Fare details are listed in the introductory Getting There & Away chapter. The service is operated by **Rīgas Jūras Līnija** (RJL; Rīga Sea Line; ☎ 720 54 60, fax 720 54 61; W www.rigasealine.lv; Eksporta iela 3a), a young company founded in 2002 which plans possible future ferry services to/from Helsinki (Finland) and the Estonian island of Saaremma.

Ferry tickets are also sold at travel agencies (see Information – Travel Agencies earlier).

**Andrejosta** (☎ 732 32 25, 950 82 75; e support.rsc@apollo.lv; Eksporta iela 1a), Rīga's yacht centre, rents out yachts from 10 Ls per day. It has a mooring depth of up to 4m.

## GETTING AROUND
## To/From the Airport

Bus No 22 runs about every 20 minutes between Rīga airport and the stop on 13 janvāra iela opposite the bus station in central Rīga. Tickets (0.20 Ls) are sold by the bus driver. A taxi to the centre should cost no more than 8 Ls.

## Bus, Tram & Trolleybus

Rīga has 123km of tram lines serving eight different routes and 23 trolleybus lines covering 217km, all operated by **TTP** (☎ 737 13 49; W www.ttp.lv; Brīvības iela 191). The usual ticket-punching system is used on trams, trolleybuses and buses too but different tickets are used on each. Tickets cost 0.20 Ls, and are sold at most news kiosks and by the driver. City transport runs daily from 5.30am to 12.30am. Some routes have an hourly night service. Updated timetables are posted on TTP's website.

## Taxi

Officially, taxis charge 0.30 Ls/km (0.40 Ls between 10pm and 6am) but as a foreigner you could get ripped off. Insist on the meter running before you set off. There are taxi ranks outside the bus and train stations, at the airport and in front of Hotel de Rome.

### Bicycle
You can hire two wheels from **Antīvās atpūtas** *(☎ 955 41 55; Pāvu iela 2)* for 2/1.50 Ls for the first/each consecutive hour. **Trase** *(☎ 728 86 17; Terbatas iela 34)* charges similar rates.

# Around Rīga

A bounty of white-sand beaches and a WWII concentration camp where the earth still groans (or rather beats) lie within easy reach of Rīga. A trifle further afield, take a walk on the wild side through pine forests and atop bogs in the lovely Ķemeri National Park (see the Kurzeme chapter for details).

## JŪRMALA
**pop 56,000**
Jūrmala (Seashore) is the combined name for a string of small towns and resorts stretching 20km along the coast west of Rīga. The beautiful fresh air and relaxed atmosphere have drawn vacationers in droves since the 19th century. In Soviet times 300,000 visitors a year from all over the USSR flooded in to boarding houses, holiday homes and sanatoriums owned by trade unions and other institutions. Today Jūrmala's long, sandy beaches backed by dunes and pine woods and its shady streets lined with low-rise wooden houses are not quite so packed. Despite warnings about swimming in the sea, everyone does (just don't swallow mouthfuls of water). Beware of ticks too (see Health in the introductory Facts for the Visitor chapter).

During Soviet times the Riga–Jūrmala highway, Latvia's only six-laner, was dubbed '10 minutes in America' because locally made films set in the USA were always filmed on it.

## Orientation
Jūrmala lies between the coast, which faces north, and the Lielupe River, which flows parallel to the coast, 1km or 2km inland. The Lielupe finally empties into the Gulf of Rīga 9km west of the mouth of the Daugava.

### ...the Earth Groans

Between 1941 and 1944 about 45,000 Jews from Rīga and about 55,000 other people, including Jews from other Nazi-occupied countries and prisoners of war, were murdered in the Nazi concentration camp at Salaspils, 15km southeast of Rīga. Giant, gaunt sculptures stand as a memorial on the site which stretches over 40 hectares. The inscription on the huge concrete bunker which forms the centrepiece of the memorial reads 'Behind this gate the earth groans' – a line from a poem written by the Latvian writer Eizens Veveris, who was imprisoned in the camp. Inside the bunker a small exhibition recounts the horrors of the camp. In its shadow lies a 6m-long block of polished stone with a metronome inside, ticking a haunting heartbeat which never stops.

To get there from Rīga, take a suburban train on the Ogre–Krustpils line to Dārziņi (not Salaspils) station. A path leads from the station to the memorial *(piemineklis)* – about a 15-minute walk.

The main townships that make up Jūrmala are, from the eastern (Rīga) end: Priedaine (inland), Lielupe, Bulduri, Dzintari, Majori, Dubulti, Jaundubulti, Pumpuri, Melluži, Asari, Vaivari, Kauguri (on the coast), Sloka (2km inland), and finally Jaunķemeri (on the coast) and ñemeri (6km inland). All except Kauguri and Jaunķemeri have train stations. The busiest part is the 4km to 5km between Bulduri and Dubulti, centred on Majori and Dzintari.

Majori's main street is the 1km-long, pedestrianised Jomas iela. Streets and paths lead through the woods on the left (north) to the beach.

## Information
The **tourist office** *(☎ 776 46 76, fax 776 46 72; ⓦ www.jurmala.lv; Jomas iela 42; open 9am-5pm Mon-Fri Oct-May, 9am-5pm Mon-Fri, 9.30am-5pm Sat & Sun June-Sept)* sells maps and arranges accommodation and guided tours. It distributes the free *Jūrmala This Week*, a quarterly listings guide.

There's a **post office** *(Jomas iela 2)* in front of the town hall and several ATMs in Majori on Jomas iela, including the one outside **Latvijas Unibanka** *(Jomas iela 46)*. Internet

RĪGA

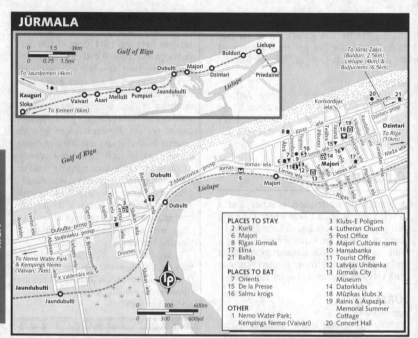

**JŪRMALA**

PLACES TO STAY
2  Kurši
6  Majori
8  Rīgas Jūrmala
17  Elina
21  Baltija

PLACES TO EAT
7  Orients
15  De la Presse
16  Salmu krogs

OTHER
1  Nemo Water Park;
   Kempings Nemo (Vaivari)
3  Klubs-E Poligons
4  Lutheran Church
5  Post Office
9  Majori Cultūras nams
10  Hansabanka
11  Tourist Office
12  Latvijas Unibanka
13  Jūrmala City
    Museum
14  Datorklubs
18  Mūzikas klubs X
19  Rainis & Aspazija
    Memorial Summer
    Cottage
20  Concert Hall

access costs 0.60 Ls per hour at Majori's **Datorklubs** *(Jomas iela; open 24hr)* and **Klubs-E Poligons** *(Slokas iela 20; open 24hr)* in Dubalti. Book your slot in advance at Datorklubs or wait at least an hour for a computer to be free of kids playing games.

### Things to See & Do

Walking the beach, dunes and woods and popping into a couple of cafés is reason enough to come to Jūrmala. Dubulti is its oldest township, while the highest **sand dunes** are at Lielupe. Further west, Vaivari is home to the wet and wonderful **Nemo Water Park** *(Nemo ūdens atrakciju parks;* ☎ 773 63 92; **e** nemo@apollo.lv; *Atbalss iela 1; admission before/after 8pm & all day Mon 5/2.50 Ls; open 11am-11pm Mon-Thur & Sun, 11am-4am Fri & Sat)*, with lots of slides, a sauna and large pool. The centre also rents out bicycles for 3/5 Ls per 30/60 minutes.

In Majori, north off Jomas iela, is poet Jānis Rainis' country cottage, where he died in 1929; it's now the museum **Rainis & Aspazija Memorial Summer Cottage** *(Raiņa un Asparijas vasarnīca;* ☎ 766 42 95; *Pliek-šāna iela 5-7; open 11am-6pm Wed-Sun,*

*closed last Friday of month).* Across Jomas iela, in the **Jūrmala City Museum** *(Jūrmalas pilsētas muzejs;* ☎ 776 47 46; *Tirgoņu iela 29; adult/child 0.50/0.20 Ls; open 11am-5pm Tues-Sun)*, you can view works by local artists and learn how the seaside resort has developed since the 19th century.

Anyone who makes it as far as Buļļuciems, the tiny town beyond Lielupe, will be rewarded by the simple but intriguing open-air **Fishery Museum** *(Jūraslīcis;* ☎ 775 11 21; *Tiklu iela 1a; admission free; open 10am-6pm Mon-Sat)*. It has exhibits (with Latvian captions) about the region's history of fishing, displayed in small cottages and linked by a planked wood walking path. If you call ahead (and speak Latvian), for a fee you can ask to taste some fish.

### Places to Stay

Jūrmala is a spread-out place, so you may have to put in a bit of legwork to find a room. The tourist office can usually guide you to accommodation in your price bracket. It also keeps a list of families that rent private rooms and can help you rent an apartment for longer stays.

## Beach Bum Hot Choice

Jūrmala isn't the only great beach on the Gulf of Rīga. Northeast of Rīga, in the opposite direction from Jūrmala, lie pristine beaches with much less traffic than those at Jūrmala. One good choice, only a 40-minute train ride from Rīga, is **Večaki**. Simply catch a suburban train (0.30 Ls) to Večaki – one runs approximately every half-hour – and follow the crowds on the straight road leading directly east to the beach. A kilometre or so north, the beach becomes nudist.

## Places to Stay – Budget

**Kempings Nemo** (☎ 773 63 92; e nemo@ apollo.lv; Atbalss iela 1; cottage beds Mon-Fri 7.50 Ls, Sat & Sun 12.50, tent pitches 1 Ls per person, car 0.50 Ls) adjoins the Nemo Water Park in Vaivari and sports little wooden cottages as well as green grass to pitch tents on.

**Baltija** (☎ 776 12 73, fax 766 18 4958; e vbaltija@groteks.lv; Kurši; singles/doubles with shared bathroom 15/25 Ls, semi-lux/lux doubles with bathroom 40/60 Ls), a former Soviet monster on nine floors, is so shabby from the outside it appears well and truly closed. Incredibly, it's not. Semi-lux doubles comprise two rooms with fridge, beige sofa and beige furnishings. Only the renovated lux rooms on the 4th floor show any sign of modernity.

## Places to Stay – Mid-Range & Top End

Many of the holiday homes or sanatoriums originally intended for Communist Party high-ups in Soviet times are quite luxurious and almost all are open to whoever chooses to stay in them today. The loveliest are in the quiet streets behind the beach, between Majori and Bulduri.

**Elina** (☎/fax 776 16 65; Lienes iela 43; doubles Sept-May 15 Ls, June-Aug 25 Ls) has five rooms inside a large wooden house; get in quick to snag one.

**Majori** (☎ 776 13 80, 776 13 90, fax 776 13 94; w www.majori.lv; Jomas iela 29; singles/ doubles with breakfast mid-Sept–mid-April 24/36 Ls, mid-May–mid-Sept from 36/54 Ls), with its green canopies and terrace café, is an attractive hotel, almost opposite Majori train station.

**Rīgas Jūrmala** (☎ 776 22 95, fax 776 16 20; e rigas_jurmala@delfi.lv; Jūras iela 23-25; unrenovated singles/doubles from 23/34 Ls, renovated singles/doubles 50/69 Ls), in Majori, is a sight for sore eyes – the 98-room renovated Soviet showpiece is bang-slap on the beach with its own swimming pool, sauna and tennis courts. Breakfast and swimming are included, and sea views command even higher prices than those listed.

**Kursi** (☎ 777 16 06, fax 777 16 05; Dubultu prospkets 30; apartments 24-56 Ls) in Dubulti, is a pleasant new place with apartments surrounding a courtyard and parking area. They come with kitchens and microwaves and rates depend on size. Prices drop in low season.

## Places to Eat

Every second building on Jomas iela offers an eating or drinking option. In summer the street is lined with beer tents and pavement terrace bars and cafés.

**Orients** (Jomas iela 33; meals 5 Ls; open 10am-midnight daily), a Middle Eastern restaurant with a great pavement terrace in Majori, is well worth a nibble. Delve into what Russians call *zakuski* – a tasty platter of salads, cold meats and smoked fish – followed by a hot saslik or fish dish with vegetables.

**De la Presse** (☎ 776 14 01; Jomas iela 57; meals 5-10 Ls; open 11am-4am daily) is one of Jūrmala's more glamorous spots to dine, people-watch on Majori's main street and dance well into the early hours in the upstairs nightclub. Its meats, cooked on an open grill in summer, are delicious.

**Salmu krogs** (☎ 776 13 93; Jomas iela 70-72) is a charming, rustic-style bar topped with a thatched roof and plenty of wooden benches around shared tables. Meats are grilled outside on the terrace.

**Jūras Zaķis** (Sea Rabbit; ☎ 775 30 05; Vienibas prospkets 1; meals 5 Ls; open noon-midnight daily), in Bulduri, is a good place to try local fish; fishing nets suspended from the ceiling support the theme. The restaurant is about 30m from the beach.

## Entertainment

In summer there are discos several nights a week in and around Majori. Look out for flyers on billboards down Jomas iela. The Nemo Water Park (see Things to See & Do earlier) organises pop concerts, disco nights and raves on summer weekends.

**Mūzikas klubs X** (☎ 928 29 78, 72 09 16; *Konkordijas iela 13; admission 0.50-1 Ls; open 5pm-midnight Mon-Thur, 1pm-6am Fri & Sat)* is a lively music club and disco, inside a red-brick building in Majori.

**Majori Cultūras nams** *(Majori Culture House; ☎ 776 24 03, 776 24 01; Jomas iela 35)* hosts films, music concerts and various art and craft exhibitions.

**Latvia Philharmonic's Concert Hall** *(Dzintari Koncertzāle)*, at the northern beach end of Turaidas iela, hosts a season of summer concerts from June to August.

## Getting There & Away

Between 5.45am and 11.10pm, two to five trains an hour run from Rīga to Jūrmala along the Ķemeri–Tukums line (see Getting There & Away under Rīga, earlier). All stop at Dubulti (0.52 Ls, 35 minutes), but not all stop at Majori (0.51 Ls, 40 minutes) and other stations.

Motorists driving into Jūrmala have to pay a toll of 1 Ls a day, at self-service machines at control posts either end of the resort. Bicycle tracks wind through pine forests from Rīga to Jūrmala; ask at the tourist office or bike hire places in Rīga for details.

## Getting Around

You can use trains to go from one part of Jūrmala to another. There are also buses along the main roads. The Nemo Water Park rents out bicycles; see Things to See & Do earlier.

Latvia's Parliament (Saeima) building, Old Rīga

Railway bridge, Daugava River, Rīga

Spire of St John's Church (Jāņa baznīca), Rīga

Busker, Old Rīga

Colourful house, Rīga

Art Nouveau architecture, Rīga

Main Square (Doma laukums), Rīga's Old Town

# Vidzeme

Vidzeme, Latvia's most scenically varied region, embraces northeastern Latvia. Its highlight, the Gauja River Valley, is sprinkled with castles and pretty landscapes – just made for exploring on foot, by canoe or from the air. A substantial wedge of it is protected by the Gauja National Park. The small towns of Sigulda, Cēsis and Valmiera are excellent bases for delving into its scenic depths, although Cēsis – slap-bang in its centre – is the only one to actually fall within the park.

Vidzeme is also home to a long sandy stretch of largely unspoilt coast along the Gulf of Rīga; Latvia's highest terrain, the Vidzeme Upland; and to Valka, one of Europe's oddest border towns.

## THE COAST

The main road from Rīga to the Estonian cities of Pärnu and Tallinn (the A1) runs close to the shore of the Gulf of Rīga for much of the 115km to the border. This is part of the infamous via Baltica (see the introductory Getting Around chapter). Soon after dividing from the Sigulda and Tartu road, 15km from Rīga, the road runs through wooded country, dotted with lakes and small villages.

**Baltezers**, a busy spot for midsummer celebrations, stands between two lakes 12km northeast of Rīga. Suburban trains on the Sigulda line stop at its station, 3km south of town. **Saulkrasti**, about 40km farther north, is a popular summer escape for Rīgans. The road meets the open sea at a sandy beach on the northern side of town.

For a scenic detour inland, head 17km east to **Bīriņi Castle** (*Bīriņu pils;* ☎ 40 66 316, 40 66 222; e *birini@latnet.lv*), a baronial manor built amid vast grounds in 1860. You can tour the house, fish and boat in Bīriņi Lake, and horse ride or picnic in the grounds of the windmill.

**Salacgrīva** is a harbour town at the mouth of the Salaca River. The **tourist office** (☎ 40 41 254; *Rīgas iela 10a; open 10am-4.30pm Mon-Fri*) runs tours to Livonian sacrificial caves along the coast. Taste the good old days at **Pie Bocmaņa** (☎ 40 71 455; *Pērmavas iela 6*), supposedly 'the most legendary fisherman's pub in town'.

The former shipbuilding town of **Ainaži** (derived from the Liv word *annagi,* meaning

## Highlights

- Cross the Gauja in a cable car for dizzying views of Latvia's 'Switzerland'
- Bomb down the Gauja Valley in a bobsled made for four
- Trace the path of the Turaida Rose from Gūtmaņis Cave to the Daina Hill Song Garden
- Canoe or raft through the Gauja Valley and sleep under the stars at night
- Learn about farming at Otte's Mill Museum near Alūksne or ride the narrow-gauge railway between Alūksne and Gulbene
- Meander around Mazsalaca's Sound Hill Park and marvel at its clever wooden dwarf sculptures

'lonely') is 1km south of Estonia. Its old naval school is now a **museum** (*Ainaži Jūrskolas memorialais muzejs;* ☎ 40 43 349; *Valdemāra iela 45; adult/child 0.30/0.20 Ls; open 10am-4pm Tues-Sat*).

## Places to Stay & Eat

**Jūras Priede** (☎ 79 54 780, 922 75 23; *Ūpes iela 56a, Saulkrasti; wooden huts around 10 Ls, tents 2 Ls*) is an attractive, well-kept camp site. Look for the sign immediately north of the bridge after crossing the Aga River.

# VIDZEME

VIDZEME

See Gauja National Park Map p267

Plenty of unremarkable hotels and motels line the coastal road between Salacgrīva and Saulkrasti.

**Bīriņu pils** (☎ 40 66 316, fax 40 66 232; e birini@latnet.lv; Bīriņi; doubles with breakfast 24-48 Ls) is the remarkable spot to sleep like a baron and breakfast beneath vaults. The 11-room hotel languishes in the grounds of Bīriņi Castle.

**Zvejnieku Sēta** (Rīgas iela 1, Salacgrīva; meals 3 Ls; open 10am-midnight daily) stands out. It has a fishing boat moored outside, fishing nets draped across its terrace and a rustic interior.

## Getting There & Away

Buses north from Rīga to Pärnu and Tallinn follow the coastal road (one hour to Saulkrasti, 1¾ hours to Salacgrīva). Suburban trains from Rīga run as far as Saulkrasti (0.70 Ls, one hour).

## MAZSALACA & RŪJIENA

There's some attractive scenery and spots renowned in Latvian folklore around Mazsalaca, 55km inland from Ainaži on the Salaca River. On the village green there is an open-air **Dinosaur Park** (Dinozauru parks; Parka iela 8; admission free). There's also the splendid park, **Sound Hill** (Skaņāis kalns; ☎ 42 51 945), 1.7km west of town, which showcases marvellous outdoor woodcarvings of gigantic proportions. Motorists can drive the length of the park or you can stroll the 2km on foot, stopping at the strategic spots. The **Werewolf Pine** is believed to turn you into a werewolf if you crawl through its roots after muttering certain incantations under a full moon. The **Stairway of Dreams**, 300m north, tells young lovers how well suited they are, while about 1km downstream from the Werewolf Pine, a spring flowing out of a rock at the **Devil's Cave** is said to have healing properties. And about 800m farther downstream, the sandstone cliff **Sound Hill** on the left bank of the river apparently throws off the odd bizarre acoustic effect. A picnic area decked out with picnic tables and benches marks the end of the trail.

In Rūjiena, 7km northeast, an enterprising bunch of businesses offer industrial tours – an ice-cream factory, a watermill, a sheep-breeding farm and a wool-processing mill are obvious highlights. The **tourist office** (☎ 42 63 278, 92 29 163; Raiņa iela 3) has a complete list of places.

The only hotel is **Tālava** (☎/fax 42 63 767, Rīgas iela 12; singles/doubles 7/10 Ls, with shower 10/18 Ls) in Rūjiena, a shabby establishment with dreary rooms.

Mazsalaca and Rūjiena are served by one suburban train daily to/from Rīga.

## SIGULDA
### pop 10,855

Known locally as the 'Switzerland of Latvia', Sigulda (formerly Segewold) is just 53km east of Rīga. The pretty town stands on the southern edge of a picturesque, steep-sided, wooded section of the Gauja Valley and is spanned by a string of medieval castles and legendary caves.

Sigulda is also a minor health resort and winter sports centre, with an Olympic bobsled run snaking down into the valley. It is the primary gateway to the beautiful Gauja National Park which fans out northeastward almost to Valmiera, extending some distance either side of the valley.

### History

Finno-Ugric Liv tribes inhabited the area as far back as 2000 BC, and by the 12th century they had built several wooden hilltop strongholds. But they were unable to prevent the German conquest in the early 13th century. In 1207, when the German crusaders were dividing up their spoils, the Gauja was chosen as the boundary in this area between the territories of the Knights of the Sword, who acquired the land south of the river, and of the archbishop of Rīga, who acquired the north side. Both built castles in prominent positions – as much to guard against each other, one suspects, as against any local uprising.

After suffering numerous wars, particularly between the 16th and 18th centuries, Sigulda developed as a country resort with the building of the Pskov–Rīga railway in 1889. The Russian owner of the local estate, Prince Kropotkin, sold off land to wealthy Rīgans to build their own country houses.

### Orientation & Information

You enter the Gauja National Park in Sigulda as you descend the hill from the town towards the river. Information panels are in Latvian and English.

VIDZEME

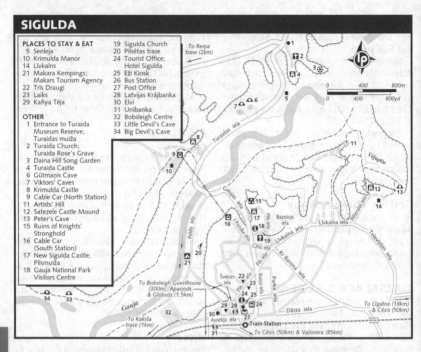

**SIGULDA**

PLACES TO STAY & EAT
5  Senleja
10  Krimulda Manor
14  Līvkalns
21  Makara Kempings;
    Makars Tourism Agency
22  Trīs Draugi
23  Laiks
29  Kafiya Tēja

OTHER
1  Entrance to Turaida
   Museum Reserve;
   Turaidas muiža
2  Turaida Church;
   Turaida Rose's Grave
3  Daina Hill Song Garden
4  Turaida Castle
6  Gūtmaņis Cave
7  Viktors' Caves
8  Krimulda Castle
9  Cable Car (North Station)
11  Artists' Hill
12  Satezele Castle Mound
13  Peter's Cave
15  Ruins of Knights'
    Stronghold
16  Cable Car
    (South Station)
17  New Sigulda Castle;
    Pilsmuiža
18  Gauja National Park
    Visitors Centre
19  Sigulda Church
20  Pilsētas trase
24  Tourist Office;
    Hotel Sigulda
25  Eži Kiosk
26  Bus Station
27  Post Office
28  Latvijas Krājbanka
30  Elvi
31  Unibanka
32  Bobsleigh Centre
33  Little Devil's Cave
34  Big Devil's Cave

To Reiņa trase (2km)

To Bobsleigh Guesthouse (300m), Aparjods & Globuss (1.5km)
To Kakiša trase (1km)
To Līgatne (18km) & Cēsis (50km)
To Cēsis (50km) & Valmiera (85km)
Train Station

The national park **visitors centre** (☎ 79 71 345, fax 79 71 344; ⓦ www.gnp.lv; Baznīcas iela 3; open 9.30am-5pm Mon, 9.30am-6pm Tues-Sun) sells park and town maps, arranges accommodation and guided tours of the park, and organises activities. It also arranges visits to local potters, weavers and bee-keepers, and in summer hosts folklore evenings.

The **tourist office** (☎/fax 79 71 335; ⓦ www.sigulda.lv; Pils iela 6; open 10am-7pm daily May-Oct, 10am-5pm daily Nov-Apr) stocks reams of information on the region.

**Unibanka** (Rīgas iela 1) has a currency exchange facility and cashes AmEx travellers cheques. There is an ATM opposite the train station and another outside **Latvijas Krājbanka** (Pils iela 1). The latter is opposite the **post office** (Pils iela 2; open 8am-6pm Mon, 8am-5pm Tues-Fri, 8am-2pm Sat).

### Sigulda Castles & Church
Little remains of the **knights' stronghold** (Siguldas pilsdrupas), built between 1207 and 1226 among woods on the northeastern edge of Sigulda. The castle hasn't been repaired since the Great Northern War, but its ruins are perhaps more evocative because of that. There's a great view through the trees to the archbishop's reconstructed Turaida Castle, on the far side of the valley.

On the way to the ruins from town, you pass **Sigulda Church** (Siguldas baznīca), built in 1225 and rebuilt in the 17th and 18th centuries; and also the 19th-century **New Sigulda Castle** (Siguldas jaunā pils), the former residence of Prince Kropotkin and now a sanatorium.

### Krimulda Castle & Manor
On the northern side of the valley, a track leads up from near the bridge to ruined **Krimulda Castle** (Krimuldas pilsdrupas), built between 1255 and 1273 and once used as a guesthouse for visiting dignitaries. A good way to reach the castle is by **cable car** (☎ 79 72 531; Poruka iela 14; adult/7-10 yrs 0.50/0.30 Ls), which crosses the valley (west of Raiņa iela) every 15 minutes between 7.30am and 6.30pm, affording splendid views of the valley. The big white building just west of the northern cable-car station is **Krimulda Manor** (Krimuldas muižas pils; Mednieku

*iela 3)*, built in 1897, confiscated by the government in 1922 and later turned into a tuberculosis hospital. Today it is a hostel (see Places to Stay) and children's sanatorium for 40-odd kids.

Buses link Sigulda bus station with Turaida and Krimulda eight or nine times daily. Bus departure times are posted at the bus station; the national park visitors centre has a printed timetable.

## Gūtmaņis' & Viktors' Caves

Below the viewing tower of Krimulda, immediately to the left of the castle as you face it, are some steep wooden steps. Walk down the 410 steps to the bottom and follow the wooden riverside path leading to **Gūtmaņis Cave** *(Gūtmaņa ala)*, in the bottom of the north side of the valley. The cave is covered with graffiti going back to the 16th century – including the coats of arms of long-gone hunters. The water from the stream flowing out of the cave is supposed to remove facial wrinkles. The cave is also meant to be named after a healer who allegedly cured the sick with water from it. This cave is most famous however, for its role in the tragic legend of the Turaida Rose (see boxed text). To get here take a Krimulda bus and get off at the Senleja stop.

**Viktors' Cave** *(Viktora ala)*, a little farther along the valley, was supposedly dug out by Viktors for Maija to sit and watch the castle gardens where he worked (see 'The Turaida Rose' boxed text).

## Turaida Museum Reserve

The centrepiece of Sigulda's **Turaida Museum Reserve** *(Turaidas muzejrezervats;* ☎/fax *79 71 402;* **w** *www.turaida-muzejs.lv; admission 1-1.5 Ls; open 9.30am-8pm daily May-Oct, 10am-5pm Nov-Apr)* is **Turaida Castle** *(Turaidas pils; open 10am-6pm daily May-Oct, 10am-5pm Nov-Apr)*, a red-brick archbishops' castle founded in 1214 on the site of a Liv stronghold. It was blown up when lightning hit its gunpowder store in the 18th century. The restored castle – whose name, Turaida, means 'God's Garden' in ancient Livonian – is better viewed from afar, but the museum inside the 15th-century **granary** offers an interesting account of the Livonian state from 1319 to 1561. Further exhibitions can be viewed in the 42m-tall **Donjon Tower** and the castle's western and southern towers.

---

### The Turaida Rose

Sigulda's local beauty, Maija, was taken into Turaida Castle as a little girl when she was found among the wounded after a battle in 1601. She grew into a famous beauty courted by men from far and wide, but she loved Viktors, a gardener at Sigulda Castle. They would meet in a cave, halfway between the two castles.

One day a particularly desperate Polish officer among Maija's suitors lured her to the cave by means of a letter forged in Viktors' handwriting. Maija offered to give the Pole the scarf from around her neck, which she said had magical protective powers, if he let her go. To prove the scarf's powers, she suggested he swing at her with his sword. Whether this was a bluff or she really believed in the scarf isn't clear. Either way, the Pole duly took his swing, killed her, and then fled the scene.

---

On the path between the castle and the road is the small wooden-spired Turaida Church (Turaidas Baznīcas; open 10am-6pm Wed-Sun May-Oct), built in 1750 and housing a small history exhibition. In the churchyard two lime trees shade the grave of the legendary Turaida Rose. The headstone bears the inscription 'Turaidas Roze 1601–1620'. Viktors himself is said to have buried Maija and planted one of the trees, then disappeared without trace. The hillside behind the church is known as Daina Hill (Dainu kalns) and shelters the Daina Hill Song Garden. The daina, or poetic folk song, is a major Latvian tradition, and the hillside is dotted with sculptures dedicated to epic Latvian heroes immortalised in the dainas collected by Krisjānis Barons; it's also Latvia's only sculpture garden.

More paths twist around the estate past the **estate manager's house**, home to an exhibition on collective farming in the 1950s; the **dog keeper's house**, where wood craft tools are displayed; the **smithy**, still operational; the **cart house**, which hosts various farming exhibitions; and the old 19th-century **sauna**. All these exhibitions are open 10am-6pm from Wednesday to Sunday from May to October.

**Kārļa Hill** *(Kārļa kalns)*, facing Turaida Castle across the ravine which the road ascends, was another old Liv stronghold.

## GAUJA NATIONAL PARK

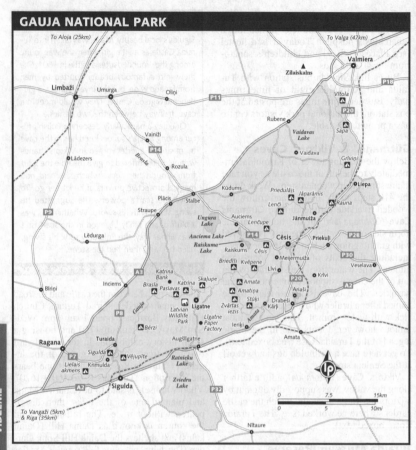

## Walking

Walking to the main sites – Sigulda Castle, Gūtmaņis' Cave and Turaida Castle – is a good way to stretch your legs. Within the Turaida Museum Reserve a series of gentle nature trails are marked, ranging from 200m to 800m in length.

A good circular walk on the castle's southern side – about 6km to and from Sigulda Church – is to **Satezele Castle Mound** (*Satezeles pilskalns*), another Liv stronghold, then to **Peter's Cave** (*Pētera ala*), on a steep bank of the Vējupīte River, and on to **Artists' Hill** (*Gleznotāju kalns*), which has an excellent 12km panorama.

On the northern bank you could walk downstream from the bridge to the **Little Devil's Cave** (*Mazā velnala*) and **Big Devil's**

Cave (*Lielā velnala*), then return along the top of the escarpment to Krimulda Castle – about 7km. The Little Devil's Cave has a **Spring of Wisdom** (*Gudrības avotiņš*). The Big Devil's Cave has black walls from the fiery breath of a travelling demon who once sheltered for a day here to avoid sunlight.

The Gauja National Park visitors centre (see Information earlier) has details of plenty more walks in the national park. Particularly interesting are its day- and night-time birdwatching and birdsong-discovery walks.

## Ballooning & Bungee Jumping

To get a different perspective on things, try a 43m-high **bungee jump** (☎ 66 40 660; ⓦ www.lgk.lv) from the cable car which crosses the Gauja. Jumps cost 13/10 Ls for the

## Canoe Trips

Vidzeme's Gauja and Salaca Rivers are both fine canoeing terrain. The 220km-long stretch between Vireši and Sigulda is particularly good, flowing through some of Latvia's best scenery with nothing more hazardous than some fairly gentle rapids. Riverside tent-camping sites dot this whole stretch; above Valmiera the river flows through almost entirely unspoilt country.

You can set up a Gauja canoe trip through many organisations. On the banks of the river in Sigulda, inside the Gauja National Park, **Makars Tourism Agency** (☎ 92 44 948, 79 73 724; 🌐 www.makars.lv; Peldu iela 1, Sigulda) arranges one- to three-day water tours in two- to four-person boats from Sigulda, Līgatne, Cēsis and Valmiera, ranging in length from 3km to 85km. Tours cost 10-39 Ls per boat including equipment, transportation between Sigulda and the tour's starting point, and camp site fees for up to four people. Tents/sleeping bags/life jackets can also be rented for 3/1/1 Ls per day, and – for the less intrepid paddler – Makars rents out canoes/two-person rubber boats/six-person rafts for 10/5/15 Ls per day.

Valmiera's **Sporta Bāze Baiļi** (☎ 42 21 861, 92 84 119, fax 42 21 922; 📧 baili@valm.lv) arranges various one-day canoe trips costing 20 Ls (24km, Valmiera–Strenči), 40 Ls (83km Valmiera–Sigulda) or 27 Ls (45km, Valmiera–Cēsis). Trips spread across two days or more cost more. Rates cover three people; life belts cost an extra 1 Ls and you can rent a tent/mat/water can if you wish for 4/1/1 Ls. Guide services are also available, including bird-watching guides.

first/subsequent jump and take place on Saturday and Sunday, May to September, from 6.30pm until the last customer has jumped.

Less stomach-turning are the scenic hot-air balloon flights organised by **Altius** (☎ 76 11 614, fax 78 60 206; 🌐 www.altius.lv). Flights are pricey: 70/100 Ls per person for 30-50/60-90 minutes in the air.

### Bobsledding & Skiing

Sigulda's 1200m-long artificial **bobsled track** (☎ 79 73 813; Sveices iela 13) was built for the former Soviet bobsleigh team. Part of the European luge championships are held here every January. In winter you can fly down the 16-bend track at 80km/h in a five-person **Vuchko tourist bob** (admission 2 Ls; open 11am-6pm Sat & Sun 1 Nov-1 March), while summer speed fiends can ride a **wheel bob** (admission 3 Ls; open 11am-6pm Sat & Sun 1 May-1 Oct). If your stomach is not up to it, scale the **viewing tower** (adult/child 0.30/0.15 Ls; open 8am-dusk daily year-round) instead for a panoramic view of the bobsled run snaking into the valley.

Sigulda sports several gentle **downhill ski slopes**, served by drag or chair lifts and snow-covered from late November until March or April. **Pilsētas trase** (350m; ☎ 94 47 713; Peldu iela 4; lift 0.25 Ls one way; open 3pm-6pm Mon-Thur, 10am-midnight Fri & Sat, 10am-10pm Sun), also known as the city ski slope; **Reiņa trase** (150m; ☎ 92 72 255;

Kalnzaķl; lift 2/5 Ls per hour/day; open 3pm-6pm & 7pm-1am Mon-Fri, 11am-6pm & 7pm-1am Sat & Sun), in Krimulda; and **Kakīša trase** (300m; ☎/fax 94 47 713; Senču iela 1; lift 0.20/0.25 Ls one way before/after 5pm; open 2pm-10pm Mon-Thur, 2pm-midnight Fri & Sat, 2pm-11pm Sun) are the primary slopes. You can hire skis, poles and boots at all three slopes for about 2-3 Ls per hour or 7-12 Ls per day. In town, Eži and Noma (see Cycling, Rollerblading & Horse Riding) also rent out all ski gear.

### Cycling, Rollerblading & Horse Riding

In summer you can rent bicycles and rollerblades from **Eži** (☎ 94 28 846; Pils iela 4a; open 10am-8pm daily May-Oct). Rental costs 5/8 Ls per day/two days.

**Turaidas muiža** (☎ 912 43 60; Turaidas iela 10) organises various horse riding activities, including treks (from 16/10 Ls per adult/child an hour) and horse-drawn carriage rides (5 Ls for four people for 20 minutes) around the national park.

### Places to Stay

Wild camping is permitted in certain designated areas in the national park – see the boxed text for details. The Makars tourism agency (see Makara Kempings) arranges B&B in private houses for 7Ls to 12 Ls per person a night.

VIDZEME

## Sleeping Beneath the Stars

Twenty-two 'wild' camp sites, which are intended for hikers and canoeists, are strung along the banks of the Gauja between Sigulda and Cēsis – the most scenic stretch of valley. They're mostly on the northern bank, but there's one opposite Katrīna Bank at Līgatne (accessible by car or on foot from Līgatne Education and Recreation Park) and a couple more on the Amata River between Zvārtas iezis and the Gauja. Both the information centre in the Līgatne park and the national park visitors centre in Sigulda can tell you where they are.

**Makara Kempings** (☎ 92 44 948, 79 73 724; W www.makars.lv; Peldu iela 1; person/tent/car/caravan 1/1/1/2 Ls; open 15 May–15 Sept), run by Makars (see the boxed text 'Canoe Trips'), is a riverside site actually in the national park. Enjoy a traditional Latvian sauna for 8 Ls per hour. Tentless guests can rent two-person tents for 2 Ls a day.

**Krimulda Manor** (☎ 79 72 232, 91 11 619, fax 79 71 721; e krimulda@ls.lv; camping 1 Ls per tent, bed in summer house 5 Ls, bed in 2-6 bedded dorm 5-7 Ls, breakfast 1 Ls), accessible via cable car (see Krimulda Castle & Manor earlier) offers excellent-value accommodation, although some might find the hospital smell a trifle unsettling (part of the place is a children's hospital).

**Senleja** (☎ 79 72 162, fax 79 70 102; Turaidas iela 4; small/large doubles without/with TV 10/15 Ls, breakfast 2 Ls), originally built for Soviet groups in the 1950s, is in the valley below Turaida Castle. Its facade is miserable but its basic rooms are clean.

**Bobsleigh Guesthouse** (Berzu iela 1a; singles/doubles 5/10 Ls) is where sports teams stay when in town for bobsledding championships. Rooms are split between two floors and bathrooms are shared between six guests.

**Hotel Sigulda** (☎ 79 72 263, fax 72 45 165; W www.hotelsigulda.lv; Pils iela 6; singles/doubles with breakfast 24/30 Ls), adjoining the tourist office, is a super-snazzy hotel with a funky pastel-pink and glass facade.

**Līvkalns** (☎ 79 70 916, 96 23 350, fax 79 709 19; W www.livkalns.lv; Pēteralas iela; doubles/triples from 25/35 Ls) is a large wooden house with a thatched roof, eight spacious rooms, luxury sauna (8 Ls per hour for two people) and lake with pavilion for tea-sipping.

**Aparjods** (☎/fax 77 05 225; W www.aparjods.lv; Ventas iela 1b; singles/doubles/triples with breakfast 25/27/35 Ls, luxury room without/with jacuzzi 40/50 Ls) is a rustic shingle-roofed place 1.5km south of town.

### Places to Eat

**Globuss** (Ventas iela 1; meals from 1 Ls) is a 24-hour supermarket with small bistro for those wanting to eat cheap. In town there's the large **Elvi** (Auseklja iela 1; open 7am-11pm daily) supermarket.

**Trīs Draugi** (☎ 79 73 721; Pils iela 9; meals from 1 Ls; open 8am-10pm daily), unusually, is a bright and sparkling place where you can be served – canteen-style – with large and tasty helpings of cheap food.

**Laiks** (☎ 79 74 640; Pils iela 8; meals 2 Ls; open 8am-2am daily), directly opposite Trīs Draugi, serves omelettes, soups, 'racy' chicken wings and other light lunchtime dishes in a pub-style setting. The bar has a pool table, darts, one-armed bandits (slot machines) and air hockey too.

**Kafiya Tēja** (☎ 79 74 032; Valdemāra iela 1) is a wonderful spot to sit in the sun, sip frothy cappuccinos and munch on sweet cakes and tarts. 'Coffee Tea' serves tea too.

**Pilsmuiža** (☎ 79 71 425; Pils iela 16; meals 3.50 Ls; open noon-2am daily), inside New Sigulda Castle, overlooks the ruins of the castle. Ask the waiter for the key to the castle tower (1937) to feast on panoramic views of the Gauja Valley.

**Aparjods** (see Places to Stay, meals around 8 Ls) dishes up delicious food in an elegant dark-wood setting with fireplace and interesting B&W photos of old Sigulda on the walls. Sample traditional herrings with curd or splash out with friends on an entire roasted piglet (108.80 Ls).

### Getting There & Away

Six to eight buses daily trundle the 50-odd kilometres between **Sigulda bus station** and Rīga (0.90 Ls, two hours).

Ten trains a day on the Rīga–Sigulda–Cēsis–Valmiera line stop at **Sigulda train station**. Fares from Sigulda include Rīga (0.86 Ls, 1¼ hours), Valmiera (1.03 Ls, 1¼ hours), Līgatne (0.33 Ls, 10 minutes) and Cēsis (0.72 Ls, 50 minutes).

## LĪGATNE
pop 1365
The village of Līgatne, in the heart of the Gauja National Park, is in itself unmomentous. During Soviet times it was known for its paper factory and little else. Some of Latvia's loveliest countryside is a mere hop, skip and jump from the village however, making it a good base from which to explore the Gauja Valley.

On the southern side of the river, about 4km west of Līgatne village and 15km northeast of Sigulda, is **Līgatne Education and Recreation Park** *(Līgatnes mācību un atpūtas parks; adult/child 1/0.50 Ls)*, a nature park where elk, beaver, deer, bison, lynx and wild boar roam in sizable open-air enclosures in the forest. A 5.1km-long motor circuit (accessible from May to the first snowfall) and a network of footpaths link a series of observation points, and there's a 22m-tall observation tower with a fine panorama. Footpaths marked out include a **nature trail with wild animals** (5.5km), a **botanical trail** (1.1km), a **wild nature trail** (1.3km) and a fun **fairy-tale trail** (900m) which winds its way through a fantastical path of 90-odd wooden sculptures.

Quality maps of the park with explanations in English are available from the **information centre** (☎ 41 53 313), not to be confused with the wooden-hut ticket office at the park entrance. The centre arranges horse riding and treks through the park.

Several sections of steep bank line the Gauja either side of Līgatne. These would hardly rate a second glance in some parts of the world, but in a flat country like Latvia they're a big deal – and they get names. The one to the north, almost opposite the wildlife park, is called **Katrīna Bank** *(Katrīnas iezis).*

### Places to Stay
One of the national park's camp sites (see the boxed text 'Sleeping Beneath the Stars' earlier in this chapter) is opposite Katrīna Bank in Līgatne. It is accessible by car or foot from Līgatne Education and Recreation Park.

**Līgatne** (☎ 41 31 321; e ligatne@rehcentrs .apollo.lv; singles/doubles/triples/quads from 13/18/21/28 Ls, sauna 15 Ls for two hours), about 4km from the village centre, is an ugly monstrosity in a beautiful setting. Its grim concrete facade appears not to have been touched since the days it served as a Communist Party holiday home, but rooms inside

are clean enough. The complex houses a rehabilitation centre as well as hotel.

### Getting There & Away
Public transport is poor. The nearest bus stop to the nature park is Gaujasmala, 2km from the entrance. Five buses daily are scheduled from Cēsis to Zvārtas iezis, but the service is erratic. You can always get a bus or suburban train to the Līgatne main road village or to Ieriķi, then walk or hitch.

Coming from the north (Straupe direction), you can catch a car ferry across the Gauja to Līgatne. A single fare is 0.40/0.20 per adult/child, plus 1 Ls per car. Boats run in summer from 6am to 11pm daily. From Līgatne village, follow the signs for 'Līgatnes Pārceltuve'.

## CĒSIS
pop 19,471
About 30km northeast of Sigulda up the Gauja Valley is the historic town of Cēsis (formerly Wenden), once the headquarters of the Livonian Order and a member of the Hanseatic League.

Today it is heralded as Latvia's most Latvian town, and is home to the country's oldest breweries. Open-air concerts are often held in summer in the castle grounds.

### Orientation & Information
The bus and train stations are on the eastern fringe. From here Raunas iela leads to the main square, Vienības laukums.

Cēsis **tourist office** (☎ 41 21 815, fax 41 07 777; w www.cesis.lv; Pils laukums 2; open 9am-6pm Mon-Sat, 10am-5pm Sun mid-May–mid-Sept, 9am-5pm Mon-Fri rest of year) is also the base for the **Vidzeme Tourism Association** (☎/fax 41 22 011; e info@vta .apollo.lv), which arranges accommodation in private homes in rural Vidzeme.

There is an ATM outside the **Latvijas Krābanka** *(Vienības laukums).* Internet access costs 0.50 Ls per hour at **Capital Datorsalons** (☎ 41 07 111; e atc@apollo.lv; Rīgas iela 7; open 9am-6pm Mon-Fri, 10am-2pm Sat).

### Castle, Museum & Park
**Cēsis Castle** *(Cēsu pils)* was founded in 1209 by the Knights of the Sword. Its dominant feature is two stout towers at the western end. To enter, visit **Cēsis History & Art Museum** *(Cēsu Vēstures un mākslas muzejs; Pils laukums*

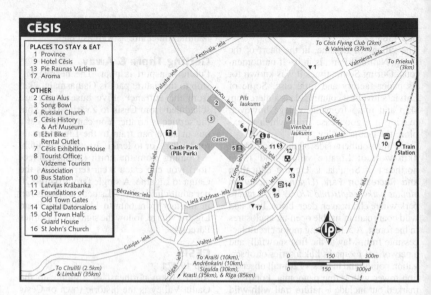

## CĒSIS

**PLACES TO STAY & EAT**
1  Province
9  Hotel Cēsis
13 Pie Raunas Vārtiem
17 Aroma

**OTHER**
2  Cēsu Alus
3  Song Bowl
4  Russian Church
5  Cēsis History
   & Art Museum
6  Ēžvi Bike
   Rental Outlet
7  Cēsis Exhibition House
8  Tourist Office;
   Vidzeme Tourism
   Association
10 Bus Station
11 Latvijas Krābanka
12 Foundations of
   Old Town Gates
14 Capital Datorsalons
15 Old Town Hall;
   Guard House
16 St John's Church

*9; adult/child 0.30/0.20 Ls; open 10am-5pm Tues-Sun)*, in the adjoining 18th-century 'new castle', painted salmon-pink. Temporary art exhibitions and chamber music concerts are held in **Cēsis Exhibition House** *(Cēsu Izstāžu nams; ☎ 41 23 557)* next to the tourist office on the same square. The yellow-and-white building housed stables and a coach house (1781) in the 18th and 19th centuries.

In pretty **Castle Park** *(Pils park)* there is a song bowl, lake and a Russian Orthodox church. On the far side from the church is the 19th-century building of **Cēsu Alus** *(Cēsis Brewery; ☎ 41 22 245; Lenču iela 9/11)*. It has brewed beer since 1590.

### Old Town
The Old Town extends south from the bottom end of Vienības laukums. Just off this square, at the top of Rīgas iela, the foundations of the Old Town gates have been excavated and left exposed. Nearby the **Old Town hall** and **guard house** *(Rīgas iela 7)* dates to 1767.

The main landmark is **St John's Church** *(Svēta Jāņa baznīca; Skolas iela)*, which dates back to 1287. Its original Gothic form has been altered. Its towers date back to 1853 and the church has some fine stained glass.

### Activities
Cyclists can hire wheels from the **Ēži bike rental outlet** *(☎ 42 81 764, 94 28 846; Pils laukums 1; open 9am-6pm Mon-Sun Apr-Sept)*. Mountain bikes cost 1/5 Ls per hour/day (3 Ls per day from the second day of hire).

In winter, skiers and snowboarders poodle down the gentle slopes and cross-country trails at **Cīrulīši** *(☎ 41 25 225, 92 75 378; e cirulkalns@e-apollo.lv; Cīrulīšu iela 70)*, on Cēsis' southwesternmost fringe. The tourist office has details of other places to ski in the region, such as **Andrēnkalni** *(10km south near Skujenes)* and **Krasti** *(some 25km farther south near Drabeši)*.

**Cēsis Flying Club** *(Cēsu Aeroklubs; ☎ 41 22 639, 94 59 578)*, 2km north of the centre on the Valmiera road, arranges flying lessons, panoramic flights, parachute jumps and gliding.

### Places to Stay & Eat
**Priekuļi** *(☎ 41 30 457; Dārza iela 2; singles/doubles 6/10 Ls)* is a hostel in Priekuļi, 3km east of Cēsis. Rooms are typically sterile and the bathrooms uninspired.

**Hotel Cēsis** *(☎ 41 22 392, fax 41 20 121; w www.danlat-group.lv; Vienības laukums 1; singles/doubles with breakfast 30/42 Ls)*, also called Danlat Hotel, gives itself three stars. The in-house restaurant serves strictly Latvian cuisine and is the top place to eat in town.

**Province** *(☎ 41 20 849; Niniera iela 6; singles/doubles 17/28 Ls, meals 2 Ls)* is a bright and sunny spot with outside seating, a popular café in a glass conservatory and five rooms up top.

**Pie Raunas Vārtiem** *(☎ 91 92 938; Rīgas iela 8; meals 2-3 Ls)* is the spot for traditional and authentic Latvian fodder in an appealing rustic setting.

Eating options in Cēsis are otherwise sparse. The odd café borders Vienības laukums. **Aroma** *(☎ 41 27 575; Lencū iela 4)* is a coffee shop with 70 types of coffee and tea.

## Getting There & Away
Cēsis bus station is served by at least hourly buses daily to/from Rīga (1.30 Ls, two hours) and about 10 daily to/from Valmiera (0.50 Ls, 45 minutes). There are also daily services to/from Saulkrasti, Limbaži, Ainaži, Valka, Rūjiena, Madona, Jaunpiebalga and Alūksne.

There are six daily trains between Cēsis and Rīga (1.30 Ls, 1¼-2 hours).

## ĀRAIŠI
Plopped on an islet in the middle of Āraiši Lake, about 10km south of Cēsis, is **Āraiši Lake Fortress** *(Āraišu ezerpils; ☎ 41 97 288; adult/child 0.60/0.20 Ls)*, a reconstruction of a settlement inhabited by ancient Latgalans in the 9th and 10th centuries. A wooden walkway leads across the water to the unusual village which was built on a low flooded islet, fortified like a hill fort and discovered by archaeologists in 1965. About 40 log houses originally stood on the site – 15 have been rebuilt in recent times.

Peering across are the ruins of **Āraiši stone castle** *(Āraišu mūra pils)*, built by Livonians in the 14th century and destroyed by troops of Russian Tsar Ivan IV in 1577. From here a path leads to a reconstructed Stone Age settlement – there's a couple of reed dwellings and earth ovens for roasting meat and fish. A Bronze Age dwelling will also be built on the lake shore. The fortress and castle, together with the 18th-century **Āraiši windmill** *(Āraišu vējdzirnavas; ☎ 41 97 288, 92 38 208, 94 61 885; open May-Nov)* signposted 1km along a dirt track from the main road, form the **Āraiši Museum Park** *(Āraišu muzejparks)*. To visit the windmill ask at the house next door.

## VALMIERA
**pop 28,732**
Valmiera (formerly Wolmar), a town of a similar size to Cēsis and about 30km north up the Gauja Valley, sits at the northeastern tip of the Gauja National Park, just outside its boundaries. It is less historic than Sigulda or Cēsis – most of its Old Town burnt down in 1944 – but does boast Latvia's best-run hostel, combined with a bonanza of wet and watery outdoor activities.

## Orientation & Information
The focus is the road bridge across the Gauja. Cēsu iela and its continuation, Stacijas iela, leads south from the bridge to the bus station (100m or so), opposite the corner of Cēsu iela, and on to the train station (2km). The centre is on the northern side of the bridge.

The **tourist office** *(☎ 42 07 177, fax 42 07 175; e tic@valmiera.gov.lv; Bruņinieku iela 2; open 7am-9pm Mon-Fri, 9am-5pm Sat May-Sept)* sells maps and arranges private accommodation.

There is an ATM outside the central **Veikals Valmiera shopping centre** *(Rigas iela 4)* and another outside **Hansa Banka** *(Rigas iela 15)*. Kick off a kid playing killer computer games to check your email at Valmiera's busy **Datocentras** *(☎ 42 81 818; e info@devia.lv; Tērbatas iela 1; open 9am-11pm daily)*. It charges 0.50 Ls per hour.

## Things to See
Valmiera's pinprick historic area stands on a point of land between the Gauja River and a tributary called the Ažkalna: **St Simon's Church** *(Svētā Sīmaņa Baznīca; Bruņinieku iela 2)* dates to 1283 and shelters a fine 19th-century organ. You can climb its church tower for a nominal fee. Along the same street are the ruins of **Valmiera Castle** founded by the Livonian Order.

Continue to **Valmiera Regional Museum** *(Valmieras Novadpētniecības muzejs; ☎ 42 32 733; Bruņinieku iela 3; adult/child 0.50/0.30; open 10am-5pm Mon-Fri, 10am-3pm Sat)*. Its collection is of limited interest but it's a good source of information on the district – if you read Latvian. The curtains rose for the first time at **Valmiera Drama Theatre** *(☎ 42 23 300; Lāčplēsa iela 4)* in 1885. The current building dates to 1987.

There's an observation tower on the hillock **Valterkalniņs**, just above the meeting of the Ažkalna and the Gauja. Across a small bridge over the Ažkalna, a loop of land surrounded by the Gauja has been preserved as a woodland **park**.

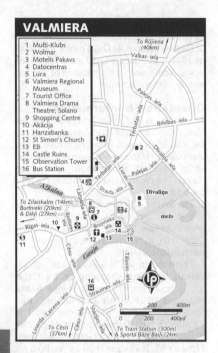

**VALMIERA**

1  Multi-Klubs
2  Wolmar
3  Motelis Pakavs
4  Datocentras
5  Luca
6  Valmiera Regional Museum
7  Tourist Office
8  Valmiera Drama Theatre; Solano
9  Shopping Centre
10  Akācija
11  Hanzabanka
12  St Simon's Church
13  Eži
14  Castle Ruins
15  Observation Tower
16  Bus Station

## Activities

In town, Eži (see Places to Stay later) rents out mountain bikes for 1/5 Ls per hour/day; helmets (0.50 Ls a day), saddle bags and seats for kids (each 1 Ls a day) are also available. The hostel sells maps, helps cyclists with itineraries, arranges private English- and German-speaking guides (20 Ls a day), and rents out sleeping bag/tents (1/3 Ls a day) for those wanting to overnight in the countryside.

Water-sport enthusiasts should touch base with Eži or Sporta Bāze Baiļi (see the boxed text 'Canoe Trips'). The latter has a short mountain-bike trail through forest and you can ski there in winter. A morning/afternoon ski pass (valid 11am-4pm/4pm-11pm) for the centre's 10 slopes costs 5/6 Ls and you can hire skis, poles and boots for 2.50 Ls per day. Snowboarding gear also costs 2.50 Ls.

## Places to Stay

**Eži** (☎ 42 81 764, 42 07 263; W www.ezi.lv; Valdemāra iela 1; dorm beds 5 Ls; breakfast 1 Ls; reception open 9am-7pm Mon-Sat, 9am-1pm Sun), wedged between the church and the river, is run by a dynamic bunch who ooze energy, speak English and understand the true meaning of customer service. Three- and six-bedded dorms – on the 2nd and 3rd floors of a red-brick water tower dating to the early 1900s – are kitted out with pine furniture and cheery furnishings. HI card holders get 10% discount.

The hostel rents out bicycles, boats and canoes (see Activities).

**Sporta Bāze Baiļi** (☎ 42 21 861, 92 84 119, fax 42 21 922; W www.baili.lv; tent sites 1.50 Ls plus 1 Ls per person, caravan sites with power 4 Ls, chalet for 4/6/7/8 people 26/36/25/44 Ls), 4km east of Valmiera centre, has self-contained wooden chalets with private bathroom, plus tent pitches and caravan sites. Breakfast/ bedding costs an extra 2/1 Ls. On site there is a sauna (3 Ls per hour, plus 1 Ls for a birch bosom). The centre rents out canoes and gear (see the boxed text 'Canoe Trips'). To reach Baiļi, go about 1.5km south along Stacijas iela from the Gauja bridge, then turn left (east) just after the Statoil station along Kauguru iela and go about 2km.

**Luca** (☎ 42 23 988, fax 94 56 899; e luca -haus@one.lv; Lucas iela 2; singles/doubles with breakfast 12/18 Ls) is a squeaky-clean guesthouse on the edge of a pretty park, with English- and German-speaking staff. The wooden house doubles as a German cultural centre and library.

**Motelis Pakavs** (☎/fax 42 81 050; Beātes iela 5; singles/doubles with breakfast 14/19 Ls) touts six very beige doubles, an equally beige in-house café, and a bar frequented by a stony-faced clientele.

**Wolmar** (☎ 42 07 301, fax 42 07 305; W www.wolmar.lv; Tērbatas iela 16a; singles/ doubles with breakfast 19/25 Ls), named after Valmiera's former German city name, is the modern, upmarket choice. Pay an extra 10 Ls an hour to be mollycoddled with a sauna and massage.

## Places to Eat & Drink

Dining options are frustratingly limited. In a nutshell, the choice is the Wolmar café (see Places to Stay) or the following.

**Solano** (Lāčplēša iela 4; meals 1-2 Ls), known for cheap but tasty traditional Latvian cuisine, is inside the drama theatre.

**Akācija** (☎ 42 33 812; Rīgas iela 10; meals 2.50-4 Ls), a busy bar with a token handful of tables, dishes up a vast array of satisfying creations. Its veal cooked in wine with mushrooms and potato pancakes is recommended.

**Multi-Klubs** (☎ 42 32 114; Tirgu iela 5; open 9pm-6am Mon-Sun) is the place to sink bar snacks and beer. Air hockey and a machine to test alcohol levels are other features of this surprisingly with-it nightclub.

### Getting There & Away
From Valmiera **bus station** (☎ 42 24 728; w www.autobusunoma.lv; Stacijas iela 1) buses run hourly between 4.55am and 7.55pm to/from Rīga (1.30 Ls, 2½ hours). Other services include 10 to 15 buses a day to/from Cēsis (0.50 Ls, 45 minutes), and eight daily to/from Rūjiena (0.80 Ls) and Valka (0.85 Ls).

The **train station** (☎ 58 27 232; Stacijas laukums) is served by five trains daily to/from Rīga (1.55 Ls, 1-3/4-3 hours) via Cēsis (0.57 Ls, 40 minutes) and Sigulda (1.03 Ls, 20 minutes).

## AROUND VALMIERA
Heading 18km northeast on the Valmiera–Valka road, you hit **Strenči**, known for the **Strenči Rapids**, 4km below the town on the Gauja. With its steep, high banks, this is reckoned to be the most scenic stretch of the entire river. To get paddling contact a canoeing centre – see the boxed text 'Canoe Trips' earlier in this chapter. The village hosts a raft festival on the third Sunday in May.

**Zilaiskalns** (Blue Hill), topped by a lookout tower 14km west of Valmiera, and **Lake Burtnieku**, about 23km north, off the Mazsalaca road, are other local beauty spots. **Burtnieki** village, on the southern edge of the lake, is known for its **horse breeding centre** (Burtnieku zirgaudzētava; ☎ 42 56 444, fax 42 56 433). When the Latvian show-jumping team isn't in training, you can ride (5 Ls per hour) or be driven around the exceptionally pretty village in a horse-drawn carriage (15 Ls). The centre is signposted 'stallis' (stables) from the village. There's a couple of B&Bs in Burtnieki where you can stay overnight.

## VALKA
**pop 6927**
Valka, about 45km northeast of Valmiera on the road and train line to Tartu in Estonia, is the Latvian (and smaller) part of the unique twin town of Valga/Valka – divided between Latvia and Estonia when the republics were declared in 1920. The border – ironically nonexistent in Soviet times – is marked by a fence and rigorously controlled by sour-faced border guards who check passports and shoo away non-Estonians and -Latvians who try to cross at the in-town borders. Foreigners and motorists have to detour 5km north to cross from Valka to Valga – just 200m apart.

The history of the 'great divide' and the 142 buildings Valka was allocated is elaborated on in the **Valka Regional Museum** (Valkas novadpētniecības muzejs; ☎ 47 22 198; Rīgas iela 64; adult/child 0.50/0.30 Ls; open 10am-5pm Mon-Fri, 10am-4pm Sat), which doubles as an unofficial tourist office.

Valka's sole hotel, **Oltrā Elpa** (☎ 47 22 280; fax 47 22 285; Zvaigžņu iela 12; singles/doubles 17/20 Ls) is brand spanking new, with tastefully furnished rooms and a decent restaurant. Saunas (8 Ls per hour) and meals (2 Ls) are also available.

### Getting There & Away
From Valka bus station, at the northern end of Rīgas iela, there are daily buses to/from Rīga (1.05-2 Ls, 3¾ hours, up to four daily) and Valmiera (0.85 Ls, four daily). There are no buses to/from Estonia; a taxi (☎ 98 71 999) to Valka from the rank in front of the bus station should cost no more than 3 Ls.

The main train station is on the Estonian side but one or two trains daily to/from Rīga (1.95 Ls; via Cēsis and Sigulda) stop on the Latvian side in Lugaži (1km off the main road, down a dirt road in the middle of nowhere).

## ALŪKSNE, GULBENE & AROUND
The primary attraction of sleepy Alūksne (pop 9954), 103km southeast of Valka and 202km east of Rīga, is Latvia's only operating **narrow-gauge railway** which runs 33km daily to Gulbene, 33km south. A diesel train makes the 1½-hour trip two to four times daily; a one-way fare costs 0.64 Ls. Updated timetables are on the Internet at w www.banitis.lv. Alūksne tourist office (see later) also has details.

Beyond that there's little to do except learn about Ernest Glueck (1654–1705), the first person to translate the Bible into Latvian, and study sermons and hymn books in Alūksne's **Ernest Glueck Bible Museum** (Ernsta Glika Bībeles muzejs; ☎ 43 23 164; Pils iela 25a; adult/child 0.40/0.20 Ls; open 10am-5pm Tues-Thur, 8am-5pm Fri, 10am-2pm Sat). Thanks to the Alūksne vicar, the Latvian versions of the New and Old Testaments

VIDZEME

were completed in 1685 and 1689 respectively. The nearby **Art Museum** (*Mākslas muzejs;* ☎ *43 21 363; Pils iela 74; adult/child 0.30/0.10 Ls; open 10am-5pm Tues-Thur, 8am-5pm Fri, 10am-2pm Sat*) is likewise worth a quick gander.

Alternatively, take a day-trip to **Otte's Mill Museum** (*Ottes dzirnavas muzejs;* ☎ *43 45 452*), a farm museum midway between Alūksne and Gulbene (as the crow flies) in Kalncempji. Granaries, a smithy, barns, a watermill, and about 4000 exhibitions and photos are among the open-air museum's exhibits. During the lively harvest festival, held the second Saturday in September, visitors can test their threshing and rope-making skills, and relax afterwards with a slab of home-made bread and mug of home-brewed beer.

Anyone driving west from Alūksne to Valmiera might consider a side trip to **Zvārtava Manor**, built in a neo-Gothic style in 1882. The park-clad estate in Zvārtava is about 2km northwest of Gaujiena, signposted off the P23. Gaujiena itself is home to **Anniņas** (☎ *43 57 101; open 9am-5pm Mon-Sat*), the house where Latvian song composer Joseph Wihtol (Jāzeps Vitols) spent most summers between 1922 and 1944 and composed some of his most important works.

**Alūksne tourist office** (☎/*fax 43 22 804;* w *www.aluksne.lv/tourism; Dārza iela 8a; open 9am-6pm Mon-Fri mid-Oct–mid-Apr, 9am-6pm Tues-Fri, 9am-3pm Sat mid-Apr–mid-Oct*) stocks plenty of information on accommodation options in and around Alūksne.

## VIDZEME UPLAND

The part-forest, part-farmed Vidzeme Upland (Vidzemes Augstiene) is sandwiched between Cēsis and Madona, 80km southeast. Hills flag the approach to **Madona**, climaxing in Latvia's highest point, **Gaiziņkalns** (312m), 10km west of the small country town.

Lakes dot the Upland, while the Gauja rises on the southern side of **Elkaskalns** (261m) near Māli. The river then flows in a big circle, east through Jaunpiebalga and Lejasciems, north past Vireši and Gaujiena to form the Latvian–Estonian border for a stretch, then southwest through Strenči and Valmiera.

The Rīga–Rēzekne–Moscow trunk road crosses the Upland from west to east (through Madona), but the north–south route from Cēsis to Madona (the P30 through Taurene and Vecpiebalga) is more scenic.

**Ērgļi**, 28km southwest of Vecpiebalga, is a small ski resort. Latvian writer Rūdolfs Blaumanis (1863–1908) was born in **Braki**, 3km east, and his former home can be visited. Traditional musical instruments are exhibited in **Meņ-eļi** (☎ *48 71 077; adult/child 0.40/0.30 Ls; open 11am-4pm Thur-Sun*), a picturesque farmstead 4km east by Lake Pulgosnis. It has a traditional sauna and bathhouse (advance reservations only), and tents can be pitched on the lake shores.

South of Madona, nature enthusiasts can discover nine lakes and several rare plant species in **Krustkalni Nature Reserve** (*Krustkalni rezervāts; 3000 hectares*); and 19 lakes, Latvia's largest bog and migrating crane population in **Teiči Nature Reserve** (*Teiču rezervāts; 19,000 hectares*), 11km southeast. Ļaudona village, wedged between the two, is a handy base for forays into either reserve. **Madona tourist office** (☎ *48 60 573, fax 48 60 581; Saieta laukums 1; open 8am-5pm Mon-Fri*) has information on both.

The northern part of Vidzeme Upland is crossed by the Rīga–Pskov–St Petersburg road (the A2).

### Getting There & Away

Buses reach into and cross the Upland from Cēsis, Valmiera and Sigulda to the north, from Rēzekne to the south, and from Rīga to the west.

# Latgale

Latvia's southeastern region is called Latgale after the Latgal (Lettish) tribes who lived here at the time of the German invasion in the 12th century. It's the main bastion of Roman Catholicism in Latvia, having been under Polish control from 1561 to 1772.

The Latgale Upland, in its far southeastern corner, is a scenic lake district with Rēzekne prominent among the medium-sized towns around its fringes. Daugavpils, southwest of Rēzekne, is Latvia's second-biggest city and has a mainly Russian population. The Daugava River flows from Daugavpils to Rīga. A number of dams and hydroelectric schemes create artificial lakes along its length, and there are a few towns of minor significance.

## DAUGAVA VALLEY

The road and railway from Rīga to Daugavpils follow the northern bank of the Daugava River fairly closely. In Ķegums, 50km east of Rīga, you can visit the hydro-electric plant and dam and visit its on-site **Daugava Electricity Museum** *(Daugavas spēkstaciju muzejs; ☎ 50 53 256; e zaliteg@ dhesk.energo.lv; Ķeguma prospekts 7–9; open 9am-4pm Mon-Fri)*. The dam was built between 1936 and 1941 and the history of electricity production in Latvia is the focus of the power-station museum.

At **Lielvārde**, 10km farther east, and **Aizkraukle**, another 20km, there are ancient castle mounds from pre-German times. Lielvārde is home to the **Andrejs Pumpurs Museum** *(Andreja Pumpura muzejs; ☎ 50 53 759; adult/child 0.50/0.20 Ls; open 10am-5pm Wed-Sun)*, devoted to the myth of Lāčplēsis and the epic poem that writer Andrejs Pumpurs wove around it (see the boxed text 'Myth of Lāčplēsis' in this chapter). The whopping stone next to the museum was once, legend has it, the mighty Lāčplēsis' bed.

The scenic ruins of a 13th-century **knights' castle**, practically sitting in the river on the confluence of the Daugava and Perse Rivers in **Koknese**, 95km east of Rīga, are famous. The riverside town has a small **tourist office** *(☎ 51 61 296, 92 75 412; e tic@koknese.apollo.lv; Blaumaņa iela 3; open 9am-5pm Mon-Fri)*, with information on the Daugava Valley.

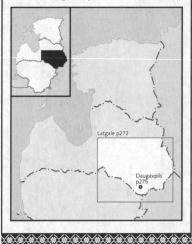

Latgale p272

Daugavpils p275

In **Krustpils**, 140km from Rīga, the railway divides and the main line heads east (away from the river) towards Rēzekne and Moscow, while the branch continues on up the river to Daugavpils. Krustpils, which has a 17th-century church and a 13th-century castle, forms a single town with **Jēkabpils** on the southern bank.

**Jēkabpils History Museum** *(Jēkabpils vēstures muzejs; ☎ 52 21 042; Rīgas iela 216b; adult/child 0.80/0.40 Ls; open 9am-5pm Mon-Fri, 10am-4pm Sat & Sun Apr-Sept, 10am-3pm Sat May-Oct)* is in the restored wing of the Krustpils castle. The museum's a fascinating **open-air section** *(☎ 52 32 501; Filozofu iela 6; adult/child 0.30/0.20 Ls; open same hours)*, with 19th-century farmstead buildings, is across the river in Jēkabpils proper.

LATGALE

# LATGALE

LATGALE

Jēkabpils offers basic rooms at **Motel Celinieks** (☎ 52 21 708; *Rīgas iela 33; doubles with shared bathroom 8 Ls*), which is a charmless pebble-dash hotel intended for road construction workers (hence the dozens of trucks parked next door).

Another choice in the region is **Pie Kaupra** (☎/fax 46-623 14; *doubles 8 Ls, meals 1.50 Ls; open 8am-midnight daily*), 62km farther east and 12km east of Viļjāni. You can sleep cheap at this red-brick, roadside motel and refuel empty stomachs in its busy bistro.

**Līvāni**, on the Rīga–Daugavpils road, is a pretty village with a **Glass Factory** (☎ 53 41 129, 53 44 540; *Zala iela 23; adult/child 0.50/0.30 Ls; open 9am-6pm Mon-Fri*) that can be visited. Since 1887 it has blown glass, which you can buy in its shop.

**Dunava**, 27km farther southeast, is the birthplace of Latvia's great poet Jānis Rainis. The village is said to be 'the cradle of the poet's soul'. The Rainis museum, **Tadenava** (☎ 52 52 522; *adult/child 0.40/0.20 Ls; open 10am-5pm Tues-Sun*), inside the house where he lived until he was four, recounts Rainis' childhood. See the Latgale Upland section later in this chapter for details of other Rainis museums in Latgale.

An alternative route to Daugavpils from Jēkabpils, is via **Gārsene**, about 50km east of Daugavpils in the gentle Saara hills, near the Lithuanian border. In winter you can ski here.

## RĒZEKNE & AROUND

Predominantly Russian Rēzekne (pop 44,000), 235km east of Rīga, forms the northwestern gateway to the Latgale Upland. The tourist bumph says the town stands on seven hills like Rome, although this is hard to see. The main street, Atbrīvoš anas alejā, runs from Rēzekne II train station (north) to the bus station (south), and crosses the central square en route. In the square's middle stands **Māra**, a statue twice destroyed by the Soviet authorities in the 1940s and only re-erected in 1992. Its inscription 'Vienoti Latvijai' means 'United Latvia'.

Regional tourist information is available at **Untumi** (☎ 46 31 255; e untumi@e-apollo.lv), a country ranch 7km northwest of town signposted off the Rīga road (the A12) where there are plenty of horses to ride (2-5 Ls per hour). Open fields surround the horse farm and there's plenty of space to pitch your tent (1 Ls per pitch) or have a picnic.

### Places to Stay & Eat

**Atpūtas bāze Sveltam** (☎ 46 98 262, 94 67 504; *open summer only*) is a lovely camp site beneath trees with a volleyball court and boats to paddle around Lake Rāzna. The site is signposted opposite the Kaunata turning along the Krāslava–Rēzekne road (P55).

**Hotel Latgale** (☎/fax 46 22 180; e lat gale@hotel.apollo.lv; Atbrīvosvanas alejā 98; *unrenovated singles/doubles 13/22 Ls, renovated doubles 30-80 Ls*), overlooking Māra, is not bad as far as Soviet-era hulks go. Prices reflect room size and extent of renovation. City maps are sold at reception.

**Little Italy** (☎ 46 25 771; *Atbrīvosvanas alejā 10; meals 3 Ls; open 11am-11pm daily*), opposite the Hotel Latgale, dishes up pizza, pasta, meats and other Italian-inspired fodder. Highlights on the badly translated menu include tunny fish and a meat assorty.

### Getting There & Away

The **bus station** (*Latgales iela 17*) has services to/from Aglona, Ludza, Daugavpils and Rīga (2.70 Ls, 4½ hours, up to six daily). The Eurolines bus from Rīga to St Petersburg stops here every second day.

**Rēzekne II train station** (*Stacijas iela*) has one train daily each way between Rīga and St Petersburg, and Moscow–Rīga. In all, there are four trains daily to/from Rīga (2.47 Ls).

The St Petersburg–Vilnius train (every second day) is the only service to stop at the southern **Rēzekne I train station** (☎ 58 83 801, 58 83 703).

## LATGALE UPLAND

The Latgale Upland (*Latgales Augstiene*), stretching south and southeast from Rēzekne, is a plateau-like area with thousands of lakes. **Lake Drīdzs** (*Dridzu ezers*) is Latvia's deepest lake at 65m. **Lake Rāzna** (*Rāznas ezers*), covering 55 sq km, is Latvia's biggest lake. Some of Latgale's prettiest scenery is around Lake Rāzna and between there and **Ezernieki**, on the eastern side of Lake Ežezers.

The Upland's highest point is **Lielais Liepukalns** (289m), 3km east of the Lake Rāzna–Ezernieki road. From the Catholic church at **Pasiene**, 8km south of Zilupe and 4km from the Russian border, there's a fine view across to the plains of Russia stretching endlessly eastward.

In **Ludza**, 25km east of Rēzekne, there's a **regional museum** (☎ 57 23 931; *Kuļņeva iela 2;*

LATGALE

## Myth of Lāčplēsis

Latvia's famous myth of Lāčplēsis runs roughly as follows: Lāčplēsis, the son of a bear mother, lived in Lielvārde. He inherited his mother's bear ears and thus was at first named Lācausis (The One With Bear's Ears). But as the young Lācausis grew stronger and was able to defend his family against wild animals, he was renamed Lāčplēsis (from *lācis* – bear and *plēst* – to tear apart).

Another, more creative variant of the myth holds that Lāčplēsis' father, rather than his mother, was actually the bear from whom he inherited his ears. Lāčplēsis' father kidnapped and impregnated a woman (Lāčplēsis' mother) and kept her trapped in his lair by means of a large stone to block her escape path. When Lāčplēsis grew up, he rolled away the stone, killed his father the bear, and rescued his mother.

Lāčplēsis' real trouble began with a witch who lived on the opposite bank of the Daugava River with her three-headed monster-son. Jealous of Lāčplēsis' prowess, the witch pitted her son against young Lāčplēsis. This three-headed monster knew Lāčplēsis' secret – that if his bear's ears (which were magic) were lopped off, Lāčplēsis could be defeated. A mighty Homeric battle ensued, in which Lāčplēsis cut off two of the monster's heads, while the monster succeeded in chopping off Lāčplēsis' ears. Their combat ended when both tumbled mortally off a cliff into the Daugava River at sunset.

open noon-5pm Mon-Sat, 10am-5pm Sun), with an open-air section demonstrating life in rural Latgale. On the first Sunday in July pilgrims flock to **Krāslava**, 45km east of Daugavpils, to celebrate St Donat's Day in the town's 18th-century Catholic church and pay homage to its patron saint.

Jānis Rainis (1865–1929) wrote some of his earliest works in Jasmuiža (also called Aizkalne), 9km west of Aglona. The **Rainis Memorial Museum** (☎ 53 54 677; adult/child 0.60/0.40 Ls; open 10am-6pm Fri-Sun) here showcases traditional Latgalian pottery as well as changing literary exhibitions devoted to the Shakespeare of Latvia. True fans will find the **Rainis House Museum** (☎ 54 22 515, 92 72 200; adult/child 0.30/ 0.15 Ls; open 10am-4pm Tues-Sat) in Berķenele, about 10km south of Daugavpils, equally interesting. The poet lived in the cottage for nine years.

### Aglona Basilica

This shimmering white, twin-towered church overlooking Lake Egles 800m south of Aglona village is Latvia's leading Roman Catholic shrine and pilgrimage site. Built in 1699, it is engulfed by a vast grass courtyard, created when Pope John Paul II visited in 1993. The disproportionately large pulpit where he addressed a congregation of thousands still stands, as does the regal archway built at the entrance to the site. One of the basilica's 10 altars guards a miraculous icon of the Virgin Mary, said to have saved Aglona from the plague in 1708.

Every year on Ascension Day (15 August) pilgrims gather here. A candlelight procession the night before precedes the religious celebration. During the Soviet era Peteris Jakovels, then dean of Aglona, was sent into forced labour after rigging up loudspeakers outside the basilica on 15 August 1959.

Aglona village, wedged between Lake Egles (east) and Lake Ciriss (west), is 35km north of Krāslava and 8km off the main Daugavpils–Rēzekne road (the A13), which crosses the western part of the lake district.

### Places to Stay & Eat

**Cakuli** (☎ 53 75 465, 91 94 362, fax 53 65 147; Ežera iela 4; bed in summer house 5 Ls, attic room with shared bathroom 8 Ls per person, singles/doubles with bathroom 15/25 Ls) is a family-run guesthouse on the shore of Lake Ciriss. Some of the rooms have a balcony with lake view. A beating in its traditional lakeside Latvian sauna (10 Ls) is an absolute must and you can rent paddleboats (3 Ls/hour).

### Getting There & Away

Public transport is limited, making a car or bicycle the only way to get around the Latgale Upland. Despite the numerous lakes, there is nowhere to hire canoes in the region. A handful of daily buses run between Rēzekne and Ludza, and several daily between Daugavpils and Krāslava, Aglona and Ludza.

Two trains run daily (in each direction) along the northern fringe of the district, on the Rēzekne–Ludza–Zilupe line, and the same on the southern fringe, on the Daugavpils–Krāslava–Indra–Robežnieki line.

## DAUGAVPILS
### pop 114,000

Daugavpils, Latvia's second-largest city, dates from 1275 and has a chequered past in which it has, at various times, been called Dünaburg by the Germans, Borisoglebsk by the Russians and Dvinsk by the Poles. Today it's a drab, post-WWII Soviet creation and so depressing to visit it's almost a national joke – a skyline of smoke stacks and the lumbering grey hulk of Daugavpils prison greet those who approach from the south. Perched on the northern bank of the Daugava River, 225km upstream from Rīga, the city acts a gateway to the decidedly lovelier Latgale Upland.

### Information

Daugavpils has no tourist office. There's an ATM outside **Hansabanka** (*Rīgas iela 22*). Internet access costs 0.30-0.50 Ls an hour depending what time you log-in at **Datoruklubs** (☎ 54 24 457; *Vienības iela 11; open 10am-6am daily*).

### Things to See

Downtown Daugavpils is a typical Soviet city centre of straight streets arranged in a strict grid, a couple of large squares, a desolate park with a black-marble **monument** to those who died in WWII (and an eternal flame that no longer burns), and a mixture of pre-WWII and Soviet era buildings. Ugly Hotel Latvija is the dominant landmark – a dramatic contrast to the white-domed **Roman Catholic church** next to it across Cietoksņa iela.

The **Regional Studies & Art Museum** (*Novadpētniecības un mākslas muzejs*; ☎ 54 24 073; *Rīgas iela 8; adult/child 0.40/0.20 Ls; open 11am-6pm Tues-Sat*), inside an Art Nouveau house guarded by two stone lions, is worth a brief visit.

Daugavpils' most remarkable feature is the huge **fortress** (*cietoksnis*; ☎ 54 26 398; *adult/child 0.20/0.10 Ls; open 8am-6pm daily*), built by the Russians in 1810 on the north-western side of town and occupied by the Soviet army until 1993. A red-brick bunker monument by the entrance states (in Russian and Latvian) that the Tatar poet Musa Jalil languished here from September to

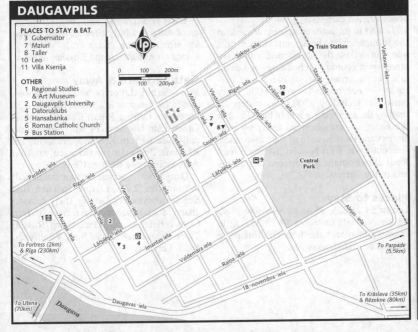

**DAUGAVPILS**

PLACES TO STAY & EAT
3 Gubernator
8 Mziuri
8 Taller
10 Leo
11 Villa Ksenija

OTHER
1 Regional Studies & Art Museum
2 Daugavpils University
4 Datoruklubs
5 Hansabanka
6 Roman Catholic Church
9 Bus Station

Train Station

Central Park

To Fortress (2km) & Rīga (230km)

To Parpade (5.5km)

To Utena (70km)

To Krāslava (35km) & Rēzekne (80km)

## Down & Out Daugavpils?

Daugavpils had 40,000 inhabitants before WWII, about two-thirds of them Latvians and one-third Russians or Poles. In 2001, 55.1% were Russian and just 16.1% Latvians (the lowest percentage of any town in Latvia), with Russian seemingly the only language used in shops, bars and on the street.

This massive shift in population took place during the Soviet era when industries located here lured mainly Russian workers. Most industries were large, specialist, all-union plants performing a single service for the whole USSR – like the 4000 people devoted to making bicycle and tractor chains or the 3500 who repaired one type of railway locomotive. When the Soviet Union collapsed, so too did these industries – and Daugavpils.

More than a decade on, the city has yet to recover. Daugavpils remains more economically depressed than other Latvian towns. Unemployment in Daugavpils city/region clocks in at 10.4/17.1%, close to the highest in the country.

October 1942, in what was then the Nazi concentration camp Stalag 340.

Tickets to the inner compound are sold at the former Soviet checkpoint. Once inside, you can follow the abandoned, run-down streets past boarded-up buildings and desolate parade areas. Part of the Soviet barracks – once home to some 6000 army personnel including 2500 army cadets attending the engineering school based within the fortress – are occupied today by pensioners and those in need of state assistance.

From town, a fairly quiet, riverside road leads 2km from the western end of Imantas iela to the fortress.

### Places to Stay
**Leo** (☎ 54 26 565, 95 48 622; Krāslavas iela 58; doubles with bathroom 19-30 Ls) is little known but offers the best comfort:price ratio in central Daugavpils.

**Paparde** (☎ 54 02 180, fax 54 11 410; e hotel.paparde@inbox.lv; Tervetes iela 17; singles/doubles with bathroom from 10/15 Ls) is a disappointingly unattractive block set in a forest near Lake Stropu. Its 15 rooms are bright and modern however. Bus No 3 and tram No 3 from the centre stop nearby.

**Villa Ksenija** (☎/fax 54 34 317; e magistr@ dpu.lv; Varšavas iela 17; singles/doubles with breakfast 35/45 Ls, luxury suite with private sauna 90 Ls) is Daugavpils' expensive, upmarket choice for those seeking luxury.

### Places to Eat
**Mziuri** (☎ 54 21 518; Mihoelsa iela 60; meals 3 Ls; open 11am-midnight daily) shines. It dishes up delicious Georgian cuisine in a stone-clad interior decorated with Georgian castles. Eating its *kuchmachi* (spicy liver cooked with pomegranate seeds) and *chanahi* (ground pork stewed with eggplant) is a definite Daugavpils highlight.

**Gubernator** (☎ 54 22 455; Lačpleša iela 10; meals 2 Ls; open 11am-midnight Mon-Fri & Sun, 11am-1am Sat), tucked in a cellar, is an unpretentious spot where you can dip into some red caviar (0.044 Ls) or munch your way through a salad weighing precisely 100g (around 0.50 Ls).

**Taller** (Viestura iela 59a; open 11am-midnight daily) is a busy beer bar with a popular street terrace and a wide variety of salads on its Latvian and Russian menu.

### Getting There & Away
From the **bus station** (☎ 54 23 000; w www .buspark.lv; Viestura iela 10) six to eight daily buses run to/from Rīga (3 Ls, 3½ hours). Other main bus services, all several times daily, are to/from Krāslava, Jēkabpils and Rēzekne. Buses also run twice daily to/from Aglona and once to/from Cēsis.

Daugavpils is served by four trains daily to/from Rīga (2.42-3 Ls, three to four hours). See the introductory Getting There & Away chapter for international rail services to/from Gomel (Belarus) and St Petersburg (Russia). Three trains daily run to/ from Vilnius (2-3 Ls, 3-4 hours).

# Zemgale

Zemgale is the region of central Latvia west of the Daugava River, between Rīga and the Lithuanian border. The region is low lying (below sea level in parts) and has a vast network of waterways. Most flow into the Lielupe River, which enters the sea between Rīga and Jūrmala – making it Latvia's most fertile farming area.

Zemgale is named after the Baltic Zemgal (Semigallian) tribes, who lived here before the 13th-century German conquest. The Semigallians, in fact, held out longer against the Germans than any other people living in the area that is now Latvia and Estonia, not being subdued until 1290. From the 16th to the 18th centuries, Zemgale (along with the Kurzeme region) formed part of the semi-independent Duchy of Courland.

Most places in Zemgale can be reached on day trips, albeit lengthy ones, from Rīga. The main road to Vilnius and Kaunas passes through Bauska, while the rail link cuts through Jelgava – a town best known for pop band Brainstorm.

Each year on the third weekend in July an evocative festival of ancient music fills the interiors and grounds of the region's most prized castles and palaces – Bauska Castle, Rastrelli's majestic Rundāle Palace and nearby Mežotne Palace.

## Highlights

- Witness one of Rastrelli's best creations after the Winter Palace in St Petersburg – Rundāle Palace
- Explore Bauska's 15th-century castle and take a tour around its museum
- Delve into the family vault of the dukes of Courland in Jelgava's baroque palace
- Sleep like a queen at Mežtone Palace or like a palace servant at nearby Rundāle

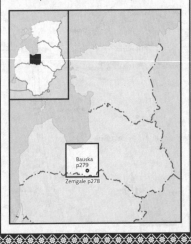

Bauska p279

Zemgale p278

## BAUSKA
### pop 10,620

Bauska is a country town with a small textile industry, 65km south of Rīga on the main Rīga–Vilnius road. It's a staging post on the way to Rundāle Palace but worth a brief stop in its own right, primarily to see its large castle.

As well as the music festival in July, Bauska Castle hosts a medieval arts festival in September.

## Orientation & Information

The city centre is on the southern side of the main road bridge that crosses over the Mēmele River. Its **tourist office** (☎/fax 39 23 797; W www.bauska.lv; Rātslaukums 1; open 9am-6pm Mon-Fri, 9am-3pm Sat) stocks lots of information on the Bauska region.

## Things to See

On a hillock between the Mēmele and Mūsa Rivers, 1km from the centre on the town's western edge, are **Bauska Castle Ruins** (Bauskas pilsdrupas; ☎ 39 23 793; open 9am-7pm daily May-Sept, 9am-6pm daily Oct). From the bus station, walk towards the centre along Zaļā iela then branch left along Uzvaras iela beside the park at the top of Kalna iela. You can also approach the ruins along any street westward off Kalna iela. The castle was built between 1443 and 1456 as a stronghold for the Livonian knights. The imposing edifice was destroyed in warfare, rebuilt as a residence for the duke of Courland in the 16th century, and destroyed again during the Great Northern War (1706).

Despite the impressive reconstruction job which was carried out in the 1970s, it is still

277

ZEMGALE

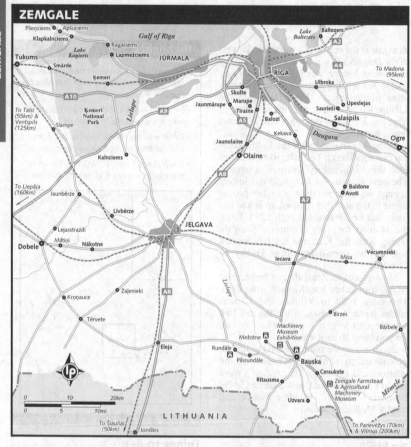

# ZEMGALE

Plieņciems · Apšuciems
Klapkalnciems · Ragaciems
*Lake Kaģieris* Lapmežciems
Tukums · Smārde
Ķemeri
*Gulf of Rīga*
JŪRMALA
*Lake Baltezers* Baltezers
RĪGA
Ulbroka
To Madona (95km)

To Talsi (55km) & Ventspils (125km)
*Ķemeri National Park*
Slampe
A10
A9
Skulte
Jaunmārupe
Marupe
Tiraine
Balozi
Ķekava
Saurieši · Upeslejas
Salaspils
*Daugava*
Ogre

Kalnciems
Jaunolaine
Olaine
A8
Baldone
Avoti
A7

To Liepāja (160km)
Jaunbērze
Līvbērze
Lejasstrazdi
Miltiņi Nākotne
JELGAVA
Iecava
Misa
Vecumnieki

Dobele
Kroņauce
Zaļenieki
A8
Tērvete
Eleja
*Lielupe*
Birzes
Bārbele

Mežotne
Rundāle
Pilsrundāle
*Machinery Museum Exhibition*
Bauska
Ceraukste

Rītausma
Uzvara
*Zemgale Farmstead & Agricultural Machinery Museum*
*Mēmele*

0   10   20km
0   5   10mi

LITHUANIA

To Šiauliai (50km)
Joniškis
To Panevēžys (70km) & Vilnius (200km)

possible to see where parts of the old castle remain. Inside, **Bauska Castle Museum** (☎ 39 23 793; adult/child 0.45/0.25 Ls; open 9am-7pm daily) displays archaeological finds and a collection of 16th- and 17th-century art.

Around the centre are several 18th- and 19th-century houses and the local **History Museum** (Bauskas novadpētniecība un mākslas muzejs; ☎ 39 22 197; e bnmuzejs@apollo.lv; Kalna iela 6; adult/child 0.30/0.20 Ls; open 10am-6pm Tues-Sun May-Oct, 10am-5pm Tues-Fri, 10am-4pm Sat & Sun Nov-Apr). A 1930s hairdressing shop and exhibition on Bauska's pre-WWII Jewish community – 15% of Bauska's prewar population – are among the exhibits. On the same street is a **synagogue** (Kalna iela 2).

## Places to Stay & Eat
**Hotel Bauska** (☎ 39 24 705, fax 39 23 027; Slimnīcas iela 7; singles/doubles 5/7 Ls, luxury doubles 10-22 Ls) has simple but adequate rooms.

**Pauze Café** (☎ 39 27 408; Zaļā iela 25; meals 2 Ls; open 10am-midnight daily), pronounced **pauza**, is popular with international visitors and is about 300m from the bus station. Good all-round dishes and plenty of beer complement a simple but tasteful decor.

## Getting There & Away
From Bauska **bus station** (☎ 39 22 477; Slimnīcas iela 11) there at least hourly buses between 5.30am and 5.30pm to/from Rīga (1.20 Ls, 1¼ hours). All long-distance buses

from Rīga to Panevėžys, Vilnius and Kaunas also stop here.

## AROUND BAUSKA

Latvian poet Plūdons (1874–1940), best remembered for his children's poetry and romantic lyrics, was born just south of Bauska in **Ceraukste**. The farmstead where he grew up is now a **house museum** (*māja muzejs; ☎ 91 94 975; adult/child 1.50/1 Ls; open 10am-6pm Wed-Sun May-Oct*). Wooden sculptures dot the garden and there is a traditional Latvian sauna.

Rural life in the 19th century is captured at the **Zemgale Farmstead & Agricultural Machinery Museum** (*Zemnieku sētas un lauksaimniecības maš imuzejs; ☎ 39 56 316; adult/child 0.40/0.20 Ls; open 10am-5pm Tues-Sun May-Oct*), a couple of kilometres farther south along the A7. Pieces of farm machinery used from the early 20th century are displayed here and at the museum's **Machinery Museum Exhibition** (*Maš inu muzeja izstāde; adult/child 0.40/0.20 Ls; open same hours*), west of Bauska on the road to Mežotne.

## RUNDĀLE PALACE

Eighteenth-century **Rundāle Palace** (*Rundāles pils; ☎ 39 62 197; ⓦ www.rpm.apollo.lv; adult/child 1.50/1 Ls; open 10am-6pm daily May-Oct, 10am-5pm daily Nov-Apr*), in

Pilsrundāle, 12km west of Bauska, is the architectural highlight of provincial Latvia. It was built for Baron Ernst Johann von Bühren (1690–1772), duke of Courland, by Bartolomeo Rastrelli, the baroque genius from Italy who created St Petersburg's Winter Palace.

Restoration to the palace began in the 1970s, with most period furnishings being bought or donated. Its facade was restored in 2001. Of the palace's 138 rooms, about 40 are open to visitors. The Gold Room (Zelta zāle) was the throne room; its ceiling paintings display the baron's virtues as a ruler. The White Room (Baltā zāle) was the ballroom. The main staircase in this wing, with multiple mirrors in its walls, is perhaps the outstanding original Rastrelli creation here.

On the ground floor of the eastern wing you can visit the palace kitchens (see Places to Stay & Eat later in this section); the western wing was for the duchess' apartments. The **Rundāle Palace Museum** (*Rundāles pils muzejs*) on the ground floor showcases paintings, silverware and other treasures from the Courland dukes' collections. In the old stables there is an interesting exhibition on Latvia's Lutheran churches in Soviet times.

A stroll through the gardens is a pleasant way to end a visit.

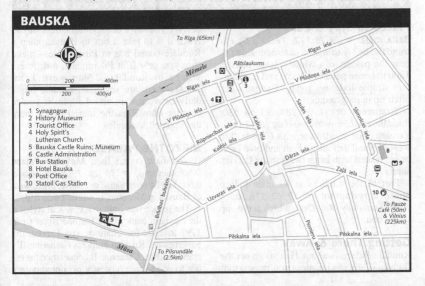

**BAUSKA**

To Rīga (65km)

0 — 200 — 400m
0 — 200 — 400yd

Mēmele
Rīgas iela
Rātslaukums
Rīgas iela
V Plūdoņa iela
V Plūdoņa iela
Rūpniecības iela
Kaleju iela
Kalna iela
Saules iela
Slimnīcas iela
Dārza iela
Zaļā iela
Uzvaras iela
Brīvības bulvāris
Mūsa
Pilskalna iela
Pionieru iela
Pilskalna iela

1 Synagogue
2 History Museum
3 Tourist Office
4 Holy Spirit's Lutheran Church
5 Bauska Castle Ruins; Museum
6 Castle Administration
7 Bus Station
8 Hotel Bauska
9 Post Office
10 Statoil Gas Station

To Pilsrundāle (2.5km)

To Pauze Café (50m) & Vilnius (225km)

## From Russia with Love

How the Italian master Bartolomeo Rastrelli came to build this splendid palace in such a remote corner of Europe, which wasn't even part of the Russian Empire at the time, is a curious tale. It begins with the marriage in 1710 of Anna Ioannovna, a niece of Russia's Peter the Great, to Frederick, Duke of Courland – no doubt an affair of state as Russia clawed its way into Poland's sphere of influence. In 1730, following Peter the Great's death, Anna of Courland found herself crowned empress of Russia.

Baltic German baron Ernst Johann von Bühren (Latvian: Bīron) had been something of a failed adventurer in Courland and Russia before becoming Anna's chief adviser (and lover) a few years before she succeeded to the Russian throne. With more interest in the trappings than the exercise of power, Anna handed over much of the management of the empire to von Bühren and a small clique of German advisers. Von Bühren's heavy-handed and corrupt style soon made him unpopular with the Russian nobility, but as long as Anna ruled Russia, the baron's star waxed. When he decided he needed a new home to go with his new status, Anna dispatched Rastrelli to Courland, and in 1736 work began on the summer palace for von Bühren, at Rundāle. It proceeded quickly with as many as 1000 people working on it at one time.

In 1737 the duke of Courland died heirless and, thanks to Russian influence, von Bühren was handed the dukedom. He then began work on an even grander Rastrelli-designed palace at Jelgava, intended as his main residence. Rundāle was put on the back burner – and came to a halt altogether in 1740 when Empress Anna died and von Bühren's enemies took their revenge, forcing him into exile for the duration of Empress Elizabeth's reign in Russia.

Only in 1763 – with a German, Catherine the Great, now on the Russian throne – was von Bühren allowed to return and finish Rundāle, also restoring the parts that had decayed in his absence. This time Rastrelli brought the Italians Francesco Martini and Carlo Zucchi, who had worked on the St Petersburg Winter Palace, to do the ceiling paintings. JM Graf, who had worked on Prussian royal palaces in Berlin, came to do the elaborate wall decorations.

In contrast to Rastrelli's initial baroque work, Rundāle, completed in 1768, was in the newer rococo style. Von Bühren was able to enjoy the palace until 1795 when, in the third Partition of Poland, Courland became Russian territory, and Catherine gave Rundāle to one of her favourites, Subov. Von Bühren managed to shift most of the fixtures and fittings to some of his other estates in Germany.

## Places to Stay & Eat

**Baltā māja** (☎ *39 23 172, 39 21 337; Pilsrundāle; bed with shared bathroom 2.50 Ls*), near the palace, is a white cottage built in 1800 to house palace servants and it still offers simple lodgings today. Campers can pitch up in its grounds.

**Straumeni** (☎ *91 09 388, 93 54 530; Rundāle; doubles with breakfast 10-12 Ls*) is a countryside guesthouse with 10 beds 3km west of Rundāle Palace. Fish and boat here, or get beaten with birch twigs in the Latvian sauna.

Part of the kitchens at Rundāle Palace house a **restaurant** (☎ *39 62 116; open 10am-6pm daily May-Oct*), which serves up tasty food.

## Getting There & Away

Rundāle Palace is about 1km south off the Bauska–Eleja road. Unless you're on a tour or have your own transport, the best way to reach it is to take a bus to Bauska, then a Rundāle-bound bus to Pilsrundāle – make sure you get off at Pilsrundāle, a different village to Rundāle, 2.5km west. From Bauska there are seven Pilsrundāle buses daily between 8am and 4.30pm; if you're coming from Rīga the tourist office there has updated schedules.

## MEŽOTNE PALACE

If you have a car then **Mežotne Palace** (*Mežotnes pils;* ☎ *39 28 796; adult/child 0.50/0.20 Ls; open 8am-5pm daily*), 11km west of Bauska in Mežotne, is worth a side trip.

The palace was built in a classical style on the northern bank of the Lielupe River from 1797 to 1802 for Charlotte von Lieven, the governess of Russian empress Catherine II's grandchildren. Catherine II bequeathed the estate to von Lieven (ancestor of contemporary writer Anatol Lieven – see Books in the regional Facts for the Visitor chapter for more information) in 1795. Agrarian reforms in 1920 transformed the family palace into an agricultural school (1921–41).

Mežotne Palace was restored in 2001 and a handful of rooms, including the dining room and grandiose Cupola Hall, can be visited. Part of the palace is a lovely live-like-royalty **hotel** *(☎ 39 28 796, ☎/fax 39 28 984; ⓔ mezotnepils@apollo.lv; singles/doubles 30/ 40 Ls)*. The surrounding 14-hectare park is landscaped English-style.

Mežotne, an ancient Zemgalian hillfort settlement, is signposted west off the northbound Bauska–Rīga road (A7).

## JELGAVA
**pop 63,000**
Jelgava, 42km southwest of Rīga, is Zemgale's biggest town. From the 16th to 18th centuries, it was the capital of the duchy of Courland and its little overseas empire. Afterwards, it was the capital of the Russian province of Courland and a place of renowned society and hospitality where gentry would gather in winter.

Unfortunately, much of Jelgava was ruined in the two world wars. But lovers of Rastrelli architecture should stop here to see the 300-room, baroque **Jelgava Palace** *(Jelgavas pils; ☎ 30 05 617; Leilā iela 2; adult/child 0.50/0.30 Ls; open 10am-4pm Mon-Fri)*, built in 1783. The palace, now Latvia's Agricultural University, houses the family vault of the dukes of Courland in its basement. The palace is beside the main river bridge on the Rīga road, a 750m walk from the central square on the eastern side of town.

Jelgava **tourist office** *(☎ 30 23 874, fax 30 21 891; Čakstes bulvāris 7)* has accommodation details.

**Hotel Jelgava** *(☎ 30 26 193, fax 30 83 005; ⓔ jelgava@apollo.lv; Leilā iela 6; singles/ doubles 8/12 Ls, renovated singles/doubles with TV 17/19 Ls)* has English-speaking staff and pleasant rooms in a lovely 1938 building near the palace.

Latvia's best-known boy band, Brainstorm (Patra Vetra), hails from the Jelgava area.

### Getting There & Away
Buses run every half-hour between Rīga and Jelgava (0.55-0.78 Ls, 1¼ hours).

One or two suburban trains an hour run from Rīga to Jelgava (0.66-0.74 Ls, 50 minutes). Some long-distance trains between Rīga and Ventspils, Siauliai, Kaunas and Vilnius also stop here.

# Kurzeme

The western region of Latvia, with coasts on both the Baltic Sea and the Gulf of Rīga, is called Kurzeme (Courland in English). Although Liepāja and Ventspils are sizable ports, Kurzeme is sparsely populated, with the northern part still heavily forested. In the south, Krievukalns on the Kursa Upland (Kurzemes Augstiene) is Kurzeme's highest point at 184m. The coastline, comprising beautiful, white-sand beaches, is untouched and home to Latvia's tiny ethnic minority, known as the Livs.

Kurzeme is very much a region apart from the rest of Latvia. When Germany signed its unconditional surrender in Berlin in 1945, the Red Army had succeeded in reconquering the whole of the Baltic states – except Courland. The region became sadly famous as the 'Courland Fortress' for the fight Latvian troops put up against the Red Army. The troops suffered heavy losses in the struggle.

Kurzeme is named after the Cours, a Baltic tribe who lived here before the 13th-century German invasion. They were an adventurous lot who would raid Scandinavia from time to time – and even, occasionally, join forces with the Vikings to attack Britain. Their leader, Lamekins, accepted Christian baptism and made a separate peace with the Pope in 1230 in order to avoid rule by the German knights of Livonia – the knights, however, refused to accept this arrangement and eventually subjugated the Cours in 1267. When the Livonian Order state collapsed under assault from Russia's Ivan the Terrible in 1561, the order's last master, Gotthard Kettler, salvaged Courland and neighbouring Zemgale as his own personal fiefdom.

Although owing allegiance to Poland, this Duchy of Courland, as it was known, was largely independent. Its capital was Jelgava (called Mitau) in Zemgale. Duke Jakob, its ruler from 1640 to 1682, developed a well-known navy, merchant fleet and shipbuilding industry, and purchased two far-flung colonies – Tobago in the Caribbean (from Britain) and an island in the mouth of the Gambia River (from African chiefs). He even laid plans to colonise Australia! His son, Duke Frederick,

## Highlights

- Drive up the Rīga–Kolka Coast road savouring its white-sand beaches and shopping at markets for freshly smoked fish
- See where the Gulf of Rīga and the Baltic Sea meet at Cape Kolka, then head south to explore the ancient land of the Livs
- Walk on top of bogs and through Latvia's oldest forest in the Slītere National Park – scale Slītere lighthouse first for an eagle's-eye view
- Snap away at eclectic sculptures in the innovative Pedvāle Open-Air Art Museum
- Discover Latvia's industrial face with a tour of the Baltic region's largest oil transhipment company in filthy-rich Ventspils

Kurzeme p283

Ventspils p291

Talsi p285

Kuldīga p294

Liepāja p296

tried to make Jelgava into a 'northern Paris' and married into the Russian royal family. The duchy was swallowed up by Russia in 1795 and governed as a province of the tsarist empire. It became part of independent Latvia after WWI.

## TUKUMS
### pop 19,465
Pleasant Tukums, 68km west of Rīga, has a **church** dating to 1670, a **castle mound** and an **art museum** (*Harmonijas iela 7*), with a collection of 1920s and 1930s Latvian art.

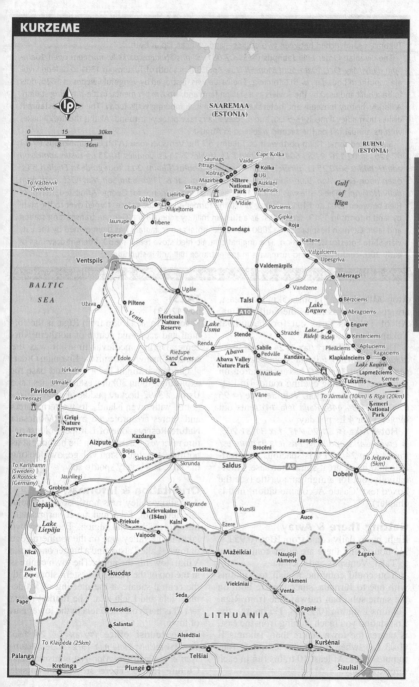

**KURZEME**

## Castle Accommodation

Tukums is sandwiched between two castles – and you can kip at both.

The Livonian Order built **Jaunpils** (☎ 31 07 081; ℯ pils@tukums.parks.lv; museum open 10am-5pm daily May-Oct, 10am-5pm Mon-Fri Nov-Apr), 34km south of Tukums, in 1301 to defend Livonia's southern boundary with Lithuania. The castle was destroyed by vengeful Swedes in 1625, only to be rebuilt and used by the Soviets as a stallion farm and, later, experimental cattle-breeding station. A library, history museum and hotel slumber within its lumbering walls today. The castle **restaurant** dishes up medieval meals (3-5 Ls), and medieval fairs take place year-round. All this theatre climaxes with its annual fair on the second weekend in August.

Signposted some 12km northwest of Tukums off the Ventspils road (A10) is **Jaumokupils** (☎ 31 07 125, 31 07 126, 91 83 604; hostel bed 7 Ls, singles 7-15 Ls, doubles 10-25 Ls; castle admission adult/child 0.50/0.25 Ls, picnicking and/or taking photos/filming 2 Ls, tour guide in English 5 Ls; open noon-6pm Mon, 9am-6pm Tues-Fri, 10am-6pm Sat & 11am-6pm Sun May-Oct, until 5pm daily Nov-Apr). The castle was built in 1901 as a hunting residence for George Armitsted, mayor of Rīga between 1901 and 1912. During WWII the former aristocratic palace, turned over to the state by land reforms in 1919, served first as a Russian military school, then German transmitting station and later, German hospital. Since 2000 the castle, hotel and restaurant has been owned by the Latvian State Forestry Commission. The original ceramic-tiled stove featuring 50 different drawings of early 20th-century Rīga and Jūrmala is in the entrance hall and is stunning.

Atop **Milzukalns** (113m), 5km northeast, are good views as far as the Gulf of Rīga. All of Tukums turns out for the annual Tukums festival in July.

The **tourist office** (☎/fax 31 24 451; W www .tukums.lv/turisms; Pils iela 3; open 9am-6pm Mon-Fri, 9am-3pm Sat) has information on Kurzeme, including cycling routes (in Latvian only) in the region. **Velo Service** (☎ 95 07 095, 64 34 448; Raiļa iela 14) rents out bicycles for 4 Ls per day.

**Hotel Arka** (☎ 31 25 747, fax 31 81 205; ℯ ervins@arka.apollo.lv; Pils iela 9; doubles/ triples from 24/36 Ls) is spacious, comfortable and has a great spiral staircase. Alternatively, opt for a night in a castle (see the boxed text 'Castle Accommodation' in this chapter).

### Getting There & Away

Eight buses daily come from Rīga (0.95 Ls, 1¼ hours) and there are other connections to Talsi, Ventspils and Liepāja.

You could combine a visit to Tukums with one to Jūrmala, since they're both on the same suburban railway line from Rīga. Tukums I station (0.99 Ls, 1½ hours), the first station you reach coming from the east, is nearer the town centre than Tukums II (1.03 Ls), where the trains terminate four minutes later. At least 10 trains run in each direction daily.

## TALSI
### pop 12,391

Peaceful Talsi, 115km from Rīga, is the cultural and economic centre of northern Kurzeme. During medieval times it was the centre of many wars with the Livonian Order.

Quiet as it might be, it's a good base for exploring. About 30km west languishes **Lake Usma**, a 3892-hectare puddle of water polka-dotted with seven islands. Its western waters and shores are protected by the **Moricsala Nature Reserve**, one of Europe's oldest nature reserves. Yachts bob in the harbour at its northwestern tip. Usma village, overlooking the lake, is a lovely spot to stay.

### Orientation & Information

A shallow valley runs north–south through the middle of Talsi making it surprisingly hilly for such a flat region. There are two lakes in the valley, one on the southern edge of town (Lake Talsu), and a bigger one (Lake Vilku) towards the north. The town centre is at the top of the valley's western slope, with the central square at the meeting of Valdemāra iela and Lielā iela. The **market** (Ezera iela 7) is north off Lielā iela in the lower part of town.

The **tourist office** (☎/fax 32 24 165; W www.talsi.lv; Lielā iela 19/21; open 10am-1pm & 1.30pm-5pm Mon-Fri) is inside Talsi Culture House. There are ATMs outside

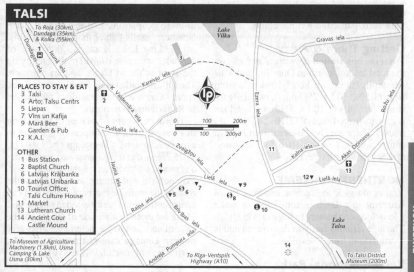

**TALSI**

PLACES TO STAY & EAT
3 Talsi
4 Arto; Talsu Centrs
5 Liepas
7 Vīns un Kafija
9 Marā Beer
  Garden & Pub
12 K.A.I.

OTHER
1 Bus Station
2 Baptist Church
6 Latvijas Krājbanka
8 Latvijas Unibanka
10 Tourist Office;
  Talsi Culture House
11 Market
13 Lutheran Church
14 Ancient Cour
  Castle Mound

KURZEME

Latvijas Unibanka *(Lielā iela 17)* and Latvijas Krājbanka *(Lielā iela 3)*.

## Things to See

There's really not a great deal to do in Talsi except wander around and enjoy the surroundings. Rising above **Lake Talsu** on the western side of town is **Pilsētas dārzs**, an ancient Cour castle mound topped by **Freedom Sun**, a statue of a man sitting Buddha-style. It was erected in 1996 in remembrance of Latvia's freedom fighters.

Above the mound, local history is documented at the **Talsi District Museum** *(Talsu novada muzejs; ☎ 32 22 770; Milenbaha iela 19; adult/child 0.50/0.30 Ls; open 11am-5pm Tues-Sun summer, 10am-4pm Tues-Sun winter)*. The museum is in a baronial manor dating to 1880.

South of town, the **Museum of Agriculture Machinery** *(Lauksaimniecības tehnikas muzejs; ☎ 32 81 343; Celtnieku iela 11; open 8am-6pm Mon-Fri; adult/child 1/0.50 Ls)* exhibits tractors from the 19th and 20th centuries.

## Places to Stay & Eat

**Usma Camping** *(☎ 63 34 500, 91 63 264, fax 36 75 486; ⓦ www.usma.lv; Priežkalni; 1km south of A10 on road to Usma village; sites 1 Ls plus 1/0.50 Ls per adult/child, beds 2.50-3 Ls, wooden cabins for two/three/four people from 10/11.50/13 Ls per cabin; open May-Oct)* is

the get-away-from-it-option for those who seek peace. You can camp here, fish, sail, row, swim and play volleyball at this lakeside site, which opened in 2002.

**Talsi** *(☎ 32 22 689, fax 22 24 596; ⓔ viesnica _talsi@e-apollo.lv; Kareivju iela 16; singles/ doubles/triples/quads 12/16/21/20 Ls)* is a Soviet-era block of 95 rooms situated atop a hill. Talsi's only hotel touts a striped yellow-and-beige exterior and a renovated interior.

**K.A.I.** *(Lielā iela 30; meals 1 Ls; open 11am-3am daily)* competes for the most kitsch spot in the Baltics. Munch on unremarkable food and watch fish bob in plastic tubes of florescence. The place has a pool table.

**Arto** *(Valdemāra iela; open 9am-9pm daily)* is a contemporary art café on the 3rd floor of the Talsu Centrs shopping centre.

**Marā Beer Garden & Pub** *(Lielā iela 16; meals 1.50 Ls; open 11am-11pm daily)* is a hip bar – at least by Talsi standards – with a lovely summer beer garden. Platefuls of food are large.

**Vīns un Kafija** *(☎ 32 81 049; Lielā iela 7; open 9am-7pm Mon-Sat)* is the place to taste and buy wine (albeit wine produced everywhere but Latvia) and coffee. It runs a beer tent out front in summer.

**Liepas** *(Lielā iela 1; meals 1 Ls; open 7.30am-9pm Mon-Sat, 9am-8pm Sun)* is a food shop and café rolled into one. Be sure to try the *platmaize*, a sponge cake topped with curd, particular to this region.

## Getting There & Away
From the **bus station** *(Dundagas iela 15)*, on the road leading north to Dundaga and Valdemārpils, there are hourly buses to/from Rīga (1.50-2.10 Ls, 2½ hours), two daily to/from Ventspils (1.10 Ls, 1½ hours) and six a day to/from Liepāja (2.10-2.45 Ls, 4½ hours). There are also buses to/from Jelgava (three hours), Kuldīga (two to 2½ hours) and Sabile (45 minutes).

## NORTHERN KURZEME
You could visit the remote northern tip of Kurzeme in a day trip from Talsi, or make a long loop on the way to Rīga or Ventspils. The area remains fairly undiscovered and is worth taking time to explore.

### Ķemeri National Park
The Rīga–Kolka coastal road (P128) twists along the Gulf of Rīga past fishing villages, sandy beaches and pine forests. Part of this coastline is protected by the Ķemeri National Park (Ķemeru nacionālais parks).

The national park was set up in 1997 and covers 42,790 hectares of forest, bog and shrubland stretching from just west of Jūrmala to Klapkalnciems, and inland to Kalnciems. Its **information centre** *(☎/fax 77 65 387; e nacionalparks@kemeri.apollo.lv; open 1 May-15 Oct)* is hidden among trees in Ķemeri, a 1930s spa town known for its sulphurous springs. The thatched-roof building (1932–33) formed part of Ķemeri Sanatorium, the main building of which – a vast white mansion built in 1936 in a classical style and empty since 1994 – is under renovation. In the park opposite, 12 cutely named bridges – Musical Bridge, Bridge of Sighs, Bridge of Caprices etc – cross the Vērš upite River.

The information centre is the starting point for **Dumbrāja laipa**, a raised plank trail (600m, 20 to 30 minutes) across rivers and through forest. A second boardwalk trail, the **Laipa Lielajā Ķemeru tīrelī** (3km, 1½ hours) crosses the large bog that fills the entire southern half of the park. The information centre arranges **bat-watching** expeditions and runs half-day **nature workshops** in summer. For birding buffs, there's **Lake Kaņieris**, home to 237 bird species nestled around 14 islets.

Fish canning and smoking remain traditional occupations in the national park. Nowhere smells fishier than **Lapmežciems**, overlooking Lake Kaņieris, 3km west of Jūrmala. Sprats are canned in the factory on the right at the village's eastern entrance. The village market sells freshly smoked eel, sprat, salmon and tuna, as does the market in **Ragaciems**, 2km north.

There are plenty of places to stay along this coastal stretch: Campers might want to avoid the Soviet-era **kempings** *(☎ 31 43 146, 31 25 358; bed in shared, unheated wooden hut and shared bathroom 2 Ls; open summer only)*, 2km north of Apš uciems, and pop across the road to the roadside car park where you can camp for free amid pretty wooded sand dunes. There are **motels** either side of the road at the eastern entrance to Ragaciems and the very modern **Lindaga café-bistro** *(☎ 31 63 544; open 10am-11pm daily)* where you can eat.

### Lake Engure to Roja
**Lake Engure**, 2km north of the fishing village of Engure, is Latvia's third-largest lake and a major bird reservation – 186 bird species (44 endangered) nest around the lake and its seven islets. The **Engure Ornithological Research Centre** *(☎ 94 74 420; Bērzciems; open by appointment only)* arranges birdwatching expeditions to the observation tower in the middle of the lake. The centre, signposted 600m north of Bērzciems village, is at the end of a 2.5km-long dirt track.

You can rent a boat to row around the lake (1/5 Ls per hour/day) from the **boat station** (laivu bāze) off the main road in Bērzciems. Boats can also be rented and a sauna indulged in at **Abragciems Kempings** *(☎ 31 61 668, 92 39 321; camp sites 8 Ls)*, a site by the sea 4km north of Engure.

At **Lake Rideļi**, a tiny lake 15km inland (west), you can visit **Rideļi Watermill**, still in operation, and munch on pancakes made with local flour at the adjoining **Cope Café & Guest House** *(☎ 31 61 373, 91 20 190; singles/doubles with breakfast 9/16 Ls, tent & adult/car 1.50/1.50 Ls)*. Boat hire costs 0.70/4.50 an hour/day.

**Roja**, 50km farther north, is another fishing town, the history of which can be found at the small **Maritime and Fishing Museum** *(Jūras un zvejniecības muzejs; ☎ 32 69 594; Selgas iela 33; adult/child 0.30/0.10 Ls; open 10am-6pm Tues-Sat)*. The most interesting exhibits are those relating to the development of Roja's collective fishing farms and state fish cannery in the 1950s.

Hotels are scarce. In Engure **Stagars** (*π/fax 31 61 477,* π *92 41 068;* e *phl@apollo.lv; Jūras iela 62; doubles/triples/quads with shared bathroom 8/12/16 Ls, doubles with bath 15 Ls)* is for the truly desperate. The **Roja Hotel** (π *32 60 209; Jūras iela 6; doubles 20 Ls),* just past the harbour, is more comfortable but often booked for conferences.

## Kolka & Cape Kolka

Kolka, Kurzeme's most northerly village, stands on the Gulf of Rīga just south of Cape Kolka (Kolkasrags) – the dividing point between the gulf and the Baltic Sea. The village is not pretty but its dramatic position on the tip of the cape is reason enough to spend time strolling along sandy beaches, over dunes and through forests. During the Soviet era the area was a military reserve, out of bounds to civilians. The place still feels like the end of the world. The cape itself (the Latvian *rags* translates literally as horn) is the point where the line of beach and dunes changes direction – making it possible to stand with one foot in the Gulf of Rīga and the other in the Baltic Sea.

**Ūš i** (π *32 77 350, 92 93 483; tent site 3 Ls, B&B 8 Ls)* has little wooden chalets with sea views and bicycles to rent. Look for the brick house, opposite the onion-domed Orthodox church on the main road at the village's northern end.

**Zitari** (π *32 47 145, 92 41 546; B&B doubles 14 Ls),* Kolka's only hotel, has clean and modern rooms and a ground-floor café *(meals 3 Ls; open 10am-midnight daily),* popular for a drink, plate of herrings (0.80 Ls) or smoked eel (2.45 Ls) after a trip to the windy cape. It neighbours the well-stocked **village shop**.

## Slītere National Park

Slītere National Park is a magnificent pocket of spectacular sand dunes and forests covering 16,360 hectares on Latvia's most savage coastal tip. Overlooking the Gulf of Riga and the Baltic Sea, the park begins at Cape Kolka and continues (5km to 10km inland from the coastline) 26km west along the Baltic Coast to Sikrags. Three of the seven coastal villages along this stretch – Kolka, Pitrags and Mazirbe – are excluded from the park, although the Kolka–Ventspils coast road (a

gravel road) goes right through it. The park's population (1300) doubles in summer when rich Rigāns flock to their summer cottages.

The park shelters deer, elk, buzzards and beaver. Rare species include the yew tree, pond turtle, golden eagle and osprey. In mid-April, during spring migration, the Kolka peninsula buzzes with 60,000-odd birds. Part of the park boundary runs close to the line of the 15km-long, 35m-high **Slītere Cliff**.

The **information centre** (π *32 81 066;* w *www.slitere.gov.lv),* inside Slītere lighthouse (see the Kolka–Ventspils Coast Road section later), runs a guide service (0.30 Ls per hour) and is the starting point for a 1.3km **nature trail** through Latvia's oldest forest. Protected since 1921, the broad-leaf forest shelters a calcium-rich bog and is prime ground for rare orchid species (which flower in June or July). Several more boardwalk trails are planned.

### The Kolka-Ventspils Coast Road

The villages along this northernmost stretch are worth exploring. Nestled among a natural wilderness of sea, sand and breathtakingly beautiful beaches and pine forests, it's as if time has stopped for its inhabitants.

In **Vaide**, 10km west of Kolka, there is little to see or do except wonder at the simple wooden houses. Elk antlers hang from the street signs and there's 518 more to be seen in the **Museum of Horns and Antlers** *(Ragu kolekcija;* π *32 44 217; adult/child 0.40/0.20 Ls; open 9am-8pm daily May-Oct)* – the collection from one man's lifetime of work as a forest warden in the national park (none are hunting trophies). You can **camp** *(0.50 Ls per person)* in the field behind the house; there's a pond, toilets and picnic tables and a small fee of 0.50 Ls per person.

**Košrags**, 6km west, is worth visiting for its 18th-century wooden buildings. Neighbouring **Mazirbe**, 18km southwest of Kolka, is home to the **Livonian People's House** *(Lībieš u tautas nams; Livlist rovkuoda in Livonian).* Currently under renovation, the 1930s building will host exhibitions on Livonian culture when it reopens. Livonian ethnographical treasures can meanwhile be viewed at the **Rundāli Museum** *(Muzejs Rundāli;* π *32 48 375; open by appointment only),* the squat, barn-like building on your right when entering the village.

**Kalēji** (π *32 48 374; doubles around 5 Ls),* a 12-bed guesthouse in a private home in

KURZEME

## The Livs

*My fatherland, You are dear to me! Where waves lap against the native shore, Where I hear my beloved mother tongue!*

**Excerpt from the Livonian hymn** *My Fatherland/Min izāmō*

The Livonians, or Livs, are Finno-Ugric peoples who first migrated to northern Latvia 5000 years ago. At the time of the 13th-century German invasion this fishing tribe inhabited the coastal regions on the eastern and western sides of the Gulf of Rīga; today a population of around 1600 is clustered in 14 fishing villages along the Livonian Coast, which stretches from Pūrciems, 11km north of Roja on the Rīga–Kolka coast road, to Lūžļa, 49km southwest of Kolka along the Kolka–Ventspils coast road. These villages are preserved under Latvian law, and it is forbidden to open a hotel, restaurant or other commercial enterprise in them.

These preservation efforts are intended to aid the cultural survival of the Livs, who are on the brink of extinction. Just 10 people or so in Latvia are native speakers of the Liv language (which is more closely related to Estonian and Finnish than to Latvian), while no more than 50 have 'Livonian' as a nationality written in their Latvian passports. Traditional Livonian songs are kept alive by Dainis and Helmi Stalti, a Liv couple who pioneered Latvia's folklore movement with their folklore ensemble Skandinieki in 1976. Liv is strictly the language of their album *Livod Iolod (Livu dziesmas/Livonian Songs)*, released in 1998.

Sadly, the younger generation of Livs, despite compulsory once-a-week classes in Liv language in schools, is much more interested in being called Latvian than Livonian; many have left their homeland for other cities in Latvia and have quickly assimilated into the surrounding Latvian culture and language. The Livonian language may well die out with the older generation.

Liv culture is celebrated each year in early August with Mazirbe's Liv festival.

---

Mazirbe, offers the chance to experience village life first-hand. It has a sauna and you can camp here. The more optimistic claim that the former Soviet barracks – a concrete complex by the sea in Mazirbe, abandoned since 1991-2 – will be turned into a luxury hotel. It could be true – or a pipe dream.

From Mazirbe a gravel road leads inland to Dundaga (see Dundaga later in this section) and Talsi. About 5km south of Mazirbe you see a sign for **Slītere Lighthouse** *(Slīteres bāka;* ☎ *32 49 215)*, 1.4km down an even dirtier track. Pay 0.30 Ls and climb 101 steps for an aerial view of the national park and Estonian island of Saaremaa. The lighthouse was built in 1849 and hosts the national park information centre.

Latvia's tallest lighthouse at 55.6m, **Miķeļ Lighthouse** *(Miķeļ bāka;* ☎ *36 81 501)*, built in 1957, is further down the coast in **Miķeļtornis**. The caretaker lives opposite the lighthouse entrance on the 1st floor; ask nicely and he'll take you up the 277 steps for yet another stunning view.

**Dundaga** Set amid three lakes, 20km from the Gulf of Rīga and 40km north of Talsi,

Dundaga is known for its **crocodile statue** *(cnr Talsu & Dinsberga iela)*. The 3m-long concrete crocodile, which lazes on a bed of stones, was given to the town by the Latvian consulate in Chicago in September 1995. The statue is in honour of Arvids von Blumenfelds, a Latvian born in Dundaga but forced to flee his home town during WWII for Australia, where he spent his days hunting crocodiles in the outback. The story goes that the film *Crocodile Dundee* was based on this Dundaga hero. As you enter Dundaga from the north, the crocodile is on your left.

**Dundaga Castle** *(Dundagas pils;* ☎ *32 42 093, 32 42 142; Pils iela 14; adult/child 0.50/ 0.20 Ls; open 10am-noon & 1pm-4pm Mon-Fri, 11am-4pm Sat & Sun)*, built in 1249 and the largest in northern Courland, can be visited. Legend has it that a fair maiden made the mistake of intruding upon a gnomes' wedding and as punishment she was walled up alive. She haunts the castle, appearing when the moon is full. Part of the castle is a music school today.

**Pūpoli** *(*☎ *32 40 100, 65 54 001;* **e** *pupoli@ dundpag.apollo.lv; tent site 2 Ls, B&B doubles 20 Ls)*, a guesthouse with a wooden terrace, has four comfortable rooms and oodles of green space for campers. It arranges berry and mushroom picking, forest walks and saunas. Pūpoli is 600m east of Dundaga centre along the Gipka road.

### Getting There & Away
Private transport is the most convenient in Northern Kurzema, but there are sporadic buses; always check return schedules before setting out. From Rīga, two buses daily serve Kolka (2.65 Ls, four hours), passing through Mērsrags and Roja.

### THE ABAVA VALLEY
The Abava River from near Kandava to its confluence with the Venta River is a popular canoe route – boats and bicycles can be rented in Kandava and Sabile. Since 1999 the valley – 30km long and 4m deep – has been protected by the **Abava Valley Nature Park**.

### Kandava
Split in two by the Abava River, Kandava is a charming, historic town, 20km south of Strazde. A mound fortified by the ancient Cours and the ruins of a **Livonian Order castle** appear to the north. From the top of the mound, there is an excellent view of the fine **stone bridge** (1875) across the Abava River – one of Latvia's oldest bridges.

Velotūre (☎ 94 15 842, 92 59 912; *Sabiles iela 6*) rents out bicycles for 4 Ls per day. Alternatively, you can try **Plosti** (☎ 31 31 349, 94 53 777; W www.plosti.lv; *Rēdnieki*), a recreational centre where you can rent bicycles, hire canoes with/without a guide to paddle down the Abava, ride horses and fish. The place also has a hostel with dorm beds (see Places to Stay & Eat).

**Pils**, a green-and-white cottage café below the castle ruins, has a wonderful fireplace in winter and sunny terrace in summer.

### Sabile & Pedvāle
Sabile, 14km downstream from Kandava, also has an **ancient fortification** mound and a 17th-century **church**. This sleepy, cobbled-street village is famed for its vineyard – listed in the *Guinness Book of Records* as being the world's most northern. A Council of Europe flag marks the famed patch of land, just one hectare in size and called **Vīna kalns** (*Wine Hill*). The only chance to taste local wine (it's impossible to buy) is at Sabile's wine festival

in July. The **tourist office** (☎ 32 52 269; *Ventspils iela 14; open 10am-3pm Mon-Fri*) has details.

**Pedvāle Open-Air Art Museum** (*Pedvāles brīvdabas mākslas muzejs*; ☎ 76 22 335; W www.pedvale.lv; *adult/child 1/0.50 Ls, guide 5/3 Ls per hour; open 9am-6pm daily May-Oct*) is 1.5km south **of the tourist office and village centre** on the northern bank of the Abava River. Many of the sculptures, installations and paintings here are in memory of those deported to Siberia and the graves of many Latvian soldiers who died during WWII can be found on the estate. Several outbuildings serve as exhibition halls and the main house is an information centre and guesthouse (see Places to Stay & Eat later).

In winter you can ski at **Zviedru cepure** (☎ 65 14 001, 91 98 283; W www.zviedru cepure.lv; *lift ticket 1/6 Ls per hour/day; open 10am-1am Mon-Thur, 9am-1am Fri-Sun winter, 10am-10pm Mon-Thur, 9am-midnight Fri-Sun summer*), a recreational centre that's 3.5km south of Sabile on the road to Matkule. You can rent ski/snowboarding gear here (2/5 Ls per hour) to whizz down its

KURZEME

two downhill runs. It also rents out boats and bikes

**Abavas rumba** is a small waterfall 4km northwest of Sabile. The **Rendas rumba**, off the Abava River at Renda, 20km downstream on a tributary called the Ivanda, falls 2m and is Latvia's highest natural waterfall.

## Places to Stay & Eat
You can camp in summer at **Zviedru cepure** (☎ 65 14 001, 91 98 283; W www.zviedru cepure.lv; Piltiņi; tent site 1.50-2 Ls). The sports centre has a small, eight-bed guesthouse too. **Plosti** (☎ 31 31 349, 94 53 777; W www.plosti.lv; Rēdnieki; dorm beds 2.50-3.50 Ls) also has a small hostel on site.

**Firkspedvāle** (☎ 32 52 249; e pedvale@ pedvale.lv; beds 5 Ls, camp sites 1 Ls) is the atmospheric guesthouse at the open-air art museum in Pedvāle. Rooms are in the attic.

**Krodziļš Dāre** (☎ 32 52 273; meals 3 Ls; open 9am-11pm daily), opposite the guesthouse, serves simple yet satisfying food inside or on a large wooden terrace overlooking the museum's artsy minigolf course, swings and seesaw.

## Getting There & Away
This area is best explored by car. From Rīga five buses daily pass through Kandava, Sabile and Renda. Kandava train station is 7km north of the town.

## VENTSPILS
### pop 44,000
Ventspils (former German name: Windau), 200km west of Rīga, is an industrial town and Latvia's busiest port. There was a Cour settlement here before the Livonian Order founded a castle in 1244. Ventspils was in the Hanseatic League from the 14th to 16th centuries, and in the 17th century Duke Jakob of Courland based his navy here. After a spell in the doldrums the town revived with the arrival of a railway from Rīga in the early 20th century.

During the Soviet era Ventspils was a key USSR port and attracted a workforce mainly from non-Latvian parts of the USSR – 32% of the population remains Russian today.

In recent years the oil-transit port town earned itself a reputation as a clean and pretty place to visit. Latvians see the city as the most dynamic outside Riga, renowned for its riches reaped from oil exports.

When in Ventspils do as locals do – drink Užavas, a light beer brewed locally.

## Orientation
The Venta River flows up the eastern side of the town then turns west for its final 2.5km to the sea. The Old Town, south of the river, was the real town centre until the Soviet navy took over the riverside area, and a new centre was created around Ganību iela and Kuldīgas iela, 750m or so farther south.

## Information
The **tourist office** (☎/fax 36 22 263; W www .tourism.ventspils.lv; Tirgus iela 7; open 8am-7pm Mon-Fri, 8am-5pm Sat, 10am-5pm Sun May-Oct, 9am-5pm Mon-Fri, 10am-3pm Sat Nov-Apr) has reams of information and reserves accommodation.

**Unibanka** (Kuldīgas iela 3), around the corner from the bus station, has a currency-exchange desk and ATM, as does **Hansabanka** (Kuldīgas iela 23 & 26) and **Baltijas Tranzītu Banka** (cnr Liela & Kuldīgas iela).

The **post office** (Jūras iela; open 8am-6pm Mon-Fri, 8am-4pm Sat) is opposite the corner of Andreja iela. Internet access costs 1 Ls per hour at **Planet Internet Club** (Andrejs iela 7; open 10am-10pm daily), on the top floor of the Andrejs Nams shopping centre. The same rates are charged at **Nozagtais Mēness** (Zvaigžļu iela 4; open 10am-6pm daily).

## Things to See & Do
There is little to see or do in the Old Town except wander its streets and absorb its 18th-century architecture. Pils iela is the main street, cutting across the Old Town from Brīvibas iela (east) to Peldu iela (west) and the castle. Peering across Brīvibas iela is the neo-Byzantine St Nicholas Russian Orthodox Church (Sv Nivolaja pareizticīgo baznīca; Plosu iela 10), built in 1901 and crowned with five onion domes. Walking west along Pils iela, you can detour south down Tirgus iela to **Rātslaukums** – a pretty cobbled square overlooked by St Nicholas Evangelical Lutheran Church (Sv Nivolaja luterāļu baznīca; Tirgus iela 2), built in 1835.

Ventspils' 13th-century **Livonian Order Castle** (☎ 36 22 031; Jana iela 17; adult/child 1/0.50 Ls; open 9am-6pm daily May-Sept, 10am-5pm daily Oct-Apr) hosts a cutting-edge interactive museum on castle history, with digital displays and two panoramic telescopes

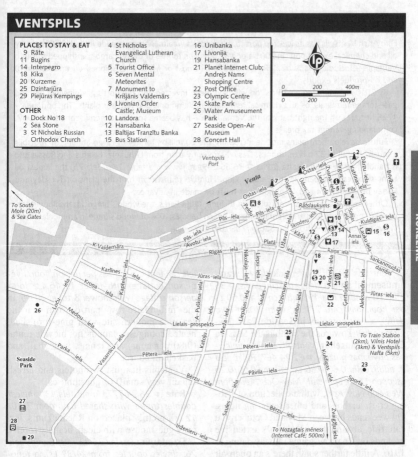

VENTSPILS

PLACES TO STAY & EAT
9  Råte
11  Bugins
14  Interpegro
18  Kika
20  Kurzeme
25  Dzintarjūra
29  Piejūras Kempings

OTHER
1  Dock No 18
2  Sea Stone
3  St Nicholas Russian
   Orthodox Church
4  St Nicholas
   Evangelical Lutheran
   Church
5  Tourist Office
7  Seven Mental
   Meteorites
8  Monument to
   Krišjānis Valdemārs
10  Livonian Order
    Castle; Museum
10  Landora
12  Hansabanka
13  Baltijas Tranzītu Banka
15  Bus Station
16  Unibanka
17  Livonija
19  Hansabanka
21  Planet Internet Club;
    Andrejs Nams
    Shopping Centre
22  Post Office
23  Olympic Centre
24  Skate Park
26  Water Amuseument
    Park
27  Seaside Open-Air
    Museum
28  Concert Hall

for visitors to enjoy an eagle's-eye view of the port and city.

From the castle, it is a two-minute walk to the Venta River. **Ostas iela**, a riverside promenade proffering interesting views of the bustling industrial port on the opposite river bank, leads east along the water. Between April and November the Hecogs Jēkabs boat sails around the mouth of the Venta River, a 45-minute trip; it departs six times daily from **dock No 18** (☎ 36 22 586; cnr Ostas iela & Tirgus iela; adult/child 0.50/0.20 Ls). The **Sea Stone** (1998), at the far eastern end of the walkway, is a massive boulder dug out from a depth of 17.5m when the port canal was deepened. It is one of several sculptures to line the scenic promenade. Look out for Feldbergs' **Seven Mental Meteorites** (1996) and

the **monument to Krišjānis Valdemārs** (2000), founder of Latvian shipping.

Ventspils' prime attraction is its coastline, which is laced with a sandy, dune-backed **beach** stretching south from the river mouth, about 2km west of the town centre. You can reach it along Viļņu iela (or Medņu iela), which branches off Vasarnīcu iela, or take bus No 10 along Lielais prospkets.

Breakwaters poke 1km or so out to sea from the mouth of the river to form Ventspils' **Sea Gates**, with a narrow entrance that makes it treacherous for shipping if there's any sea running. A popular pastime is to walk or cycle 1km from the northern end of the beach, along the **South Mole** (Dienvidu mols) walkway, to the lighthouse at the end of the southern breakwater.

## Filthy-Rich Ventspils

Filthy-rich Ventspils has its ice-free port to thank for its wealth. Moscow made it the USSR's primary oil and chemical export port. In 2001 alone 37.9 million tonnes of transit cargo transhipped through Ventspils – including 11% of all Russia's crude-oil (most of which gets shipped on to Rotterdam) and oil-products exports.

By 2010 an estimated €420 million will have been invested into the port's gas pipeline, oil- and gas-storage terminals, oil and chemical terminals, and ammonia and fertiliser plants. The port area – 1728 hectares on the right bank of the Venta River – has been a special economic zone since 1997, commanding various tax breaks.

Future development plans include increasing the 20 million tonnes of cargo arriving in Ventspils annually by rail to 32 million tonnes. Gas oil arrives by train from Lithuania, Belarus and Russia and is handled by **Ventspils Nafta** (tours ☎ 36 66 259; W www.vnafta.lv; Talsu iela 75) the largest oil trans-shipment company in the Baltic region. Humble tourists can tour the plant on Tuesday and Friday between 1pm and 4pm; bookings must be made in advance.

Other industrial giants at Ventspils port include **Kālija Parks**, the world's biggest transhipping terminal of potassium salt; and **Ventamonjaks**, which handles 10% of world's trade in ammonia. Prime views can be enjoyed from the South Mole and Ostas iela.

Ventspils' beach is overlooked by a **water amusement park** (Ūdens atrakciju parks; ☎ 36 65 853; Mednu iela 19; adult/child 1/0.50 Ls per hour, day card 2/1 Ls; open 10am-8pm daily), a vast complex in **Seaside Park** (Piejūras parks). Towards the south is the **Seaside Open-Air Museum** (Ventspils jūras zvejniecibas brīvdabas muzejs; ☎ 32 24 467, Riņķu iela 2; adult/child 0.60/0.30 Ls, railway 0.50/0.25 Ls; open 11am-6pm daily May-Oct, 11am-5pm Wed-Sun Nov-Apr), with a collection of fishing craft, anchors and other seafaring items. On weekends between May and October you can ride around the museum's extensive grounds on a narrow-gauge railway dating to 1916. A little farther south there's an **open-air concert hall** (Vasarnīcu iela). Bus Nos 6 and 11 run here regularly from Lielais prospkets.

Boarders, bladers and BMX bikers can leap around in the region's only **Skate Park** (Skeitparks; ☎ 36 22 172; Sporta iela 7-9; admission free; open 24hr), kitted out with 18 jumps. Ice skaters can twirl around the city's ice-skating rink, inside the modern **Olympic Centre** (☎ 36 21 996; Sporta iela 7-9; skating 1 Ls per hour, skate rental adult/child 0.50/0.20 Ls), host to Latvia's national Eurovision final in 2002 and potential host for the 2003 Eurovision Song Contest. The sports complex has a **sauna** (2 Ls per person per hour) too.

### Places to Stay

**Piejūras Kempings** (☎ 36 27 925, fax 36 27 991; W www.camping.ventspils.lv; Vasarnicu iela 56; tent site 1.50 Ls per person, four/five-person cottage with toilet 10/15 Ls, four-person cottage with shower & toilet 20 Ls), in the 'millionaire row' part of town near the sea, is a modern site with pine-furnished, heated cottages, a laundrette, bicycle rental (0.80 per hour) and tennis, volleyball and basketball courts.

Ventspils has just two hotels and a rash (albeit very small) of guesthouses.

**Rāte** (☎ 36 24 777; Annas iela 13; singles/doubles/triples with shared bathroom 7/10/12 Ls), prettily placed on Rātslaukums, is a cosy guesthouse with clean, homely rooms.

**Dzintarjūra** (☎/fax 36 22 719; Ganību iela 26; singles/doubles from 24/32 Ls), a renovated, Soviet-era hotel poetically called 'Amber Sea', is Ventspils' premier hotel.

**Vilnis** (☎ 36 68 880, fax 36 65 054; W www.vilnis.lv; Talsu iela 5; singles/doubles from 25/44 Ls), the other side of the Venta River near the busy port, is a service-orientated block targeted primarily to business travellers.

### Places to Eat

**Bugins** (☎ 36 80 151; Lielā iela 1/3; meals 4 Ls; open 10am-midnight daily), with its log-cabin interior, booth tables and rustic knick-knacks strung everywhere, is as hip as you'll get in provincial Latvia. A feast of shashliks, soups, salads and omelettes fill its vast menu.

**Kurzeme** (☎ 36 24 180; Jūras iela; dishes from 2 Ls; open 8am-11pm daily) is a modern coffee shop with glass tables, sparkling furnishings and mirrored windows.

**Kika** (☎ 36 21 285; *Kuldīgas iela 23; open 8am-10pm daily*) touts a jolly decor and is a jolly nice place for coffee and cake.

**Interpegro** (*Annas iela 1; open 8am-midnight daily*) is a central supermarket.

## Entertainment

**Landora** (☎ 36 22 481; *Lielā iela 2; meals 3 Ls; disco open 11pm-5am Thur-Sat*) is decorated with fishing nets and junk from the sea. Live bands play here Saturday from 11pm.

**Livonija** (☎ 36 22 287; *Talsu iela 8; open 10pm-6am*) is a nightclub. Another club above **Kurzeme** (see Places to Eat earlier) rocks into the early hours, and a **bowling nightclub** adjoins the Dzintarjūra hotel.

## Getting There & Away

Ventspils' **bus station** (☎ 36 22 789; *Kuldīga iela 5*) is served by hourly buses to/from Rīga (2.70 Ls, 2½-four hours); two daily to/from Liepāja (1.95-2.45 Ls, three hours) and Talsi (1.10 Ls, 1½ hours); and up to four to/from Kuldīga (0.90 Ls, 1½ hours), Dundaga (1.20 Ls) and Jelgava (2.90-3 Ls, 4¾-5½ hours) via Kandava and Tukums.

Two trains run daily to/from Rīga (2.17 Ls, 4¼ hours) from the **train station** (*Dzeizce/nieku iela*), on the Rīga road 2km east of the centre, across the river.

**VV Line LV** (☎ 36 07 358, fax 36 07 355; ₩ www.vvline.com; *Plostu iela 7*) runs seasonal ferries six times weekly from **Ventspils ferry terminal** (☎ 36 07 357; *Plostu iela 7*) to Västervik in Sweden. See under Sea in the introductory Getting There & Away chapter for details. In Ventspils, **Latvia Tours** (☎ 36 25 413, fax 36 07 037; ⓔ venta@laviatours.lv; ₩ www.latviatours.lv; *Ganību iela 8*) also sells tickets.

## KULDĪGA

### pop 13,335

Kuldīga, 54km southwest of Ventspils, is a picturesque town on the Venta River. It was an important Cours settlement and most likely the Cour capital at the time of the 13th-century German invasion. Later Kuldīga (then called Goldingen) became an important stronghold of the Livonian Order, and in its heyday served as the capital of the Duchy of Courland (1596–1616). But the town suffered greatly in the Great Northern War (1700–21) and never quite regained its former importance.

Kuldīga throws its annual town festival in mid-July.

## Orientation & Information

The Venta River flows up the eastern side of town and is crossed by the bridge that leads out to the Rīga road. The old part of the town centre is within 500m or so west and southwest of the bridge. The newer part of the centre focuses on Pilsētas laukums, 500m west along Liepājas iela.

The **tourist office** (☎/fax 33 22 259; ₩ www.kuldiga.lv; *Baznīcas iela 5; open 9am-5pm Mon-Sat, 10am-2pm Sun mid-May–mid-Sept, 9am-5pm Mon-Fri rest of year*) is helpful. You'll find an ATM outside **Hansabanka** (*Liepājas iela 15*) and a **post office** (*Liepājas iela 34*) nearby.

## Old Town

A central point from which to explore is **Rātslaukums**, the old town-hall square, so called because of the **17th-century town hall** (*Rātslaukums 5*). The new town hall, built in 1860 in Italian Renaissance style, is at the southern end of the square and Kuldīga's **oldest house** – built in 1670, reconstructed in 1742 and renovated in 1982 – stands here on the northern corner of Pasta iela.

From Rātslaukums, Baznīcas iela leads north to the Lutheran **St Katrīna's Church** (Sv Katrīnas baznīca), built in 1655 and largely rebuilt in the 1860s and 1960s. The wooden altar and pulpit date from 1660 and the large organ, which has 996 pipes, from 1712. Another fine church, the 1640 Roman Catholic **Holy Trinity Church** (Sv Trisvienības baznīca; Raiļa iela), with an ornate baroque/rococo interior, is also a short way off Rātslaukums, along Liepājas iela – the main old-town street.

From Baznīcas iela a bridge leads across the Aleksupīte, a tributary of the Venta, to a **water mill** (1807). Across the river is the site of the **Livonian Order Castle**, built from 1242 to 1245 but ruined during the Great Northern War (1700–21). The **castle watchman's house** (*Pils iela 4*) was built in 1735 to protect the ruins. Legend has it that the house was the site of executions and beheadings and the stream behind the house ran red with the victims' blood. Today all that remains of the castle are a few mounds and ditches. In

KURZEME

**KURZEME**

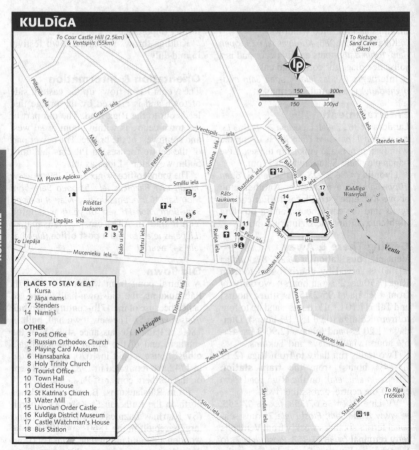

# KULDĪGA

To Cour Castle Hill (2.5km) & Ventspils (55km)

To Riežupe Sand Caves (5km)

0    150    300m
0    150    300yd

Pīteres iela

Grants iela

Mālu iela

Pētera iela

Ventspils iela

Alunāna iela

Upes iela

Krasta iela

Stendes iela

Baznīcas iela

M Plavas Aploku

Smilšu iela

Baznīcas iela

▥ 5

🏨 12

13

17

Kuldīga Waterfall

Rāts-laukums

1 🏨

Pilsētas laukums

🏨 4

Kalna iela

14
▼

15

16 ▥

Pils iela

iela

Liepājas iela

Liepājas iela

§ 6

7 ▼

11

Pasta iela

Diķu

To Liepāja

🏨
2  3

Balo iela

Putnu iela

Raiņa iela

8
10

§
9

To Liepāja

Mucenieku iela

Rumbas iela

Venta

Dzirnavu iela

Annas iela

Jelgavas iela

Alekšupīte

Ziedu iela

Skrundas iela

Stacijas iela

To Rīga (165km)

Sūru iela

🚌 18

**PLACES TO STAY & EAT**
1  Kursa
2  Jāņa nams
7  Stenders
14  Namiņš

**OTHER**
3  Post Office
4  Russian Orthodox Church
5  Playing Card Museum
6  Hansabanka
8  Holy Trinity Church
9  Tourist Office
10  Town Hall
11  Oldest House
12  St Katrina's Church
13  Water Mill
15  Livonian Order Castle
16  Kuldīga District Museum
17  Castle Watchman's House
18  Bus Station

the grounds the **Kuldīga District Museum** (*Kuldīgas novada muzejs*; ☎ 33 22 364; Pils iela; adult/child 0.40/0.20 Ls; open 11am-5pm Tues-Sun) is inside a house built in Paris in 1900 to house the Russian pavilion at the World Exhibition.

From Pils iela there's an excellent view of the Venta and the **Kuldīga waterfall**, which is only a metre or two high but stretching the width of the river – at 275m it's said to be Europe's widest waterfall. You can fish and swim here and, when the water's low, you can walk across the top of the falls.

Away from the Old Town, there is a small **Playing Card Museum** (*Spēļu kāršu muzejs*; ☎ 33 24 347; Smilš u iela 10; adult/child 0.40/0.10 Ls; open 10am-4pm Mon-Sat).

## Other Attractions
The large **old castle hill** (*pilskalns*), 2.5km north of town on the western bank of the Venta, was the fortress of Lamekins, the Cour who ruled much of Kurzeme before the 13th-century German invasion. Legend has it that the castle was so staggeringly beautiful – copper pendants hanging from the roof glistened in the sunlight and tinkled in the wind – that invaders were magnetically drawn to it. To get to the hill follow Ventspils iela then Virkas iela, north from the centre, then take the right fork off Virkas iela.

Immediately after crossing the old bridge – the eastern extension of Baznīcas iela – turn left to get to **Riežupe Sand Caves** (*Smilšu alas*; ☎ 33 26 236, 33 23 604; adult/child 2/1 Ls; open 11am-5pm daily May-Oct), 5km farther along unpaved Krasta iela in Riežupe. The labyrinthine caves can be visited by candle-light; they're a chilly 8°C so bring a warm sweater. The forested area around the caves is equipped with picnic tables and outdoor games.

## Places to Stay & Eat

**Kursa** (☎ 33 22 430, fax 33 23 671; Pilsētas laukums 6; singles/doubles from 12/16 Ls) is your quintessential, unrenovated, Soviet-era block.

**Jāņa nams** (☎ 33 23 456, fax 33 23 785; Liepājas iela 36; doubles with breakfast 22-40 Ls), a cosy, 18-room hotel, has a sauna and funky in-house café.

Staff at the tourist office have a list of Kuldīga cafés; ask them about restaurants and they will proudly tell you that the town doesn't have any! A handful of uninspiring places to snack dot Liepājas iela.

**Stenders** (☎ 33 22 703; Liepājas iela 3; meals 2 Ls; admission for concerts 1.50 Ls; open 11am-10pm Sun-Thur, 11am-4am Fri & Sat), the town's hippest joint, is housed in a 18th-century granary. Live bands often play here.

**Namiņš** (☎ 33 22 697; Kalna iela 25a; open 11am-midnight daily), near the river and castle, serves an assortment of light dishes on the terrace (summer) or in front of the fire (winter). The café sells Rīga-bridge tickets – see Getting There & Away.

## Getting There & Away

From the **bus station** (☎ 33 22 061; Stacijas iela) six to 10 buses daily run to/from Rīga (2.20 Ls, three to four hours), six daily to/from Liepāja (1.10-1.55 Ls, 2¼ hours) and up to four daily to/from Ventspils (0.90 Ls, 1½ hours).

Motorists must buy a 0.50 Ls ticket to cross the old road bridge (the Rīga road) across the Venta in the town centre. Looping around town to cross the river at the new bridge (the Ventspils road) instead is free. Namiņš sells tickets (see Places to Stay & Eat earlier).

## LIEPĀJA

pop 89,400

Liepāja, 205km west of Rīga and 111km south of Ventspils on the Baltic Coast, is Latvia's third-largest city. Like Ventspils it has an ice-free harbour. Founded by the Livonian Order in the mid-13th century, the city only really took off with the deepening of the harbour and arrival of a railway track in the 19th century. It became a communi-cations centre with an undersea cable to Copenhagen laid in the 1860s, and was home to a passenger shipping service to North America before WWI. Between the two world wars there were ship-repair and aircraft-building industries.

Though lacking in sightseeing attractions, Liepāja (former German name: Libau) has a pleasant beachfront, a spate of fun places to drink and dine at, and a naval port built by Russian Tsar Alexander III in 1890 and used as a Soviet military base until the early 1990s. Bizarrely, the local city council markets Liepāja today as the place where wind is born!

In August the city hosts Latvia's largest rock festival, Liepājas Dzintars (Amber of Liepāja).

South of the city, nature enthusiasts can find peace, tranquillity and lots of birds in **Pape**, a village wedged 45km south between the sea and **Lake Pape**. Horses run wild here and there's an **open-air museum**.

## Orientation & Information

Liepāja occupies the neck of land (about 2km to 3km wide) between Lake Liepāja and the sea. The city straddles Tirdzniecības Canal, the narrow canal flowing from the lake to the sea. The former naval port, and train and bus stations sit north of the canal, and the city centre south.

The **tourist office** (☎/fax 34 80 808; W www.liepaja.lv; Lielā iela 11; open 9am-6pm Mon-Fri, 9am-5pm Sat), inside the Liva Hotel, offers a limited amount of English-speaking help to visitors.

There is an ATM outside the Liva Hotel and others can be found outside **Hansabanka** (Kuršu laukums 11 & Graudu iela 40). The **post office** (cnr Pasta iela & Radio iela) is a block west of Lielā iela. You can access the Inter-net for 1 Ls an hour at **Tikls** (☎ 34 27 503; Peldu iela 32/34; open 24hr) or **Netlogs** (☎ 34 24 717; Peldu iela 16; open 10am-6pm Mon-Fri, 10am-3pm Sat).

## City Centre

The large, 1742–58 Lutheran **Holy Trinity Church** (Sv Trīsvienības baznīca; Lielā iela 9), on the eastern side of Liepāja's main street, has a fine interior. Next door at Lielā iela 5 shimmers the ornate pale-blue facade of a fine 19th-century **townhouse** beautifully

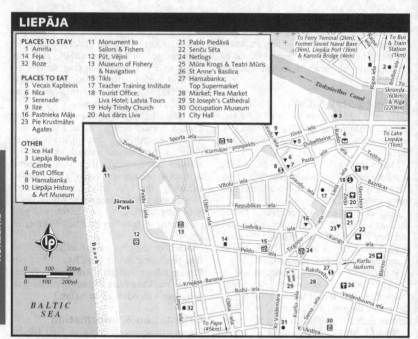

# LIEPĀJA

| PLACES TO STAY | 11 | Monument to | 21 | Pablo Piedāvā |
| 1 | Amrita | | Sailors & Fishers | 22 | Senču Sēta |
| 14 | Feja | 12 | Pūt, Vējini | 24 | Netlogs |
| 32 | Roze | 13 | Museum of Fishery | 25 | Mūra Krogs & Teatri Mūris |
| | | | & Navigation | 26 | St Anne's Basilica |
| PLACES TO EAT | 15 | Tikls | 27 | Hansabanka; |
| 5 | Vecais Kapteinis | 17 | Teacher Training Institute | | Top Supermarket |
| 6 | Nīca | 18 | Tourist Office; | 28 | Market; Flea Market |
| 7 | Serenade | | Liva Hotel; Latvia Tours | 29 | St Joseph's Cathedral |
| 9 | Ilze | 19 | Holy Trinity Church | 30 | Occupation Museum |
| 16 | Pastnieka Māja | 20 | Alus dārzs Liva | 31 | City Hall |
| 23 | Pie Krustmātes | | | | |
| | Agates | | | | |

| OTHER | | |
| 2 | Ice Hall |
| 3 | Liepāja Bowling |
| | Centre |
| 4 | Post Office |
| 8 | Hansabanka |
| 10 | Liepāja History |
| | & Art Museum |

## Other Attractions

renovated in 2002. The **Teacher Training Institute** (*Liepājas Pedagoģiskais Institūts*) fills the street's western side.

About 700m from the bridge, Lielā iela becomes pedestrianised Tirgoņu iela. South of this are Liepaja's busy **market** (*tirgus*) selling fruit and vegetables, and **flea market** (*mantu tirgus*) which sells everything from second-hand tables to pirate CDs, DVDs, both on Kuršu iela. The large church opposite is the Roman Catholic **St Joseph's Cathedral** (*Sv Jāzepa katedrāla*). If you cut east through the market you reach Kuršu laukums, an elongated square over which 16th-century **St Anne's Basilica** (*Sv Annas basilica*), a red-brick edifice built in 1587 with a sky-high steeple, resides.

The **Occupation Museum** (*Okupāciju režīmos*; ☎ *34 20 274; Ukstiņa iela 79; adult/child 0.30/0.15 Ls; open 10am-5pm Tues-Sun*) is a Liepāja highlight. Captions are in Latvian but no words are needed to explain the powerful photographs and images of the 1939–40 deportations to Siberia (an estimated 2000 people from Liepāja were deported) and the fight for independence in 1991.

The monumental red-brick building immediately west of the bridge crossing the canal is a **bowling centre**, a former warehouse. You can ice-skate at the **ice hall** (*Ledus halle;* ☎ *34 81 840; Brīvības iela 3/7*), across the bridge on the northern side of the canal. The rink is open to the public for short sessions two to four times daily; a schedule is posted outside. Otherwise, it is home to the city's star ice-hockey team, Eastern European Hockey League champions in 2002. Tickets to games cost 0.80-2.50 Ls.

Between the city centre and the sea, the architecture becomes predominantly wooden. Inside one such two-storey mansion is the **Museum of Fishery & Navigation** (*Zvejniecības un ku-niecības muzejs;* ☎ *34 26 996; Hikes iela 9; adult/child 0.30 Ls; open 10am-5pm Wed-Sun*).

A collection of carved amber ornaments 1500 years old is showcased in the **Liepāja History & Art Museum** (*Liepājas vēstures un mākslas muzejs;* ☎ *34 22 327; Kūrmājas prospekts, 16/18; adult/child 0.50/0.30 Ls; open 10am-5pm Wed-Sun Sept-May, 11am-6pm Wed-Sun June-Aug*). At the seaside end of the

## Naval Port Tour

In 1908 Liepāja – along with St Petersburg, Odessa, Tallinn and Rīga – was one of the Russian Empire's five largest commercial ports. From 1951 until 1956 and between 1967 and 1991 it was a closed Soviet naval base. When Latvia assumed complete control of the port following the final withdrawal of Soviet troops in 1994, half-sunk Russian submarines and vessels littered its waters. Today, an estimated seven million tonnes of cargo a year passes through Liepāja port – an ice-free port and special economic zone since 1997.

But poignant reminders of Liepāja's military past remain. To get to the formal naval township, cross **Karosta Bridge** (1906). Some 300m north, along Atmodas bulvāris, is the **Naval Officers' Assembly House** (1898–1907), used by the tsar's naval officers until 1915. The Liepāja Symphony Orchestra performs here today. Two blocks east on Katedrāles iela is the magnificent **St Nicholas' Russian Orthodox Cathedral** (1900-03), the outside walls of which bear the entire weight of the staggeringly large edifice. Prior to independence, the Soviet navy's sailing club used it as their club house.

same street is a **monument** to sailors and fishers who died at sea.

The **beach**, west of the city centre and backed by dunes and the wooded **Jūrmala Park**, is long, clean and sandy. But few swim here – which may be due to reports that several hundred thousand tonnes of toxic waste and unexploded bombs were dumped off Liepāja by the Soviet navy after WWII, or to the warning sign (in English) on the beach that reads 'objects which resemble amber could wash ashore on the beach and cause burns'.

### Places to Stay

**Liva Hotel** (☎ 34 20 102, fax 34 80 259; W www.liva.lv; Lielā iela 11; singles 12-35 Ls, doubles 18-45 Ls) is scarcely recognisable as the Soviet ghetto it once was. Everything about the place is renovated and sparkles.

**Roze** (☎/fax 34 21 155; e roze@arcu.lv; Rožu iela 37; singles 26-38 Ls, doubles 34-50 Ls), a lovely guesthouse in a traditional wooden house near the sea, is a stone's throw from Jūrmala Park and touts a rash of stylish rooms.

**Feja** (☎ 34 22 688, fax 34 81 447; Kurzemes iela 9; singles 26-38 Ls, doubles 34-50 Ls), a turreted red-brick guesthouse, offers standard rooms with all the mod cons and a couple of luxury suites. The entrance is on Peldu iela.

**Amrita** (☎ 34 03 434, fax 34 80 444; W www.amrita.lv; Rīgas iela 7; singles 40-50 Ls, doubles 50-65 Ls, presidential suite 205 Ls), Liepāja's most upmarket accommodation, is topped off by a two-floor presidential suite. Rooms for lesser mortals are decorated in a 'cosy Scandinavian style' (so says the hotel's marketing bumph).

### Places to Eat

**Pie Krustmātes Agates** (Zveju iela 4/6; meals 1 Ls; open 8am-11pm daily) is a real gem. The canteen-style spot dishes up mains for 0.35 Ls in a lovely rustic setting, decorated with cartwheels, dried flowers, pumpkins and the like.

**Vecais Kapteinis** (Old Captain; ☎ 34 25 522; Dubelsteina iela 14; meals 6 Ls; open 10am-1am daily), in a stunning timber-framed building dating to 1773, dishes up all the Latvian favourites, like grey peas with bacon served in a pot, and homemade dumplings. Sturgeons swim around in a tank waiting to be eaten (21 Ls).

**Pastnieka Māja** (☎ 34 07 521; Brīvzemnieka iela 53; meals 6 Ls; open noon-midnight Mon-Thur, noon-2am Fri & Sat, 11am-midnight Sun) is the other hot spot for dining. The vast mansion, set back off the road, sports a spacious wooden veranda and a bold and colourful, jolly interior.

**Nīca** (☎ 34 80 011; Graudu iela 31), a stylish mix of old and new, and **Ilze** (☎ 34 26 724; Graudu iela 23) are popular cafés. **Serenade** (cnr Graudu iela & Pasta iela) is a sweet spot for cakes.

Don't forget the **market** (Kuršu laukums) for fresh fruit and vegies, and the **Top** (Kuršu laukums 11) supermarket for dried foodstuffs.

### Entertainment

Cinema as well as theatre venues and programmes are listed in Liepāja This Week, a weekly eight-page entertainment magazine –

KURZEME

pick up a free copy at the tourist office. In summer open-air concerts are held at **Pūt, Vējini** (☎ *34 25 268*), an outside theatre in Jūrmala Park.

**Alus dārzs Līva** (☎ *34 20 102; Rozu laukums; open noon-2am daily May-Oct*), a contemporary beer bar in a pavilion next to the **Liva Hotel**, is a fine spot for lapping up summer sun and Latvian beer.

**Senču Sēta** (☎ *34 25 453; Stendera iela 13a; open 10am or 11am-midnight Tues-Thur & Sun, 11am-3am Fri & Sat*) touts a flower-filled beer garden.

**Mura Krogs & Teatri Muris** (☎ *34 80 202; Bāriņu iela; open 10am-midnight daily*) is an alternative theatre and bar set in a cobbled courtyard town. Food is named after plays and theatre performances take place twice weekly.

**Pablo Piedāvā** (☎ *34 81 555; Zivju iela 4/6;* W *www.pablo.lv; adult/child 0.50-2.50 Ls; open 11am-6am daily*), a popular music club and rock café, is the leading venue for live music.

### Getting There & Away

Liepāja's **bus & train stations** (☎ *34 27 552; Rīgas iela*) are rolled into one, linked by tram No 1 with Lielā iela in the town centre.

There are daily bus services at least hourly to/from Rīga (2.65 Ls, 3½ hours direct, four to 4½ hours via Kalnciems, five to 5½ hours via Jelgava, and seven hours via Tukums); and six buses daily to/from Kuldīga (1.10-1.55 Ls, 2¼ hours), Talsi (2.10-2.45 Ls, 4½ hours) and Ventspils (1.95-2.45 Ls, three to 3¾ hours). Updated timetables are online at W www.liepaja-online.lv/lap.

If you are thinking of getting the train, there are four services daily to/from Rīga (2.95-3.40 Ls, 4¾-6 hours).

In town, **Latvia Tours** (☎ *34 27 172, fax 34 07 058;* W *www.latviatours.lv; Lielā iela 11*), inside the Liva Hotel, sells tickets for ferries and Eurolines buses.

**Terrabalt** (☎ *34 27 214, 34 25 756, fax 34 87 404;* W *www.terrabalt.lv; Pier No 46*) runs ferries from Liepāja to Karlshamn (Sweden) and Rostock (Germany). Ferries depart to Karlshamn three times weekly (17½ hours); seats cost 38 Ls, beds in two-/four-bed cabins cost 60/67 Ls. There's a 5 Ls port tax per person and it costs 7/46 Ls to transport a bicycle/car.

Terrabalt ferries to Rostock depart twice weekly (seven hours). A seat costs €80 and beds in two-/four-bed cabins cost €110/140; port tax is €10. It costs €10/115 to transport a bicycle/car.

On both routes children aged three to 15 pay approximately 50% less.

## SKRUNDA & AROUND

Skrunda (pop 4226), 58km east of Liepāja and 150km from Rīga, is of zero interest beyond the fact that it was a Soviet military town. The USSR's westernmost early-warning **radar station**, ever alert to track incoming nuclear missiles, was built here. Although Russian forces officially withdrew from Latvia in mid-1994, some 500 Russian military personnel remained at Skrunda until 1999 when Russia officially passed control of the area to Latvia. Today, a solitary Latvian guard is the only sign of life at the station, which has been abandoned and is slated to be destroyed. The complex is 5km north of town on the road to Kuldīga; it is set off the road, down a dirt track next to the Kombināts bus stop.

**Bojas**, 25km west of Skrunda and 6km south of Aizpute on the road to Kalvene, is the setting for a **Forest Museum** (Meža muzejs; ☎ *34 48 054; adult child 0.50/0.20 Ls; open 10am-5pm Tues-Sun mid-May–mid-Sept, 10am-4pm Mon-Fri rest of year*). While its 17 rooms outline the story of how people used to live in the forest, they also provide a colourful guide to the flowers and fauna of Latvia. So wallow in nature and wander around the pond.

JONATHAN SMITH

# Lithuania

## HIGHLIGHTS

- Get lost in the narrow, cobbled heart of beautiful, baroque Vilnius

- Get sweaty in the Curonian Spit's unique beachside sauna then make a dash into the icy Baltic Sea

- Go crazy in party-loving Palanga – drink the night away and watch the sun rise over its famous pier

- Go boating on the serene lakes that dot the magnificent Aukštaitija National Park

- Gaze in wonder at the eerie Hill of Crosses in Šiauliai

# Facts about Lithuania

'May our love for Lithuania burn in our hearts, so that Lithuanian unity will blossom forever…'
**Lithuanian National Anthem**
**Vincas Kudirka, 1858–99**

Rebellious, quirky and vibrant; Lithuania is Europe's best-kept secret. Shoved successively between Russian pillar and Nazi post, tenacious little Lithuania stunned the world when it played David and Goliath with the might of the Soviet Union – and won its independence just over a decade ago. Today, the nation that vanished from the maps of Europe is back, with high hopes of joining the European Union (EU) and the North Atlantic Treaty Organization (NATO). The 5 January 2003 election turnout was low due to cold weather. There was a shock victory for the challenger in Lithuania's presidential election, Rolandas Paksas, over the incumbent, Valdas Adamkus. With 99% of the votes counted, Lithuania's Central Election Commission said Mr Paksas, of the right-wing Liberal Democrats, had won 54.9%, compared with 45% for Mr Adamkus. Mr Paksas, aged 46, mounted an aggressive campaign, promising a better life for Lithuanians, tough on law and order, and his campaign even involved a daring stunt flight in formation with two other planes underneath a low bridge.

But this is a country with a colourful history, once boasting an empire stretching from the Baltic to the Black Sea. Its raw pagan roots fuse with Catholic fervour, the Polish inheritance that sets it apart from its Baltic brothers.

Vilnius is strange in an eccentric and quirky way. It's a small city with astonishing contrasts – eerie shadowy courtyards, eccentric artist community, disturbing history and beautiful baroque. Lithuania's natural treasures – including the forests of the south, the magical Curonian Spit and Nemunas Delta on the coast – glitter. The Hill of Crosses near Šiauliai and the controversial Soviet sculpture park in southeastern Lithuania both vie for attention.

## HISTORY

Lithuanians certainly have a sense of irony: they led the Baltic push for independence and they are credited with causing the collapse of the Soviet Union; then, at their first democratic elections, in 1992, they voted in the ex-communist Lithuanian Democratic Labour Party (LDDP)!

Presidential elections followed in 1993, the year the last Soviet soldier left the country, and former Communist Party first secretary Algirdas Brazauskas won with 60% of the vote. But change was under way. In the space of three years, Lithuania's currency, the *litas*, replaced the Russian rouble, Lithuania joined the NATO Partnership for Peace programme and in 1995 Lithuanian became the official language and an association agreement was signed with the EU. The EU forced Lithuania to abolish the country's controversial death penalty in 1998.

Lithuania has made friends with its neighbours by settling border squabbles, including with Russian-owned Kaliningrad. The border treaty was still not resolved in 2002 – when Lithuanian Prime Minister Algirdas Brazauskas made an official visit to Kaliningrad. Lithuania has suggested that Russia should make an agreement with the EU over visas, while saying it's not opposed to visa-free connection. It was not until July 1999 that an age-old dispute with Latvia over maritime borders was finally resolved.

Talks between Lithuania and the EU about the country's EU membership began in 1999. The Ignalina nuclear power plant remains the thorn in the EU's side. Lithuania will not be able to join the EU without decommissioning both its reactors. Lithuania has agreed to decommission one of its two reactors by 2005, with the help of a €10 million grant under the PHARE assistance program, and has agreed to close down the other by 2009.

The country's national pride swelled at the Sydney Olympics in 2000, as the Lithuania team – including its beloved basketball players – snatched two gold medals and three bronze. Around this time, Lithuania presented Moscow with a €21 billion bill, the estimated cost of Soviet occupation. In 2001 Lithuania took over as annual chair of the Council of Europe Committee of Ministers at its 109th session in Strasbourg and the Dalai Lama paid a visit.

The *litas* was pegged to the euro instead of the US dollar in February 2002, and US president George Bush welcomed Lithuania

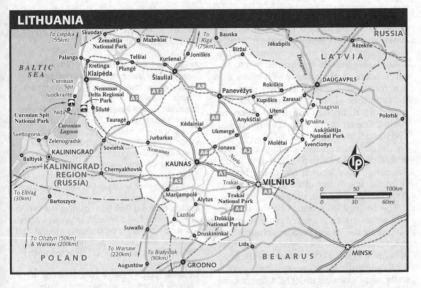

into NATO. Lithuania sees its role in NATO as interpreter between the West and former USSR satellite states, as well as offering military medical officers for peace-keeping missions.

By mid-2002 Lithuania had closed 26 of its 31 chapters for EU entry. Lithuania has focused on stopping its subsidies for farmers – in line with EU policy. It must also bring its infrastructure, eg, transport links, up to scratch before it can complete its application for EU membership.

## GEOGRAPHY

Lithuania can be described in two words: flat and fertile. It's the largest of the Baltic countries: 65,200 sq km and dotted with lush forests, 4000 lakes and a 100km-wide lowland centre. Its neighbours are Latvia in the north, Belarus in the southeast, and Poland and the Kaliningrad Region (Russia) in the southwest. Its four main regions are Aukštaitija (Upper Lithuania), the east; Žemaitija (Lower Lithuania), the west; Dzūkija, the south; and Suvalkija or Sūduva, the southwest. The central flat plain is flanked by two higher areas exceeding 150m above sea level. The eastern area straddling the Belarus border has the country's highest point at Juozapinės (294m). The other is the Žemaitija Upland, which spreads over the north west and reaches a height of 234m.

Half of Lithuania's short Baltic Coast lies along the Curonian Spit (Kuršių Nerija), the region's most mesmerising natural feature. It is a sand bar stretching 98km long, and only 4km wide, with sand dunes up to 60m high.

Behind the spit is the wide (up to 35km) Curonian Lagoon, which the Nemunas River flows into.

## ECOLOGY & ENVIRONMENT

That warm glow of happiness you feel in Lithuania may have to do with the Ignalina nuclear power plant, 120km north of Vilnius. It is a Soviet-era reactor similar in design to the infamous, and deadly, Chornobyl plant in the Ukraine, site of the world's worst nuclear disaster in 1986. This has not worried Lithuania, which is the most nuclear power–dependent country in the world: 80% of its electricity comes from the plant, near the Belarus border. Experts rank it among the world's most dangerous nuclear installations, a claim hotly denied by Lithuania. Despite the EU spending €236 million in the last decade to improve safety, it now wants the plant shut down completely, at a cost of €3.2 billion – which Lithuania says it can't pay (see the boxed text 'Ignalina' in the Eastern & Southern Lithuania chapter).

Worryingly, police seized 20kg of deadly uranium only in 2002, a decade after it was stolen from Ignalina by bogus workers.

But the main environmental challenge facing Lithuania today could also affect the ecosystem of the entire planet. A deadly race against time is under way to stop the entire Baltic Sea being poisoned by chemical weapons sunk during WWII when Soviet forces sank several German ships off the Lithuanian–Latvian border, 70 nautical miles off Klaipėda. The lethal weapons could cause an international environmental disaster if they seep out of the 40,000 bombs and mines decomposing on the sea bed. This could happen in just five years. Scientists have known about the bombs since the war – but discovered as late as 2000 that they were in danger of leaking.

The Butinge oil terminal on the western Lithuanian coast has sparked protests among environmentalists and economists alike. Due to several oil spills, the largest being 60 tons of oil in November 2001, which shut Butinge for four months, it has operated only sporadically since opening in 1999. Current controversy rages over the huge losses the terminal has incurred, plus the fact it cost €266 million to build.

The Latvian Green Party is leading protests against plans to build a new paper factory in the Aukštaitija National Park region and new hydropower dams in the Nemunas Delta, which are also being cited as possible alternative power sources to Ignalina.

As the move to fully-fledged capitalism charges along, there is currently the question of where to put all those discarded soft-drink cans and fast-food wrappers. Landfill sites are filling up and, increasingly, people dump their rubbish illegally in the countryside.

## NATIONAL PARKS & RESERVES

Lithuania has five national parks, five nature reserves and 394 areas under varying degrees of control, which are home to some rare wildlife. The highlight is the Curonian Spit National Park, which protects an outstanding sand spit, lagoon and towering dunes in western Lithuania. This natural wonder, which Unesco declared a World Heritage site in 2000, boasts rare species of mammals, birds and butterflies. Elks, wild boars and even a tiny number of European bison roam in the country's forests, while the Nemunas Delta wetlands are a twitcher's heaven, being an important breeding area for hundreds of species of birds.

More information on some of the parks and their wildlife habitats can be found in the regional chapters.

**Aukštaitija National Park** 300 sq km in north eastern Lithuanian lake district near Ignalina – lakes, rivers, forest, walking, canoeing; park centre at Palūšė

**Čepkeliai Nature Reserve** 85 sq km on Belarus border south of Marcinkonys – Lithuania's biggest marsh, bird habitat, forest

**Curonian Spit (Kuršių Nerija) National Park** 26,473 hectares on the Curonian sand spit south of Klaipėda – a special environment of high dunes, pine forests, beaches, lagoon and sea coast; park headquarters and information centre in Smiltynė

**Dzūkija National Park** 550 sq km of the Varėna-Druskininkai forest in south Lithuania – forests, historic settlements on Nemunas River at Merkinė and Liskiava; park headquarters at Marcinkonys, accommodation at spa town, Druskininkai

**Kamanos Nature Reserve** 36 sq km, west of Naujoji Akmenė in northwestern Lithuania near Latvian border – upland bogs, bird, plant and mammal habitat; limited access

**Nemunas Delta (Nemuno Deltos) Regional Park** 35,000 hectares on the east coast of the Curonian Lagoon – a unique delta of waterways, dikes, polders and islands with varied bird life; park administration in Silutė and information centre in Rusnė

**Trakai National Park** 80 sq km around Trakai, west of Vilnius – lakes, castles, historic town

**Viesvilė Nature Reserve** 32 sq km, west of Jurbarkas, southwestern Lithuania – river basin, forest and marshland

**Žemaitija National Park** 200 sq km in north-western Lithuania – forests, Lake Plateliai, Žemaičių Kalvarija Catholic shrine centre; information centre in Plateliai

**Žuvintas Nature Reserve** 54 sq km around Žuvintas Lake near Marijampolė, southwestern Lithuania – important bird and plant habitat

## GOVERNMENT & POLITICS

Since 1992, when the constitution was approved, Lithuania has been an independent, democratic republic. Its first free elections raised international eyebrows when the LDDP won a majority in the 141-seat Seimas (Parliament). Former communist Algirdas Brazauskas became the head of state – president – in 1993 but the government was dogged by corruption scandals.

Presidential elections in January 1998 were a watershed in Lithuanian politics.

Wild card – and US citizen – Valdas Adamkus, a 71-year-old Lithuanian emigre, gained victory with a slim majority. Having lived in the US since his parents fled the Soviets in 1944, there were hopes he would inject some American life into the failing economy (see the boxed text 'All the President's Men & Women' in the introductory Facts about the Region chapter).

Adamkus appointed a member of the ruling Conservative Party, 43-year-old Rolandas Paksas, as his prime minister in 1999. The popular Vilnius mayor and champion stunt pilot won instant approval as 'the people's choice'.

Unfortunately, Paksas' days were numbered. He resigned over the controversial sale of the state-owned Butinge oil refinery to a US firm in October 1999. The move shocked the nation when he revealed how the deal meant Lithuania would cover the refinery's €426 million debt to buyer Williams International. As a result, Williams gained a 33% stake. (See Economy later.)

Paksas was briefly replaced by unpopular Andius Kubilius of the ruling Homeland Union (conservative) Party, until the elections of October 2000. The conservative faction lost out to the Social Democratic Coalition, which won 31% of the vote and holds 52 seats in the Seimas, headed by former president Algirdas Brazauskas. Paksas, chairman of the Lithuanian Liberal Union, became prime minister again.

Brazauskas was touted as a potential candidate for the presidential elections in December 2002 but controversy dogged his private life, leaving the path clearer for popular Adamkus.

## ECONOMY

Postindependence was a painful time for Lithuania as the Baltic economic underdog. Initially inflation ran at 1000% and thousands of jobs were lost from inefficient heavy industry.

By 1996 Lithuania's inflation rate – at 35% – was still higher than that of its neighbours. Years of Soviet bureaucracy left Lithuania unable to adjust to free-market reforms and the first round of privatisation of state-owned enterprises was virtually restricted to Lithuanian buyers. But Lithuania was the first post-Soviet Baltic state to open a stock exchange, in 1993.

Lithuania's initial poor economic performance was further exacerbated by the collapse of the country's banking system in 1995–96. Around 400 million Lt went astray amid allegations of corruption.

But miracles do happen. Lithuania clawed its way back to become the Baltic top dog. Praised by the International Monetary Fund as 'dynamic, liberal and open', the economy is one of the world's fastest growing: GDP growth was 5.9% in 2001. Lithuania's GDP grew by 6.8% in the third quarter of 2002 thanks to an increase in domestic consumption, growing investment and increased confidence. Also Lithuania's four telecommunications companies invested €188 million into new technologies and network development. Inflation clocked in at 2.1% in 2001, but the country remains dogged by high unemployment, estimated at 11% in 2002. Wages remain low with average monthly salaries of €284. Naturally this supply of cheap, skilled labour made Lithuania a magnet for foreign investment, attracting €3216 million from abroad in 2001. A campaign to lure international cash in 1997 focused on the country's low operating costs, cheap workforce and its location at the region's transport hub between East and West. Large-scale privatisation in 1997–98 earned Lithuania €600 million from foreign investment – the most rapid growth of investment in the Baltics. In July 1998, 60% of Lietuvos Telekomas (Lithuanian Telecom) was sold for €544 million to a Swedish-Finnish consortium. In October 1999, the US energy company Williams International gained a 33% stake in the Mažeikių Nafta oil refinery (despite the latter reporting losses of €26 million in 1998).

Just as things were going well, the Russian economic crisis of 1998 rocked the Baltics. Lithuania fell into a deep recession. Growth shrank by 4.1%. However, forward-thinking Lithuanians diversified into new EU electronic, chemical and manufacturing markets. By 2000 growth was a respectable 3.3%. In 2000 €110 million was pumped into Vilniaus Bankas from a Scandinavian consortium, making it the second-largest foreign investment in Lithuania. That same year, Lithuania joined the World Trade Organization. In February 2002, the *litas* was pegged to the euro at 3.4528 to 1 – ending a seven-year peg to the US dollar – to make exports competitive and show determination to join Europe. The *Wall Street Journal* recently published the Index of Economic Freedom, listing Lithuania among the top scorers, with 'the most improved economy in the history of the index'.

But many rural areas are in terminal decline. Lithuania has the questionable boast of the world's highest suicide rate, which is fuelled by rampant alcoholism and soaring unemployment (unofficially as high as 30%) in the countryside. The EU has already pumped in €18 million for regeneration projects.

## POPULATION & PEOPLE

Lithuania has the most ethnically homogeneous population of the three Baltic countries, with Lithuanians accounting for 81% of the 3.6 million people. About 8% are Russian, 7% Polish and 0.1% Jews.

Lithuanians are descendants of the Balt tribes who inhabited roughly the area of modern Lithuania. They spread into the southeastern Baltic area, along with other Balt tribes who settled modern Latvia, Poland and the Kaliningrad Region, from the south and east in about 2000 BC. By the 13th century the tribes in Lithuania were basically two groups that are now referred to as Lithuanians (in the southeast) and Samogitians (in the northwest).

The Lithuanian diaspora is the biggest of the peoples of the Baltic countries, due to emigration for political and economic reasons in the 19th and early 20th centuries and the brutal history of WWII. More than three million Lithuanians live abroad, including an estimated 800,000 in the USA, mainly in Chicago. Other communities exist in Canada, South America, Britain and Australia. More than 250,000 Jews were deported by the Soviets in 1944.

A public education centre for Roma people was set up in 2000 in Vilnius as part of a government-funded project to integrate them into Lithuanian society.

Under the citizenship law of December 1991, all residents who lived in Lithuania before 3 November 1989 were granted citizenship. People who have moved there since will have to stay 10 years before they can become citizens. Nonethnic Lithuanians have to pass a language test to get jobs dealing with the public.

## EDUCATION

The first school opened in Lithuania in Vilnius Cathedral in 1397, followed by a host of elementary and parish schools. Vilnius University – the country's first – opened in 1579 and is still the flagship state institution. Others include Vytautas Magnus University in Kaunas, founded by the Lithuanian diaspora of the United States, and Klaipėda University. Until 1998, Vilnius was still the only place to get a degree. Since then, nine state universities, five academies and four colleges have sprung up, alongside a variety of private research centres and institutions.

More than 80% of pupils go on to further education (many also working full time), a far higher number than in the other Baltic countries. Education still lags behind European standards, with outdated equipment and years of underfunding, despite 6.7% of GDP being allocated to education in 1999, roughly €400 per pupil per year. Teachers earn €213, 25% less than the national monthly average salary.

## ARTS
### Music

Lithuania is the jazz giant of the Baltics. Two noteworthy musicians are the sparkling pianist Gintautas Abarius and the more cerebral saxophonist Petras Vysniauskas. Equally famed in both Lithuania and abroad is the Ganelin Trio, whose avant-garde jazz stunned the West when discovered in the 1980s.

Home-brand pop music is dominated by girl band Mango and boy band B'avarija. The latter was disqualified from the 2002 Eurovision Song Contest line-up for prereleasing its track *Mes Cia* (We All) under another name; according to the contest rules, the song must be original. Group Skamp, which came 13th in the 2001 Eurovision contest, with *You Got Style*, plays mainstream hip-hop, while G&G Sindikatas mixes purer street sounds. DJs Mamania and Element are proof that dance music has arrived in Lithuania.

Expect popular electronic pop-rock from Lemon's Joy and hard rock from Rebel Heart. Lithuania's leading soloists include female blues singer Arina, who has been popular for more than a decade, and Andrius Mamontovas, who sang back-up vocals for Bryan Ferry during his 1999 European tour and is one of the best-loved artists in Lithuania, his signature song being *Laužo āviesa* (Fire Light). Vilnius-based Bix pioneered the use of brass in the Lithuanian pop scene in the early 1990s.

The romantic and folk-influenced Mikalojus Konstantinas Čiurlionis is Lithuania's leading composer from earlier periods. Two of his major works are the symphonic poems *Miske* (In the Forest) and *Jūra* (The Sea), written between 1900 and 1907. Čiurlionis wrote many piano pieces, notably played and recorded by contemporary Lithuanian parliament chairman Vytautas Landbergis.

Saulius Sondeckis, conductor of the Lithuanian Chamber Orchestra, and opera tenor Virgilijus Noreika are prominent late-20th-century musicians.

## Literature

The first major fiction in Lithuanian was the poem *Metai* (The Seasons) by Kristijonas Donelaitis, describing the life of serfs in the 18th century. A high mark in the 19th century was Antanas Baranauskas' poem *Anykščių silelis* (Anykščiai Pine Forest), written in 1860–61, which uses the forest as a symbol of Lithuania and bemoans its destruction by foreign landlords.

From 1864 Lithuanian literature was severely handicapped by Russia's insistence on the Cyrillic alphabet for all publishing. Jonas Mačiulis (1862–1932), known as Maironis, was the poet of the Lithuanian national revival. His nationalist, romantic *Pavasario balsai* (Voices of Spring), which was published in 1895, was the beginning of modern Lithuanian poetry. Vincas Mykolaitis-Putinas, a priest who left the priesthood in the 1930s, is probably the leading literary figure of the 20th century. He wrote poetry as well as prose but his outstanding work is *Altorių sesėly* (In the Altars' Shadow), a three-volume novel.

Several major Polish writers grew up in Lithuania and regarded themselves as partly Lithuanian. Among them are Adam Mickiewicz, the inspiration of 19th-century nationalists, whose great poem *Pan Tadeusz* begins 'Lithuania, my fatherland…', and the contemporary writers Czesław Miłosz (winner of the 1980 Nobel prize) and novelist Tadeusz Konwicki. Miłosz, poet, essayist and critic, has translated Lithuanian *dainas* (Baltic folk rhymes) into French and written about intellectuals and the Soviet occupation of the Baltic states in the last chapter of *The Captive Mind*.

Among novelists at the fore of contemporary Lithuanian literature is Antanas Skėma. His semiautobiographical novel *Balta drobule* (White Linen Shroud; 1954), recounting a childhood in Kaunas, then emigration to Germany and New York, pioneered flow of consciousness in Lithuanian literature. Realist novelist and short story writer Ričardas Gavelis sent shock waves through the literary world with his novels *Vilnius Poker* (1989) and *Vilnius Jazz* (1993), which openly criticised and mocked the defunct Soviet system and mentality. Equally controversial was the story of a priest's love affair with a woman, *Ragana ir lietus* (The Witch and the Rain) by Jurga Ivanauskaitė, which was immediately banned on publication in 1992. Jurgis Kunčinas is another name that provoked controversy.

Poets to look out for include Lithuanian emigre Alfonsas Nyka-Niliūnas (born near Utena in 1919), who writes in both Lithuanian and English, Henrikas Radauskas and Jonas Aistas (1904–73).

## Visual Arts

Lithuania has a thriving contemporary art scene. Artists in Vilnius are the brains behind the tongue-in-cheek Republic of Užupis, which hosts alternative art festivals, fashion shows and exhibitions in its breakaway state. Some 19km north of Vilnius, at a site claimed to be the exact geographic centre of Europe, international artists, led by Lithuanian sculptor Gintaras Karosas, have created the unique Europos Parkas sculpture park, which is home to a very large TV sculpture!

Photography has achieved international recognition. Vytautas Stanionis was the leading postwar figure, while artists Antanas Sutkus and Algirdas Kairys used the medium as social criticism. Vitalijus Butyrinas' famous series *Tales of the Sea* uses abstract expressionism to make powerful images.

From Lenin to rock legend, Konstantinas Bogdanas is famed for his heroic bronzes of communist heroes, which now languish in the Soviet sculpture park in southeastern Lithuania – and then for creating the world's only bust of musician Frank Zappa, proudly displayed in Vilnius.

In contrast, respected Vilnius sculptor Stanislovas Kuzma was persecuted by the KGB and forced to flee the capital during the Soviet period. His creations include *The Feast of the Muse* (1982), a trio of golden faces which peer down from the entrance of the Academic Drama Theatre in Vilnius, *Pietà* (1995) in Antakalnio cemetery and the three saints which stand atop Vilnius Cathedral.

Mikalojus Konstantinas Čiurlionis (1875–1911) achieved international recognition with his romantic and symbolic paintings in gentle, lyrical tones. A depressive genius, he was also a major composer. There's a good book on his life and work by former Lithuanian president Vytautas Landsbergis: *MK Čiurlionis – Time and Content* is well illustrated with many of Čiurlionis' paintings, scores, letters and writings.

Two artists who achieved major standing, although their work is not specifically Lithuanian, were the Vilnius-bred Jews Isaak Levitan (a landscape painter who holds an important place in Russian 19th-century art) and Jacques Lipchitz (a 20th-century sculptor).

## Folk Art

The carved wooden crosses that cover Lithuania are both a beautiful expression of religious fervour and a striking nationalistic statement. They are placed at crossroads, cemeteries, village squares and at the sites of extraordinary events. Pagan symbols of suns, moons and plants are also intertwined, making the totems a unique cultural contradiction. Vincas Svirskis (1835–1916) was the master; there's a fine collection of his carvings in the National Museum in Vilnius. In the Soviet period, such work – with its religious overtones – was banned, but it survived to amazing effect at the Hill of Crosses near Šiauliai.

## Film & Theatre

The Lithuanian film industry, though small, is flourishing. Audrius Stonys has won acclaim in Europe with his documentaries shown at festivals worldwide. Film director Šarūnas Bartas (born in Šiauliai in 1964) made two documentaries before moving on to feature-length films: *Trys Dienos* (Three Days; 1991) was followed by the silent B&W movie *Koridorius* (The Corridor; 1995), which won acclaim at several film festivals in Europe, including Cannes. Algimantas Puipa won at the Stockholm Film Festival in 1998 with *The Necklace of Wolf's Teeth*. His *Elsie from Gilija* has received international recognition.

Theatre has grown from subversive roots. It went underground following a Tsarist ban –

and is now an international force. Theatre festival LIFE, held in Vilnius each year, attracts an impressive list of global big names. Among the resident directors of the festival is respected theatre director Eimuntas Nekrosius, whose unconventional productions including adaptations of Shakespeare's *Richard III*, *Macbeth* and *Hamlet* and Chekhov's *Uncle Vanya* made Lithuanian theatre known throughout the world.

Contemporary and controversial is Vilnius-based Oskaras Korsunovas, whose works such as *Old Woman*, *Shopping and Fucking* and *PS Files OK* have done the theatre festival circuit, including Edinburgh and Avignon. Other names to watch include young Gintaras Varnas and Rimas Tuminas.

## SOCIETY & CONDUCT

With their emotional natures and tendency towards mysticism, Lithuanians could be described as the Italians of the Baltic region. They are fiercely proud of their national identity, as a backlash from the brutal attempts to eradicate it and memories of their long-lost empire.

Their pride in being the (disputed) geographical centre of Europe shows in their willingness to speak English, German and even Russian, in stark contrast to Latvia and Estonia.

There are strict rules regarding conduct. When visiting a Lithuanian bring an odd number of flowers – even-numbered bouquets are for the dead! Never shake hands across a doorway, as it is believed to bring bad luck, and always maintain eye contact when toasting your host, otherwise they will think you are shifty.

Western excesses are infiltrating this strongly Catholic country. Once banned, strip joints and casinos are opening their dubious doors. The state estimates they will add 25 million Lt to the country's coffers.

Guzzling grog in the streets is illegal. Anyone caught with a bottle of beer al fresco will be fined 50 Lt and repeat offenders face a month behind bars.

## Treatment of Animals

Animal sacrifice may have been the norm in pre-Christian Lithuania, but this pagan tradition thankfully died a more peaceful death. Animals are regarded generally with love and respect by the pet-loving Lithuanian people.

The stork, for example, is revered traditionally as protector of the home (see the boxed text 'Storking' in the introductory Facts about the Region chapter). The only sticking point is that the minute the first flurries of snow hit the streets, fur is *de rigueur* for wrapping up warm in. The city of Kaunas has the country's only zoo, which claims to encourage breeding species rather than just gawping at furry things in cages.

## RELIGION

Lithuania was the last pagan country in Europe, and was only baptised into Roman Catholicism in 1387, two centuries after Estonia and Latvia. This explains why so much of its religious art, national culture and traditions have raw pagan roots. The 16th-century religious Reformation sent a wave of Protestantism across Lithuania (and Poland, which was united with Lithuania in the Commonwealth), but in the 1570s this was reversed by the Counter-Reformation. During the

Soviet years, Catholicism was persecuted and hence became a symbol of nationalistic fervour. Churches were seized, closed and turned into 'museums of atheism' or used for other secular purposes by the state, and most priests and other leading figures in the church were sent to Siberia. During the drive for independence the church grew in power as a key player in the political struggles.

Other minorities include Orthodox believers, Lutherans (who also suffered at the hands of the Soviets), Jews (see the boxed text 'Jerusalem of the North' in the Vilnius chapter), Evangelical Christians and the Romuva movement, which is a pagan revivalist belief system based on a profound respect for nature. The Romuva symbol is a holy oak tree with a flame and there are a few hundred worshippers in Lithuania (see the boxed text 'Paganism vs Christianity' in the Facts about the Region chapter). The smallest religious community in Lithuania numbering only several hundred are the Karaites people.

# Facts for the Visitor

This chapter is specific to Lithuania. For more general information on travelling in the Baltics see the introductory Facts for the Visitor chapter.

## SUGGESTED ITINERARIES
The following suggestions may help you plan your visit.

**Two days** Vilnius, with a trip to Trakai.

**One week** A few days in the capital combined with a day trip to Trakai or the Soviet sculpture park, plus a couple of days either hiking and canoeing in the Aukštaitija National Park or discovering the dunes on the Curonian Spit.

**Two weeks** Vilnius to Klaipėda, the gateway to the Curonian Spit. Explore the dunes near Nida, sweat it out in the seaside sauna in Smiltynė, then head down the mainland to Rusnė and explore the backwaters of the Nemunas Delta by boat. Double back, go to the eerie Hill of Crosses near Šiauliai via Orvydas Garden, the Soviet missile base and Lake Plateliai. Back to Vilnius via Kaunas.

## PLANNING
The introductory Facts for the Visitor chapter has general information for planning your trip.

### Maps
For details of maps of the region, see the introductory Facts for the Visitor chapter. Lithuania is best covered by the Lietuva Road Map (1:500,000), published by Rīga-based map publisher Jāņa sēta (see Maps under Orientation in the Rīga chapter). It includes small inset city maps of Šiauliai, Panevėžys, Vilnius, Kaunas and Klaipėda. It's sold in TIC offices and kiosks for 8 Lt. Jāņa sēta's individual city plans (miesto planas) cover Vilnius, Kaunas and Klaipėda at a scale of 1:25,000, with a 1:10,000 inset of the centre and Palanga (1:15,000), Šiauliai and Panevėžys (1:20,000). These cost 6 Lt. to 8 Lt.

The Vilnius-based map publisher Briedis produces various maps (not as well distributed or updated as regularly as Jāņa sēta maps). Briedis' *Atlasas* is sold in large bookshops and petrol stations.

## RESPONSIBLE TOURISM
Fragile Neringa (Curonian Spit), along with the rest of Lithuania, should command the respect of visitors. Tourists are urged to enjoy the natural beauty without dropping litter, lighting fires in unauthorised areas or disturbing plants and wildlife.

## TOURIST OFFICES
Lithuania has a network of tourist offices (TICs), coordinated by the **Lithuanian State Department of Tourism** (☎ 5-262 2610, fax 5-212 6819; ℮ info@tourism.lt; ⓦ www .tourism.lt; Vilniaus gatvė 4/35, LT-2600 Vilnius). For a list of its representatives overseas, see Tourist Offices in the introductory Facts for the Visitor chapter. Details of individual city/town/area information offices are given in the relevant chapters.

For more information on Lithuania's three Unesco World Heritage awards (Neringa, Vilnius Old Town and the tradition of cross crafting), visit the Vilnius-based **Lithuanian National Commission for Unesco** (☎/fax 5-210 7340; ℮ unesco@taide.lt; Šv Jono gatvė 11) or visit ⓦ www.unesco.org.

## VISAS & DOCUMENTS
See the introductory Facts for the Visitor chapter or check the Ministry of Foreign Affairs website ⓦ www.urm.lt.

## EMBASSIES & CONSULATES
### Lithuanian Embassies & Consulates
Lithuanian diplomatic representation in other countries includes:

**Australia** *Consulate:* (☎ 02-9498 2571) 40B Fiddens Wharf Rd, Killara, NSW 2071

**Belarus** (☎ 017-285 2448, fax 017-285 3337, ℮ ambasada@belsonet.net) Zacharova ulitsa 68, 220088 Minsk

**Canada** (☎ 613-567 5458, fax 613-567 5315, ℮ litemb@storm.ca) 130 Albert St, Suite 204, Ottawa, Ontario K1P 5G4

**Czech Republic** (☎ 02-572 101 22, fax 02-572 101 24, ℮ ltembcz@mbox.vol.cz) Pod Klikovkou 1916/2, 1500 Praha 5, Czech Republic

**Denmark** (☎ 39-636 207, fax 39-636 532) Bernstorffsvej 214, DK-2920 Charlottelund, Copenhagen

**Estonia** (☎ 631 4030/4053, fax 641 2013, ℮ amber@anet.ee) Uus tänav 15, 0100 Tallinn

**Finland** (☎ 09-608 210, fax 09-608 220, ℮ embassy@liettua.pp.fi) Rauhankatu 13a, 00170 Helsinki

**France** (☎ 01 48 01 00 33, fax 01 48 01 03 31,
  e amb.lituanie@magic.fr) 14 blv Montmartre,
  75009 Paris
**Germany** (☎ 030-890 6810, fax 030-890 681 15,
  e botschaftlitauen@t-online.de)
  Katharinenstrasse 9, D-10711 Berlin
**Israel** (☎ 3-528 8514, fax 3-525 7265) Top Tower
  14th floor, Dizengoff 50, Suite 1404, Tel Aviv
  64332
**Latvia** (☎ 732 1519, fax 732 1589,
  e lithemb@ltemb.vip.lv) Rūpniecības iela 24,
  1010 Rīga
**Norway** (☎ 22-558 150, fax 22-556 730) Gimle
  Terrace 6, Oslo 0244
**Poland, Romania & Bulgaria** (☎ 02-625 3368,
  fax 02-625 3440, W www.waw.pdi
  .net/~litwa_amb) aleje Szucha 5, 00-580
  Warsaw
**Russia** (☎ 095-291 1698, fax 095-202 3516)
  Borisoglebsky per 10, 121069 Moscow
  *Consulate in Kaliningrad:* (☎ 0112-551 444,
  fax 0112-216 651) Proletarskaja 133,
  Kaliningrad
  *Consulate in St Petersburg:* (☎ 812-314 58 57,
  fax 812-315 89 91, e ltconsul@mail
  .wplus.net) Gorokhovaya ulitsa 4, 190000 St
  Petersburg
**UK** (☎ 020-7486 6401/2, fax 020-7486 6403,
  W www.users.globalnet.co.uk/~lralon) 84
  Gloucester Place, London W1U 6AU
**USA** (☎ 202-234 5860, fax 202-328 0466,
  W www.ltembassyus.org) 2622 16th St NW,
  Washington, DC 20009
  *Consulate in New York:* (☎ 212-354 7849, fax
  212-354 7911, e lrgkn@msn.com, 420 Fifth
  Ave, New York, NY 10018
  *Consulate in Chicago:* (☎ 312-397 0382, fax
  312-397 0383) 211 E Ontario St, Suite 1500,
  Chicago, IL 60611

## Embassies & Consulates in Lithuania

Foreign embassies in Vilnius (☎ 5) include:

**Australia** *Consulate:* (☎/fax 212 3369,
  e aust.con@post.omnitel.net) Karmelitų
  gatvė4/12
**Belarus** (☎ 266 2200, fax 266 2211,
  e bpl@post.5ci.lt) Mindaugo gatvė 13
**Canada** (☎ 249 6853, fax 249 6898,
  e vilnius@canada.lt) Gedimino prospektas 64
**Czech Republic** (☎ 266 1040/1, fax 266 1066,
  W www.mfa.cz/vilnius) Tilto gatvė 1/2
**Denmark** (☎ 215 3434, fax 231 2300,
  W www.denmark.lt) Kosciuš kos gatvė 36
**Estonia** (☎ 278 0200, fax 278 0201,
  e sekretar@estemb.lt) Mickevičiaus gatvė 4a
**Finland** (☎ 212 1621, fax 212 2463,
  e finemb.vilnius@post.omnitel.net) Klaipėdos
  gatvė 6, 3rd floor

**France** (☎ 212 2979, fax 212 4211,
  e ambafrance.vilnius@diplomatie.gouv.fr)
  Švarco gatvė 1
**Germany** (☎ 265 0272, fax 213 1812,
  e germ.emb@takas.lt) Sierakausko gatvė 24
**Latvia** (☎ 213 1260, fax 213 1130,
  e lietuva@latvia.balt.net) Čiurlionio gatvė 76
**Norway** (☎ 272 6926, fax 272 6964,
  W www.norvegija.lt) Poš kos gatvė 59
**Poland** (☎ 270 9001, fax 270 9007,
  e ambpol@tdd.lt) Smėlio gatvė 20a
**Russia** (☎ 272 1763, fax 272 3877,
  e rusemb@rusemb.lt) Latvių gatvė 53/54
**UK** (☎ 212 2070, fax 272 7579,
  W www.britain.lt) Antakalnio gatvė 2
**USA** (☎ 266 5500, fax 266 5510,
  W www.usembassy.lt) Akmenų gatvė 6

## CUSTOMS

Customs regulations are subject to change;
see the introductory Facts for the Visitor
chapter for some general pointers. In Vilnius,
the **customs department** (☎ *212 6415, fax 212
4948;* e *info@cust.lt;* W *www.cust.lt; Jakš to
gatvė 1/25)* has up-to-date information.

You can import duty free: 1L of spirits,
2L of wine or champagne, 3L of beer and
200 cigarettes or 250g of tobacco. But if
you arrive any way other than by sea or air
the quotas are smaller. Upon entering, you
must declare foreign currency in cash above
10,000 Lt and upon exiting, amounts over
5000 Lt.

Lithuania limits the export of amber, but
a few souvenirs should be okay providing
their value doesn't exceed €266. You need
a Culture Ministry permit, and pay 10% to
20% duty, to export artworks over 50 years
old. For further information contact the
**Committee of Cultural Heritage** (☎ *272
4005; Snipiš kių gatvė 3, Vilnius).*

## MONEY

Lithuania introduced its own currency, the
*litas* (plural: *litų*), on 25 June 1993. It replaced the *talonas* (coupon), the transitional
currency used during the phasing out of the
Soviet rouble in Lithuania. The *litas* (Lt) is
divided into 100 *centų* (singular: *centas*). It
comes in 10 Lt, 20 Lt, 50 Lt, 100 Lt, 200 Lt
and 500 Lt notes and 1 Lt, 2 Lt and 5 Lt coins
and the virtually worthless *centų* coins. It
was pegged to the US dollar at a rate of 4 Lt
to $1 for seven years and in February 2002
pegged to the euro. In early 2003 exchange
rates were the following.

| country | unit | | litų (Lt) |
|---------|------|---|-----------|
| Australia | A$1 | = | 1.88 |
| Canada | C$1 | = | 2.12 |
| euro zone | €1 | = | 3.47 |
| Sweden | 1 SKr | = | 0.38 |
| UK | UK£1 | = | 5.30 |
| USA | US$1 | = | 3.22 |

## POST & COMMUNICATIONS
### Post
Lithuania's postal system is quick and cheap. Letters/postcards cost 1.70/1 Lt internationally and 1/0.80 Lt domestically. Mail to the USA takes about 10 days, to Europe about a week. EMS is the cheapest express mail service; find it in Vilnius at the **main post office** (*paš tas;* ☎ *616 759; Gedimino prospektas 7*).

### Telephone
The Lithuanian telephone network was digitalised in 2002 and all the area access codes were changed. If you are in doubt about a code check **Lietuvos Telekomas** (*Lithuanian Telecom;* ⓦ *www.telecom.lt*). To call other cities in Lithuania, dial ☎ 8, wait for the tone, then dial the area code and telephone number.

To make an international call dial ☎ 00 before the country code. To call Lithuania from abroad, dial ☎ 370 then the area code, follow with the city code and telephone number. To call other cities in Lithuania, dial ☎ 8, wait for the tone, then dial the city code.

All blue public phones are card-only, sold in denominations of 50/75/100/200 units costing 9/13/16/30 Lt. Lithuanians do seem to have their mobile phones surgically attached to their ears though.

No self-respecting Lithuanian would be seen without a mobile phone surgically attached to their ear. A communications revolution is under way – more than 800,000 Lithuanians owned mobiles at the end of 2001 compared with 15,000 in 1996. The leading mobile companies in Lithuania are **Bitė** (ⓔ *info@bite.lt;* ⓦ *www.bite.lt*), **Omnitel** (ⓔ *info@omnitel.net;* ⓦ *www.omnitel.lt*) and **Tele 2** (ⓔ *tele2@tele2.lt;* ⓦ *www.tele2.lt*) in Lithuanian only, all of whom offer prepaid SIM cards as well as a monthly subscription system. Mobile numbers are preceded by the number 8, followed by a three-digit code, then five digits starting with the number 6, for example, ☎ 8-298-6xxxx. Mobile telephone numbers are listed in full in this guide.

**Emergency Services** Nationwide emergency numbers are ☎ 01 for fire, ☎ 02 for police and ☎ 03 for ambulance.

### Email & Internet Access
Logging on gets easier by the day as Internet cafés grow like mushrooms (as they say in Lithuania!) in Vilnius (2 Lt to 8 Lt per hour). Outside the capital, prices and speeds are higher and slower respectively.

## DIGITAL RESOURCES
Handy sites specific to Lithuania include:

ⓦ **www.tourism.lt** Well researched and informative home page of the Lithuanian State Department of Tourism

ⓦ **www.travel.lt** Handy tips for exploring the countryside, from the Tourism Fund of Lithuania

ⓦ **www.vilnius.lt** Brilliant up-to-the-minute guide to the capital, with good news archives

ⓦ **www.online.lt** Complete index of Lithuanian Internet resources, *Yellow-Pages* style, plus cheeky and detailed city guides to Vilnius, Klaipėda and Kaunas

ⓦ **www.inter.banga.lt** Every news and information link you will ever need for culture and current affairs

## BOOKS
Vilnius-based publishing house **Vaga** (☎ *5-249 8392; Gedimino prospektas 50, Lt-2600 Vilnius*) publishes books in English. Vilnius hosts the largest book fair in the Baltics; this has taken place each spring for the last three years.

In the USA, Lithuanian-focused titles are available at **The Baltic Bookshelf** (☎/fax *410-721 34 11;* ⓔ *balticbook@aol.com;* ⓦ *www .geocities.com/balticbook; PO Box 3314, Crofton, MD 21114*) and from the **Lithuanian Research and Studies Center** (☎ *773-434 4545; 5600 Claremont Ave, Chicago, IL 60636*). In Australia, contact the **Lithuanian Studies Society at the University of Tasmania** (ⓔ *a .taskunas@utas.edu.au; PO Box 777, Sandy Bay, Tasmania 7006*).

### History & Politics
*Lithuania – Independent Again: The Autobiography of Vytautas Landsbergis* (1998) by Anthony Packer & Eimuntas Sova is a highly readable autobiography of one of Lithuania's most admired and respected politicians (and musicians). The scene outside parliament on 13 January 1991 is just one of the dramatic

moments in Lithuanian history that Landsbergis brings vividly to life.

*Showdown – The Lithuanian Rebellion and the Break Up of the Soviet Union* (1997) by Richard J Krickus, and SC Rowell's *Lithuania Ascending: A Pagan Empire within East-Central Europe 1295–1345* both look at the southernmost Baltic nation from a political perspective.

In Lithuania, *Forest of the Gods* by dramatist Balys Sruoga is a powerful account of the author's time spent in the Stutthof Nazi concentration camp in the early 1940s. The book was censored for many years and only published in 1957, 10 years after Sruoga's death. *Hell in Ice* is the firsthand account of Lithuanian Onutė Garbstienė, who was deported to Siberia in 1941 along with her two small children.

*The Book of Sorrow* (1997) by Josif Levinson (born 1917) is a moving account of a childhood spent in the Dzūkija region, southern Lithuania, and the murder of the author's father in 1941. *In Lithuanian Wood* by Wendell Mayo is a set of moving short stories examining the Nazi and Soviet eras.

*Lithuania – Past, Culture, Present* (1999), published by Baltos Lankos and edited by Saulius Žukas, is a beautiful, hardback book presenting the history of Lithuania up until the present day. The equally weighty *The Old Lithuanian Sculpture (Senoji Lietuvių Skulptūra)* (1995) by R Paknio Leidykla presents the development of Lithuania's treasured roadside shrines and crosses through the ages. *Guide to Lithuania's Baroque Monuments* (1996), published by the Council of Europe, is for anyone interested in architecture or churches. *Of Gods and Holidays: The Baltic Heritage* (1999) is a revealing look at Lithuania's Pagan roots.

For an eclectic collection of black-and-white photographs of past and present Lithuania, look out for *Lithuanian Photography: Yesterday and Today* (2001). No prizes for guessing what the authoritative tome *The History of the Lithuanian Language* (1998) by Zigmas Zinkevičius is about.

### Fiction

*Bohin Manor* by Tadeusz Konwicki, a leading modern Polish writer who was born in Lithuania, is set in the aftermath of the 1863 uprising. Like Estonian novelist Jaan Kross, Konwicki uses the past to comment on more contemporary events, evoking the tensions between locals, their Russian rulers and a Jewish outsider, as well as the foreboding and mysterious nature of the Lithuanian backwoods.

Published locally, *Lithuania in Her Own Words: An Anthology of Contemporary Lithuanian Writing* (1997) is edited by Laima Sruoginis. *Lithuanian Literature* (1997) edited by Vytautas Kubilius is a good background read.

The works of several contemporary Lithuanian poets are available in English. *The Theology of Rain* is a collection of poems by Alfonsas Nyka-Niliūnas, and *Four Poets of Lithuania* (1995) is about the emergence of postmodernism in Baltic poetry. The poems in both collections are selected and translated by Jonas Zdanys, son of a Lithuanian emigre who has himself authored some 20 poetry collections. The voice of Australia's Lithuanian diaspora is represented by Lidija Simkutė, whose family fled the Žemaitija region during WWII. Her recent creation is the bilingual poetry collection *Spaces of Silence* (1999).

## NEWSPAPERS & MAGAZINES

Some Western newspapers, mostly German or American titles, are sold at upmarket hotels in Vilnius, Kaunas and Klaipėda. The British *Financial Times* is available for 15 Lt. For regional news, the English-language *Baltic Times* has the area sewn up. It costs 4 Lt from kiosks or hotels, or is free from TICs. A brilliant source of cultural and current affairs features is the Lithuanian Airlines in-flight magazine *Lithuania in the World*, found at Littera bookshop in Vilnius for 9 Lt, or indeed on a plane. *City Paper* (w www.balticsww .com), a mix of high-brow business news and country guide, is found at good hotels. The *In Your Pocket* city guides to Vilnius (published every two months) and Klaipėda/Kaunas (annual) are crammed with essential insider information and cost 8 Lt from TICs and hotels.

Locally, the most popular Lithuanian newspaper is *Lietuvos Rytas*, favoured by its many advertisements, classifieds and entertainment listings. Other dailies include *Respublika*, *Lietuvos Aidas* and Kaunas' daily *Kauno Diena*. The smaller, *Financial Times* (*Lietuvos Žinios*) is a business newspaper with an English-language summary, published fortnightly. *Jerusalem of Lithuania* is published in Yiddish, Lithuanian,

Russian and English, and is sold at the State Jewish Museum in Vilnius.

Lithuanian-inspired publications published and distributed overseas include *Lithuanian Papers* (e a.tuskunas@educ.utas.edu.au), an annual journal published by the Lithuanian Studies Society at the University of Tasmania (see Books earlier), and *Bridges* (☎ 703-390 0498, e contact@javlb.org), 11876 Sunrise Valley Dr, Suite 201 Reston, VA 20191, USA, a Lithuanian-American news journal published 10 times a year.

For details of publications covering all three Baltic countries, see the introductory Facts for the Visitor chapter.

## RADIO & TV
Lithuania has seen a rash of new private TV and radio stations. State station Lithuanian TV faces competition from several commercial channels, including Baltic TV, which screens CNN news in English at midnight and World Net at 1pm. Newcomers LNK TV and TV3 are popular for showing American films, soap operas and concerts.

Popular M1 (106.8 FM), the first independent radio station to broadcast in Soviet times, has launched a sister station, M1 Plus (106.2FM), dedicated to music.

Upbeat commercial channel Radiocentras (101.5 FM) is a favourite, as well as Lithuanian Radio 1 (102.6 FM) and Lithuanian music station Lietus (103.1).

Radio Vilnius (102.6FM) has local news in English at 10pm and Voice of America at 10.30pm. The BBC World Service (95.5 FM) is available 24 hours a day, as is Radio France Internationale (98.3 FM). Znad Wilii is an independent Polish-Russian language channel (103.8 FM).

## GAY & LESBIAN TRAVELLERS
The scene is still low-key. For general information, chat rooms and guides get in touch with the **Lithuanian Gay League** (☎ 5-233 3031; PO Box 2862, Vilnius, LT-2000; w www.gay.lt).

The country's first gay club, **Men's Factory** (☎ 5-231 0687; e vgc@takas.lt) in Vilnius, opened as recently as 2000.

## DANGERS & ANNOYANCES
There have been some disturbing reports of anti-Semitic attacks. Be assured these are rare and the majority of Lithuanians are friendly and polite. The older generation appears to hold antiquated views on gay people and those from ethnic backgrounds.

## PUBLIC HOLIDAYS & SPECIAL EVENTS
Lithuania's national holidays are:

**New Year's Day** 1 January
**Independence Day** 16 February – Nepriklausomybės diena; anniversary of 1918 independence declaration
**Good Friday**
**Easter Monday**
**Mothers' Day** First Sunday in May
**Statehood Day** 6 July – commemoration of coronation of Grand Duke Mindaugas, 13th century
**All Saints' Day** 1 November
**Christmas** Kalėdos 25, 26 December

Lithuania also celebrates a host of commemorative days, such as the Day of the Lithuanian Flag (1 January), St Casimir's Day (4 March), Earth Day (20 March), Partisans' Day (fourth Sunday in May), Black Ribbon Day (23 August) and the Genocide Day of Lithuanian Jews (23 September). People still officially work on these days but the national flag flutters outside most public buildings and private homes.

Lithuania's most important cultural events include its national song festival, midsummer celebrations and the Baltika folk festival. For background to these events see the special section 'The Power of Song'. In Vilnius, the **Lithuanian Folk Culture Centre** (☎ 5-261 1190, 5-261 2540, fax 5-261 2607; e lfcc@lfcc.lt; w www.lfcc.lt/kc/indexen.htm; Barboros Radvilaitės gatvė 8, LT-2600 Vilnius) has information on most leading cultural events, which include:

**February**
**Horse Race** First Saturday of the month, on Lake Sartai in Dusetos, near Utena, if the lake is frozen, otherwise in the town
**Užgavėnės (Mardi Gras)** Animal, bird and beast masquerades in towns and villages of Žemaitija

**March**
**St Casimir's Day** Held on 4 March. Lithuania's patron saint's day, with the Kaziukas crafts fair in Vilnius around this date.
**Birstonas Jazz Festival** Held late March in evennumbered years. Three-day jazz event, with top Lithuanian and foreign musicians.

**April**

**Kaunas International Jazz Festival** Four-day festival, with acts in Kaunas and Vilnius, attracting top jazz musicians from all over the world.

**May**

**LIFE International Theatre Festival** A week-long theatre festival in Vilnius, attracting avant-garde theatre companies from Europe.

**July**

**Vilnius Summer Music Festival** A week-long summer festival of street theatre, dancing, masked parades and craft fairs in the streets of Vilnius' Old Town.

**Žemaičių Kalvarija Church Festival** First week of the month. Thousands of pilgrims from all over Lithuania flock to the Žemaičių Kalvarija to celebrate this week-long church festival.

**Klaipėda Sea Festival** Late July. Celebrations in the port city; 2002 was the 750th anniversary.

**September**

**Vilnius City Days** Mid-month. Three days of musical and cultural events in theatres, concert halls and in the streets of Vilnius.

**October**

**Vilnius Jazz Festival** One of eastern Europe's leading contemporary jazz gatherings, held in Vilnius.

**November**

**Vėlinės (All Souls' Day)** Held on 2 November. Commemoration of the dead, with visits to cemeteries.

## ACTIVITIES

Lithuania is a land known for its love of nature. People were still worshiping ancient oak trees a mere six centuries ago – and these days they take regular pilgrimages out to the luscious lakes and forests in their free time.

Boating, berrying and bird-watching are all uplifting pursuits. Travellers can cycle into the wilderness, sweat in traditional saunas and experience the frozen joys of ice-fishing or skiing.

For more details see the introductory Facts for the Visitor chapter or individual destination chapters.

## ACCOMMODATION

For general information on staying in camping grounds, hotels and B&Bs, as well as home and farmstays, see the introductory Facts for the Visitor chapter.

The **Lithuanian Hostels Association** *(Lietuvos nakvynės namai; ☎ 5-215 4627, fax 5-212 0149; ⓦ http://filaretai.8m.com; Filaretų gatvė 17, Vilnius LT-2001)* is based at the largest hostel it runs, the Filaretai Hostel. The association runs a second hostel, the Old Town Hostel, in Vilnius' Old Town, and has affiliated hostels in Klaipėda, Ignalina and the village of Zervynos in the Dzūkija National Park in southern Lithuania. A bed in a shared room costs 10 Lt to 40 Lt a night. Linen is usually included and Hostelling International (HI) members get a small discount in some hostels. The association sells HI cards (valid for one year) for 30 Lt at its Filaretai hostel.

For B&Bs, with or without a Lithuanian host, check out Litinterp in Vilnius, Klaipeda and Kaunas via the website ⓦ www.litinterp.lt (see destination chapters for details).

Lithuanian camping grounds are basic, cheap (5 Lt to 20 Lt to pitch a tent, 15 Lt to 30 Lt for a wooden cabin) and generally rundown. Moves are under way by the Lithuanian Tourist Board to spruce up facilities.

## FOOD & DRINKS

Long, miserable winters are to blame for the hearty, waist-widening diet based on potatoes, meat and dairy products.

Lithuanian food is epitomised in the formidable zeppelin *cepelinai*, an airship-shaped parcel of thick potato dough, filled with cheese, *mesa* (meat) or *grybai (*mushrooms). It comes topped with a sauce made from onions, butter, sour cream and bacon bits. Another artery-furring favourite is grated potatoes and carrots baked in the oven and served with sour cream, *kugelis*. *Koldūnai* is hearty ravioli stuffed with meat, mushrooms or *kopūstai* (cabbage), served with sour cream.

Lithuanians are not afraid of eating the less savoury bits of animals: *liežuvis*, cow's tongue, is considered a delicacy, and they pork out on smoked pig's ears, trotters or fried pork innards, *vėdarai*.

Pancakes come in various types, sweet or savoury, and are eaten at any time of the day. *Blyneliai* (small pancakes), *varskõčiai* (curd pancakes) and *bulviniai blyneliai*, made with grated potato, come stuffed with meat, *varske* (cheese curd), or fruit and chocolate.

Common Lithuanian starters include *silkė* (herring), *sprotai* (sprats), mushrooms, salads and soups. *Saltibarsčiai*, a cold beetroot soup served with boiled potatoes, is garishly pink in colour.

Lithuanians create a new dish to mark special occasions. *Sakotis* is a metre-tall, Christmas tree–shaped cake that's covered with long spikes (made from a rather dry, sponge-cake mixture) which is generally served at weddings. Christmas is another major culinary feast. Dinner on 24 December consists of 12 different vegetarian dishes, one of which is *kūčiukai* – cubed biscuits made from dough and poppy seeds and served in poppy-seed milk.

Beer is *alus* in Lithuanian – the best local brands are Utenos and Kalnapilis. No drink would be complete without the bar snack, *kepta duona*, which reaches new fattening heights with deep-fried bread heaped in garlic (see the boxed text 'Beer Talk' in the Central Lithuanian chapter). Lithuanians also drink *midus* (mead), such as Žalgiris and Suktinis, which are as much as 60- proof, and *gira*, made from fermented grains or fruit and brown rye bread. The more sober-minded should look out for *stakliskes*, a honey liqueur, or *starkas* made from apple- and pear-tree leaves.

General information on eating in the region is given in the introductory Facts for the Visitor chapter. The Language chapter at the back of this book includes words and phrases useful when ordering a meal. Anyone wanting to build their own zeppelins should invest in the cookery book *Lithuanian Traditional Foods* (1998), compiled by Birutė Imbrasiene.

## ENTERTAINMENT

Lithuania has a well-deserved reputation as the Baltic queen of contemporary jazz, theatre and the avant-garde. All three Baltic capitals host a rich repertoire of classical music and opera festivals, but it is Lithuania which boasts the most renowned, ranging from the LIFE International Theatre Festival to the Kaunas International Jazz Festival.

Offsetting such classicism are the fun theme bars, offbeat clubs and low-key dance parties, providing the traveller with a rare opportunity to mingle with the local arts scene. Kaunas is particularly well known for its bohemian arty set, in contrast to the seaside resort of Palanga, where bars, clubs and all-night discos are mainstream. Nightlife in Vilnius has developed in recent years. You can pose in trendy, expensive house clubs, enjoy nostalgic Soviet-theme clubs, let your hair down in studenty live music joints or dance till dawn at warehouse rave parties, costing between 5 Lt and 25 Lt. The fledgling gay scene boasts one club, Men's Factory in Vilnius, which is also popular with trendy heterosexuals.

There are also one-off rock, pop, folk, jazz and blues concerts – by visiting foreign stars as well as local artists. Websites to watch are Ⓦ www.classicalmusic.lt and Ⓦ www.cinema.lt (Lithuanian only).

## SPECTATOR SPORTS

Basketball is akin to religion in Lithuania. The worshipped national team has won bronze medals in the last three Olympic Games. It came within seconds of pulling off the basketball coup of the century by almost defeating the American Dream Team at the Sydney 2000 Games.

Žalgiris Kaunas is top of the domestic league. It won the European Cup in 1997, knocked the USA out of the World Championships in 1998 and bounced its way to victory in the final of the 1999 EuroLeague (Europe's equivalent of the USA's NBA) before crashing out of the 2001 European Championships in Turkey.

Lithuania's best-known basketball players include Sarūnas Marčiulionis ('Roony' to his friends), the first Lithuanian to play in the NBA in 1989 and Arvydas Sabonis (nicknamed 'Sabas'), indisputably one of the game's greatest centres. Both men were among the Lithuanian line-up at the 1992 Barcelona Olympics, wearing psychedelic tie-dyed T-shirts sponsored by the Grateful Dead rock band!

Marčiulionis and Sabonis have since set up basketball schools – and luxury hotels – in Vilnius and Kaunas respectively. Sabonis' €30 million contract with NBA team Portland ended in 2001, but he rejoined that same year. If you want to find out more information on these players check out Ⓦ www.eurobasket.com – it's a great site for basketball lovers.

Popular Lithuanian ice-skaters Margarita Drobiazko and Povilas Vanagas controversially lost out on medals both at the Salt Lake City Winter Olympics and the Ice Dancing World Championship in 2002, amid accusations of biased judges. But their woe has raised the profile of the sport in Lithuania.

World champion cyclist Diana Žiliūtė won the Tour de France in 1999 and silver at the Sydney 2000 Olympics.

## SHOPPING

Amber – pine resin fossilised 50 million years ago – is one of Lithuania's treasures. It washes up on beaches and is captured in fishing nets – especially around Klaipėda and along the Curonian Spit (see the boxed text 'Baltic Gold' in the introductory Facts about the Region chapter). Modern amber jewellery costs anything from 10 Lt to 1600 Lt; there are particularly fine amber galleries in Vilnius and Nida.

Other Lithuanian arts and crafts adorn the artisan stalls that line the length of Vilnius' Pilies gatvė. Pottery bells, woven wicker baskets, wooden toys and painted eggs are traditional Lithuanian gifts. *Verbos,* which can be up to 1m tall, are Lithuania's equivalent of palms. They are decorated with dried flower arrangements, and are found in abundance at the Kaziukas Fair, held in Vilnius around St Casimir's Day (4 March) or sold at Sauluva (see Shopping in the Vilnius chapter).

Vilnius has two main markets, Gariūnai, to the west off the Kaunas road, and Kalvarijų, just north of the city centre, where you can join the scrum of babushkas jostling for all manner of bargains. They are both open till noon Tuesday to Sunday. Gariūnai has a staggering selection of second-hand vehicles and black-market CDs. Minibuses marked 'Gariūnai' or 'Gariūnų Turgus' ferry shoppers from the train station road every morning. By car it's 11km along Savanorių prospektas from Vilnius centre.

The largest indoor shopping and recreation centre in the Baltics, **Akropolis** (☎ 484 848; ⓦ www.akropolis.lt; Ozo 25), boasts an ice-rink in its centre, bowling alley and parking for 1800 cars. It has five screens at the vast new €10 million multiplex, north of Vilnius.

The European companies that jointly built and financed Akropolis began building another shopping mall outside Kaunas in April 2002. A German entrepreneur is the mastermind of the project, which is being carried out by Dutch multinational Ahold and its Scandinavian subsidiary ICA. They will start work on another complex in Klaipėda in 2004, once the Kaunas mall is complete.

# Vilnius

☎ 5 • pop 600,000 • elevation 184m

Bizarre, beautiful and bewitching; the city of Vilnius seduces visitors with Old Town charm. Its chocolate-box Baroque and skyline littered with the spires of Orthodox and Catholic churches are intoxicating. Indeed, it is so decadent and fragile that Unesco has declared this, Europe's largest Baroque Old Town, a World Heritage site. But there's more to this devilishly attractive capital than meets the eye. There is an underlying oddness that creates its soul.

Where else could there be the world's only statue of psychedelic musician Frank Zappa? Or a self-proclaimed, albeit unofficial, independent republic inhabited by artists and dreaming bohemians? Where else is there the spirit of freedom and resistance that existed during Soviet occupation? There are reminders of loss and pain everywhere, from the tragic horror of the KGB's torture cells to the ghetto in the centre of all this beauty where the Jewish community lived before their mass wartime slaughter.

Strange bars glow inside dark courtyards and crumbling archways frame the life of the narrow, cobbled streets. But change is under way. There are big plans for this little city using foreign cash and local vision. But new business and infrastructure won't disguise the curious charm of eccentric, soulful Vilnius, which lies 250km inland in Lithuania's southeast corner.

## HISTORY

According to legend, Vilnius was founded in the 1320s when the Lithuanian grand duke Gediminas, camping on a hunting trip, dreamt of an iron wolf that howled with the voices of 100 wolves. His interpretation was to build an impregnable city as mighty as their cry. In fact, the site had been occupied at least 1000 years before and may also have been a political and trade centre.

Fourteenth-century Vilnius was built on Gediminas Hill, with its upper and lower castles and townspeople's houses protected by a moat, walls and towers against the knights of the Teutonic Order, who attacked at least six times between 1365 and 1402. The knights' defeat by joint Lithuanian-Polish forces at Grünwald, in 1410, ushered in a period of

## Highlights

- Make a wish at the cathedral's secret spot, then hike up Gediminas Hill to the tower for sunset over the city spires
- Get lost in the cobbled streets of the Old Town, not missing Pilies gatvė, the Gates of Dawn and the university's 12 courtyards
- Become a temporary citizen of the artists' Republic of Užupis, the Montmartre of Vilnius, with a drink on Užupio Kavinė's 'seaside' terrace
- Cruise the blue lagoon round Trakai Castle in a yacht
- Marvel at the treasure trove of religious jewels on display at the Applied Art Museum

Vilnius pp318-19
Central Vilnius pp322-3
Jewish Quarter p329
Trakai p343 ● ✪

prosperity in which Vilnius extended south into what's now the Old Town, and many Gothic buildings were erected.

The castles were rebuilt, and the cathedral founded inside the lower one. Following attacks by Tatars from the south, 2.4km of defensive wall was built (1503–22).

In the 16th century, Vilnius was one of the biggest cities in Eastern Europe, with a population of about 25,000. It blossomed with fine buildings in the late-Gothic and Renaissance styles as the Lithuanians, Žygimantas I and II, occupied the Polish-Lithuanian throne. Polish Jesuits founded Vilnius University in 1579 and made the city a bastion of the Catholic Counter-Reformation. Lithuania had a subordinate position in the Polish-Lithuanian state in the 17th century; and Vilnius in Poland's 'golden age'. Under Jesuit influence, Baroque architecture arrived.

Nineteenth-century Vilnius was a refuge for Polish and Lithuanian gentry dispossessed by the region's new Russian rulers. This made it a focus of the Polish national revival, in which Vilnius-bred poet Adam Mickiewicz was a leading inspiration. Neither of the 1830–31 and 1863–64 Polish uprisings succeeded here but Vilnius University was shut all the same by the tsarist authorities.

In the second half of the 19th century industrialisation arrived and railways were built. Vilnius became an important Jewish city, with around 75,000 Jews in its 160,000 population in the early 20th century, earning it the name 'Jerusalem of Lithuania'.

During WWI Vilnius was occupied by Germany for over three years. In the aftermath of the war civil unrest broke out between Bolshevik, Polish and Lithuanian forces. When the fighting died down, Vilnius found itself in an isolated corner of Poland. It was now essentially a Polish and Jewish city, with the street names in Polish and the Lithuanians a small minority of the population.

Stalin handed Vilnius to Lithuania after the Red Army entered Poland in 1939, but WWII saw another three-year German occupation. Most Vilnius Jews were killed in its ghetto or in Paneriai Forest. Vilnius' population fell from 209,000 to 110,000, and the city was badly damaged in the six-day battle when the Red Army recaptured it.

New residential and industrial suburbs sprang up around the city after WWII, populated by Lithuanians from the countryside and immigrant Russians and Belarusians. Russians account for about 19% of the city's population today, Poles for some 4% and Belarusians, less than 1%.

Vilnius was the chief focus of Lithuania's push for independence from the Soviet Union in the late 1980s and early 1990s. In 1989 a human chain was formed as a protest against Soviet occupation – it stretched from Tallinn to Vilnius. But the fight for independence took a tragic turn on 13 January 1991. Soviet troops stormed the city's TV

installations, killing 12 and wounding many more that were there to defend them. The brutality of the attack against unarmed civilians brought the Lithuanians' plight to the attention of the west – and sparked the end of Red Army rule.

The independence years saw Vilnius struggling to become a European city. In 1994 the Old Town was honoured with Unesco World Heritage status, bringing EU cash (millions of euros) into the city centre for renovation. In 2000 flamboyant Artūras Zuokas, from the Liberal Union Party, was elected Vilnius mayor at the age of 32. His radical plans for the city raised eyebrows among conservative factions but he played a major role in raising the city's status internationally by, among other things, advertising Vilnius abroad for the first time and inviting potential foreign investors to the city.

In 2002 the city's prospects got a boost when the European bank agreed to a €10 million loan for new rail links, an Old Town bypass and new highways linking Vilnius to Kiev and Minsk. The same year saw work begin on the controversial reconstruction of the Jewish ghetto (see the boxed text 'Jerusalem of the North' later).

## ORIENTATION
The centre of Vilnius is on the south side of the Neris River. Its heart is Katedros aikštė (Cathedral Square), with the cathedral on the north side and Gedimino kalnas (Gediminas Hill) rising behind. South of Katedros aikštė are the cobbled Old Town streets *(senamiestis)*; to the west, Gedimino prospektas cuts straight across the newer part of the centre to parliament. The train and bus stations are beyond the Old Town's southern edge, 1.5km from Katedros aikštė.

The city has tourist signs in English and Lithuanian pointing to sites around the Old Town, making it impossible to get lost!

### Maps
Quality road maps, city maps and atlases published by Briedis and Jāņa sēta (see the Maps section in the Lithuania Facts for the Visitor chapter) are sold in most bookshops, fuel stations and at the tourist information centre at Vilnius airport. Jāņa sēta's 2001/02 *Vilnius City Plan* (1:25,000), which includes a city centre map (1:10,000), costs 8 Lt.

VILNIUS

# VILNIUS

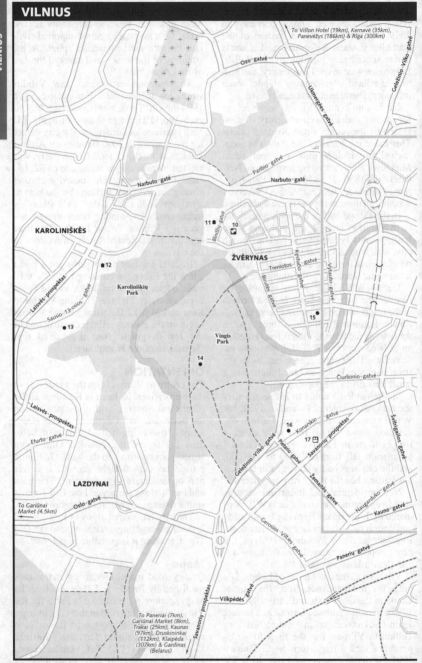

To Villon Hotel (19km), Kernavė (35km), Panevėžys (186km) & Rīga (300km)

Ozo gatvė

Ukmergės gatvė

Geležinio Vilko gatvė

Panibio gatvė

Narbuto gatė

Narbuto gatė

KAROLINIŠKĖS

11 ☗  10 ⌂

Blindžių gatvė

ŽVĖRYNAS

Treniotos gatvė

Kęstučio gatvė

Birutės gatvė

Vytauto gatvė

🏠 12

Karoliniškių Park

Laisvės prospektas

Sausio 13-osios gatvė

● 13

15 ●

Vingis Park

14 ●

Čiurlionio gatvė

Laisvės prospektas

Efurto gatvė

16 ●  Konarskio gatvė

Savanorių prospektas

Švitrigailos gatvė

LAZDYNAI

Geležinio Vilko gatvė

Pelanio gatvė

17 ☒

Žemaitės gatvė

To Gariūnai Market (4.5km)

Oslo gatvė

Naugarduko gatvė

Kauno gatvė

Gerosios Viltes gatvė

Savanorių prospektas

Vilkpėdės

gatvė

Panerių gatvė

To Paneriai (7km), Gariūnai Market (8km), Trakai (25km), Kaunas (97km), Druskininkai (112km), Klaipėda (307km) & Gardinas (Belarus)

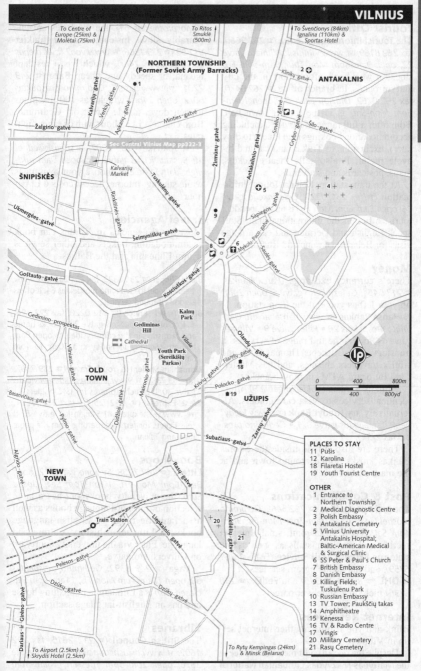

VILNIUS

**To Centre of Europe (25km) & Molėtai (75km)**

**To Ritos Smuklė (500m)**

**To Švenčionys (84km) Ignalina (110km) & Sportas Hotel**

NORTHERN TOWNSHIP
(Former Soviet Army Barracks)

ANTAKALNIS

Kalvarijų gatvė
Verkių gatvė
Apkasų gatvė

Klinikų gatvė

Žalgirio gatvė

Minties gatvė

Žirmūnų gatvė

Antakalnio gatvė

Smelio gatvė
Grybo gatvė
Šilo gatvė

See Central Vilnius Map pp322-3

ŠNIPIŠKĖS

Kalvarijų Market

Tuskulėnų gatvė

Ukmergės gatvė

Rinktinės gatvė

Šeimyniškių gatvė

Sapiegos gatvė

Saulės gatvė

Mykolo paso gatvė

Goštauto gatvė

Kosciuškos gatvė

Gedimino prospektas

Kalnų Park

Gediminas Hill

Cathedral

Youth Park (Sereikiškių Parkas)

Vilnia

Olandų gatvė

Filaretų gatvė

Krivių gatvė

OLD TOWN

Vilniaus gatvė

Maironio gatvė

Basanavičiaus gatvė

Pylimo gatvė

Didžioji gatvė

Polocko gatvė

UŽUPIS

Zarasų gatvė

Subačiaus gatvė

NEW TOWN

Algirdo gatvė

Rasų gatvė

Liepkalnio gatvė

Sukilėlių gatvė

Train Station

Pelesos gatvė

Dzūkų gatvė

Dzūkų gatvė

Dariaus ir Girėno gatvė

**To Airport (2.5km) & Skrydis Hotel (2.5km)**

**To Rytų Kempingas (24km) & Minsk (Belarus)**

0     400     800m
0     400     800yd

VILNIUS

## INFORMATION
### Tourist Offices
The **Tourist Information Centre** (☎ 262 9660, fax 262 8169; W www.vilnius.lt; Vilniaus gatvė 22; open 9am-6pm Mon-Thur, 9am-5pm Fri) stocks a wealth of information on the city and surrounds. Its **branch office** (☎ 262 6470, fax 262 0762; Didžioji gatvė 31; open 10am-6pm Mon-Sat) is in the former town hall. Both offer a full range of services, including accommodation bookings (see Places to Stay later), excursions to Trakai, and car and bicycle rental. It also sells theatre tickets, maps, postcards and souvenirs.

At the train station, **Kelvita Tourist Information** (☎/fax 231 0229; Geležinkelio gatvė 16; open 8am-6pm Mon-Fri) is an independent tourist office in the international hall. Staff speak English and German and can arrange visas for Belarus, Ukraine and Russia.

### Money
There's **currency exchange** (Parex Bankas; ☎ 213 5454; Geležinkelio gatvė 6; open 24hr) on your left as you exit the train station.

**Hansa Bankas** (W www.hansabank.lt; Gedimino prospektas 26 • Pilies gatvė 9 • Vilniaus gatvė 16) offers the full range of services. It transfers money, accepts Thomas Cook and AmEx travellers cheques, and has Master-Card/Eurocard ATMs in most branches.

**Vilniaus Bankas** (Vokiečių gatvė 9) offers identical services to Visa card holders. Alternatively, try **Kredyt Bank** (W www.kredyt bank.lt; Liejyklos gatvė 3/1 • Gedimino prospektas 2/33).

There are also ATMs inside the Snoras Bankas kiosks dotted around town and at the main post office.

### Post & Communications
The **main post office** (☎ 262 5468; Gedimino prospektas 7; open 7am-7pm Mon-Fri, 9am-4pm Sat) has a pizza joint, small Internet section and souvenir stalls as well as the state-run **Express Mail Service** (EMS; ☎ 261 6759), and fax and telegram services.

**DHL** (☎ 8-800 22 345) and **FedEx** (☎ 230 6795) pick up and deliver parcels.

### Internet Resources
Blink and you'll miss another Internet set-up in Vilnius.

Despite the one-off 5 Lt membership fee at the **Martynas Mažvydas Lithuanian National Library** (☎ 249 7023; e biblio@lnb.lrs.lt; Gedimino prospektas 51), the machines are unbearably slow. Instead, aim for funkier **VOO2** (☎ 279 1866; W www.voo2.lt; Aš menos gatvė 8; open 24hr), which has a resident iguana; or speedy and cheap **Bazė** (☎ 249 7701; W www.base.lt; Gedimino prospektas 50/2; open 24hr), which has 100 machines hidden down a side street off Gedimino. Both charge 4 Lt an hour with cheaper night rates.

At **Spausk** (☎ 265 2002; e spausk@eunet .lt; Basanavičiaus gatvė 18; open 9am-midnight daily) you can choose your own tunes while surfing. Internet access costs 6 Lt per hour.

### Travel Agencies
Most travel agencies in Vilnius can book accommodation, tickets and other services within Lithuania and the Baltics.

**Baltic Clipper** (☎ 231 2323, fax 231 2324, W www .baltic-clipper.lt) Gedimino prospektas 64. It offers a good all-round service.

**Baltic Travel Service** (☎ 212 0220, fax 222 196, e lcc@bts.lt) Subačiaus gatvė 2. It books home and farmstays in the countryside. It's open 8am to 6pm Monday to Friday and 10am to 4pm Saturday.

**Lithuanian Student & Youth Travel** (☎ 239 7397, fax 239 7386, W www.jaunimas.lt) Basanavičiaus gatvė 30. It has cheap fares for ISIC holders.

**West Express** (☎ 212 2500, fax 212 5321, W www.westexpress.lt) Stulginskio gatvė 5. It sells tickets for ferries departing from Klaipėda, Rīga and Tallinn.

### Bookshops
**Littera** (☎ 268 7258; Šv Jono gatvė 12; open 9am-6pm Mon-Fri, 10am-3pm Sat, closed Sun), the university bookshop, has a large selection of foreign-language books as well as a fantastic range of English-language books on Lithuanian history, culture and language. Enter via the university courtyard on Universiteto gatvė.

**Vaga** (☎ 249 8392; Gedimino prospektas 50; open 10am-7pm Mon-Fri, 11am-4pm Sat, closed Sun) is a Lithuanian publishing house and has an English-language section.

### Libraries
The **British Council** (☎ 212 2615, fax 212 1602; W www.britishcouncil.lt; Vilniaus gatvė 39/6; open 2pm-5pm Tues-Fri, 10am-3pm

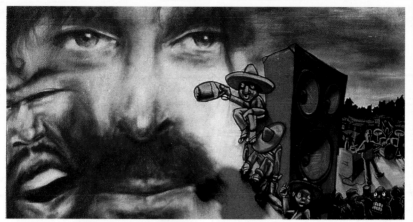

Frank Zappa mural, Kalinausko gatvė, Vilnius

St Anne's Church (Onos bažnyčia), Vilnius

JONATHAN SMITH

Cathedral bell tower, Vilnius

CRAIG PERSHOUSE

Vilnius Cathedral

JONATHAN SMITH

Flower seller, Gedimino prospektas, Vilnius

*Sat)*, in the House of Teachers, has British papers and magazines.

The **American Centre** (☎ 266 0330, fax 212 0445; ⓦ www.usembassy.lt; Pranciskonų gatvė 3/6), inside a 15th-century Franciscan monastery, has an **information resource centre** *(open 2pm-5pm Tues-Thur)* where you can scan the latest American newspapers and magazines.

There is a library inside the **Centre Culturel Français** (☎ 312 985, fax 312 987; ⓔ info@ centrefrancais.lt; Didžioji gatvė 1; library open 1.30pm-6.30pm Mon-Fri, 10am-3pm Sat).

## Laundry

Get your smalls whiter than white at **Palūstrė** (☎ 233 4567; Savanorių prospektas 11a; open 7am-7pm Mon-Fri, 7am-2pm Sat), which does service washes or use the machines yourself.

## Left Luggage

There are left luggage rooms *(bagažinė)* inside the **bus station** *(bag per day 3 Lt; open 5.30am-9pm Mon-Fri, 7am-9pm Sat)* and **train station** *(basement; bag per day 2 Lt)*.

## Medical Services

The **Baltic-American Medical & Surgical Clinic** (☎ 234 2020; ⓦ www.baclinic.com; Antakalnio gatvė 124; open 24hr), inside Vilnius University Antakalnis hospital, and the **Medical Diagnostic Centre** (☎ 270 9120; Grybo gatvė 32; open 8am-7pm Mon-Fri, 9am-3pm Sat) both offer an English-language service.

The German-Lithuanian pharmacy, **Vokiečių vaistinė** (☎ 212 4232; Didžioji gatvė 13; open 8am-7pm Mon-Fri, 10am-6pm Sat & Sun) stocks the best range of Western medicines. **Gedimino Vaistinė** (☎ 261 0135; Gedimino prospektas 27; open 24hr) is open 24 hours a day and stocks a wide range of medicines. The staff only speak Lithuanian so you'll have to mime your complaint!

## Emergency

For an ambulance, call ☎ 03.

The International Police Commission has English-, French-, Russian- and German-speaking staff for foreigners who are victims of crime. Ring ☎ 726 159, ☎ 716 221 or ☎ 02 in an emergency.

## WALKING TOUR

Cathedral Square (Katedros aikštė) is a good starting point for exploring. Tour the cathedral, then walk up the path through the park, next to the square, to Gedimino Tower (Gedimino bokstas) on top of Gediminas Hill (Gedimino kalnas). From the top of the tower there are views across the entire city – the Old Town to the south, Gedimino prospektas to the west in the newer part of town, Three Crosses Hill (Trijų kryžių kalnas) to the east and the river stretching north.

From here, hike into the Old Town along Pilies gatvė. This street, together with Didžioji gatvė and Aušros Vartų gatvė, forms the main single axis of the Old Town down to the Gates of Dawn (Aušros Vartai).

Save some time for a stroll along Gedimino prospektas, through the newer part of central Vilnius to parliament.

North and east of the cathedral you'll find the Applied Art Museum, SS Peter & Paul's Church and Three Crosses Hill. South of the cathedral there is the university and its 12 courtyards and the artistic Užupis district, which are well worth a stroll.

If time is short, the little money you'd spend on a taxi to the TV Tower and Gariūnai market would be well spent.

## GEDIMINAS HILL

Vilnius was founded on the 48m-tall Gediminas Hill (Gedimino kalnas). The red-brick tower dates back to the 13th century. It was part of the 14th-century defences of the upper of the two Vilnius castles. The original tower was one tier higher than the 20m-tall edifice that stands there today. Its walls were ruined during the 1655–61 Russian occupation but it was restored in 1930. It houses the **Vilnius Castle Museum** (Vilnius pilies muziejus; ☎ 261 7453; Arsenalo gatvė 5; adult/child 4/2 Lt; open 11am-5pm Tues-Sun Nov-Apr, 10am-7pm Tues-Sun May-Oct). A model of the castle as it was in the 14th century is among the displays. An exhibition centre in the **Lower Castle Museum** (Žemutinės pilies muziejus; ☎ 262 9988; Katedros gatvė 3a; adult/child 4/2 Lt; open 9am-5pm Mon-Fri) displays the archaeological excavation of the Royal Palace. The Renaissance began in Vilnius with the building of the Royal Palace of the Grand Dukes of Lithuania on the grounds of the Lower Castle (1520–30). In 1795 czarist Russia occupied Vilnius and the entire Lithuania. Very soon the greater part of the buildings of the Lower Castle as well as the city defence wall were demolished.

VILNIUS

# CENTRAL VILNIUS

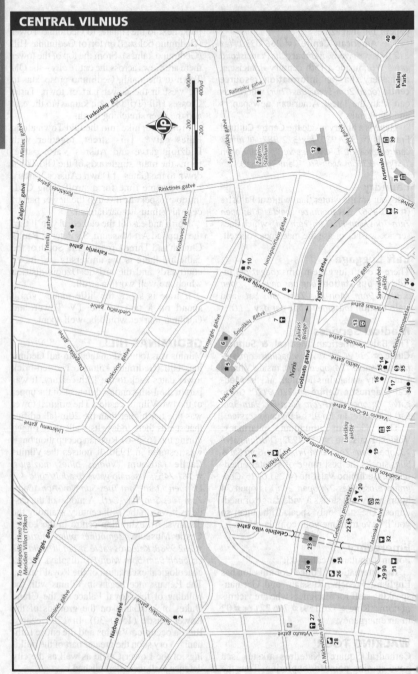

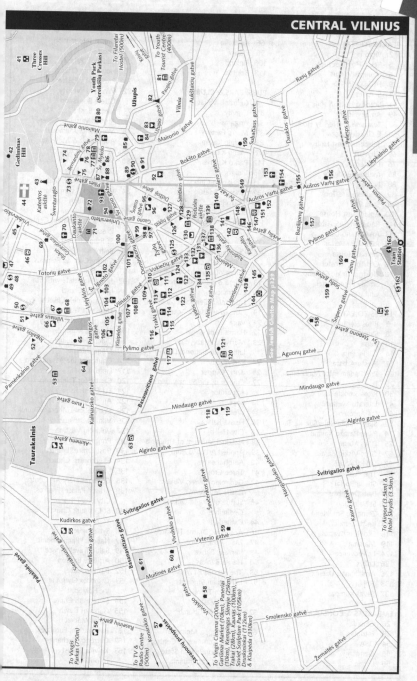

# CENTRAL VILNIUS

**PLACES TO STAY**

2  Victoria
5  Reval Hotel Lietuva
6  Naujasis Vilnius
9  Holiday Inn
11  Šarūnas
15  Scandic Hotel Neringa
49  Ambassador
58  Teacher's University Hostel
59  E-Guest House
60  Telecom Guest House
69  CityPark
76  Litinterp
85  Mabre Residence
88  Narutis
89  Shakespeare Too
98  Stikliai
100  Apia Guest House
141  Radisson SAS Astorija
143  AAA Mano Liza
145  Rūdninkų Vartai
148  Grybas House
156  Old Town Hostel
158  Elektros Tinklų Statybos
159  Smiley Face Hostel
160  Gintaras

**PLACES TO EAT**

3  Ritos Slėptuvė
8  San Marco
10  Kuba
14  Čili Picerija
17  Presto Arbata
20  Prie Parlamento; Ministerija
29  Iki
30  Ritos Smoklė
45  Literatų Svetainė
51  Da Antonio
52  Sue's Indian Raja/Sue Ka Tai
74  Pilies Pasažo Kavinė
75  Pilies Menė
87  Gero Viskio Baras
97  Stikliai Aludė
99  The PUB
103  Stiklių Bočiai
107  Balti Dramblai
109  St Valentino
111  Žemaičių Smuklė
113  Keisti Ženklai
116  Skonis ir Kvapas
119  Maxima
124  La Provence
126  Lokys
128  Amatininkų Užeiga
133  Finjan
137  Savas Kampas

**EMBASSIES & CONSULATES**

26  Canada
28  Estonia
54  USA
55  Germany
56  Latvia

66  Australia
96  France
106  Finland
118  Belarus

**PUBS, BARS & CLUBS**

4  Geležinis Vilkas
31  Gravity
32  Angaras
37  Men's Factory
83  Užupio Kavinė
92  Mano Kavinė
112  Parko Kavinė
115  Indigo
131  Lithuanian Club
132  Twins O'Brien
136  Brodvėjus
146  Bix
151  Soho

**OTHER**

1  Kalvarijų Market
7  St Raphael's Church
12  Palace of Concerts & Sports
13  Opera & Ballet Theatre
16  Pharmacy
18  Lithuanian Genocide Museum
19  Lithuanian Music Academy
21  Vaga
22  Hansa Bankas
23  Martynas Mažvydas Lithuanian National Library
24  Parliament
25  Baltic Clipper
27  Church of the Saint Virgin's Apparition
33  Bazė
34  West Express
35  Hansa Bankas
36  City Hall
38  National Museum of Lithuania
39  Applied Arts Museum
40  Amphitheatre
41  Three Crosses
42  Gediminas Tower; Vilnius Castle Museum
43  Statue of Grand Duke Gediminas
44  Cathedral
46  Academic Drama Theatre
47  Main Post Office
48  Vilniaus Bankas
50  Hansa Bankas
53  The Holocaust Museum
57  Lithuanian Student & Youth Travel
61  Flower Market
62  Romanovs' Church
63  Spausk
64  Frank Zappa Memorial
65  Jewish Community Centre; Vilna Gaon;Jewish State Museum of Lithuania

67  Tourist Information Centre
68  Radvilos' Palace
70  Holy Cross Church
71  President's Palace
72  Vilnius University; Littera Bookshop
73  Hansa Bankas
77  Amber Museum-Gallery
78  Mickiewicz Memorial Apartment & Museum
79  St Michael's Church
80  St Anne's Church
81  Stiklo Karoliukai
82  Angel of Užupis Statue
84  Orthodox Assumption Virgin Church
86  Sauluva
90  Tourist Information Centre
91  Russian Gallery
93  St John's Church
94  Belfry
95  Centre Culturel Français
101  Holy Spirit Church
102  Jesuit Noviciate with St Ignatius' Church
104  St Catherine's Church
105  House of Teachers;British Council; Vartai Gallery
108  Theatre, Music & Cinema Museum
110  Onmi Internet
114  Church of the Assumption
117  Lietuva
120  Centre for Tolerance
121  EU Commisson
122  American Centre
123  Evangelical Lutheran Church
125  Vilnaus Bankas
127  Vokiečių Vaistinė
129  Photography Gallery
130  Post Office (Branch)
134  St Nicholas' Church
135  VOO2
138  Contemporary Art Centre
139  Artists' Palace; Freskos; City Bus Tours
140  St Casimir's Church
142  Youth Theatre
144  Synagogue
147  National Philharmonic
149  Baltic Travel Service
150  Artillery Bastion
152  Basilian Gates
153  Orthodox Church of the Holy Spirit
154  St Teresa's Church
155  Gates of Dawn
157  Halės Market
161  Bus Station; Eurolines
162  Currency Exchange
163  Kelvita Tourist Information

## KATEDROS AIKŠTĖ

This square is the main meeting point for skateboarding kids, strolling lovers, bands of babushkas and everyone else!

To make your dreams come true, find the tile marked *stebuklas* (miracle). It marks the spot where the human chain between Tallinn and Vilnius ended. Two million Lithuanians joined it to protest at Soviet occupation in 1989. To make a wish, do a clockwise 360-degree turn on the tile. You must search for this elusive tile yourself as it is forbidden by superstition to reveal its location in the square.

In the 19th century, markets and fairs were held here. A moat ran around what is now the square's perimeter – roughly where Vrublevskio and Sventaragio streets are today – and ships could sail almost to the cathedral door. Within the moat were walls and towers, the only remaining parts of which are the 57m-tall **belfry**, standing alone near the west end of the cathedral (a favourite rendezvous point), and a few excavated remains behind the cathedral.

At the eastern end of the square is a **statue** of Grand Duke Gediminas and his horse. It is built on an ancient pagan site – the remains of which were found when the foundations were dug. A ritual stone was discovered, believed to have been for pagan offerings. Behind Gediminas, **Sereikiskės** and **Kalnų Parks** lead to Three Crosses Hill.

### Cathedral

This important national symbol was originally used for the worship of Perkūnas, the Lithuanian thunder god. Much later in its turbulent history it was used by the Soviets as a picture gallery. It was reconsecrated in 1989 and Mass has been celebrated daily ever since.

The first wooden cathedral was built here in 1387–88. A grander edifice was constructed under Grand Duke Vytautas in the 15th century. It was initially in Gothic style, but has been rebuilt so often, as architectural fashions have changed, that its old form is unrecognisable. The most important restoration was completed from 1783 to 1801, when the outside was completely redone in the classical style that remains today. The white **brass statues** of Sts Helene, Stanislav and Casimir on top of the cathedral are replicas of the original wooden versions added in

1793. They were destroyed under Stalin's regime in 1956 and not resurrected until 1996. Helene, who holds a 9m gold cross, and her saintly companions are a distinctive landmark, clearly visible from the far western end of Gedimino prospektas.

The statues on the south side facing the square are Lithuanian dukes; those on the north side are apostles and saints. The interior retains more of its original aspect, though the entrances to the side chapels were harmonised in the late 18th century.

The **Chapel of St Casimir** is the showpiece. It's at the eastern end of the south aisle (built 1623–36) with a Baroque cupola, coloured marble and granite on the walls, white stucco sculptures, and fresco scenes from the life of St Casimir, a 15th-century grand duke (1458–84) who was canonised in 1602 and is the patron saint of Lithuania. Take a moment to discover the bizarre laughing Madonna. She is beautifully crafted inside the chapel, overlooking the silver coffin of Casimir.

Religious jewels, worth €11 million, were discovered in the cathedral in 1985 after being hidden in the walls by Russian soldiers in 1655. Fearing they would be seized by the Soviets, they remained a secret – until 1998 and are now a must-see exhibition at the Applied Arts Museum.

### MUSEUMS

The **National Museum of Lithuania** (*Lietuvos nacionalinis muziejus;* ☎ 262 9426; W *www.lnm.lt; Arsenalo gatvė 1; adult/child 4/2 Lt; open 10am-5pm Wed-Sun*), in an old arsenal building 100m north of the cathedral, has historical and ethnographic exhibits looking at Lithuanian life up to the pre-WWII independence period. **Prehistoric Lithuania** (☎ 262 9426; *Arsenalo gatvė 1; adult/student 4/2 Lt; open 10am-5pm Tues-Sun*) has opened in a wing of the old arsenal, recreating the lives of ancient tribes.

At the **Applied Arts Museum** (*Taikomosios dailės muziejus;* ☎ 262 8080; *Arsenalo gatvė 3a; admission 8 Lt; open 11am-6pm Tues-Sat, 11am-4pm Sun*) precious stones vie with gold and silver to make this exhibition truly a treasure. The folk art and cross carvings upstairs should not be missed.

The **Theatre, Music & Cinema Museum** (*Lietuvos teatro, muzikos ir kino muziejus;* ☎ 262 2406; *Vilniaus gatvė 41; open noon-6pm Tues-Fri, 11am-4pm Sat*) has borrowed a

Čiurlionis backdrop from Kaunas' Čiurlionis museum to add to its fascinating display of memorabilia from stage and screen.

## OLD TOWN

The largest Old Town in Eastern Europe deserves its Unesco World Heritage status. The area stretching 1.5km south from Katedros aikštė was built up in the 15th and 16th centuries, and its narrow, winding streets, hidden courtyards and lavish old churches retain the feel of bygone centuries. The Old Town's main axis is along Pilies, Didžioji and Aušros Vartų gatvė. Its approximate boundary, starting from Katedros aikštė, runs along Stuokos-Gucevičiaus, Liejyklos, Vilniaus, Trakų, Pylimo, Bazilijonų, Šv Dvasios, Boksto, Maironio, Radvilaitės and Sventaragio streets – an area of roughly a square kilometre.

### Pilies Gatvė

Cobbled Pilies gatvė (Castle Street) is the main entrance to the Old Town from Katedros aikštė. It is the hub of Vilnius' bar and café life. Craft stalls line the southern part of the narrow street. Until the 19th century, Pilies gatvė was separated from what's now the square by the lower castle wall which ran across its northern end. Only a gate in the wall connected the two. Notice the 15th- to 17th-century brickwork of Nos 4, 12 and 16 towards the northern end of the street.

### Vilnius University

Founded by Jesuits in 1579 on the instigation of the Polish king Stefan Batory in the Counter-Reformation, the university was run by Jesuits for two centuries and became one of the greatest centres of Polish learning. It produced many notable scholars from the 17th to early 19th century, but was closed by the Russians in 1832 and didn't reopen until 1919. Today it has about 14,000 students and the library houses five million books. The world's first **Centre for Stateless Cultures** (☎/fax 268 7293; e statelesscultures@centras .lt; Universitato gatvė 5) or those that have no army nor navy, including Yiddish, Roma and Karaimic cultures, is in suite No 23 of the history faculty.

The university's 12 courtyards are indicative of the need to explore in Vilnius. Hidden but linked, they are accessed by passages and gates from the surrounding streets. The south-

ern gate on Šv Jono gatvė brings you into Didysis or Skarga Courtyard. Inside is **St John's Church** (Šv Jono bažnyčia), founded in 1387 well before the university arrived. It now has an outstanding 18th-century Baroque main façade and a fine interior. Its 17th-century **bell tower**, standing on the south side of the courtyard, is a distinctive feature in the Vilnius skyline. The galleries around three sides of this courtyard are in the early 17th-century Mannerist style, which formed the transition from Renaissance to Baroque.

The arch through the 16th-century building opposite St John's leads to Pocobuto Courtyard, with an old two-domed **observatory** whose late 18th-century façade is adorned with reliefs of the zodiac.

### Daukanto Aikštė

The exit from the university's Sarbievijus Courtyard to Universiteto gatvė brings you into the square opposite the former Bishops' Palace – now the **President's Palace**, rebuilt in the classical Russian Empire style early in the 19th century. The palace was used by both Napoleon, when he was advancing on Moscow, and by his Russian adversary, General Mikhail Kutuzov, when he was chasing Napoleon back to Paris. Free guided tours (in Lithuanian only) run on Friday and Saturday, and must be booked in advance through the **President's Office** (☎ 266 4154, 266 4025; w www.president.lt).

### Mickiewicz Memorial Apartment & Museum

'Lithuania, my fatherland…' is, oddly, Poland's national romantic masterpiece. It's not so surprising when you realise it was Polish poet Adam Mickiewicz (1798–1855) who wrote the infamous line from his poem 'Pan Tadeusz'. He grew up near Vilnius and studied at the university (1815–19) before being exiled for anti-Russian activities in 1824. His old rooms are now a museum (Mickevičiaus Memorialinis Butas-Muziejus; ☎ 261 8836; Bernardinų gatvė 11; open 10am-5pm Tues-Fri, 10am-2pm Sat & Sun). He wrote the poem 'Gražina' in these rooms in 1822. His work inspired Polish nationalists in the 19th century.

### St Michael's & St Anne's Churches

Opposite the eastern end of Bernardinų gatvė is 17th-century **St Michael's Church** (Šv

Mykolo bažnyčia; ☎ 261 6409; Šv Mykolo gatvė 9; open 11am-5pm Mon, 11am-6pm Wed-Sun), now a museum focusing on 1918–90 architecture. Nearby is the privately operated **Amber Museum-Gallery** (Gintaro Muziejus-Galerija; ☎ 262 3092; W www.amber.lt; Šv Mykolo gatvė 8; open 10am-7pm daily), which has various Jurassic Park–style insect exhibits and some fine jewellery pieces – some to admire, some to buy.

Across Maironio gatvė stands the fine 16th-century **St Anne's Church** (Šv Onos bažnyčia; ☎ 261 1236; Maironio gatvė 8; mass held at 6.30pm & 7.30pm Mon-Fri, 9am, 11.30am & 6.30pm Sat & Sun), the jewel of Lithuanian Gothic architecture with its sweeping curves, delicate pinnacles and 33 different types of red brick. According to legend, Napoleon was so enamoured of it, he wished he could take it back to Paris in the palm of his hand. The buildings adjoining St Anne's were part of a mostly 16th-century **Bernardine monastery** (like St Michael's) and also part of the Old Town's defensive wall. A **statue of Mickiewicz** stands beside St Anne's.

## Didžioji Gatvė

Didžioji gatvė (Main Street) continues south from Pilies gatvė, where it widens into **Rotušės aikštė** (Town Hall Square), which was, for a long time, one of the centres of Vilnius life. Markets were held here from the 15th century, when this was a crossroad to Kraków and Rīga. The old Town Hall in the middle of the square has stood since at least the early 16th century, but its classical exterior dates from 1785 to 1799. It is now the **Artists' Palace**.

The oldest Baroque church in Vilnius is the large **St Casimir's** (Šv Kazimiero bažnyčia; ☎ 212 1715; Didžioji gatvė 34), built by the Jesuits from 1604 to 1615. Its dome and cross-shaped ground plan defined a new style for 17th-century Lithuanian churches. Under tsarist rule St Casimir's was taken over by the Russian Orthodox church and given an onion dome, removed in 1942. It spent two decades as a museum of atheism under Soviet rule.

## Aušros Vartų Gatvė

This is the oldest and most charming street in Vilnius. Flanked by churches of different denominations, it was lucky to survive the Soviet regime. They renamed it Gorky Street before deciding to bulldoze it – and

the famous Gates of Dawn – to make way for a Moscow–Minsk road.

Near the northern (lower) end there's a late-Baroque archway known as the **Basilian Gates** (Aušros Vartų gatvė 7), forming the entrance to the decrepit Holy Trinity Basilian monastery complex. On the eastern side of the street is the big, pink, domed 17th-century **Orthodox Church of the Holy Spirit** (Šv Dvasios cerkvė; Aušros Vartų gatvė 10), the chief Russian Orthodox church of Lithuania. The preserved bodies of three 14th-century martyrs – Sts Anthony, Ivan and Eustachius – lie in a chamber at the foot of a flight of steps in front of the altar (you can even see their feet peeping out). Catholic **St Teresa's Church** (Šv Teresės bažnyčia; Aušros Vartų gatvė 14), further south, is early Baroque (1635–50) outside and elaborate late Baroque inside. Below its entrance is a sinister chamber for the dead – awkward should a wedding procession meet a funeral party coming out of the cellar.

**Gates of Dawn** At the top of Aušros Vartų gatvė, the 16th-century **Gates of Dawn** (Aušros Vartai) are the only one of the original nine in the town wall still intact.

A door on the eastern side opens onto a staircase that leads up to a little 18th-century chapel directly over the gate arch. This houses a supposedly miracle-working **icon of the Virgin**, reputed to have been souvenired from the Crimea by Grand Duke Algirdas in 1363, though more likely dating from the 16th century. It is revered by the deeply Catholic Polish community, to whom the chapel is known as the Ostrabramska, and is said to be one of Eastern Europe's leading pilgrimage destinations. A replica of the icon, which was repainted in the 17th or 18th century, adorns a chapel in St Peter's in Rome. Beggars, babushkas and impromptu worshippers make up the bustling, devout crowds. A surviving length of the Old Town fortification wall leads east.

## Artillery Bastion

Follow the old wall around from the Gates of Dawn on to Šv Dvasios gatvė, then continue north, you will reach the Artillery Bastion (Artilerijos bastėja; ☎ 261 2149; Boksto gatvė 20/18; admission 2 Lt; open 10am-5pm Wed-Sun). This 17th-century fortification houses a collection of old weaponry and armour. At dusk, lovers come here to watch the sunset.

## Jerusalem of the North

One of Europe's prominent Jewish communities flourished in prewar Vilnius (Vilna in Yiddish). Nazi and Soviet brutality virtually wiped it out. Now the Jewish quarter is being rebuilt – amid raging controversy in a country still haunted by the spectre of anti-Semitism.

The history of Vilnius is indebted to Jewish culture. Three thousand Jews settled in Vilnius eight centuries ago at the invitation of Gediminas. Vilnius rabbi and scholar, Gaon Elijahu ben Shlomo Zalman (1720–97), led opposition to the widespread Jewish mystical movement Hassidism. In the 19th century, Vilnius become a centre for the European Jewish language, Yiddish. Famous landscape artist Isaak Levitan (1860–1900) and, later, the sculptor Jacques Lipchitz (1891–1973) were Vilnius Jews. The city's Jewish population peaked on the eve of WWI at almost 100,000 (out of 240,000 in Lithuania).

Plagued by discrimination and poverty, the Jewish community diminished in the interwar years when Vilnius was a provincial outpost of Poland. Despite this Vilnius blossomed into the Jewish cultural hub of Eastern Europe, and was chosen ahead of the other Yiddish centres, Warsaw and New York, as the headquarters of the Yiddish-language scientific research institute YIVO in 1925 (the institute stood west of the Old Town on Vivulskio gatvė). Jewish schools, libraries, literature and theatre flourished. There were 100 synagogues and prayer houses and six daily Jewish newspapers.

Today there are just 5000 Jews in Lithuania, 80% of which live in Vilnius. During the Perestroika years an estimated 6000 Jews left Lithuania for Israel. In mid-1996, following years of bickering, Germany agreed to pay €1 million to Lithuania to compensate holocaust survivors and victims of Nazi persecution. Further media attention was focused on the community in June 1999 when the Holocaust Museum in Washington apologised for selling a satirical CD entitled *Songs of Kovno (Kaunas) Ghetto*. The lyrics blamed Lithuania for the death of a community, sparking off old debates about whether Lithuanian sidekicks were as cruel and merciless in the Vilnius holocaust as their German masters.

In 2002 Lithuania handed hundreds of Torah scrolls that survived the Holocaust to Israelis in a ceremony in Vilnius. The move was an apology to Israel for the part Lithuanians played in the devastating massacre of most of the country's 240,000 Jews.

### Jewish Quarter & Ghettos

The Jewish quarter lay in the streets west of Didžioji gatvė. Today the street names Žydų (Jews) and Gaono (Gaon) are among the few explicit reminders of this. The Great Synagogue (1572) and its famous Strashun Library (1902) stood at the western end of Žydų gatvė; the site is home to a nursery school today.

Virtually all Vilnius' Jewish organisations, except communist ones, were dissolved when the Soviet Union took over eastern Poland in September 1939. Many Jewish leaders were deported. Meanwhile Polish Jews fleeing the Nazis arrived here as refugees. Vilnius fell to the Nazis two days after their invasion of the USSR on 22 June 1941. In the next three months some 35,000 Jews – almost half those in the city – were murdered in **Paneriai Forest** (see the Around Vilnius section later), before a ghetto was established in a small area north of Vokiečių gatvė, which was the heart of the **Jewish quarter**. This first ghetto – known as the **Small Ghetto** – was liquidated after 46 days and its inhabitants killed at Paneriai; a memorial plaque outside Gaono gatvė 3 remembers the 11,000 Jews marched to their death from this ghetto between 6 September and 20 October 1941. At Žydų gatvė 3, outside the former home of **Gaon Elijahu**, is a memorial bust, erected in 1997 on the 200th anniversary of the death of the sage who could recite the entire Talmud by heart at the age of six.

Vilnius' **Large Ghetto**, created on 6 September 1941 south of Vokiečių gatvė, lasted until the general liquidation of ghettos on Himmler's orders in September 1943, when 26,000 people were killed at Paneriai and a further 10,000 herded off to concentration camps. About 6000 Vilnius Jews

## Jerusalem of the North

escaped. The single gate of the main ghetto stood at what's now Rūdninkų gatvė 18, marked with a plaque bearing a detailed map of the former ghetto. The former **Judenrat** (ghetto administration building) was at Rūdninkų gatvė 8; its courtyard shelters a commemorative plaque to 1200 Jews selected to be sent to Paneriai.

### Jewish Quarter Controversy

Restoration of the Jewish ghetto is planned at a cost of €32 million. The Great Synagogue, the area around Žydų gatvė, and plots in Rūdninkų gatvė and near the French embassy between Švarco and Šv Jono gatvės are earmarked for reconstruction. It is both a tribute to the perished community and a resurrection of the lost culture. Despite the plans being formally adopted by parliament in 2000, there has been outspoken opposition. Most controversially, MP Vytautas Sustauskas claimed Lithuania would 'be turned into slaves of the Jews' in an outrageous outburst which has inflamed simmering anti-Semitic sentiment. And as the project would develop much of the remaining lucrative property in the Old Town, there is little hope of it fizzling out. For more information, contact the **Centre for Tolerance** (☎ 663 818; Naugarduko gatvė 11), the rebuilding nerve-centre.

### Jewish Ghetto

1 Gate to Small Ghetto
2 Memorial Bust; House of Gaon Elijahu Ben Shlomo Shlomo Zalman (1720-97)
3 Site of former Great Synagogue (1572) & Strashun Library (1902)
4 Judenrat
5 Gate to Large Ghetto
6 Synagogue (1894)
7 Centre for Tolerance

To Jewish Community Centre (500m) & Jewish State Museum (500m)
Dominikonų
Traku
Gaono gatvė (Gaon St)
Stiklių gatvė
Volteku gatvė
Žydų gatvė (Jewish St)
(Freedom St)
0    150    300m
0    150    300yd
SMALL GHETTO
Didžioji gatvė (German St)
Naugarduko
Žemaitijos
Ašmenos
Šiaulių
Rūdninkų
LARGE GHETTO
Ligonines
Small Ghetto (6 Sep – 21 Oct 1941)
Large Ghetto (6 Sep 1941 – 23 Sep 1943)
Pylimo
Karmelitų
Adikių gatvė

### Jewish Museums, Synagogues & Cemeteries

One of the few Vilnius ghetto survivors helped found the **Lithuanian State Jewish Museum of Vilna Gaon** (Lietuvos valstybinis Vilniaus Gaono žydų muziejus; ☎ 261 7907; admission by donation; open 2pm-6pm Mon-Fri) inside the **Jewish Community of Lithuania** (☎ 261 3003; W www.litjews.org; Pylimo gatvė 4; admission free; open 10pm-5pm Mon-Fri). Powerful B&W photographs recount the Holocaust and guided tours of Jewish Vilnius in English can be arranged. A visit to the **Holocaust Museum** (☎ 262 0730; Pamėnkalnio gatvė 12; admission by donation; open 9am-5pm Mon-Thur, 9am-4pm Fri) is equally moving. The exhibition is a stark reminder of the true horror suffered by Lithuanian Jews in an 'unedited' display of horrific images and words.

Modern Vilnius' only **synagogue** (☎ 261 2523; Pylimo gatvė 39) was built in 1894 for the wealthy, and it survived only because the Nazis used it as a medical store. Restored in 1995, it is used by a small Orthodox community for services at 8.30am and 7pm.

The Soviets liquidated several Jewish cemeteries in the 1950s. The **old Jewish cemetery** where Rabbi Gaon Elijahu was originally buried was ripped up in 1957 and turned into a sports stadium (Žalgiris Stadium). The maceivas (tombstones) were recycled in the city as paving stones; the steps leading up Tauro Hill to the Trade Union Palace on Mykolaičio-Putino gatvė were originally built from Jewish gravestones. In 1991 the Jewish community retrieved many of these desecrated maceivas. Gaon Elijahu is now buried in the **new Jewish cemetery**, north of Vingas Park in the Virsuliskės district (entrance on Ažuolyno gatvė).

## Old Town – West

There are four sizable Catholic church and monastery complexes, all created by different monastic orders, within 200m of the corner of Vilniaus and Dominikonų gatvė. All chiefly date from the 17th- and 18th-century Baroque era. Among them, the **Holy Spirit Church** (Šv Dvasios bažnyčia; ☎ 262 9595; cnr Dominikonų & Šv Ignoto gatvė; admission free; open 6.30pm-7pm daily, services at 7am, 3pm & 6pm Mon-Sat, 8am, 9am, 10.30am, 12pm, 1.30pm & 6pm Sun) is Vilnius' primary Polish church (1679). Once attached to a Dominican monastery, it has a splendid gold and white interior and a labyrinth of cellars concealing preserved corpses. The two towers of the peach and creamy-white **St Catherine's Church** (Šv Kotrynos bažnyčia; Vilniaus gatvė 30) were once part of a Benedictine monastery. Opposite sits the city's colourful **Theatre, Music & Cinema Museum** (see Museums earlier).

Symbolic of the extravagant renovation that has been sweeping through the Old Town in recent years was the reconsecration in mid-1999 of the Franciscan **Church of the Assumption** (Trakų gatvė 9/1). Dubbed 'Sands Church' after the quarter in which it stands, this 15th-century church (1421) served as a hospital for the French army in 1812 and as state archives from 1864 to 1934 and 1949 to 1989. The building was returned to the Archbishopric of Vilnius only in 1995 and in turn to the Franciscan friars in 1998.

Other churches include the **Jesuit Noviciate with St Ignatius' Church** (Šv Ignoto bažnyčia; Šv Ignoto gatvė) and the fine little **St Nicholas' Church** (Šv Mikalojaus bažnyčia; ☎ 261-8559; Šv Mikalojaus gatvė; admission free; services 4pm Thur & Sat, 8.30am Sun). The latter was founded by German merchants and is Lithuania's oldest Gothic church, dating from 1320 (before Lithuania's conversion). The extensively renovated **Evangelical Lutheran Church** (Evangelikų liuteronų bažnyčia; ☎ 212 3792; Vokiečių gatvė 20; services 9.30am & 11am Sun), dating from 1553, is in a courtyard and is home to Vilnius' tiny Protestant community. Under the Soviet regime a concrete floor divided the church into a workshop and a basketball court.

**Radvilos' Palace** (Radvilų rūmai; ☎ 212 1477; Vilniaus gatvė 41; admission 3 Lt; open noon-6pm Tues-Sat, noon-5pm Sun), the 17th-century residence of Jonusas Radvila (1612–55), houses the foreign fine arts section of the Lithuanian Art Museum.

## EAST OF GEDIMINAS HILL

You could be in danger of crossing a border without realising it when you walk across the Vilnia River into Užupis. The area dubbed the Montmartre of Vilnius has declared itself an independent republic! (See the boxed text 'Rebels with a Cause').

### Three Crosses

The landmark Three Crosses (Trys kryžiai) stand majestically atop (you guessed it) Three Crosses Hill (Trijų kryžių kalnas), just east of Gediminas kalnas. Crosses are said to have stood here since the 17th century in memory of three monks who were martyred by crucifixion on this spot. The remains of three crosses lie in the shadow of the erect ones. These are the original hill monuments which the Soviets bulldozed after World War II. In the spirit of Lithuania the people rebuilt them but left the twisted remains of the originals as a historical reminder of oppression. Walk up to them through Kalnų Park from Kosciuskos gatvė.

### SS Peter & Paul's Church

Don't be fooled by the uninspiring exterior of SS Peter & Paul's Church (Šv Petro ir Povilo bažnyčias; ☎ 234 0229; Antakalnio gatvė 1; open daily), the Baroque interior will leave you breathless. Thousands of ornate white sculptures, created by Italian sculptors from 1675 to 1704, crowd the church, which was founded by the Lithuanian noble Mykolas Kazimieras Paca (his tomb is on the right of the porch as you enter and his portrait hangs on the left of the altar).

### Rasų & Military Cemeteries

Vilnius' Rasų and Military Cemeteries (Sukilėlių gatvė) face each other in the southeast of the Old Town. Founded in 1801, Rasų cemetery is the resting place of Vilnius' elite, including artists and politicians. More interesting, however, is the small, unkempt military cemetery opposite, where the heart of the Polish Marshal Jósef Piłsudki, responsible for Poland's annexation of Vilnius in 1921, lies. His mother shares his heart's grave. His body is buried in Kraków.

## Rebels with a Cause

The cheeky streak of rebellion that pervades Lithuania has flourished in the bohemian heart of Vilnius. A revolution has taken place – without a single drop of blood being spilled. The artists, dreamers, drunks and squatters of the notorious Užupis quarter have declared a break-away state.

The Republic of Užupis was officially, in an unofficial sense, born in 1998. The state now has its own tongue-in-cheek president, anthem, flags and constitution, which ends 'Don't conquer. Don't defend. Don't surrender' in typically bizarre fashion. The declaration was originally a light-hearted protest at soaring property prices in the historic Old Town, which pushed the artistic community into run-down Užupis. Now the area, which is separated from the rest of Vilnius by the Vilnia River (Lithuanian for 'beyond the river'), is a model for alternative living. Each April Fool's Day since independence was declared, citizens of the Republic of Užupis celebrate their bizarre and wholly unofficial state. 'Border' guards wearing comical outfits stamp passports at the main bridge and President Romas Lileikis makes speeches in the quarter's small focal square. It is here, at the intersection of Užupio, Maluno and Paupio streets that the Angel of Užupis statue was unveiled in 2002. The Dalai Lama, on his second visit to Lithuania in 2001, was granted honorary citizenship and said he wanted the sound of the Angel's horn to travel across the world. The headquarters and self-proclaimed 'Mecca' is Užupis Kavinė, which overlooks the river, affectionately known as Užupis seaside. Three art galleries now grace the crumbling streets, which are in the middle of a face-lift. Vilnius mayor, young and dynamic Artūras Zuokas, coincidentally recently moved to the 15th-century area, also known as 'Little Havana'.

## NEW TOWN

The area known as the New Town (Naujamiestis) stretches 2km west of the cathedral and the Old Town; it was mostly built in the 19th century.

### Gedimino Prospektas

Sandwiched between the cathedral's dramatic skyline and the silver-domed Church of the Saint Virgin's Apparition is the main street of modern Vilnius. Gedimino prospektas' 1.75km length is dotted with shops, a theatre, banks, hotels, offices, government buildings, parliament and a few park squares. Laid out in 1852, it has had 11 name changes since. The tsarists named it after St George, the Poles after Mickiewicz, and the Soviet rulers first after Stalin, then Lenin.

Reconstruction work began in 2002, planting trees and giving it a general make-over. The cobbles may prevent trolleybuses being able to run the length of Gedimino prospektas in future, and it is likely they will be rerouted to avoid the main street altogether.

**Savivaldybės Aikštė** The **City Hall** (☎ 212 6977; W www.vilnius.lt; Gedimino gatvė 9; open 9am-5pm daily) is on the eastern side of this square at the corner of Vilniaus gatvė; the seat of the government occupies the north side. Above Vilniaus gatvė, down towards the river, is the large modern **Opera & Ballet Theatre** (Operos ir Baleto Teatras; ☎ 262 0636; W www.opera.lt; Vienuolio gatvė 1).

**Lukiškių Aikštė** It was here that Vilnius' infamous statue of Lenin towered over the people (see the boxed text 'Stalin World' in the Eastern & Southern Lithuania chapter).

The large building (1890) facing this square, which was called Lenin Square after the statue, at Gedimino prospektas 40, used to be the headquarters of the Lithuanian KGB, and during the Nazi occupation, the Gestapo. Part of it is used as the state prosecutor's office and state archives today.

The remainder houses the horrific **Museum of Genocide Victims** (Genocido aukų muziejus; ☎ 249 6264; Aukų gatvė 2a; open 10am-6pm Tues-Sun 15 May-14 Sept, 10am-4pm Tues-Sun 15 Sept-14 May). Many of the museum guides are former inmates, and will show you around the cells where they were tormented. Inside two locked cells (Nos 16 and 18) are the remains of KGB victims found buried in a mass grave in Tuskulenai Park. Memorial plaques honouring those who perished in 1945 to 1946 adorn the outside of the building. Call in advance if you want a tour (Lithuanian and Russian only); illustrative captions in the cells are in English.

**VILNIUS**

## The Killing Fields

The remains of prisoners who were shot have since been found buried in Tuskulenai Park, a popular picnic spot in Vilnius until 1994 when the KGB graveyard was discovered. The park is now known as the 'killing fields'.

The remains belong to partisans who put up an armed resistance against Soviet rule from positions in the surrounding forests. The KGB shot them from 1944 to 1947. Of the 706 bodies discovered, only 43 have been identified. Their remains will stay locked in cell Nos 16 and 18 until a suitable resting place can be found.

The site, signposted 'Tuskulėnų dvaro memorialo teritorija', is open only from 10am to 10pm on 1 and 2 November. To get to the killing fields, take trolleybus No 8, 12, 17 or 18 to Žirmūnai and get off at the stop after the roundabout on Žirmūnų gatvė.

**Parliament** The concrete slabs with mangled barbed wire and angry slogans daubed on them are poignant reminders of Lithuania's recent violent past. It was here, and at the TV & Radio Centre and TV Tower, that barricades were erected on 13 January 1991 to protect parliament (Seimas) from Soviet troops. Thousands of people gathered at the building. The barricades to the north of the parliament building were left in place until December 1992, when the last Russian soldier left Vilnius.

The classical building next to parliament is the **Martynas Mažvydas Lithuanian National Library**. Trolleybus No 7 from the train station, or No 3 from the Gedimino stop on Vrublevskio gatvė near the cathedral, will take you along Jasinskio gatvė, a block south of Gedimino prospektas. For parliament, get off at the Tiltas stop just before the river or the Liubarto stop just after it.

### South of the River
**Romanovs' Church** (*Basanavičiaus gatvė*) is an eye-catching Russian Orthodox church built in 1913 which sports pea-green onion domes. A little further down is a **flower market** (*Basanavičiaus gatvė 42; open 24hr*). A **kenessa** (*Liubarto gatvė 6*), a traditional prayer house of the Karaites, Lithuania's smallest ethnic minority, is west of Jasinskio gatvė.

Rock-and-roll legend **Frank Zappa** (*Kalinausko gatvė 1*) is immortalised in a 4.2m-high bronze bust – flanked by a swirling psychedelic mural. It is the world's first/only memorial to the off-beat American who died from cancer in 1993. It was erected in 1995 by the Lithuanian Frank Zappa fan club after a long dispute with various authorities, who found the whole idea completely preposterous.

### Vingis Park
Just over 1km southwest of parliament, at the western end of Čiurlionio gatvė, is the wooded Vingis Park (Vingio parkas). It is surrounded on three sides by the Neris and has a big stage, the usual setting for the Lithuanian Song Festival. If you don't want to walk all the way from the city centre, take trolleybus No 7 from the train station or No 3 from the Gedimino stop on Vrublevskio gatvė, near the cathedral. Get off at the Kęstučio stop (the second after the bridge over the river), then walk over the footbridge from the end of Treniotos gatvė.

### TV & Radio Centre
Like the more distant TV Tower (see later), the TV & Radio Centre (*cnr Konarskio gatvė & Pietario gatvė*), near the southeastern edge of Vingis Park, was stormed by Soviet tanks and troops in the early hours of 13 January 1991. A group of wooden crosses stand outside the centre as a memorial to the many martyrs of Lithuania's independence campaign.

### North of the River
The neglected north bank of the Neris is undergoing a radical transformation, the brainchild of Vilnius mayor Artūras Zuokas. A new business district, dubbed 'Sunrise Valley', is being built to create an information technology sector with brand- new office and retail space and a new, relocated municipal building to boot. Holiday Inn kickstarted the changes by opening its plush new hotel in 2002. The same year, work also started on the first of two new bridges linking the centre to the business district.

North of the Neris there are numerous examples of Soviet architecture. The imposing relics date from the Khrushchev to Gorbachev eras. **St Raphael's Church** (*Šv Rapolo bažnyčia*), on the northern side of Žaliasis tiltas (Green Bridge) over the Neris, has a fine Baroque interior.

## Beginning with A

'We want to show the world how a little nation fought for its independence; show how dear, how valuable, independence itself is.'
**Juozas Aleksiejūnas, Tour Guide, Museum of Genocide Victims.**

Juozas Aleksiejūnas is in his 80s. He is a tour guide at the Museum of Genocide Victims, which is in the former headquarters and prison of the KGB in Vilnius. He is also a former inmate of this house of horrors where blood still stains the walls of the cramped cells in which prisoners lived and died. His story is a proud but harrowing one.

Aleksiejūnas joined the partisan resistance movement in 1944, just after Soviet rule was re-established in Lithuania. As one of the country's estimated 40,000 'forest brothers', he roamed the forests in the Molėtai area, 75km north of Vilnius, with five other 'brothers'. His official task was to steal identity forms from the local passport office to pass on to fellow partisans.

On 26 March 1945, he was betrayed. He was arrested by the KGB and tried for anti-Soviet activities. In less than an hour he was found guilty and his ordeal in Vilnius' KGB prison, notorious for its high security and inhumane disciplinary measures, began.

Between 1944 and 1953, 200,000 Lithuanians passed through the Soviet prisons. The one in Vilnius was used for equally sinister purposes by the Gestapo during the Nazi occupation; its execution ward, various torture chambers and 9m-square cells where up to 20 prisoners were kept at any one time all remain today.

Aleksiejūnas was interrogated and tortured for a week. 'How many of you are there?' and 'Who is your leader?' were the questions fired at him. Prisoners did not have names. They were called 'Beginning with A', 'Beginning with B' and so on to ensure prisoners knew as little about each other as possible. Inmates who attempted conversation were sent to an isolation cell, stripped to their underwear and rationed to 300g of bread and half a litre of water a day.

Inmates who refused 'to talk' to KGB officers during interrogation were sent to the infamous 'soft cell'. Its walls were heavily padded to muffle the hideous human cries and the sound of beatings. Prisoners were put in straitjackets and forced to sit in the pitch-black, silent cell until their spirit broke. Aleksiejūnas survived the soft cell hell.

After three days in the 'wet room' he lost consciousness. This 8 x 10m punishment cell had a sunken floor covered with cold water, which turned to ice in winter. In the centre was a slippery metal pedestal, 30cm in diameter, which was the prisoners' only refuge from the wet floor.

Juozas Aleksiejūnas was later moved to Vokiski prison in Vilnius. On 29 June 1945, he was deported to Vorkuta, Siberia, where he spent five years in a hard labour camp followed by a further five years in a high security prison. In 1955 he was released on parole. But he was not allowed to leave Vorkuta and had to report twice a month (which he did for nine years) to the prison's special commander. His Lithuanian wife, Jane, whom he married in 1943 (but had barely seen since), joined him in Vorkuta where their first son was born. The Aleksiejūnas family was allowed to return home to Vilnius in 1963.

**Antakalnis Cemetery**, off Karių kapų gatvė in the northern region of Antakalnis, is said to be one of the most beautiful graveyards in Eastern Europe. Those killed by Soviet special forces outside the parliament on 13 January 1991 are buried here, along with seven border guards killed by Soviet forces at the Medininkai border crossing with Belarus in 1991. A sculpture of the Madonna cradling her son stands in memorial to them. On All Saints' Day (1 November) hundreds of people light candles by the graves out of respect for the dead.

## TV TOWER

This 326m-tall tower *(Televizijos Bokstas;* ☎ *245 8877;* Ⓦ *www.lrtc.lt; Sausio 13-osios gatvė 10; admission 15 Lt; open 10am-9pm daily)* is symbolic of Lithuania's strength of spirit. On 13 January 1991, Soviet special forces (OMON) tanks and troops killed 12 people here. Lithuanian TV kept broadcasting until the troops came through the tower door. Carved wooden crosses and candles now stand as memorials to the victims and on 13 January hundreds of people light candles at this spot. The tower houses a small exhibit

VILNIUS

about those who died. Every year fairy lights are strung on the tower to create the world's largest Christmas tree!

**Paukščių takas** (Milky Way; ☎/fax 252 5338; open 10am-10pm daily) is a revolving restaurant inside the tower with panoramic views of the city. The fearless can do Europe's highest **bungee jump** from the tower (☎ 8-284 171 67; rates per jump 250 Lt).

To get to the tower, take trolleybus No 16 from the train station or No 11 from Lukiskių aikštė to the Televizijos Bokstas stop on Laisvės prospektas. A trip here takes you into the heart of Vilnius' Soviet-era high-rise suburbs.

## SOVIET BARRACKS
The shabby barracks were home to the 107th Motorized Rifle Brigade until 31 December 1992, when the Red Army pulled out. Once an unwanted reminder of Soviet occupation, the 63-hectare site is undergoing a rebirth as, ironically, a new business park for budding capitalism.

The skeletons of 2000 Napoleonic soldiers were dug up as underground cables were being laid in 2002. Archaeologists since say the remains of up to 40,000 men could lie on the site – a mass grave created after the soldiers died of starvation and injuries while retreating from the Russian army. The bones have been taken to Vilnius University for archaeologists to catalogue, while the Lithuanian authorities quibble with the French authorities on where and when the remains should be laid to rest.

## EXHIBITIONS
Lithuanian and foreign avant-garde artists are exhibited at the **Contemporary Art Centre** (Šiuolaikinio meno centras; ☎ 262 3476; e info@cac.lt; Vokiečių gatvė 2; open 11am-7pm Tues-Sun, closed Mon). Another funky gallery is the **Russian Gallery** (Rusų meno galerija; ☎ 212 3236; Bokšto gatvė 4/2; open 12pm-6pm Tues-Sun, closed Mon).

The **Centre Culturel Français** (☎ 312 985, fax 312 987; e info@centrefrancais.lt; Didžioji gatvė 1) boasts some original and experimental exhibitions as well as some cultural events.

**Stiklo Karoliukai** (☎ 215 3875; w www .karoliukai.svetaine.lt; Paupio gatvė 2) is the latest gallery space that is located on the Užupis block.

## ORGANISED TOURS
For city tours, it's not hard to miss the funky bright yellow bus parked on Rotušės aikštė. It's 10 Lt for a one-hour tour of the Old Town (daily except Monday and Tuesday) at one of five departure times. Advance telephone bookings are required (☎ 738 625)

**Vilnius City Tour** (☎ 8-699 54064, ☎/fax 615 558; w www.vilniuscitytour.com) organises daily walking tours in English, costing 60 Lt, departing from Katedros aikštė at 10am, 3pm and 6pm daily.

Informative and moving tours of Jewish Vilnius are organised by the Lithuanian State Jewish Museum (see the boxed text 'Jerusalem of the North' earlier).

## SPECIAL EVENTS
Vilnius enjoys a rich pageant of festivals. They include:

**Užgavėnės** A pagan carnival celebrated on Shrove Tuesday (Mardi Gras) in February to mark the end of winter
**Kaziukas crafts fair** Held in the Old Town to celebrate St Casimir's Day on 4 March
**Lygiadienis** Another pagan carnival celebrating spring equinox in March
**International Life Theatre Festival** Takes over Kalnų Park in mid-May
**Vilnius Festival** Annually brings classical music concerts to numerous Old Town courtyards in June
**St Christopher's Summer Music Festival** A week in July
**Vilnius Days** An international street festival in mid-September

## PLACES TO STAY – BUDGET
### Camping
Five kilometres from Trakai, **Kempingas Slėnyje** (☎/fax 8-528 51 387; Totoriš kes village; doubles 60 Lt, triples 70-80 Lt, suites 130 Lt, apartments 250 Lt) has a sauna, sandy beach, paddleboat, boat rental and hot air balloon rides. You can even pitch a tent here too.

### Hostels
**Old Town Hostel** (☎ 262 5357; e oldtown hostels@delfi.lt; Aušros Vartų gatvė 20-15; dorm beds member/nonmember 32/34 Lt) has 25 beds which fill up quickly. It's a two-minute signposted walk from the train and bus stations and the Old Town. Lovely Livijus, who runs the place, boasts free Internet

and cheap car rental. It's the place to meet travellers and socialise.

**Filaretai Hostel** (☎ 215 4627, fax 212 0149; e filaretai@post.omnitel.net; Filaretų gatvė 17; dorm beds 24 Lt, doubles/triples 32/28 Lt), like Old Town Hostel, is affiliated with the Lithuanian Hostels Association and is equally fine and friendly. It's a kilometre east of the Old Town in funky Užupis district. It has a washing machine and satellite TV. Linen is included but there is a 5 Lt charge added to the first night's accommodation, and breakfast (optional) is 6 Lt. To get here take bus No 34 from outside the bus and train stations to the seventh stop. Both the Filaretai and Old Town Hostels can arrange sauna and canoeing trips.

**Youth Tourist Centre** (Jaunųjų turistų centras; ☎ 261 1547, fax 262 7742; Polocko gatvė 7; dorm beds 24 Lt), near Filaretai Hostel, has 16 cheap but cheerful rooms that are simply equipped and clean. Little English is spoken.

**Teacher's University Hostel** (☎ 213 0509, fax 216 2291; Vivulskio gatvė 36; singles 65 Lt, doubles 27-28 Lt, triples 24-27 Lt, suites 130 Lt) is on the Old Town's western fringe. It has a motley selection of rooms and is a cheap, if drab, choice.

Close to the train and bus stations, **Smiley Face Hostel** (☎ 213 9477; Sodų gatvė 13; singles/doubles/triples 60/80/120 Lt) is seedy but handy for anyone turning up late at night and needing a room.

**Elektros Tinklų Statybos** (☎ 216 0254, fax 329 079; Šv Stepono gatvė 11; dorm beds 24 Lt; reception open 8am-3pm Mon-Fri) is just as run-down but friendlier, with 55 beds and shared bathroom and kitchen.

### B&Bs

**Litinterp** (☎ 212 3850, fax 212 3559; w www.litinterp.lt; Bernardinų gatvė 7-2; singles/doubles from 80/120 Lt; open 8.30am-5.30pm Mon-Fri, 9am-3pm Sat) arranges B&B accommodation in the Old Town. It also arranges accommodation in Klaipėda, Nida, Palanga and Kaunas and rents cars. Bookings can be made via the Internet.

The main **Tourist Information Centre** (☎ 262 9660, fax 262 8169; w www.vilnius.lt; Vilniaus gatvė 22; open 9am-6pm Mon-Thur, 9am-5pm Fri) also provides accommodation in private homes in the Old Town. It costs from 70 Lt for a bed in a family house with

shared bathroom to 250 Lt for a room in an apartment.

**Apia Guest House** (☎ 212 3426, fax 212 3618; e apia@takas.lt; Šv Ignoto gatvė 12; singles 240 Lt, doubles 260-320 Lt) is small and charming. The rates include breakfast.

### Hotels

**Gintaras** (☎ 273 8011, fax 213 3881; e reservation@hotelgintaras.lt; Seinų gatvė 14; singles/doubles/quads 80/110/200 Lt) proves the old adage of location, location, location – as there's nothing else going for it except being slap bang in front of the train station. The former Soviet ghetto has brightened up its lobby but its rooms are still shabby. The saving grace is the price. As with everything in close range of the station, security is not the best here.

**Hotel Skrydis** (☎ 232 9099, fax 230 6498; e vilnius-airport@post.omnitel.net; Rodūnios kelias 8; singles/doubles/triples from 50/60/70 Lt), at the airport, has a melee of rooms with or without private bathroom, renovated or not renovated, with a mixture of prices to reflect this.

### PLACES TO STAY – MID-RANGE

If looks aren't important to you then former Soviet hotels could be the answer to your Vilnius price dilemma. They generally won't break the bank for a night's sleep. But – as with all good things – this won't last long. Prices are already rising as renovations sweep through their floors.

### Old Town & Gedimino Prospektas

**At the Ambassador** (☎ 261 5460, fax 212 1716; e info@ambassador.lt; Gedimino prospektas 12; singles/doubles/suites 240/280/360 Lt) is located in a prime spot but the less-than-friendly staff don't do this dimly lit hotel any favours.

**Narutis** (☎ 212 2894, fax 262 2882; e narutis@5ci.lt; Pilies gatvė 24; singles/doubles/suites 320/400/650 Lt) is housed in an historic red brick town house dating from 1581. It has classy rooms decked out in wood.

**Telecom Guest House** (☎ 236 7150, fax 265 2782; e hotel@telecom.lt; Vivulskio gatvė 13a; singles/doubles/suites 250/300/430 Lt) is one of Vilnius' best-kept accommodation secrets.

**E-Guest House** (☎ 266 0730, fax 233 5710; w www.e-guesthouse.lt; Ševčenkos gatvė 16; doubles/apartments 180/240 Lt) is a quirky hi-tech hotel offering free Internet connection in each room and a rent-a-laptop service!

## North of the River

The fabulously ugly Lietuva hotel has risen like a phoenix from the flames with its remarkable transformation into the swanky **Reval Hotel Lietuva** (e sales@revalhotels .com; Konstitucijos gatvė 20; singles from €110, doubles €130-175, suites €175-350). It was due to open in May 2003. Gone is the seedy Soviet landmark – instead this is the ultimate in luxury in the heart of Vilnius' evolving business sector.

**Naujasis Vilnius** (☎ 273 9595, fax 273 9500; e hotel@hotelnv.lt; w www.hotelnv.lt; Ukmergės gatvė 14; singles/doubles 340/400 Lt), next door to Lietuva, is a towering hotel with renovated rooms.

There are a few smaller, cosier options.

**Victoria** (☎ 272 4013, fax 272 4320; e hotel@victoria.lt; Saltoniskių gatvė 56; singles/doubles/quads 192/232/320 Lt) has comfortable rooms in the historic Žvėrynas district.

**Pušis** (Pine Tree; ☎ 268 3999, fax 272 1305; e pusis@pusishotel.lt; Blindžių gatvė 17; singles/doubles/suites 70/130/180 Lt) is a good no-frills choice and only a short walk away from Vingis Park.

## PLACES TO STAY – TOP END

Vilnius boasts a divine selection of hotels for the well-heeled (and well-walleted) traveller.

## Old Town & Gedimino Prospektas

The Old Town's narrow streets have several charming family-run places tucked away.

**AAA Mano Liza** (☎ 212 2225, fax 212 2608; w www.hotelinvilnius.lt; Ligoninės gatvė 5; doubles/luxury suites from 320/560 Lt) has real double beds, making it an elegant romantic hide-away in this late 19th-century building (1885).

**Rūdninkų Vartai** (☎ 261 3916, fax 212 0507; e rudvar@takas.lt; Rūdninkų gatvė 15/46; singles/doubles/suites from 305/350/530 Lt), near Mano Liza, has comfortable rooms built around a courtyard.

**Grybas House** (☎ 212 1854, fax 212 2416; w www.grybashouse.com; Aušros Vartų gatvė 3a; suites 320-540 Lt) is in a courtyard off Aušros Vartų gatvė. The prices of the 10 suites here depend on the view (a courtyard view is the priciest). Breakfast is served in the

cosy cellar bar and the host family arranges city tours in English.

**Scandic Hotel Neringa** (☎ 261 0516, fax 261 4160; e neringa@scandic-hotels.com; Gedimino prospektas 23; singles 375-570 Lt, doubles 550-670 Lt) has seen few changes over the past 35 years. Now it boasts a sauna, Jacuzzi, airport shuttle bus and conference hall. Its restaurant is a blast from the Soviet past. See it to believe it!

**Mabre Residence** (☎ 212 2195, fax 212 2240; e mabre@mabre.lt; Maironio gatvė 13; singles/doubles/suites from 320/460/580 Lt) is an enchanting choice in a former Orthodox monastery. Its rooms are off the tourist trail yet central.

**Shakespeare Too** (☎ 266 1626, fax 266 1627; w www.shakespeareetoo.lt; Pilies gatvė 34; singles/doubles/suites from 360/560/720 Lt), a bizarre, Shakespearean-themed hotel in the heart of the Old Town. Each room is individually furnished.

**CityPark** (☎ 212 3515, fax 261 7745; w www.citypark.lt; Stuokos-Gucevičiaus gatvė 3; singles/doubles/suites from 360/480/660 Lt) is within coughing distance of the cathedral.

**Stikliai** (☎ 262 7971, fax 212 3870; w www .stikliaihotel.lt; Gaono gatvė 7; singles/doubles/ suites from 600/660/840 Lt) is the cream of the crop, tucked down a picture-postcard cobbled street in the old Jewish quarter and named after the glass blowers who had their workshop in the 17th-century pad on Stikliai gatvė (Glass Blowers St).

**Radisson SAS Astorija** (☎ 212 0110, fax 212 1762; e reservations.vilnius@radisson SAS.com; Didžioji gatvė 35/2; singles/doubles from 784/880 Lt) is a mint-green classical wonder overlooking St Casimir's Church.

## North of the River

**Holiday Inn** (☎ 210 3000, fax 210 3001; e holiday-inn@ibc.lt; Šeimyniš kių 1; singles/ doubles/suites 483/587/656 Lt) is everything you'd expect – sleek, with contemporary grandeur. It is well placed in the area set to become Vilnius' business district.

**Šarūnas** (☎ 272 3888, fax 272 4355; w www.hotelsarunas.lt; Raitininkų gatvė 4; singles/doubles/suites from 360/420/460 Lt) is east of the Žaliasis bridge. It is the creation of Lithuanian basketball god Sarūnas Marčiulionis.

**Karolina** (☎ 245 3939, fax 216 9341; e hotel@karolina.lt; Sausio 13-osios gatvė 2;

singles/doubles from 80/100 Lt) sports a bowling alley and is a favourite for groups and for business types.

## Out of Town
Le Meridien Villon (☎ 273 9600, fax 273 9730; e lemeridienvillon@post.omnitel.net; singles/doubles/suites from 480/560/680 Lt) is a 200-room haven 19km north of Vilnius on the Rīga road. Next to a lake and surrounded by forests, this sumptuous palace has its own ballroom, nightclub, casino and shuttle bus to the city centre.

## PLACES TO EAT
Whether it's curry, *kepta duona* (fried bread sticks oozing garlic) or *cepelinai* (gut-busting meat and potato dish shaped like a zeppelin) you want, Vilnius has a mouth-watering selection of international and local cuisine. Traditional food has survived the Western dining take-over bid and it's still the cheapest place for a Baltic blow-out with budget binges for as little as 20 Lt. The prices for a full meal here include starter, main dish and dessert, but exclude drinks.

## Lithuanian
Ritos Smuklė (Rita's Tavern; ☎ 277 0786; e smukle@rita.lt; Žirmūnų gatvė 68; meals 30-40 Lt; open 10am-midnight daily) is a Lithuanian institution north of the city. Hog down on smoked pigs' ears (9.60 Lt) while the spit roast turns. Owner Rita Dapkutė is an American-Lithuanian and her restaurant is strictly Lithuanian-only dishes and ingredients. No Coca-Cola in sight. Folk bands play at weekends. Take bus No 12 from outside the cathedral to the Žirmūnai stop.

Žemaičių Smuklė (☎ 261 6573; Vokiečių gatvė 24, Old Town; meals 30-100 Lt; open 11am-midnight daily) offers wild boar, pheasant or venison. It's a meat-eater's paradise. Take shelter from the snow or sun in the atmospheric cellars with hearty beer snacks. Reservations are needed in summer.

Lokys (The Bear; ☎ 262 9046; Stiklių gatvė 8; meals from 30 Lt) is a Vilnius institution with beaver on the menu set in a maze of cellars in the Old Town.

Stiklių Bočiai (☎ 625 141; Šv Ignoto gatvė 4/3; meals 35 Lt upwards; open 11am-midnight daily) is a medieval maelstrom of folk music, pig-roasting and beer, served by charming, knicker-bockered waiters in a banquet hall.

Stiklių Aludė (☎ 262 4501; Gaono gatvė 7; meals 40-100 Lt; open 11am-midnight daily) is a beer cellar/restaurant serving giant-sized *cepelinai* from traditionally-dressed maidens.

## European
Who says the English can't cook? These British-run places have revolutionised the dining scene. The PUB (☎ 261 8393; w www .pub.lt; Dominikonų gatvė 9; meals 13-20 Lt; open until 5am Fri & Sat) will satisfy the largest appetites. Gorge on good old shepherd's pie or fish and chips. Prie Parlamento (☎ 249 6606; w www.prieparlamento.lt; Gedimino prospektas 46; meals 25-35 Lt; open 8am-3am daily, until 5am Fri & Sat) is a more upmarket expat haunt. Its divine chocolate brownies, juicy steaks and full English breakfasts cure all homesickness.

Offsetting these is a host of colourful offbeat eating places.

Savas Kampas (☎ 212 3203; Vokiečių gatvė 4, Old Town; lunch 10 Lt; open 10am-1am daily, until 3am Fri & Sat) is a friendly joint with hearty Lithuanian food. It's a local favourite and a good meeting place.

Ritos Slėptuvė (☎ 262 6117; Gostauto gatvė 8; meals 25-40 Lt; open 7.30am-4am Fri & Sat) is an underground, in-your-face, all-American diner. Authentic tortillas, steaks and burgers compete with brilliant breakfasts (try the delicious banana bread) with as much coffee as you can drink.

La Provence (☎ 261 6573; Vokiečių gatvė 24; meals 45-100 Lt; open daily 10am-midnight) has an elegant French menu, with such delights as snails, scallops and lime sorbet.

Literatų Svetainė (☎ 611 889; Gedimino prospektas 1; meals 50 Lt) is where the Polish-Lithuanian poet and Nobel Prize winner, Czesław Miłosz, watched the Red Army march into Vilnius in June 1940. Today exquisite Scandinavian food and impeccable service make this a top spot.

The Stikliai restaurants are the most decadent and pricey in Vilnius. The restaurant inside the hotel, Stikliai (☎ 262 4501; Gaono gatvė 7; meals from 100 Lt; open daily noon-midnight), specialises in French cuisine as well as caviar pancakes in lavishly furnished surroundings.

## International
Finjan (☎ 261 2104; Vokiečių gatvė 18; meals 12-25 Lt; open daily 11am-midnight) is where

you can smoke a water pipe (20 Lt) or enjoy the weekend belly dancing while stuffing good, cheap Middle Eastern food such as pitas filled with falafel, smothered in searingly hot chilli sauce.

**Balti Drambliai** (☎ 262 0875; *Vilniaus gatvė 41; meals 15-20 Lt; open daily 11am-midnight)* is vegetarian heaven and offers an exhaustive menu of cheap vegan and veggie delights from all cuisines.

**Sue's Indian Raja/Sue Ka Tai** (☎ 262 3802; *Jogailos gatvė 11/2; meals 40-70 Lt; open daily noon-11pm)*, oddly, serves both Indian and Thai. Good for vegetarians.

**Freskos** (☎ 261 8133; *Didžioji gatvė 31; meals 40 Lt; open daily 11am-midnight)* offers an experimental menu against a theatrical backdrop in the heart of the Old Town.

## Cafés
**Skonis ir Kvapas** (☎ 212 2803; *Trakų gatvė 8; open daily 9.30am-11pm)* has an astonishing selection of fragrantly named teas, posh salads (7 Lt) and decadent cakes (4 Lt).

**Presto Arbata** (☎ 262 1967; *Gedimino prospektas 32a; open 7am-10pm Mon-Thur, 7am-midnight Fri & Sat)* has delights such as fresh prawn salads (8 Lt), frothy coffee and blackcurrant cheesecake (3.60 Lt).

**Pilies Menė** (☎ 261 2552; *Pilies gatvė 8; open daily 10am-midnight)* nearby is a popular and cheap eating and drinking spot with a pavement terrace and 33 *blyneliai* (pancake) varieties (4 Lt to 8 Lt), such as decadent ones stuffed with bananas and dripping in chocolate sauce.

Choose **Keisti Ženklai** *(Strange Signs;* ☎ 261 0779; *Trakų gatvė 13; meals 20 Lt)* for large tasty meals at reasonable prices.

**Pilies Pasažo Kavinė** (☎ 243 6221; *Pilies gatvė 6; meals 20 Lt; open daily 11am-11pm)* is a hidden treasure with hearty *kepta duona* (deep-fried bread with garlic) and a lovely tiled fireplace to snuggle up by.

**Amatininkų Užeiga** (☎ 261 7968; *Didžioji gatvė 19/2; meals 30 Lt; open 8am-5am Mon-Fri, 11am-5pm Sat & Sun)* serves hearty Lithuanian stews, grilled fish and creamy pancakes until dawn.

## Pizzerias
The Lithuanian love affair with the humble pizza continues unabated.

**Čili Picerija** (☎ 231 2462; *Didžioji gatvė 5 & Gedimino prospektas 23; pizza under 15 Lt;*

*open daily 8am-midnight)* is a pizza staple with 21 types to choose from.

**Da Antonio** (☎ 262 0109; *Vilniaus gatvė 23;* ☎ 261 8341; *Pilies gatvė 20; meals 30 Lt; open daily 10am-11pm)* serves classic Italian favourites.

**St Valentino** (☎ 231 4198; *Vilniaus gatvė 47/18; meals 50 Lt; open daily 7.30am-11pm)* is a classier rival.

**Kuba** (☎ 790 526; *Šeimyniš kių 3a; meals 10 Lt; open 8.30am-midnight daily)* is a classy canteen offering fabulous fodder in a sleek setting just north of the river. It boasts inspiring salads, good Italian dishes and pancakes. The meals are charged according to their weight.

## Self-Catering
Milk straight from the cow's udder, homemade honey and smoked eel are some of the culinary delights at **Kalvarijų Market** *(Kalvarijų 6; open 7am-noon Tues-Sun).* **Halės Market** *(Bazilijonų gatvė; open sunrise-noon)* is near the train station. It's a straggly hive of kiosks selling food and clothing.

**Iki** *(Žirmūnų gatvė 2; open daily 8am-10pm)* and **Maxima** *(Mindaugo gatvė 11; open daily 8am-midnight)* are two central supermarkets, both totally Western in stock and service.

## ENTERTAINMENT
The tourist office publishes an events list. *Vilnius In Your Pocket* and the *Baltic Times* also publish entertainment listings.

## Bars & Nightclubs
Vilnius' nightlife is a laid-back affair as most places are pub, restaurant and club all rolled into one. Vokiečių gatvė is where the nightlife begins. The road is lined with pubs and some of the best clubs in town are within staggering distance. Come summer, the pretty, recently renovated street is a wash with trendy young things swigging bottled beer and looking gorgeous in the many contemporary bars that spring up down the central grassed area.

**Prie Parlamento** (☎ 249 6606; [w] www .prieparlamento.lt; *Gedimino prospektas 46; open until 5am Fri & Sat)* and **The PUB** (☎ 261 8393; [w] www.pub.lt; *Dominikonų gatvė 9; open until 5am Fri & Sat)* are top places; the latter has live bands playing most weekends.

**Bix** *(Etmonų gatvė 6),* formed by the Lithuanian hard-rock band of the same name, has avant-garde, industrial-style decor and remains a favourite among the city's young and fun crowd.

**Užupio Kavinė** (☎ 212 2138; *Užupio gatvė 2; meals 30 Lt; open daily 11am-10pm*) is tucked well away from the Old Town's trampled tourist trail. Its riverside terrace and artsy clientele are unmatched and it serves good food too.

**Gero Viskio Baras** (*Pilies gatvė 28*) has a cramped dance floor, so watch your wallet.

**Parko Kavinė** (☎ 212 0609; *Trakų gatvė 11/2*) has a brilliantly bizarre tree-lined cellar and park benches to swig beer on!

**Twins O'Brien** (☎ 212 0808; *Vokiečių gatvė 8*) does a mean Guinness stew alongside a pint of the black stuff.

**Soho** (*Aušros Vartų gatvė 7*) is a comfy night spot/gallery newly opened by the former owner of the successful British joints.

**Contemporary Art Centre** (*Vokiečių gatvė 2*) has a smoky hide-out bar filled with arty Lithuanian luvvies!

**Mano Kavinė** (☎ 215 300; *Bokš to gatvė 7; meals 20 Lt; open 11am-11pm daily*) is a funky/studenty hang-out. Try pronouncing its cocktail called 'Neprisikashkopustelaujancho punch' after drinking one!

**Gravity** (*Jasinskio gatvė 16; admission 25 Lt; open 10pm-6am Thur-Sat*) has happening DJs, exotic cocktails and a thumping house all night. But forget your smelly combat trousers – dress up as there's a London-style door policy.

Two bars, local DJs, live music, and discos make **Brodvėjus** (*Mėsinių 4; admission 10 Lt*) a must.

**Lithuanian Club** (*Vokiečių gatvė 8; open until 4am daily*) is sweaty stuff as it's rammed to the hilt with funky young things.

**Indigo** (*Trakų gatvė 3/2; women/men 5/10 Lt; open 9am-3am daily, until 5am Fri & Sat*) is a dubiously flashy, Old Town joint touting a retro canteen on the ground floor, dance floor on the 2nd, cocktail bar on the 3rd and a courtyard outside.

**Ministerija** (*Gedimino prospektas 46; open 6pm-3am daily, until 5am Fri*) is a mainstream nightclub in the cellar of Prie Parlamento. It has jazz sessions and student nights.

**Geležinis Vilkas** (*Lukiskių skg 3*) is a bit of an institution here. It boasts a strange combination of the Soviet theme, erotic dancing and a swimming pool!

## Cinemas

The **Lietuva** (☎ 262 3422; *Pylimo gatvė 17; admission 12 Lt*) has the largest screen in Lithuania and there's also **Vingis** multiplex (*Savanorių 7; admission 12 Lt*).

**Akropolis** (☎ 484 848; ⓦ *www.akropolis .lt; Ozo 25*) has five screens at the vast new €10 million multiplex, north of Vilnius. The largest indoor shopping and recreation centre in the Baltics also boasts an ice-rink in its centre, a bowling alley and parking for 1800 cars.

The **Centre Culturel Français** (☎ 312 985, fax 312 987; ⓔ *info@centrefrancais.lt; Didžioji gatvė 1*) hosts a week-long French film festival every autumn.

**The PUB** (☎ 261 8393; ⓦ *www.pub.lt; Dominikonų gatvė 9; open until 5am Fri & Sat*) screens English-language films, Lithuanian basketball matches and Sky Sports on a big screen in its courtyard in summer.

## Classical Music, Opera, Ballet & Theatre

The Lithuania Chamber Orchestra, Kaunas State Choir (Kauno valstybinis choras) and Lithuanian State Symphony Orchestra (Lietuvos valstybinis simfoninis orkestras) all have excellent reputations.

**Opera & Ballet Theatre** (☎ 262 0636; ⓦ *www.opera.lt; Vienuolio gatvė 1*) hosts big concerts. Its resident companies perform a wide range of classical opera and ballet.

**National Philharmonic** (*Nacionalinė filharmonija;* ☎ 262 6802; ⓦ *www.filharmonija .lt; Aušros Vartų gatvė 5; kasa open 11am-7pm daily, closed Mon*) sells tickets inside the kasa.

**Lithuanian Music Academy** (*Lietuvos muzikos akademija;* ☎ 261 0144; *Gedimino prospektas 42*) has performances from mid-June to mid-September, as do **St John's Church** and **St Casimir's Church** in the Old Town, and the university courtyards, while the National Philharmonic breaks for summer. The Vilnius String Quartet performs in the courtyard of Grybas House (see Places to Stay earlier) every Wednesday (free admission).

**Academic Drama Theatre** (*Akademinis dramos teatras;* ☎ 262 9771; ⓦ *www.teatras .lt; Gedimino prospektas 4*) and the **Youth Theatre** (*Jaunimo teatras;* ☎ 616 126; *Arklių gatvė 5*) are the main theatres staging Lithuanian and foreign plays (in Lithuanian).

VILNIUS

## SHOPPING

Most days, Pilies gatvė is transformed into a bustling arts and crafts market. Some traders sell their wares during the week here too; the painters always hang out at the southern end of Pilies.

**Sauluva** (Pilies gatvė 22), in a courtyard, sells *Verbos* (traditional woven dried flowers crafted to celebrate Palm Sunday), as well as wooden toys, amber jewellery, hand-made puppets and glassware.

**Sancta**, opposite the entrance to St Teresa's Church (Aušros Vartų gatvė 12), sells religious relics.

The **Amber Gallery** (☎ 212 1988; Aušros Vartų gatvė 9) has exquisite honey-coloured jewellery.

## GETTING THERE & AWAY

See the introductory Getting There & Away chapter for details on links with countries outside the region.

## Air

The only domestic flight is with Lithuanian Airlines (LAL). The seasonal (mid-May to mid-September), once weekly Vilnius–Palanga flight costs 115/195 Lt for a one way/return.

LAL and Rīga-based Air Baltic fly six times weekly (on Tues, Wed, Thur) to/from Rīga. A one-way ticket costs about 936 Lt, a return ticket about 1061 Lt.

LAL and Estonian Air both have daily flights (except during weekends) to/from Tallinn. A one-way ticket costs around 870 Lt, while a return ticket would be about 1000 Lt.

If you are buying an international air ticket in Vilnius, you should shop around for the cheapest fare. If you are 26 or under, try the Lithuanian Student and Youth Travel (see Information section earlier). Most of the major airlines – including **Estonian Air** (☎ 273 9022; e vilnius@estonian-air.ee), **LAL** (☎ 252 5555; w www.lal.lt), **Finnair** (☎ 233 0810), **SAS** (☎ 239 5500) and also **Lufthansa** (☎ 230 6031) – have an office at the airport. **Air Lithuania** (☎ 213 1322; e avia@iti.lt; Šitrigailos gatvė 26) is in town.

In town West Express, Baltic Clipper and Baltic Travel Service travel agencies can arrange flights and check prices – see Information earlier in this chapter. Or check website w www.airlines.lt.

## Bus

The **bus station** (autobusų stotis; ☎ 216 2977) is south of the Old Town at Sodų gatvė 22, next to the train station. Inside the gleaming ticket hall, tickets can be bought at window Nos 1 to 6, which are open between 5.30am and 5.30pm. Timetables of local and international buses are helpfully displayed on a large board. If you're still confused, head to the information centre (open 6am to 9pm), where English-speaking staff can guide you in the right direction – literally.

**Eurolines** (☎ 215 1377, fax 215 1376; w www.eurolines.lt; open 5.30am-9.30pm Mon-Sat, 5.30am-11am & 2pm-9.30pm Sun) is based inside the main hall. It sells tickets for Eurolines international destinations to Scandinavia, UK, other European countries and Moscow, as well as tickets for other bus companies. You can also buy ferry tickets to Sweden, Germany and Finland.

Out on the platform, the left-hand side is for buses to nearby destinations (including Trakai); pay on board. On the right-hand side you'll find the long-distance buses; you need a ticket unless the bus is in transit, in which case you may have to scrum for a seat when it pulls in. When you buy a ticket at the station, your seat number (vieta) and platform number (aikstele) are marked on the ticket.

The bus station also boasts a branch of Iki supermarket, left luggage, a Vilniaus Bankas ATM and a chemist.

Bus timetables change frequently. For up-to-date information check the website w www.autobusai.lt. Buses to destinations within the Baltics include:

**Druskininkai** 14.50 Lt, two hours, 125km, four direct daily

**Ignalina** 8.70 Lt, three hours, 110km, one daily

**Kaunas** 11.50 Lt, two hours, 100km, about 20 daily

**Klaipėda** 38 Lt, five to seven hours, 10km, eight daily

**Lazdijai** 17.50–18.50 Lt, three hours, 150km, three to five daily

**Molėtai** 6.50–7.50 Lt, 1½ hours, 75km, five daily

**Palanga** 41 Lt, six hours, 340km, about nine daily

**Panevėžys** 14–16 Lt, 2¼ hours, 186km, about 12 daily

**Rīga** 40 Lt, six hours, 290km, two daily

**Šiauliai** 23–27 Lt, 4½ hours, 220km, 12 daily

**Tallinn** 90 Lt, 12 hours, 600km, two daily

**Trakai** 3 Lt, 45 minutes, 28km, about 30 daily

## Getting the Last Laugh

When independence was won in 1991, the Balts set about destroying the painful reminders of their Soviet past. Streets were renamed, hammer and sickle emblems unscrewed, and the hated Lenins, Stalins and other Red Army monuments axed with a vengeance and hurled on the scrap heap of history.

Today, the Soviet era is the source of derision as one big uncomfortable joke. Lithuanian people flock in their thousands to the Soviet sculpture theme park at Grūtas to have their photographs taken with the once-formidable Big Brother statues of Lenin and Stalin.

Accusations of cashing in on Lithuania's dark history have been largely ignored by the park, and other ventures such as nightclub *Geležinis Vilkas*, where Machine Gun Anna struts her stuff in front of a predominantly local crowd. Vodka is downed from Soviet canteen mugs, black-bread sandwiches are served by waitresses in yet more Soviet military attire, and there's a model MiG fighter plane on the dance floor.

Then there is Frank Zappa. The statue of the American rock-and-legend, said to be the first of its kind in the world, was created by a Lithuanian sculptor prized for his Soviet realist statues. Unlike the stony-faced Soviet times though, even the authorities seem to have a sense of humour these days. At the inauguration ceremony in 1995 of the statue dedicated to a man famed for his anti-establishment songs, the Vilnius Municipality sent along the local police orchestra to play. It seems the Baltic people might be getting the last laugh after all.

## Train

The **train station** (*Geležinkelio stotis;* ☎ 233 0087, 233 0086; *Geležinkelio 16*) is next to the bus station.

Tickets for domestic trains are sold in the domestic ticket hall, to the left as you face the main station building. Tickets for international destinations are sold in the international ticket hall, to the right of the building; window No 28 is for tickets to Western Europe while the **informacija window** (*No 22; open daily 6am-midnight*) doles out information (but only in Lithuanian or Russian) and sells train schedules (*Vilniaus stoties keleivinių traukinių tvarkar-astis*).

Buying your return-journey ticket in advance is particularly recommended if, for example, you are travelling to St Petersburg (where you still have to queue for hours at a ticket booth reserved specially for foreigners). International train tickets are sold in town at Lithuanian Student & Youth Travel and West Express (see Information earlier).

There is no rail link between Vilnius and Tallinn. One train runs daily from Vilnius to Rīga (46 Lt, eight hours, 300km), one train runs every other day to Sestokai (three hours, 198km, Warsaw-bound train) and there are between one and three trains daily to Moscow (14 hours, 944km). Website W www.litrail.lt has details of all the constantly changing services. The other direct daily services from Vilnius within the Baltics include the following.

**Ignalina** 9.50 Lt, two hours, 110km, seven trains (one terminating at St Petersburg)
**Kaunas** 9.80 Lt, 1¼–2 hours, 100km, 13 to 16 trains
**Klaipėda** 25.40 Lt, five hours, 350km, three trains
**Šiauliai** 24.10 Lt, 4½ hours, 200km, five to eight trains
**Trakai** 2.80 Lt, 40 minutes, 28km, seven trains

## Car & Motorcycle

Numerous 24-hour petrol stations run by the Western oil companies Neste, Shell, Statoil and Texaco selling Western-grade fuel, including unleaded and diesel, are dotted at strategic points all over the city and across the country. In town, try **Statoil** (*Gostauto gatvė 13 & Geležinio vilko 2a*).

Most Western car manufacturers are represented in Vilnius and sport showrooms and repair services.

If you hire a car and intend to cross the border in a Lithuanian-registered car, different insurance rules apply and must be checked with the hire company. Anyone crossing into Lithuania must buy insurance at the border (up to 94.7 Lt), as Lithuania is not part of the International Transport Insurance System. Car rental companies in Vilnius include:

**Avis** (☎ 230 6820, fax 230 6821, e avis@avis.lt) Dariaus ir Girėno gatvė 32a
Branch: (☎/fax 232 9316) Vilnius airport
**Budget** (☎ 230 6708, fax 230 6709, e budget@budget.lt) Rodūnios Kelias 2

Europcar (☎ 212 0207, 212 2739, fax 212 0439,
  🅔 city@europcar.lt) Stuokos-Gucevičiaus 9-1
  Branch: (☎/fax 216 3442) Vilnius airport
Hertz (☎ 272 6940, fax 272 6940, 🅔 hertz@
  hertz.lt) Kalvarijų gatvė14
  Branch: (☎/fax 232 9301) Vilnius airport
Litinterp (☎ 212 3850; 🅔 vilnius@litinterp.lt)
  Bernardinų gatvė 7-2
Rimas Rent a Car (☎/fax 277 6213, 8-698 21 662,
  🅔 rimas.cars@is.lt)
  Charismatic Rimas rents cheap self-drive cars
  or you can hire a car with an English-speaking
  driver.
Old Town Hostel (☎ 262 5357, 🅔 oldtown
  hostels@delfi.lt) Aušros Vartų gatvė 20/15
  Old Town Hostel has a Saab for 80-100 Lt a day.

## GETTING AROUND
## To/From the Airport
**Vilnius airport** *(oro uostas;* ☎ *230 6666;*
🅦 *www.vilnius-airport.lt; Rodūnė skelias 2,
Kirtimai)* is about 5km south of the centre, off
Dariaus ir Girėno gatvė. Bus No 1 runs between the airport and train station; bus No 2
runs between the airport and the northwestern suburb of Seskinė via the Žaliasis bridge
across the Neris down to Lukiskių aikštė.

A taxi from the airport to the city centre
should cost you no more than 15 Lt.

### Bus, Trolleybus & Minibus
Public transport dinosaurs in the shape of
ancient buses rumble through Vilnius alongside their slightly better sisters, the trolleybuses. To ride one is a bargain fare of 0.80
Lt (if bought from one of the many news
kiosks dotted about town, 1 Lt when bought
from the driver). A monthly pass costs 35 Lt
and most routes run from about 5.30am or
6am to around midnight. Unpunched tickets
warrant a 20 Lt on-the-spot fine.

Minibuses shadow most bus and trolleybus routes, are quicker and pick up/drop off
passengers anywhere en route (not just at
official bus stops); expect to pay about 2 Lt
to the driver after boarding. Their route and
number are displayed on the front and you
just flag them down.

Check 🅦 www.vilniustransport.lt for up-
to-date details in English, Lithuanian and
Russian.

### Taxi
Taxis officially charge between 1 Lt and
1.30 Lt per kilometre. Cars with meters are
the most efficient and offer the least chance

## On Their Bikes

Lithuanians are not known for their love of
cycling. But one scheme tried to put pay to
lethargy across the capital. The brainchild of
wacky Vilnius mayor Artūras Zuokas was to
give the city 400 orange bikes for people to
use – then put back. That was the idea anyway. At the end of the first day of the exper-
iment in summer 2001 in supposedly 'crime-
free' Vilnius, the police rounded up 38 of
them, with only one of them intact enough to
ride again. Entrepreneurs were openly selling
them or repainting them. Miles of bicycle
tracks were painted on Vilnius streets and the
mayor was so determined people would use
them that bikes can now be rented for a symbolic fee of 1 Lt a day from the main Tourist
Information Centre on Vilniaus gatvė. To see
new – and crazier – ideas brewing you can
watch the mayor at work on the webcam he
set up in his office, at 🅦 www.vilnius.lt.

of you getting ripped off. A five-minute journey across town should cost no more than 10
Lt and it's worth bartering before you set off.

Taxi ranks are numerous. These include:
outside the train station; in front of the old
Town Hall on Didžioji gatvė; in front of the
Contemporary Art Centre on Vokiečių gatvė;
and outside the Radisson SAS Astorija hotel.

The cheapest type of taxis are those you
book by telephone (☎ 215 0505, 261 6161,
277 7777).

# Around Vilnius

## PANERIAI
Lithuania's brutal and tragic history is
starkly portrayed at this site of Jewish mass
murder. The WWII Nazi death camp of
Paneriai is 10km southwest of central Vilnius. Over 100,000 people were murdered
in this forest between July 1941 and July
1944; some 70,000 of them were Jews from
Vilnius and its surrounds. About half the
city's Jewish population – about 35,000
people – had already been massacred here
by the end of the first three months of the
German occupation (June to September
1941) at the hands of Einsatzkommando 9,
an SS killing unit of elite Nazi troops.

VILNIUS

Lithuanian accomplices are accused of doing at least as much of the killing as their German overseers.

The forest entrance – now more of a wooded site – is marked by a memorial, the **Panerių memorialas**. The text in Russian, dating from the Soviet period, remembers the 100,000 'Soviet citizens' killed here. The memorial plaques in Lithuanian and Hebrew – erected later – honour the 70,000 Jewish victims.

A path leads down to the small but shocking **Paneriai Museum** (*Panerių muziejus;* ☎ 264 1847, 260 2001; Agrastų gatvė 15; open 11am-6pm Wed-Sat). There are two monuments here – one Jewish (marked with the Star of David), the other one Soviet (an obelisk topped with a Soviet star). From here there are paths leading to a number of grassed-over pits among the trees where, from December 1943, the Nazis lined up some 300 to 4000 victims at a time and methodically shot them in the back of the head. After the bodies fell, they were covered with sand to await the next layer of bodies. The Nazis later burnt the exhumed corpses of their victims to hide the evidence of their crimes. One of the deeper pits, according to its sign, was where they kept those who were forced to dig up the corpses and pulverise the bones.

### Getting There & Away
There are about 20 suburban trains daily (some terminating in Trakai or Kaunas) from Vilnius to Paneriai station (0.90 Lt, 20 minutes). From the station, on Agrastų gatvė, it is a 1km walk southwest along Agrastų gatvė straight to the site.

If driving, beware the total lack of signs. Take Savanorių prospektas until the E28 highway.

### TRAKAI
☎ 528 • pop 6111
The old Lithuanian capital, Trakai, with its two lakeside castles, is 28km west of Vilnius. Gediminas may have made it his capital in the 1320s, while Kęstutis certainly made it his base later in the 14th century. The castles were built to fend off the German knights. Today Trakai – the centre of the Trakai National Park spanning 8200 hectares – is a small, quiet town in an attractive country area of lakes and islands. Each July, the Trakai

**TRAKAI**

1 Island Castle;
  Trakai History Museum
2 Boats to Campsite
  & Diving Club
3 Kibininė
4 Karališkas Sodas
5 Prie Pilies
6 Nendre
7 Galvė
8 Kenessa
9 Karaites Ethnographic
  Museum
10 Trys Langai
11 Žalgiris Yacht Club
12 Liepsnelė Guest House
13 Peninsula Castle
14 Trakai Information Centre
15 Church
16 Hotel Trakų
17 Tourist Information Centre
18 Židinys
19 Ancient Castle Hill
20 Bus Station

Lake Galvė

To Trakų Sporto
Bazė (500m), Slėnyje
Hostel & Camping
(4km) & Kaunas (72km)

Lake
Luka

Lake
Totoriškių

Lake
Kretuvo gatvė
Kranto gatvė
Karaimų gatvė
Trakų gatvė
Maironio gatvė
Birutės gatvė
Vytauto gatvė
Mindaugo gatvė
Janonio gatvė

To Birštonas
(76km)

To Train
Station (250m)

To Lakštas Country
Tourism Centre (5km)
& Vilnius (28km)

(8/  16 07  14 57  1857)  (9)  16 00  1745
16 17  1717          16 40      18 25
16 51  16 40          17 10 — 19 10

Festival fills the park with song, dance and music. Most of the town stands on a 2km-long, north-pointing tongue of land between Lake Luka to its east and Lake Totoriskių to its west. A third lake, Lake Galvė, opens out from the northern end of the peninsula. Motorists have to pay a 5 Lt daily entrance fee to the park in summer.

## Information
The **Trakai Information Centre** (☎ 51 934; Vytauto gatvė 69; e trakaitic@is.lt, w www.trakai.lt; open 9am-12pm, 12.45pm-6pm Mon-Fri, 10am-3pm Sat, closed Sun) has friendly staff that give out oodles of information on what's happening locally.

**Tourist Information Centre** (☎/fax 51 934; e trakaitic@is.lt; Vytauto gatvė 69; open 9am-6pm Mon-Fri, 10am-3pm Sat) sells maps and guides of Trakai and books accommodation.

## Peninsula Castle
The ruins of Trakai's peninsula castle, destroyed in the 17th century, are at the north end of town, in a park near the eastern shore. It is thought to have been built from 1362 to 1382 by Grand Duke Vytautas' father, Kęstutis.

## Karaites
The peninsula is dotted with old wooden cottages, many of them built by the Karaites (Karaimai) – a Judaist sect originating in Baghdad which adheres to the Law of Moses. Their descendants were brought to Trakai from the Crimea by Vytautas (around 1400) to serve as bodyguards. Only 12 families (60 Karaites) still live in Trakai and their numbers are dwindling rapidly, prompting fears that Lithuania's smallest ethnic minority could die out. On the western side is the **Karaites Ethnographic Museum** (Karaimų etnografinė paroda; Karaimų gatvė 22; open 10am-6pm Wed-Sun; closed Mon & Tues). A few doors down there's an early-19th-century **Kenessa** (Karaite prayer house; Karaimų gatvė 30).

## Island Castle
The painstakingly restored, red-brick Gothic castle, which stands on an island in Lake Galvė, probably dates from around 1400 when Vytautas found he needed stronger defences than the peninsula castle afforded. It is linked to the shore by footbridges. The

triangular outer courtyard is separated by a moat from the main tower, which has a cavernous central court and a range of galleries, halls and rooms, some housing the **Trakai History Museum** (☎ 58 246; adult/student 8/3.50 Lt; open 10am-7pm daily). The museum charts the history of the castle and its prominence as a major holy site in Lithuania. Concerts and plays are held in the castle in summer.

## Activities
It is possible to take a yacht trip on Lake Galvė or rent your own paddle or rowboat. Bartering with one of the boat-owners by the lake should get a boat for 15 Lt per hour or a yacht for 60 Lt per hour.

The **Žalgiris Yacht Club** (☎ 52 824; Žemaitės gatvė 3) has yachts to rent. For waterbikes, jet skis and speedboats try the **Trakų Sporto Bazė** (Trakai Sports Base; ☎ 55 501, fax 55 387; Karaimų gatvė 73). It also rents out bicycles.

## Places to Stay
**Slėnje Hostel & Camping** (☎/fax 51 387; 2-/4-person tent sites 5/7 Lt, dorm beds 20 Lt, rooms 60-220 Lt) is on the northern side of Lake Galvė off the road to Vievis, 4km out of Trakai. You can pitch your tent by the lake or stay in wooden cabins or the hostel, which has a sauna and diving club, rents boats and fishing equipment and can even arrange trips over Trakai in a hot-air balloon.

**Galvė** (☎ 51 345; Karaimų gatvė 41; beds 24-28 Lt) is a wooden home with a lake view but it's basic with shared showers and toilet.

**Liepsnelė Guest House** (☎ 52 221; Žemaitės gatvė 2; dorm beds 20 Lt; open May-Oct) has four- to six-bed basic dorms and views to die for.

**Trakų Sporto Bazė** (Trakai Sports Base; ☎ 55 501, fax 55 387; Karaimų gatvė 73; singles/doubles/suites 72/120/160 Lt), a former training camp for Lithuania's sporting heroes, has all the facilities, including a gym, sauna, pool and more, but the rooms are worn-out!

**Lakš tas Country Tourism Centre** (☎ 590 43, 8-298 16 533) is a farm which ecotourists with their own set of wheels or a sturdy set of hiking boots should head for, some 5km east of Trakai in Varnikų Forest. You can camp here, stay in a wooden cabin or in the comfort of the main farmhouse. From Trakai, follow the Vilnius road to Lentvaris, then turn left (north) along

Rubežiaus gatvė. The third road on the left leads to the farm.

**Hotel Trakų** (☎ 55 505, fax 55 503; e hotel .traku@takas.lt; Ežero gatvė 7; singles/doubles 220/280 Lt), top of the lot, sits alongside Lake Totoriskių. The rooms are comfortably furnished and have all the mod cons. The hotel has a lovely lakeside restaurant, open to nonguests too, with a summer terrace.

## Places to Eat
Several cafés and restaurants dot the Vytauto gatvė-Karaimų gatvė axis.

Check out **Nendre** (☎ 55 808; Karaimų gatvė 46; meals from 15 Lt; open 10am-11pm daily) for cheap food and crazy interior design with the odd live band thrown in.

**Židinys** (Vytauto gatvė 91; meals 15 Lt; open daily 11am-midnight), between the bus station and the peninsula castle, affords pretty views over Lake Totoriskių from its outside terrace.

**Trys Langai** (☎ 21 445; Karaimų gatvė 20a; meals 20 Lt; open daily 9am-midnight) also has pretty lake panoramas.

**Kibininė** (☎ 55 865; Karaimų gatvė 65; meals 20 Lt; open daily 10am-10pm) serves the piping hot house speciality of traditional Karaite pasties (kibinai) served with a bread-based drink, similar to gira.

**Karališ kas sodas** (Royal Garden; ☎ 55 749; Karaimų gatvė 57; open daily 11am-10pm) is a quaint bar sheltered in the pea-green painted wooded house a few doors away from Kibininė.

**Prie Pilies** (☎ 53 489; Karaimų gatvė 53a; meals from 25 Lt; open 12pm-midnight daily), overlooking Lake Galvė, is buzzing in summer with newlyweds having their photograph taken.

## Getting There & Away
More than 30 buses daily, between 6.55am and 10pm, run from Vilnius bus station to Trakai and back (3 Lt, 45 minutes). There are also seven trains daily between 5am and 8pm (2.80 Lt, 40 minutes).

## CENTRE OF EUROPE
Lithuania is proud of its claim to have the centre of Europe 25km north of Vilnius off the Molėtai highway (it's odd that they marked the spot with a glum-looking rock). Despite claims to the contrary, the French National Geographical Institute pronounced its central position in 1989 at this bleak little spot, lying at a latitude of 54° 54 and longitude of 25° 19. The large round rock is inscribed with the four points of the compass and the words 'Geografinis Europos Centras'. To get to Europe's disputed centre, turn left off the Vilnius–Molėtai road at the sign saying 'Europos Centras'; the rock is on the left side, on a small hill opposite a red cross put up by the Lithuanian temperance movement.

Some 17km from the centre of Europe off the Utena road is the **Centre of Europe Museum** (Europos centro muziejus; ☎ 237 7077; w www.europosparkas.lt; adult/student/child 10/8/6 Lt; open 9am-sunset daily). Leading contemporary sculptors, including Sol Le-Witt and Dennis Oppenheim, show works in wooded parkland (bring mosquito repellent in summer). The sculpture park was the brainchild of Lithuanian sculptor Gintaras Karosas in response to the centre of Europe tag. He is responsible for the TV maze. Every year international workshops are held here, attracting artists from all over the world.

## Getting There & Away
From Vilnius, minibuses marked 'Europos parkas' leave daily from the bus stop on Kalvarijų gatvė for the Centre of Europe Museum or take trolleybus No 10 to the Žalgirio stop or bus No 36 to the end of the line. By car, head north along Kalvarijų gatvė until you reach the Santasriskių roundabout, then bear right towards Žalieji ežerai, following the signs for 'Europos parkas'.

## KERNAVĖ
Kernavė, 35km northwest of Vilnius, is thought to have been the site of the 1253 coronation of Mindaugas, who united Lithuania for the first time. There are four old castle mounds in rural surroundings, and archaeologists have uncovered part of a medieval town nearby – 196.2 hectares of which is protected by an **Archaeological and Historical Reservation** (Archeologijos ir istorijos rezervatas), dubbed the 'Pompeii of Lithuania'. There is also a reservation **museum** (☎ 382-47 385, fax 47 391; e kernave.muziejus@is.lt; Kerniaus gatvė 4; open 10am-5pm Wed-Sun Apr-Oct; 10am-3pm Wed-Sun Nov-Mar). Kernavė is in the Neris Valley, reached by a road through Dūkstos from Maisiagala on the main road north to Ukmergė.

# Eastern & Southern Lithuania

The deep, magical forests of the eastern and southern corners of Lithuania are a tree-hugger's paradise. Some of the most spectacular scenery in the Baltic region is found in these wildernesses with a lake district which extends into Belarus and Latvia.

Aukštaitija National Park is Lithuania's oldest – and best-loved – natural wonder and is framed by the 900-sq-km Laboranas-Pabradė Forest. Close-by, the fresh air turns to hot air as nestled beside the natural splendour is possibly the most dangerous nuclear installation in the world; the infamous Ignalina nuclear power station is at the centre of much debate both nationally and internationally.

Dzūkija, in the far south, is the biggest national park, surrounded by the 1500-sq-km Druskininkai-Varėna Forest. Nearby, on the Nemunas River, is the spa resort of Druskininkai and a controversial Soviet sculpture theme park.

## AUKŠTAITIJA NATIONAL PARK
☎ 386 • elevation 150m

In beloved Aukštaitija National Park (Aukš-taitijos nacionalinis parkas; admission 2 Lt) it's clear where Lithuania's love of nature arose. The natural paradise of deep, whispering forests and blue lakes put a spell on this once-Pagan country. Glaciers sculpted the 400-sq-km area, which was given national park status in 1974.

Around 70% of the park comprises pine, spruce and deciduous forests; inhabited by elk, deer and wild boar. The highlight of Aukštaitija (Lithuanian for highlands) is the labyrinth of lakes – 126 in total. Great views can be enjoyed from the hilltops (up to 200m) around the park's deepest lake, Lake Tauragnas (60.5m deep), on the north-eastern outskirts of the park. A short trail leads to the top of 155m **Ledakalnis** (Ice Hill), from where there's a panorama of some six or seven lakes. One of the park's prettiest lakes is Baluosas, which covers 442 hectares and is surrounded by woods on all sides plus it supports seven islands (one of which has its own small lake). The park is home to 194 bird and 60 animal species – including rare white-tailed and golden eagles.

## Highlights

- Ski, canoe, hike or windsurf while watching out for white-tailed and golden eagles in Aukštaitija National Park
- Serenade a loved one with Čiulionis' music in the spa town of Druskininkai and take a cruise to Liskiava
- Sweat out your stresses in Zervynos Hostel's sauna or go mushrooming in the forests of Dzūkija National Park
- Shiver in the shadow of Ignalina nuclear power station and learn what all the fuss is all about in its surreal information centre
- See stars in the night sky from Molėtai Astronomical Observatory
- Shake Lenin's hand and rub shoulders with Lithuania's Soviet past at the world's only sculpture theme park

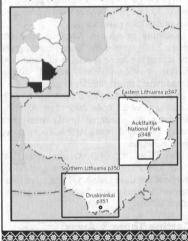

The Trainiskis Wildlife Sanctuary (including Lake Baltys and Lake Gruodiskės) and Ažvinčiai Forest (4603 hectares, home to many 150- to 200-year-old pine trees) are protected zones which can only be visited with park guides. Canoeing and camping along the lakes and connecting rivers are popular activities, as is walking the park's many trails. Mushroom and berry picking is permitted in designated forest areas (see the boxed text 'Mushrooming' later).

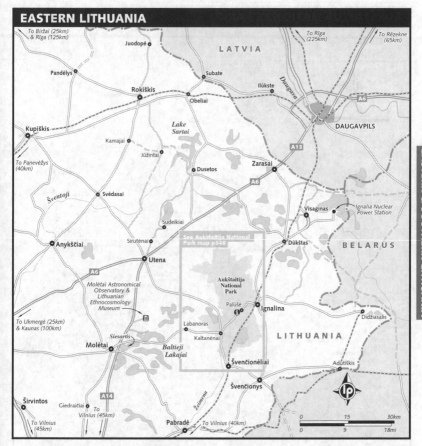

**EASTERN LITHUANIA**

*To Biržai (25km) & Rīga (125km)*
*To Rīga (225km)*
*To Rēzekne (65km)*

LATVIA

Juodopė
Pandėlys
Subate
Ilūkste
Rokiškis
Obeliai
Daugava
Kupiškis
Kamajai
Lake Sartai
DAUGAVPILS
Jūžintai
A13
*To Panevėžys (40km)*
Dusetos
Zarasai
Švedasai
A6
Šventoji
Sudeikiai
Visaginas
*Ignalia Nuclear Power Station*
Anykščiai
Sirutėnai
Dūkštas
BELARUS
Utena
*See Aukštaitija National Park map p348*
A6
Aukštaitija National Park
*Molėtai Astronomical Observatory & Lithuanian Ethnocosmology Museum*
Palūšė
Ignalina
Didžiasalis
*To Ukmergė (25km) & Kaunas (100km)*
Labanoras
Siesartis
Kaltanėnai
LITHUANIA
Molėtai
Baltieji Lakajai
Švenčionėliai
Adutiškis
Širvintos
Giedraičiai
*To Vilnius (45km)*
Švenčionys
*To Vilnius (45km)*
Pabradė
*To Vilnius (40km)*

0   15   30km
0   9   18mi

There are a hundred settlements within the park – some dating back to the 18th century – five of which, **Šuminai**, **Salos II**, **Vaišnoriškės**, **Varniškės II** and **Strazdai** are protected ethnographic centres. **Ginučiai** boasts a 19th-century **watermill**. Northwest of Ginučiai lies the village of Stripeikiai, which is popular with visitors for its **Ancient Bee-keeping Museum**. The park has several ancient fortification mounds *(pili-akalnis)* such as the Taurapilio mound on the southern shore of Lake Tauragnas, and some quaint old wooden architecture, including a fine wooden **church** and **bell tower** (c. 1750) – pictured on the one litas banknote – at Palūšė. Around Lake Lūsiai is a **wooden sculpture trail** depicting Lithuanian folklore.

Detailed maps of the park are available from the **Tourism Centre** (☎/fax 53 135, 52 891; e anp@is.lt), opposite Lake Lūsiai (literally 'Wild Cat Lake') in **Palūšė**, 5km southwest of Ignalina. The centre arranges walking treks and backpacking trips by boat. Park guides cost 30 Lt per hour (Russian language). The centre rents boats/canoes for 5/10 Lt per hour, tents cost 5 Lt to 8 Lt per day and bicycles cost 30 Lt per day. You can windsurf, kayak, ski, play tennis, fish or ride in a horse sled. Camping and hiking gear can also be hired.

Visitors to Aukštaitija must buy a permit from the Tourist Centre (2 Lt). Unaccompanied children under 16, littering, lighting fires and drunken behaviour are all forbidden in the park.

EASTERN & SOUTHERN LITHUANIA

# AUKŠTAITIJA NATIONAL PARK

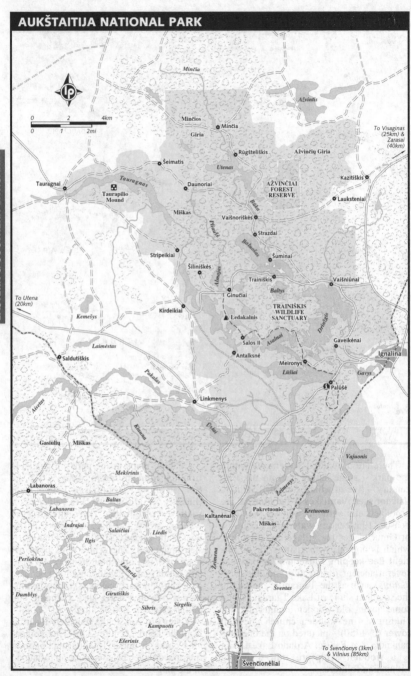

Minčia

To Visaginas
(25km) &
Zarasai
(40km)

Minčios
Minčia
Giria
Rūgšteliškis
Ažvinčių Giria
Šeimatis
Utenas
Kazitiškis
Tauragnai
Tauragnas
Daunoriai
AŽVINČIAI
FOREST
RESERVE
Laukstenai
Taurapilio
Mound
Miškas
Vaišnoriškės
Stripeikiai
Strazdai
Šiliniškės
Šuminai
Trainiškis
Vaišniūnai
Ginučiai
Baltys
Kirdeikiai
Ledakalnis
TRAINIŠKIS
WILDLIFE
SANCTUARY
Asalnai
Gaveikėnai
Salos II
Ignalina
Antalksnė
Meironys
Lūšiai
Gavys
To Utena
(20km)
Kemešys
Laimestas
Saldutiškis
Palūšė
Pakalas
Linkmenys
Ūsiai
Kiauna
Vajuonis
Gasiulių
Miškas
Mekšrinis
Labanoras
Baltas
Žeimenys
Kretuonas
Labanoras
Indrajai
Salaičiai
Liedis
Kaltanėnai
Pakretuonio
Miškas
Ilgis
Perioksna
Laknele
Žeimena
Šventas
Dumblys
Girutiškis
Sibris
Sirgėlis
Kampuotis
Ešerinis
To Švenčionys (3km)
& Vilnius (85km)
Švenčionėliai

## Places to Stay

The centre at Palūšė has rooms starting at 20 Lt and 4-bed dorms for 40 Lt. It runs 16 **camp sites** within the park; pitching a tent costs 7 Lt per person per day (5 Lt per day for stays of more than four days). It also offers summer lodging in **wooden cabins** with shared facilities from 15 Lt per night. 'Comfort' double rooms (60 Lt) with bathroom are also available.

The park offers B&B accommodation, including **Ginučiai watermill** (☎ 36 419; bed in 10-bed dorm 20 Lt, doubles/triples 50/60 Lt), which has rooms with shared kitchen and bathroom.

**Maximovas** (beds 50 Lt), a family home in Ginučiai village, offers B&B in a lakeside, wooden cottage.

**Ignalina Hostel** (fax 52 118; Mokyklos gatvė 4; dorm beds 14 Lt) is a 68-bed hostel run by the Lithuanian Hostels Association. It has shared rooms with communal showers.

**Lithuanian Winter Sports Centre** (☎ 54 193; Sporto gatvė 3; 1-room/2-room apartments 30/60 Lt) has apartments in Ignalina.

The centre operates a ski lift (6 Lt per hour) and has sleds/ski equipment for hire (also 6 Lt per hour). In summer you can hire boats (5 Lt per hour). From the centre of Ignalina, cross the railway line and follow Budrių gatvė for 2km until you reach the *Lietuvos Žemios sportos centras* sign (on the right).

## Getting There & Away

Either hop in the car or jump on one of six daily trains from Vilnius to Ignalina (9.60 Lt, two hours, 110km). Once in Ignalina, either take a taxi (pay about 5 Lt), wait for one of the sporadic buses from the bus station directly opposite or walk!

There is one bus daily from Vilnius (via Molėtai, Panevėžys and Marijampolė), two buses to/from Kaunas (19.50 Lt, four hours) and three to/from Utena.

## VISAGINAS & IGNALINA NUCLEAR POWER STATION
☎ 386 • pop 30,000

Visaginas was built as recently as 1975 for the workers of Ignalina AE (Ignalinos Atominė

### Ignalina

Ignalina looks uncannily like Springfield's nuclear power station in *The Simpsons* and, according to scientists, it's just as safe. If that isn't enough to send a shiver down the spine then knowing it's the same design as the Chernobyl reactor, site of one of the world's worst nuclear disasters in 1986 in the Ukraine, certainly will.

Ignalina, 120km north of Vilnius, has two RMBK reactors which supply 80% of Lithuania's energy. Unlike reactors in the West, these reactors are graphite-cooled and have no containment system. If an accident occurs (like the explosion at Chernobyl), there is an increased chance of the emissions escaping into the atmosphere. One of them is already past its sell-by-date but safety upgrades keep it humming along. Political meltdown is the current worry. Lithuania reluctantly signed an EU agreement to close one reactor by 2004. The EU wants the other shut by 2009 – or Lithuania will not be welcomed into Europe. Already €236 million of European money has been pumped into Ignalina AE to bring safety standards on par with western levels – but Lithuania says it will cost €3.2 billion to close it and dispose of the redundant radioactive material. Now Lithuania insists it will take until 2020 to shut it completely – adding fuel to an already hot fire.

At Ignalina AE's **information centre** (☎/fax 29 911, 29 719; e info@mail.iae.lt; open 8am-5pm daily) a spokesman insisted it was safe and ruled out any repeat of Chernobyl because of design modifications. However, there have been several radioactive 'incidents' since 1990. Despite which the international press reports expressing fears about the safety of the site were dismissed as 'alarmist'.

Despite Europe's fears, Lithuanians strongly oppose shutting the plant. Where else will they find cheap electricity? How will the 5000 workers and the entire town of Visaginas cope with the loss of their livelihoods?

To visit the site, see a video in English, Russian or Lithuanian about Ignalina and play with a scaled-down model of the plant, ring the information centre before turning up. Take a shuttle bus from Visaginas if you have no private transport.

SOUTHERN LITHUANIA

Elektrinė; nuclear power station). The bizarre lakeside frontier was designed for energy specialists seconded from Russia to oversee Ignalina AE's construction (confusingly not in the town of Ignalina itself, which is 50km south of Visaginas).

Once called Sniečkus, after the head of the Lithuanian Communist Party, the Soviet toy town, which is full of identical-looking blocks of flats amid a forest, is circled by a ring road where buses shuttle 5000 shift workers between Visaginas and the plant, 2km east of the town centre.

In the town centre a Geiger counter records the day's radiation level which is not a reassuring sight. Russian is the main language spoken here as workers flooded in from the former USSR.

Staying the night should only be attempted if you've missed the last train home! **Aukštaitija** (*☎/fax 31 346; Veteranų gatvė 9; rooms 250 Lt*) is the only option. Its grim so-called 'luxury' singles and doubles are astonishingly overpriced.

There are six daily trains to/from Vilnius to Visaginas (12.50 Lt), via Ignalina (9.60 Lt), two buses to/from Kaunas (19.50 Lt)

and one bus to Ignalina from Vilnius (8.70 Lt one-way).

## MOLĖTAI
**☎ 383**

The small town of Molėtai, 75km north of Vilnius and 30km west of the Aukštaitija National Park, is the centre of another lake district. There's a handful of **camp sites** on Siesartis and Baltieji Lakajai Lakes, 6km to 9km eastwards.

There are spectacular views of Molėtai's lake-studded landscape and the stars above Lithuania from the **Molėtai Astronomical Observatory** (*☎ 45 444; e mao@astro.lt*) built on Kaldiniai Hill (193m) in the **Labanoro Regional Park**. The observatory boasts the largest telescope (25 tonnes) in northern Europe. Book in advance for evening visits to see the night stars, or for guided tours in English.

Explore hell, heaven and earth at the unique **Lithuanian Ethnocosmology Museum** (*Lietuvos etnokosmologijos muziejus; ☎ 45 424, 45 423*), next door to the observatory. Even the floors in the lift are labelled with planets in this bizarre exhibition exploring man's relationship, spiritual and physical, with the cosmos. For opening hours, times of tours and to book an English-speaking guide it's advisable to ring in advance. If you ask nicely you can book its rooftop telescope (a mini version of the one at the observatory).

To reach the observatory and museum, follow the Molėtai–Utena road for 10km, then turn right at the 'Lietuvos ethnokosmologijos muziejus' sign and follow the dirt track for 4km.

Five buses run daily from Vilnius to Molėtai (6.50-7.50 Lt, 1½ hours). A local bus runs sporadically between the museum and Molėtai.

## UTENA
☎ 389 • pop 36,000

Utena, 34km north of Molėtai, is one of the oldest towns in Lithuania, dating from 1261. It is rightly famous for the Utenos beer brewed here. There's a **tourist office** (☎/fax 54 346; e turizmas@utena.omnitel.net; Utenio aikštė 5; open 9am-5pm daily) in town.

The village of Sirutėnai, 5km north of Utena on the road to Sudeikiai, has the curious **Bells & Arts Museum** (☎ 47 434), set up by a local sculptor in defiance of Krushchev's orders to destroy all wayside shrines, crosses and churches in the 1970s. Today it houses some 300 bells of all shapes and sizes. Every Saturday in summer, Atlanka (as the tower is known locally) is flooded with newlyweds having their photos taken in front of the fairy-tale tower. While you're here look out for the fascinating pile of Soviet propaganda heaped up high outside the sculptor's work shed, opposite the brick tower.

Some 34km northeast of Utena is the village of **Dusetos**, famous for its annual horse race held on the frozen surface of **Lake Sartai**. The race dates back to 1865 and attracts horse enthusiasts, musicians and folk artists from all over the region. It is held on the first Saturday of February.

## DRUSKININKAI
☎ 313 • pop 21,700

Spa town Druskininkai is the oldest – and most famous – health resort in Lithuania. As the first rays of summer appear, expect a flood of people seeking miracle cures for

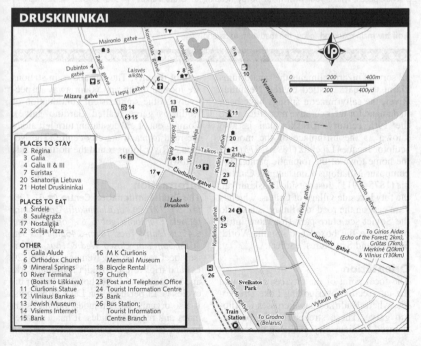

DRUSKININKAI

PLACES TO STAY
2 Regina
3 Galia
4 Galia II & III
7 Euristas
20 Sanatorija Lietuva
21 Hotel Druskininkai

PLACES TO EAT
1 Širdelė
8 Saulėgraža
17 Nostalgija
22 Sicilija Pizza

OTHER
5 Galia Aludė
6 Orthodox Church
9 Mineral Springs
10 River Terminal (Boats to Liškiava)
11 Čiurlionis Statue
12 Vilniaus Bankas
13 Jewish Museum
14 Visiems Internet
15 Bank
16 M K Čiurlionis Memorial Museum
18 Bicycle Rental
19 Church
23 Post and Telephone Office
24 Tourist Information Centre
25 Bank
26 Bus Station; Tourist Information Centre Branch

To Girios Aidas (Echo of the Forest; 2km), Grūtas (7km), Merkinė (20km) & Vilnius (130km)

Lake Druskonis

Sveikatos Park

Train Station   To Grodno (Belarus)

## Stalin World: Scandal and Sculptures

Headline-grabbing Grūtas Park opened amid continued controversy on 1 April 2001. Dubbed Stalin World, this collection of bronze sculptures once stared down Big Brother-style at the oppressed people of Lithuania in parks and squares across the country. Daring entrepreneur, local 'mushroom king' millionaire Viliumas Malinauskas, won the loan of the hated objects from the Ministry of Culture in 1999. The former head of a collective farm, who made his fortune canning mushrooms hence the irreverent nickname, set about turning part of his 200-hectare estate into the exhibition centre for 75 Communist relics. A wooden path runs through the site which was built to resemble a Siberian concentration camp. Among the exhibits are watch towers and barbed wire. An eerie Russian radio plays in the background and a single 'prison train' carriage inside which Jews were herded for deportation to Siberia stands at the entrance.

Then there are the Lenins and Stalins and other Communist heroes which were once a reminder of Soviet ideology. Best known, is the Lenin, which stood until 1955 on Lukiškių aikštė, outside the KGB headquarters. The decapitated statue of Lenin and Kapsukas, founder of the Lithuanian Communist Party, was the handiwork of sculptor Konstantinas Bogdanas who later created the tribute to Frank Zappa.

They look harmless enough, indeed they are used as backdrops for trendy wedding photographs, but their resurrection created mixed reactions, understandable in a country which lost a third of its people during the Soviet occupation. The park with its ice-cream stall, playground littered with canons, mini zoo for children and restaurant has been branded a diabolical version of Disney. Memories of firing squads and whole villages massacred provoked accusations of trivialising the horrors. But Viliumas Malinauskas, whose father spent 10 years in Siberian camps, said: 'This is a place reflecting the painful past of our nation which brought pain, torture and loss. One cannot forget or cross out history – whatever it is'.

Lithuania may be coming to terms with the venture. It attracted 100,000 visitors in its first official year open and 5000 people attended the park's anniversary party, held on 1 April 2002, fittingly, the national Day of Liars. An actor dressed as Lenin strolled around the park before making a Communist-style speech. Make your own mind up by heading to **Grūto Parkas** (☎ 313-55 511; e hesona@ druskininkai.omnitel.net; adult/child 5/2 Lt; open 9am-sunset daily). Call in advance for an English-speaking guide. Grūtas is 7km east of Druskininkai; entering the village from the south, turn left (west) off the main road and follow the road 1km to its end.

all sorts of bizarre ailments the sanatoriums claim to treat. Nestled on the Nemunus River, the salty mineral springs have been in demand for their curative properties since the 19th century. Druskininkai is also known as the birthplace of the modern sculptor Jacques Lipchitz (1891–1973), and the home town of the romantic painter and composer Mikalojus Konstantinas Čiurlionis (1875–1911). Just outside Druskininkai, the tiny lakeside village of Grūtas, which is 7km east on the road to Vilnius, is home to the Soviet sculpture park (for more information see the boxed text 'Stalin World: Scandal and Sculptures' earlier).

### Orientation

The focal point of the city centres around the intersection overlooking Lake Druskonis, where Kudirkos gatvė crosses Čiurlionio gatvė. These streets and the pedestrianised Vilniaus alėja make up the central area of the city. The bus and train stations are located 450m and 600m away respectively on the southeastern continuation of Kudirkos gatvė (called Gardino gatvė). Coming out of either station, turn left along the road to reach the city centre. The Nemunas River loops round the northern side of town.

### Information

The **Tourist Information Centre** (☎ 52 198, fax 51 777; e druskininkutib@post.omni tel.net; Čiurlionio gatvė 65; open 10am-6.45pm Mon & Tues, 10am-6.45pm Fri & Sat, 10am-5pm Sun; closed Wed & Thur) organises boat tours of the Nemunas River (20 Lt) and trips to the Dzūkija National Park, and rents boats (5 Lt per hour) and water bicycles (7 Lt per hour) on Lake Druskonis. It also organises accommodation, and sells maps and regional guides. It has a smaller **branch** (☎ 52 984; Gardino gatvė 1; open

Kaunas Castle (Kauno pilies), Kaunas

Hill of Crosses, Šiauliai

Fishing cottage, Nida

Lithuanian architecture, Palanga

Colourful carving, Juodkrantė

Wooden weathervanes, Nida

Palanga seaside resort

## Creations of Čiurlionis

The prolific work of Lithuania's finest painter and musician is enough to bring out the culture vulture in everyone. Born in Varena (1875–1911), he spent his childhood in Druskininkai. Among his achievements, he wrote Lithuania's first symphony *In the Forest*, created piano pieces and conducted and composed string quartet pieces. Oh yes, and he also put paint to canvas and produced romantic masterpieces, theatre backdrops and some exquisite stained glass. He organised one of Lithuania's first art exhibitions in 1907. But as with many creative geniuses he succumbed to the depression which dogged him throughout his life. He died of pneumonia at the age of 35 – after achieving in this short span what many could not have accomplished in an entire lifetime.

*8.30am-12.30pm & 1.15pm-5.15pm Mon-Fri)* at the bus station.

You can change money at a number of banks in the city centre – at Kudirkos gatvė 33, Vilniaus gatvė 16 or at Čiurlionio gatvė 4a where there's also **Visiems Internet** place. There's also a **post and telephone office** *(Kudirkos gatvė 39)* in town.

### Things to See & Do
A **statue** of Čiurlionis stands at the northern end of Kudirkos gatvė. Lithuania's most talented painter and musician lived most of his childhood 400m west of it, in what is now the **MK Čiurlionis Memorial Museum** *(☎ 52 755; Čiurlionio gatvė 41; adult/student 2/1 Lt; open noon-6pm Tues-Sun)*. Mikalojus Konstantinas Čiurlionis' contribution to national culture cannot be underestimated (see the boxed text 'Creations of Čiurlionis'). Piano concerts are held here in summer and the Days of MK Čiurlionis festival takes place in September.

The **Jewish Museum** *(☎ 56 077; Sv Jokūbo gatvė 17; open noon-5pm Tues-Thur)* is a branch of the Lithuanian State Jewish Museum in Vilnius housing exhibitions in commemoration of the Druskininkai-born sculptor Jacques Lipchitz. Prior to WWII, one third of Druskininkai's residents were Jewish.

**Girios Aidas** (Echo of the Forest), 2km eastwards at Čiurlionio gatvė 102, was built

to give the impression of floating, by using a wooden house supported by a single pedestal. It contains the **forest museum** *(open noon-6pm Tues-Sun)* which is a living nature exhibition.

### Places to Stay
You'll find that many prices are slashed during the winter between October and May so it is worth bartering.

**Hotel Druskininkai** *(☎ 52 566, fax 52 217; Kudirkos gatvė 43; singles/doubles US$15/25)* has really gone for the drab, post-Soviet look.

**Euristas** *(☎ 52 254; Vilniaus alėja 22; doubles 80-100 Lt)* has nice Scandinavian-style rooms housed in a green, wooden building off Druskininkai's main pedestrian avenue.

**Sanatorija Lietuva** *(☎ 51 200, fax 55 490; Kudirkos gatvė 45; singles/doubles from 172/304 Lt)* is ranked among the top health resorts in the former USSR. It offers medicinal mud baths and massage.

**Galia** *(☎ 52 809; Maironio gatvė 3; singles/doubles 70/240 Lt)* is an upmarket venture with two sister hotels **Galia II** and **Galia III** *(☎ 55 696; Dubintos gatvė 3 & 4; singles/doubles 120/200 Lt)*, near the Beer Bar.

**Regina** *(☎ 59 060, fax 59 061; e reservation@regina.lt; Kosciuškos gatvė 3; singles/doubles 200/280 Lt)* is the brightest new offering in town.

### Places to Eat
Food options are limited in Druskininkai.

**Sicilija Pizza** *(☎ 51 865; Taikos gatvė 9; meals 15 Lt)* offers 60 varieties for addicts.

Strolling down Vilniaus alėja, you'll find a handful of cafés and bars.

**Saulėgrąža** *(☎ 52 254; Vilniaus alėja 22; meals 20-30 Lt)* stands out as an arty bar with good Lithuanian- and American-style food.

**Širdelė** *(Maironio gatvė 16; meals 20-30 Lt)* is a cosy home-style restaurant tucked inside a yellow wooden house.

**Nostalgija** *(Čiurlionio gatvė 55; meals 15-30 Lt)* has a lovely lakeside terrace and a botanical restaurant serving excellent Lithuanian fodder.

### Getting There & Away
In summer, a steam boats ploughs the Nemunas River between Druskininkai and Liskiava (see Getting There & Away in the Dzūkija National Park section).

There are four direct buses (14.50 Lt, two hours, 125km) daily to/from Vilnius. There are six buses daily via Alytus to/from Kaunas (13.20 Lt, two to three hours); and one each to/from Palanga and Klaipėda (39.50 Lt, via Kaunas), Šiauliai (via Kaunas) and Panevėžys.

For buses to/from Grodno (Gardinas in Lithuanian) in Belarus see the introductory Getting There & Away chapter.

There is no train service to Druskininkai.

## DZŪKIJA NATIONAL PARK
☎ 310

Dzūkija National Park is the perfect place to evict a few gnomes from their mushroom homes. This lush paradise is a popular spot for mushroom picking and berrying, both Lithuanian traditions and trades (see the boxed text 'Mushrooming').

Covering an area of 550 sq km, the park is Lithuania's largest with four-fifths covered by dense pine forest, much of which is protected under the park's 20 different nature reserves. Between Marcinkonys and the Belarus border is the **Čepkeliai Nature Reserve**, protecting Lithuania's biggest marsh (5858 hectares) and wildlife sanctuary containing primeval flora and fauna. A number of villages within the park, including **Zervynos** which is midway between Varėna and Marcinkonys, are ethnographic reserves. **Liskiava**, 10km northeast of Druskininkai, on the left bank of the Nemunas, has remnants of a 14th-century hilltop castle that figures in several Lithuanian folk tales. The village church and former Dominican monastery (1704–20), is famous for its seven rococo-style altars. **Merkinė**, 10km farther down the Nemunas (at its confluence with the Merkys River), also dates back to the 14th century. These villages are a creative seedbed for the traditions of folk carving, weaving and pottery.

The **National Park Headquarters** (☎ 44 466, fax 44 471; e dzukijanp@is.lt; Miškininkų gatvė 61) are in Marcinkonys. The **Tourist Information Centre** (☎ 57 245; Vilniaus gatvė 2, Merkinė; open 8am-5pm Mon-Fri, 8am-3.45pm Sat) provides information on the park's various walking, cycling and water-based trails.

For five years between 1918 and 1923, a small band of 50 armed men declared the **Republic of Perloja** (a small town 10km west of Varėna) and protected the town

from the retreating German Army and the Red Army. It is a source of great pride in the town still today.

Falling just outside the boundaries of the national park, 22km northeast of Marcinkonys and 58km northeast of Druskininkai, is **Varėna**. Founded in the 15th century when Grand Duke Vytautas built a hunting lodge here, it is also the birthplace of MK Čiurlionis. The main road (A4) leading from Varėna to Druskininkai is lined with sculpted wooden 'totem' poles and sculptures, erected in 1975 in commemoration of the 100th anniversary of Čiurlionis' birth.

### Places to Stay

The national park information centres arrange home-stay accommodation in villages around the park and distribute maps marked up with the six camp sites located in the park.

**Zervynos Hostel** (☎ 39 583, 8-287 50826; bunk beds 10 Lt) is affiliated to the Lithuanian Hostels Association. This is a rural idyll. Owner Artūras (speaks no English) has two wooden turn-of-the-20th-century cottages, one with wood-burning stove, the other with no heating. Both have basic bunks and no electricity or washing facilities (bathe in the river and pee in the bushes). Meals are an additional 5 Lt. The traditional sauna burnt down! However, sauna fans can be reassured another has been built and is operational for 50 Lt. Artūras organises mushrooming and berrying expeditions in the surrounding forests, rents out two-person canoes (40 Lt per day) and organises canoeing trips along the Ūla River. If you call in advance, he will meet you at Zervynos train station. By car, Zervynos Hostel is at the end of a 3km-long gravel road, signposted off the main Varėna–Marcinkonys road (take the right fork at the end).

### Getting There & Away

Between May and October a steamboat ploughs its way along the Nemunas between Druskininkai and Liskiava (20 Lt, one hour). The boat departs daily (except Monday) at 2.30pm from Druskininkai Port and returns three hours later. Otherwise there are four or five buses daily between the two places.

There are also a few buses a day from Druskininkai to Merkinė and vice versa. A whole lot more buses – including the four between Druskininkai and Vilnius, and most of

## Mushrooming

Mushrooming is a blooming business in Lithuania, particularly in the heavily forested Varėna region which, come August and September, is carpeted with the little white and yellow buttons. The forests lining the Varėna–Druskininkai highway (A4) and the Zervynos forests – best known for sand dunes, beehive hollows and substantial *grybas* (mushroom) populations – both make good *grybaula* (mushroom hunting grounds).

The crinkle-topped, yellow *chanterelle* and stubby *boletus* are among the edible wild mushroom varieties that are hunted. They are exported to Italy, Germany and other parts of Europe. The less common *baravykas*, with its distinctive brown cap, is a stronger-tasting mushroom that usually ends up stuffed inside a *cepelinai*, or dried and stored away until Christmas Eve when it is served as one of the 12 *kucios* (vegetarian dishes) traditionally eaten on 24 December. Picking and selling mushrooms provides the main source of income in the Varėna region, the going rate is 13 Lt per kilogram.

*Warning: Never venture into the forest to mushroom without a local guide as there are deadly poisonous species.*

those between Druskininkai and Alytus (or Kaunas) – stop at the Merkinė intersection (Merkinės kryžkelė), 2km east of Merkinė town centre.

There are six daily trains to/from Vilnius, stopping at Zervynos (Marcinkonys-bound) taking two hours (8.70 Lt).

## THE SOUTHWEST

The nearest town to the infamous Polish border is **Lazdijai**, 43km northwest of Druskininkai, on the road to Suwałki (Poland). The **Tourist Centre** (☎ 318-51 160; e *ltic@centras .lt; Vilniaus gatvė 1*) makes accommodation bookings, or try **Hotel Žibintas** (☎ 318-51 269; *Nepriklausomybės alėja 5*).

The town of **Šeštokai**, 18km north of Lazdijai, is one end of another Lithuania–Poland border crossing, this time for the Šeštokai–Suwałki railway. The main approach to the Kalvarija–Suwałki border crossing with Poland is through **Marijampolė**, where there's the **Hotel Arvi** (☎ 343-54 581; e *arvim@mari.omnitel.net; Kudirkos gatvė 24; singles/doubles 260/360 Lt*). Make accommodation bookings at the privately-run **Marijampolė Information Centre** (☎ 343-51 109, fax 343-56 825; e *jotva@mari.omnitel .net; Kudirkos gatvė 41*). In Marijampolė there is an **Ethnographic Museum** (☎ 343-93 042; *Vytauto gatvė 31*) and the **Museum of Urban Architecture** (☎ 343-56 288; *Basanavičiaus gatvė 18*) which is a lot of fun.

Shallow Lake Žuvintas, 30km north of Lazdijai and 20km southeast of Marijampolė, and its surrounding marshes covering some 4127 hectares, form part of the **Žuvintas Nature Reserve**. The reserve was established in 1937 and protects an important breeding ground for birds. Bird-watching guides, boats and tours are organised by the Dzūkija National Park TIC or the local **Tourist Information Centre** (☎ 315-35 404, fax 338 565; e *tour.info@alytus.omnitel.net; Rotušės 14a, Alytus*).

### Getting There & Away

Buses run to Marijampolė and Kalvarija from Kaunas, and to Lazdijai from Druskininkai, Kaunas and Vilnius. Four trains run to Šeštokai from Kaunas, via Marijampolė, one from Vilnius (on even days). For details on crossing into Poland see the introductory Getting There & Away chapter.

# Central Lithuania

Three of Lithuania's five largest cities lie in a triangle in the centre of the country – Kaunas, Panevėžys and Šiauliai.

The central Lithuanian region also has one of the country's strangest monuments – the Hill of Crosses, a national pilgrimage site near Šiauliai.

## KAUNAS
☎ 37 • pop 415,800

Kaunas has a reputation as a sprawling urban city and a hotbed of post-Soviet mafia. Think again. This vibrant city, the second largest in Lithuania, is a thriving cultural and industrial centre with a beautiful Old Town.

Legend has it that Kaunas, which lies 100km west of Vilnius at the confluence of the Nemunas and Neris Rivers, was founded by the son of two tragic young lovers. Beautiful maiden Milda let the Holy Eternal Flame go out while caring for her lover Daugerutis. They were sentenced to death by vengeful gods, thus they fled to a cave and gave birth to Kaunas.

Archaeologists insist the city dates from the 13th century and until the 15th century was in the frontline against the Teutonic Order on Lithuania's western frontier. The Order was defeated by the Lithuanian/Polish alliance at Grünwald, in 1410.

Kaunas became a successful river trading town in the 15th and 16th centuries. German merchants were influential here, and there was a Hanseatic League office. Its strategic position is the main reason it was reduced to ashes 13 times before WWII – when it once again received a battering. Today, it is still a river port with a sizable student population, some fine architecture and plenty of museums.

## Orientation

Kaunas' historic heart is the square, Rotušės aikštė, sitting between the Nemunas and Neris Rivers. Pedestrianised Vilniaus gatvė runs 900m east from Rotušės aikštė to meet the city's main axis, Laisvės alėja, also pedestrianised, which heads 2km east.

The life of modern Kaunas revolves around the streets of Laisvės alėja and Donelaičio gatvė, where most shops, galleries, museums, places to eat and the main

## Highlights

- Stroll Kaunas' Old Town streets, trek up Laisvės alėja to St Michael the Archangel Church and see what made the city blush
- Donate a devil to Kaunas' diabolical Devil Museum
- Ride a piece of mobile history on one of Europe's few remaining funiculars
- Pay tribute to Jews massacred at the Ninth Fort Nazi death camp
- Pretend you're on an 18th-century Lithuanian farmstead at Rumšiškės
- Plant your own cross amid thousands of others at the Hill of Crosses near Šiauliai
- Rediscover your inner child at the Panevėžys Puppet Theatre

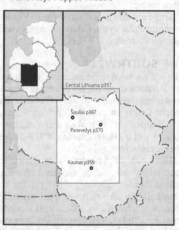

hotels are located. The bus and train stations are 900m and 1.25km, respectively, south of the eastern end of Laisvės alėja, down Vytauto prospektas.

**Maps** Jāņa sēta publishes the *Kaunas City Plan* (1:25,000), sold in most bookshops. A pocket-sized version of the same map is published in the combined Kaunas/Klaipeda *In Your Pocket*, an annual guide available from most hotels, art galleries and news kiosks for 8 Lt.

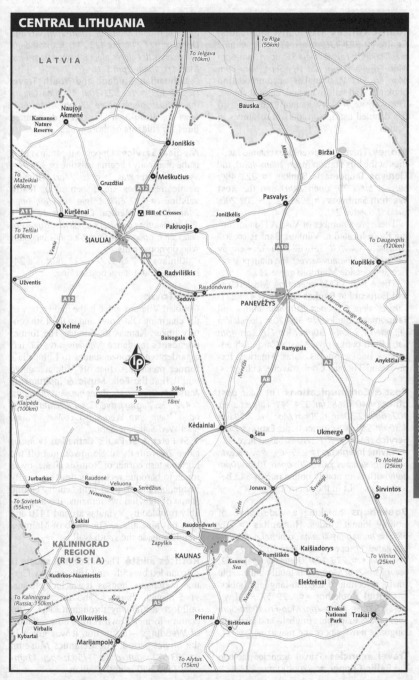

## Information

**Tourist Offices** The Tourist Information Centre (☎ 323 436, ☎/fax 423 678; e turiz mas@takas.lt; Laisvės alėja 36; open 9am-6pm Mon-Fri, 9am-3pm Sat Apr-Sept; 9am-6pm Mon-Fri Oct-Mar) makes accommodation bookings, and sells maps and regional guides. The website w www.kaunas.lt (in English) has detailed listings on tourism resources in Kaunas.

**Money** There are currency exchange facilities at the **bus station** (open 10am-4pm), the **Lietuvos Taupomasis Bankas** (☎ 322 460; Laisvės alėja 79; open 24hr) and the **Best Western Santakos** (☎ 302 702, fax 302 700; Gruodžio gatvė 21).

There are a number of Visa ATMs including those located at **Vilniaus Bankas** (☎ 307 016; w www.vb.lt; Laisvės alėja 82 • cnr Šv Gertrūdos & Vilniaus gatvės), the main post office and outside Maironio gatvė 117.

There are ATMs accepting MasterCard and Eurocard at **Bankas Snoras** (☎ 424 211; Laisvės alėja 60; open 8am-8pm daily) and **Taupomasis Bankas** (☎ 307 203; Donelaičio 76; open 7.30am-7.30pm Mon-Fri, 8am-4pm Sat). Both banks give MasterCard cash advances. Bankas Snoras cashes American Express and Thomas Cook travellers cheques.

**Post & Communications** The main **post office** (☎ 401 368, fax 324 341; Laisvės alėja 102; open 7.30am-6.30pm Mon-Fri, 7.30am-4.30pm Sat) is a Soviet treat. **Express Mail Service** (EMS; ☎ 401 378) is based here.

**Kavinė Internetas** (☎ 225 364; w www.cafe net.ot.lt; Vilniaus gatvė 26; open 10am-10pm daily) offers an hourly online rate of 5 Lt before noon; 7 Lt in the afternoon.

**Bookshops** Stocking a wide range of Lonely Planet guides, **Humanitas** (☎ 209 581; e humanitas@kaunas.omnitel.net; Vilniaus gatvė 11; open 10am-7pm Fri-Sat, 11am-4pm Sun • ☎ 226 124; Donelaičio gatvė 52; open 9am-7pm Mon-Fri) is totally unbeatable for its selection of English-language books.

**Central Bookshop** (☎ 229 572; Laisvės alėja 81; open 10am-7pm Mon-Fri, 10am-5pm Sun) stocks maps plus English- and German-language newspapers and magazines.

**Travel agencies** Travel agencies include the **Baltic Clipper** (☎ 320 300, fax 223 471; e bc@baltic-clipper.lt; Laisvės alėja 61/1; open 9am-6pm Mon-Fri, 10am-2pm Sat) and **Delta** (☎ 424 211, fax 423 211; e info@delta -interservis.lt; Laisvės alėja 88; open 9am-6pm Mon-Fri, 10am-2pm Sat).

**Lithuanian Student and Youth Travel** (☎ 202 303, ☎/fax 322 303; e kaunas@jauni mas.lt; Ožeskienės gatvė 27; open 9am-6pm Mon-Fri, 10am-2pm Sat) offers discounted fares for students or those under 26.

**Medical Services** Opposite the train station is the pharmacy **Lucerna vaistinė** (☎ 324 444; Vytauto prospektas 2; open 24hr). Homeopathic medicines are dispensed at **Teatro vaistinė** (☎ 222 681; Laisvė alėja 89; open 24hr). **Kaunas Medical Centre** (☎ 313 440; e kmc@kaunas.omnitel.net; Savanorių prospektas 284; open 8am-6pm Mon-Fri) has staff who do house calls.

**Klinikos** (☎ 733 377, ☎ 733 360) is a 24-hour medical emergency service.

## Old Town

Cobbled Vilniaus gatvė is the main artery of the charming Old Town and in the 13th century linked Kaunas to Vilnius. The former **president's residence** (Vilniaus gatvė 33) has a garden with bronze statues to Lithuania's former presidents. Just off Vilniaus gatvė you'll find the **Folk Music & Instruments Museum** (Lietuvos tautinės muzikos muziejus; ☎ 422 295; Kurpių gatvė 12; adult/child 2/1 Lt; open 10am-5pm Wed-Sun Oct-May; 11am-6pm Wed-Sun June-Sept).

**St Peter & St Paul's Cathedral** (Vilniaus gatvė 26) with its single tower, just off the northeastern corner of Rotušės aikštė, owes much to baroque reconstruction, especially inside, but the original 15th-century Gothic shape of its windows remains. It was probably founded by Vytautas around 1410 and now has nine altars. The **tomb** of Maironis stands outside the south wall.

**Rotušės aikštė** The old **central square** is surrounded by 15th- and 16th-century German merchants' houses. It was lucky to survive Soviet planners who threatened to bulldoze a highway through it. The 17th-century former Town Hall is now a **Palace of Weddings** – a function it was given in the Soviet period. The **Ceramics Museum** (☎ 203 572; adult/child 11/5 Lt; open 11am-5pm Tues-Sun) is in the cellar.

# KAUNAS

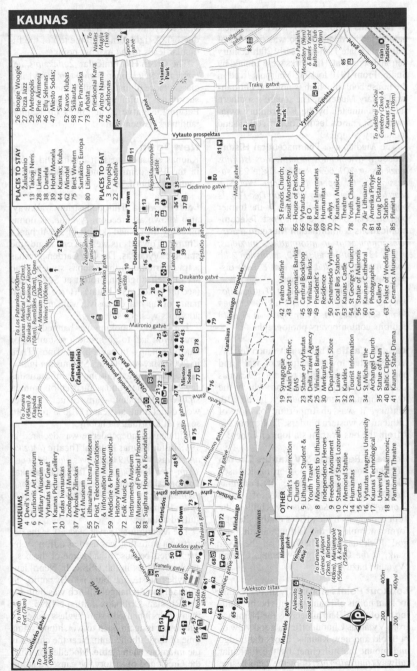

**MUSEUMS**
4 Devil's Museum
6 Čiurlionis Art Museum
7 Military Museum of
    Vytautas the Great
11 Kaunas Picture Gallery
20 Tadas Ivanauskas
    Zoological Museum
37 Mykolas Žilinskas
    Art Museum
55 Lithuanian Literary Museum
57 Post, Telecommunications
    & Information Museum
59 Medicine & Pharmaceutical
    History Museum
72 Folk Music &
    Instruments Museum
82 Museum of Political Prisoners
83 Sugihara House & Foundation

**PLACES TO STAY**
1 Žaliakalnio
13 Takioji Neris
28 Lietuva
38 Daniela
39 Hotel Monela
44 Kaunas; Kuba
62 Minotel
75 Best Western
    Santakos; Europa
80 Litinterp

**PLACES TO EAT**
3 Pompeja
22 Arbatinė
26 Boogie Woogie
27 Pizza Jazz
29 Metropolis
36 Prie Akmenų
46 Elfų Seksmas
47 Miesto Sodas;
    Siena
52 Kavos Klubas
58 Skilautas
71 Pas Prancišką
73 Arbata
    Prieškoniai Kava
74 Antrоi Namai
76 Carlstonas

**OTHER**
2 Christ's Resurrection
    Church
5 Lithuanian Student &
    Youth Travel
8 Monuments to Lithuanian
    Independence Heroes
9 Freedom Monument
10 Statue of Stasis Lozoraitis
12 Memorial Statue
14 Humanitas
15 Fortas
16 Vytautas Magnus University
17 Kaunas Technological
    University
18 Kaunas Philharmonic;
    Pantomime Theatre
19 Synagogue
21 Main Post Office;
    EMS
23 Statue of Vytautas
24 Delta Travel Agency
25 Vilniaus Bankas
30 Merkurijus
    Department Store
31 Laisvė
32 Kankles
33 Tourist Information
    Centre
34 St Michael the
    Archangel Church
35 Statue of Man
40 Baltic Clipper
41 Kaunas State Drama

42 Teatro Vaistinė
43 Lietuvos
    Taupomasis Bankas
45 Central Bookshop
48 Vilniaus Bankas
49 President's
    Residence
50 Senamiesčio Vyninė
51 Local Bus Station
53 Kaunas Castle
54 St George's Church
56 Statue of Maironis
60 Kaunas Cathedral
61 Photographic
    Gallery
63 Palace of Weddings;
    Ceramics Museum
64 St Francis Church;
    Jesuit Monastery
65 House of Perkūnas
66 Vytautas Church
67 B O
68 Kavinė Internetas
69 Humanitas
70 Avilys
77 Kaunas Musical
    Theatre
78 Youth Chamber
    Theatre
79 Air Lithuania
81 Amerika Pirtyje
84 Long Distance Bus
    Station
85 Planeta

**CENTRAL LITHUANIA**

In the southwest corner stands a **statue of Maironis** (1862–1932), a Kaunas priest named Jonas Mačiulis who was the poet of Lithuania's late 19th- and early 20th-century nationalist revival. His works were banned by Stalin. From 1910 to 1932 Maironis lived in the house behind, which is now the **Lithuanian Literary Museum**. The square's southern side is dominated by the 17th-century twin-towered **St Francis Jesuit Church**, college and monastery complex.

The **Medicine & Pharmaceutical History Museum** *(Medicinios ir farmacijos istorijos muziejus;* ☎ *201 569; Rotušės aikštė 28; admission 1 Lt; open 11am-5pm Wed-Sun March-Nov; 10am-4pm Wed-Sun Dec-Feb)* is both gruesome and fascinating. In the former post office stables there is the **Post, Telecommunications & Information Museum** *(Pašto, telekomunikaciju ir informatikos muziejus;* ☎ *321 131; Rotušės aikštė 19; admission 2 Lt; open 10am-6pm Wed, Thur, Sat & Sun)* displaying lots of old telephones.

The **Photographic Gallery** *(Fotografijos galerija;* ☎ *321 789; Rotušės aikštė 1; open 11am-6pm Tues-Fri, 11am-5pm Sat & Sun)* exhibits contemporary photographs.

**Kaunas Castle** There's not much left! A reconstructed tower, sections of wall, and part of a moat are all that remain of Kaunas Castle (Kauno pilies) around which the town originally grew. Founded in the 13th century, it was an important bastion of Lithuania's western borders. Trolleybus No 7 from the bus or train stations ends here.

**House of Perkūnas & Vytautas Church** Off the southeastern corner of Rotušės aikštė, the curious House of Perkūnas *(Perkūno namas;* ☎ *209 259; Aleksoto gatvė 6; open 11am-4pm Sat & Sun)* was built in the 16th century as trade offices on the site of a former temple to the Lithuanian thunder god, Perkūnas. Just beyond, on the river bank, is the Gothic-style Vytautas Church (Vytauto bažnyčia).

**Lookout Points** Apparently there are nine lookout points of Kaunas. Don't bother finding all of them! The hill across the Nemunas from Vytautas Church offers a good view of both old and new Kaunas. Cross the bridge and mount the hill either by the funicular railway *(funikulierius)* or by the steps beside

it. A ride on the funicular costs a bargain 0.50 Lt (you can buy tickets from the conductor). A right turn from the top of the funicular leads to the lookout point.

The **Green Hill funicular** *(Žaliakalnis; admission 0.50 Lt; open 7am-11pm daily)* is a classic piece of history and is one of the few surviving funiculars in Europe. From Putvinskio gatvė 22 it glides up Kaunas landmark, Green Hill.

## New Town

Kaunas expanded east from the Old Town in the 19th century, and the modern city centre was born.

**Laisvės alėja** This pedestrian walkway, also known as Freedom Avenue, is dominated by the domed skyline of **St Michael's Church**. Towards its western end stands the **statue of Vytautas**. The **City Garden** now has a tragic tribute to the Kaunas student who set himself alight in protest at Soviet rule (see the boxed text 'Kaunas Heroes'). Remnants of an old defensive wall and tower adorn its western side.

For 10 years smoking was banned on this street (you had to go inside a restaurant or bar to light up – or pay a 200 Lt fine!) Then in 2000 Mayor Vytautas Sustauskas butted in – and permitted puffing again. Statistics say half of men and a quarter of women smoke in Lithuania – any casual observer would put that at nearer 100% for both sexes. It's virtually a hobby.

Lithuanian independence was declared in 1918 inside **Kaunas Musical Theatre** *(Muzikinis teatras;* ☎ *200 933; Laisvės alėja 91; open 10am-6pm Tues-Sun)*. The **Tadas Ivanauskas Zoological Museum** *(Tado Ivanausko zoologijos muziejus;* ☎/fax *229 675; Laisvės alėja 106; open 11am-6pm Tues-Sun)* exhibits 13,000 stuffed animals.

The **Merkurijus** *(Laisvės alėja 60)* is the department store that was used as a film set by the Soviets because it had some of the best-stocked shelves in the USSR. In Nepriklausomybės aikštė, the blue neo-Byzantine **St Michael the Archangel Church** was built for the Russian Orthodox faith in 1895. For many years it housed a stained glass museum, but now it is again open to worshippers, this time of the Catholic faith. Near the church is the infamous **Man statue**. Modelled on Nike the Greek god of victory, he caused a storm

## Kaunas Heroes

Beloved Lithuanian pilots **Steponas Darius** and **Stanislovas Girėnas** grace the 10 Lt banknote. Immortalised by their daring quest for world record glory, they died on 15 July 1933, 7186km short of completing the longest, non-stop transatlantic flight. Two days after setting off from New York, 25,000 people gathered at Kaunas airport for their triumphant return. They never arrived. Their orange plane *Lituanica* crashed in Germany. The wreckage is displayed at Kaunas Military Museum. Fifty thousand people attended their funeral. After being embalmed, then hidden during Soviet occupation, the bodies finally came to rest at Aukštieji Šančiai Cemetery in 1964.

Kaunas-based Japanese diplomat **Chiune Sugihara** saved 12,000 Jewish lives between 1939 and 1940. He issued transit visas to stranded Polish Jews who faced being forced into Soviet citizenship. When the Soviets annexed Lithuania and ordered all consulates be shut he asked for a short extension. Dubbed 'Japan's Schindler', he disobeyed orders for 29 days by signing 300 visas per day, and handed the stamp to a Jewish refugee when he left. The **Sugihara House & Foundation** was opened in 2000 with a small museum in the actual home he lived in. Sugihara, who died in 1986, was honoured in 2001 with cherry trees planted in the Vilnius street bearing his name and also at the former Japanese embassy in Kaunas.

The spirit of resistance was encompassed by the partisan **Forest Brothers** who fought against Soviet occupation. The **Museum of Exiles and Political Prisoners** in Kaunas documents their fight. Led by Jonas Žemaitis-Vytautas (1909–54), 100,000 men went into Lithuania's forests to battle the tyrannical regime. A third were killed, the rest captured and deported. Fighting continued until 1954 when the last partisan was shot. Across Lithuania crosses are placed at battle sites to honour their fight for freedom.

One of the most desperate anti-Soviet actions was the suicide of Kaunas student **Romas Kalanta**. On 14 May 1972 he doused himself in petrol and set fire to himself in protest at tyrannical communist rule. A suicide note was found in his diary. A monument called Field of Sacrifice was unveiled in May 2002 on the spot where he died. The work is by Lithuanian sculptor Robertas Antinis.

of controversy when his glorious pose exposing his manhood was unveiled.

Behind the Man statue is **Mykolas Žilinskas Art Museum** (☎ 222 853; *Nepriklausomybės aikštė 12; open 11am-5pm Tues-Sun*) which boasts the only Rubens in Lithuania. The **Museum of Political Prisoners** (*Rezistencijos ir tremties muziejus;* ☎ 323 179; *Vytauto prospektas 46; open 10am-4pm Thur- Sun*) documents partisan struggles (see the boxed text 'Kaunas Heroes').

**Vienybės aikštė** Unity Square houses the main buildings of Kaunas Technological University (Kauno technologijos universitetas) which has 14,000 students, and the smaller Vytautas Magnus University (Vytauto didžiojo universitetas), refounded in 1989 by an émigré Lithuanian, Lucija Baskaus-kaitė. On the northern side of Donelaičio gatvė are monuments to Lithuanian independence heroes, an eternal flame surrounded by carved crosses and the **Freedom Monument** (Laisvės paminklas). This is dated 16 February 1918, which is the day

Lithuania declared independence. During the Stalin era it was hidden and finally replaced on 16 February 1989.

The **Military Museum of Vytautas the Great** (*Vytauto didžiojo karo muziejus;* ☎ 320 939; *Donelaičio gatvė 64; open 10am-5pm Wed-Sun*) stands on the northern side. This is not just a military museum, it also covers Lithuania's history from prehistoric times to the present day. Of particular interest is the wreckage of the aircraft in which Steponas Darius and Stasys Girėnas died while attempting to fly nonstop from New York to Kaunas in 1933 (see the boxed text 'Kaunas Heroes'). The pair are buried in the **Aukštieji Šančiai Cemetery** (*Asmenos gatvė 1*) and there is a **memorial statue** (*Sporto gatvė*) to them, east of the centre.

In the same building, but with its own entrance at the back, is the **Čiurlionis Art Museum** (*Čiurlionio dailės muziejus;* ☎ 204 446; *Putvinskio gatvė 55; open 11am-5pm Tues-Sun*), Kaunas' leading museum pictured on the 20 Lt banknote. It has extensive collections of the romantic paintings of Mikalojus

Konstantinas Čiurlionis (1875–1911), one of Lithuania's greatest artists and composers, as well as Lithuanian folk art and 16th- to 20th-century European applied art.

There's a **statue** (Donelaičio 60) honouring the exiled Lithuanian politician Stasys Lozoraitis (1924–94) who, despite losing against Algirdas Brazauskas in the 1993 presidential elections, was known as the 'president of hope'. He worked tirelessly in Rome and then Washington as Lithuanian ambassador during the Soviet occupation. He was reburied in Kaunas in June 1999.

The **Devil's Museum** (Velnių muziejus; ☎ 221 587; Putvinskio gatvė 64; open 11am-5pm Tues-Sun) has a bizarre collection of 2000 diabolical devil statuettes collected by landscape artist Antanas Žmuidzinavičius (1876–1966). Note the satanic figures of Hitler and Stalin, formed from tree roots, performing a deadly dance over Lithuania.

**Kaunas Picture Gallery** (☎ 200 520; Donelaičio gatvė 16; open 11am-5pm Tues-Sun) houses a tribute to Jurgis Mačiūnas, the father of the avant-garde movement Fluxus.

## Parks

**Vytautas Park** (Vytauto parkas) occupies the slope up from the end of Laisvės alėja. The Ažuolynas is a lovely park stretching more than 1km farther east from the stadium. South of Vytautas Park is **Ramybės Park**. In 1995, a statue commemorating those who fought for Lithuanian independence (1919–22) was unveiled here. Ramybės Park was home to the Old City Cemetery until the Soviets tore up all the graves, including that of the unknown soldier, in the 1960s. **Panemunės Park** (Panemunės parkas), on the southern side of the river about 1.5km farther east, is mostly pine woods. You can reach it by catching bus No 29, which goes south down Vytauto prospektas.

## Other Attractions

**Ninth Fort, Jewish Ghetto & Synagogue** Lithuania's brutal history was at some of its darkest here. The Ninth Fort (IX Fortas; ☎ 377 750; Žemaičių plentas 73; admission 4 Lt; open 10am-6pm Wed-Mon, 10am-4pm Wed-Sun, Dec-Feb), on Kaunas' northwestern outskirts, was built in the late 19th century to fortify the western frontier of the tsarist empire. In WWII, the Nazis made it a death camp. An estimated 80,000

people, including most of Kaunas' Jewish population, were butchered here. Later it was used as a prison and place of execution by Stalin's henchmen. Monumental sculptures mark the site of the mass grave.

The museum has exhibits on the Nazi horrors against Jews, and also includes material on Soviet atrocities against Lithuanians. Take bus No 35 or 23 from the bus station to the IX Fortas bus stop, 7km out of town, follow the pedestrian underpass for 700m. Alternately, take minibus No 93, 96 or 46 from the centre.

The WWII Jewish ghetto is on the western bank of the Neris, in the area bounded by Jurbarko, Panerių and Demokratų streets. Close to Laisvės alėja is Kaunas' only operational **synagogue** (Ožeskienės gatvė 17). Beside it stands a memorial to some 1600 children who were killed at the Ninth Fort. The remains of two other synagogues can still be seen nearby at Zamenhofo gatvė 7 and 9.

**Sugihara House** East of the centre, Sugihara House & Foundation (☎ 332 881; W www.sugihara-foundation.com; Vaižganto gatvė 30) is a tribute to Japanese consul Chiune Sugihara who saved the lives of countless Jews (see the boxed text 'Kaunas Heroes').

A mini 'hill of crosses' stands further east on Barsausko gatvė.

**Pažaislis Monastery** This fine example of 17th-century baroque architecture is 9km east of the centre, near the shores of the Kaunas Sea (Kauno marios) – the large artificial lake created by damming (for hydro-electricity) the Nemunas on the eastern side of Kaunas. The highlight is the monastery church with its 50m-high cupola and sumptuous Venetian interior, made from pink and black marble brought from Kraków in Poland. It has frescoes on the walls and ceilings. The monastery has had a chequered history; passing from Catholic to Orthodox control, then back to Catholic, before being used as a psychiatric hospital for part of the Soviet era. It has been under restoration since the 1960s.

One of the best times to visit the monastery is during the Pažaislis Music Festival (Pažaislio muzikos festivalis), held here each year in summer. Take trolleybus No 5, 9 or 12 to the terminus on Masiulio gatvė, a few hundred metres before the monastery. Call in advance for year-round, guided tours (☎ 756 485; open 11am-5pm daily, shorter in winter).

## Activities

Adrenalin junkies can fly, glide, parachute or go ballooning at **Darius and Girėnas Airport** (☎ 391 548; Veiverių gatvė 132), 2km from the centre. For information on general activities in Lithuania, see the introductory Facts for the Visitor chapter.

## Special Events

The highlight in Kaunas' social diary is the four-day **jazz festival** (ⓦ www.kaunasjazz.lt) each April. Top toe-tapping musicians from around the world belt out tunes at the largest jazz event in the Baltic region.

For classical fans, the **Pažaislis Music Festival** has concerts in the courtyards and churches of Pažaislis Monastery each year between May and August.

## Places to Stay – Budget & Mid-Range

There are no hostels in Kaunas, which makes budget beds scarce.

**Litinterp** (☎ 228 718, mobile ☎ 8-699 14690, fax 425 120; ⓦ www.lintinterp.lt; Gedimino gatvė 28/7; singles/doubles/triples from 70/120/180 Lt; open 8.30am-5.30pm Mon-Fri, 9am-3pm Sat) comes to the rescue with B&B rooms. It also rents bicycles. Take trolleybus No 7 or 1 from the bus station and get off at the third stop.

Former Soviet hotels are the cheapest places to stay in the centre.

**Hotel Monela** (☎ 221 791, fax 224 480; Laisvės alėja 35; singles/doubles 98/156 Lt) is not as grim as its exterior suggests and it has clean, simple rooms. Breakfast is included in the rates.

**Lietuva** (☎ 205 992; ⓔ metropol@takas.lt, Daukanto gatvė 21; singles/doubles 120/160 Lt) is nearby. The rates here include breakfast.

**Takioji Neris** (☎ 306 100, fax 205 289; ⓔ takneris@takas.lt; Donelaičio gatvė 27; singles/doubles from 180/220 Lt) has renovated rooms and all the mod cons.

Out of town, the Yacht Club's motel **Burės Yacht Baltosios Club** (☎ 370 422; ⓔ jachtklubas@takas.lt; Gimbutienės gatvė 35; rooms 50-180 Lt) has rooms. Take trolleybus No 5 from the bus station to the end of the line then walk the remaining 1.5km to the lakeside.

## Places to Stay – Top End

Kaunas has some good hotels – including the appropriately named **Kaunas** (☎ 750 850, fax 750 851; ⓔ hotel.kaunas@takas.lt; Laisvės alėja 79; doubles/suites from 320/500 Lt). This swanky pillow parlour, dated 1892, boasts two rooms that have glass-walled bathrooms overlooking Laisvės alėja.

**Daniela** (☎ 321 505, fax 321 632; ⓔ daniela@kaunas.omnitel.net; Mickevičiaus gatvė 28; singles/doubles from 320/410 Lt) is a retro-chic hotel owned by basketball hero Arvydas Sabonis.

**Best Western Santakos** (☎ 302 702, fax 302 700; ⓔ office@santaka.lt; Gruodžio gatvė 21; singles/doubles 360/480 Lt), in the Old Town, houses Europa nightclub, popular for the jazz nights held in its cellar.

**Minotel** (☎ 229 981, fax 220 355; ⓔ minotel@kaunas.omnitel.net; Kuzmos gatvė 8) is tucked away in a nice spot in the Old Town.

**Žaliakalnio** (☎ 321 412, fax 733 769; ⓔ reception@greenhillhotel.lt; Savanorių prospektas 66; doubles/suites 300/500 Lt) is the new kid on the hotel block. Located on top of Green Hill, it's the prime place for New Year's Eve celebrations.

**Nakties Magija** (☎ 797 923; Skroblų gatvė 3; singles/doubles from 220/280 Lt) is 1km out of town and has pleasant rooms.

## Places to Eat

Dining in Kaunas is pleasantly affordable in comparison to Vilnius.

**New Town Kuba** (☎ 209 932; Laisvės alėja 79; meals 10-15 Lt; open 9am-midnight daily) is a split-level canteen and bar.

**Miesto Sodas** (☎ 424 424; Laisvės alėja 93; meals 20-30 Lt; open till midnight) is the trendiest spot in town with cool club **Siena** (open till 4am weekends) located down in the basement.

**Elfų Sėlmas** (☎ 201 727; Laisvės alėja 85; meals 20 Lt; open till 4am weekends) serves cheap Lithuanian nosh in its bizarre elfin-themed restaurant by day, by night it's a lively drinking hangout.

**Boogie Woogie** (☎ 422 404; Laisvės alėja 76; meals 25-35 Lt) serves hearty American-style meals.

**Arbatinė** (☎ 323 732; Laisvės alėja 100; meals 15 Lt; open 8.30am-7.30pm Mon-Fri, 10am-6pm Sat) will set Vegan pulses racing with its dairy- and meat-free policy.

**Metropolis** (☎ 209 220; Laisvės alėja 68; meals 25-35 Lt) is the latest addition to Laisvės alėja and serves European and Lithuanian dishes along with posh pizza.

**Pompėja** (☎ 422 055; Putvinskio gatvė 38; meals 25 Lt), set in a fake Italian villa at the foot of the Green Hill (Žaliakalnis) funicular, has flame-grilled meat and fish on lava stones.

**Čarlstonas** (☎ 202 993; Kęstučio gatvė 93; meals 50-100 Lt) does a mean paella and features exotic things such as jellied eels and brains.

**Prie Akmenų** (☎ 323 517; Laisvės alėja 21; open till midnight) serves up cheap pizza and beer deals (10 Lt) overlooking St Michael's Church.

**Pizza Jazz** (Laisves alėja 68; pizza 9-17 Lt) is Kaunas' pioneering fast-food chain.

**Old Town** In a traditional setting, **Pas Pranciska** (☎ 203 875; Zamenhofo gatvė 11; meals 15-25 Lt) serves delicious home-made soups, juicy steaks and roast beef.

**Skiliautas** (Rotušės aikštė 26; meals 20 Lt) is tucked away in a tiny courtyard and is where you can savour local food then drink with local bohemians.

**Kavos Klubas** (Valančiaus gatvė 19) is heaven for coffee lovers with a huge selection of aromatic coffee beans.

**Arbata Prieskoniai Kava** (Vilniaus gatvė 29) is a tea-lover's equivalent to Kavos Klubas.

## Entertainment

Check daily newspaper *Kauno Diena* for listings.

**Pubs & Nightclubs** Student hangout **B O** (Blue Orange; Muitinės gatvė 9; open till 2am weekends, till midnight weekdays) is a laid-back place to go for a beer.

**Fortas** (Donelaičio gatvė 65; open until 5am Fri & Sat, til 2am Sun-Thur) has a heady combination of live Irish jigs, cheap bar food and Guinness.

**Amerika Pirtyje** (Vytauto prospektas 7) is an American-inspired club with DJs spinning Euro-pop until 4am. **Europa** (Gruodžio gatvė 19) is a more refined alternative in the basement of Best Western Santakos.

**Los Patrankos** (Savanorių prospektas 124) has a state-of the-art sound system and space for 1500 clubbers. You can have a beer while bowling at **Straikas** (☎ 409 000; Draugystės gatvė 6a).

**Avilys** (☎ 203 476; Vilniaus gatvė 34; meals 40 Lt upwards; open until 2am weekends) is where you can wash down mussels stewed in beer for 28 Lt or indulge in chocolate beer truffles for 1 Lt each. Avilys also serves up award-winning home-brewed beers.

**Cinemas** Plush new **Planeta** (☎ 338 330; Vytauto prospektas 6) has taken Kaunas into the 21st century with surround sound and top English-language films with Lithuanian subtitles.

**Kanklės** (☎ 229 569; Laisvės alėja 36) and more modern **Laisvė** (☎ 205 203; Laisvės alėja 46) are scruffy joints bang in the middle of Laisvės alėja showing Hollywood blockbusters.

**Classical Music, Opera & Theatre** The main classical concert hall is **Kaunas Philharmonic** (Kauno filharmonija; ☎ 200 478; Sapiegos 5; admission 8-20 Lt; open 2pm-6pm daily).

**Kaunas Musical Theatre** (Muzikinis teatras; ☎ 200 933; Laisvės alėja 91; admission 8-20 Lt; open 10am-6pm Tues-Sun) is where operas are staged at 6pm Monday to Friday and 5pm Saturday and Sunday.

**Kaunas State Drama Theatre** (Akademinis dramos teatras; ☎ 224 064; Laisvės alėja 71) has one of Lithuania's most original companies; it also has a second, smaller **theatre** (Kęstučio gatvė 64).

**Youth Chamber Theatre** (Jaunimo kamerinis teatras; ☎ 228 226; Kęstučio gatvė 74a; open 2pm-6pm Mon-Sat) is known for its alternative theatre.

**Pantomime Theatre** (Pantomimos teatras; ☎ 225 668; Ožeskienės gatvė 12) shows more light-hearted plays.

## Shopping

Souvenirs and antiques can be found in many galleries along quaint Valančiaus gatvė. Laisvė alėja is lined with boutiques and familiar chain stores. On the A1 outside Kaunas, building has started on an enormous shopping mall which will have space for 3500 cars, nightclubs as well as a bowling alley.

## Getting There & Away

Bus and train connections to/from countries outside the Baltics are covered in the introductory Getting There & Away chapter.

**Air** Ten kilometres north of the Old Town in the suburb of Karmėlava is **Kaunas airport** (☎ 399 307; *Savanorių prospektas*). International flights to/from here are operated by **Air Lithuania** (*Aviakompanija Lietuva; fax 228 176;* [W] *www.airlithuania.lt; Kestučio gatvė 69 •* ☎ *541 400; Kaunas airport*). It flies, via Palanga (115/194 Lt, one way/return), to Hamburg, Oslo, Billund and Kristianstad.

**Bus** The long-distance **bus station** (☎ 409 060; *Vytauto prospektas 24*) caters to domestic and international travel. Ticket booths are open 4.30am to 9pm and the **information window** is in the main booking hall. Kautra bus company runs buses throughout Lithuania. Nippy microbuses to/from Vilnius arrive/depart from platform 12. Left luggage is open 7am to 9pm.

International tickets are sold inside the **International Booking Office** (*Tarptautinių autobusu bilietų kasa;* ☎ *322 222; open 7.30am-7pm Mon-Fri, 7.30am-3pm Sat, 7.30am-8pm Sun*). International destinations served by direct bus to/from Kaunas include Amsterdam, Berlin, Bratislava, Brussels, Grodno, Minsk, Paris, St Petersburg, Vienna and Warsaw.

Daily services within the Baltics to/from Kaunas include the following.

**Druskininkai** 13.20 Lt, two to three hours, 130km, six buses via Alytus
**Ignalina** 19.50 Lt, four hours, 200km, two buses
**Klaipėda** 22-28 Lt, 3-3½ hours, 210km, 10 buses
**Lazdijai** 12.80 Lt, two hours, 100km, three buses
**Marijampolė** 7 Lt, 1-1½ hours, 55km, about nine buses
**Palanga** 35 Lt, 3½ hours, 230km, about 11 buses
**Panevėžys** 13.50 Lt, 2 hours, 110km, about 20 buses
**Rīga** 28.80 Lt, 4½-5½ hours, 280km, one bus
**Šiauliai** 17.50 Lt, three hours, 140km, 20 buses
**Tallinn** 100 Lt, 12 hours, 575km, one daily bus
**Vilnius** 11.50 Lt, two hours, 100km, about 20 buses

**Train** Kaunas **train station** (☎ 372 260; *Čiurlionio gatvė 16*) is at the southern end of Vytauto prospektas.

Between 13 and 16 trains make the trip to/from Vilnius daily (9.80 Lt, two hours). There are four daily Kaunas–Sestokai trains and one Vilnius–Sestokai train (once daily on even days), connecting with the Sestokai–Suwałki train into Poland and passes through

Kaunas, as does a daily Moscow train (see the introductory Getting There & Away chapter for more information).

There are two daily trains to/from Klaipėda (23.40 Lt, six hours); one daily to/from Rīga (22 Lt, five hours); and three daily to/from Šiauliai (14.10 Lt, three hours).

**Car & Motorcycle** Cars and bicycles can be rented from **Litinterp** (☎ 228 718, mobile ☎ 8-699 14690, fax 425 120; [W] *www.lintinterp.lt; Gedimino gatvė 28/7*).

**Boat** Sadly the Kaunas–Nida hydrofoil is no longer in existence. Those with sea legs should not despair as there's a summer cruise (May 15 to October 1) along the Nemunas River down to the Open Air Museum at Rumšiškės. The boat leaves **Kaunas Sea Terminal** (Kaunas Marios Prieplauka) at 11am and returns to Kaunas at 4pm. The day trip costs 12 Lt for adults, children under the age of seven go free. To get there take trolleybus No 5 or 9.

## Getting Around
Minibus No 120 links Kaunas airport with Šv Gertrudos gatvė in the centre of town for a 1 Lt ride.

Buses and trolleybuses run from 5am to 11pm. Minibuses run later.

Trolleybus Nos 1, 5 and 7 all go north from the train station along Vytauto prospektas, west along Kęstučio gatvė and Nemuno gatvė, then north on Birstono gatvė. Returning, they head east along Šv Gertrūdos gatvė, Oželkienės gatvė and Donelaičio gatvė, then south down Vytauto prospektas to the train station.

To get a taxi, call ☎ 366 666.

## AROUND KAUNAS
### Rumšiškės
Go back in time at the **Open-Air Museum** (☎ 346-47 392, 47 569; *open 10am-6pm Wed-Sun May-Oct; 10am-6pm Fri, Sat & Sun in winter, must be arranged in advance*) in Rumšiškės. Four villages, with 18th- and 19th-century buildings, represent the four main regions. Here you will find entire farmsteads, a chapel, a roadside inn and a barn theatre, which hosts folklore performances in summer. In the museum workshop, potters, weavers and joiners demonstrate their crafts. Guided tours in English are available.

**CENTRAL LITHUANIA**

Rumšiškės is 20km east of Kaunas, about 2km off the Vilnius road. To get here take a Vilnius-bound bus from Kaunas, and get off at the Rumšiškės stop – a 2km walk to the museum.

## Birstonas

Some 40km south of Kaunas on the Nemunas River is the small spa town of Birstonas. It hosts a three-day jazz festival in spring during even-numbered years, which brings out Lithuania's top jazz musicians and many of their fans.

## ŠIAULIAI

☎ 41 • pop 147,000 • elevation 151m

Lithuania's fourth largest city tends to be overshadowed by the infamous Hill of Crosses 10km north. But despite this – and plague, fires and battles – Šiauliai has survived its troubled history to become an eccentric, thriving city 140km north of Kaunas – and the main centre of the northwestern region of Žemaitija – known as Samogitia.

Šiauliai was founded in 1236 at the site of a great battle. The Knights of the Sword, returning north from a raid, were defeated at the Battle of Saulė by the Samogitians. Together with the Teutonic knights they finally occupied Samogitia in 1398, but a rebellion in 1408 led to a joint Lithuanian and Polish campaign against the knights and they were decisively defeated at Grünwald in 1410.

Šiauliai began to grow in the 16th century but was destroyed by fire in 1872. The town's dwindling economy was given a boost in 1995 when the former Žokniai military airport, abandoned by the Soviet army in 1993, was transformed into a free economic zone.

## Orientation

Today, the centre is small enough to walk round, the main north–south street being Tilžės gatvė, with the bus station towards its southern end and the tall SS Peter & Paul's Church, on Pergalės aikštė, near its northern end, almost 1km away.

The main east–west axis is Vilniaus gatvė, which crosses Tilžės gatvė 300m south of the church and is pedestrianised for over 500m either side. A small clock tower in the little square where the two streets meet is a good orientation point and a favourite local meeting place.

## Information

The **Tourist Information Centre** (☎ 523 110, fax 523 111; ⓦ www.siauliai.lt; Vilniaus gatvė 213; open 9am-6pm Mon-Fri, 10am-3pm Sat) sells maps and guides, takes accommodation bookings and arranges excursions to the Hill of Crosses.

Cash advances can be made at **Šiaulių Bankas** (Tilžės gatvė 149). There are Visa ATMs next to the tourist information centre and at **Vilniaus Bankas** (Tilžės gatvė 157). There is an ATM which accepts MasterCard and Eurocard (Bankas Snoras booth) in front of the bus station; in the lobby of the Šiauliai hotel; and outside **Taupomasis Bankas** (Dvaro gatvė 85).

The **post office** is at Aušros alėja 42. **West Express** (☎ 523 333, fax 524 978; Vasario 16-osios gatvė 48) is an agent for Lithuanian Airlines. The **Baltic Travel Service** (☎ 429 502) has a branch inside the Šiauliai hotel.

For Internet access, head to **Tinklas** (☎ 526 503; Auštros alėja 11) which has terminals for 2 Lt per hour and a resident snake.

## Town Centre

**SS Peter & Paul's Church** (Šv Petro ir Povilo bažnyčia), overlooking Pergalės aikštė, was constructed between 1595 and 1625, from the proceeds of the sale of four-year-old bulls donated by local farmers. It has a 75m-tall spire, which is Lithuania's second highest. **St George's Church** (Dubijos gatvė) was built for the local Russian garrison in 1909, but is Catholic today. Another distinctive landmark of the city is the mammoth **sundial** (cnr Salkausko gatvė & Ežero gatvė), topped by a bronze statue of an archer in what has become known as 'Sundial Square'. It was built in 1986 to commemorate the 750th anniversary of the Battle of Saulė. Opposite the central market, a **monument** marks the spot where participants of the 1863 uprising were hung.

Šiauliai has an eccentric collection of museums, including the **Radio & Television Museum** (☎ 524 399; Vilniaus gatvė 174; adult/child 2/1 Lt; open 10am-6pm Tues-Fri, 11am-4pm Sat); a **Bicycle Museum** (☎ 524 395; Vilniaus gatvė 139; adult/child 2/1 Lt; open 10am-6pm Tues-Fri, 11am-4pm Sat); the **Cat Museum** (☎ 523 883; Žuvininkų gatvė 18; adult/child 2/1 Lt; open 11am-5pm Wed-Sun); a **Photography Museum** (☎ 524 396; Vilniaus gatvė 140; adult/child 2/1 Lt; open 10am-6pm Tues-Fri, 11am-4pm Sat);

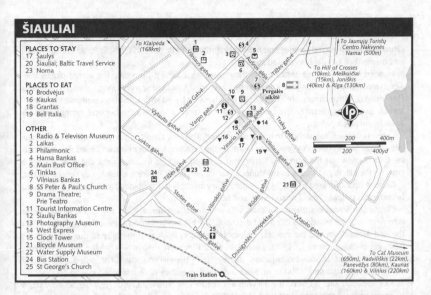

**ŠIAULIAI**

PLACES TO STAY
17  Šaulys
20  Šiauliai; Baltic Travel Service
23  Norna

PLACES TO EAT
10  Brodvėjus
16  Kaukas
18  Grantas
19  Bell Italia

OTHER
1  Radio & Televison Museum
2  Laikas
3  Philarmonic
4  Hansa Bankas
5  Main Post Office
6  Tinklas
7  Vilniaus Bankas
8  SS Peter & Paul's Church
9  Drama Theatre;
   Prie Teatro
11  Tourist Information Centre
12  Šiaulių Bankas
13  Photography Museum
14  West Express
15  Clock Tower
21  Bicycle Museum
22  Water Supply Museum
24  Bus Station
25  St George's Church

and the **Water Supply Museum** (☎ 525 571; Vytauto gatvė 103; adult/child 2/1 Lt; open 8am-5pm Mon-Fri).

## Hill of Crosses
Described as the 'Mecca of Lithuania', the sight of thousands upon thousands of crosses covering this hillock has inspired many pilgrimages. Large and tiny, expensive and cheap, wood and metal, the crosses are devotional, to accompany prayers, or finely carved folk art masterpieces. Others are memorials, tagged with flowers, a photograph or other mementoes in memory of the deceased, and inscribed with a sweet or sacred message.

Traditional *koplytstulpis*, wooden sculptures of a figure topped with a little roof, intersperse the crosses, as do magnificent sculptures of the Sorrowful Christ (Rūpintojėlis). Easter brings the biggest flocks of pilgrims.

Souvenir traders sell crosses in the car park, if you want to add your own.

The Hill of Crosses (Kryžių kalnas) is 10km north of Šiauliai, 2km east off the road to Joniškis and Rīga, in the village of Jurgaičiai.

There are eight buses daily from Šiauliai bus station to Joniškis, and eight to Rīga. Get off at the Domantai stop and walk the 2km track to the hill. Look for the sign 'Kryžių kalnas 2' on the A12. If you want to

head north after visiting the Hill of Crosses, it may be better to wait for a bus on the main road here and not bother going back into Šiauliai (try to check the schedules before leaving Šiauliai). A taxi costs 25 Lt one way.

## Places to Stay
**Jaunųjų Turistų Centro Nakvynės Namai** (☎ 523 992; Rygos gatvė 36; dorm beds 15 Lt) is a hostel that offers beds in shared rooms.

**Šiauliai** (☎ 434 554, fax 438 339; Draugystės prospektas 25; singles/doubles 60/80 Lt) is spectacularly ugly but has great views being 14-storeys high!

**Norna** (☎/fax 429 326; Tilžės gatvė 126) is the gleaming white hotel opposite the bus station.

**Šaulys** (☎ 520 812, fax 520 911; Vasario 16-osios gatvė 40; singles/doubles/triples from 150/200/270 Lt) has a sauna and pool.

## Places to Eat
Šiauliai has some surprisingly good hangouts. **Brodvėjus** (☎ 500 412; Vilniaus gatvė 146; meals 20 Lt) is popular for pizzas upstairs and has a bar open until midnight downstairs.

**Café Kaukas** (Tilžės gatvė 144; snacks 15 Lt) serves cheap eats and **Prie Teatro** (Tilžės gatvė 151) has decadent ice-cream cocktails (4-8 Lt).

**Bell Italia** (☎ 520 866; Vilniaus gatvė 167; meals 20-30 Lt) serves delicious Italian food – 'Viagra Pizza' is guaranteed to fire you up!

CENTRAL LITHUANIA

## Double Cross

Once symbols of sacred fervour and national identity, both Pagan and Catholic; cross crafting is the embodiment of Lithuanian contradiction.

Handed down from master to pupil, the crosses were carved from oak; the sacred pagan tree. They were made as offerings to gods, draped with food, coloured scarves (for a wedding) or aprons (for fertility). Once consecrated by priests, they became linked with Christian ceremonies in unmistakable sacred significance. The crosses, which measure up to 5m, then became symbols of defiance against occupation.

Legend interweaves history as to how it came about. There are almost as many myths as crosses. Some claim it was built in three days and three nights by the bereaved families of warriors killed in a great battle. Others say it was the work of a father who, in a desperate bid to cure his sick daughter, planted a cross on the hill. Pagan traditions tell stories of sacred fires being lit here and tended by celestial virgins.

Crosses first appeared in the 14th century. They multiplied after bloody anti-Tsarist uprisings to become this potent symbol of suffering and hope.

During the Soviet era planting a cross was an arrestable offence – but pilgrims kept coming to commemorate the thousands killed and deported. The hill was bulldozed at least three times. In 1961 the Red Army destroyed the crosses, sealed off the tracks leading to the hill and dug ditches at its base, yet overnight more crosses appeared. In 1972 they were destroyed after the immolation of a student in protest at Soviet occupation. But by 1990, the Hill of Crosses comprised a staggering 40,000 crosses, spanning 4600 sq m. Since independence, they have multiplied maybe 10 times. In 1993 Pope John Paul II graced the hill with a sculpture of a crucified Christ. New crosses now stand to commemorate those who perished in the 2001 Twin Towers attack in New York. The spirit continues, the hill grows and the sound of the crosses rattling in the wind becomes yet more sobering.

The ancient pre-Christian craft was given Unesco status in 2002 as a World Heritage tradition.

**Grantas** (☎ 427 902; Visinskio gatvė 41; meals 40 Lt) is a British pub serving hearty meals in a cosy basement.

## Entertainment

Spend an evening at the **Drama Theatre** (☎ 432 940; Tilžės gatvė 155) or watch an English-language film at **Laikas** (☎ 525 208; Vilniaus gatvė 172).

## Getting There & Away

Šiauliai has quite good bus and train connections with other parts of Lithuania, as well as with Rīga and Tallinn; the Rīga–Simferopol, Vilnius–Rīga and Lviv–Rīga trains pass through Šiauliai.

**Bus** Many daily services leave Šiauliai from the **bus station** (☎ 528 058; Tilžės gatvė 109), including the following.

Kaunas 17.50 Lt, three hours, 140km, 20 buses
Klaipėda 20 Lt, 2½ hours, 155km, six buses
Mažeikiai 9 Lt, 1½ hours, 80km, about 12 buses
Palanga 18 Lt, 2½ hours, 150km, about 10 buses
Panevėžys 9 Lt, 1½ hours, 80km, 12 buses
Rīga 14.50 Lt, 2½-3 hours, 130km, eight buses

Tallinn 8½ hours, 440km, one bus
Vilnius 24-27 Lt, 4½ hours, 220km, 12 buses

**Train** The station (☎ 430 652; Dubijos gatvė 44) has daily services to/from Šiauliai including the following.

Kaunas 14.10 Lt, four hours, three trains
Klaipėda 14.50 Lt, 3¾ hours, six trains
Rīga 2-2½ hours, one to three trains
Vilnius 24.10 Lt, 4½ hours, six trains

## RADVILIŠKIS

☎ 422 • pop 21,000

The grimy railway town of Radviliškis, 22km southeast of Šiauliai, is notable only as the central hub of the rail network.

However, the 55km stretch of road between Radviliškis and Panevėžys has some interesting stops, not least neighbouring **Šeduva**, 10km further southeast. Šeduva is an official 16th-century architectural monument. A windmill marks the entrance to the tiny village, housing **Šeduvos Malūnas** (☎ 56 300; doubles 100 Lt), which is a restaurant that serves good Lithuanian food and has a 10-room hotel attached. Šeduva has a beautiful yellow **Baroque church** and an **Ethnographic Museum** (*Veriskių 7; open 9am-4pm Tues-Fri, 9am-1pm Sat*) in an old tannery.

The **Daugyvenė Cultural History Museum** (☎ *51 747*) is 2km further along the Panevėžys road (A9) in Pakalniškiai village. Neighbouring village Kleboniškiai boasts the **Rural Life Museum** (☎ *63 674; admission 3 Lt; open 9am-6pm Tues-Sun*).

The hotel **Prie Ežero** (☎ *44 430; singles/ doubles 118/140 Lt*) sits by a pretty lake in Raudondvaris.

### Getting There & Away

About 12 buses a day run between Šiauliai and Panevėžys, via Radviliškis. There are buses every half an hour to/from Radviliškis and Šeduva and one a day to/from Vilnius.

There's six to eight daily trains to/from Vilnius (16.40 Lt, 2½ hours), three daily to/from Kaunas (12.50 Lt, three hours) and six daily to/from Klaipėda, via Šiauliai, (15.90 Lt, 2½ hours).

### ANYKŠČIAI
☎ 381 • pop 13,000

Lovely Anykščiai sits on the confluence of the Sventoji and Anyksta Rivers. Fanning out eastwards are 76 lakes, the largest of which – Rubikiai (968 hectares) – is speckled with 16 islands.

This sleepy town is best known for its enormous, record-breaking boulder showcased in pine forest, and for its now defunct narrow-gauge railway (see the boxed text 'End of the Line?').

In town, the neo-Gothic **St Mathew's Church** (1899–1909), with its two 79m-tall, silver capped steeples – the tallest in Lithuania – is also a landmark. According to legend, the devil tried to destroy the church with a boulder that he brought from the depths of hell. But on the morning of his attack, the cock sang earlier than usual, prompting the devil to drop the rock 10km south of Anykščiai in the forest. The **Puntukas Stone** is 5.7m tall, 6.7m wide, 6.9m long and weighs 265 tonnes and has a tribute to pilots Darius and Girėnas carved into it. **Tourist Information** (☎/fax 59 177; e anyksciai.turizmas@is.lt; Gegužes gatvė 1; open 10am-6pm Mon-Fri, 10am-3pm Sat) gives complicated directions to get to it.

**Hotel Puntukas** (☎ *51 345; Baranausko aikštė 8; singles/doubles/triples 40/70/90 Lt*),

---

### End of the Line?

An era of train travel ended in summer 2001 when the narrow-gauge railway chugged its last. It now lies quietly rusting, instead of providing a vital local lifeline for the remote villages linking Anykščiai with Panevėžys (60km west).

The 750mm-wide tracks are all that remain of an extensive narrow-gauge rail network built in the late 1890s as a cargo link to the wide-gauge railways. The first section, operational from 1895, snaked for 125km from Senčionėliai (a major stop on the St Petersburg–Warsaw line) to Pastavy in present-day Belarus. A second section linking Senčionėliai to Panevėžys (144km) opened in 1901. Permission was consequently granted to extend the tracks farther north from Panevėžys to Rīga (Latvia) and farther eastwards into Belarus from Pastavy to Mogilov. During WWI the Germans made great use of the network which fell into decline after WWII.

Groups can hire the train (500 Lt) for a journey and the tourist information office in Panevėžys does one-off organised excursions (10 Lt). But unless cash is found, the line will remain a tourist attraction rather than the twice-daily local link it was intended to be.

---

on the central square behind the bus station, has basic rooms.

### Getting There & Away

The **bus station** (☎ *51 333; Vienuolio gatvė 1*) is opposite the tourist office. Services to/from Anykščiai include Panevėžys (three to eight daily), Vilnius (six daily) and Kaunas (13 daily).

### PANEVĖŽYS
☎ 45 • pop 134,000

Known as the 'Chicago of Lithuania' for crime and mafia dealings, Panevėžys has done some serious work on its image recently. Emerging from post-Soviet industrial collapse, it now boasts a prestigious theatrical tradition, a charming riverbed lake and a thriving art scene.

Panevėžys, Lithuania's fifth largest city, lies 140km north of Vilnius on the Nevėžis River and on the Rīga highway. It was founded in 1503 and it claims to be the most

**CENTRAL LITHUANIA**

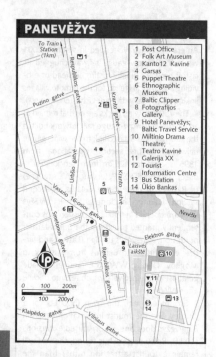

**PANEVĖŽYS**

To Train Station (1km)

1 Post Office
2 Folk Art Museum
3 Kanto12 Kavinė
4 Garsas
5 Puppet Theatre
6 Ethnographic Museum
7 Baltic Clipper
8 Fototgrafijos Gallery
9 Hotel Panevėžys; Baltic Travel Service
10 Miltinio Drama Theatre; Teatro Kavinė
11 Galerija XX
12 Tourist Information Centre
13 Bus Station
14 Ūkio Bankas

Lithuanian (Lithuanians make up 94% of its population). It is still largely a manufacturing base.

## Orientation
You can walk around Panevėžys. At the centre is north–south **Laisvės aikštė**, dissected at its northern end by east–west Elektros gatvė and its southern (and narrower) end by Vilniaus gatvė. Basanavičiaus gatvė runs north to the Rīga road and south to Kaunas and Vilnius. The train station is 2km northwest of the centre, the bus station is a 10-minute walk westwards on Tilžes gatvė.

## Information
The **Tourist Information Centre** (☎ 508 081, fax 508 080; e pantic@takas.lt; Laisvės aikštė; open 10am-6pm Mon-Fri, 9am-2pm Sat) has friendly English-speaking staff who arrange trips on the narrow-gauge railway, book accommodation and sell regional guides.

There's a Vilniaus Bankas ATM at Kranto gatvė 2, and an ATM accepting Master-Card/Eurocard inside the lobby of **Ūkio Bankas** at Laisvė aikštė 15.

There's also a **post office** (☎ 464 445; Respublikos gatvė 6) in town.

**Baltic Clipper** (☎ 468 407; Vasario 16-osios gatvė 19a) and **Baltic Travel Service** (☎ 435 919; Hotel Panevėžys, Laisvės alėja 26) offer flights, bus tickets and tours.

Cultural centre **Garsas** (☎ 468 833; Respublikos gatvė 30) has Internet facilities, a nightclub, an arty bar and a cinema showing English-language movies.

## Things to See
Triangular-shaped pedestrianised **Laisvės aikštė** is a pleasant central tree-lined spot surrounded by bars, cafés and shops. At its northern end lies a **river bed**, with a small bridge and sculptures.

The **Ethnographic Museum** (☎ 461 973; Vasario 16-osios 23; adult/child 2/1 Lt; open 11am-6pm Tues-Sat) is just along the road from the Baltic Clipper.

The **Folk Art Museum** (Kranto gatvė 21; open 11am-5pm Thur-Sun) is housed in the city's oldest building dated 1614.

**Fototgrafijos Gallery** (☎ 467 551; Vasario 16-osios 11; open 11am-7pm Wed-Sat, 11am-6pm Sun) exhibits contemporary photography.

## Places to Stay & Eat
**Hotel Panevėžys** (☎ 501 601, fax 435 117; e info@hotelpanevezys.lt; Laisvės aikštė 26; singles/doubles/suites 120/160/270 Lt) squats at the northern end of the Laisvės aikštė. Its landmark Soviet ugliness is infamous but it's the only hotel in the centre!

### Beer Talk

Northern Lithuania is the home of barley-malt beer. Ale-makers keep to ancient recipes and rituals that are almost 1000 years old. Among the many home-brewed delights are Utenos Beer, Kalnapilis, Ragutis and Gubernija.

You can visit the Panevėžys **Kalnapilis brewery** (☎ 505 280; w www.kalnapilis.lt; Taikos aleja 1; 1hr tour 4 Lt), tours can be arranged through the TIC. The latter can also advise on the annual two-day Biržai Beer Festival (e tic.birzai@post.omnitel.net), a fiesta of beer-keg throwing and general drunken behaviour 65km north of Panevėžys.

**Galerija XX** *(☎ 438 701; Laisvės aikštė 7; meals 10-15Lt)* serves you up huge potato pancakes.

**Teatro Kavinė** *(Laisvės aikštė 5)* is a block northwards at the theatre with meals on the summer terrace for 15 Lt.

**Kanto12 Kavinė** *(☎ 468 983; Kanto gatvė; meals 30 Lt)* serves Lithuanian food.

## Entertainment

**Miltinio Drama Theatre** *(☎ 584 596; Laisvės aikštė 5; admission 8-10 Lt)* is named after its legendary local stage director Juozas Miltinis. Performances are in Lithuanian.

The **puppet theatre** *(☎ 511 236; Respublikos gatvė 30; admission 2-3 Lt)* is the only travelling cart theatre in Lithuania.

## Getting There & Away

From the **bus station** *(☎ 463 325; Savanorių aikštė 5)*, there are buses to/from Vilnius (14-16 Lt, 2¼ hours, about 9 daily), Kaunas (13.50 Lt, two hours, 20 daily), Šiauliai (9 Lt, 1-1½ hours, 12 daily), Rīga via Bauska (17 Lt, four hours, six daily) and Tallinn via Rīga (59 Lt, eight hours, three daily). There are two daily trains to Šiauliai via Radviliškis and no direct route to Vilnius or Kaunas.

# Western Lithuania

The 'Sahara of Lithuania', a stretch of sand dunes sculpted by wind and time called the Curonian Spit (Kuršių Nerija), is the jewel of this short coastline. This anorexic and fragile natural phenomena (it's 97km long and no more than 4km wide) protects the largest inland body of water, the Curonian Lagoon, from the restless Baltic Sea. These tall dunes, wild white beaches and pine forests give the Spit a touch of pure magic, which Unesco recognised as a World Heritage landscape in 2000.

Four traditional fishing villages are clustered on the spit, known collectively as Neringa, while the southern half of the Curonian Spit is Russian territory, forming part of the Kaliningrad region. Just north, Lithuania's third largest city and major port, Klaipėda, is the gateway to all this beauty. The seaside resort of Palanga is the place to party. Nearby the Žemaitija National Park is steeped in ancient folklore, while the Orvydas Garden is a bizarre open-air art gallery of stone carvings.

Meanwhile, the Nemunas River finishes its winding journey through Lithuania in the Nemunas Delta Regional Park, flanked by the Curonian Lagoon. It's a wondrous wetland providing an important resting spot for migrating birds.

## ŽEMAITIJA UPLAND
☎ 448

Northwest Lithuania, historically called Samogitia, is today known as Žemaitija, or Lower Lithuania – in contrast to the northeast of the country, which is Aukštaitija (Upper Lithuania). Samogitians, as western Lithuanians are still called today, are known for their strong sense of ethnic identity. The highest point in Žemaitija is Medvėgalis (234m).

### Plungė

Plungė is one of the main towns of the area. It lies on the Klaipėda–Kretinga–Šiauliai railway and just off the Palanga–Kretinga–Šiauliai road. A major attraction in Plungė is the vast neo-classical manor house and estate, which was home to the Oginski family in the 19th century, and today is home to the **Žemaitija Art Museum** (☎ 54 731).

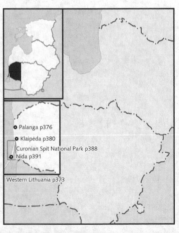

○ Palanga p376
○ Klaipėda p380
Curonian Spit National Park p388
○ Nida p391
Western Lithuania p373

### Žemaitija National Park

This 200-sq-km park is enshrined in fables of devils, ghosts and buried treasure amid its thick carpet of fir trees.

Stunning **Lake Plateliai** (Platelių ežeras), renowned for its seven islets and seven ancient shore terraces, was carved by a glacier. Legend would have it that it was swept into the sky with a storm before dropping where it lies now after the magic words 'Ale plate

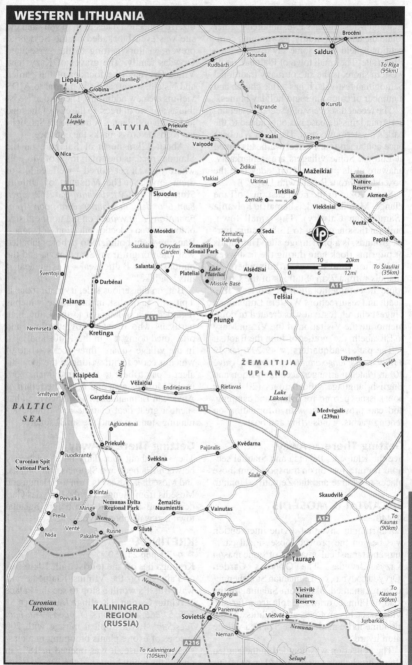

# WESTERN LITHUANIA

To Rīga (95km)

LATVIA

Broceni
Saldus
Skrunda
A9
Rudbārži
Liepāja
Grobina
Jaunlieģi
Venta
Nigrande
Kursīši
Lake Liepāja
Nica
Priekule
Kalni
Ezere
Vaiņode
A11
Židikai
Mažeikiai
Kamanos Nature Reserve
Ylakiai
Ukrinai
Tirkšliai
Skuodas
Žemalė
Akmenė
Viekšniai
Mosėdis
Žemaičių Kalvarija
Seda
Venta
Šaukliai
Orvydas Garden
Žemaitija National Park
Papilė
Salantai
Plateliai
Lake Plateliai
Alsėdžiai
Šventoji
Darbėnai
Missile Base
0    10    20km
0    6    12mi
To Šiauliai (35km)
Telšiai
Palanga
A11
Nemirseta
Kretinga
A11
Plungė
Minija
Užventis
Venta
Klaipėda
Vėžaičiai
Endriejavas
Rietavas
ŽEMAITIJA UPLAND
Smiltynė
Gargždai
A1
Lake Lūkstas
BALTIC SEA
Agluonėnai
Medvėgalis (239m)
Priekulė
Pajūralis
Kvėdarna
Juodkrantė
Švėkšna
Curonian Spit National Park
Šilalė
Skaudvilė
Pervalka
Kintai
Žemaičių Naumiestis
Vainutas
A12
Preila
Mingė
Nemunas Delta Regional Park
Nemunas
To Kaunas (90km)
Nida
Ventė
Rusnė
Šilutė
Pakalnė
Juknaičiai
Curonian Lagoon
Pagėgiai
Viešvilė Nature Reserve
To Kaunas (80km)
KALININGRAD REGION (RUSSIA)
Panemunė
Sovietsk
Viešvilė
Nemunas
Jurbarkas
Neman
A216
To Kaliningrad (105km)
Šešupė

WESTERN LITHUANIA

lej' (the rain goes wide) were uttered. Every June, on Midsummer's Eve, hundreds gather round the lake and, in July, a swimming competition is held here. Some say it was once a Pagan site. The small town of **Plateliai**, on its western shore, is the site of many traditional Samogitian festivals. It has a fine church and a number of camp sites and holiday homes.

The recent discovery of a secret Soviet underground missile base has only added to the park's mysterious charm. The Cold War base once contained four nuclear warheads aimed at Europe. Some villagers are, remarkably, unaware of its presence even today (see the boxed text 'From Russia with Love?').

Some 20km to the northeast, just off the Plungė–Mažeikiai road, is Ūemaičių **Kalvarija** (Samogitian Calvary). This small town, built on the site of 9th- to 13th-century burial grounds, is a pilgrimage site. Thousands of pilgrims flock here during the first week of July to climb the seven hills where 20 chapels form a 7km 'Stations of the Cross' route in commemoration of Christ's life, death and resurrection. Western Lithuania's biggest church festival was created to commemorate the Visitation of the Virgin Mary to Elizabeth, the mother of John the Baptist.

The **park headquarters** (☎ 49 231, fax 49 337; ℮ znp@plunge.omnitel.net; Didžioji gatvė 10) in Plateliai arranges accommodation and English-language guided tours (20 Lt per hour), issues permits for fishing and camping, and can provide you with information on renting yachts, windsurfing and boats.

## Getting There & Away

See the Klaipėda, Palanga and Šiauliai sections for information on transport from those places to Plungė and the Žemaitija Upland.

## SALANTAI & MOSĖDIS
☎ 440

Local rumour says that divine intervention was behind the prolific, obsessional carvings and fantastical creations of stone mason Kazys Orvydas. The **Orvydas Garden** (Orvydų sodyba), or 'Lithuanian Stonehenge' as its nicknamed, 5km from Salantai on the road to Plungė, draws people from far and wide to see his grottoes, arches, huts and the monuments he made for the Salantai village churchyard.

The collection was hoarded in the garden after Khrushchev's wrath turned on religious objects during the 1960s. But most of the bizarre collection dates to the 1980s and the site was even blockaded by the Soviets to prevent visitors getting to the persecuted Orvydas family. The graves of Kazys and Vilius Orvydas (the founder of the garden and his eldest son) and a memorial to AIDS victims are new additions. The garden is visible as a grove of trees, to the east of the road just south of Salantai. A traditional Samogitian roadside cross marks the entrance.

About 12km north of Salantai, on the Skuodas road, is the small town of Mosėdis where you can get stoned – well see lots of them anyway! The **Museum of Unique Stones** (☎ 76 291; Salantų gatvė 2; open 8am-6pm daily in summer; 8am-noon, 1pm-5pm Mon-Fri in winter) on the northern side of town has an eclectic collection – of stones. Ranging from boulders to pebbles labelled with their origin from Scandinavia and the bottom of the Baltic Sea – it is unclear if this is a joke!

But, on the serious side, its main focus is a pit with an obelisk in the middle, which is regarded as a monument to the Lithuanian partisans who resisted Soviet rule – and often died doing it – in the 1940s and '50s. In the village square, three rocks – one of which is carved with writing in the local dialect – pay tribute to the Samogitians born in the Mosėdis area and urges the return of American-Lithuanians. The village itself has spent a great deal of time and trouble arranging stones around the small square.

## Getting There & Away

There are about four daily buses each way between Klaipėda and Skuodas (via Salantai and Mosėdis). Buses also run to Salantai and Mosėdis from Plungė. For the Orvydas Garden get off at the last stop before Salantai town and walk about 1km.

## KRETINGA
☎ 445 • pop 21,250

Kretinga lies off the tourist trail, 10km east of Palanga, on the Vilnius–Klaipėda railway. But it's worth a stop to see the **Palace & Winter Garden** at **Kretinga Museum** (☎ 53 505, 51 366; admission 4 Lt; open 10am-6pm Tues-Sun). It's a tropical mirage with 200 species of exotic plants blooming in a classical glasshouse. It was opened in 1875 in one of the many homes of the Tyszkiewicz

## From Russia with Love?

Deep in the forests of Žemaitija National Park a secret Soviet underground missile base has been discovered. It once housed mighty nuclear missiles – with enough power to destroy most of Europe. The 22m-long R12 rockets with 3m-long warheads were smuggled into the heart of Lithuania so that they were in range of their targets – Britain, Norway, West Germany, Turkey and Spain.

This terrifying arsenal lay hidden from the Lithuanian people for the best part of 40 years. The base, a circular underground centre was flanked by the four missile containers, only visible from the ground by their domed tops. The James Bond-style pad, which lies 10km south of idyllic rural village Plateliai, was equipped with electrical and radio stations, and control rooms. Ten thousand soldiers were secretly drafted in from USSR satellite states to construct the base in 1960. It was home to the 79th Rocket Regiment until 1978 – when the missiles mysteriously disappeared and the base was left to rot. During its history the base was put on red alert during the 1968 Czechoslovakia aggression and deployed rockets to Cuba during the crisis in September 1962. The military town for the soldiers stands nearby.

For a tour, ring the Žemaitija National Park HQ in Plateliai before setting out as it's not always open. Entrance is 4 Lt and an English-speaking guide can be booked for 20 Lt. By car take the road to Plateliai off the A11 (Kretinga–Šiauliai road), follow signs to Plateliai, then turn off at Plokštinė. It's 5km from here to the Raketine Baze (missile base). It's unsurprisingly difficult to find (it's meant to be secret!) without private transport but there are sporadic local buses to/from Plateliai, get off at the Plokštinė sign and hike the rest.

family of Polish nobles. A fire devastated it in 1915 and in 1940 an invading Soviet Army destroyed it. Now, extensive restoration has made this treasure into perhaps the most appealing restaurant in the Baltics. The museum itself has thousands of exhibits from the region including wooden crosses and old photographs.

The remains of a **Franciscan Monastery**, damaged in WWII and never restored, and the **Church of the Annunciation** are close to the palace.

**Vienkiemis** (☎ 46 425; doubles 100 Lt), a guesthouse overlooking a small lake on the northern edge of Kretinga at Padvariai, can arrange fishing and sailing on the lake.

**Pajūrio egzotika** (☎ 44 423, 44 413) in Žibininkai, is a brewery that makes Juozas beer to the recipe of a 16th-century duke.

## PALANGA
☎ 460 • pop 19,550
Palanga is a small resort town that has a split personality – it's a quiet pensioner's paradise in winter and a heaving all-night party place in summer. During the warmer months, tourists from all over Lithuania and overseas flock to the famous 10km sandy beach that is backed by dunes and pine woods.

You'll find Palanga (if you don't hear it first) 25km north of Klaipėda and 18km south of the Latvian border. Blink and you'll

miss another hotel or bar opening, yet despite the crowds and encroaching neon, it still retains its traditional charms with wooden houses on the tree-lined heart of the action, Basanavičiaus gatvė.

## History
Although it appears there are no ancient remains now, Palanga apparently dates back to the 12th century. Lying on what was for centuries a very short stretch of Lithuanian Coast, between German (or Prussian) territory to the south and German- or Polish-dominated territory to the north, Palanga has often been Lithuania's only port – or potential port, for it was completely destroyed by the Swedish army in 1710. It developed as a resort in the 19th century and during the Soviet era the city was one of the leading hot spots.

## Orientation
Vytauto gatvė, the main street, runs parallel to the coast about 1km inland. The striking, red-brick Catholic church, on the western side of the street, is roughly the middle of town. The tourist office and bus station are a few steps east of it at Kretingos gatvė. Basanavičiaus gatvė – pedestrian-only between 11am and midnight in summer – heads east–west from the town down to the little pier of which Palanga residents are so proud. Lined with bars, restaurants and hotels it's the

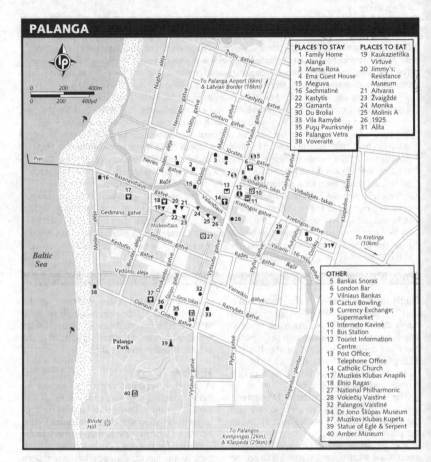

PALANGA

| PLACES TO STAY | PLACES TO EAT |
|---|---|
| 1 Family Home | 19 Kaukazietiška |
| 2 Alanga | Virtuvė |
| 3 Mama Rosa | 20 Jimmy's; |
| 4 Ema Guest House | Resistance |
| 15 Meguva | Museum |
| 16 Šachmatinė | 21 Aitvaras |
| 22 Kastytis | 23 Žvaigždė |
| 29 Gamanta | 24 Monika |
| 30 Du Broliai | 25 Molinis A |
| 33 Vila Ramybė | 26 1925 |
| 35 Pušų Paunksnėje | 31 Alita |
| 36 Palangos Vėtra | |
| 38 Voveraitė | |

OTHER
5 Bankas Snoras
6 London Bar
7 Vilniaus Bankas
8 Cactus Bowling
9 Currency Exchange;
   Supermarket
10 Interneto Kavinė
11 Bus Station
12 Tourist Information
   Centre
13 Post Office;
   Telephone Office
14 Catholic Church
17 Muzikos Klubas Anapilis
18 Elnio Ragas
27 National Philharmonic
28 Vokiečių Vaistinė
32 Palangos Vaistinė
34 Dr Jono Šliūpas Museum
37 Muzikos Klubas Kupeta
39 Statue of Eglė & Serpent
40 Amber Museum

hub of Palanga's entertainment. Klaipėdos plentas, the main road between Klaipėda and the Latvian border, skirts the town to the east.

**Maps** Jāņa sēta's *Palanga* town plan map (1:15,000) features detailed maps of Palanga and neighbouring Sventoji; a pocket-size map of Palanga is also included in the *Klaipėda/Kaunas In Your Pocket* guide.

## Information

The **Tourist Information Centre** (*turizmo informacijos centras*; ☎/fax 48 822; ℮ palanga turinfo@is.lt; Kretingos gatvė 1; open 8am-8pm daily May-Oct; 9am-1pm & 2pm-6pm Nov-Mar) books accommodation and sells maps and guides. It adjoins the tiny bus station.

There's a **post office** (☎ 48 506; Vytauto gatvė 53; open 9am-1pm & 2pm-6.30pm Mon-Fri, 9am-1pm & 2pm-4pm Sat) in town and also an **Express Mail Service** (EMS; ☎ 315 031) available. Faxes can be sent/received from the adjoining **telephone office** (☎ 48 048, fax 48 225; open 7am-10pm daily).

There is an ATM accepting MasterCard inside the telephone centre as well as at **Bankas Snoras kiosks** (cnr Vytauto & Jūratės gatvė; open 24hr • Basanavičiaus gatvė). Visa and MasterCard can be used at **Vilniaus Bankas** (☎ 49 140; Vytauto gatvė 61; open 8am-5pm daily) and **Lietuva Taupomasis Bankas** (Jūratės gatvė 15).

Pharmacy-wise, there's **Palangos vaistinė** (Vytauto gatvė 33; open 9am-8pm Mon-Fri, 9am-6pm Sat & Sun) which was used as the

WESTERN LITHUANIA

local KGB headquarters between 1944 and 1951 and also a **German pharmacy** *(Vokiečių vaistinė; Vytauto gatvė 86; open 9am-9pm Mon-Fri, 10am-9pm Sat, 11am-9pm Sun)*.

Surf the information superhighway at **Interneto Kavinė** *(☎ 53 411; Vytauto gatvė 97; open 9am-8pm daily)* for an exorbitant 12 Lt per hour.

## Beaches

Watch where you're wandering, Palanga boasts areas for carefree nudists. Men and women experience the joys of nature at separate spots near where River Ronžė joins the sea.

The naked truth is that Palanga's beach has enough sand for everyone – clothed or otherwise. It boasts fine white sands flanked by pine-covered dunes. Everyone appears to ignore warnings not to bathe in the sea by gleefully splashing in the Baltic waves and leaping off the end of the pier.

Bouncy castles, water slides and trampolines pepper the area round the pier. Toys for adults – jet skis, motorboats etc – can be hired on the section accessible via Žvejų gatvė or you can pretend to be in California and play beach volleyball within spitting distance of the pier.

From the end of Basanavičiaus gatvė, a wide boardwalk leads over the dunes to Palanga's majestic wooden **pier**. It was completely rebuilt in 1997 after being reduced to bare stumps by a fierce storm in 1993, then battered again by Hurricane Anatoly in 1999. By day, street vendors sell popcorn, *ledai* (ice cream), *desrainiai* (hot dogs), *alus* (beer) and *gira* (a sweet mead drink), making it all rather fun. Come dusk, families and lovers gather here to watch the sunset and have their photograph taken.

## Botanical Park & Museums

Lush greenery and swans gliding on peaceful lakes make this a haven from the town centre. The Botanical Park (Palangos botanikos parkas), stretching from Vytauto gatvė to the beach at the southern end of town, surrounds the late 19th-century palace of the Tyszkiewicz family. The gardens were designed by French landscape artist Edward André in the 19th century.

The sweeping classical palace is now an excellent **Amber Museum** *(Gintaro muziejus; ☎ 53 501; Vytauto gatvė 17; admission 5 Lt;*

*open 11am-7pm Tues-Sun)*. Inside there are 20,000 examples of honey-coloured Baltic gold, some with prehistoric insects and plants preserved inside them Jurassic Park-style. There is information in English and a beautiful selection of amber jewellery.

The park includes a rose garden (behind the palace), a couple of lakes, a **statue of Eglė and the serpent**, and **Birutės kalnas** (Birutė Hill), thought to have once been the site of a pagan shrine. According to legend, the shrine was tended by vestal virgins, one of whom, Birutė, was kidnapped and married by Grand Duke Kęstutis. The hill is now topped by a 19th-century chapel.

Palanga's other museum of interest is the **Dr Jono Šliūpas Memorial House** *(☎ 54 559; Vytauto gatvė 23; open 11am-5pm Wed-Sun)*, featuring local history. There's a small photographic display inside the **Resistance Museum** *(Basanavičiaus gatvė 19; open 3pm-5pm Wed, Sat & Sun)*.

## Special Events

Palanga hosts its grand opening of the summer season on the first Saturday of June. The season's close, held the last Saturday in August, is likewise marked by a massive street carnival, song festival, market and pop concert.

## Places to Stay

Prices in Palanga change like the wind. Prices listed are for the high season, which runs from May to September. Come winter, prices are slashed by 50% or more. In summer, it is practically impossible to get a room for the night unless you've booked well in advance.

### Places to Stay – Budget

**Camping** The pick of a grotty bunch **Palangos Kempingas** *(tent sites 5 Lt, cabins 10-15 Lt)* is 2km out of Palanga on the Klaipėda-Palanga highway (A13). It has basic wooden cabins. There's a shop selling a few meagre provisions amid the gardens.

**Homestays** B&B can be arranged through **Litinterp** *(☎ 411 814, 311 490, fax 411 815; e klaipeda@litinterp.lt; Šimkaus gatvė 21/4; open 8.30am-5.30pm Mon-Fri, 10am-3pm Sat)*. Singles/doubles start at 80/140 Lt and advance bookings can be made through its Klaipėda, Kaunas or Vilnius offices.

The **family home** (☎ 57 076; Nėries gatvė 24; beds 10 Lt), west of the Catholic church and 300m from the sea, classes itself as a hostel by offering travellers a bed for the night. Ring in advance.

A handful of other private houses on this street and on the northern section (between Nėries and Jūratės) of Birutės alėja also have rooms to rent in summer; look for signs reading nuomojami or kambariai (rooms).

**Hotels** Rest homes – large, grey blocks formerly reserved for members of Soviet organisations – are an inexpensive option.

**Meguva** (☎ 48 839, fax 48 819; Valančiaus gatvė 1; singles/doubles/triples from 40/50/45 Lt) is tucked behind the red brick church in the centre of town.

**Ema Guest House** (☎ 48 608; Jūratės gatvė; doubles/triples/quads 35/50/60 Lt) is another cheap but basic option.

**Kastytis** (Mickevičiaus gatvė 8; doubles/triples 150/220 Lt) is a large, ugly place with reasonable rooms; and triples which are as spacey as apartments for groups.

**Gamanta** (☎ 48 885, fax 48 889; e info@gamanta.lt; Plytų gatvė 7; singles/doubles/suites 180/200/400 Lt), close to the bus station, has all the mod cons.

There are some good luxury hotels, including the following.

**Du Broliai** (Two Brothers; ☎ 40 040, fax 52 889; Vytauto gatvė 160; doubles 300 Lt ● ☎ 48 047; Kretingos gatvė 36; doubles 300 Lt) is popular for its friendly service.

**Vila Ramybė** (☎/fax 54 124; Vytauto gatvė 54; doubles 100-200 Lt) stands out from the crowd with good music, good food and good ambience. Rates include a continental breakfast on the terrace.

**Mama Rosa** (☎ 48 581, ☎/fax 48 580; Jūratės gatvė 28a) is also charming.

**Voveraitė** (☎ 52 532, ☎/fax 53 422; Meilės alėja 24; doubles in June 250 Lt, in July & Aug 400-500 Lt) is ideally positioned within a whisper of the beach. It has seven rooms, a 24-hour pizzeria, plus a bar and nightclub open until 6am.

**Tauras** (☎/fax 49 111; Vytauto gatvė 116; singles/suites from 180/240 Lt) has a warm wooden nautical feel and a bargain, 50 Lt per hour sauna. You can also hire a bicycle for 6 Lt per hour or 30 Lt/day.

Top-notch hotels that will stretch the wallet even further, include **Pusų Paunksnėje**

(☎ 49 080, fax 49 081; e pusupaunksneje@palanga.omnitel.net; Dariaus ir Girėno gatvė 25; doubles 300-800 Lt), a beautiful wooden tavern owned by Lithuanian basketball hero Arvydas Sabonis.

**Palangos Vėtra** (☎ 53 579; Daukanto gatvė 35; doubles 300-800 Lt) is a vision of Scandinavian glass and wood.

**Sachmatinė** (☎ 48 296, fax 51 655; Basanavičiaus gatvė 45; doubles 300-800 Lt) is pride of place in party territory.

**Alanga** (☎ 49 318, fax 49 316; e alanga@palanga.omnitel.net; Nėries gatvė 14; doubles/suites 120/190 Lt) is a blushing pink delight with the added bonus of babysitters and a lovely restaurant!

## Places to Eat

Palanga has lots of options so you can afford to be choosy. The food focus is on Basanavičiaus gatvė which is lined with the good, bad and ugly of Palanga's own particular brand of kitsch dining; from fake Hawaiian sunshades to Wild West taverns. Those seeking peace and tranquillity should head for the outside terrace restaurants at achingly cool Villa Rambyė, Pusų Paunksnėje, Palangos Vėtra and Sachmatinė (see Places to Stay earlier) which are among the best places to eat in town; expect to pay 35 Lt upwards a head.

Places known for their traditional tavern feel, Lithuanian beers and rustic snacks, along Basanavičiaus gatvė, include the following.

**Monika** (Basanavičiaus gatvė 12; meals 25 Lt) serves hearty sweet or savoury pancakes in a wooden cabin.

**Molinis A** (Basanavičiaus gatvė 8; meals 20 Lt; open until 2am daily) is close to **1925** (Basanavičiaus gatvė 4; meals 25 Lt) which chucks in live music.

**Aitvaras** (☎ 52 042; Basanavičiaus gatvė 17; meals 30 Lt) is a classy glasshouse with excellent fish dishes and posh pizzas.

**Jimmy's** (Basanavičiaus gatvė 19; meals 30 Lt; open May-Sept only) has American-style chicken wings, potato skins, BBQ pork ribs and a no smoking policy, despite which it's a favoured hang-out.

The rest of town has some tasty spots including the following.

**Alita** (☎ 48 199; Kretingos gatvė 54; meals 20 Lt) is a bar-café that has a non-smoking room, owned by the Lithuanian champagne manufacturers.

**Žvaigždė** *(☎ 54 198; Daukanto gatvė 6; meals 20 Lt; open 11am-midnight daily)* serves downright decadent *blyneliai* (pancakes) and is the ideal spot for a Lithuanian lunch on the verandah, in the garden or around the swimming pool.

**Kaukazietiška Virtuvė** *(Mickevičiaus gatvė 8; meals 30 Lt)* flame-grills fiery Caucasian *šašlykas* (shashlik).

## Entertainment
The Tourist Information Centre (see Information earlier) knows what's on where. Watch out for posters on street corners or outside the **National Philharmonic** *(Nacionalinė filharmonija; Vytauto gatvė 82)*, which is opposite the defunct Naglis Cinema.

Palanga hosts many summer music festivals.

The **Open-air concert hall** *(Vasaros koncertų salė; ☎ 52 210; Vytauto gatvė 43)* is the main venue for classical concerts.

**Muzikos Klubas Kupeta** *(Daukanto gatvė 24)* is where live rock, folk, jazz and blues takes to the stage.

**Muzikos Klubas Anapilis** *(☎ 51 951; Basanavičiaus gatvė 3)* draws a bohemian crowd for live music until midnight.

**Elnio Ragas** *(☎ 53 505; Basanavičiaus gatvė 25)* serves steaming wild boar (35 Lt) to large men with large beers at this rustic joint.

**Sachmatinė** *(☎ 48 296; Basanavičiaus gatvė 45; open 9pm-5am Wed-Sat, 9pm-4am Sun)* goes wild at weekends and is Palanga's hottest night spot (see also Places to Stay, earlier).

**Cactus Bowling** *(☎ 53 288; e cactusbowling@takas.lt; Vytauto gatvė 98)* has two bars, seven lanes and a Mexican restaurant. Olé!

## Getting There & Away
You can reach Palanga by road or air. Services are much more frequent in summer.

**Air** Palanga airport is 6km from the town centre on the main road north. Air Lithuania flies weekly to/from Vilnius (see Getting There & Away in the Vilnius chapter). International flights, to Hamburg, Oslo, Billund and Kristianstad, (see the introductory Getting There & Away chapter) are handled by Air Lithuania and Lithuanian Airlines (LAL).

**Air Lithuania** *(☎ 53 431; open 7.15am-10pm Mon-Fri, 6am-10pm Sat)* has an airport office. Contact **LAL** *(☎ 5-275 2585, 5-275 2588; e info@lal.lt)* at its Vilnius office.

**Bus** The bus station *(☎ 53 333; Kretingos gatvė 1)* is bang in the town centre. *Mikroautobusai* (microbuses) to/from Klaipėda (3 Lt, 45 minutes) depart from one of the tiny platforms approximately every 20 minutes. Other daily services to/from Palanga include the following.

Kaunas 35 Lt, 3½ hours, 230km, about 11 buses
Klaipėda 3 Lt, 45 minutes, 25km, every 20 minutes
Kretinga 20 minutes, 10km, every 15 minutes
Rīga (via Liepāja) 5½ hours, 318km, one bus
Šiauliai 2½ hours, 150km, about 10 buses, via Panevėžys and Plungė
Vilnius 41 Lt, six hours, 340km, about 9 buses

**Train** Kretinga is the nearest train station and it is served by three daily trains to/from Vilnius, three to/from Klaipėda, two to/from Radviliškis, and one to/from Kaunas.

## Getting Around
Bus No 2 runs to/from the airport, roughly every hour from 6am to 10pm. Timetables are posted at its town centre stop, on Požėlos gatvė behind the bus station. Bus No 1 runs the length of the town (via the same stop on Požėlos gatvė), but is erratic and infrequent. The main taxi stand is on Požėlos gatvė, behind the bus station, or call *(☎ 54 103, 51 777)*.

You can hire a bicycle from Tauras for 6 Lt per hour or 30 Lt/day.

## KLAIPĖDA
☎ 46 • pop 202,500
Sea port Klaipėda is the gateway to the lush natural beauty of the Curonian Spit. But as Lithuania's third largest city it certainly has some little gems of its own. Most notably it was once the German town of Memel, and some of the Germanic flavour and architecture still remain along with the famous bell tower.

Lying 315km west of Vilnius, beside the narrow strait where the Curonian Lagoon opens into the Baltic Sea, it connects Lithuania to Scandinavia via cargo and passenger ferry routes.

Despite being destroyed in WWII, the city is a pleasant place, which celebrates its nautical heritage with a flamboyant Sea Festival each year in July.

# KLAIPĖDA

To Klaipėda University (300m), Melnragė (4km), Morena (4km),
Giruliai (8km), Pajūris (8km), Palanga (30km) & Kretinga (35km)

**PLACES TO STAY**
2  Klaipėda Travellers' Hostel
7  Radisson SAS
11  Litinterp; Mėja
20  Prūsija
21  Viktorija; EuroRenta
27  Hotel Klaipėda; Hertz; Krantas Travel; Ost Reise; Scandlines
34  Europa Palace
38  Astra

**PLACES TO EAT**
3  Bambola
9  Garazas
10  Kitas Krantas
14  Iki
18  Forena; Taupomasis Bankas
19  Boogie Woogie
22  Bambola; Lombardas
31  Rasytė
42  Bistro Bonton
44  Fotogalerija
45  Galerija Peda

**OTHER**
1  Bus Station
4  Krantas Travel
5  Statue
6  Žemaitija
8  West Express
12  Juodojo Katino Smuklė
13  Klaipedos Knygos
15  Conservatoire
16  Picture Gallery
17  Bitas Internet
23  Lietuvos Telekomas
24  Main Post Office
25  Clock & Watch Museum
26  Musical Theatre
28  Meridianas
29  Žvejų
30  Buru Užeiga
32  Vilniaus Bankas
33  Kurpiai
35  Klaipėda Theatre
36  Drama Theatre
37  Old Castle Port
39  Simon Dach Fountain; Statue
40  Taupomasis Bankas
41  Baltic Clipper
43  Klaipėda City Library
46  Lithuania Minor History Museum
47  Tourist Information Centre
48  Baroti Gallery; Bohema
49  Blacksmith's Museum
50  Market
51  Old Castle

Dariaus ir Girėno gatvė

Train Station

Priestočio gatvė

To Godūnas Hotel (300m & Lithuanian Student and Youth Travel (350m)

Šiaulių gatvė

Nėries gatvė

Sodų gatvė

Butkų Juzės gatvė

Janonio gatvė

Lietuvnynkų aikštė

Vilties gatvė

Daukanto gatvė

Mažvydo Sculpture Park

Herkaus Manto gatvė

Kanto gatvė

Daukanto gatvė

To Skandalas (400m)

Šiaulių gatvė

Mažvydo alėja

Donelaičio gatvė

Kauno gatvė

Vytauto gatvė

Donelaičio aikštė

To Kaunas (213km)

Puodžių gatvė

Simkaus gatvė

H Manto gatvė

Danės krantinė

Liepų gatvė

Vytauto gatvė

Jūros gatvė

Naujoji Sodo gatvė

Danės River

Uosto gatvė

Danės gatvė

Danės gatvė

Curonian Lagoon

Žvejų gatvė

Teatro gatvė

Kepėjų gatvė

Kurpių gatvė

Turgaus gatvė

Tiltų gatvė

Vežejų gatvė

Old Town

Didžioji Vandens gatvė

Tomo gatvė

Teatro aikštė

Daržų gatvė

Šaltkalvių gatvė

Aukštoji gatvė

Taikos prospektas

Pilies gatvė

Turgaus aikštė

To Smiltynė (500m), Hotel Palva, Neringa, Maritime Museum, Aquarium & Dolphinarium

To New River Port (3km), Šilutė (48km), Shipping Terminals & Sovetisk (100km)

0  150  300m
0  150  300yd

WESTERN LITHUANIA

## History

There was probably a fishing village here – settled by ancient Balts at the mouth of the Danė river – before the German crusaders arrived in the region, but Klaipėda has been a predominantly German town, called Memel, for nearly all its history. A castle was founded here in 1252 by the Livonian Order and transferred, along with its surrounding settlement, to the Teutonic Order in 1328.

Memel was the northernmost town of the territory ruled by, firstly, the Teutonic Order (until its demise in the 16th century), then the Duchy of Prussia, the order's successor state. From 1871 to WWI, it was part of a united Germany that stretched as far west as the borders of France and Switzerland.

The town has been plundered and destroyed several times by war, in the 13th and 14th centuries when the Teutonic Order and Lithuania were at war. In 1678 it was reduced to ashes by Sweden. Up to the 17th-century, brick and stone houses were forbidden, because, it was reasoned, they would survive the city's fall and provide cover for an enemy.

By WWI, Memel had 30,000 inhabitants – an even ratio of Germans and Lithuanians. Under the Treaty of Versailles at the end of WWI, the town, the northern half of the Curonian Spit and a strip of land (about 150km long and 20km wide) along the eastern side of the Curonian Lagoon and the northern side of the Nemunas river, were separated from Germany as an 'international territory'. An autonomous government was established and a French garrison stationed there. This 'Memel Territory' remained in a kind of stateless limbo until January 1923, when Lithuanian troops marched in and annexed it. In 1925 Memel officially became Klaipėda for the first time.

Hitler annexed the territory in March 1939 – his last land grab before WWII began. The Nazis used the harbour as a submarine base and in January 1945, whole sections of the town were flattened in the bombardment leading to its capture by the Red Army. There were only eight survivors left in the besieged town after mass evacuations to Germany and Kaliningrad.

After WWII, Klaipėda was rebuilt, repopulated (mainly by Lithuanians and Russians) and developed into an important Soviet city on the back of shipbuilding and fishing. In 1982 the first international ferry, Klaipeto Mukran was built as a military tool, and later used solely for trade.

Today, only a handful of Germans live in or around Klaipėda which in 2002 hosted celebrations for its 750th anniversary.

## Orientation

The Danė River flows westward across the city centre and enters the Curonian Lagoon 4km from the Baltic Sea. The key street axis is the single, long, north–south Manto gatvė (north of the river), Tiltų gatvė (for its first 600m south of the river) and Taikos prospektas.

The heart of the old part of town lies within the 400m south of the river, mostly west of Tiltų gatvė. Most hotels, the train and bus stations, and many other services are north of the river.

Smiltynė, the northern tip of the Curonian Spit, lies about 500m off the mouth of the Danė, across the narrow channel which forms the northern end of the Curonian Lagoon.

**Maps** Jāņa sēta publishes useful city plans of Klaipėda (1:25,000) and Palanga (1:15,000), available from most news kiosks in Lithuania for 6.40 Lt.

## Information

**Tourist Offices** The **Tourist Information Centre** (*Klaipėdos turizmo informacijos centras;* ☎ 412 186, fax 412 185; @ kltic@takas.lt; Tomo gatvė 2; open 8.30am-5.30pm Mon-Fri, 9am-2pm Sat; closed Sat Oct-Apr) sells maps and locally published guidebooks, arranges hotel accommodation and guided tours (100 Lt for a three-hour city tour for one to 40 people).

Independent souls should pick up a copy of *Klaipėda/Kaunas In Your Pocket*, an annual city guide published in English and German, and sold in hotels and news kiosks for 8 Lt.

**Money** For cash advances on both Visa and MasterCard visit **Vilniaus Bankas** (☎ 310 333; Turgaus gatvė 15 ● ☎ 310 925; Daržų gatvė 13). It also cashes American Express travellers cheques.

**Taupomasis Bankas**, which gives cash advances on Visa, cashes Visa travellers cheques and offers Western Union money transfers, has Visa at Manto gatvė 4 (☎ 410 479) next to Forena restaurant which is also a 24-hour currency exchange. There's also a branch on the corner of Turgaus gatvė and Teatro gatvė (overlooking Teatro aikštė).

**Post & Communications** The main **post office** (☎ 315 014; Liepų gatvė 16; open 8am-7pm Mon-Fri, 9am-4pm Sat) has an **EMS** (☎ 315 031) service. Phone calls can be made from public cardphones on the street or from a cardphone inside the **Lithuanian Telecom** (Lietuvos telekomas; ☎ 411 033; Manto gatvė 2; open 9am-10pm daily) office.

**Internet Resources** Get surfing at **Bitas Internet** (☎ 411 049; Šaulių 4) for 2 Lt per hour.

Public online access is also possible at **Klaipėda City Library** (Klaipėdos miesto biblioteka; ☎ 314 723; Turgaus gatvė 8; open 10am-7pm Mon-Fri, 10am-5pm Sat) for the bargain one-off payment of 5 Lt. You can then use the computers every day for a year (book first).

**Travel Agencies** Accommodation bookings and excursions can be booked through **Mėja** (☎ 310 295, fax 411 815; Simkaus gatvė 21-8) and **Baltic Clipper** (☎ 312 312, fax 312 057; Turgaus gatvė 2).

**Lithuanian Student and Youth Travel** (☎ 314 672, fax 314 669; ℮ klaipeda@jaunimas.lt; Janonio gatvė 16) offers discounted air, plane and bus tickets.

**West Express** (☎ 310 311; ℮ office@westexpress.lt; Daukanto gatvė 20) offers the friendliest service and local travel advice.

Tickets for ferries from Klaipėda to Kiel and Karlshamn are sold by **Krantas Travel** (☎ 395 111, fax 395 222; ⓦ www.krantas.lt/travel; Lietuvininkų gatvė 5; open 8am-7pm Mon-Fri, 10am-5pm Sat). It also has a small **branch office** (☎ 314 375) inside Hotel Klaipėda, as does **Ost Reise Service** which also sells ferry tickets.

**Bookshops** A selection of English-language books about Lithuania and some paperbacks can be found at **Centrinis Knygynas** (☎ 411 594; Turgaus aikštė 2). **Klaipėdos Knygos** (Manto gatvė 9) is under renovation. Foreign-language newspapers are sold inside **Lombardas** (Manto gatvė 1).

## Old Town

Much of central Klaipėda was wrecked in WWII, so there are only bits of the German town left. But there are some restored streets in the oldest part between the river and Turgaus aikštė. Along Kurpių gatvė and Kepėjų gatvė east of Tiltų gatvė, are a number of rebuilt **old houses**. You can rent **paddle boats** on the southern bank, on the western side of the Tiltų gatvė bridge.

The focus of the Old Town is **Teatro aikštė** (Theatre Square), west of Tiltų gatvė. On its northern side stands the fine classical-style **Klaipėda Theatre** built in 1857, damaged in WWII and since restored. Hitler stood on the theatre balcony in 1939 and proclaimed the *Anschluss* (incorporation) of Memel into Germany to the crowds in the square.

In front of the theatre stands the **Simon Dach Fountain**, named after the 17th-century German poet (1605–59), born in Klaipėda, who became the focus of a well known circle of Königsberg writers and musicians.

On a pedestal in the middle of the fountain stands the **statue of Äennchen von Tharau**, the subject of a famous German wedding and love song, originally written in the East Prussian dialect. The words of the song were originally ascribed to Dach, but it's now thought that another member of the same Königsberg circle, the composer and cathedral organist Johann Albert, wrote them. The original early 20th-century statue and fountain, symbols of Memel, did not survive WWII, but replicas were put in place in 1989 by the Äennchen von Tharau Society, founded in Germany for the purpose.

Before WWII, Klaipėda's market used to stretch west from Teatro aikštė to the far side of Pilies gatvė. West of Pilies gatvė you can make out the site of Klaipėda's old **castle**, south of Žvejų gatvė, still protected by its moat which has an outlet into the southern side of the Danė.

**Baroti Gallery** (Baroti Galerija; ☎ 313 580; Aukštoji gatvė 3/3), two blocks south of Teatro aikštė, is partly housed in a converted fish warehouse (1819). Its exposed timber style, known as *Fachwerk*, is typical of German Memel. There are a few more **Fachwerk Buildings** around this part of town – a particularly fine one is at Sukilieliu gatvė 18. Around the corner from the gallery is the **Lithuanian Minor History Museum** (Mažosios lietuvos istorijos muziejus; ☎ 410 524; Didžioji Vandens gatvė 6; adult/ child 2/1 Lt; open 10am-5.15pm Tues-Sat), which has over 50,000 items tracing the early history of

Lithuania. Information is in both German and Lithuanian.

Amid the Old Town's crumbling streets is the cute **Blacksmith's Museum** *(Kalvystės muziejus; ☎ 410 526; Šaltkalvių gatvė 2/2a; open 10am-6pm Tues-Sat)*, housed in a former smithy. Ornate crosses are displayed in the courtyard and wrought-iron candlesticks fill the interior.

## North of the River

There's a **riverside park** along the northern bank of the Danė, immediately east of the Tiltų/Manto gatvė bridge. Liepų gatvė was once, for a brief spell, called Adolf-Hitler-Strasse. Manto gatvė was Hermann-Göring-Strasse. The **Picture Gallery** *(Paveikslų galerija; ☎ 213 319; Liepų gatvė 33; adult/child 3/1.5 Lt; open noon-6pm Tues-Sun)* and sculpture garden was formerly the German cemetery.

Gothic to nuclear clocks tick-tock inside the **Clock & Watch Museum** *(Laikrodžių muziejus; ☎ 410 415; Liepų gatvė 12; adult/child 4/2 Lt; open noon-6pm Tues-Sat, noon-5pm Sun)*. Unique carillon concerts are hosted in the back yard of the clock museum on summer weekends at noon; the 48 bell carillon is actually inside the 44m-tall bell tower of the neighbouring **post office** and is the largest musical instrument in Lithuania. The post office is worth a visit for its brilliant red-brick exterior and colourful stained glass windows.

A 3m-tall, granite **statue of Martynas Mažvydas** (c. 1510–63), author of *Catechisms* – the first book to be published in Lithuanian in 1547 – was unveiled here on the book's 450th anniversary in September 1997. The statue was sculpted by Lithuanian sculptor, Regimantas Midvikis. During the late 19th century, when printing books in the Lithuanian alphabet was banned (the official alphabet was Cyrillic), writers followed Mažvydas' example by printing their books in Königsberg (Kaliningrad) and smuggling them into Lithuania.

The main site of **Klaipėda University** *(Manto gatvė 84)* is 1km north of the centre.

## Smiltynė

Smiltynė is only a hop, skip and a jump away across the thin strait that divides Klaipėda from its achingly beautiful coastal sister.

Once disembarked from the pedestrian ferry, Smiltynė has one of nature's best playgrounds to explore with beaches, high dunes, pine forests and a collection of exhibitions and museums. The more adventurous can partake in a traditional sauna (5Lt) which is stuffed to the gills when it opens at weekends before cooling off with a quick – and invigoratingly healthy – dash into the Baltic Sea.

Smiltynė is easy to reach, with regular ferries making the five-minute crossing from the Old Castle Port in Klaipėda to the ferry landing on the eastern side of Smiltynė, 2km from the tip of the peninsula.

The headquarters and information centre of the Curonian Spit National Park (see the following section) is also in Smiltynė.

**Things to See** The biggest crowd-pleaser on Smiltynė (after the nudist beaches) is the **Maritime Museum, Aquarium & Dolphinarium** *(Jūrų muziejų, akvariumą ir delfinariumas; ☎ 490 751; ☎/fax 490 750; ⓔ olga@ juru.muziejus.lt; museum & aquarium adult/ student 6/3 Lt; open 10.30am-6.30pm Tues-Sun June-Aug; 10.30am-5.30pm Wed-Sun May & Sept; 10.30am-4.30pm Sat & Sun Oct-Apr)*. Smiltynė's showpiece is set in a 19th-century fort, built by the Prussian army in 1865 to 1971. Sea lion performances (admission 4 Lt) are at 11.15am and 1.15pm, and dolphin shows (10/5 Lt per adult/child) are at noon and 3pm. The dolphinarium has five bottle-nosed dolphins and the aquarium has tropical fish and fish from the Curonian Lagoon and the Baltic Sea, and a coral and shell display.

The **wrecked rowing boat** of Gintaras Paulionis (1945–94), the first Lithuanian to cross the Baltic Sea in a rowing boat, is on display. The Klaipėda fisherman set off on 28 June 1994, and arrived in Sweden some three weeks later. So pleased was he that he crossed the treacherous stretch of water that he did it again homeward-bound. During the return journey, his boat capsized and he drowned in the same storm that claimed 800 lives aboard the *Estonia* ferry in September 1994.

The fortress itself was intended to protect Klaipėda from naval attack, but advances in military technology rendered it obsolete by the end of the 19th century. In WWII the Germans used it as an ammunition store, then blew it up in 1945 as the Red Army was moving in to take Klaipėda. It was reconstructed for its present purpose in the 1970s.

To get there follow the little road which heads north from the pedestrian landing point. It's a 1.5km stroll – or if your sea legs are still wobbly let a horse and cart take the strain for 25 Lt.

Along this road there are a number of interesting local exhibitions. The **Curonian Spit National Park Nature Museum** *(Kuršių nerijos nacionalinis parkas gamtos muziejus ekspozicija;* ☎ *391 109; Smiltynė plentas 12, 10 & 9; admission 2 Lt; open 11am-6pm Wed-Sun May-Oct),* 200m from the ferry landing, gives an introduction to the flora, fauna and landscape of the spit. It is housed in three traditional wooden summerhouses – painted yellow, green and brown respectively.

About 700m farther is a display of veteran fishing vessels *(žvejybos laivai-veteranai).* Next along is an **ethnographic sea fishermen's farmstead** *(etnografinė pajūrio žvejo sodyba)* with a small collection of traditional 19th-century, wooden fishing houses.

**Beaches** Simply grab your Speedos and amble down the pleasant tracks which cut through cool pine forests across the spit's 1km wide tip. The bleached white sands run the whole of the western length of the 98km spit.

It's forbidden to wander off the beaten track in case of disturbing the lattices of intertwined branches which help prevent the sand from shifting. Sections of beach signposted *'Moterų pliažas'* are meant for women only; sections marked *'Vyrų pliažas'* are for men. A *'bendras pliažas'* is a mixed beach. Walk off the ferry and straight ahead across the car park, then bear left as if heading towards Nida; almost immediately on your right a large sign marks a smooth footpath that leads through pine forest to the sauna, women's beach (1km), mixed beach (700m) and men's beach (900m). Nude or topless bathing is the norm on the single-sex beaches.

**Activities** Fishing trips can be organised, and all the tackle bought, at **Žūklė** *(☎ 8-298 44605; Aukštoji gatvė 8),* a fishing shop and club in Klaipėda Old Town.

The really friendly adrenaline-junkies at **Klaipėda Skydiving Club** will put you up for the night at their clubhouse before pushing you out of a plane. Ring Gintaras on *(☎ 99-29 062;* e *gintarasr@yahoo.com)* to book a skydive.

## Places to Stay

**Hostels** Relocated from the Old Town, **Klaipėda Travellers Hostel** *(☎ 211 879, 8-685 33104;* e *jskuodaite@yahoo.com; Butkų Juzės gatvė 7/4; dorm beds/doubles 32/80 Lt)* is now within a whisper of the bus station and a two-minute walk (with a heavy rucksack) from the train station. Beds are in two small dorms, sleeping a total of 12 people, and there's one double room. There's bike rental (20 Lt per day), car rental (pay per kilometre), free Internet, and owner Jurda will take you on tours of Orvydas Garden, the missile base and Nida.

**Homestays** Bookings can be made through **Litinterp** *(☎ 411 814, 311 490, fax 411 815;* e *klaipeda@litinterp.lt; Šimkaus gatvė 21/4; open 8.30am-5.30pm Mon-Fri, 10am-3pm Sat),* which offers B&B singles/doubles in Klaipėda from 70/140 Lt a night.

**Town Centre Hotels** The top of the best-price pile is **Viktorija** *(☎ 400 055, fax 412 187; Šimkaus gatvė 2; singles/doubles/triples/quads/quins 40/60/80/85/100 Lt, doubles with bath 120 Lt),* but it's also bottom of the nice pile. It's central, shabby and dirt-cheap.

**Prūsija** *(☎ 412 081, fax 412 078; Šimkaus gatvė 6; singles/doubles 160/180 Lt),* a block north of Viktorija, is a bizarre place with an eclectic bunch of gilded mirrors on the walls, a reception that is seldom staffed and a restaurant serving Caucasian food.

**Hotel Klaipėda** *(☎ 394 372, fax 404 373;* e *hotel@klaipeda.omnitel.net; Naujoji Sodo gatvė 1; singles/doubles/suites from 180/260/350 Lt)* is a magnificent red-brick monstrosity. The landmark former 12-storey Intourist Hotel squats just north of the Danė River. Recent renovations have given the hotel a contemporary boost and more luxurious facilities.

There are international standard hotels, including the nautical-themed **Radisson SAS** *(☎ 490 800, fax 490 815;* e *juest.klaipeda@ radissonsas.com; Sauliu gatvė 28; singles/doubles 644/732 Lt).*

**Godūnas Hotel** *(☎/fax 310 901;* e *godunas@klaipeda.omnitel.net; Janonio gatvė 11; singles/suites 150/190 Lt)* has reasonable rooms with real double beds (not just two singles pushed together) and all mod cons.

**Europa Palace** *(fax 612 000; Teatro gatvė 1; singles/doubles 320/520 Lt)* is in a prime spot, on the pretty Teatro aikštė and close to the Smiltynė–Klaipėda ferry landing. It has 35 elegant rooms with heated bathroom floors.

**Astra** (*☎ 313 849, fax 216 420; Pilies gatvė 2; singles/doubles from 200/260 Lt*) is spitting distance from the Old Castle Port on the edge of the Old Town and has lovely rooms assuring a sound night's sleep.

**Seaside Hotels** Overlooking the beach amid pretty pine forests, **Pajūris** (*☎ 490 154, fax 490 142; Šlaito gatvė 18a; e giruliai@pajuris.lt; singles/doubles/triples 100/140/200 Lt*) is 8km north of Klaipėda in the suburb of Giruliai. Get there on minibus No 4 from Manto gatvė.

**Morena** (*☎ 351 314, fax 351 331; e admin@morenahotel.lt; Audros gatvė 8a, Melnragė; singles & doubles 100 Lt, suites 150 Lt*), near the coast, 4km north of the centre, is a small, family-run hotel offering wood-panelled rooms in the attic.

**Hotel Palva** (*☎ 391 155, fax 391 155; e info@palva.lt; Smiltynės gatvė 19; singles/doubles 80/130 Lt*), under *remontas* (renovation) for years, has finally re-opened as a hotel. The summer mansion slumbers on the water's edge, across the Curonian Lagoon in Smiltynė.

## Places to Eat
**Restaurants & Cafés** Not only the best place to eat in Klaipėda, **Kurpiai** (*☎ 410 555; Kurpių gatvė 1a; meals 35-60 Lt; open noon-3am daily*) is one of Lithuania's best bars (hell no – it's the best). Funky live jazz is played every night while you sample tender, juicy steaks and fish dishes. This place is heaving at weekends so get in well before 9pm when the tunes get going. You won't want to leave.

**Skandalas** (*The Scandal; ☎ 411 585; Kanto gatvė 44; meals 40 Lt; open noon-2am daily*) is a brash American dream, part Wild West, part Mae West. You can't beat it though for its steaks as big as states smothered in creamy sauces with potato wedges. Prices rise by 30% after 6pm.

**Bambola** (*☎ 312 213; Manto gatvė 1; open 11am-10pm Sun-Thur, 11am-midnight Fri & Sat • Nėries gatvė 10 near the bus and train stations; open 11am-10pm daily*) is an eatery Klaipėda is famed for in Lithuania. It is a fantastic pizzeria touting over 40 different pizzas (*picos*) and lasagne.

**Galerija Peda** (*Footprint Gallery; ☎ 410 710; Turgaus gatvė 10*), a stylish place inside an art gallery, is perfect for light evening snacks (8 Lt to 18 Lt), sweet-centred *blyneliai* and live jazz concerts at the weekend until midnight.

**Bistro BonTon** (*☎ 410 567; Turgaus gatvė 4/2; meals 20 Lt*) is a popular place serving many a cheap fill in a cheerful setting.

**Fotogalerija** (*Tomo gatvė 7; meals 15-25 Lt*), in the heart of the Old Town, is more quirky with a wooden ceiling and typical Memel beamed walls serving light Lithuanian pancakes of all types and fillings.

**Rasytė** (*☎ 412 728; Tiltų gatvė 6; meals 25-45 Lt*) dishes up a disco as well as food and a bar with a leafy courtyard which is popular in summer.

Manto gatvė has an array of eateries.

**Garazas** (*☎ 411 445; Manto gatvė 13; meals 30 Lt; open 10am-midnight daily*) is a bizarre themed café-cum-bar with car seats arranged around tables on oil drums, waiters in mechanics' dungarees and a collection of spanners on the walls.

**Kitas Krantas** (*☎ 217 365; Manto gatvė 11; meals 25 Lt*) is just as stylish as Garazas, and is the place where the city's cool young beauties sip cocktails and hang out.

**Boogie Woogie** (*☎ 411 844; Manto gatvė 5; meals 30 Lt; open until 2am daily*) is a hugely popular (but not spectacular) place serving American and European fodder.

**Forena** (*☎ 314 476; Manto gatvė 4; meals 40-100 Lt; open 7am-1am daily*) serves excellent Italian cuisine in its smart upmarket restaurant.

**Fast Food & Self-Catering** Self-caterers can stock up at **Iki** (*Mažvydo alėja 7/11; open 8am-10pm daily*), a Western-run supermarket.

## Entertainment
**Bars & Nightclubs** Klaipėda's Old Town seems to boast more traditional beer bars than any other place in Lithuania. Popular haunts include **Žvejų** (*Kurpių gatvė 8; open 10am-10pm daily*) overlooking the river; and close by **Buru Užeiga** (*Kepuju gatvė 17*).

**Meridianas** is an old sailing ship turned bar, moored on the river by the Manto gatvė bridge, which looks more like its rotting than rocking these days.

**Juodojo Katino Smuklė** (*Black Cat Pub; Mažvydo alėja 1*) is a cosy, dark wood bar filled with people having fun!

**Bohema** *(☎ 314 446; Aukštoji gatvė 3/3)* is a friendly place to sip a beer with a fabulous courtyard terrace sheltered by the Fachwerk beams of the Baroti Gallery.

**Kurpiai** *(☎ 410 555; Kurpių gatvė 1a; open noon-3am daily)* is where local 'Lithuanian Louis Armstrong' Kango is known for his amazing sax life!

**Theatre** At the **Drama Theatre** *(Dramos teatros; ☎ 314 453; Teatro aikštė 2)* the shows start at 7pm (except Monday).

The **Musical Theatre** *(Muzikinis teatras; ☎ 410 556; Danės krantinė 19)*, just north of the river, is home to the **Klaipėda Philharmonic** *(☎ 410 576; open 11am-2pm & 4pm-7pm Tues-Sun)*.

## Getting There & Away

For information on buses to/from Poland and Belarus, and ships to/from Germany, see the introductory Getting There & Away chapter.

**Air** The nearest airport is north of Palanga (see Palanga Getting There & Away). In Klaipėda, **West Express** *(☎ 310 311; e office@westexpress.lt; Daukanto gatvė 20)* sells Air Lithuania tickets.

**Bus** Klaipėda **bus station** *(☎ 411 547; Priestočio gatvė)* is 150m from the train station, about 1.5km north of the river and 750m east of Manto gatvė.

The Klaipėda–Kaunas–Vilnius highway is among the best in the Baltics, with some eight buses to/from Vilnius (32-38 Lt, six hours) and 10 buses to/from Kaunas (22-28 Lt, three hours) ploughing this route daily.

Most buses to Juodkrantė and Nida do not depart from the bus station, but from the ferry landing on the Curonian Spit at Smiltynė. The schedules are posted at the stop at Smiltynė, but it is better to ask at the information window at the bus station. In summer, microbuses to Nida (via Juodkrantė) run every half-hour from the ferry landing.

Daily services to/from Klaipėda include the following.

**Druskininkai** (via Kaunas) 39.50 Lt, 5½ hours, 273km, one bus
**Jurbarkas** (via Šilutė) 16 Lt, 2½ hours, 146km, three buses
**Kretinga** 3 Lt, 1¼ hours, 32km, every half an hour

**Liepāja** (via Palanga) 11.50 Lt, 2¾ hours, 98km, four buses
**Mažeikiai** 19 Lt, 2½-3 hours, 108km, six buses (one via Plungė)
**Nida** 7 Lt, 1½-2 hours, 48km, two buses from the bus station, plus microbuses every half-hour from Smiltynė
**Palanga** 3 Lt, 45 minutes, 25km, around 20 buses, plus microbuses every half-hour in summer
**Rīga** 35 Lt, six to seven hours, 310km, two buses (one via Liepāja and Palanga)
**Šiauliai** 20 Lt, 2½ hours, 155km, six buses

**Train** The **train station** *(☎ 313 677; Priestočio gatvė 1)*, 150m from the bus station, has an unusual, tall, helmeted clock tower.

Daily there are three trains to/from Vilnius (25.40 Lt, five to nine hours), via Kaunas; six trains to/from Šiauliai (14.50 Lt, 3¼ hours) originating in Radviliskis, and Kretinga (30 minutes); and one train to/from Tauragė (10.90 Lt, 3½ hours), and three to/from Šilutė (5 Lt, 1¼ hours).

**Ferry** See the introductory Getting There & Away chapter for schedules and fares on the passenger ferries to/from Kiel and Mukran in Germany, and Karlshamn in Sweden.

For information and bookings contact **Krantas Travel** *(☎ 395 111, fax 395 222; w www.krantas.lt/travel; Lietuvininkų gatvė 5; open 8am-7pm Mon-Fri, 10am-5pm Sat)*.

Routes to Copenhagen, Fredericia, and Aarhus in Denmark, and Århus in Sweden are mainly for cargo but there are some places for passengers. For information and bookings contact **Krantas Shipping** *(☎ 395 111, fax 395 222; Perkėlos gatvė 10)*. For the Mukran ferry, contact **Scandlines** *(☎ 310 561; room 108 Klaipėda Hotel)*; or **DFDS Baltic Line** *(☎ 496 400, 496 480, fax 496 499; Minijos gatvė 180)* in Klaipėda.

State-owned **Klaipėda Port** *(Klaipėdos Nafta: w www.spk.lt)* is the most northerly ice-free port – the water won't freeze even at minus 25°C.

## Getting Around

**Bus** No 8 from the Geležinkelio Stotis stops outside the train station, runs south to Pergalės aikštė then down Manto gatvė through the city centre to the Turgaus stop, on Taikos prospektas. Minibuses follow the same route.

**Car & Motorcycle** Inside Hotel Klaipėda, **Hertz** *(☎ 310 737; e klaipeda@hertz.lt)* has a branch. **Unirenta** (☎ 312 613, fax 313 100; ⓔ office@unirenta.lt; Tomo gatvė 7) and **EuroRenta** (☎ 382 121; ⓔ rent@eurorenta.lt; Šimkaus gatvė 2) are two local companies offering competitive rates.

Litinterp and the Klaipėda Travellers Hostel both offer cheap car rental (see Places to Stay earlier).

**Ferry** The main Smiltynė ferry leaves from the **Old Castle Port** (Senoji perkėla; ☎ 314 257; Žvejų gatvė 8), on the southern bank of the Danė River, 100m west of the Naujoji Uosto/Pilies gatvė bridge. It docks on the eastern side of Smiltynė, at the start of the road to Nida and 1.5km south of the Maritime Museum.

Timetables are posted at the ticket office (kasa) but pilots ignore them and leave early if ferries are full. Ferries sail to/from Smiltynė every half an hour between 6.30am and 2.15am June to August. The rest of the year, there is at least one ferry an hour until 2am. The crossing takes 10 minutes. Complicated ferry ticket fees have been scrapped. Foot passengers ride for free while cars are charged at 20 Lt each. Pay on the ferry. In summer, Old Castle Port ferries are pedestrian only.

The **New River Port** (Naujoji perkėla; ☎ 310 974; Nemuno gatvė 8), 3km south of the mouth of the Danė, is for vehicles. Ferries sail half-hourly from 6.50am to 8.30pm Monday to Friday, and 7.30am to 9.30pm Saturday and Sunday (hourly in winter). On the Curonian Spit this ferry docks 2.5km south of the ferry landing at Smiltynė.

Bus No 1 continues down to the New River Port from its stops in Klaipėda city centre. Get off at the New River Port stop.

# Curonian Spit National Park

☎ 469 • pop 2528

The heady scent of ozone and pine are at their headiest on this thin tongue of sand. Waves from the Baltic Sea pound one side, the Curonian Lagoon laps the other. The winds and tree-felling have sculpted the Curonian Spit (Kuršių Nerija in Lithuanian; Kurische Nehrung in German) over time. But this precious natural treasure is by nature a fragile one – being made up of millions of grains of constantly shifting sand. As the dunes creep closer to the Baltic Sea there are fears it may disappear within two centuries.

In 1991 the Curonian Spit National Park was formed to protect the dunes, lagoon and the surrounding Baltic Sea. Lush pine forests filled with deer, elk and wild boar cover 70% of the spit, the dunes make up a quarter of it while only 1.5% is urban. The main industry is tourism, which ironically is also a major environmental threat. Fishing was traditionally the main source of income and fishermen still smoke their catch to an old Curonian recipe today.

The entire Curonian Spit was Prussian or German territory until WWI. The northern half was annexed by Lithuania, along with the rest of the 'Memel Territory', in 1923. It still has a magnetic attraction for returning German exiles who once lived on the spit and now enjoy holidays here instead. During the Soviet era the hotels were earmarked for communist *apparatchiks* (high ranking officials) and their families. Today, it is held in universal affection by Lithuanians.

The southern half of the spit is Russian, and a road runs the whole length to Kaliningrad, the main city in the neighbouring Russian-owned Kaliningrad region. The main settlement on the Lithuanian side is Nida, a quaint summer resort just north of the Russian border which, like the other settlements on the sheltered lagoon coast – Juodkrantė, Pervalka and Preila – began life as a fishing village. These four villages form the Neringa administrative district. The good, sandy and rugged beaches are all on the west coast of the spit. Facing the widest part of the Baltic Sea, the waters here can get quite rough during spring and autumn storms when amber is washed up onto the shore. Don't bathe in the lagoon; it's polluted.

The Curonian Spit National Park covers an area of 26,473 hectares, some 16,700 hectares of which comprise water. Its forests are home to 37 different mammal species, 10 of which are rare – including, in 2002, elk (only 30), roe (210) and wild boar (120). More than 200 species of birds flutter overhead (54 of them rare), and 470 types of butterfly.

Visitors must pay a 3 Lt fee to enter the park (car and driver 15 Lt). Even if you are travelling by bus, this fee is still obligatory (the driver will wait while you buy a ticket at the roadside kiosk). The speed limit for

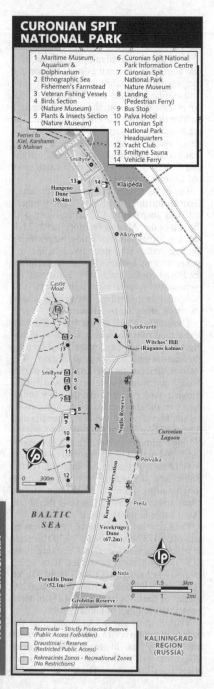

## CURONIAN SPIT NATIONAL PARK

1  Maritime Museum, Aquarium & Dolphinarium
2  Ethnographic Sea Fishermen's Farmstead
3  Veteran Fishing Vessels
4  Birds Section (Nature Museum)
5  Plants & Insects Section (Nature Museum)
6  Curonian Spit National Park Information Centre
7  Curonian Spit National Park Nature Museum
8  Landing (Pedestrian Ferry)
9  Bus Stop
10  Palva Hotel
11  Curonian Spit National Park Headquarters
12  Yacht Club
13  Smiltynė Sauna
14  Vehicle Ferry

Ferries to Kiel, Karshamn & Mukran

SEE INSET

Smiltynė

13  14  Klaipėda

Hangeno Dune (36.4m)

Alksnynė

Castle Moat

Juodkrantė

Witches' Hill (Raganos kalnas)

Smiltynė  4  5  6  7  8  9  10  11  12

Nagls Reserve

Curonian Lagoon

Pervalka

Karvaičiai Reservation

Preila

BALTIC SEA

Vecekrugo Dune (67.2m)

Parnidis Dune (52.1m)

Nida

Grobštas Reserve

0  300m

0  1.5  3km
0  1  2mi

Rezervatai - Strictly Protected Reserve (Public Access Forbidden)
Draustiniai - Reserves (Restricted Public Access)
Rekreacinės Zonos - Recreational Zones (No Restrictions)

KALININGRAD REGION (RUSSIA)

cars in the national park is 40km/h through villages and 60km/h or 70km/h on the open road; cars have to be parked in designated parking areas. Beware of the occasional elk crossing the road. Culprits caught damaging the flora or fauna, disturbing nests during nesting and migration, pitching a tent, lighting a fire or walking on the dunes risk a 300 Lt fine. Other spit rules: only walk on marked tracks and don't pick flowers; they help to stabilise the sands (see the boxed text 'Shifting Sands & Delicate Dunes').

## Information

The headquarters of the Curonian Spit National Park (*Kursių Nerijos nacionalinis parkas;* ☎/fax 46-391 113; e info@nerija.lt; *Smiltynės plentas 18*) is about 1km from Smiltynė ferry port. The excellent **Tourist Information Centre** (*Informacijos centras;* ☎ 46-391 177, 46-402 257, ☎/fax 46-391 179; e kinfo@takas.lt; Smiltynės plentas 11; open 8am-4pm Mon-Fri Sept-May; 8am-4pm Mon-Fri, 10am-4pm Sat May-Sept) is next door to the nature museum in Smiltynė. It shows films, arranges guides and excursions, and distributes an abundance of information about the park.

There are small tourist offices in Nida and Juodkrantė or go to the superb website w www.nerija.lt.

## Getting There & Away

The Klaipėda–Smiltynė ferry (see Klaipėda Getting There & Away earlier) is the main access route to the Curonian Spit. From Smiltynė, microbuses, timed to coincide with ferry arrivals/departures, plough the route between Smiltynė and Nida, passing through Juodkrantė. Some buses (but not all) stop in Pervalka and Preila too.

Between June and August, buses run hourly from 7.15am to 11.15pm. Journey time between Smiltynė and Juodkrantė/Nida is 30/50 minutes; a single fare to Nida is 7.50 Lt. The daily Smiltynė–Kaliningrad bus also stops at Juodkrantė. There are reports of travellers being charged four times the price when paying in *litų* rather than roubles on this journey.

In the low season, buses become less regular – running every two hours between 7.15am and 9.15pm. Your best bet is to team up with other Juodkrantė/Nida-bound travellers and share a taxi ride there. Barter before

## Shifting Sands & Delicate Dunes

Lithuanian legend has it that motherly sea giantess Neringa created the spit. She lovingly carried armfuls of sand in her apron to form a protected harbour for the local fishing folk. The truth is almost as enchanting, the spit being formed 5000 or 6000 years ago as the waves and winds of the Baltic Sea let sand accumulate in its shallow waters near the coast. The result is a grandeur and original beauty found absolutely nowhere else.

Massive deforestation in the 16th century started the sands shifting. Trees were felled for timber, leaving the sands free to roam unhindered at the wish of the strong coastal winds. At a pace of 20m a year, the sands swallowed 14 villages until the 19th century.

Dubbed the 'Sahara of Lithuania' due to its desert state – drastic action was needed. In 1768 an international commission set about replanting. Today this remains a priority of the national park authorities. Deciduous forest (mainly birch groves) covers 20% of the national park; coniferous forest, primarily pine and mountain pine trees, constitutes a further 53%. Alder trees can be found on 206 hectares (3% of the park's area). The spit lattices of branches and wooden stakes have pinned down the sand. But Hurricane Anatoly ripped through the spit in 1999, further damaging the dunes. In 2000, the year it became a World Heritage site, Unesco officials granted the spit $30,000 to repair the damage and build special paths to stop people walking on them. A further $20,000 is sought to renovate 100 traditional fishermen's houses in and around Nida.

But the sands are still moving – 5½m north in 2002. Slowly the spit is drifting into the Baltic Sea. There are problems with tourism as 1.5 million people visit the dunes each year. The threat of forest fire and people straying off the designated paths is consequently high. Also the Russian side will not release maps of their half of the spit as it is a military area and officially secret.

Meanwhile the dunes are shrinking -winds, waves and humans have reduced them by 10m in 30 years. Its precious beauty may yet be lost forever.

---

setting off, a fare per person to Juodkrantė is around 10 Lt per person (that does not including the 3 Lt per person entrance fee to the national park).

Note that the spit's only petrol station near Nida is shut so fill up in Klaipėda.

## JUODKRANTĖ
☎ 469 • pop 600

Sleepy little Juodkrantė (former German name: Schwarzort) is 20km south of Smiltynė on the east (lagoon) coast of the spit. Holiday homes, a few shops, žuvis (smoked fish) outlets, a **post office** (Kalno gatvė 3) and the main bus stop and pier (both opposite Liudviko Rėzos 8) make up the tiny village centre.

A kilometre south there's a red-brick German **Evangelical-Lutheran church** (Liudviko Rėzos 56), dating from 1885, and some prettily painted, old wooden cottages.

In 1854 to 1855 and 1860, amber was excavated in the village in three separate little clusters – 2250 tonnes in all. At the northern end there's an area around a fishing harbour known as Amber Bay, just north of which is sheltered Lithuania's largest colony of grey heron-cormorants. The spit is about 1.5km wide at this point and the fine stretch of forest – good for spotting elk that emerge from cover in the early morning and evening – is among the loveliest you will find on the peninsula.

If you go into the woods, be sure of a big surprise…in the form of devils, witches and ghouls skulking on **Witches' Hill** (Raganos kalnas). Fantastical and grotesque wooden carvings from Lithuanian folklore line this sculpture trail which veers from fairytale to nightmare. It's signposted immediately south of Liudviko Rėzos 46. Children love it.

From Juodkrantė, a **coastal cycling path** leads the whole way to Nida. The first 2km are lined with stone sculptures created for the 1997 to 1999 'Earth and Water' International Sculpture Symposium.

## Information
A small **tourist office** (☎/fax 53 490; e juodkrante@neringa.lt; open 9am-5pm Tues-Sat May-Sept) is inside Hotel Ažuolynas.

Postcards and German-language books on Neringa are sold at the **shop** (Liudviko Rėzos 13) inside a 1920s fishing cottage.

WESTERN LITHUANIA

## Places to Stay

Ask around to see if anyone knows of cheap rooms available – local people will often let you stay in their home for about 40 Lt a night.

**Smilga** *(☎ 53 283; Kalno gatvė 18; beds from 35 Lt; open May-Sept)* is cheap but not cheerful. It's a 20-room, run-down place with double, triple and quad rooms, offering nothing more than a night's sleep. It's only open in the height of summer.

**Ažuolynas** *(☎ 53 310, fax 53 316; Liudviko Rėzos 54; singles/doubles May-Sept 179/228 Lt)*, in the southern part of the village, is Juodkrantė's most modern former rest home. It boasts a swimming pool, gym and outdoor concert venue.

**Santauta** *(☎ 53 167; Kalno gatvė 36; singles/doubles/triples 60/90/150 Lt)* has minimalist rooms.

**Kurena** *(☎ 53 101; Liudviko Rėzos 10; doubles from 250 Lt)* is a brand new, tasteful haven with proper double beds.

**Vila Flora** *(☎ 53 024; Kalno gatvė 7a; singles/doubles 160/240 Lt)* is just as nice, with a decent café.

**Eglių Slėnis** *(Fir Valley; ☎/fax 53 364; Kalno gatvė 28; singles/doubles/quads from 120/220/300 Lt)* is a large, modern block, with giant-sized rooms kitted out with a kitchen, TV and (in most cases) balcony.

## Places to Eat

Eating options are limited; self-caterers should stock up on provisions in Klaipėda before arriving. Family-run restaurants, where simple but good Lithuanian home cooking can be sampled, include the following.

**Pamario takas** *(Liudviko Rėzos 42; meal 25 Lt; open until midnight)* in a quaint fishing cottage close to the end of the Witches' Hill trail.

**Žvejonė** *(☎ 53 280; Liudviko Rėzos 30; open until midnight)* has chairs in a flower-filled garden.

For a smoked fish or two, head for one of the numerous *žuvis* outlets that dot the length of Liudviko Rėzos – from north to south.

## JUODKRANTĖ TO NIDA

Just south of Juodkrantė the road switches from the eastern side of the peninsula to the western. Between the two main settlements are two smaller villages, **Pervalka** and **Preila**, both on the east coast and reached by side roads from the main road. These tiny fishing

villages are comparatively new, formed in the 19th century by the peoples of the once neighbouring villages, Karaičiai and Naujieji Nagliai, after shifting sands forced them to flee. Records show that Naujieji Nagliai became nothing more than a mountain of sand in 1843. Reforesting the area at the time cost the Prussian government more than half a million marks.

**Vecekrugas dune**, the highest dune on the whole peninsula, 67.2m high at the last count, is near Preila. It is covered with forest pines. The ridge on which it stands, known as Old Inn Hill (Senosis smuklės kalnas), was named after an inn that once stood at the foot of the dune. The entire area is protected as the **Karvaičiai Reservation**, a 3043 hectare area – a few pockets are accessible to the public.

## NIDA
☎ 469 • pop 2000

Lovely Nida is an old-fashioned fishing village surrounded by natural beauty. The allure of sparkling lagoon waters, yellow sands, hazy pine forests and wooden cottages with fishing nets strung outside have made it the hub of the spit. Each year 50,000 tourists swamp this tiny village.

Nida (former German name: Nidden) is the largest settlement on the Lithuanian half of the Curonian Spit, 48km from Klaipėda and just 3km from the Russian border. It has a harbour where a hydrofoil used to cross the lagoon to Kaunas. White-sand beaches are a 2km walk away through pine forest – or there's a shuttle bus in summer from pier to beachfront. Just to the south stand some of the most impressive dunes on the peninsula, including Parnidis Dune (Parnidžio kopa) which has steps up to its 52m high summit where there's a sundial and stunning views of rippling, untouched dunes.

A colony of mainly East Prussian artists from the late 19th century drew inspiration from here. It developed as a tourist resort and there were five hotels by the 1930s, when the German writer Thomas Mann (1875–1955) had a summer home built here. In 1968, French philosopher Jean Paul Sartre (1905–80) was granted special permission by Khrushchev to spend some time on the dunes.

Nida may stretch for 2km but its centre is at the southern end, behind the harbour. Three roads link the village to the main road. The southernmost of these is Taikos

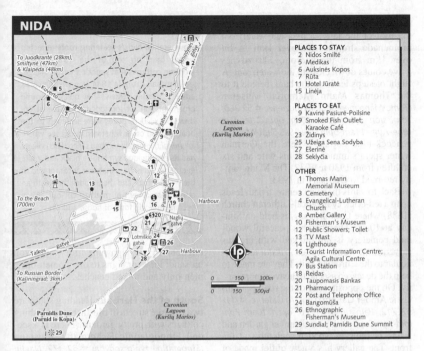

**NIDA**

**PLACES TO STAY**
2  Nidos Smiltė
5  Medikas
6  Auksinės Kopos
7  Rūta
11 Hotel Jūratė
15 Linėja

**PLACES TO EAT**
9  Kavinė Pasiurė-Poilsinė
19 Smoked Fish Outlet;
   Karaoke Café
23 Židinys
25 Užeiga Sena Sodyba
27 Ešerinė
28 Seklyčia

**OTHER**
1  Thomas Mann
   Memorial Museum
3  Cemetery
4  Evangelical-Lutheran
   Church
8  Amber Gallery
10 Fisherman's Museum
12 Public Showers; Toilet
13 TV Mast
14 Lighthouse
16 Tourist Information Centre;
   Agila Cultural Centre
17 Bus Station
18 Reidas
20 Taupomasis Bankas
21 Pharmacy
22 Post and Telephone Office
24 Bangomūša
26 Ethnographic
   Fisherman's Museum
29 Sundial; Parnidis Dune Summit

To Juodkrantė (28km),
Smiltynė (47km)
& Klaipėda (48km)

Curonian
Lagoon
(Kuršių Marios)

To the Beach
(700m)

Harbour

To Russian Border
(Kaliningrad; 3km)

Harbour

Parnidis Dune
(Parnidio Kopa)

Curonian
Lagoon
(Kuršių Marios)

0      150      300m
0      150      300yd

gatvė, which leads straight to the village heart. Coming from Klaipėda (north), you enter Nida along Kuverto gatvė; turn right onto Pamario gatvė to reach the centre.

## Information

The **Tourist Information Centre** (☎ 52 345, fax 52 538; e agilainfo@is.lt; Taikos gatvė 4; open 9am-8pm Mon-Sat, 9am-3pm Sun June-Aug; 10am-6pm Mon-Fri 1 Sept-May), inside the **Agila Cultural Centre** (kultūros centras; Taikos gatvė 4), arranges homestay accommodation from 150 Lt per room with a 5 Lt booking fee. Or ask for Laime's apartments for 35 Lt per person; and excursions (111 Lt in Russian, Lithuanian and German).

You can change money, get cash advances on Visa and MasterCard, and exchange Thomas Cook and American Express travellers cheques at **Taupomasis Bankas** (☎ 52 241; Taikos gatvė 5), next to the police station. There is a Visa ATM inside Hotel Jūratė; the ATM inside the blue Bankas Snoras booth next to Naglių gatvė 27 accepts MasterCard.

The **post and telephone office** is at Taikos gatvė 15. There's also a **pharmacy** (vaistinė; Taikos gatvė 11; open 8.30am-8.30pm daily

May-Sept) in town. Take your own suncream as it's in short supply on the spit.

## Things to See & Do

Chill out. Go for walks, relax and enjoy yourself. During the spring and autumn storms, amber is washed up on the shores. In the depths of winter the frozen lagoon is dotted with people ice fishing, warming themselves by drinking vodka. In summer you can hire paddle boats from a small wooden hut at the southern end of Lotmiškio gatvė, or jet skis from the dunes on the beach that kiss the other side of the peninsula. Alternatively, opt for a trip aboard a handsome replica of a **kurėnai** (☎ 8-689 93335; July and August only), a traditional 19th-century fishing boat; the boat departs from the harbour. There are outlets with **bicycles** to hire around almost every street corner in Nida centre. Romantic horse-drawn carriage rides cost 15 Lt for 15 minutes.

**North of the Harbour** Gorgeous views of the windswept dunes – a sight that takes your breath away – can be had at the harbour, from the end of the jetty next to the derelict main harbour building (*priepaulka*). From the foot of the jetty, a pleasant waterfront promenade stretches for over 1km. A bit over 1km from the harbour, Skruzdynės gatvė comes down close to the waterfront. A flight of steps leads up the bank beside it to the **Thomas Mann Memorial Museum** (*Tomo Mano memorialinis muziejus; ☎ 52 260; admission 2 Lt; open 10am-6pm Tues-Sun June-Aug; 11am-5pm Tues-Sat Sept-May*), a peacock-blue cottage where the German writer spent summers with his wife and six children from 1930 to 1932. The Mann family returned to Germany in 1933.

Back towards the town centre, a path leads up to a red-brick **Evangelical-Lutheran church** (1888) where Catholic mass is held on Sunday at 10am. The church's peaceful woodland cemetery is pin-pricked with crosses carved from wood – called *krikstai* and particular to the Curonian Spit. They are made to help the deceased ascend to heaven more easily. On the opposite side of the road is a fantastic **Amber Gallery** (*Gintaro Galerija; ☎/fax 52 712; Pamario gatvė 20; open 10am-7pm mid-Apr–Sept*) with a small amber garden and a line of unusual wooden sculptures at the front. The gallery has a new **outlet** made of glass, straddling the ends of an ancient wooden boat just behind the harbour.

Heading back towards the harbour there's a **Fisherman's Museum** (*Gyventojų Verslų Ekspozicija; Kuverto gatvė 2; open 11am-5pm Wed-Sun, May-Sept*), which traces the development of Nida's fishing industry with an exhibition of tools, nets and B&W photographs.

**West of the Harbour** All westward routes lead ultimately to the beach on the far side of the peninsula. One good way is to turn right (north) off Taikos gatvė, opposite the post office. The street bends sharply left after 150m and climbs. Just over 400m along this bit, a path leads up the hill to a **lighthouse** on the right, which is the highest point in the area. If you continue a farther 700m along the path, behind the lighthouse, you'll come out on a good, straight path leading back down to the main road and, 400m beyond that, to the beach.

A less adventurous option is to follow Taikos gatvė westwards until it meets the main Smiltynė–Nida road, then continue in the same direction along a paved footpath

## Seafaring Weathercocks

Nowhere are Nida's seafaring roots reflected better than on top of the 19th-century wooden cottages that speckle the spit village.

A Prussian ruling in 1844 saw weathercocks arrive to identify vessels. They quickly became ornamentation for rooftops too. Made of tin, these 60 x 30cm plates were fastened to the boat mast so other fishermen could see where a *kurėnai* (Neringa boat) had sailed. Each village had its own unique symbol – a black and white geometrical design – that was incorporated in the weathercock and then embellished with an eclectic assortment of mythical cut-outs. They became an early form of house address.

(signposted) through pine forest until you hit sand; look for signs to the women-only, men-only and mixed beaches.

**South of the Harbour** Heading south are two or three streets of old-fashioned fishing cottages with pretty gardens. There is a second **Ethnographic Fisherman's Museum** (*Etnografinė žvejo sodyba; ☎ 52 372; Naglių gatvė 4; admission 1 Lt; open 11am-7pm Tues-Fri May-Sept; 11am-5pm Tues-Sat Sept-May*) inside an old fishing cottage with rooms arranged as they were in the 19th century.

Beyond Lotmiškio gatvė there's a path that leads along the coastline then through a wooded area and up the spectacularly high and bare dunes that you can see from the village via a flight of 180 wooden steps. From the top of the steps, a track leads to **Parnidis dune** – 7km long and the park's most impressive chain of unforested dune (hence the reason why much of it is, in fact, a reservation strictly off-limits to the public). Parnidis peaks at 52m and is topped with a **granite sundial** featuring the old Lithuanian calendar.

The unique panorama of sand, both coastlines, the forests to the north, and a mixture of sand and forests to the south is heart-stopping and unforgettable. You can explore in any direction from here, but the Kaliningrad border is 3km south – it's made pretty obvious by the signs and Lithuanian border guards there to stop you straying into Russian territory.

## Places to Stay

Prices in Nida fluctuate wildly between winter and summer; high-season prices (June, July and August) are listed below. Camping is forbidden in the park.

The **Tourist Information Centre** (☎ 52 345, fax 52 538; e agilainfo@is.lt; Taikos gatvė 4; open 9am-8pm Mon-Sat, 9am-3pm Sun June-Aug; 10am-6pm Mon-Fri 1 Sept-May) arranges accommodation in private homes from 35 Lt to 150 Lt per night (one-room apartment). Rooms in a private home or wooden summerhouse with bath and linen start at 35 Lt. Clean, modern **public showers** (Taikos gatvė 29; rates 5 Lt; open 10am-8pm daily) are in the town centre. If these are full try **Nida Yacht Club** (☎ 52 828) at the harbour end of Taikos gatvė.

**Nidos Pušynes** (☎ 52 221; Pušynes gatvė 123; huts per person 20 Lt, doubles/suites 230/400 Lt) is sought-after for its position overlooking the lagoon, close to Thomas Mann's residence at the northern end of Skruzdynės gatvė. Breakfast is an extra 18 Lt. Even better, it has a handful of beachside **wooden huts** for the adventurous (and poor!).

**Medikas** (☎ 52 985; Kuverto gatvė 14; doubles/triples 120/130 Lt) is a good option for bargain hunters.

**Nidos Smiltė** (☎ 52 221; Skruzdynės gatvė 2; doubles 40-230 Lt), 300m south, has dirt-cheap and large, modern and consequently more expensive rooms.

**Hotel Jūratė** (☎ 52 300; Pamario gatvė 3; singles/doubles 150/200 Lt) is in the right location in the centre of Nida and has old-fashioned rooms.

The pick of Nida's collection of former Soviet rest homes, includes **Rūta** (☎ 52 367; Kuverto gatvė 15; singles/doubles 158/316 Lt), a former rest home of the Communist Party, has uninspiring rooms close to the beach.

**Auksinės Kopos** (☎ 52 212; Kuverto gatvė 17; singles/doubles from 105/130 Lt), opposite, is a sprawling rest home with a nice outdoor swimming pool and crisp, clean rooms.

**Linėja** (☎ 52 390, fax 52 718; Taikos gatvė 18; e lineja@pajuris.lt; singles/doubles from 120/150 Lt) has clean, chintzy rooms, a bowling alley and all mod cons in a package-holiday style concrete block.

## Places to Eat

**Smoked fish outlets** (Rūkyta žuvis) include the **shop** (open 10am-10pm summer) at the bus station; and at Naglių gatvė 18 where there's also the karaoke bar which is only just big enough for the microphone let alone punters.

**Židinys** (☎ 51 123; Kopų gatvė 1a; meals 20 Lt) is a non-smoking, friendly place off the tourist trail serving pastas, soups and Lithuanian staples.

**Ešerinė** (☎ 52 757; Naglių gatvė 2; meals 25-40 Lt; open 10am-midnight daily) is an odd but attractive Hawaiian-style wooden building with grass for its roof. Munch on typical Lithuanian *fermentinis sūris* (sticks of cheese) while watching the sun sink behind the dunes.

**Kavinė Pasiurė-Poilsine** (Kuverto gatvė 2; open 10am-midnight daily), another lovely spot at which to dine or drink while watching the waves lap, is next to the Fisherman's Museum.

**Užeiga Sena Sodyba** (☎ 52 782; Naglių gatvė 6; meals 30 Lt) serves Lithuanian fare in a flowery garden only in summer (note the swans on the gable).

**Linėja** (Pamario gatvė 7; meals 40 Lt), the restaurant not the hotel, is the place to try for a touch of upmarket cuisine, with imaginative dishes.

**Seklyčia** (☎ 52 945; Lotmiškio gatvė 1; meals 50-70 Lt; open 9am-midnight daily) is a Scandinavian-style haven with views of the dunes and an excellent (if pricey) fish menu. Believe everything you hear – the *kepta duona* is the best in Lithuania (and the lobster probably is as well at 85 Lt!).

## Entertainment

Discos, films, art exhibitions and other sporadic cultural events are hosted by the **Agila Cultural Centre** (kultūros centras; Taikos gatvė 4). Friday nights are disco nights in the centre's café-bar. Look for posters outside advertising events. Nida hosts the International Folk Music Festival each June. **Bangomūša** (Naglių gatvė 5; open until midnight) is a bright blue delight. Failing that, singing karaoke at the small and simple outdoor café, tucked next to the smoked fish outlet at Naglių gatvė 18, can be entertaining!

**Reidas** (Naglių gatvė 20) is an appealing bar with a pool table.

## Getting There & Away

You can reach Nida by bus or private vehicle from Klaipėda, or Smiltynė, at the northern tip of the Curonian Spit, or Kaliningrad (via Zelenogradsk). The Lithuanian border post is on the main road, immediately south of the closed petrol station at the corner of Taikos gatvé. The Russian border post is 3km further south; don't even think about crossing without the necessary Russian visa and paperwork (see Visas & Documents in the introductory Facts for the Visitor).

**Bus** Buses arrive and depart from the **bus station** (☎ 52 472; Nagliy gatvé 20). All Juodkrantė-bound buses continue to Nida. From Nida there are microbuses every half-hour to/from Smiltyně (1¼ hours) between 6.15am and 11.15pm (until 8pm from September to May); and a couple of buses daily from Klaipėda bus station (1½-2 hours). Buses tend to leave when they're full rather than stick rigidly to the timetable.

## CURONIAN LAGOON (EAST COAST)

The low-lying, marsh-dotted eastern side of the Curonian Lagoon (Kursiy marios) is described as 'the end of the world'. Remote and rural, there is little to reveal its historical Prussian/German roots. Unlike the western coast, this area has scarcely been touched by tourism. Summer skies offer magnificent views of the spit's white dunes across the lagoon. In winter, the lagoon – up to 12km wide in places – freezes and the ice becomes speckled with ice-fishermen waiting patiently for a *stinta* (smelt) to bite.

The main town of the region is **Šilutė** (German: Heydekrug; pop 25,000), 48km from Klaipėda on the Sovietsk road and railway. There's the small **Šilutė Museum** (☎ 441-62 209; Lietuvininky gatvé 36; admission 1 Lt; open 9am-5pm Tues-Sat).

Beyond that, this small and sleepy town serves as a gateway into the extraordinary **Nemunas Delta** where the Nemunas River ends its 937km journey from its source in the Minsk Upland in neighbouring Belarus, by splitting into numerous tributaries and spilling into the Curonian Lagoon. In the heart of the Delta is the fishing village of **Rusnė**, where the main stream divides into three – the Atmata, the Pakalnė and the Skirvytė. As with the lagoon, the Nemunas Delta freezes most winters, setting its hardy residents in extreme weathers. Spring flooding is common and merciless.

Inland, the pinprick hamlet of **Agluonénai**, midway between Šilutė and Klaipėda, offers travellers a fabulous opportunity to discover a real Russian sauna *(banya)* – see the boxed text 'Some Like it Hot' in the introductory Facts for the Visitor chapter.

Run by a friendly, mildly eccentric owner, the rustic **Karčema** *(Inn;* ☎ *46-442 277)* has two Russian saunas (big/small 40/30 Lt per hour) sheltered in a traditional wooden farmstead covering five hectares. Each sauna houses 10 to 15 people and is kitted out with a pool and separate 'cooling down' room. There's an outside bar that serves grilled *šašlykas* and has tables made from millstones under the trees. Other facilities include a sandy volleyball court, small lake and forest marked with hiking trails. You can even stay the night – there are two rooms for 80 Lt. Karčema is set off the road; approaching the village from the north, look for a red granite sculpture set on a small hillock.

# Nemunas Delta Regional Park

☎ 441 • pop 4000

The savage yet serenely beautiful landscape of the Nemunas Delta (Nemuno Deltos) is, in fact, a soggy cluster of islands, covering 30,000 hectares and protected since 1992 under the Nemunas Delta Regional Park (Nemuno Deltos Regioninis Parkas). One-fifth of the park is water.

The largest island, **Rusnė Island**, covers 4800 hectares and increases in size by 15cm to 20cm a year. Some 270 of the 325 bird species found in Lithuania frequent the park, many of which can be spotted from the **observation towers** at Naikupé, Uostadvaris and Rusnė on Rusnė Island. Rare species are among the one million birds that pass through the station each migratory period (see the boxed text 'Nemunas Bird Life').

From **Rusnė**, the largest village on the island, there are seasonal boats across the lagoon to Nida.

Boat is the main form of transport in the park, dubbed 'Lithuania's Venice', particularly between March and mid-May when spring floods plunge about 5% of the park under water. In 1994 exceptionally severe flooding saw the waters rise to 1.5m in places.

A depth of 40cm to 70cm is the norm most years, during which villagers are transported both in and out of the park by an amphibious tractor. Dike-protected polders cover the park, the first polder being built in 1840 to protect Rusnė village. The **water-pumping station** at Uostadvaris dates from 1907 and can be visited upon request. Many lower polders are still flooded seasonally and serve as valuable spawning grounds for various fish species (there are some 60 in the park) and a resting place for migratory birds.

Another intriguing point is **Ventė**, on the tip of the south-pointing promontory of the delta. Known locally as Ventės Ragas (World's Edge), a Teutonic Order castle was built here in the 1360s to protect shipping in the area. However, the castle and its church collapsed within a couple of hundred years. In the church's case, at least, this was due to the severity of the storms on this isolated point – as indicated by Ventė's German name, Windenburg (Windy Castle). The church was rebuilt but wrecked again by storms in 1702. Its stones were used a few years later to build the church at **Kintai**, a town 10km farther north on the regional park's northeastern boundary. In 1837, a wooden tower (lit by an oil lamp) was built at Ventė, which was replaced in 1862 by the lighthouse that still stands today. The old German cemetery can still be seen on the shore of the lagoon at Ventė.

The edge of the world – **Ventės Ragas** – is a sparsely inhabited area. There are just a few fishers' houses and a lighthouse at the tip – which can be either beautifully tranquil or beautifully wild. The main attraction of Ventė, besides its dramatic nature and uplifting isolation, is the important **Ornithological Station-Museum**. The first bird-ringing station was established in Ventės Ragas in 1929, but it was not until 1959 to 1960 that large bird traps were installed here. Today, zig zag, snipe, cobweb and duck traps are all used to temporarily ensnare the birds before they are ringed. The station banded its millionth bird in 1998. About 200 different species have been observed at the centre, including the white stork which favours Ventė as its prime breeding ground.

From Ventė, you can hire a boat to sail west across the Curonian Lagoon to Nida, or east to the delta settlement of **Mingė** (also called Minija after the river that forms the

### Nemunas Bird Life

The Nemunas wetlands are a twitcher's heaven. Many rare birds breed in the lush marshes around Rusnė including rare black storks, white-tailed eagles, black-tailed godwits, pintails, dunlin, ruff and great snipe.

It is also an important area for migratory waterfowl as the Arctic–European–East African bird migration flight path cuts through it. But it's not just a stop-over or feeding site – the park is a breeding ground for 169 species of birds, and some, for example, the pintail, don't breed anywhere else in Lithuania.

Rare aquatic warblers, corn-crakes black-headed gulls, white-winged black terns and great crested grebes have their biggest colonies in the Delta. One million birds pass over the **Ventės Ragas Ornithological Station** (☎ 441-54 480), 66km south of Klaipėda at the end of the Kintai–Ventė road. About 70 of them are trapped and ringed for research into world migration habits.

main 'street' through the village). No more than 100 people live in Mingė and only two families still speak Lietuvinkai, an ethnic dialect of Lithuanian, distinct to the delta which has all but died out. The 19th-century riverside houses are made of wood with reed roofs and are protected as architectural monuments. A good way to explore this area is by bicycle; from Mingė a **cycling track** runs around **Lake Krokų Lanka** – the largest lake in the park at 4km long and 3.3km wide.

The **headquarters of the Nemunas Delta Regional Park** (☎/fax 75 050; @ ndrp@silute .omnitel.net; Lietuvininkų gatvė 10) is in the centre of Šilutė, and there is a helpful **information centre** (☎ 58 154; Pakalnės gatvė 40a; open 8am-5pm daily June-Aug; 8am-5pm Mon-Fri in winter) in Rusnė; despite its supposed street address, the latter is way off the beaten path; follow the 'Rekreacinis-Informacinis centras' signs from Rusnė. Both centres organise informative bird-watching and fishing trips, and boat tours with a local English- or German-speaking guide that take you along the park's many waterways. It will also arrange farmstay accommodation (see Places to Stay), sell you a licence to fish in the park (10 Lt per day) and organise boat trips to Nida.

WESTERN LITHUANIA

## Places to Stay & Eat

**Camping & Farmstays** It is possible to camp in the Nemunas Delta Regional Park in official **camp sites** *(tent sites 20-50 Lt)*. The park also organises accommodation on farms, mainly in Rusnė, 8km west of Šilutė for 20 Lt to 50 Lt per night. It's the best way to experience the park especially with delicious home cooking thrown in, which is worth the additional cost.

**Ventaine** *(☎ 44 525)* is a camp site on the shore of the lagoon in Ventė; the park HQ in Šilutė will book your place and give directions.

**Hotels – In the Park** At Ventės Ragas, **Ventė Tourist Centre** *(☎ 44 534; tent sites per person 20 Lt, doubles with shower 100-200 Lt)* is privately-run and extremely popular due to its lagoon views and pleasant, modern rooms.

**Hotels – Outside the Park** In Šilutė there's a cheap **youth hostel** *(☎ 51 806, ☎/fax 51 804; Lietuvninkų gatvė72; dorm beds 30 Lt)* with 30 beds.

**Nemunas** *(☎ 52 345; Lietuvninkų gatvė 70; rooms per person 75 Lt)* is Šilutės one hotel, with single, double and triple rooms.

**Vilkėnų malūnas** *(☎/fax 48 371; suites 120-150 Lt)* is ideal as a base for exploring the area. It's in the village of Švėkšna, 12km east of Agluonėnai and about 24km north of Šilutė. It is housed in an old water mill. The rooms are comfortable. Breakfast is an additional 16 Lt and there's a tennis court (10 Lt), paddle boats to hire (4 Lt to 8 Lt) and a Russian-style sauna (40 Lt per hour).

**Laigebu** *(☎ 59 690, ☎/fax 52 232; singles/ doubles 100/200 Lt, with half-board 110/220 Lt)*, about 15km east of Šilutė in Žemaičių Naumiestis, is a large and modern building overlooking a lake. It's surrounded by forest and attracts a fair number of tour groups, but is appealing nonetheless. The hotel has a sauna, and rents bicycles and river boats (10 Lt per hour).

**Juknaičiai** *(☎ 58 973, ☎/fax 52 758; Beržų gatvė 3; rooms per person from 45 Lt)*, in Juknaičiai, 8km south of Šilutė, has fabulous interior design harkening to a bygone era. Its winter garden is a must-see, as is its salt room – a room built entirely from salt and used for medicinal treatments (sitting amid the four salt walls is apparently 'good for the blood'). Its wooden façade is the work of Grecevičius, a contemporary Palanga architect considered to be among Lithuania's most innovative.

## Getting There & Away

Getting to the area without your own wheels can be really tough going. To Šilutė there are there are 10 buses a day from Klaipėda (6.50 Lt), five from Kaunas (20.50 Lt, 180km) and four from Vilnius (32 Lt, 280km) in summer. There are fewer buses in winter making it unsuitable for a day trip. From Šilutė there are sporadic buses to Rusnė.

## Getting Around

Boat is the best means of exploring the delta (it's 8km from Pakalnė to Kintai by boat but 45km by road). The main routes follow the three main Delta tributaries – the Atmata (13km), Skirvytė (9km) and Pakalnė (9km) Rivers – which fan out westwards from Rusnė.

Boats can be hired with a boatman-guide in Rusnė at the park information centre. In Ventės Ragas, the **Ventė Tourist Centre** *(☎ 44 534)* can help you to rent a boat to explore the Delta or sail to Nida; a boat for up to 15/30 people costs 250/600 Lt a day.

# Language

## ESTONIAN

Estonian belongs to the Baltic-Finnic branch of the Finno-Ugric languages. It's closely related to Finnish and, distantly, to Hungarian. The complex grammar of Estonian make it a difficult language to learn – try your luck with 14 cases, declining adjectives and no future tense. Added to this is a vocabulary with no link to any other language outside its own group, save recent borrowings.

A comprehensive and radical reform of the language was undertaken in the early 1900s by Johannes Aavik, somewhat de-Germanising the grammar and adding thousands of new terms. Another language reformer, Johannes Veski, criticised Aavik's liberal borrowing from Finnish, and proceeded to augment the vocabulary by using Estonian roots to create new words. It's a process that is continuing to this day as new Estonian words are inven-ted to suit modern needs. All the same, the last few years have seen an increase in the liberal use of English words in place of their more complicated Estonian translations, or adding Estonian verb endings to English words, eg, in order to *surfima* the Web or *e-mailima* your friends, you need to *klikima* the mouse often!

You're unlikely to pick up more than a smattering of Estonian in a short visit, but knowing a few basic words and phrases will go down well with the people you meet. For trivia buffs, Estonian boasts the word with the most consecutively repeated vowel: *jäääär*, which means 'edge of ice'.

## Alphabet & Pronunciation

Estonian lacks a few letters of the English alphabet but has some extra ones of its own. The alphabet is as follows: **a b d e f g h i j k l m n o p r s š z ž t u v õ ä ö ü**.

Note that š is counted as a separate letter from s, ž from z, õ and ö from o, ä from a, and ü from u. The alphabetical order becomes important if you're using a dictionary or any other alphabetical list; words beginning with ä, for instance, are listed near the end of alphabetical lists, not after a. When pronouncing a word, the emphasis is always on the first syllable. Letters are generally pronounced as in English. The following may present difficulties:

| | |
|---|---|
| a | as the 'u' in 'cut' |
| b | similar to English 'p' |
| g | similar to English 'k' |
| j | as the 'y' in 'yes' |
| š | as 'sh' |
| ž | as the 's' in 'pleasure' |
| õ | somewhere between the 'e' in 'bed' and the 'u' in 'fur' |
| ä | as the 'a' in 'cat' |
| ö | as the 'u' in 'fur' but with rounded lips |
| ü | as a short 'you' |
| ai | as the 'i' in 'pine' |
| ei | as in 'vein' |
| oo | as the 'a' in 'water' |
| uu | as the 'oo' in 'boot' |
| öö | as the 'u' in 'fur' |

## Greetings & Civilities

| | |
|---|---|
| Hello. | *Tere.* |
| Good morning. | *Tere hommikust.* |
| Good day/Good afternoon. | *Tere päevast.* |
| Good evening. | *Tere õhtust.* |
| Good night. | *Head ööd.* |
| Goodbye. | *Head aega* ('**hey**-ahd ei-gah') or *Nägemiseni.* |
| Yes. | *Jah.* |
| No. | *Ei.* |
| Excuse me. | *Vabandage.* |
| Please. | *Palun.* |
| Thank you/Thanks. | *Tänan/Aitäh.* |

## Language Difficulties

| | |
|---|---|
| Do you speak English? | *Kas te räägite inglise keelt?* |
| I don't speak Estonian. | *Ma ei räägi eesti keelt.* |
| I don't understand. | *Ma ei saa aru.* |

## Getting Around

| | |
|---|---|
| airport | *lennujaam* |
| bus station | *bussijaam* |
| port | *sadam* |
| railway station | *raudteejaam* |
| stop (eg, bus stop) | *peatus* |
| bus | *buss* |

| | |
|---|---|
| taxi | takso |
| train | rong |
| tram | tramm |
| trolleybus | trollibuss |
| | |
| express | ekspress |
| fast | kiir |
| fast train | kiirrong |
| passenger train | reisirong |
| diesel train | diiselrong |
| suburban or local (train or bus) | linnalähedane |
| electric train | elektrirong |
| transit (bus) | transiit |
| | |
| arrival/ arrival time | saabub/ saabumine |
| departure/ departure time | väljub/ väljumine |
| every day | iga päev |
| even dates | paaris päevad |
| odd dates | paaritu päevad |
| except | välja arvatud |
| not running/ cancelled | ei sõida |
| through/via | läbi/kaudu |
| ticket | pilet |
| ticket office | piletikassa/kassa |
| advance-booking office | eelmüügikassa |
| soft class/deluxe | luksus |
| sleeping carriage (soft class) | magamisvagun |
| compartment (class) | kupee |

## Around Town

| | |
|---|---|
| bank | pank |
| castle | loss |
| church | kirik |
| city centre | kesklinn |
| currency exchange | valuutavahetus |
| department store | kaubamaja |
| hotel | hotell |
| market | turg |
| post office | postkontor |
| room | tuba |
| shop | kauplus/pood |
| stamp | mark |
| telephone | telefon |
| | |
| Where? | Kus? |
| How much? | Kui palju? |
| There is/are ... | On ... |
| There isn't/aren't ... | Ei ole ... |
| cheap | odav |
| expensive | kallis |
| open | avatud/lahti |

| | |
|---|---|
| closed | suletud/kinni |
| break (eg, for lunch) | vaheaeg |

## Food

| | |
|---|---|
| bar | baar |
| bill | arve |
| cafe | kohvik |
| canteen/cafeteria | söökla |
| restaurant | restoran |
| snack bar | einelaud |
| | |
| beef stroganoff | biifstrogonoff/ böfstrooganov |
| black bread | leib |
| butter | või |
| caviar | kalamari |
| cheese | juust |
| chicken | kana |
| desserts | magusroad |
| fish | kala |
| fruit | puuvili |
| grilled 'chop' | karbonaad |
| ice cream | jäätis |
| kebab | šašlõkk |
| meat (red) | liha |
| meat/main dishes | liharoad |
| mushroom | seen |
| national dishes | rahvusroad |
| pancake | pannkook |
| potato | kartul |
| salad | salat |
| sausage | vorst |
| soup | supp |
| starters | eelroad |
| steak | biifsteek |
| vegetables | köögivili |
| white bread | sai |
| | |
| water | vesi |
| mineral water | mineraalvesi |
| juice | mahl |
| tea | tee |
| coffee | kohv |
| milk | piim |
| sugar | suhkur |
| | |
| beer | õlu |
| brandy | konjak |
| champagne | šampus |
| vodka | viin |
| wine | vein |

## Time, Date & Numbers

| | |
|---|---|
| today | täna |
| yesterday | eile |
| tomorrow | homme |

| | |
|---|---|
| Sunday | *pühapäev* |
| Monday | *esmaspäev* |
| Tuesday | *teisipäev* |
| Wednesday | *kolmapäev* |
| Thursday | *neljapäev* |
| Friday | *reede* |
| Saturday | *laupäev* |
| | |
| January | *jaanuar* |
| February | *veebruar* |
| March | *märts* |
| April | *aprill* |
| May | *mai* |
| June | *juuni* |
| July | *juuli* |
| August | *august* |
| September | *september* |
| October | *oktoober* |
| November | *november* |
| December | *detsember* |

| | | |
|---|---|---|
| 1 | | *üks* |
| 2 | | *kaks* |
| 3 | | *kolm* |
| 4 | | *neli* |
| 5 | | *viis* |
| 6 | | *kuus* |
| 7 | | *seitse* |
| 8 | | *kaheksa* |
| 9 | | *üheksa* |
| 10 | | *kümme* |
| 11 | | *üksteist* |
| 12 | | *kaksteist* |
| 13 | | *kolmteist* |
| 14 | | *neliteist* |
| 15 | | *viisteist* |
| 16 | | *kuusteist* |
| 17 | | *seitseteist* |
| 18 | | *kaheksateist* |
| 19 | | *üheksateist* |
| 20 | | *kakskümmend* |
| 25 | | *kakskümmend viis* |
| 30 | | *kolmkümmend* |
| 40 | | *nelikümmend* |
| 50 | | *viiskümmend* |
| 60 | | *kuuskümmend* |
| 70 | | *seitsekümmend* |
| 80 | | *kaheksakümmend* |
| 90 | | *üheksakümmend* |
| 100 | | *sada* |

## Health & Emergencies

| | |
|---|---|
| doctor | *arst* |
| hospital | *haigla* |
| ambulance | *esmaabi* |
| police | *politsei* |

| | |
|---|---|
| chemist | *apteek* |
| toilet | *tualett* |

## LATVIAN

Latvian is one of only two surviving languages of the Baltic branch of the Indo-European language family. Even more than Estonians, the speakers of Latvian regard their language as an endangered species – only about 55% of the people in the country, and just over 45% of the inhabitants of the capital, Rīga, speak it as their first language. The east and west of the country have some dialect differences from standard central Latvian.

Latvian and Lithuanian have a lot of vocabulary in common but are not quite close enough to each other to be mutually intelligible. They began to develop as separate languages around the 7th century AD.

### Alphabet & Pronunciation

The Latvian alphabet is as follows: a b c č d e f g ģ (Ģ) h i j k ķ l ļ m n ņ o p r s š t u v z.

Note that č, ģ, ķ, ļ, ņ, š and ž are counted as separate letters from c, g, k, l, n, s and z. Letters are generally pronounced as in English except:

| | |
|---|---|
| c | as the 'ts' in 'bits' |
| č | as the 'ch' in 'church' |
| ģ | as the 'j' in 'jet' |
| j | as the 'y' in 'yes' |
| ķ | as 'tu' in 'tune' |
| ļ | as the 'lli' in 'billiards' |
| ņ | as the 'ni' in 'onion' |
| o | as the 'a' in 'water' |
| š | as the 'sh' in 'ship' |
| ž | as the 's' in 'pleasure' |
| ai | as the the 'i' in 'pine' |
| ei | as in 'vein' |
| ie | as in 'pier' |

A macron (eg, ā) has the effect of lengthening the vowel it's placed over:

| | |
|---|---|
| ā | as the 'a' in 'barn' |
| ē | as the 'e' in 'where' |
| ī | as the 'i' in 'marine' |
| ū | as the 'oo' in 'boot' |

### Greetings & Civilities

| | |
|---|---|
| Hello. | *Labdien/Sveiki.* |
| Good morning. | *Labrīt.* |

| | |
|---|---|
| Good day/Good afternoon. | *Labdien.* |
| Good evening. | *Labvakar.* |
| Good night. | *Ar labu nakti.* |
| Goodbye. | *Uz redzēšanos/Atā.* |
| Yes. | *Jā.* |
| No. | *Nē.* |
| Excuse me. | *Atvainojiet.* |
| Please. | *Lūdzu.* |
| Thank you. | *Paldies.* |

## Language Difficulties

| | |
|---|---|
| Do you speak English? | *Vai jūs runājat angliski?* |
| I don't speak Latvian. | *Es nerunāju latviski.* |
| I don't understand. | *Es nesaprotu.* |

## Getting Around

| | |
|---|---|
| airport | *lidosta* |
| railway station | *dzelzceļa stacija* |
| train | *vilciens* |
| bus station | *autoosta* |
| bus | *autobuss* |
| port | *osta* |
| taxi | *taksometrs* |
| tram | *tramvajs* |
| trolleybus | *trolejbuss* |
| stop (eg, bus stop) | *pietura* |
| petrol | *benzīns/degviela* |
| | |
| express | *ekspresis* |
| fast | *ātrs* |
| fast train | *ātrvilciens* |
| passenger train | *pasažieru vilciens* |
| diesel train | *diiselrong* |
| suburban or local (train or bus) | *piepilsētu* |
| electric train | *elektrovilciens* |
| transit (bus) | *tranzīts* |
| | |
| arrival/ arrival time | *pienāk/ pienākšanas laiks* |
| departure/ departure time | *atiet/ atiešanas laiks* |
| every day | *katru dienu* |
| even dates | *pāra datumos* |
| odd dates | *nepāra datumos* |
| except | *izņemot* |
| not running/ cancelled | *nekursē/atcelts* |
| through/via | *cauri* |
| | |
| ticket | *biļete* |
| ticket office | *kase* |
| advance-booking office | *iepriekšpārdošanas kases* |

| | |
|---|---|
| soft class/deluxe | *mīksts/luksus* |
| sleeping carriage (soft class) | *guļamvagons* |
| compartment (class) | *kupeja* |

## Around Town

| | |
|---|---|
| bank | *banka* |
| castle | *pils* |
| church | *baznīca* |
| city centre | *centrs* |
| currency exchange | *valūtas maiņa* |
| department store | *universālveikals* |
| hotel | *viesnīca* |
| market | *tirgus* |
| post office | *pasts* |
| room | *istaba* |
| shop | *veikals* |
| stamp | *pastmarka* |
| telephone | *telefons* |
| | |
| Where? | *Kur?* |
| There is/are ... | *Ir ...* |
| There isn't/aren't ... | *Nav ...* |
| How much? | *Cik?* |
| cheap | *lēts* |
| expensive | *dārgs* |
| open | *atvērts* |
| closed | *slēgts* |
| break (eg, for lunch) | *pārtraukums* |

## Food & Drinks

| | |
|---|---|
| bar | *bārs* |
| bill | *rēķins* |
| cafe | *kafejnīca* |
| canteen/cafeteria | *ēdnīca* |
| restaurant | *restorāns* |
| snack bar | *bufete* |
| | |
| beef stroganoff | *stroganovs* |
| black bread | *rupjmaize* |
| butter | *sviests* |
| caviar | *kaviārs/ikri* |
| cheese | *siers* |
| chicken | *vista* |
| coffee | *kafija* |
| desserts | *saldie ēdieni* |
| fish | *zivs* |
| fruit | *augļi* |
| grilled 'chop' | *karbonāde* |
| ice cream | *saldējums* |
| juice | *sula* |
| kebab | *šašliks* |
| meat (red) | *gaļa* |
| meat/main dishes | *gaļas ēdieni/otrie ēdieni* |
| milk | *piens* |

| | | | |
|---|---|---|---|
| mineral water | *minerālūdens* | 10 | *desmit* |
| mushroom | *sēne/šampinjons* | 11 | *vienpadsmit* |
| national dishes | *nacionālie ēdieni* | 12 | *divpadsmit* |
| pancake | *pankūka* | 13 | *trīspadsmit* |
| potato | *kartupelis* | 14 | *četrpadsmit* |
| salad | *salāti* | 15 | *piecpadsmit* |
| sausage | *desa* | 16 | *sešpadsmit* |
| soup | *zupa* | 17 | *septiņpadsmit* |
| starters | *uzkoda* | 18 | *astoņpadsmit* |
| steak | *bifšteks* | 19 | *deviņpadsmit* |
| sugar | *cukurs* | 20 | *divdesmit* |
| tea | *tēja* | 25 | *divdesmit pieci* |
| vegetables | *saknes/dārzeņi* | 30 | *trīsdesmit* |
| water | *ūdens* | 40 | *četrdesmit* |
| white bread | *baltmaize* | 50 | *piecdesmit* |
| | | 60 | *sešdesmit* |
| beer | *alus* | 70 | *septiņdesmit* |
| brandy | *konjaks* | 80 | *astoņdesmit* |
| champagne | *šampanietis* | 90 | *deviņdesmit* |
| vodka | *degvīns* | 100 | *simts* |
| wine | *vīns* | | |

## Time, Date & Numbers

| | |
|---|---|
| today | *šodien* |
| yesterday | *vakar* |
| tomorrow | *rīt* |
| | |
| Sunday | *svētdiena* |
| Monday | *pirmdiena* |
| Tuesday | *otrdiena* |
| Wednesday | *trešdiena* |
| Thursday | *ceturtdiena* |
| Friday | *piektdiena* |
| Saturday | *sestdiena* |
| | |
| January | *janvāris* |
| February | *februāris* |
| March | *marts* |
| April | *aprīlis* |
| May | *maijs* |
| June | *jūnijs* |
| July | *jūlijs* |
| August | *augusts* |
| September | *septembris* |
| October | *oktobris* |
| November | *novembris* |
| December | *decembris* |
| | |
| 1 | *viens* |
| 2 | *divi* |
| 3 | *trīs* |
| 4 | *četri* |
| 5 | *pieci* |
| 6 | *seši* |
| 7 | *septiņi* |
| 8 | *astoņi* |
| 9 | *deviņi* |

## Health & Emergencies

| | |
|---|---|
| toilet | *tualete* |
| chemist | *aptieka* |
| doctor | *ārsts* |
| hospital | *slimnīca* |
| ambulance | *ātrā palīdzība* |
| police | *policija* |

## LITHUANIAN

Lithuanian is another surviving language of the Baltic branch of the Indo-European language family. Because many of its forms have remained unchanged longer than those of other Indo-European languages (which cover most of Europe and a fair bit of Asia) Lithuanian is very important to linguistic scholars; it's said to be as archaic as Sanskrit in its grammatical forms. It is also open to free borrowings from other tongues when deemed necessary, as phrases like *ping pong klubas* and *marketingo departamento direktorius* demonstrate.

Žemaičiai or Low Lithuanian, spoken in the west, is a separate dialect from *Aukštaičiai* or High Lithuanian, spoken in the rest of the country.

## Alphabet & Pronunciation

The Lithuanian alphabet is as follows: a b c
č d e f g h i/y j k l m n o p r s š t u v z ž.

The i and y are partly interchangeable and y comes straight after i in alphabetical lists. Note that č, š and ž are separate letters from c, s and z. Letters are generally pronounced as in English except the following:

| | |
|---|---|
| c | as 'ts' |
| č | as 'ch' |
| y | between the 'i' in 'tin' and the 'ee' in 'feet' |
| j | as the 'y' in 'yes' |
| o | as the 'oa' in 'boat' |
| š | as 'sh' |
| ž | as the 's' in 'pleasure' |
| ei | as the 'ai' in 'pain' |
| ie | as the 'ye' in 'yet' |
| ui | as the 'wi' in 'win' |

Accent marks above and below vowels (eg, ā and ė) all have the general effect of lengthening the vowel:

| | |
|---|---|
| ā | as the 'a' in 'father' |
| ę | as the 'ai' in 'air' |
| ų | as the 'oo' in 'boot' |
| ū | as the 'oo' in 'boot' |
| ė | as the 'a' in 'late' |

## Greetings & Civilities

| | |
|---|---|
| Hello. | Labas/Sveikas. |
| Good morning. | Labas rytas. |
| Good day/Good afternoon. | Laba diena. |
| Good evening. | Labas vakaras. |
| Good night. | Labanakt. |
| Goodbye. | Sudie or Viso gero. |
| Yes. | Taip. |
| No. | Ne. |
| Excuse me. | Atsiprašau. |
| Please. | Prašau. |
| Thank you. | Ačiū. |

## Language Difficulties

| | |
|---|---|
| Do you speak English? | Ar kalbate angliškai? |
| I don't speak Lithuanian. | Aš nekalbu lietuviškai. |
| I don't understand. | Aš nesuprantu. |

## Getting Around

| | |
|---|---|
| airport | oro uostas |
| bus station | autobusų stotis |
| port | uostas |
| railway station | geležinkelio stotis |
| stop (eg, bus stop) | stotelė |
| bus | autobusas |
| taxi | taksi |
| train | traukinys |
| tram | tramvajus |
| trolleybus | troleibusas |

| | |
|---|---|
| express | ekspresas |
| fast | greitas |
| fast train | greitasis traukinys |
| passenger train | keleivinis traukinys |
| diesel train | dyzelinis traukinys |
| suburban or local (train or bus) | priemiestinis/vietinis |
| electric train | elektrinis traukinys |
| transit (bus) | pravažiuojantis |
| departure/ departure time | išvyksta/ išvykimo laikas |
| arrival/ arrival time | atvyksta/ atvykimo laikas |
| every day | kasdien |
| even dates | porinėmis dienomis |
| odd dates | neporinėmis dienomis |
| except | išskyrus |
| not running/ cancelled | nekursuoja |
| through/via | sper |
| ticket | bilietas |
| ticket office | kasa |
| advance-booking office | išankstinio bilietų pardavimo kasa |
| soft class/deluxe | minkštas/liuksas |
| sleeping carriage (soft class) | miegamasis |
| compartment (class) | kupė |

## Around Town

| | |
|---|---|
| bank | bankas |
| castle | pilis |
| church | bažnyčia |
| city centre | centras |
| currency exchange | valiutos keitykla |
| department store | universalinė parduotuvė |
| hotel | viešbutis |
| market | turgus |
| post office | paštas |
| room | kambarys |
| shop | parduotuvė |
| stamp | pašto ženklas |
| telephone | telefonas |
| Where? | Kur? |
| There is/are ... | Yra ... |
| There isn't/aren't ... | Nėra ... |
| How much? | Kiek? |
| cheap | pigus |
| expensive | brangus |
| open | atidaryta |
| closed | uždaryta |
| break (eg, for lunch) | pertrauka |

## Food & Drinks

| | |
|---|---|
| bar | *baras* |
| bill | *sąskaita* |
| cafe | *kavinė* |
| canteen/cafeteria | *valgykla* |
| restaurant | *restoranas* |
| snack bar | *bufetas* |
| | |
| beef stroganoff | *befstrogenas* |
| black bread | *duona* |
| butter | *sviestas* |
| caviar | *ikrai* |
| cheese | *sūris* |
| chicken | *vištiena* |
| desserts | *saldumynai* |
| fish | *žuvis* |
| fruit | *vaisiai* |
| grilled 'chop' | *karbonadas* |
| ice cream | *ledai* |
| kebab | *šašlykas* |
| meat (red) | *mesa* |
| meat/main dishes | *mėsos patiekalai* |
| mushroom | *grybai* |
| national dishes | *nacionaliniai patiekalai* |
| pancake | *blynas* |
| potato | *bulvė* |
| salad | *salotos/mišrainė* |
| sausage | *dešra* |
| soup | *sriuba* |
| starters | *užkanda* |
| steak | *bifšteksas* |
| vegetables | *daržovės* |
| white bread | *batonas* |
| | |
| water | *vanduo* |
| mineral water | *mineralinis vanduo* |
| juice | *sultys* |
| tea | *arbata* |
| coffee | *kava* |
| milk | *pienas* |
| sugar | *cukrus* |
| | |
| beer | *alus* |
| brandy | *konjakas* |
| champagne | *šampanas* |
| vodka | *degtinė* |
| wine | *vynas* |

## Times, Date & Numbers

| | |
|---|---|
| today | *šiandien* |
| tomorrow | *rytoj* |
| yesterday | *vakar* |
| | |
| Sunday | *sekmadienis* |
| Monday | *pirmadienis* |
| Tuesday | *antradienis* |
| Wednesday | *trečiadienis* |
| Thursday | *ketvirtadienis* |
| Friday | *penktadienis* |
| Saturday | *šeštadienis* |
| | |
| January | *sausis* |
| February | *vasaris* |
| March | *kovas* |
| April | *balandis* |
| May | *gegužė* |
| June | *birželis* |
| July | *liepa* |
| August | *rugpjūtis* |
| September | *rugsėjis* |
| October | *spalis* |
| November | *lapkritis* |
| December | *gruodis* |

| | |
|---|---|
| 1 | *vienas* |
| 2 | *du* |
| 3 | *trys* |
| 4 | *keturi* |
| 5 | *penki* |
| 6 | *šeši* |
| 7 | *septyni* |
| 8 | *aštuoni* |
| 9 | *devyni* |
| 10 | *dešimt* |
| 11 | *vienuolika* |
| 12 | *dvylika* |
| 13 | *trylika* |
| 14 | *keturiolika* |
| 15 | *penkiolika* |
| 16 | *šešiolika* |
| 17 | *septyniolika* |
| 18 | *aštuoniolika* |
| 19 | *devyniolika* |
| 20 | *dvidešimt* |
| 25 | *dvidešimt penki* |
| 30 | *trisdešimt* |
| 40 | *keturiasdešimt* |
| 50 | *penkiasdešimt* |
| 60 | *šešiasdešimt* |
| 70 | *septyniasdešimt* |
| 80 | *aštuoniasdešimt* |
| 90 | *devyniasdešimt* |
| 100 | *šimtas* |

## Health & Emergencies

| | |
|---|---|
| doctor | *gydytojas* |
| hospital | *ligoninė* |
| ambulance | *greitoji pagalba* |
| police | *policija* |
| chemist | *vaistinė* |
| toilet | *tualetas* |

# Glossary

## Abbreviations
Est – Estonian     Lith – Lithuanian     Ger – German
Lat – Latvian     Fin – Finnish     Rus – Russian

**aikštė** – square (Lith)
**aludė** – beer cellar (Lith)
**aludos sodas** – beer garden (Lith)
**alus** – beer (Lat, Lith)
**alus dārzs** – beer garden (Lat)
**apteek** – pharmacy (Est)
**aptieka** – pharmacy (Lat)
**arve** – bill (Est)
**Aukštaitija** – Upper Lithuania
**autobusų stotis** – bus station (Lith)
**autoosta** – bus staion (Lat)

**baar** – pub, bar (Est)
**babushka** – grandmothers/pensioner ladies in berets (Rus)
**bagāžas glabātava** – left-luggage room (Lat)
**bagažinė** – left-luggage room (Lith)
**bāka** – lighthouse (Lat)
**Baltic glint** – raised limestone bank stretching from Sweden across the north of Estonia into Russia
**Baltijas jūra** – Baltic Sea (Lat, Lith)
**baras** – pub, bar (Lith)
**baznīca** – church (Lat)
**bažnyčia** – church (Lith)
**biļete** – ticket (Lat)
**bilietas** – ticket (Lith)
**BKA** – West Estonian Archipelago Biosphere Reserve
**brokastis** – breakfast (Lat)
**bulvāris** – boulevard (Lat)
**bussijaam** – bus station (Est)

**ceļš** – railway track, road (Lat)
**cent (s), centų (pl)** – Lithuania's unit of national currency, 100 centų equalling 1 *litas*
**centras** – town centre (Lith)
**centrs** – town centre (Lith)
**Chudskoe Ozero** – Lake Peipsi (Rus)
**Courland** – Kurzeme

**daina** – short, poetic, oral song or verse (Lat)
**datorsalons** – Internet café (Lat)
**dievas** – sky god
**dzelzceļa stacija** – train station (Lat)

**dzintars** – amber (Lat)
**ebreji** – Jews (Lat)
**Eesti** – Estonia (Est)
**Estija** – Estonia (Lith)
**Estland** – Estonia (Ger)
**ežeras** – lake (Lith)
**ezerpils** – lake fortress (Lat)
**ezers** – lake (Lat)

**gatvė** – street (Lith)
**geležinkelio stotis** – train station (Lith)
**gintara** – amber (Lith)
**grāmata** – book (Lat)
**grynieji pinigai** – cash (Lith)

**hommikusöök** – breakfast (Est)

**iela** – street (Lat)
**iezis** – rock, bank (Lat)
**Igaunija** – Estonia (Lat)
**infokeskus** – information centre (Est)
**informacija** – information centre (Lith)
**informācijas centrs** – information centre (Lat)
**interneta kafenica** – Internet café (Lat)
**internetas kavinė** – Internet café (Lith)
**interneti kohvik** – Internet café (Est)

**järv** – lake (Est)
**jõgi** – river (Est)
**jūra** – sea (Lat, Lith)
**juut** – Jews (Est)

**kalnas** – mountain, hill (Lith)
**kalns** – mountain, hill (Lat)
**kämping** – camp site (Est)
**kanklės** – zither (Lith)
**kannel** – zither (Est)
**katedra** – cathedral (Lith)
**katedrāle** – cathedral (Lat)
**kelias** – road (Lith)
**kelionių biuras** – tourist office (Lith)
**kempingas** – camp site (Lith)
**kempings** – camp site (Lat)
**kepta duona** – deep-fried, black-bread garlic sticks (Lith)

**kesklinn** – town centre (Est)
**kiirtee** – highway, motorway (Est)
**kindlus** – fortress (Est)
**kino** – cinema (Est, Lat, Lith)
**kirik** – church (Est)
**knyga** – book (Lith)
**Kokle** – zither (Lat)
**kortelė** – credit card (Lith)
**krediitkaart** – credit card (Est)
**kredītkarte** – credit card (Lat)
**krogs** – pub or bar (Lat)
**Kuržemė** – Kurzeme (Lith)
**Kurische Nehrung** – Curonian Spit (Ger)
**Kurisches Haff** – Curonian Lagoon (Ger)
**Kurland** – Kurzeme (Ger)
**Kurshskaya kosa** – Curonian Spit (Rus)
**Kurshsky zaliv** – Curonian Lagoon (Rus)
**Kursių marios** – Curonian Lagoon (Lith)
**Kursių nerijos/Neringa** – Curonian Spit (Lith)

**Läänemeri** – Baltic Sea (Est)
**laht** – bay (Est)
**laipa** – boardwalk, plank way (Lat)
**LAL** – Lithuanian Airlines
**Läti** – Latvia (Est)
**lats (s), lati (pl)** – Latvia's unit of national currency
**Latvija** – Latvia (Lat, Lith)
**Latvijas Ceļš** – Latvian Way; centre-right political party (Lat)
**laukums** – square (Lat)
**Leedu** – Lithuania (Est)
**lennujaam** – airport (Est)
**Lettland** – Latvia (Ger)
**līcis** – bay (Lat)
**lidosta** – airport (Lat)
**Lietuva** – Lithuania (Lat, Lith)
**linnuvaatlus torn** – bird-watching tower (Est)
**litas (s), litų (pl)** – Lithuania's unit of national currency
**Litauen** – Lithuania (Ger)
**Litva** – Lithuania (Rus)
**Litwa** – Lithuania (Pol)
**looduse õpperada** – nature trail (Est)
**looduskaitseala** – nature/landscape reserve (Est)
**looduspark** – nature park (Est)
**loss** – castle, palace (Est)

**mägi** – mountain, hill (Est)
**merevaik** – amber (Est)
**meri** – sea (Est)
**mets** – forest (Est)

**Metsavennad** – Forest Brothers resistance movement (Est)
**mežs** – forest (Lat)
**midus** – mead (Lith)
**miske** – forest (Lith)
**mitte suitsetada** – no smoking (Est)
**muuseum** – museum (Est)
**muzejs** – museum (Lat)
**muziejus** – museum (Lith)

**nacionālais parks** – national park (Lat)
**nacionalinio parko** – national park (Lith)
**naktinis klubas** – nightclub (Lith)
**nakts klubs** – nightclub (Lat)
**nauda** – cash (Lat)

**õllekelder** – beer cellar (Est)
**õlleterrass** – beer garden (Est)
**õlu** – beer (Est)
**ööklubi** – nightclub (Est)
**oro uostas** – airport (Lith)
**osta** – port (Lat)

**pakihoiuruum** – left-luggage room (Est)
**park** – park (Est)
**parka** – park (Lith)
**parks** – park (Lat)
**paš to ministerija** – post office (Lith)
**pasts** – post office (Lat)
**Peipaus ežeras** – Lake Peipsi (Lith)
**Peipsi järv** – Lake Peipsi (Est)
**Peko** – pagan god of fertility in Setu traditions (Est)
**perkėla** – port (Lith)
**Perkūnas** – god of thunder
**peronas** – platform (Lith)
**perons** – platform (Lat)
**perroon** – platform (Est)
**Pihkva järv** – Lake Pskov (Est)
**pilet** – ticket (Est)
**pilies** – castle (Lith)
**pils** – castle, palace (Lat)
**pilsdrupas** – knights' castle (Lat)
**pilskalns** – castle mound (Lat)
**pirts** – sauna (Lat)
**plats** – square (Est)
**plentas** – highway, motorway (Lith)
**postkontor** – post office (Est)
**prāmju osta** – ferry terminal (Lat)
**prieplauka** – ferry terminal (Lith)
**prospects** – boulevard (Lat)
**prospektas** – boulevard (Lith)
**Pskovskoe Ozero** – Lake Pskov (Rus)
**pubi** – pub, bar (Est)

**puiestee** – boulevard (Est)
**pusryčiai** – breakfast (Lith)
**raamat** – book (Est)
**raekoda** – town/city hall (Est)
**raha** – cash (Est)
**rahvuspark** – national park (Est)
**rātsnams** – town/city hall (Lat)
**raudteejaam** – train station (Est)
**rąžė** – river (Lith)
**reisisadam** – ferry terminal (Est)
**remontas** – repair, renovation (Lith)
**remonts** – repair, renovation (Lat)
**reserveerimine** – reservation (Est)
**Reval** – Tallinn (Ger)
**rezervāts** – reservation (Lat)
**Riigikogu** – Parliament (Est)
**roopad** – mountain (Est, Lat)
**rotušė** – town/city hall (Lith)
**rūmai** – palace (Lith)

**saar** – island (Est)
**sadam** – port (Est)
**Saeima** – Parliament (Lat)
**santīms (s), santīmi (pl)** – Latvia's unit of national currency, 100 santīmi equals 1 *lats*
**sąskaita** – bill (Lith)
**saun** – sauna (Est)
**Seimas** – Parliament (Lith)
**senamiestis** – Old Town (Lith)
**Setu** – ethnic group of mixed Estonian and Orthodox traditions; pagan god of fertility in Setu traditions
**Setumaa** – territory of the Setu people in southeastern Estonia and Russia (Est)
**sild** – bridge (Est)
**smuklė** – tavern (Lith)
**soo** – bog, swamp (Est)
**šoseja** – highway, motorway (Lat)
**sporta bāze** – 'sports base' dating to Soviet era (Lat, Lith)
**sularaha** – cash (Est)

**süstamatk** – cathedral (Est)
**taimetoitlane** – vegetarian (Est)
**Tallina** – Tallinn (Lat)
**Talinas** – Tallinn (Lith)
**Tallinna** – Tallinn (Fin)
**talong** – ticket (Est)
**tänav** – street (Est)
**tee** – road (Est)
**tiibur** – hydrofoil (Est)
**tilts** – bridge (Lat)
**tiltas** – bridge (Lith)
**trahter** – tavern (Est)
**tualetas** – toilet (Lith)
**tualete** – toilet (Lat)
**tualett** – toilet (Est)
**turg** – market (Est)
**tirgus** – market (Lat)
**turgus** – market (Lith)
**tūrisma birojs** – tourist office (Lat)
**turismikeskus** – tourist office (Est)

**upe** – river (Lat)

**vaistinė** – pharmacy (Lith)
**väljak** – square (Est)
**vanalinn** – Old Town (Est)
**Vanemuine** – ancient Estonian song god (Est)
**vecpilsēta** – Old Town (Lat)
**Vecrīga** – Old Rīga (Lat)
**veļetārietis** – vegetarian (Lat)
**vegetarinis** – vegetarian (Lith)
**via Baltica** – international road link (the E67) linking Estonia with Poland
**Vilna** – Vilnius (Ger)
**Viļņa** – Vilnius (Lat)
**Viro** – Estonia (Fin)

**Wilno** – Vilnius (Pol)

**žydų** – Jews (Lith)

# LONELY PLANET

You already know that Lonely Planet produces more than this one guidebook, but you might not be aware of the other products we have on this region. Here is a selection of titles that you may want to check out as well:

**St Petersburg Map**
ISBN 1 86450 179 0
US$5.99 • UK£3.99

**St Petersburg**
ISBN 1 86450 325 4
US$15.99 • UK£9.99

**Russian Phrasebook**
ISBN 1 86450 106 5
US$7.95 • UK£4.50

**Europe on a Shoestring**
ISBN 1 74059 314 6
US$24.99 • UK£14.99

**Poland**
ISBN 1 74059 082 1
US$19.99 • UK£12.99

**Scandinavian Phrasebook**
ISBN 1 86450 225 8
US$7.99 • UK£4.50

**Russia & Belarus**
ISBN 1 74059 265 4
US$29.99 • UK£18.99

**Moscow**
ISBN 1 86450 359 9
US$18.99 • UK£10.99

**Denmark**
ISBN 1 74059 075 9
US$17.99 • UK£12.99

**Scandinavian Europe**
ISBN 1 74059 318 9
US$24.99 • UK£14.99

**Sweden**
ISBN 1 74059 227 1
US$19.99 • UK£12.99

**Finland**
ISBN 1 74059 076 7
US$21.99 • UK£13.99

**Available wherever books are sold**

# Index

## Abbreviations

Est - Estonia

Lat - Latvia

Lith - Lithuania

## Text

Österby (Est) 181
Otepää (Est) 164-6, **165**

## P

Padise (Est) 141-2
painting
　Estonia 104-5
　Latvia 220-1
Pakri Islands (Est) 139
Palanga (Lith) 375-90, **376**
Paldiski (Est) 140-1
Palmse (Est) 145
Palūšė (Lith) 347
Paneriai (Lith) 342-3
Panevėžys (Lith) 369-71, **370**
Panga (Est) 198
Pärnu (Est) 200-7, **204**
Pasiene (Lat) 273
Pažaislis Monastery (Lith) 362
Pedvāle (Lat) 289-90
people 34-5
Pervalka (Lith) 390
photography 51-2
　books 109-10
Piirisaar (Est) 174
Pikk jalg (Est) 124
Pirita (Est) 126
Pirita Tee (Est) 125
Piusa (Est) 172
plants 30, 98, 126, 144
Plungė (Lith) 372
Podnieks, Juris 226
Põide (Est) 192-3
politics 32
　Estonia 99-100
　Latvia 216-17
　Lithuania 302-3
pollution 29-30
Põlva (Est) 166-7
population 34-5
　Estonia 100-2
　Latvia 219
　Lithuania 304
postal services 48
　Estonia 108-9
　Latvia 223
　Lithuania 310
Prangli (Est) 139
Preila (Lith) 390
President's Palace (Lith) 326
public holidays 57-8
　Estonia 111-12
　Latvia 227
　Lithuania 312-13
Pühajärv (Est) 164
Pühalepa Church (Est) 184
Pürksi (Est) 181

**Bold** indicates maps.

Pumpurs, Andrejs 271
Purtse (Est) 149

## R

radio 51
　Estonia 111
　Latvia 227
　Lithuania 312
Radviliškis (Lith) 368-9
Raekoja Plats (Est) 119-22
rafting 60
Rainis, Jānis 254, 274
Rainis Memorial Museum (Lat) 274
Rastrelli, Bartolomeo 279, 280
religion 39-40
　Estonia 106
　Latvia 221
　Lithuania 307
responsible tourism 38-9, 43
　cultural considerations 38-9
　Latvia 222
Rēzekne (Lat) 273
Riežupe sand caves (Lat) 294-5
Riflemen statue (Lat) 237
Rīga (Lat) 230-56, **232**, **234**, **238**
　accommodation 243-4
　attractions 235-42
　entertainment 247-50
　food 245-7
　shopping 241, 250
　travel to/from 250-2
　travel within 252-3
Ristna (Est) 188
road distances **85**
Roja (Lat) 286-7
rollerblading
　Sigulda (Lat) 263
Rõuge (Est) 169
Ruhnu (Est) 209
Rūjiena (Lat) 259
Rumpo Peninsula (Est) 182
Rumšiškės (Lith) 365-6
Rundāle Palace (Lat) 279-80
Rundāli Museum (Lat) 287
Rusnė (Lith) 394

## S

Saaremaa (Est) 190-9, **191**
Saarnaki (Est) 189
Sabile (Lat) 289-90
Sabonis, Arvydas 314
safe travel 56-7, 86
　Lithuania 312
　money 47
　women travellers 55
St Anne's Church (Lith) 326-7
St John's Church (Est) 171, 210
St John's Church (Lat) 239, 266

St Katrīna's Church (Lat) 293
St Mathew's Church (Lith) 369
St Michael's Church (Lith) 326-7
St Nicholas Church (Lith) 123
St Olaf Church (Est) 123
St Peter & St Paul's Cathedral (Lith) 358
St Peter's Church (Lat) 239
St Saviour's Church (Lat) 237
SS Peter & Paul's Church (Lith) 330, 366
Salacgrīva (Lat) 257
Salantai (Lith) 374
Saulkrasti (Lat) 257
saunas 61, 128
scams 56-7
sculpture 38
　courses 62
Seaside Open-Air Museum (Lat) 292
Semonova, Uljana 229
Šeštokai (Lith) 355
Setumaa (Est) 171-3
shopping
　Estonia 113
　Latvia 229
　Lithuania 315
Šiauliai (Lith) 366-8
Sigulda (Lat) 259-64, **260**
Sillamäe (Est) 150-1
Šilutė (Lith) 394
skiing 59-60
　Andrēnkalni (Lat) 266
　Cīruliši (Lat) 266
　Ērgļi (Lat) 270
　Ignalina (Lith) 349
　Krasti (Lat) 266
　Otepää (Est) 164-5
　Sigulda (Lat) 263
　Valmiera (Lat) 268
　Zviedru Cepure (Lat) 289-90
Skrunda (Lat) 298
sky-diving
　Smiltynė (Lith) 384
Slītere National Park (Lat) 287-9
Smiltynė (Lith) 383-4
Song Bowl (Est) 125
Soomaa National Park (Est) 211-12
Sõrve Peninsula (Est) 198
Southern Hiiumaa (Est) 189-92
Soviet rule 22-3
special events, see festivals, public holidays
Strenči (Lat) 269
Sugihara, Chiune 361
Suur Munamägi (Est) 169
Suure-Jaani (Est) 211
Suuremõisa (Est) 184
Sviby (Est) 181
swimming 128

# Boxed Text

# MAP LEGEND

## CITY ROUTES

| | |
|---|---|
| Freeway ......... Freeway | ═ ⊐ ⊐ ⊐ ......... Unsealed Road |
| Highway ......... Primary Road | ......... One Way Street |
| Road ......... Secondary Road | ......... Pedestrian Street |
| Street ......... Street | ⊓⊓⊓⊓⊓⊓ ......... Stepped Street |
| Lane ......... Lane | ⊐ ═ ═ ═ ......... Tunnel |
| ......... On/Off Ramp | ═══════ ......... Footbridge |

## REGIONAL ROUTES

| |
|---|
| ═══════ ......... Tollway, Freeway |
| ═══════ ......... Primary Road |
| ......... Secondary Road |
| ......... Minor Road |

## BOUNDARIES

| |
|---|
| ▬ ▬ ▪ ▬ ▪ ......... International |
| ▬ ▬ ▪ ▪ ......... State |
| ▬ ▬ ▬ ......... Disputed |
| ▬▬●▬▬ ......... Fortified Wall |

## HYDROGRAPHY

| | |
|---|---|
| ......... River, Creek | ......... Dry Lake; Salt Lake |
| ......... Canal | ......... Spring; Rapids |
| ......... Lake | ......... Waterfalls |

## TRANSPORT ROUTES & STATIONS

| | |
|---|---|
| ─────○── ......... Train | ─────🚪 ......... Ferry |
| ........... ......... Underground Train | ─ ─ ─ ─ ─ ......... Walking Trail |
| ──Ⓜ── ......... Metro | • • • • • • • ......... Walking Tour |
| ▬▬▬▬▬ ......... Tramway | ─ ─ 🚲 ─ ......... Cycling Trail |
| ╫──╫──╫ ......... Cable Car, Chairlift | ......... Path |

## AREA FEATURES

| | | |
|---|---|---|
| ......... Building | ......... Market | ......... Beach | ......... Campus |
| ......... Park, Gardens | ......... Sports Ground | + + + ......... Cemetery | ......... Plaza |

## POPULATION SYMBOLS

| | | |
|---|---|---|
| ✪ **CAPITAL** ......... National Capital | ● **CITY** ......... City | ● Village ......... Village |
| ◉ **CAPITAL** ......... State Capital | ● Town ......... Town | ......... Urban Area |

## MAP SYMBOLS

| | | |
|---|---|---|
| ▪ ......... Place to Stay | ▼ ......... Place to Eat | ● ......... Point of Interest |

| | | | |
|---|---|---|---|
| ✈ ......... Airport | ⊟ ......... Cinema | 🏛 ......... Museum | ⛷ ......... Ski Field |
| ⚓ ......... Anchorage | ▢ ......... Embassy, Consulate | ▣ ......... National Park | ▥ ......... Stately Home |
| ⊖ ......... Bank | ✛ ......... Hospital | ✚ ......... Police Station | ☎ ......... Telephone |
| 🚏 ▣ ......... Bus Stop, Terminal | ▣ ......... Internet Cafe | ▤ ......... Post Office | ▣ ......... Theatre |
| ▣ ......... Castle | ⚲ ......... Lighthouse | ▤ ......... Pub or Bar | ❶ ......... Tourist Information |
| ⌂ ......... Cave | ☀ ......... Lookout | ▣ ......... Ruins | ▣ ......... Winery |
| ▤ ▣ ......... Church | ▲ ......... Monument | ▣ ......... Shopping Centre | ▣ ......... Zoo |

*Note: not all symbols displayed above appear in this book*

---

# LONELY PLANET OFFICES

## Australia
Locked Bag 1, Footscray, Victoria 3011
☎ 03 8379 8000  fax 03 8379 8111
email: talk2us@lonelyplanet.com.au

## UK
10a Spring Place, London NW5 3BH
☎ 020 7428 4800  fax 020 7428 4828
email: go@lonelyplanet.co.uk

## USA
150 Linden St, Oakland, CA 94607
☎ 510 893 8555  TOLL FREE: 800 275 8555
fax 510 893 8572
email: info@lonelyplanet.com

## France
1 rue du Dahomey, 75011 Paris
☎ 01 55 25 33 00  fax 01 55 25 33 01
email: bip@lonelyplanet.fr
www.lonelyplanet.fr

**World Wide Web: www.lonelyplanet.com *or* AOL keyword: lp**
**Lonely Planet Images: www.lonelyplanetimages.com**